D1713528

A POLITICAL HISTORY

of NATIONAL CITIZENSHIP

and IDENTITY IN ITALY,

1861–1950

Sabina Donati

STANFORD UNIVERSITY PRESS

STANFORD, CALIFORNIA

Stanford University Press
Stanford, California

Published with the support of the Swiss National Science Foundation and the
Maison de l'Histoire, Université de Genève.

Library of Congress Cataloging-in-Publication Data

Donati, Sabina, author.
A political history of national citizenship and identity in Italy, 1861-1950 /
Sabina Donati.
    pages cm
Based on the author's thesis (doctoral)—Graduate Institute of International
Studies, Geneva.
Includes bibliographical references and index.
ISBN 978-0-8047-8451-1 (cloth : alk. paper)
    1. Citizenship—Italy—History—19th century. 2. Citizenship—Italy—
History—20th century. 3. National characteristics, Italian—History—19th
century. 4. National characteristics, Italian—History—20th century. 5. Italy—
Politics and government—19th century. 6. Italy—Politics and government—
20th century. I. Title.
JN5591.D63 2013
323.60945'09041—dc23
                                        2012039000
ISBN 978-0-8047-8733-8 (electronic)
Typeset by Bruce Lundquist in 10/12 Sabon

A mamma e papà
ed ai miei fratelli

Do you see how great a responsibility the orator has in
historical writing? [...] For who does not know history's
first law to be that an author must not dare to tell anything
but the truth? And its second that he must make bold to
tell the whole truth? That there must be no suggestion of
partiality anywhere in his writings? Nor of malice?

*Videtisne, quantum munus sit oratoris historia? [...] Nam
quis nescit, primam esse historiae legem, ne quid falsi
dicere audeat? Deinde ne quid veri non audeat? Ne qua
suspicio gratiae sit in scribendo? Ne qua simultatis?*

—Cicero, *De Oratore*, trans. E. W. Sutton, vol. 1
(London: Heinemann; Cambridge, Mass.: Harvard
University Press, 1959).

"Now say,
would it be worse for man on earth if he were not a citizen?"
"Yes," I replied, "and here I ask for no proof."

*"Or dì: sarebbe il peggio
per l'omo in terra, se non fosse cive?"
"Sì," rispuos'io; "e qui ragion non cheggio."*

—Dante Alighieri, *The Divine Comedy*,
trans. C. S. Singleton, vol. 3
(Princeton: Princeton University Press, 1977).

Contents

Contents

PART TWO

HISTORICAL EVOLUTION DURING THE FASCIST EPOCH

(1922–1945)

⊥

Acknowledgments

This is a book about Italy, its citizens, foreigners and Others. It is a book on *italianità* and national membership that I have been fortunate to write as an Italian woman, born and bred in Italy, but also as a foreigner and resident alien abroad, having been living outside the Italian peninsula for more than twenty years. The gestation of this volume has therefore been shaped by a personal mix of academic experiences, migratory life and *italianità* at home and abroad.

The research, writing and publication of this work would not have been possible without the generous financial support of several institutions, providing me with academic subsidies, research grants and fellowships. I am most grateful to the Fonds National Suisse de la Recherche Scientifique for its aid to publication as well as for a *chercheurs débutants* grant that allowed me to spend one full year in the Italian historical archives. I also wish to express my thanks to the Maison de l'Histoire of the Université de Genève for its funding toward production and publication costs; and to acknowledge my appreciation to the Tokyo Foundation and to the Graduate Institute of International and Development Studies, Geneva, for their annual fellowships and grants.

As a long and rewarding journey this project has benefited from the insightful advice, thought-provoking comments and continuous encouragement of many people. My greatest debts of gratitude go to Andre Liebich (Graduate Institute), whose profound knowledge and generously sharp insights provoked me to reflect on many interrelated historical aspects of citizenship and national identity from the very early stages of this work; I cannot find words to thank him for his devoted intellectual presence. I am also most thankful to Peter Sahlins (University of California, Berkeley) for his useful critiques and remarks on how to rethink the citizenship-nationhood nexus and for sharing his expertise on legal-jurisprudential histories of citizenship; as well as to Bruno Arcidiacono (Graduate Institute) for his early advice to incorporate European comparisons into my research. The work has also grown along the way and progressed a great deal thanks to the intellectual contribution of three perceptive reviewers, whose powerful mix of effective criticism and keen revision suggestion has been extremely beneficial.

Aron Rodrigue (Stanford Humanities Center) and Davide Rodogno (Graduate Institute) have been very special sources of help and advice for me, particularly in the most demanding phases of the publication process. At Stanford University Press I wish to express my gratitude to Norris Pope for his kindness and expert guidance, Thomas Finnegan for his precious copy editing and the entire Press for the magic of turning a blossom into a flower, a final manuscript into a book.

Among my colleagues at Webster University Geneva I would like to thank all faculty and staff, and express my gratefulness to the Department of International Relations and to Alexandre Vautravers.

All the archival and documentary research was carried out in Italy, where I spent twelve months collecting invaluable historical material on the various citizenship issues recounted in this volume. Unique and most gratifying, this research in the peninsula was then coupled with further collection of sources that I was privileged to carry out for a number of years in the inspiring settings of Swiss libraries. In Rome I wish to thank Leopoldo Nuti for his warm welcome at the Università di Roma Tre. The staffs of the Italian libraries and of the depository archival institutions have also afforded me with inestimable assistance, for which I am truly indebted. Special words of appreciation go to the personnel of the Biblioteca e Archivio della Camera dei Deputati, for assisting me in the collection of Italian parliamentary debates; to Eugenio Pauselli and his friendly colleagues at the Biblioteca del Ministero dell'Interno, for their help in finding ministerial and judiciary material on naturalization files; to Alessandro Gionfrida and Giovanni Sargeri at the Ufficio Storico dello Stato Maggiore dell'Esercito, for all the information and assistance in finding the sources pertaining to Italy's colonized and occupied territories; to Maria Pina Di Simone and the staff of the Archivio Centrale dello Stato, for their gentleness in answering all my numerous questions; to Stefania Ruggeri at the Archivio Storico Diplomatico del Ministero degli Affari Esteri, for her gracious help. Special thanks go as well to the librarians of the Graduate Institute, to those of the Bibliothèque de Genève, and to the staff of the Dépôt des Bibliothèques Universitaires, for their patience and rapidity in finding all the books that I needed.

I cannot name all the kind friends and peers who throughout the years have supplied me with not only intellectual but also emotional support, often despite our long-distance friendships. I want to thank wholeheartedly those I was fortunate to meet: in England, when doing my undergraduate studies at the University of London Queen Mary and Westfield College; in France, while joining the Erasmus exchange program at the

Université François Rabelais of Tours; in Switzerland, when doing my postgraduate degree and Ph.D. studies at the Graduate Institute; in Italy, while carrying out the research for this project and, before then, when living there with my family.

In different ways, the multinational and multicultural body of my students has also been a source of inspiration in thinking and writing about notions of citizenship, foreignness and national identity from the very international city of Geneva. On one side of the lake, my thoughts go to all the nationalities represented at Webster University, where I teach modern European history and research methodologies. On the other side of the lake, a particular thought for the asylum seekers arriving in the canton and to whom I had the chance to teach French within the Asylum/ Insertion program of the Geneva Republic.

Italian journalist and dear friend Benedetta Gentile has also marked my academic life in a special way, and I am most grateful for her advice.

Giovanni Arcudi, Cristiano d'Orsi, Gemma Zanellato, Manuela Alberti, Maria Holzmann, Liz Ravelo, Sophie Davaris and Lucia Raffaelli deserve distinctive mention.

Finally, a special thought to my family and relatives in Italy, for their love and care. As I have been living more years abroad than in peninsular Italy, my notion of "home" has necessarily changed and evolved. Yet, "between the here and there," the presence and the assurances of my family members have been indelible and constant factors, providing me with an inestimable foundation of belonging. My parents and my brothers as well as my late grandparents have always been a source of enthusiasm and encouragement; my sisters-in-law and my niece, a source of refreshing creativeness.

Any mistakes or inaccuracies in this work are my own. In addition, all translations are mine, unless otherwise stated.

Abbreviations Used in the Main Text

ACC	Allied Control Commission
AMG	Allied Military Government
AOI	Africa Orientale Italiana
CIAF	Commissione Italiana di Armistizio con la Francia
CIE	Cittadinanza italiana egea (Aegean Italian citizenship)
CIL	Cittadinanza italiana libica (Libyan Italian citizenship)
CIS	Cittadinanza italiana speciale (Special Italian citizenship)
CITC	Cittadinanza italiana in Tripolitania e Cirenaica (Italian citizenship of Tripolitania and Cyrenaica)
CLN	Comitato di Liberazione Nazionale
CTLT	Cittadinanza del Territorio Libero di Trieste (Citizenship of the Free Territory of Trieste)
EU	European Union
FIAT	Fabbrica Italiana Automobili Torino
Gabap	Gabinetto—Armistizio Pace
MAE	Ministero degli Affari Esteri
MP	Member of Parliament
ONMI	Opera Nazionale Maternità e Infanzia
RSI	Repubblica Sociale Italiana
SAOI	Sudditanza dell'Africa Orientale Italiana (Subjecthood of Italian East Africa)
SC	Sudditanza coloniale (Colonial subjecthood)

SIL   Sudditanza degli indigeni della Libia
           (Subjecthood of the indigenous peoples of Libya)

TLT   Territorio Libero di Trieste (Free Territory of Trieste)

UN   United Nations

USA   United States of America

USSR   Union of Soviet Socialist Republics

A POLITICAL HISTORY

of NATIONAL CITIZENSHIP

and IDENTITY IN ITALY,

1861–1950

Introduction

Dante's allegorical journey through Hell, Purgatory and Paradise—*The Divine Comedy*—was written by Italy's supreme poet during his melancholic years of forced political exile, while coming to know, away from Florence, "how salt is the taste of another's bread, and how hard the path to descend and mount by another man's stairs."[1] The most famous Florentine citizen in history—a White Guelph, "born and grew up on the fair stream of Arno, at the great town"[2] and so actively involved in Florentine political affairs as to achieve the position of prior (one of the six highest magistrates)—was obliged to take the road of exile after the opposing faction of the Black Guelphs took power in 1301. Charged with graft and hostility against the pope, he was sentenced to death and, consequently, never returned to his birthplace, dying in the city of Ravenna in 1321. Throughout his life, he defined himself, frequently, as "*Florentinus et exul inmeritus*" (a Florentine and an undeserved exile) and made reference, recurrently, in his works, to his profound longing for return as well as to his severe disapproval of his co-citizens' warring hostile politics.[3]

Almost five and a half centuries after Dante's death, in the historical context of the Italian Risorgimento and of the Roman Question, the famous General and Left Deputy Giuseppe Garibaldi contemplated, in a nervous state of mind and probably under the influence of the most radical wing of his party, taking an extreme measure as a way of discrediting the Italian king's government and of countering its action against him: to acquire American citizenship and thus lose automatically his Italian *status civitatis* and parliamentary position. More precisely, irritated by the Italian government's decision to arrest him and confine him at Varignano after the disastrous campaign against French and Papal troops at Mentana in 1867, Garibaldi asked the American consul at La Spezia, William T. Rice, whether he could be recognized as an American citizen.[4] In this way, he could then invoke the protection of his new state and be rescued from the "unjust" act the Italian government and the

Savoy monarchy had performed against his person. Eventually, though, Garibaldi's decision to acquire a foreign nationality on mere instrumental political grounds was not realized in practice. In fact, the general did not pursue the matter further—thus, avoiding a probable scandal that would surely have widened the already large breach that divided the revolutionary Left from the moderate Right on the Roman Question.[5]

The biographical episodes concerning Dante Alighieri on the one hand and Giuseppe Garibaldi on the other draw attention, from different angles, to an "invisible factor" linking the exiled poet to medieval Florence and the arrested general to the 1861 Kingdom of Italy. This intangible "umbilical cord" connecting individuals to a political community—be that a Greek *polis*, the Roman empire, the Christian medieval city-state, or the modern territorial nation-state—has an age-old name going back to ancient times: citizenship.[6]

How can one define this concept? Debate has emerged around this notion in numerous disciplines and from various perspectives, but so far no universally accepted definition has been formulated.[7] Indeed, citizenship has meant and continues to mean a variety of things. Jurists, for instance, see it primarily as a legal status, tend to call it synonymously with the term "nationality" and refer basically to state membership—that is, the formal membership of a person in a political community.[8] By contrast, liberal political thinkers perceive it particularly as a status enjoyed equally by everyone who is a member of a state's citizenry, emphasizing the justification of the individual's entitlements and the equality of all citizens as rights-bearing persons.[9] This latter view, though, has attracted criticism. And in fact, so-called communitarians have shifted their attention to the primacy of the community and to the individual's active participation in the business of rule, thus defining citizenship as a role that the *civis* assumes by participating in the determination of the common good—that is, by "ruling and being ruled," as Aristotle's *zoon politikon*.[10] In addition to these perspectives, the notion under consideration has been conceived as being, and providing, an identity: thus, seen through the lens of psychology, it is an important expression of individual self-understanding because it helps us define ourselves as well as determine to whom we are alike and from whom we are different.[11] Finally, as sociologists have persuasively argued, it is also an identity that provides a source of unity, of shared solidarity and of social inclusion thanks to its "integrative function" vis-à-vis previously excluded groups within mainstream society.[12]

Undoubtedly, all these theoretical debates draw attention to a fundamental factor: citizenship is a multifaceted and dynamic idea that defies any single and unilateral explanation. Broadly speaking, it can be seen as an institution that, as Pietro Costa has already argued, is made up of five fundamental elements: the individual, rights, duties, sense of belonging and political community.[13] These are five large parameters that delimit the concept and can be regarded as "the core components of citizenship" and "the elemental structures of its semantic field."[14] Most importantly and as a contribution to the ongoing theoretical discussions, citizenship is an evolving notion that adjusts and adapts itself to a variety of historical epochs, political regimes and diverse societies. For this reason, it possesses a plethora of semantic meanings that vary according to the context in which the concept has developed. This is why, to use Costa's terminology based on studies concerning the logic of language, it is not unfounded to see citizenship as "an indexical expression," namely, shifting from context to context; it is a word defining different things at different times, making the concept highly flexible in historical perspective.[15]

Recently, there has been an explosion of interest in this theme. The plethora of publications, the emergence of specialized journals such as *Citizenship Studies*—which is currently leading the international debate on academic analysis of this topic—as well as the increasing discussions within the various national political arenas and the international press demonstrate the current topical importance of the subject. In fact, a venerable institution, citizenship is also a contemporary topic constantly emerging and reemerging within current affairs because it is an issue that touches, directly or indirectly, on a variety of fundamental questions. For instance, it is an element that follows the birth, life and death of states (the process of statehood); it contributes to the existence and survival of nations (the process of nationhood); it is linked to many political, socio-economic, cultural and military matters including international emigration and immigration, accommodation of minorities, allocation of welfare benefits, identity, national security. Finally, from a specifically European point of view, the topic has also acquired much relevance following the epochal recent events of the creation of post-Soviet nation-states, German reunification and the deepening and widening process of EU integration.

From a scholarly perspective, this ongoing interest is clearly testified by the existence of an extensive and growing literature. For example, the classical works of Derek Benjamin Heater and Peter Riesenberg as well as the edited publication of Danilo Zolo and the studies of Salvatore Veca and Enrico Grosso are just a few examples of a very long list.[16] Authors from distinct academic backgrounds have been intrigued by so many diverse facets of citizenship that one can now find a wealth of analysis pertaining to a wide spectrum of civic matters, ranging from a person's moral right to become a citizen of a state[17] to new conceptualizations of citizenship models as "transnational" or "postnational" membership within a globalized world[18]; from the extension of citizenship rights to minority groups for recognition of cultural difference within contemporary political entities[19] to whether patriotism is the name of a virtue or the name of a vice[20]; alongside pages on how symbolic historical reparations such as apologies can be acts of inclusionary, but also exclusionary, politics of cultural citizenship.[21]

So although the notion has been the object of much and multisided inquiry, the specific research field concerning "national citizenship in historical perspective" is still at its inception and has so far focused mainly on the French, German and British experiences.[22] Lately the Scandinavian countries too have been studied from a citizenship and nationhood viewpoint, with the inclusion of a short historical account.[23] Yet the existing literature regarding this specialized field is still lacunary as far as the Italian case study is concerned, and relatively few English-language publications are available on the topic. Italy's *status civitatis* has in fact been examined mainly by Italian legal scholars, sociologists and political scientists[24] while Italian contemporary historians have so far concentrated in particular on citizenship and migration issues as in Guido Tintori's rigorous research.[25] Also, the concise English-language accounts that have discussed the Italian historical experience are limited in scope as they examine only specific aspects. Ferruccio Pastore, for instance, has mainly focused on the way Italian governmental policies concerning nationality have been closely determined by questions of historical emigration and impacted on contemporary immigration.[26] Turning to the context of European integration and to the link between citizenship and identity in post–World War Two republican Italy, scholar Mathias Koenig-Archibugi has studied notions of nation building and the practice of Italian citizenship within a setting of partisan mediation and ideological polarization.[27] Finally, the research carried out by Pamela Ballinger has brought to light the little-known question of Italian repatriation and decolonization after the Second World War with a special focus on nationhood and citizenship issues.[28] However, no in-depth monographic analysis has been carried out to date on Italian citizenship and national identification that could provide readers with a much-needed comprehensive examination, in historical perspective and not limited to an Italian-language readership.

Our book takes up this challenge since it aims at filling the scholarly lacuna. As a history of Italian national citizenship, it necessarily has an "*a quo*" and an "*ad quem*." The *a quo* of our historical journey (i.e., the starting point) is the 1861 birth of the unified Italian kingdom—that is, the political unification of the country under the Savoy monarchy. The *ad quem* (i.e., the point of arrival) is 1950, representing the first period after the end of Savoy Italy and the birth of the Italian Republic. By taking these two historical years as the beginning and end of our voyage, this work focuses on the genesis of Italian monarchical subjecthood in 1861, on its historical developments throughout the liberal and fascist eras and on its end in 1946 with proclamation of the Republic of Italy and the birth and first developments of postwar Italian republican citizenship.

This broad periodization, covering almost ninety years of national history and going across pre- and post-1922 Italy, has been chosen in order to emphasize origins and evolutions of our theme, analyzed in the *longue durée*. This is an approach that allows researchers to stress continuities and discontinuities in their historical narratives, and in this way contribute to a wider historiographical debate that has been taking place especially among Italian historians since the end of the Second World War. These academic discussions, also explained in detail by Stefan Berger and Roberto Pertici,[29] touch on national history writing and its links with national identity formation following an "uncomfortable past" as the Duce's dictatorship and the tragedy of the Second World War. In particular, whereas some Italian historians such as Benedetto Croce, Adolfo Omodeo and Luigi Salvatorelli have argued about a basic discontinuity between Fascism and the Italian nation-state created by the Risorgimento, other historians such as Antonio Gramsci and Fabio Cusin (as well as Piero Gobetti and Guido Dorso, before them) have interpreted Fascism as the logical outcome of Italian national history.[30] Since the debate has been enriched throughout the postwar decades with a plurality of other historical discourses and national narratives,[31] it can be fruitful to provide, with our book, further findings about continuities and discontinuities between liberal and fascist Ital(ies) with the objective of adding food for thought on this historiographical roundtable.

Largely based on extensive archival research carried out in Italy (at the Archive and Library of the Italian Chamber of Deputies, at the Diplomatic Archive of the Ministry of Foreign Affairs, at the Historical Archive of the Italian Army and at the State Central Archive), this study examines the policies, debates and formal notions of citizenship in the peninsula with a view to grasping the vision of Italian national identity that they illuminate. Being a *political* history, this monograph is not a study in the legal theory, doctrine and jurisprudence of Italian citizenship. Instead, by differentiating and analyzing modes of acquisition and modes of exercise of national citizenship, it provides a systematic inquiry of the various citizenship policies and discourses that were successively formulated in the Italian kingdom as a recently unified national state, as a liberal constitutional entity granting differentiated rights to its female and male population, as a country of immigration and of emigration and as a late colonial power. It also covers the citizenship strategies that were introduced by monarchical Italy during the fascist era—this time, as an aspiring totalitarian state forging its female and male citizenry, as an expansionist fascist power aiming at creating a Second Roman Empire, and as an occupied and divided country after 8 September 1943. Third, it encompasses the initial civic developments in post–World War Two Italy, in this case as a republican state subject to the Allied peace settlement and trying to face its fascist past while embarking on the democratic road. Finally, highlighting precedents, continuities and breaking points within Italian national history, this work incorporates elements of comparison with other European experiences as well, and by drawing numerous times on French, British and German citizenship traditions it aims at bringing out fully the specificity of the Italian case study.

Clearly, the underlying premise of this book, implicitly mentioned at the beginning of the preceding paragraph (i.e., the relationship between citizenship and national identity), calls for further important clarifications—particularly, in light of academic discussions concerning the citizenship-nationhood nexus and involving Rogers Brubaker's and Patrick Weil's findings and writings.[32] Also, the historical perspective of this study combined with European comparisons requires further explanations of two fundamental factors: the historicity of the concept of citizenship as well as the terminological variety that characterizes discourses about "citizenship," "nationality" and "subjecthood" in different languages and countries.

The essential assumption underpinning our inquiry is that citizenship and national identity—citizenship and nationhood—are linked and related to each other in fundamental ways. Citizenship is indeed a precious source for examining and understanding the vision(s) of national self-identification developed in a country; as an academic field of study, it can therefore say a lot about notions and conceptions of the nation as well as notions and connotations of what it means to be part of that specific nation. To explain these assertions, we invite our readers to ponder what we can call "the mirror and pencil metaphors"—constituting and shaping the entire framework of this book on the history of Italian national citizenship and identity. As a *mirror*, citizenship can well reflect nationhood—although at times, and not automatically. More particularly, and bearing in mind Weil's well-demonstrated confutation of Brubaker's argument pertaining to France and Germany,[33] it is important to stress that citizenship principles and norms (i.e., *jus sanguinis*, *jus soli*, naturalization, residence and marriage) do *not* reflect nationhood *in themselves* and *by themselves* because there is no causal link between national identity and nationality laws. In effect, as pertinently illustrated by Weil, enshrinement of the rule of descent and of the territorial principle into a country's citizenship regime is subject to "legal transfers" and "imitations" between and among juridical traditions, across countries and across epochs—"legal transplants" that have nothing to do with concepts of the nation.[34] So, by looking at a citizenship rule, one cannot deduct and presume that such a norm is to be explained and attributed to specific cultural idioms of national self-identification because juridical principles and legal rules are independent from notions of national identity. Yet—and this is the point we want to make to revive, complicate and extend this lively debate—if one looks not at the norm in itself but at contingent use, appropriation, adaptation and application of a specific membership policy by the authorities of a country within a specific historical context and vis-à-vis different subjects, then one can uncover many interesting insights about concepts and definitions of a particular nation. In other words, a norm might well have been borrowed from another legal tradition and been shaped by the work of jurists, with no connections whatsoever to discourses regarding national belonging. In this respect, more evidence will also be provided from the Italian case study to give further strength to Weil's assertions within a broader European perspective. But when the work of jurists is used for realizing specific political objectives, or is differentially applied in a particular country according to the contexts and the subjects, or is discussed in broad political arenas, then one can indeed come across a reservoir of elements to understand many aspects and languages of national identification. So, it is the use and adoption of an apparently neutral and silent juridical norm within a particular context by specific authorities that, in certain cases, and in tandem with more explicit political and parliamentary debates pertaining to citizenship, can reflect, as a *mirror*, notions of membership in a nation.

Besides being a mirror for historical analysis, citizenship can well be a *pencil* for the historian. In fact, one can argue that citizenship is an academic source that can help the scholar sketch, visualize and draw the contours and content of national identity as they were shaped and defined by citizenship rules, policies and discourses at precise moments of national history. To be Italian, to become Italian and to exercise rights and duties in the peninsula as Italian citizens meant very different things at specific points of the historical journey carried out in this book. Metaphorically, the changing laws and debates concerning citizenship can certainly be useful pencils for researchers when trying to give form to and grasp the historically evolving and changeable meanings of *italianità*. Here, we are actually moving from "the Brubaker-Weil debate" to extend the scope of the citizenship analysis well beyond and incorporate a wider examination of the concept, both as a status in law and as a practice, in relation to the complex notion of national belonging within various historical contexts. In this way, we aim at applying to the Italian case study the broad, multidimensional and fruitful approach recently used to similarly discuss citizenship and national identity in twentieth-century Germany, notably in the collection of essays edited by Geoff Eley and Jan Palmowsky.[35]

So, to return to our two metaphors, both as a mirror and as a pencil for scholars citizenship can indeed shed valuable light on notions and visions of national identification. It does touch on meanings of Italian-hood in a significant way—Italianhood, Italianness, *italianità* and national identity being synonymous terms indicating the collective phenomenon of national belonging, sometimes distinguishable from, more often blurred with, other identities of the self. "National identity and the nation," says Anthony D. Smith, "are complex constructs composed of a number of interrelated components—ethnic, cultural, territorial, economic and legal-political. They signify bonds of solidarity among members of communities united by shared memories, myths and traditions that may or may not find expression in states of their own."[36] Also, as pointed out by Anna Triandafyllidou, as a collective and social identity, national identification is inherently dynamic, interactive, contextual, contested and evolving with time.[37] Our systematic and thorough study of Italian citizenship will attempt to grasp—with the help of mirrors and pencils—such a relational and collective phenomenon. Finally, since we will look at and discuss notions of nationhood in the Italian peninsula, it is pertinent to emphasize from the start the distinction between the terms *national identity* and *national character*, by referring in particular to the recent research by Silvana Patriarca on the history of the discourse(s) about the Italians' national character from the nineteenth century until the present day.[38] As already noted by this scholar, the two expressions have been and are often used interchangeably; yet they do not mean the same thing. In fact, "national character" refers to those objective dispositions made of moral and mental traits of a population (i.e., vices and virtues), while the expression "national identity" tends to incorporate a more subjective dimension of self-identification.[39] In our book, the major focus is on national identity, although at times some references are also made to the national character of Italy's population, especially when our findings might speak directly or indirectly to other scholarly works and related debates.

Having explained and justified the premise of our work, we now discuss two further concluding points concerning our historical perspective enriched with comparisons with other European countries. The first point refers to the aforementioned historical variety of meanings hidden behind use of the same word (citizenship), applied in different epochs. The term *citizenship* has in fact been employed over the centuries to mean numerous things with diverse contents. To take an example: the four-teenth-century medieval Florentine citizenship enjoyed by Dante was very different from the nineteenth-century membership status of Garibaldi as a deputy of the newly created Italian nation-state. Also, if one looks at the situation today, one can add that both statuses differ in many ways from the twenty-first-century citizenship enjoyed, for instance, by Italians in their increasingly multicultural country. The same term—*cittadinanza* (citizenship)—is employed in the three cases; but in the first, the term refers to collective rights and duties acquired through participation in a guild; in the second, to an individualized legal status enjoyed in a modern territorial kingdom; in the third, to membership within a contemporary democratic republic. A similar argument could indeed be made in reference to how the word *citizenship* was used in post-1861 Italy during the liberal and fascist epochs—studied in this book—or in any other country during other periods. Therefore, it is exactly this historical semantic diversity that calls for the ability of the historian to study "the word (citizenship)" and "the concept attached to that word" in a precise point in history, by analyzing both elements (the word and the concept) within their context and by neutralizing the scholar's human temptation of giving explanations and of making judgments on the basis of his or her contemporaneous conceptions of citizenship.[40]

As for linguistic and terminological varieties across countries, one should bear in mind that the terms *citizenship*, *nationality* and *subjecthood*—all essential for this research on the Italian case study—have been, and are being, applied in some languages either with peculiar meanings or, in certain cases, interchangeably—thus causing confusion and calling for some clarification.[41] Surely, a preliminary overview of these multiple uses—in Germany, Great Britain, France and Italy—is also useful before starting our historical journey in the peninsula.

Historically, in German legal terminology, there has been a fundamental difference between the use of *Staatsbürgerschaft* (meaning active participatory citizenship) and the more neutral term *Staatsangehörigkeit* (referring to formal state membership and deprived of any democratic connotation as the other term has). However, recent legislative bills in Germany tend now to use the two concepts interchangeably. Also and most interestingly, the formal relationship of *Staatsangehörigkeit* has always been dissociated from *Nationalität*—the latter being conceived as ethno-national belonging and referring to nation membership as a prepolitical category.[42]

This semantic differentiation between *Staatsangehörigkeit* and *Nationalität*, which still continues in present-day German discourse, has not characterized the history of the same terms in Great Britain and in France. In the English and later British state, the central concept of belonging was not "citizenship" but "subjecthood," the latter being based on the notion of allegiance owed by the subject to the Crown. The term *citizenship* has in fact lacked any relevant role, and even though it was used in English during the Middle Ages to denote the relationship of the individual to a city, it has remained a vague and fluid notion on the state and national levels. This was due in particular to the usual practice of replacing the ancient Roman concept of "citizen" with the English word *subject* while trying to accommodate Roman law into English legislation. So, absent in national discourse for centuries, the term *citizenship* would be introduced for the first time in British law only in 1948 with formulation of a new "citizenship of the United Kingdom and colonies" alongside the various citizenships of the self-governing dominions—and most confusingly, from a terminological point of view, within the framework of (one) unifying "British nationality" (the latter being used, since 1914, as a synonym with "subjecthood"). The English legal term *nationality* has, in fact, kept a neutral and different meaning from the German concept of *Nationalität*, replacing basically the word *subjecthood*—although, in international law, the English word *nationality* is also used interchangeably with *citizenship*, meaning state membership; thus explaining why today "British subjects," "British citizens" and "British nationals" could be one and the same category of people.[43]

In France, by contrast, the words *citoyen* (citizen) and *sujet* (subject), which had coexisted without any confrontation for centuries, were separated in abstract terms with the events of 1789. In fact, following the French Revolution, the notion of *citoyen*, as the active and participatory individual, was idealized and put at the core of the new revolutionary nation—now making the term indissoluble from the concept of popular sovereignty while delegitimizing the word *sujet* and using it pejoratively with a connotation of passivity. The terminological issue, though, which concerns us here, was to be complicated by the fact that the word *citoyen* was not deprived of a certain ambiguity due to an inherent "duality" that, formulated by the Abbé Sieyès and enshrined in a 1789 law, "divided" the concept of citizenship into "passive" and "active" variants. The first linked all citizens without distinction to the political nation; the second was reserved only for those who were eligible to participate in formulating the laws of the nation via political suffrage.[44] In addition to this, the word *nationalité* (nationality), applied before 1789 as meaning national feelings, from the 1880s became a legal term used in the same sense as the German *Staatsangehörigkeit*—that is, in the sense of state membership. So the French words *nationalité* and *citoyenneté* came to be used as synonyms—thus leading to a semantic fusion made possible because of the political definition of French nationhood and the fusion of the concepts of state, nation and sovereign people that took place in 1789 and that distinguished the French experience from its German counterpart.[45]

Finally, in the Italian language the word *cittadinanza* (citizenship) seems to have appeared for the first time in the fourteenth century as meaning the quality of citizen in a city; it is only at the end of the eighteenth century, following the French Revolution, that the term acquired the signification of being a member of a modern sovereign state.[46] By contrast, the relatively more recent term *nazionalità* (nationality), used since the nineteenth century, came to be applied with a peculiar double meaning that was to be retained in post-unification Italy as well. In particular, as will emerge clearly from this study, it was used as synonymous with "citizenship" (meaning juridical state membership) but also as a general cultural term indicating "the belonging of an individual to a nation" (*"appartenenza alla nazione"*) in analogy with the German use of *Nationalität* and deprived of any legal connotations. Moreover, in the chapters that follow, historical evidence demonstrates that in the post-1861 Savoy kingdom the words *sudditanza* (subjecthood), *cittadinanza* and *nazionalità* were very often applied interchangeably—thus making any possible semantic differentiation an interesting historical task.

Clearly, all these uses (abuses and misuses) of the words under consideration should be borne in mind. Also, the fact that these terms have been applied, and still are, as synonyms should be taken into account. Finally, it is important to remind our readers that unless clearly specified and explained, we have also employed the words interchangeably, as was largely done in liberal and fascist Italy; however, in many instances we have made a great effort to convey the historicity of a term by attempting to give its exact meaning as it was shaped in a particular context of Italian history. In this way, even though "the terminological problem" persists, at least we have faced it rather than avoid it. After all, writing in the Middle Ages, the Italian jurist Bartolus of Saxoferrato argued that "today [in the fourteenth century] we use this vocabulary [citizenship] broadly and improperly."[47] Surely, his comment is still very much valid for us as well, living in the twenty-first century.

Ready, now, to start our historical journey, we can delineate its detailed content. The book is divided into nine chapters, arranged in chronological and thematic order. Chapter One explores, for the first time in the scholarly literature as far as we are aware, the origins of Italian monarchical subjecthood and focuses on the 1859–1865 period since the territorial annexations that ultimately led to proclamation of the Italian kingdom in March 1861 and final approval of the first national Italian Civil Code in 1865 marked the genesis of Italian national citizenship in a profound way.

After bringing to light the birth of Italian monarchical subjecthood, this study then analyzes its historical evolution throughout the liberal decades (Part One) and during the fascist era (Part Two). Part One (Chapters Two through Five) covers the years from 1866 to 1922. In particular, Chapter Two explores Italian national citizenship from a female and a male perspective, thus focusing on gender issues, making Italian women

visible within our history and redressing an important imbalance that
has characterized citizenship studies for a long time. Chapter Three in-
vestigates citizenship policies vis-à-vis Italy's categories of foreigners (i.e.,
Italiani non regnicoli and non-Italian aliens), looking at the country's
little-known historical immigrants and discussing the related notions of
alienhood and Italianness. To complete this picture, the citizenship provisions and debates pertaining to Italian emigrants and to their settled
communities abroad are the subject of Chapter Four, which not only
adds further insights on the concept of *italianità* but also links Italy's civic
policies concerning emigration with those that were introduced vis-à-vis
immigration. Finally, by exploring the developments that took place following liberal Italy's expansionism in Africa and in the Mediterranean
Sea, Chapter Five examines the nonmetropolitan dimension of Italian
citizenship and looks at how the Italian state incorporated the native populations living in its African colonies, at the partially unknown policies
vis-à-vis those living in its Mediterranean occupied territories and at the
discourse(s) formulated on these civic issues before Mussolini took power.

After analyzing the historical evolution of Italian citizenship in the liberal period, this study concentrates on the major continuities and breaking
points pertaining to the citizenship issues and provisions that characterized the Italian peninsula during the entire fascist era—therefore not only
throughout the Duce's ventennium (1922–1943) but also during the relatively less-studied six hundred days of the Republic of Salò (1943–1945).
These twenty-three years of Italian history are covered in Part Two (Chapters Six through Eight)—avoiding the usual (and antihistorical) hole that
is made by jumping over the republican experience of Salò and going directly from the fascist ventennium to the 1946 birth of the Italian Republic. Chapters Six and Seven concern the years of Mussolini's premiership
and dictatorship in the peninsula, from October 1922 to July 1943. More
particularly, female citizenship and its male counterpart are explored and
discussed in Chapter Six, where, in line with the corresponding chapter on
liberal Italy, emphasis is put on gender issues within the specific historical
context of fascism. Leaving the peninsula, Chapter Seven is then entirely
devoted to the citizenship system introduced by Mussolini in Italy's African colonies and to the still largely neglected civic accommodation of the
populations living in all the European Mediterranean lands that were annexed or occupied by the regime until 1943. The aim is to discuss legislation and official discourse in comparison with the previous liberal colonial
variant. Finally, by focusing on citizenship issues in the Italian peninsula
following the fall of Mussolini's regime, the armistice of September 1943
and the division of the country, Chapter Eight delves into the civic developments of those controversial months of Italian history up to the end of
World War Two.

Having gone through liberal and fascist Ital(ies), this study then concludes our historical account on post-unification Italian monarchical subjecthood by dealing with the latter's death and by discussing the birth and first developments of Italian democratic republican citizenship. This is the topic of Chapter Nine, which examines the end of Italian subjecthood following the referendum of June 1946, the gradual shrinking of Italian citizenship due to the 1947 peace settlement with the Allies and the first defining characteristics of postwar Italian republican *status civitatis*.

From monarchical subjects to republican citizens and in comparison with other Europeans, the Italians have gone through a complex and fascinating process of national self-identification, which, analyzed in all chapters in its dynamic, evolving and sometimes contested forms, will then be discussed fully in the conclusion of the book.

CHAPTER ONE

National Risorgimento,
the Piedmontese Solution
and the Origins of Italian Monarchical
Subjecthood (1859–1866)

In March 1861, after almost thirteen centuries of political fragmentation and multiple states, the divided Italian peninsula was unified under the House of Savoy and the Italian kingdom proclaimed from the city of Turin. This Italian state stretched from the Western Alps to Sicily and excluded, for important reasons of international politics, the Venetian and the Roman provinces that remained under Austrian and pontifical rule until 1866 and 1870 respectively. Even though realized in a "truncated" way, the national ideal of political unification was finally achieved, thanks to a combination of skilled diplomatic negotiations, Piedmontese dynastic aspirations, French military interventions and mounting nationalist hopes.[1]

The historical developments leading to a unified Italy under the Savoy King Vittorio Emanuele II shaped and determined not only the Italian process of attaining independent statehood but also the origins of the national citizenship link that came to unite the "divided" peoples of the peninsula. In particular, the period from 1859 to 1866 establishes the historical roots of the post-unification juridical membership status that will subsequently develop throughout the liberal and the fascist epochs. The purpose of this first chapter is therefore to focus on this eight-year period of pre- and post-unification Italian history with a view to discussing the genesis and the first characteristics of the national civic bond uniting the Italians of the 1861 state within a peculiar context of internal divisions—linguistic, economic, social and mental—that were also enriched with specific racial considerations. In this way, the still relatively unknown and distant origins of to-day's Italian citizenship will finally emerge fully from the dust of archives and of public libraries.

I.I. THE SAVOY ROAD TO POLITICAL UNIFICATION AND THE
BIRTH OF ITALIAN MONARCHICAL SUBJECTHOOD (1859–1861)

The nineteenth-century period of Italian Risorgimento saw the burgeon-
ing of a variety of nationalist political programs that aimed in different
ways and through different means to accomplish the political unification of the Italian peninsula. These diverse nationalist projects ranged,
among others, from radical revolutionary republicanism—as personified
by Giuseppe Mazzini—to liberal Catholic patriotism—as represented by
Vincenzo Gioberti—to moderate liberal monarchism—as symbolized
by Camillo Benso di Cavour.

"Patriot and democrat, prophet and politician,"[2] the Genoese Mazzini
(1805–1872) strove for an Italy that in his view had to become a unitary and democratic republic, free from foreign occupation and enjoying statehood within the highest objective of contributing, with all other
nation-states, to the development of humanity. This optimistic and idealist program was a radical one and had to be carried out through both
education and popular insurrection.[3] The Piedmontese cleric Vincenzo
Gioberti (1801–1852), by contrast, a liberal-catholic, supporting neo-
Guelphian principles and seeking to reconcile a commitment to Italian
independence with loyalty to Catholicism, called for establishment of an
Italian confederation of existing rulers and states under the guidance and
the leadership of the pontiff.[4]

Eventually, both patriotic programs—the Mazzinian and the Giober-
tian—were to be overturned by events as the final outcome of the various revolutionary movements of the nineteenth century in the peninsula
demonstrated: on the one hand, popular insurrections lacked means, co-
ordination and common "patriotic" agendas; on the other hand, the Pope
would never declare war against a Catholic country (Austria) in the name
of Italian nationalism. And in fact, the road that ultimately led in a successful way to Italian statehood was the Savoy solution under the leadership of Vittorio Emanuele II and of his skillful Prime Minister Cavour.
The Savoy moderate program was characterized by a piecemeal approach
to Piedmontese leadership in the Italian peninsula and by a gradual project of political unification through Piedmontese territorial expansions to
be realized via international alliances, military aid, diplomacy, war and,
ultimately, the organization of plebiscites.[5]

Interestingly, had Mazzini's or Gioberti's visions been realized in practice—as to make unified Italy a republic, in the first case, and a confederation of states, in the second—their respective forms of statehood would
have led to two different citizenship links uniting all the populations
of the peninsula. In the first case, the Italians would have been linked
through a republican citizenship bond, similar, probably, to the status

that was enshrined in the 1849 constitution of the short-lived Roman Republic, where, after the flight of Pius IX to Gaeta, Mazzini's ideals were put into action and Mazzini himself elected as triumvir.[6] In the second case, on the contrary, since the peninsula would have become a political confederation under papal authority, the populations would have kept the current subjecthood related to each state and, probably, enjoyed an additional federal juridical link of pontifical loyalty—uniting all of them to the pope.

The history of Italian citizenship, though, was to take another course—ensuing from the actual historical process of Italian statehood as it took place between 1859 and 1861 under the Savoy dynasty. The reader will recall that in 1859 the Italian peninsula was divided into seven states: the Kingdom of Sardinia, the Austrian Kingdom of Lombardy-Venetia, the Duchy of Modena, the Duchy of Parma, the Grand Duchy of Tuscany, the Papal State and Legations as well as the Kingdom of the Two Sicilies. Because of the existence of these seven political territorial entities, an inhabitant of the Italian peninsula was linked to one of seven sovereigns via seven juridical links of subjecthood, according to the state from which the person originated. This is why, traveling to and across the pre-unification states of northern Italy, one encountered the "Piedmontese subjects" or "*regnicoli*" of King Vittorio Emanuele II, the "Austrian subjects" of Emperor Franz Joseph, the "Modenese subjects" of Duke Francesco V as well as the "Parmese subjects" of the regent Duchess Luisa Maria and of her son the Duke Roberto I.[7] Also, moving down the center and the south of the Italian boot, the same traveler found the "Tuscan subjects" of Grand-Duke Leopoldo II, the "Pontifical subjects" of Pope Pius IX and, finally, the "subjects of the Kingdom of the Two Sicilies" living in the Bourbon state of King Francesco II. Each of these populations enjoyed a status that was regulated according to the civil codes and legislation of the various Restoration states and, each link of subjecthood made a person, automatically, a foreigner in another state of the peninsula.[8]

Following the 1859 outbreak of hostilities against Austria, the Franco-Piedmontese victories in Magenta and Solferino as well as the subsequent armistice and treaties of Villafranca and Zurich (drawn up by the French and the Austrian emperors without any consultation with Turin), Piedmont was allowed to annex the region of Lombardy in December 1859. In the meantime, the power vacuum created by Austrian withdrawal and by the flight of the old rulers from Parma, Modena, Tuscany and the Papal Legations made possible conversion of local elites in central Italy to the idea of a union with the Kingdom of Piedmont. Within this context, Cavour's diplomatic negotiations, tacit approval by Napoleon III in exchange of Nice and Savoy, creation of pro-Piedmontese provisional governmental authorities in the pre-unification states and the results of national plebiscites carried out *in loco* through male universal suffrage led, in March 1860, to incorporation of Parma, Modena and Tuscany into the Savoy state as well as to the latter's annexation of the pontifical province of Bologna in the Romagne region. Finally, after the expedition of the Thousand Red Shirts led by Garibaldi as well as Cavour's risky, but successful, plan to recapture the initiative by sending Piedmontese troops headed by the king as well as by rapidly organizing further national plebiscites in the South, the Savoy state incorporated Sicily and the Neapolitan provinces in December 1860 and, in the same month, completed this territorial expansionist process with annexation of the pontifical provinces of Marche and Umbria. By March 1861, the first national parliament was elected; Vittorio Emanuele II was recognized as king of Italy and the European powers were notified of the official proclamation of *il Regno d'Italia* (the Kingdom of Italy).[9]

As the geographical borders of the Savoy state were gradually being extended in this way in 1859 and 1860, not only lands but also populations came under the sovereignty of Vittorio Emanuele II. Consequently, the already mentioned pre-unification subjecthood links that embodied the *status civitatis* of the populations living in each ex-Italian state went through a fundamental transformation on the basis of the so-called phenomenon of collective naturalizations—referring to the change of citizenship of an entire population after a territorial change has taken place. In fact, with only some minor individual exceptions, all the inhabitants of the annexed provinces became subjects of the Savoy king and lost their previous membership status.[10]

In particular, the people of annexed Lombardy—holding Austrian subjecthood—became *sudditi* (subjects) of Vittorio Emanuele II, except those who opted for keeping their Austrian juridical link (within one year from the ratification of the 1859 Zurich treaty) and emigrated to a part of the Austrian empire. A similar fate was also reserved for the pontifical subjects living in the annexed provinces of Romagne, Marche and Umbria as these inhabitants became *sudditi* of the Savoy House, except those who could provide explicit proof of wanting to keep their pontifical subjecthood (for instance, by accepting a governmental function in a commune that was still under papal rule). This means that with the exclusion of very limited individual cases in which the liberal principle of giving priority to the person's will was taken into account, all these people living in the north and in the center of the peninsula became Savoy subjects *en masse*. Finally, the populations of Parma, Modena and Tuscany as well as those of the Bourbon Kingdom of the Two Sicilies acquired the monarchical subjecthood of the Savoy dynasty, but contrary to the Austrian Lombards and to the just-mentioned pontifical subjects, they were not given the right of option because the Duchies of Parma and Modena, the Grand-Duchy of Tuscany and the Southern Kingdom disappeared with their final incorporation into the Savoy state and were abolished together with their pre-unification citizenship status. Clearly, within this context the inhabitants concerned could not have been granted a right of option because their previous subjecthood no longer existed and there was no alternative membership status to opt for.[11]

In short, while the Savoy state expanded geographically, the demographic circle of its subjects grew accordingly as the legal status uniting the residents of the Italian lands was now Savoy monarchical subjecthood. This means that both the historical process of Italian statehood and the genesis of Italian national post-unification citizenship are directly linked to the Restoration state (and to the dynasty) that took the lead and accomplished successfully the political unification of Italy. This is why, from a strictly juridical point of view, the 1861 Kingdom of Italy is "the ex-Piedmontese kingdom with a new name" (*Regno d'Italia*) and with new borders.[12] And this is why, as shown by our findings, the 1861 Italian monarchical subjecthood (*sudditanza del Regno d'Italia*) is former Piedmontese subjecthood—as it had been extended from Piedmont-Sardinia to all the new provinces—with a new name, acquired with the official proclamation of March 1861.[13] A juridical continuity exists, therefore, between the two membership statuses; however, from the historian's perspective, such legal continuity is also enriched with a "new" national flavor because from March 1861 Savoy monarchical subjecthood was no longer Piedmontese but Italian. It is the historical change of name (from Kingdom of Piedmont to Kingdom of Italy) that brings about a new national era for the *sudditanza* of the peninsula, although from the standpoint of international law both the 1861 state and its related monarchical subjecthood are not new entities.

So, when the first national parliament proclaimed the birth of *il Regno d'Italia*, the people who were united under Vittorio Emanuele II became *sudditi italiani* (Italian subjects), or as they were also called, *regnicoli* of the Italian kingdom. Similarly to many countries in other epochs, the expression *cittadini* (citizens) was applied as well and used as a synonymous word despite the fact that from a historical standpoint the term *cittadinanza* (citizenship) should refer to a more substantial and "thicker" status, involving the active participation of the individual, than the word *sudditanza* (subjecthood), which usually connotes an idea of passive relationship between the sovereign and the subject.

As *sudditi italiani*, they now shared the same national monarchical bond that, from a theoretical point of view, was based on the traditional principle of "allegiance" owed by the subjects to their sovereign and making the sovereign, in return, provide them with "protection." This special abstract relationship, created around what we can call the "allegiance-protection binomial," is common to monarchical states and draws its origins from the ancient feudal tenet of allegiance that the writer Robert Kiefé defines in this way: "Allegiance is the feudal obligation of fealty and obedience which a vassal owes to his overlord, an obligation which has its counterpart in the protection, guardianship, that the lord owes to his vassal."[14]

In other words, between the sovereign and the subject—"the legal superior and the legal inferior"—there is a double and reciprocal tie that binds them mutually since "*protectio trahit subjectionem et subjectio protectionem*"; the King's guardianship entails the subjects' duty of obedience vis-à-vis the monarch and, *ex adverso*, the subjects' loyalty entails the monarch's protection.[15] Obviously this is a royal link that, even though imagined, nonetheless unites all subjects of a territory to the same king, as well as distinguishing in a very clear way the *sudditi* (subjects) from the *stranieri* (aliens). In fact, the obligation of allegiance owed to the Crown is not expected from foreigners, although the latter have to respect the laws of a country if they emigrate there.[16]

Savoy monarchical subjecthood was therefore the first institutional cement binding the populations of the peninsula together, the first *national* juridical link that started uniting the twenty-two million Italians of the 1861 state after centuries of political fragmentations.

1.2. LEFTOVERS FROM THE RESTORATION PERIOD: CIVIC DIVISIONS IN THE UNIFIED PENINSULA (1861–1865)

Despite the creation of a politically united Italy and the initial civic merger of the Italians, the post-1861 *regnicoli* continued to be "divided" paradoxically from a citizenship perspective that has been overlooked by historians and that will finally be brought to light. This issue concerns the fact that geographic civic divisions persisted for another five years of post-unification history because of important legal and administrative civic frontiers that were to be dismantled only in 1866.

During this period, the Italians were in fact subject to a variety of citizenship (or subjecthood) norms, some of which were applied in the entire Savoy state in a uniform way (because they had been extended to all the annexed provinces) whereas others were in force only regionally according to the political geography of the pre-unification ex-Italian states. This peculiar application of "national" and "regional" provisions was due to the fact that in the aftermath of the 1861 proclamation the young and weak Italian nation-state had to face a plethora of pressing problems menacing its very existence (e.g., the brigands' war in the South, high military expenses, serious budget deficits) and therefore had to postpone the national legislative unification that was needed to unite the peninsula—internally—by introducing and extending the same laws over the entire country. Consequently, until 1865, when national legislative unification was finally approved, most of the civil norms of the pre-1859 Restoration states were kept in force in unified Italy.[17]

This factor created a very peculiar situation around the country because the unifying link of Italian monarchical subjecthood—stretching over the entire Savoy state—found itself face to face with the divisive pre-1859 citizenship arrangements that were still in force after 1861 and that applied differently in say, Milan, Pisa or Palermo, according to the legislation of a particular area of unified Italy. At the same time as the Italians were pooled together through one and the same national tenet of allegiance, they were being separated by the numerous and diverse civic rules that, inherited from the pre-unification era, reproduced basically the ancient divisions of the past.

For instance, until 1865, even though all the inhabitants of the unified country were *sudditi italiani*, how a person was ascribed Italian subjecthood at birth differed according to geography. Monarchical subjecthood was in fact transmitted *jure sanguinis* in the entire territory of the 1861 state, and therefore a child born to an Italian father (or in certain limited cases to an Italian mother) was a subject; however, the extent to which the *jus soli* principle could be applied in combination with the rule of descent varied. More particularly, since birth on Italian soil did not have a bearing on the child's membership status according to the still-valid civil code of Parma and to the grand-ducal laws of Tuscany, children born from a foreign father, say, in the northern city of Piacenza and in Florence were aliens at birth and kept their foreign status all their life unless they naturalized. Hence, in this part of the unified peninsula, the *jus sanguinis* rule was applied in an exclusive way. By contrast, in the areas of Piedmont, Romagne, Marche and Umbria, where the Sardinian code was applicable, the children of foreign parents were *sudditi italiani* at birth upon specific conditions (i.e., the child was born in the kingdom and the father had been living in Italy for ten consecutive years), whereas the same offspring, born in the Italian territories that were once part of the ex-Duchy of Lucca and of the ex-Kingdom of the Two Sicilies, would be alien at birth but with a right to claim the quality of national within one year after attaining the age of twenty-one. This means that in Turin, Lucca, Naples and Palermo the *jus sanguinis* rule was complemented with elements of *jus soli* and that the latter differed according to the city concerned.[18]

A fundamental consequence of this variety in ascribing monarchical subjecthood is that the concepts of *suddito* and *straniero* (subject and foreigner) were not being defined uniformly during the first five years of post-unification Italy. Consequently, the national concept of *italianità* was being shaped in a nonhomogeneous way. Also, whereas children of foreign parents would be automatically drafted in those parts of the peninsula in which the Sardinian code was in use (because they were subjects at birth upon certain conditions), those living in Lucca's territories and in the southern Italian provinces did not, because they were aliens—and only by making a declaration within one year after majority would they have become subjects, and thus potential soldiers. As a result, the national and nationalizing system of the barracks could be avoided by some, and the duty of dying for one's country be shared in an unequal way. And in fact, as shown by archival evidence, the children of foreign fathers who were "wrongly" drafted in southern Italy during the 1861–1865 period claimed the right to have their names erased from the recruitment list because the civil code of the Kingdom of the Two Sicilies—still in force in those lands—allowed them to do so. Eventually, all their claims were successful (and therefore the exemption from the draft was granted) because as "noncitizens" these children of foreign fathers did not have the duty to do military service.[19]

Two further examples that show the regional and anti-unitary application of citizenship provisions between 1861 and 1865 concern the issue of naturalization of first-generation immigrants on the one hand, and of loss of status on the other. Since an 1859 (Piedmontese) law regarding acquisition of monarchical subjecthood via naturalization had been extended during the annexation period over the peninsula, the distinction made by pre-1859 Piedmontese authorities between naturalization of "non-Italian foreigners" and that of "the Italians of the other [nonannexed] provinces" continued to be applied in 1861 within the entire Savoy kingdom.[20] This topic—concerning non-Italian immigrants and so-called *Italiani non regnicoli*—will be analyzed in great detail in Chapter Three. What interests us here is that the specific requirements that had to be fulfilled by non-Italian immigrants in order to become subjects of Vittorio Emanuele II differed within the 1861 Savoy state according to the norms that were valid in the city or in the village where the foreigner lived. For instance, aliens living in the south of the peninsula could naturalize after only one continuous year of domicile if they had rendered important services to the state, distinguished themselves for a special talent or bought property in the kingdom. Alternatively, they could become *sudditi* after fulfilling the requirements of ten consecutive years of residence and economic independence, or of five years of residence and marriage with a subject. By contrast, in the northern region of annexed Lombardy, where apparently

Austrian rules still regulated the naturalization process, foreigners could acquire subjecthood by getting a job in the civil service, by starting a profession that required ordinary domicile in the country, or after ten continuous years of stay. Also, if none of these requirements could be fulfilled, the person could then ask directly Italian political authorities to make a discretionary decision on the basis of the foreigner's patrimony, industry and moral conduct. Finally and most importantly, in the geographical areas of Piedmont, Romagne, Marche and Umbria, where the Sardinian code was the rule, the naturalized Italians who left the country for more than one year (without the permission of the sovereign) could be denaturalized, whereas this was not the case for those who had acquired Italian subjecthood in the other parts of the kingdom.[21] So the naturalization process—necessary for foreigners to become Italian—differed according to the legal landscape of the unitary state, and therefore the concepts of "alienhood" and of "becoming a national" were variable notions.

The issue concerning loss of subjecthood by all *sudditi* was also defined regionally. In fact, whereas the *regnicoli* of the 1861 state would lose their Italian monarchical status in many parts of the kingdom if the individual naturalized abroad, accepted a public job for a foreign country without the authorization of the Italian government or took permanent domicile overseas with no intention of returning, those who originated from Lombardy—still subjected to severe Austrian emigration legislation—would additionally lose their *sudditanza* after living outside the country for ten years, or after only five years if they had moved abroad with their family.[22] Finally, whereas an Italian subject from Turin who naturalized abroad without the sovereign's permission did not cease having the duties and responsibilities related to his original subjecthood (hence the person was not exempted from doing military service), his Neapolitan compatriot who acquired other status abroad (even without the permission of his government) lost the quality of subject, and with it the rights and duties attached to it. This means, again, that losing the "*qualité d'Italien*" was delineated in disparate ways around the country and that the national responsibility of serving the state through compulsory conscription was circumvented—with important consequences for a unifying idiom of Italian nationhood.[23]

Within this peculiar context, an Italian parliamentary commission asked in January 1865, "How can we not feel ourselves disheartened by this bitter variety of laws that makes the Italians of the various provinces almost foreigners among themselves?"[24]

The political borders that had disappeared within the peninsula following national Risorgimento continued to exist between 1861 and 1865—replaced, basically, by the invisible civil frontiers, leftovers from the Restoration period and still drawn and sanctioned by law. This anti-unitary situation had to be brought to an end, and soon, especially now that, as the patriotic writer and politician Massimo D'Azeglio wrote in his autobiographic work, "it is necessary to make the Italians if one wants to have Italy; and [...], once they are made, then indeed Italy will do by itself."[25]

1.3. STARTING TO "MAKE THE ITALIANS" THROUGH A UNIFYING SYSTEM OF NATIONAL CITIZENSHIP (1865–66)

Since the civic divisions and the variety of legal systems described here made the Italians a divided people in a politically unified country, the successive liberal governments of the Destra Storica (Historical Right)—from the premiership of Cavour (March–June 1861) to that of Alfonso Ferrero della Marmora (1864–1866)—discussed at great length the importance of achieving legislative unification with a view to strengthening Italy's recently acquired status as a nation-state. In particular, harmonized application of the same laws, codes and citizenship provisions at the national level was seen as a state instrument to link the country and the people, as railways were similarly being built to link the territories of the various provinces of the peninsula. Train tracks would unite by cutting across and sewing up the geographical lands of the country; identical civic norms around the country would unite by dismantling the invisible legal borders within the circle of the national citizenry.

The great attention given by the young Italian state to civil legislative unification and to introduction of unitary citizenship arrangements as part of a larger legislative project of unifying the civil, penal and commercial branches of domestic law emerges by looking at the numerous proposals that were made at the time in order to formulate a new civil code for the unitary state. In fact, between 1861 and 1863, the subsequent ministers of justice Giovanni Battista Cassinis, Vincenzo Miglietti and Giuseppe Pisanelli presented three bills before parliament for approval of new national civil norms that would abolish the normative particularisms and regionalisms still in force around the peninsula. Later, in November 1864, as none of these projects had reached the final parliamentary stage and the imminent transfer of the Italian capital to Florence made the issue even more urgent (since Tuscany was still largely and exceptionally ruled by uncodified Roman law), Italy's new minister of justice, Giuseppe Vacca, made a fourth and final proposal. The latter, based on the previous three, was eventually approved by both chambers of parliament in February and March 1865 and, by entering into force on 1 January 1866, finally abrogated the legal mosaic of Restoration provisions explored in the previous section of this chapter.[26]

Interestingly, the official discourse of those years emphasized consistently the link between national political unification and the need to have a single civil code with the same citizenship rules that would be shared by all *regnicoli* of the Italian kingdom. Opening the floor at the chamber of deputies on 24 November 1864, Minister Vacca made the point very clearly:

[T]he need for legislative unification is universally regarded as an indispensable element in firmly cementing Italian unity. And to tell the truth, badly can one have unity of the kingdom when the quality of Italian citizen is acquired in a different manner in the various parts in which Italy was divided in the past; when the status of persons is governed by a diversity of laws in the various provinces; [...] lastly when the citizen, accused of a misdeed, does not find the same guarantees in the whole territory of the State.[27]

Peninsulawide citizenship rules would therefore be a key tool to fortify Italian integration, whereas the still-persistent implementation of myriad pre-unification norms was only "a flagrant negation" of national unification.[28] In effect, not only did the current legal mosaic remind Italy of its former political divides but it also contributed to continuation of those past fragmentations by legally preventing amalgamation of the populations of the Italian state.[29] Hence, as Senator Diodato Pallieri argued in the high chamber, it was about time to get rid of all the "clashing codes and Bourbon, Pontifical, Austrian laws etc. and to replace them with legislation which, be one and Italian."[30]

These nationalist arguments were so widespread that numerous other voices sang in unison from the parliamentary benches to convey the same political message: for instance, in the words of deputy Raffaele Conforti, a unitary code would make Italy "completely united" and finally "a nation."[31] It would lead to "practical accomplishment of the unity of our fatherland," exclaimed deputy Giuseppe Massari,[32] and it would consolidate "the unity of the Italians' civic life, the nationality, the unity of the homeland," as Pisanelli put it.[33] This was an urgent and vital step to be taken especially because, as minister Vacca emphasized in another speech, Italy had recently achieved its political unification and therefore lacked the old traditions of national statehood enjoyed by other European powers.[34] Also, as deputy Antonio Mordini argued, there existed a special need to unify Italy's internal laws and rules because of the contemporary context in which a mounting menace of anti-unitary (Austrian and Pontifical) reactions destabilized, from outside, the recently created Italian kingdom.[35] And finally, as reiterated in a contemporary senatorial report, the introduction of a statewide code was a measure not only to make all Italians citizens of a same fatherland but also to tell Italy's European partners that nothing could stop the country from continuing to pursue the road of national unity.[36] Formulation of a single text containing uniform citizenship arrangements would therefore contribute to strengthening the political, cultural and social dimensions concerning the interrelated processes of Italian statehood and Italian nationhood.

The citizenship provisions that were eventually approved in 1865 and implemented from January 1866 were quite similar, and in some cases identical, to those that had been in force in the pre-unification period in numerous Restoration states. In fact, while criticizing the anti-unitary aspect of geographic application of all the various codes of the previous decades, the 1861 Italian authorities emulated and magnified most of their content (with a predilection for liberal and generous rules), this being due to their century-old developments, their Napoleonic source and their ancient Roman origins. This means, therefore, that in line with Weil's point on the way nationality laws work, "legal borrowings" and "imitations" did take place in the Italian peninsula as well.[37]

In particular, and to take only one example but an eloquent one, pertaining to transmission of Italian citizenship via the *jus sanguinis* and *jus soli* principles, we shall demonstrate—in reference again to "the Brubaker-Weil debate"—how the French innovation of embracing the rule of descent in the 1804 civil code had an impact on the Italian peninsula and, most importantly, that the Italian emulation (in line with its French model) was not "ethnically motivated" but based on the assumption that "family links" transmitted through "the pater familias" were more important than the principles of territorial subjecthood and *jus soli*.[38] And finally, to extend our inquiry, a discussion will follow to show how the choice and the combination of specific juridical norms in Italy's first national civil code started drawing specific contours of the concept of *italianità* so as to make the latter more open and less exclusive than the contemporary post-unification notion of Germanness. In this way, some important aspects of the specificity of the Italian case study shall begin to emerge within a broader European comparative perspective.

In 1865, the Italian state continued to ascribe monarchical subjecthood (equally called *cittadinanza italiana*, Italian citizenship) according to the rule of bloodline, as it had been doing since 1861. In fact, by applying the principle of paternal transmission of nationality as the first norm and of maternal *jus sanguinis* as a secondary rule (only if the father was unknown), children of Italian nationals were Italians at birth—no matter whether they were born in the kingdom or abroad. Moreover, should both parents be unidentified, Italian citizenship was conferred exceptionally *jure soli* in order to avoid statelessness (*apolidìa*).[39]

During the debates that led to legislative approval, the choice in favor of *jus sanguinis* was tied at the time to a critique of unconditional *jus soli*, and in fact no one actually contemplated automatic attribution of

Italian citizenship at birth to every person born in the kingdom. Speaking respectively on 16 and 17 February 1865, deputies Pisanelli and Mancini emphasized and criticized the feudal connotation of the *jus soli* rule and argued that taking the territorial norm as the first, the only and the supreme citizenship principle meant, basically, going backwards—that is, returning to feudalism and to the time when man was "an accessory of soil."[40] Making all children born in Italy automatically Italian at birth (including those of foreign immigrants) was therefore considered an inferior norm and associated with a historical epoch that should no longer be emulated. By contrast, the rule of descent was praised at great length during parliamentary discussions, and here again Mancini was very eloquent on this point. Seeing the transmission of citizenship *jure sanguinis* as the "hyphen" uniting the-child-the-father-the-family-and-the-nation (no matter the infant's birthplace), the Italian deputy and professor intoned a *magnificat* on the rule of descent that has remained memorable in the annals of the Italian parliament. As he put it:

Man is born member of a family and, since the nation is an aggregate of families, man is a citizen of the nation to which belongs his father, his family. The place where a person is born, the one where a person has domicile or residence has no value or meaning. And worthy of praise be the novel Code which has paid homage to this great principle by proclaiming Italian the person born in whichever place to an Italian father, namely to an Italian family.[41]

So, as this passage demonstrates, transmission of nationality via bloodline was seen as the supreme citizenship norm and explicitly upheld by drawing, as in France in 1804, on discourses emphasizing the priority of the *jus familiae* over the feudal *jus soli*—the former originating from Roman law and spread through continental Europe via the French civil code, the latter coming from England. In other words, by adding Italian historical evidence to Weil's already mentioned argument, we see clearly that past and foreign legal borrowings constantly took place, and continue to take place, within the formulation of nationality laws.[42] Also, it is clear that embracing the rule of descent—in Italy as in France—had no ethnic connotations but was a way of reviving Roman law.

To criticize unconditional *jus soli*, though, and to put emphasis upon the link *jus-sanguinis*-the-child-the-father-the-nation, did not mean that the rule of descent should be used on its own on the peninsula. Italian citizenship did not have to be attributed, exclusively, to children of Italian parents. In fact, the 1865 authorities diluted the rule of bloodline with some elements of territoriality. In our previous section we emphasized that the extent to which the *jus soli* rule was applied between 1861 and 1865 varied around the country and ranged from "total absence" (i.e., second-generation immigrants born in Italy could become Italian only through naturalization) to a "relatively substantial extent" (i.e., the same second generations were aliens at birth but had a right to become Italian at majority) to a "large extent" (i.e., Italian citizenship was ascribed at birth if the double requirement of the child's birth and the father's decennial domicile applied). In 1865, the liberal state approved and blended the second and third of these solutions by also adding more generous modifications to extend the group of second generations issued from immigration with a right to acquire Italian membership status. More particularly, if a child of a foreign father was born in the kingdom and the father had been living in Italy continuously for ten years, the infant was Italian at birth, with a right to claim the quality of foreigner in a declaration to be made within one year from majority. Also, if the father lacked the decennial domicile, the child born in the kingdom was an alien but had a right to acquire Italian citizenship at majority by making a declaration, or alternatively by accepting a public job with the Italian government, joining the army or navy, or responding to a call to arms.[43]

During the debates, neither Mancini nor any other deputies or senators proposed to have an exclusive reliance on the *jus sanguinis* principle and to erase, for this reason, any trace of *jus soli* from the proposed text. Some considerations about territoriality had to be reflected in the citizenship arrangements—although, as Pisanelli reiterated on 16 February 1865, the rule on descent was to have a predominant position.[44] Taking the floor on the same day, the Sicilian lawyer and future prime minister Francesco Crispi gave an initial impression of being in favor of granting Italian *status civitatis* by using the *jus soli* norm in a more extensive way: "[C]itizenship, gentlemen, is given by the soil in which one is born; every individual born in the kingdom of Italy is an Italian citizen."[45] However, Crispi did not explain or make any particular defense of his assertion and did not argue, as one would have expected, in favor of conferring citizenship at birth upon all children born in the kingdom from foreign fathers; in fact, he simply accepted the proposition that they could claim Italian citizenship at majority.[46] Also, in the already mentioned projects of civil codes presented by Miglietti and Pisanelli in 1862 and 1863, an interesting provision was incorporated concerning not only the second generations issued from foreign immigrants but also the third. In particular, a child born in the kingdom from a foreign father (also born in the kingdom, or with ten years of domicile) would have been Italian at birth with a right to opt for foreignness by making a declaration within one year from majority.[47] Therefore, by contemplating the so-called rule of double *jus soli*, these two proposals put great emphasis on territorial considerations. However, this latter norm was not reproduced in the final text of the 1865 code, and on the basis of the archival material that we were able to gather, it seems that neither the proponents nor the various parliamentarians who studied Pisanelli's and Miglietti's texts defended, disapproved or even mentioned this issue.[48] Also, despite the references made to the previous post-unification projects of civil codes during the final discussions of 1865, nothing was said in parliament about these specific provisions—not even by Pisanelli himself, who, as we have seen, proposed the text (inclusive of double *jus soli*) but did not refer to it two years later when discussing Vacca's subsequent project. Surely, the imminent transfer of the Italian capital from Turin to Florence and the urgency to approve legislative unification of the country as soon as possible explain the fact that not all citizenship questions were covered and that several of them were actually skipped during the hearings.

According to our findings, we can therefore conclude that the superiority of the *jus sanguinis* rule over the feudal territorial norm of unconditional *jus soli* was indisputable in the peninsula and that no proposition was made to attribute citizenship at birth on the basis of this second tenet alone. Italian authorities, though, did not defend exclusive use of *jus sanguinis* but combined it with elements of territoriality. The extent to which the rule of descent was diluted with the principle of *jus soli* was quite substantial in the final text of 1865 as explored above.

This situation makes the nineteenth-century Italian case study very different from the contemporary post-unification German counterpart. In fact, on the basis of Brubaker's account on citizenship in Germany and of Andreas Fahrmeir's revisionist work, we know that attribution of German citizenship, enshrined in the 1870 North German Federation's citizenship code, in the contemporary legislation of each individual German state, and in the 1871 policy replacing the words "North German" with the term "Imperial," did not include, in any form, *jus soli* at birth for children of non-German aliens born in Germany.[49] This means that the category of offspring issued from non-German immigration remained foreigners indefinitely (unless the individual naturalized under specific conditions). Also, this German citizenship situation points to the fact that the notion of being German in the initial post-unification period was being shaped in a more exclusionary way than the notion of being Italian during the same epoch. In fact, in stark contrast with the German example, 1865 Italy endorsed a relatively inclusive definition of national citizenship that, together with the *jus sanguinis* rule, took into account the presumption that birth combined with long years of settlement in the country as well as with civil and military service rendered to the state were sufficient factors to transform aliens into Italians. So, we can argue that in 1865 the Italian citizenship policy pertaining to *jus sanguinis* in combination with *jus soli* made the concept of "being Italian" much more inclusive than its German counterpart shaped by contemporary German citizenship arrangements. It is the presence of the territorial principle of *jus soli* on the peninsula and its absence in Germany that made the difference; clearly, the contours of *italianità*, as drawn by these initial citizenship rules, were more flexible, open and receptive of elements of foreignness than the corresponding contours characterizing Germanness.

1.4. NATIONAL UNIFICATION, RACIAL THINKING AND *ITALIANITÀ*

The civic Italian unity that started in 1861 (with introduction of a single monarchical subjecthood) and that was given a boost in 1866 (with implementation of a single civil code) was by no means uncomplicated and uncontested. In fact, since the beginning it took a very peculiar form because it occurred not only within a well-known context of regional, linguistic, social and economic divides often emphasized by scholars of Italian history[50] but also within a background of "racial representations of the South" and of "mental divisions" within the peninsula as recently discussed by Aliza S. Wong.[51]

Throughout the first years of territorial unification, and in the subsequent decades as well, the inhabitants of the Italian South (the Mezzogiorno) were often considered, imagined and depicted as disturbing "Others" in some official quarters.[52] In particular, drawing on a pre-1861 European reservoir of intellectual representations of southern Italy as "non-European" and "barbarous," various Italian voices around the country saw southerners as being "backward" and "inferior." For example, in October 1860, after being sent to the South by Cavour, the head administrator Luigi Carlo Farini wrote to the Piedmontese prime minister: "But my friend, what kind of lands are these . . . ! What barbarity! This is not Italy! This is Africa: the Bedouin, in comparison to these hicks, are the flower of civil virtue."[53]

These words were not rarely used. And in fact almost three years later, in February 1863, Italian General Nino Bixio argued in a letter to his spouse that the southern region of Puglia had to be "depopulated" and its people "sent to Africa to make them civilized."[54] Finally, among other officials who were sent to, or fought against brigandage in, the South, Alessandro Bianco di Saint Jorioz stands out for having said, "Here we are among a population who, although in Italy and born Italian, seems to belong to the primitive tribes of Africa."[55] Clearly, references to race and racial considerations, including all the related stereotypes, were neither unknown nor absent in Italy at the time. Racial thinking and the discourse of race, meaning by these broad terms "racialized and racist ways of seeing the world and representing it,"[56] were phenomena that did not spare the Italian boot. Most importantly, distinct racial formulations were being addressed by some nationals vis-à-vis a part of Italy's citizenry since the beginning of the unification process.

This metaphorical language of difference, rich in negative tropes and images, was also combined with specific discussions regarding the actual political union of the country, which, according to these discourses, was taking place between an economic and moral vanguard north, on the one side, and a Mezzogiorno whose lack of development simply echoed the vices and uncivilized level of its populace, on the other. Within this intellectual and political context (which will lead in the immediately subsequent years to debates concerning the so-called Southern Question), discourses were multiple and varying as they ranged from explicit objections made by some northerners who saw unification as "distasteful" and "perilous" to a language legitimizing the "civilized and moral rule" of the north over the south, to metaphors of the Mezzogiorno as a "plague" or "gangrene" that needed systematic and comprehensive treatment from the northern surgeon.[57] Thus by using our findings in conversation with the scholars mentioned here, we can emphasize the fact that, "united" by the juridical bond of monarchical subjecthood, the Italians of 1861 became part of a national collectivity that, although it combined national unity with regional diversity, was at the same time in tension with its "internal others" and at times even racialized them.

In some important additional discourses concerning regionalism in general, the notion of post-1861 *italianità* was considered large enough to accommodate all the diverse regional identities of the peninsula. For instance, speaking in 1864, the minister of public education, Francesco De Sanctis, said: "Becoming Italians we do not have to cease being Neapolitans. Italy can be proud of having at its breast the richest differences that render proud the Lombard, the Tuscan, the Neapolitan, the Piedmontese, the Roman, the Sicilian; it is a nation that has in itself the richness of many nations."[58] From this perspective, Italianness was therefore perceived as being an inclusive concept that would welcome all the cultural richness of the country. Inclusive and all-embracing, though, it was questioned since the very first years through the racialized idioms discussed in these pages.

This is a fundamental point that is also in line with the recent revisionist work edited by Alberto Burgio, confuting a previous Italian historiographical vulgate that has basically depicted the history of Italy and of its national state as immune to any racialization and racial ideology, and therefore a unique and gentle case compared to other European national experiences.[59] The southerner, typically seen in previous centuries as diverse and primitive, was an "external other" in the pre-unification epoch because at that time the various kingdoms in the South were states not yet incorporated into a politically united Italy. From 1861 onward, though, this otherness became "internal"[60] and, arguably, a significant mental and intellectual factor of tension and divisiveness within the unifying nature of national citizenship. So, since its institutional birth, the union of all populations of the peninsula through monarchical subjecthood had to face and compete with all these factors within a context of contrasting and simultaneous discourses on inclusiveness and exclusiveness.

1.5. CONCLUSION

The origins of today's Italian national citizenship go back to the nineteenth century and to the historical as well as geographical process of statehood that took place in the peninsula under King Vittorio Emanuele II. The once-divided Italian populations were in fact gradually united around the tenet of Savoy monarchical allegiance and from March 1861 transformed into *sudditi italiani*, sharing the same monarchical bond at the national level throughout the entire *Regno d'Italia*. This unifying link of subjecthood, though, was to be menaced—as soon as Italy was unified politically—by the corrosive effect of certain divisive civic provisions, which were inherited from the Restoration past and continued to be applied in the unified country on a geographical basis. The legal regional arrangements touching upon the life of the twenty-two million *regnicoli* of the Italian kingdom made the concept of *italianità* a variable and unequal notion, thus putting the process of statehood and nationhood in peril. This is why, within the context of national Risorgimento, the young Italian state strove to introduce a single civil code that, by containing the same citizenship provisions for all the Italians of the kingdom, would contribute to realization of the institutional objective of making the Italians, now that Italy had been made. National citizenship policies were therefore seen—since the beginning of Italian post-unification history—as a fundamental component of the country's domestic policy to consolidate the recently acquired status as a nation-state by fortifying the internal cohesion of the national citizenry. The enormous task of shaping a new "Italian" membership status from the former Piedmontese, Parmese, Modenese, Tuscan, Austrian Lombard, Pontifical and Bourbon links of subjecthood was just beginning. . . . It was indeed an enormous and formidable task, bearing in mind that besides regionalism, the unifying notion of one Italian monarchical subjecthood was being complicated by the presence of persistent mental divisions that tended to racialize southern Italian citizens and make them internal others.

At this point of our analysis, we can take the reader to the First Part of the book, explore specific historical developments of Italian national citizenship as they took place throughout the liberal period from 1866 until 1922 and provide further citizenship aspects that, as we shall demonstrate in subsequent chapters, can shed light in different ways on the multiple links and relations between national citizenship and national identity.

PART ONE

Historical Developments During the Liberal Period
(1866–1922)

CHAPTER TWO

"Becoming Visible"

Italian Women and Their Male Co-Citizens
in the Liberal State

The history of the civic umbilical cord linking the Italian subjects to their
state is a "divided" history—as in many other countries—since women
and men have been part of it on different terms. Most importantly, when
women would appear formally absent from this history, they were, in
fact, present: the only thing is that they could not be seen because their
citizen status was in the shadow of their fathers, brothers, husbands and
sons. Citizenship—understood both as a mode of acquisition and a mode
of exercise—has touched the lives of women and men in various ways
and through distinct paths. For instance, throughout the centuries and
until recently, wives and mothers—in contrast to husbands and fathers—
were discriminated against in nationality matters concerning loss of citizen status and maternal *jus sanguinis*; also, with regard to the extension
of civil, political and social rights, female and male co-citizens did not go
through the same dynamic of inclusion and exclusion.

By looking at the Italian case study between 1866 and 1922, this chapter aims at analyzing and discussing Italy's citizenship policies, throughout the liberal decades, vis-à-vis its female nationals without forgetting
the other history of citizenship: the one concerning the Italian male counterpart. After all, womanhood and manhood are relational categories,
and if "talking about women without talking about men is like clapping
hands with one hand only," the opposite is also true.[1] Hence, the importance of making women "visible" within the history of Italian citizenship
and of studying female and male perspective(s) together.[2] Also, to grasp
the extent to which Italian female membership status shared similarities
with, but also differed from, that of contemporary women elsewhere,
parallels and contrasts will be drawn with the British and French cases.
And finally, in line with our previous pages, the chapter will complement

the analysis on national citizenship by discussing the presence and the persistence of racial thinking in the peninsula throughout the entire liberal period.

2.1. "AS A WIFE AND AS A MOTHER I HAVE NO COUNTRY": LOSS OF NATIONALITY AND IRRELEVANCE OF MATERNAL *JUS SANGUINIS*[3]

During the liberal epoch, in comparison with their male counterparts, Italian women enjoyed a *sui generis* status since they could neither retain their nationality regardless of whom they married nor pass it on to their children. In fact, in being wives they had to follow the nationality of their husbands, in line with the Latin maxim *uxor statum mariti sequitur*, and therefore had a "dependent nationality," derived from the male spouse's membership status.[4] Also, as mothers they could not transmit their citizenship to the next generation except under very specific conditions. Hence, from the perspective of these two precise nationality matters, one can say that, as a general rule, the history of citizenship in the liberal decades was a history of "effective statelessness" for many women.[5]

More particularly and in practical terms, an Italian woman kept her Italian nationality upon marriage only if the husband was Italian. By marrying an alien, she would be automatically stripped of her original nationality—the only exception being if wife would have become stateless because no transmission of citizenship was allowed by the marriage legislation in force in the husband's country of origin. Having lost her Italian nationality because of her foreign spouse, the ex-Italian wife had then a right to reacquire it only when the husband died and upon condition of either residing already in the kingdom or returning to the peninsula and making, in both cases, an explicit declaration. Also, during the marriage union (between two Italians or between an Italian woman and a foreigner), wives were obliged to change nationality if the husband decided to naturalize abroad—unless the woman kept her residence in the peninsula. And wives could not naturalize of their own initiative since married women were not allowed to acquire a citizenship other than what was held by the husband, even in case of personal separation between the two spouses. As aliens, these former Italians had no automatic right to live in Italy, were subject to the laws concerning foreigners (including the norms on expulsion from the country for reasons of public security) and lost basically all rights attached to Italian female *status civitatis*. These norms—largely inherited, like many others, from the legal traditions of the pre-unification period, from the Napoleonic code and from Roman law—were enshrined in the first national civil code of unified Italy in 1865 and continued to be in force throughout the entire liberal epoch as they were also incorporated into the subsequent Italian citizenship law of 1912.[6]

In the capacity of parent as well, the position of Italian women was inferior to that of men because as a general rule children of Italian mothers were attributed Italian nationality at birth if the father was Italian; this meant that the offspring of an Italian woman and an alien father was an alien at birth (except when the *jus soli* rule could be applied if the alien father had ten years of domicile in the kingdom, as we saw in the previous chapter). The only exceptional application of maternal *jus sanguinis* in the peninsula was when the husband could not pass his citizenship on to the children because he was unknown, stateless or a foreigner who was not allowed to transmit his status to the offspring born outside his country of origin because of state legislation at home (thus making the children stateless).[7]

The contrast with the nationality policies reserved to Italian husbands and fathers could not be more evident. In fact, an Italian male citizen who married a foreign woman did not lose his original status but naturalized his wife by making her an Italian citizen upon condition that she was resident in the kingdom. Also, until 1912, an Italian husband made an (ex-foreign) wife Italian for life, since the woman had to keep her Italian nationality during her widowhood as well—a situation that would change toward the end of the liberal period as widows were then able to reacquire their original status by transferring their residence abroad. Finally, contrary to their female counterparts, Italian husbands saw no restrictions to the individual freedom of applying for naturalization abroad and, as we have seen, determined the citizenship status of their children because paternal descent was the primary rule applied by the liberal state in this matter.[8]

Clearly, these citizenship provisions pointed to an important reality: Italian women—in contrast to their male co-citizens—had no country and no national identity to hold independently and to transmit *from a legal point of view*. Italian females did of course have a country and a national identity, like anyone else originating from the peninsula; yet there was no state recognition of this on the same terms as for males. This is why we believe that the expression "effective statelessness" (meaning literally "without a state" and deprived, in this case, of its humanitarian dimension) is appropriate when thinking and talking about women and nationality during those years of Italian national history.

Seen from a wider European perspective, though, this Italian situation was by no means unique. The position of female nationals in liberal Italy paralleled in fact the condition of contemporary women in many other countries. British-born female subjects, for instance, were deprived of their British nationality upon marriage to a non-British man. Also, unless their children were born on British soil and the rule of *jus soli* was applied, the offspring was alien. British membership status, as regulated by the British Nationality Act of 1730 and by the British Nationality and Status of Aliens Act of 1914, was therefore shaped by norms concerning women that were similar to those of the Italian peninsula. The only minor difference from the Italian case, introduced in Great Britain in 1914, was to allow British female subjects to retain their nationality if their husbands relinquished British nationality *after* marriage.[9] Generally speaking, in France as well wives and mothers shared the same Italian and British paths since upon marriage they took the citizenship of their foreign spouse (and lost their original one with a right to reacquire it only during widowhood) and, upon the birth of their children, saw French male lineage prioritized. These norms, enshrined in the 1804 Napoleonic code, continued to be in force in the French Hexagon during the period of liberal Italy—although, from the 1920s, following the end of the First World War, things started changing gradually in favor of French female independence upon marriage. As a result, in November 1922 the French senate approved a bill (which was to become law in 1927) allowing French women marrying aliens and alien women marrying Frenchmen to have the right to choose whether to take their husband's nationality (and no longer the obligation as before).[10]

The persistent differentiated citizenship norms concerning wives and husbands on the one hand, and mothers and fathers vis-à-vis their children on the other, were regarded as so obvious across the European continent during the nineteenth and early twentieth centuries as to be taken almost for granted by the liberal Italian authorities who were legislating on these matters or discussing and writing about them at the institutional, academic or professional level. The provisions concerning the changes of nationality by married women were so clear and unquestionable, said an Italian senatorial authority in 1911, that they could not raise objections.[11] Similarly, the norms regarding transmission of citizenship by descent and the superiority of paternal *jus sanguinis* could even have been erased from legislation, argued other state representatives, because they reflected a principle on which "it was superfluous" to legislate.[12]

But why was the contrast between the norms concerning female nationals and those related to the male counterpart considered obvious? Which widespread principles and concerns did the citizenship provisions mirror? The rules concerning the women of the peninsula, like those touching on the nationality of females in many other countries, were seen as necessary to uphold and realize in practice the deeply rooted "principle of family unity" according to which the domestic household, created through the institution of marriage, was a primary state cell and a social entity to be kept united through the husband/father's traditional authority *and* nationality status. In particular, by defining the nationality of all family members through marital and paternal citizenship (that is through the *status civitatis* of the male adult within the couple), the authorities saw to it that the family remained united from a legal point of view, whereas if individuals held different nationalities within the same household, the latter would disintegrate. Multiplicity of citizenship(s) under the same roof was seen as a dangerous social phenomenon that would not only alter the juridical relations among the family members but erode the links underpinning the marital union and complicate the exercise of traditional male authority that characterized husband-wife, as well as father-children, relations.[13] Hence, it was in the name of domestic union that *both parents* and *all children* had to hold one and the same citizenship; it was in the name of domestic union that, upon marriage, a husband would transmit his status to the wife (regardless of her will) and that, on the birth of the couple's children, fatherhood (rather than motherhood) would determine the babies' status.

The two nationality issues—transmission to the wife and to the offspring—were linked to each other, and the latter was actually a consequence of the former. In effect, as shown by archival evidence, the doctrine of "family union" provided theoretical justification not only for the supremacy of marital citizenship over the wife's nationality but also for the predominance of paternal *jus sanguinis* over maternal transmission of citizenship to the next generation.[14] The secondary literature concerning female citizenship in general seems to have focused mainly on the first aspect (loss of the wife's original status) and to have overlooked the second issue (how to explain the predominance of paternal lineage).[15] The two must be explained by making reference to the same principle because, as various Italian ministerial and parliamentary authorities emphasized during the liberal years, the tenet of domestic unity could not allow a difference of citizenship, whether between the husband and the wife *or* between the father and the minor children. These two nationality issues shared therefore common theoretical underpinnings.[16]

At this point one could ask why the male adult, rather than the female, was prioritized in this context. Historically, within the juridical traditions of the Italian peninsula and back to the ancient Romans, the husband had constantly been regarded as the "natural" head of the family: "the true and unique head."[17] It was he who gave the surname to his wife and children; it was his residence that determined residence for his minor offspring; it was he who exercised the *potestas* over the latter as well as represented it in all civil acts. As a consequence, argued a contemporary scholar in liberal Italy, it was "logical" that the husband's/father's nationality should be extended to the whole family unit.[18]

Also, "for reasons of convenience, of concord and of morality" the female spouse had to share the same citizenship as her husband (just as she shared the same marital life with him): "ethical reasons" justified the "disappearance" of the wife's nationality within the couple and her total dependence on the husband's membership status.[19] The subordinated nationality of women—as wives and mothers—was, therefore, linked to questions of social harmony, concord, moral integrity and ethics. Within this context, it is interesting to ask how the notions of citizenship and of womanhood were directly related to all the latter social and ethical concepts. In view of providing an answer, we will draw on a recent dynamic theoretical debate concerning the impact of the institution of marriage on female nationality as well as the place of women in the history of citizenship in general—not as individuals entirely excluded from it but as persons who have been "part of it" as "dependent citizens," "subjected" to the rule of men on the basis of the widely held belief that this was necessary for preserving peace.[20]

The conceptual link between keeping tranquility within society on the one hand, and imposing certain "legitimate" legal restrictions on the status of married women on the other, was shaped by the conviction that by introducing legal norms that kept the woman subordinated to the husband's nationality, one protected society from the presumed negative consequences of a wife's independence of will. In particular, the belief was widespread that by maintaining the wife's citizenship derivative of and dependent on the husband's status the male could control and ensure the sexual fidelity of his spouse—thus avoiding "the specter of anarchy" in society that adultery had been evoking for centuries.[21] The question regarded especially the social disorder that would be generated through procreation of children by adulterous married women, offspring that *in legal terms* would be the children of the woman's legal husband. This, in turn, would not just cause psychological distress for all persons concerned but also jeopardize the social stability maintained by producing only legitimate heirs who guaranteed orderly transmission of property from one generation to the other.

Indeed, one set of marriage legislation mirroring these fears was represented, for instance, by the adultery laws that treated and punished the infidelity of the wife differently from infidelity on the part of the husband. As Italian Senator Cristoforo Mameli argued in 1865:

[...] greater gravity [is imputed] to the wife's adultery because the latter proves greater corruption of heart and renunciation of every virtuous sentiment by the woman; because nature manifests with certain signs the wife's infidelity; because the fruits of her illicit loves are mostly dependent upon the husband and the legitimate offspring.[22]

Apart from the norms specifically concerning adultery, other marriage provisions reflected the same anxiety about "social anarchy," for instance those restraining the wife's liberty with regard to her freedom of domicile and, as we shall see in the subsequent sections of this chapter, those concerning some civil rights such as freedom of movement and disposal of property. All these norms empowered the husband to constrain the wife's liberty and made him "the master of her physical space" in order, ultimately, to "protect his proprietary right over her body" and to "avoid social disorder by ensuring her fidelity." Logically, the fact of depriving wives and mothers of an "independent nationality" followed the same reasoning and was justified on the basis of the same social necessity.[23]

The related arguments concerning family unity and social peace were clearly in stark opposition with the universalist liberal principles of equality, of individual rights and of no obligations without consent that were very much cherished during those years in the Italian peninsula as elsewhere. Obviously, liberalism could not be at ease within these discourses. And yet, throughout the liberal period, sophisticated arguments could be heard in some Italian quarters to justify women's dependent nationality by using, ironically, liberal political notions of consent, knowledge and obligation—as contract theorists had done in previous centuries. As an Italian senatorial authority put it in 1911 when talking about the change of nationality by the wife upon marriage: "[...] there exists no doubt about the goodness of the principle; it meets the *consortium omnis vitae* within the married couple and it involves obviously a non-coercive, voluntary acquisition for women, who, by consenting to marriage, accept also this natural consequence."[24]

So, by marriage, a contract freely entered into, the woman was presumed to accept "willingly" the change of her nationality because the latter was a resulting corollary of that contract. Clearly, an important underlying liberal assumption took place here: women were seen as autonomous and fully informed agents who knew the consequences of marriage before their union, and upon choosing to marry they automatically consented to the corresponding obligations (including change of citizenship status). As the scholar Kif Augustine-Adams recently emphasized, where *knowledge* of facts, of consequences and of alternatives existed, the obligation to change citizenship was not seen as an imposition on the woman's will; the wife's dependent citizenship was thus "a condition voluntarily entered into, with notice of the consequences."[25] Put simply, women *knew* about the foreign nationality of their future husband before getting married; they therefore consented to the change of their status by *deciding* to marry an alien. The irony, though, was that men were never asked to choose between marriage and keeping their citizenship and that women were therefore faced with a stark choice that men never had.

In 1865 and in 1912, the liberal legislator was unanimous in defending the principle of the unity of nationality within the family (in the case of mixed marriages), without showing any particular concern for the liberal tenet of individual will. The only instances in which references were made to liberalism concerned the further change of nationality by women not upon marriage but, subsequently, in case the husband naturalized abroad during the period of the marital union.

For example, in 1865 Deputy Mancini criticized the fact that the status of the Italian wife had to change, obligatorily, when the Italian husband acquired a foreign citizenship. According to the parliamentarian, this was "an inexcusable offence to the principle of liberty" against Italian women (and their children) as well as a symbol of "dependence" and "subordination."[26] Mancini's liberal argument, though, remained isolated since no further speeches were made along this line. Also, the deputy limited his intervention only to the case of Italian women who had to become foreigners after naturalization of their Italian husbands abroad and did not apply the same liberal principle to the foreign wife who had to become Italian after naturalization of her foreign husband in Italy.[27] Furthermore, when talking about foreign women keeping their Italian nationality in case of widowhood, Mancini proposed to amend the text of the civil code by erasing the requirement of domicile in the Italian kingdom and letting the widow keep Italian membership status no matter where the woman lived.[28] Surely, as committee members Carlo Cadorna and Vincenzo Niutta argued, the widow should have been left free, in the name of liberty and of individual will, to go back to her original citizenship by changing her domicile rather than being obliged to keep Italian citizenship all her life.[29] So Mancini's liberalism vis-à-vis female nationality issues was not consistent and appears to have been used instrumentally and for demographic purposes so as to make sure that Italy would lose the least number of citizens.

During the debates leading to the 1912 Italian citizenship law, the wife's will was not considered to be a primary factor either. At one point in the discussions, Senator Pasquale Fiore proposed to condition at least the female change of status during the marital union on the woman's explicit declaration.[30] After all, if a woman knew when she got married that she would have to sacrifice her citizenship once and consented to this with marriage, she could not know in advance that her husband would naturalize abroad and impose on her a further automatic change of nationality. However, in 1912 as in previous years, the principle of the unity of the family was prioritized and the proposition was therefore rejected, with these words:

If the Italian husband becomes a foreign citizen, the wife loses her Italian citizenship provided always that she acquires the one of her spouse. It may be painful, it may sometimes mean an act of violence vis-à-vis the woman's will, but between two evils, one should choose the minor one. It is better to do violence to the wife's will than split the family unity from which the law expects so many beneficial effects, both legally and morally.[31]

This official discourse of the Italian liberal state concerning its female population shared many similarities with what was pronounced in other countries. For instance, speaking on behalf of the British government in the debate on the 1914 British Nationality Bill, Lewis Harcourt argued that to allow a woman to retain her own nationality "when she deliberately marries an alien" would be "departing from the practice of the whole civilised world."[32] Also, a select committee, set up in Great Britain to discuss a 1922 bill concerning the nationality of married women, reiterated the priority that had to be given to the husband's/father's nationality by using sharp metaphorical language that deserves full citation.

The Committee . . . cannot overlook the fact that by marriage a woman is merged in the unit of the family, and that within the family it is at present the husband who is head, who bears its legal responsibilities such as the maintenance of the wife, the children and the home, and whose occupation in most cases is the decisive factor as to where that home is to be established, and who among other things gives his nationality to the children. It is their opinion therefore that in this important sphere of family life the nationality of the husband should be the governing factor and determine the nationality of the wife. If two ride a horse one must ride in front.[33]

Official discourses, though, were also linked to specific national concerns that were absent in the Italian peninsula and present in other countries. For example, the situation of British married women as it stood in the early 1900s affected in particular poor women such as those living in the East End of London. As the MP William Samuel Glyn-Jones explained during the debates over the 1914 act, they were "British-born Jewesses who are married to Jews who have not become naturalized and have lost their British nationality in consequence."[34] Nationality matters were therefore linked to immigration issues and, in this case, to the British governmental objective of controlling Jewish immigration to Britain from Eastern Europe (as also reflected in a previous Aliens Act of 1905).[35] In addition to this migration dimension, female citizenship norms were to be determined in Great Britain by the wider imperial necessities perceived by the British government, especially from 1914 onward. Since the 1914 British Nationality Act introduced the concept of "common imperial allegiance to the Crown" and defined all individuals born within "His Majesty's dominions and allegiance" as British subjects anywhere in the empire, it had been a "British principle" since then that changes to the nationality laws in Great Britain would be made in agreement with all the dominions and later the British Commonwealth. As the various British governments regarded common nationality laws within the empire as a way of strengthening the latter's cohesion, they were unwilling to alter married women's nationality status in the metropole and make a breach in this legislative uniformity. The imperial connotation of British nationality policy had, therefore, a negative impact on the emancipation of women in this respect, and women's nationality had to be sacrificed across the Channel not only to the unity of the family—as in Italy—but also to the unity of the empire. And in fact, only after Canada destroyed the empirewide system of direct allegiance to the British Crown by passing the Canadian Citizenship Act of 1946 would the United Kingdom finally change the status of British-born women by providing in 1948 that marriage would have no effect on a British woman's nationality.[36]

In the case of early-twentieth-century France, debates on mixed marriage and on the nationality of female citizens were to be related not only to general feminist claims but also to nationalist anxieties touching on demographic urgencies—aggravated later on by the high number of French casualties of the First World War combined with a low national birth rate. As a traditional country of immigration, France had always had a high percentage of mixed marital unions, which meant that the thousands of French women, born and resident in France, who married aliens became aliens themselves in their own country. This loss of "French nationals," though, started to be seen as absurd and at odds with the demographic situation of France right after the 1914–1918 conflict. Also, as a massive social phenomenon touching on the lives of many Frenchwomen, this legal situation became more visible in the Hexagon and criticism more vocal, especially because numerous women lost their nationality automatically (sometimes even without knowing it), and with it many other entitlements, including the right to take up certain jobs that only French nationals could do. So from 1919, thanks to the mobilization of the *Congrès du conseil national des femmes françaises* and of the French parliament, various bills were discussed reflecting a blend of feminist demands and nationalist/populist fears.[37]

To conclude, Italian females, as subjects of the Italian kingdom, enjoyed a secondary position within the family both as wives of husbands and mothers of children. Their lack of an independent nationality that could be retained upon marriage and transmitted to the next generation was seen as necessary in the interest of the family and of society. As a general rule, an Italian woman acquired Italian nationality at birth from her father (and not from her mother); she would keep it upon marriage and transmit it to the children only through an Italian husband. From this perspective, wives and mothers, contrary to their male counterparts, had no state that would recognize, *by law and without exceptions*, their national identity. Women living in contemporary Great Britain and France generally shared this same nationality issue, although the respective national paths and official discourses were different, at times, from the Italian ones.

To be able to hold and keep their own nationality on the same terms as their respective male co-citizens, women would have to wait a certain period of time in the three countries mentioned in this chapter according to the respective national contexts: 1975 in Italy, 1948 in the United Kingdom and 1927 in France. The same is also true for acquiring the right to transmit nationality equally, by maternal *jus sanguinis*, although this would be achieved later in the twentieth century in all three cases: 1983 in Italy and in the United Kingdom, 1973 in France.[38] In the next section we set aside these two nationality issues and focus on the actual content of female *status civitatis* as it was shaped during the liberal decades.

2.2. CONTENT OF CITIZENSHIP:
THE PECULIAR FEMALE PATH TO CIVIC INCLUSION

When one speaks of the civil, social and political content of citizenship, one usually refers to civil entitlements such as freedom, in general, and freedom of residence, of association and of owning property in particular; to active and passive political rights (i.e., the right to vote and to be elected); to social claims, understood in terms of access rights to public services (i.e., schools, hospitals) and in terms of transfer of income (i.e., maternity leave, child allowances, pensions, unemployment benefits).

The classical account of the British sociologist Thomas Humphrey Marshall on the gradual expansion of citizenship through successive acquisition of civil, political and social rights in the eighteenth, nineteenth and twentieth centuries respectively has been criticized from a feminist perspective for being simply androcentric. Women have been put at the margins of his history of citizenship since the citizen that the scholar had in mind was the British working-class man.[39] The chronology and the conditions of female inclusion as full members of a community have differed generally from those concerning male nationals. For instance, whereas acquisition of full civil rights by men has generally preceded universal manhood suffrage and the latter has usually been achieved before the introduction of welfare social rights, this order is upset in the case of women. A number of social rights such as maternity protection and interdiction of night shifts were introduced for them before they attained the right to vote; also, several important civil rights were refused to wives until well into the second half of the twentieth century. In comparison with men, women have therefore been latecomers as full members of the national community and have gone through a distinct dynamic of inclusion.[40]

Our findings and related literature concerning the Italian case study confirm the argument. As we shall demonstrate below, whereas Italy's male citizenry was granted full civil rights before achieving universal suffrage, this was not to be the case for Italian women. Also and most significantly, Italian male citizens acquired civil entitlements *and* voting rights during the liberal period, but Italian women did not. Finally, in contrast with their male counterparts, Italian female nationals were awarded some social rights, as mothers, before the civil and political content of their citizenship had run its full course.

Before taking the reader through these three citizenship dimensions, one final caveat deserves consideration: there is a difference between *formal recognition* of a right according to the law of a country and the *actual practice and exercise* of that specific right by the individual. A person could be granted a certain entitlement by the state but not be able to exercise it for a variety of reasons: lack of implementation by the institutions, high illiteracy among the population, economic and social backwardness within the country, corruption and illegality in the organization and running of political elections. Indeed, no serious study of the civil, political and social aspects of citizenship in liberal Italy can overlook this point: the legal recognition of certain rights was seriously undermined by an unfavorable social and political context that characterized the young and weak post-1861 Italian state.

For instance, in liberal Italy the bureaucratic and state apparatuses were notoriously slow in implementing legislation and policy across the entire peninsula; civil and social citizenship rights in particular were to be the first victims of such slowness and lack of implementation by state institutions. The country was also notoriously known for a social plague that was to be a gangrene in large parts of the citizenry body throughout the entire liberal period: illiteracy.[41] Obviously this social factor could only have a negative impact on the whole concept of citizenship, no matter the dimension through which one analyzes it. In addition, the economic backwardness of the country as a whole and of certain Italian southern areas in particular was well known.[42] Surely, what it meant to be a citizen and to hold rights in a country where lack of bread was the rule rather than the exception for the majority of the population requires a lot of imagination. Finally, despite the liberal constitutional guarantees formally introduced with the *Statuto Albertino* (i.e., the constitution of the kingdom at the time) and with a variety of post-1861 national laws, one should not overlook the fact that illegalities were not rare during political elections; witness striking opposition voters from the electoral lists, letting absent people and even the dead become electors, accepting violence outside polling stations . . . in short, making the unique citizen-ship act of casting a vote something rather peculiar in Italy.[43] It goes without saying that the gap between recognition and exercise of rights must be kept in mind when reading the following sections on the content of female and male citizenship(s).

2.2.a. Civil Rights

Throughout the liberal epoch, Italian women and men enjoyed, equally, the legal recognition of a number of important civil entitlements that were extended to the entire peninsula without distinction of sex. For instance, the right to individual liberty, to an inviolable domicile, to freedom of press and to freedom of association were all enshrined in the constitution of the country and enjoyed by all, including female and male Italian Jews who, first emancipated in the Kingdom of Piedmont-Sardinia in 1848, saw their right to equality recognized in the post-unification period as well and, contrary to the Restoration epoch, were finally allowed to move out from ghettos and integrate within the social, economic and intel-lectual life of the country.[44] Also, daughters living in the peninsula had the same property rights as their brothers since female and male children could inherit their father's patrimony, equally, in legitimate succession.[45]

The supposed equality of sexes reflected in these provisions was, how-ever, gravely undermined in the norms concerning married women. So whereas male citizens were universally entitled to full civil rights, not all Italian women were. In fact, a wife did not enjoy the same civil rights as her husband with regard to property entitlements, testamentary freedom, liberty to make civil contracts and freedom of movement. In particular, even though married women could own and inherit property, they needed the expressed approval of their husband (so-called marital authorization) to administer and bequeath their private fortune independently, take out a mortgage, cash in capital, administer a bank account autonomously and get a passport to travel abroad or emigrate.[46] The husband exercised, therefore, a sort of "legal guardianship" over his partner, similar to that needed by minor children and the mentally handicapped. This factor—female incapacity in the sphere of civil rights upon marriage—was again a characteristic of female citizenship status in many other European coun-tries, such as contemporary France, where in this respect French women held the same inferior position as their Italian counterparts in comparison with their male co-citizens.[47]

Towards the end of the liberal era—following the First World War and the contribution Italian women made during the conflict by massively substituting for male labor—it seemed that state recognition of women's participation in the workforce during the years 1915–1918 would lead to female emancipation in the peninsula. And in fact, in 1919 the liberal state sanctioned the right of women to administer their personal property by abolishing the husband's authorization needed by the wife to complete a variety of economic transactions.[48] However, apart from the fact that Italian women would have to wait until post-1946 republican Italy to see all the other restrictions finally erased from national legislation, this extension of rights to Italian females, in acknowledgment of their involvement in the war effort, did not go beyond the limited sphere of civil entitlements. This becomes clearer in the section following.

2.2.b. Political Rights

Formal recognition of civil rights was granted to Italian women partially and gradually, but the one concerning female political entitlements was completely absent in the Italian kingdom during the liberal period. This factor was to make the status of women in the peninsula stand out in opposition not only to the situation of Italian men but also to the status of contemporary British women in their country.

Even though in a slow and gradual manner, Italian male citizens acquired universal suffrage, at the local and national levels, during the liberal decades. Extension of the male franchise was in fact incorporated into the various political agendas of successive Left governments whose objective was, among others, to introduce democratic reforms and, by widening the citizenry's participation in political life, attempt to shorten the gap between "legal" and "real" Italy. In 1889, to start with, Francesco Crispi's government abolished the previous provisions that had restricted the male electorate in administrative elections on the basis of census considerations (i.e., property ownership and payment of taxes) and allowed all Italian male citizens of twenty-one years of age and over to acquire local political rights. Male universal suffrage was therefore achieved *at the local level* in the nineteenth century.[49]

For gradual enfranchisement of men in *national* parliamentary elections, more time and stages were needed by the liberal state. In fact, first applied in the plebiscites that had sanctioned the annexations of the ex-Italian states to the Savoy kingdom in 1859–60, universal male suffrage was not embraced by the 1861 Italian authorities and male national voting rights were restricted until 1881 to men who had enough education to be independent and enough income to be interested in maintaining social order, namely, to Italian males of at least twenty-five years of age who could read and write, owned property and could pay forty lire per year in taxes. Subsequently, after the circle of the male electorate was extended in 1882—under the government of Agostino Depretis—by reducing the age qualification to twenty-one and the taxpaying obligation to nineteen lire, further democratic steps were taken and universal male suffrage finally achieved in 1912 during the premiership of Giovanni Giolitti. Through a major reform bill that surprised his colleagues within the Italian parliament, the Turinese premier allowed all male citizens of at least age thirty to vote without any census or capacity requirements (including, therefore, a large mass of illiterates) as well as giving voting rights to those aged twenty-one and over who had served in a military corps, passed the exam at the end of the third year of elementary school or, as previously, paid taxes or owned property. In this way, male suffrage came to include the southern peasantry—a large and easily manipulable rural electorate—who would have neutralized the contemporary increasing strength of hostile voters (and in particular of the more radical industrial workers of northern Italy). Finally, following the catastrophe of World War One and with a view to giving more representation to those social classes that had suffered most from the hardships of the war, the government of Francesco Saverio Nitti extended the male franchise in 1919 even further by letting all men participate in political elections from the age of twenty-one (rather than thirty) and all soldiers who had served during the conflict, from the age of eighteen.[50]

The contrast with the political citizenship of their female counterparts could not be more evident since, during the same decades, Italian women did not enjoy, explicitly and directly, any political right and had to content themselves with being only "indirect citizens" (that is, represented, in the local and national public spheres, by their fathers, husbands, brothers and sons). Female local suffrage was not actually unknown in the peninsula because in the pre-1861 period women had the right to vote at the local level on the basis of census considerations in the Grand Duchy of Tuscany and in the Austrian Kingdom of Lombardy-Venetia.[51] With the proclamation of the 1861 Italian state, this was no longer to be the case and women would have to wait until the fascist period to see some of them cast their first vote at municipal elections. As for national political rights, they would not be able to go to the polling stations until 1945, when universal adult suffrage was finally introduced under the government of Ivanoe Bonomi. Indeed, the only explicit political right to which women were entitled up to 1922 concerned those female nationals who could participate in political life through men by using the women's property census to habilitate the respective father or husband to vote, in case the male electors alone could not fulfill the census requirement.[52]

As we have said, the economic and social contribution of Italian women to the war effort in 1915–1918 gave way to some optimism concerning eventual improvement of the legal position held by Italian female citizens in the peninsula. Hopes, though, were to be satisfied partially only within the sphere of civil rights, while being totally frustrated as far as female franchise was concerned. In this respect, a parliamentary bill was presented and approved in the lower chamber in 1919; thus showing that a large portion of Italian deputies supported electoral reforms to incorporate women into the electorate. However, the Italian senate failed twice to pass the legislation, and therefore women remained disenfranchised for the entire liberal era. In the same year, male suffrage was being extended to new categories of citizens and made more universal to take into account soldiers who had fought at the front; female citizens who had nevertheless contributed to the war national effort were denied any political participation since no sympathetic and favorable majority could be found in the upper parliamentary chamber.[53]

The continuous disenfranchisement of Italian women throughout the entire liberal era stands out not only in comparison with the gradual extension of voting rights to Italian men but also in comparison with the situation of contemporary British women. In Great Britain, some categories of female citizens had enjoyed municipal voting rights since 1869, when widows and spinsters who were householders were entitled to participate in local elections in England and Wales. By 1907, when the local suffrage disqualification of married women was ultimately removed, British female subjects had been granted the right to vote in practically all local elections, were in most cases eligible to hold the offices for which they might vote and could now concentrate on securing the parliamentary franchise. This last, contrary to the Italian case study, was largely achieved beyond the Channel in 1918. In fact, following the First World War and thanks in particular to a long British tradition of liberalism as well as to the strength of the British feminist movement, women thirty years of age were permitted to vote for members of the English Parliament if they came within any of certain categories: they already enjoyed municipal suffrage; or were wives of men having the municipal franchise; or were graduates of a university; or were engaged in Red Cross, nursing or other national service at home or abroad. True, they still had to win a reduction in the age qualification and the right to sit as members of Parliament themselves; yet, contrary to their Italian sisters living in the peninsula during the same period, they did have some say in British public life.[54]

2.2.c. Social Rights

The specificity of the female path to inclusion emerges clearly if one also explores the third dimension of citizenship under study: social entitlements. Truly, one aspect of social membership (i.e., access rights to public services, and in our case to schools) was shared in similar ways by women and men living in the peninsula. The right to education was in fact formally guaranteed at the same time for both sexes without distinction, though also, sadly, not implemented without distinction. However, if one looks at other aspects of social citizenship (in particular at transfer of income under the schemes of maternity leave and social insurance), one notices a gender difference with regard to chronology of inclusion and inferiority of status.

The right to education, to start with, was formally acquired, equally, by female and male children in successive stages, in 1861, 1877 and 1912. Post-unification Italy did therefore try to tackle the social problem of illiteracy, although with very limited results. More particularly, with the 1859 (Piedmontese) Casati Law, which was extended to the whole peninsula after unification, elementary education was first made free. Then, in 1877, with the approval of the Coppino Act passed under the Left government of Depretis, it also became compulsory for children between the ages of six and nine. This was indeed an important policy, which however remained a dead letter in many areas of the country since parents preferred sending their children to the fields rather than to school (*pauvreté oblige*); the local administrations, which were in charge of organizing and supporting primary education, were very keen on economizing at the expense of popular literacy; and finally, very few inspectors were appointed to check on application of these educational provisions. Later on, in 1911–12, a further Education Reform Act was introduced under the government of Giolitti, specifically with the aim to complement the simultaneously approved legislation concerning universal manhood suffrage. Yet even though the responsibility to organize primary education was transferred from the villages to the province and other improvements were introduced for better schooling, the Italians would have to wait for the fascist period and for the famous Gentile Reform of 1923 for more fundamental changes within this field.[55]

If one now turns to other social rights bestowed on the Italians in the peninsula during the liberal decades, one sees that the situation was formally and substantially different for women and men. First, female workers were disadvantaged compared to their male counterparts since so-called Workers' Mutual Aid Societies (*Società Operaie di Mutuo Soccorso*)—nonstate organizations replacing a weak and absent Italian state in the management of social insurance schemes, unemployment subsides and pensions—were mainly monopolized by men, did not usually allow women to have access to more remunerative jobs and to most social benefits, or just excluded them altogether.[56]

Also, despite the fact that from 1898 onward the Italian state attempted to participate directly and more actively in formulation of social policies following the example of Bismarckian Germany, numerous social provisions concerned mainly the positions of male workers and male heads of the household—thus making women acquire social rights "in weakened forms or dependent upon the spouse."[57] The first Italian welfare state was therefore not only "particularistic" and "occupational" (to use Ugo Ascoli's expressions) but also "gender biased." It was "particularistic" and "occupational" in the sense that social policies were applied according to the group and also because social provisions were granted not to all citizens (which would have made the welfare state universalist) but only to those individuals who had a job—for example, the industrial working class and agricultural workers.[58] It was "gender biased" since women were either absent from state policy or treated as dependent on their husbands. To a large extent this was also the case in Great Britain, where, for instance, the social policies affecting women that were formulated by the liberal government of the years 1906–1914 in the field of national health and unemployment insurance reflected the assumption that the male spouse should maintain the household and therefore treated adult women as dependents of men.[59]

Finally, although some social rights were granted directly to Italian female nationals as workers, these social entitlements were bestowed later upon them than upon men—mainly in the twentieth century—and were seriously undermined for various reasons. For instance, a factory act, designed more to meet the requirements of employers rather than of women, was passed to regulate the work of females in 1902; also, mothers had to wait until 1910 to see the creation of the first National Maternity Fund. The latter obliged factory female employees to stop working during the first month after childbirth and granted a right to both married and unmarried women to a maternity allowance. However, despite the fact that the essential principle according to which the state should participate in financing the fund alongside female workers and employers was accepted for the first time, the shortcomings of this legislation were numerous. In effect, as there were delays in payment, nonpayment by employers and general lack of enforcement by the authorities, women were often left defenseless.[60]

Besides the similarity that we have mentioned between the social citizenship of Italian female nationals and that held by contemporary British women, one final aspect should be highlighted to contrast the two cases. The relation between the social and political aspects of the content of citizenship varied between the Italian and the British examples. In fact, when child and maternal infant welfare services were introduced in Great Britain in the 1900s and maternity benefits in 1911 thanks to pressure from organized women, British female citizens already held political rights at the local level, and as they realized that the benefits were paid to the father in his capacity as head of the household, they lobbied and succeeded in 1913 to obtain direct payment to mothers.[61] Clearly by having a say in the public sphere and by being more vocal and organized than their Italian female counterparts, they could put forward their claims more effectively and be more successful than the women of the peninsula. This specific aspect confirms that there is no universal story about gender and citizenship, and that the timing and dynamic of women's inclusion as well as the relations between the civil, social and political aspects of their citizenship content need to be told from different national contexts.[62]

To conclude, within Italy's peculiar context, which hindered the flourishing and expansion of civil, political and social rights for men and women indistinctly, the content of Italian female *status civitatis* was different from that enjoyed by Italian male nationals. Being entitled to partial civil rights if married, lacking any direct political rights and enjoying very few and limited social entitlements, Italian women were second-class citizens and holders of a status that can be defined as "halfway citizenship."[63] In comparison with their British sisters, their position appeared to be even lower in some important respects. Next we discuss why the number and the content of Italian women's rights were constantly inferior to the ones held by men—expanding and enriching with further insights our previous discussion concerning the nationality of women as wives and mothers.

2.2.d. *Understanding the sui generis Content of Female status civitatis*

Womanhood was valued during the liberal period for its reproductive and nurturing role as well as for representing a unique and complementary element within Creation. As a senatorial authority put it before the high chamber:

Just think that the soldiers who fight our wars are procreated by the female, formed by the blood, and fed with the milk, of the female. Think that the first and last word that is uttered by the human lip is mom. Just think that if the male is the most beautiful flower of creation, the female is its perfume [signs of assent].[64]

However, despite their central roles, women were treated differently by law compared to men, and the latter's content of citizenship was clearly "thicker" than what was held by the former. How can one explain the Italian state's differentiated policy with regard to content of citizenship?

If we focus on married women first and we bear in mind our previous discussion on wives' loss of nationality and on mothers' *jus sanguinis*, it is not difficult to understand the reasons and the theoretical principles that explain why, upon marriage, female nationals were obliged to see some of their rights restricted. As scholar Giovanna Zincone has emphasized, if one looks at the evolution of civil, political and social rights in the peninsula, one notices that in all three dimensions women acquired them with an important delay and the common and recurrent reason for this late acquisition was "the capsulizing of women in subordinate position within the family unit."[65] Married women acquired individual rights much later because this was seen as destabilizing family unity by weakening the role of the husband as the unique head of the household.[66]

Admittedly, in some Italian quarters various objections were raised during the liberal era against the particular limited content of the wife's status. For instance, in 1865, in reference to marital authorizations, some representatives spoke in favor of allowing wives to administer their property autonomously—as they used to do in the Austrian Kingdom of Lombardy-Venetia. According to one deputy, the various fears surrounding the emancipation of women were unfounded since the presumed negative inconvenience of eroding family links by letting women administer their fortune without the consent of their husband did not stand close scrutiny. On the contrary, disorder was more likely to take place by imposing such a humiliating obligation on the woman.[67] Also, why should only the wife be obliged to such limitation of freedom, insisted another state official?[68] In his words, either both spouses had to ask for an authorization from a tribunal or, if men were left free to dispose of property, then women as well should have been able to do so. The principle of sexual equality required it.[69] Finally, in reference to political entitlements, another parliamentary representative defended the case of granting (married and unmarried) women the right to have a *direct* voice in the Italian parliament through a personal and explicit vote rather than by an implicit and tacit one that, according to the traditional argument, was exercised through male relatives.[70]

Yet the concept of family union was too strongly rooted and widespread within state discourse concerning content of citizenship to be put aside. For instance, as Minister Vacca argued in 1865 in justifying the necessity of keeping marital authorization, the latter was incorporated into Italian policy, "with wise advice, given that we have recognized in this [factor], a tribute to marital authority and a pledge of concord and harmony between the spouses."[71] This point was to be upheld until 1919, when, as we have seen, the liberal state finally abolished this civil restriction for married women. Moreover, as emphasized recently by the scholar Ursula Vogel, traditionally the husband was regarded as the person who supported, protected and *represented* the wife in the public sphere.[72] Consequently, women did not need to acquire voting rights in order to be represented and should not participate directly because in the name of the unity of marriage a woman could not have interests distinct from those of her husband.[73] This explains the situation of Italian women as nonvoters as well as the aforementioned "franchise disqualification" of British married women at local elections before 1907.

The reference to the principle of family union and to the particular case of married women was, though, only one aspect of a larger debate concerning womanhood and content of citizenship in general, and touching on a variety of additional arguments that were raised in the peninsula during the liberal decades. These arguments regarded specifically "economic concerns," "the public-private dichotomy," "female nature" and "Italy's immaturity and unripe context" for female emancipation despite the latter's strongly supported claims.

With regard to the argument about economic concerns, it is instructive to learn that some state authorities used it during the liberal epoch to criticize and object even to the principle of equality reflected in the provisions concerning civil rights of daughters and sons in legitimate succession. Speaking in 1865 in reference to this issue, Deputy Giuseppe Panattoni proposed to exclude daughters from inheritance in exchange for compensation.[74] This would have kept property undivided within the family and avoided continuous partition of land and factories, which usually led to less profit and caused serious consequences for the economy in general and for agriculture in particular. Important economic considerations were at stake here.[75] Clearly, mention of compensation to be given to the propertyless daughter was a timid sign of consideration vis-à-vis the dignity of women. Yet the sentiment of the whole proposition reflected a nostalgic approval for those inheritance systems that had characterized many parts of Europe since the thirteenth century and that, by favoring brothers over sisters, or as in most cases the eldest son exclusively (the system of primogeniture), hindered the economic independence of women.[76] Ultimately, Panattoni's amendment was not approved; however, his objections show that translation of the liberal tenet of individual equality into the language of civil rights met with some opposition when the individuals under discussion were female nationals and the economy could have been influenced negatively.

As regards the other arguments, they were mainly put forward and discussed together in relation to the general enfranchisement of Italian women. Discussing this issue repeatedly in the 1880s and 1910s, a number of parliamentary authorities emphasized the fact that exercise of a public function such as the right to vote was incompatible with the position of women within society: "Even if [the woman] can vote with perfect intelligence and with full independence, she is not called to this duty because of her social being."[77] Women's place was not in the public realm; this was a social axiom because of the traditional and undisputable dichotomy between "the private and the public sphere" that automatically relegated women in domestic life to care for the house, the husband and the children. But why did Italian officialdom see the social mission of a female citizen to be exclusively at home? Minister and deputy Giuseppe

Zanardelli provides us with a clear answer when arguing in 1880 that all female virtues for which women were so admired (i.e., tenderness, passion, spontaneity) and that originated from the fact that a woman's heart governed her mind and a woman's imagination overcame her reason were not appropriate for the exercise of public civic duties.[78] A difference of nature existed, therefore, between women and men, and this same difference justified the female obligation to be at home. By remaining in the domestic realm women were not excluded from politics; in fact, so argued the minister, the most noble part of female citizenship within political life was not voting or being elected but "molding characters, . . . inspiring the love of country and the nobility of feelings, . . . supporting and giving strength in the exercise of public virtues, directing the minds and the hearts towards those shining ideals to which . . . turn[ed] [a woman's] thought."[79] In other words, to give birth, educate, inspire and support the man who will take part in public life. Female nationals would keep their dignity not in a "senate of women"—a very interesting image used at that time—but in the private sphere.[80]

Finally, although numerous speeches were made in the peninsula in favor of introducing female suffrage (especially in 1912, when the right to vote was extended to illiterate men),[81] several influential voices argued strongly that it was not yet the right moment to grant it since the country was not ready for female emancipation, from a social and institutional point of view.[82] Obviously, in the name of justice and equality between men and women, female exclusion from the politically active citizenry appeared to some as a disturbing feature of Italian society. As maintained by a parliamentarian in 1912, this exclusion was informed basically by a "traditional prejudice" that regarded political participation as a "sexual" rather than a "human right" to be held by each individual.[83] Also, from 1913 onward, how could one grant the right to vote to illiterate male citizens and still deny it to women in general, and to cultivated women in particular? "We give the suffrage to the uneducated; could we still deny it for long to women?" asked Deputy Carlo Schanzer bluntly.[84] And from another bench: "I will never be able to persuade myself that one should deny a cultured woman what one gives to an ignorant man."[85] Clearly, the legal inferiority of female nationals could not be more striking; after all, argued several other senators, if not at the national level, why not enfranchise women at least at the local level?[86]

Ultimately, women never got the right to vote in the liberal period. For some representatives, male universal suffrage was already, per se, a new political and social experience that demanded a particular effort by the Italian state to accommodate a new electorate; obviously, such effort would have been more complicated with the even larger extension of the active citizenry brought about by enfranchisement of women.[87] Also, as others stated, time was still needed before Italy could bestow political rights on its female population and emphasis was put on making women's emancipation a gradual process. Speaking in 1912, President of the Council of Ministers Giolitti was quite clear when he maintained that he was not in favor of introducing female suffrage straightaway at that moment because a different order had to be followed: first, reforms were needed to improve the civil condition of women within the family, and then after this one could grant them local political rights and finally national political suffrage. Female emancipation had to take place slowly and step by step.[88] Subsequently, from 1918 onward even the widespread argument concerning the large contribution of women to the war effort did not lead successfully to female suffrage. Feminist claims were in fact not fully embraced at the senatorial level and the bill was ultimately rejected.[89]

To conclude: the limited content of Italian citizenship enjoyed by women during the liberal period reflected a variety of concerns and points of view, in particular the well-known doctrine of family union as well as general arguments linked to economic imperatives, to the distinctive social spheres and distinct natures of womanhood and manhood and to the unripe historical and social contexts of the post-1861 liberal state. The civic emancipation of women had still a long way to go.

2.3. ITALY'S FEMALE AND MALE CITIZENS AND RACIAL THINKING THROUGHOUT THE LIBERAL DECADES

2.3.a. The Persistence of National Discourses about Southerners, Civilization and Race

As we saw in the previous chapter, racial representations were not absent in the peninsula at the time of unification. In fact, the Italian citizens of the South were often perceived and depicted as inferior and racialized Others in domestic discourse. Interestingly, these specific formulations continued throughout the liberal decades and intensified, especially from 1875 onward, in reference to political discussions concerning the Southern Question. Also, in the late nineteenth and early twentieth centuries, debate was to be enriched with Italian anthropological and physiognomic discourses on racial theories.[90] Thus, the concept of *italianità* as reflected in the citizenship issues examined here did not have just an important gender dimension. It also continued to be challenged by specific language and tropes about the Italian race that concerned Italian women and men alike and touched on additional sensitive issues of identity, equality and difference. This rhetoric did not make any specific distinction between female and male citizens as it referred broadly to the Italians of the South in general. However, it is clear that both groups were targeted since both made up the southern people. It is therefore instructive to enrich our analysis once more by drawing directly on this related scholarly debate.

As emphasized by Wong, the Southern Question was one of the first domestic issues to be tackled by the young Italian nation-state, as well as giving rise to a plurality of arguments among northern and southern politicians and writers who attempted to examine the economic and perceived cultural and moral underdevelopment of the Mezzogiorno from a variety of historical, political and sociological standpoints.[91] The purpose of these sensitive national discussions was twofold: to understand the roots and the origins of a very complex matter that involved reflection about abject poverty, corrupted elites, mafia and *camorra* (Neapolitan organized crime); and to inform the government in Rome so as to bring about action and reforms. However, these debates would also go beyond the goals cited here, contributing—even if indirectly and unintentionally—to the persistence of negative stereotypes about Southerners, still circulating today.[92]

For instance, in those lively discussions, which could vary in content and linguistic tone, the binary opposition between "barbarity" and "civility" was often used. Writing in the mid-1870s on the North-South divide, Neapolitan historian Pasquale Villari described one component of Italy's citizenry (i.e., the inhabitants of the Mezzogiorno) as living basically in a "semi-barbarous status," constantly struggling in misery and protesting against this social desolation by adhering to brigandage.[93] Also, in making further observations on the actual process of Italian political unification, Villari frankly addressed "the northerners" by saying "either you manage to civilize us, or we will manage to render you barbarians."[94]

This specific language, pointing out the barbarity of the Southern Italians, was also used by historian and senator Niccola Marselli in the mid-1880s in emphasizing that all the Italians had a responsibility to participate in the strengthening process of national unification: the Italians in the north, who had to help to civilize their southern counterparts, and the Italians in the south, who were meant to elevate themselves toward civic progress and modernity.[95] In fact, as Marselli put it, "there exist[ed] in Italy, especially in the Mezzogiorno . . . entire social strata to redeem and to civilize."[96] Finally, at times these discourses were also enriched with the medical metaphor by which, as a linguistic device, the south was portrayed as a dangerous and risky disease that really threatened the health and well-being of the entire Italian boot. On the basis of this reasoning, then, northern doctors would be called on either for "amputating the gangrened limb" or "to cure it and make possible the southern rising to

European civilization."[97] So throughout the liberal epoch, the notion of national citizenship, which as we have seen incorporated an important gender flavor, was also to be complicated and contested by discourses pertaining to the uncivilized and barbarous status of the Southern Italian citizens (women and men alike).

Subsequently, during the late nineteenth century and the beginning of the twentieth, these divisive considerations and talks came to be coupled with additional racial theories that, put forward by Italian anthropologists, became quite widespread across the country.[98] In particular, seeking to grasp the contemporary problems of the Mezzogiorno through notions of race and biology, these theoretical arguments added an important dimension to ideas of diversity and difference formulated within Italian circles. However, as theories they were also to be criticized because, based as they were on several scientific methods that purported to give them some authority, they were founded on the researcher's prejudices too—so as to lead to very biased and nonscientific conclusions.[99]

According to this anthropological perspective, represented by northern and southern scholars such as the influential Giuseppe Sergi, Cesare Lombroso, Enrico Ferri, and Alfredo Niceforo, Italy was basically peopled by two races: a primitive Mediterranean racial element living south of the River Tiber, and an advanced Aryan group living in the north. The southerners belonged, therefore, to a different racial stock from that of northerners. In more detail, the leading theory of Sergi—formulated on the basis of cranial morphology—saw the peninsula as being inhabited by Mediterraneans (or Italics, "*Italici*") whose origin was Euro-African and by Aryans ("*Arii*") whose origins were Euro-Asian. The first race was predominant in the more disordered societies of the destitute South, the second in the more civic-minded and affluent North.[100] In Lombroso's research too, the racial variations of the Italian population alongside notions of criminality and savagery were regarded as fundamental criteria for understanding the southern issue and the problematic of "making Italy."[101]

So, by reexamining the question of the Mezzogiorno, these anthropologists saw race as the major cause of southern decadence and attempted to explain how biology shaped the political and collective features of Italy's inhabitants. Consequently, the northerners were perceived from a biological standpoint as more predisposed to civic responsibility within stable societies while the southerners could only be lethargic parasites and indolent individualists living in disorganized political communities.[102] Furthermore, it was race that could explain notions of civilization and progress as well as the causes of the uncivilized realities in the South. As a result, racial determinism basically explicated the Southern Question. In fact, within this rhetoric, the backwardness of the Mezzogiorno was an unavoidable and inevitable biological factor; race was a lens of analysis to predict criminality, mafia and camorra, and it was a marker of southern inferior civilization.[103] Also, and most interestingly, while being defended, these theories were used by some writers and intellectuals either in a negative way, to underline how the 1861 union of the northern and southern regions was "forced and not beneficial" to either part of the country, or in a more positive way, to emphasize the importance of racial mixing in "making every difference nonexistent" or "even making a stronger race" out of the merger of the two races.[104]

Not all these discourses—those inspired by the Southern Question and the ones later enriched with anthropological racial considerations—were accepted equally across the country. For instance, we know that sociologist Napoleone Colajanni criticized the divisive impact of the medical metaphor on the widening of the gap between the north and the south, arguing that it was actually the whole peninsula that was ill.[105] Also, others could not help but discern a certain ironical paradox of a European southern country criticizing its own south by using the same tropes and figurative language that had been used, and were being used, by northern European nations in describing Italy as a whole as an underdeveloped neighbor.[106] Lastly, apart from the fact that the categories of race formulated here were criticized in some quarters for being ambiguous and often left undefined, several other sociologists attacked, as already noted, the scientific methods used by these anthropologists, their incomplete data and their superficial analysis.[107] Nonetheless, these racial theories did enjoy popularity at the time, and they did influence academics, politicians and policy makers alike. This is because, as the scholar Patriarca has already pointed out,[108] metaphors do not simply enrich our language but also structure our thinking and shape our actions.

Thus throughout the liberal years the unifying institution of Italian national citizenship not only had a separated history for women and men but was also confronted with divisive talks and writings concerning barbarous and uncivilized Italians (women and men coming from the South) and with divisive theories on the Italian race in general. Racial thinking was not absent in nineteenth and early-twentieth-century Italy, and as we have emphasized in this section, it complicated the notions of national citizenship and Italianness in a significant way. As internal Others in a unified Italy, Southern citizens (female and male) were regarded by some as internal aliens and, as such, not really an integral part of Italy's national citizenry. They were Italians from a legal point of view; their Italianness was very much contested and represented in a peculiar way.

In the next and final section we explore another aspect that complicated even more the concepts of *cittadinanza* and *italianità* during the liberal age.

2.3.b. The Presence of Anti-semitic Prejudices and Language in the Peninsula

As we have seen in this chapter, following the proclamation of the secular kingdom of Italy under the Savoy monarchy, the many freedoms that were enshrined in the constitution were recognized for all Italian citizens no matter their religious affiliation, including (female and male) Jews. However, this equality did not mean the absence of anti-Semitic feelings, talk and attitudes in some quarters of the Italian peninsula. Indeed, during the end of the nineteenth century and the beginning of the twentieth anti-Semitism was by no means nonexistent in Italy, being actually deeprooted in a certain clerical tradition, and especially among the Jesuits of the most influential Catholic biweekly, *Civiltà cattolica*.[109]

Surely, the Italian Catholic clergy and its most radical and vocal anti-Semitic members were a tiny minority of the Italian citizenry; yet they enjoyed a prominent role as sermon preachers, educators and intellectual shepherds, thus influencing—directly or indirectly—literate public opinion and the less-educated masses alike.

In a systematic analysis of the most authoritative Church-linked Catholic press throughout the liberal decades of the 1880s and 1890s, David I. Kertzer provides a wealth of evidence about the major anti-Semitic discourses that were circulating in Italy, as elsewhere, through these press articles.[110] These discourses, like the ones pertaining to Southerners, targeted the Italian Jewish community as a whole without making any specific distinction between women and men. However, it is clear that both female and male Italian citizens were concerned as Jews, as Italians and as Italian Jews. Discussing some of this rhetoric here is therefore particularly instructive as it brings to light further challenging factors that make the already composite and complicated notions of Italian citizenship and identity even more disputed and contested.

For instance, according to the same Jesuit periodical the Jews were a foreign race and could not really be "Italian." "Oh how wrong and deluded," wrote *Civiltà cattolica* in 1880,

are those who think that Judaism is just a religion, like Catholicism, Paganism, Protestantism, and not in fact a race, a people, and a nation! While it is certain that others can be, for example, both Catholic and either Italian, French or English . . . or Protestant and a member of whatever country or nation . . . it is a great error to believe that the same is true of the Jews. For the Jews are not only Jews because of their religion . . . they are Jews also and especially because of their race.[111]

Along the same vein, one could read similar language ten years later: the Jews "formed a foreign nation in the nations where they resided, a sworn enemy of the nation's well-being. . . . Although they may live in

France, in Germany, in England, they never become French, or German, or English, but remain Jews and nothing but Jews."[112] This argument could well imply the same negative views vis-à-vis those in Italy too, despite the fact that, as rightly pointed out in recent historiography, the Jews of the peninsula were Italians, spoke neither Yiddish nor Ladin and, arguably, since Risorgimento had become Italian even more rapidly than the rest of the population because of the Jews' important role and growing activities in the political, social, economic and intellectual life of the newly unified country.[113]

Moreover, according to the anti-Semitic Catholic rhetoric, the citizenship rights granted to the Jews following their emancipation in the peninsula, as elsewhere, were a "mistake" because if the Jews were left "too free" they would immediately become hostile "persecutors" in the country where they lived and would basically take control of politics, the economy, the financial sector and the press, thus becoming a "menace."[114] As *Civiltà cattolica* put it in 1880:

The Jews—eternal insolent children, obstinate, dirty, thieves, liars, ignoramuses, pests and the scourge of those near and far— . . . immediately abused [their new-found freedom] to interfere with that of others. They managed to lay their hands on . . . all public wealth . . . and virtually alone they took control not only of all the money . . . but of the law itself in those countries where they have been allowed to hold public offices.[115]

Echoing these words a few years later, a Milanese Catholic daily would make a similar point by stating that the Jew

is the possessor of the gold . . . and so the Jew is the ruler of the world. This is why the Jews are our masters, dear readers, precisely our masters. You can find the Jews in the Senate, in Parliament, in Public Administration, in the Chamber of Commerce, in journalism, having more or less changed their first and last names, *but always Jews to the core!*[116]

This is why, in line with all these discourses, it was appropriate, even urgent, to reintroduce restrictive legislation on the civil liberties and citizenship rights that the Jews now enjoyed together with the other citizens.[117] After all, if by their religion and nature the Jews "[could] not and must not live among others as any other people in the world . . . do,"[118] perhaps even the reintroduction of ghettos was to be contemplated again. . . .

Besides the virulent anti-Semitic press campaign taking place in the 1880s and 1890s, some anti-Semitic discourses continued to be formulated in Italy during the liberal years of the twentieth century as well. Most telling is the fact that the *Protocols of the Elders of Zion* was published in the peninsula in 1921 with two Italian editions being made possible by the intellectual work of Monsignor Umberto Benigni (with a number of supplements to the bimonthly *Fede e Religione*) and of former seminarist and fascist Giovanni Preziosi (bringing out another edition).[119] This anti-Semitic book was presented by its proponents in Italy, as it had been elsewhere, as newly discovered "evidence" of a meeting held by a secret international directorate of Jews planning world conquest. It was a forgery and an invented story, which however was to become the principle source of the anti-Semitic myth of a "universal Jewish conspiracy to dominate the world."[120]

On the basis of a combination of long-standing *traditional* religious Catholic views and nineteenth-century *modern* anti-Semitic language, then, one part of Italy's population (i.e., female and male Jews) was seen in some circles as being not completely Italian, as not deserving all the citizenship rights enjoyed at the time in the secular Savoy kingdom of Italy, and as representing a dangerous group within the Italian unified citizenry. Belonging to a "foreign" race, roughly thirty-five to forty thousand "untruthful and false" Italian citizens were part of a national citizenry whose *italianità* was not totally immune to the anti-Semitic virus spreading across the European continent.[121] This virus circulated in liberal Italy particularly through the press and publications; yet it did not have an essential and central place in the political life of the country and did not lead at the time to the creation of a political and organized movement in the peninsula as was the case in other contemporary European countries such as Germany, Austria-Hungary and France.[122] The anti-Semitism of the liberal decades, scattered in some influential Catholic quarters well before the fascists took power, was characterized by prejudicial attitudes and verbal hostility against a minority on the basis of a mélange of old Church views and modern anti-Semitic themes. Among the former we should mention in particular the Catholic references to "demonic race" for having killed Jesus, "obstinate children" for not wanting to convert, "Jewish terrible smell" going back to *foetor judaicus* to be evaporated with baptism, etc. Among modern themes, we should instead ponder citizenship emancipation leading to "Jewish domination," the "disproportionate" powerful position of the Jewish citizens despite being a minority in their countries and "secret Jewish conspiracy" against Christian societies.[123]

2.4. CONCLUSION

Readers of Giuseppe Mazzini might recall that the final words in his *Duties of Man* refer interestingly to women and to their inferior position in civil, political and social terms:

And I will point out to you [Italian working-men], in bidding you farewell, another Duty, not less solemn than that which obliges us to found a Free and United Nation. Your emancipation can only be founded on the triumph of one principle,

the unity of the Human Family. To-day, half of the human family, the half from
which we seek inspiration and consolation, the half to which is entrusted the
first education of our children, is, by a singular contradiction, declared civilly,
politically, and socially unequal, and is excluded from this unity. It is for you [...],
in the name of religious truth, to protest in every way and upon every occasion
against this negation of unity.[124]

Mazzini's words are particularly apposite when thinking about the citizenship of Italian female subjects living throughout the liberal decades.
As we have tried to show in this chapter, Italian women were not treated
equally to the other half of the national citizenry, and the juridical cord
linking female nationals to the Italian state was rather peculiar. A woman
was legally recognized as an Italian citizen usually if her father was Italian. Her legal status could not be transmitted to her foreign husband,
nor kept for herself upon marriage, nor passed on to her progeny (unless
under exceptional circumstances). Women did not therefore have "a nationality of their own," to paraphrase the title of a recent monograph.[125]
Moreover, the content of their status was constantly less substantial than
the one held by Italian men (single or married). Women's citizenship was
thus "thinner" than the *status civitatis* enjoyed by male nationals.

This means that the contours and the content of the notion of "being
Italian," as drawn and shaped by the citizenship legislation discussed in
the first two sections of this chapter, and reflected too in the related official discourses, are not the same for all Italian subjects living in liberal
Italy. In fact, our findings show that *italianità* did not only mean to origi-
nate from the territories of the peninsula annexed to the Savoy kingdom
and involving certain boundaries determined by a specific combination
of *jus sanguinis* and *jus soli*, as explained in our previous chapter. It also
meant different things to the male and female halves of the Italian population. Women were in a peculiar position in relation to the concept of
Italianness because, *qua* women, they did not have a country and a related national identity recognized without exception by the national legislation of their state. Also, no full-fledged legal recognition was granted
to them with regard to civil, social and political rights to be exercised independently rather than in the constant shadow of Italian male relatives.
This is why, from a gender perspective, it is not unfounded to talk about
a notion of *italianità* that is dual as well as multiple and that takes into
account the shared aspects with male citizenship but also the differences
between the two groups.

As further explained in the third section of the chapter, throughout
the liberal years the concept of Italian national citizenship was enriched
not only with a fundamental gender facet but also with considerations
pertaining to the *italianità*, or rather the non-*italianità*, of certain categories of nationals. In fact, in some quarters of the peninsula (female and

male) Italian Southerners were often portrayed as uncivilized, savage, barbarian and non-European. Also, in certain Catholic milieux, Italian (female and male) Jews were regarded as a foreign race and as undeserving holders of citizenship rights. Therefore, as this chapter demonstrates, the notion of Italianness—delineated so far with the help of citizenship provisions, debate and official rhetoric—was shaped by gender arguments, by racial talk pertaining to women and men in the South, and by anti-Semitic thinking and writing about Jewish women and men.

In the next chapter we continue our historical journey and discuss issues of immigration and alienhood that bring to light further significant aspects of Italian national citizenship and Italian national identity.

CHAPTER THREE

Foreign Immigration, Citizenship and *Italianità* in the Peninsula

Italiani non regnicoli, *Non-Italian Immigrants and Notions of Alienhood*

The Outsiders—the foreigners, those belonging to other political communities—are part and parcel of the definition of nationhood. The identity of a nation is conditioned, defined, redefined and transformed by the presence of the external Others because it has a dynamic "double-edged character": it is based on a set of common (cultural and civic) elements that link the members together *from within*; it presupposes difference and awareness of others from which the nation seeks to differentiate itself *from without*. Thus, national consciousness necessarily involves commonality with our fellow members—the ins—and difference from the nonmembers—the outs. It involves "oneness" and "otherness" at once.[1]

The outsiders to whom we shall refer in this chapter are two special groups of foreign immigrants who made up the category of *stranieri* (aliens) in the Italian kingdom during the liberal period, namely the "*Italiani non regnicoli*" and "non-Italian aliens." In particular, by exploring liberal Italy's citizenship legislation and discourses vis-à-vis these two groups of newcomers as well as extending the analysis over the second generations born in the peninsula up to 1922, this chapter demonstrates two things in relation to national identity. First, it shows that Italian citizenship policy in tandem with related debate on first-generation immigration reflected, clearly, specific Italian traditions of nationhood that are to be discussed thoroughly. Second, and from another angle, it argues that the citizenship rules pertaining to the second generations drew specific contours around the notion of Italianness that are to be compared again with those of the contemporary German counterpart.

3.1. HISTORICAL CONTEXT AND DEFINITIONS:
ITALIAN AND NON-ITALIAN IMMIGRATION

During the liberal epoch, Italy was mainly an emigration country. This is an aspect of post-unification history that we will explore in the next chapter of the book and that, as the existing literature demonstrates, has been thoroughly studied from a variety of perspectives.[2] Yet less known to the public in general and overlooked by historians in particular[3] is the fact that the Italian kingdom witnessed two interesting types of immigration during the liberal decades, which, although unimportant in size compared to the emigration flows of the Italians from the 1880s to the 1910s, had a political and economic significance as well as an essential impact on state official discourses concerning the concept of *italianità*. Indeed, thanks to the presence in the country of these two entirely different types of foreigners from whom Italian national identity could be conceptualized and in some cases differentiated, the Italian state set the tone and the terminology that were to characterize the debate(s) on alienhood and Italianness throughout the liberal years.

The first type of immigration, which we can call "national" or "Risorgimentalist," involved arrival and settlement of Italian political émigrés who were forced to leave their original countries (the Austrian empire and the pontifical state) because of their personal political views and desertion within Austrian and pontifical troops—when several Italian lands were still under "the priest of Rome" and the "Caesar of Vienna," to use sarcastic and colorful expressions of that time.[4] Mainly a political type of migratory movement (although economic considerations were also involved), it originated from the territories that had not been incorporated into the 1861 Italian kingdom. It was, therefore, a type of national immigration directly linked to the ideology of truncated Risorgimento and whose historical origin went back to the pre-1859 kingdom of Piedmont, when the "Italians" of the other Restoration states of the peninsula found refuge in the Savoy state to escape their respective "tyrannical" governments. Interestingly, the size of this category of migrants followed the geography of post-1861 Italian statehood, and as Italy extended its political borders through the annexations of 1866, 1870 and 1919 the group under study shrank automatically. This peculiar shrinking character was because, as we have already seen in Chapter One, following the territorial expansion of the Savoy kingdom the populations who inhabited the annexed lands became subjects of the Italian king through the system of collective naturalizations. In 1866 and in 1919, they also enjoyed a right of option, guaranteed under specific conditions and similar to the one granted to the Austrian Lombards in 1859. Consequently, these immigrants—

who became *sudditi* (subjects) of the Savoy monarch and who therefore changed their status from *non regnicoli* to *regnicoli*—no longer qualified as foreigners.[5]

The second type of immigration, by contrast, was unrelated to the process of Italian unification (although a number of these foreigners had also taken part in the Risorgimento battles and expeditions).[6] Indeed, it was primarily a financial, economic and commercial type of migration, made up to a great extent of well-off and cultivated entrepreneurs, merchants and financial backers many of whom had actually moved to the peninsula during the pre-unitary period and settled there by 1861.[7] As an Italian senatorial authority emphasized in 1905, whereas France and the United States were destination countries for a large exodus of not always "desirable" emigrants, Italy enjoyed a highly educated, rich and socially prestigious form of immigration.[8]

Although completely different in terms of typology, the two international movements of arrivals were curiously related to each other: the first migratory phenomenon gave name to the other. In fact, since the first group consisted of "immigrants of Italian nationality" (the latter concept of Italian nationality meaning, here, nation membership and *not* state membership), the rest was automatically called "immigration of non-Italian nationality." Alternatively and synonymously, whereas the former were named *Italiani non regnicoli* or just "Italians," all the other aliens were automatically referred to as "non-Italians" or *stranieri* (foreigners). Legally speaking, both categories were made of individuals holding foreign citizenship(s). But the former were "special aliens" who shared, to various degrees and for a variety of reasons, some traits of *italianità* with the Italian subjects of the 1861 kingdom; the latter were "outright foreigners"—if we may use this expression.[9]

How the general notion of Italian nation membership was defined by the liberal state to determine whether an immigrant was, or was not, an *Italiano non regnicolo* is worth analyzing in depth for its evident relevance to the central topic of this book. Which were the elements of commonality that these special immigrants shared with the subjects of the Italian kingdom? What factors made them Italian? Obviously, if one was not a *non regnicolo*, then one would have automatically qualified as a non-Italian. Thus, by defining the *italianità* of the first group, one could understand the total alienhood of the second.

Unfortunately, no precise and unanimously accepted definition of the first category was provided by Italian authorities throughout the liberal era. For instance, Italy's legislation contained a variety of expressions: "Italians who do not belong to the Kingdom of Italy" (*Italiani non appartenenti al Regno d'Italia*); "citizens of the other Italian provinces" (*cittadini delle altre province italiane*); or "individuals of Italian

nationality" (*individui di nazionalità italiana*). Yet no further specifica-
tions were given in the laws about who these Italians were.[10] During the
parliamentary hearings, senators and ministers alike were not more precise than their approved provisions and, as they stated clearly on several
occasions, preferred to leave the definitional issue to the various interpretations of Italian courts and tribunals, in charge of deciding on the
italianità of the immigrant, case by case.[11] These interpretations, though,
were not always consistent, and a high level of elusiveness could also be
found in the documents issued by ministerial authorities as well as by
Italian judiciary bodies such as the Council of State and by legal and consultative organs providing juridical assistance and expertise to the state
administration, such as the Council of Diplomatic Disputes within the
Ministry of Foreign Affairs.[12]

Clearly, the lack of a precise definition made the tasks of the competent
authorities at times rather difficult—as some archival documentation demonstrates—because no unequivocal guiding principles were set.[13] Nevertheless, the multiple (and scattered) geographical, cultural and historical
references that we were able to find during our research and that were
made directly or indirectly, explicitly or implicitly, by Italian officialdom
to say whether a particular migrant was a *non regnicolo* provide interesting insights for historical analysis of Italian nationhood.

On the basis of these discourses, we can argue that the notion of Italianness—reflected in the image of the *non regnicoli*—was clearly based on the
concept of the pre-political and cultural nation defined in opposition to,
and distinct from, the territorial and institutional framework of Italian
statehood. Also most interesting is to have discovered that liberal Italy had
an idea of *italianità* that was very extensive; it incorporated not only the
"nation in search of a state" that achieved and completed its Risorgimento
process in 1861, 1866, 1870 and 1919 (as well as losing some populations to France in 1860) but also other Italian-speaking peoples who had
some links with the peninsula and with the historical development of Italian nationhood but whose countries (or lands) of provenance were under
neither Austrian (and Austro-Hungarian) rule nor pontifical sovereignty.
This means that the category of the *Italiani non regnicoli* was much wider
than the already mentioned group of political immigrants that had moved
to the Savoy kingdom for political reasons linked to national Risorgimento. It included a variety of other aliens, as we shall demonstrate below.

As regards the arrivals who originated from the "unredeemed lands"
(*terre irredente*) of Venice (before 1866) and of Rome (before 1870),
they were considered to be of "Italian nationality" on the basis of geographical and historical considerations, for linguistic reasons and on account of the liberal patriotic opposition between freedom and tyranny.
The *Veneti* and *Romani* who emigrated to the 1861 kingdom were thus

Italians because, as some parliamentarians also emphasized before the 1866 annexation, they came from lands that "belonged" traditionally to Italy; their idiom was the Italian language, although spoken with different accents; and ideologically they were patriotic exiles who had escaped oppression to join the "free Italian provinces."[14]

These criteria of *italianità* were also explicitly mentioned, or tacitly implied, vis-à-vis the immigrants who had left some other "unredeemed" territories under Austro-Hungarian domination that were to be either annexed right after the First World War or the subject of unending territorial negotiations and not ceded to the Italian liberal state. For instance, in 1887 an Italian judicial body maintained that the term *non regnicoli* was not related just to the inhabitants who had arrived from the Eternal City and from the Venetian lagoon but also to the migrants who came from the city of Gorizia, in the Oriental Alps. This was justified by the city being in a territory that was Italian from ethnographical, historical and geographical points of view.[15] Also, before the incorporation of Venice into the Savoy state, a deputy actually referred to the *Istriani*—those coming from the Istrian peninsula—as part of the group of special foreigners under study.[16] Bearing this in mind, it does not come as a surprise that later on, in a parliamentary debate held in 1903, an explicit reference was also made to Trieste; the Italian lower chamber recognized as an *Italiano non regnicolo* an immigrant who was born in Vienna from a German family and who had been resident in the Adriatic city—thus interpreting the geographical criterion in an extensive way, by taking residence (rather than birth) as a sufficient criterion.[17] From Trieste to Fiume, the mental journey was not long, and in fact in 1912, in the name of a general concept of "geographical and ethnographical Italy," the Court of Appeal of Ancona defined an Austrian immigrant—who had studied and graduated in Florence—as a *non regnicolo* because the person was born in what was then the Hungarian county of Modrus-Fiume.[18] Finally, whereas in 1899 Senator Augusto Pierantoni listed not only the *triestino* (from Trieste) but also the *trentino* (from the city of Trento) as *non regnicoli* of the Italian kingdom,[19] on one previous occasion the Italian-speaking émigrés from *Tirolo*—the largely German-speaking Süd-Tirol that Italian nationalists preferred calling Alto Adige—were also mentioned on the basis of a linguistic consideration.[20] In fact, as Benedetto Cairoli argued in the lower chamber before the province of Venice was ceded by Vienna, some dangerous arrivals suspected of having been paid by the Austrian government for their political activities in Italy, were caught by the Italian police; yet, the deputy emphasized, "they had neither a Venetian accent, nor a Tirolese accent; they were foreigners."[21] Since no archival findings at our disposal rectify or criticize Cairoli's blunt statement, one can argue that those who came from Tirolo (before the 1919 annexation to Italy) and who spoke Italian (although with a particular accent) were not completely foreigners in the eyes of the liberal state but qualified as *Italiani non regnicoli.*

Apart from the references to lands and peoples of the Austro-Hungarian empire, the group of these special immigrants was also linked to the recent loss of Savoy and Nice in 1860 when Cavour sacrificed the two provinces to France in exchange for tacit consent from Napoleon III to the Piedmontese incorporation of central Italy. However, according to our sources, the migrants who came from Savoy did not qualify as "special aliens" because, as was explained in a decision made by an Italian Court in 1896, the Savoy region was not Italian—from a geographical point of view (i.e., the Alps separated it from the peninsula) or an ethnic perspective (i.e., French was the language spoken by the population). Thus, without any consideration of the historical link with Italy's royal family, some liberal authorities regarded the immigrants who originated from French Savoy as "outright foreigners."[22] By contrast, since a parliamentary official argued in 1863 that the incoming inhabitants from Nice (Nizza) had to be regarded as *Italiani non regnicoli* and we did not find any other document modifying this view, we presume that the liberal state excluded at times the *Savoiardi* but included the *Nizzardi* into its concept of Italian nationhood.[23]

The *non regnicoli* continued to be defined in an extensive way throughout the liberal era. In fact, the notion of Italianness came to incorporate not only the aforementioned ex-pontifical, Austro-Hungarian and French subjects of "Italian nationality" but also a variety of other foreigners who originated from some "Italian" historical territories, whose mention is illuminating for understanding the boundaries of the Italian nation as drawn by post-1861 Italian state representatives. For instance, talking in the upper chamber in 1869, Senator Pier Silvestro Leopardi made specific allusions to the *Italiani non regnicoli* who had emigrated from the Swiss Canton of Ticino. As he put it, this canton was an ancient Italian territory and the *Ticinesi* were a people who shared common origins with the Italians of the peninsula.[24] Also, continued two judicial authorities, since these Italian-speaking immigrants were not as foreign in the post-1861 Savoy kingdom as a German or a Frenchman would be from a "natural *italianità*" that the latter aliens lacked, the *Ticinesi* deserved to be part of this special group.[25] Besides the *Ticinesi*, though, one had to consider the *Maltesi* (from Malta) and the *Corsi* (from Corsica) as well, who from "obvious" linguistic and historical considerations enjoyed the same title of special *stranieri* (special aliens). After all, Italian was still largely spoken in the two islands and both territories had previously been under Roman rule, and in the case of Corsica under Genoese domination as well.[26] Finally, this category was so inclusive as to incorporate the emigrants of the Republic of San Marino too—that is, the inhabitants of a state whose history had not always been linked with the political developments of the rest of the peninsula. These outsiders who arrived from the small Adriatic Republic were defined as *non regnicoli* as shown by a document of 1905 concerning the case of a number of *Sanmarinesi* resident in the Italian province of Forlì (in the Romagna region) and exercising the profession of district municipal doctors.[27] Unfortunately, the document does not explain why they belonged to the "Italian family"; it just implies so. However, under the dust of parliamentary archival materials, we were able to find some additional post-unification documentation where one can read that the *Sanmarinesi* were part of the "Italian nation" on the basis of cultural and linguistic factors and that, in contrast with the "unhappy Italian brothers" who before the completion of Risorgimento had been under "tyrannical" foreign domination (Austrian and pontifical rule), those from San Marino enjoyed a privileged position since "they [were] free like us and more than us."[28] Also, these "inhabitants of Mount Titano," the highest of San Marino's seven hills, were "veterans of Latin patriotism" and thus sharing a common historical background with the *regnicoli* of post-unification Italy.[29]

Admittedly, the expanding boundaries of this special group of aliens (and therefore of the corresponding broad notion of Italianhood) were the subject of debate, especially among the various courts involved, and interpreted with some flexibility: for some, the rules concerning these *stranieri* (foreigners) were to be applied only to the Italians of Venice and Rome. For others, a difference had to be drawn between the provinces that had some hope of being annexed and those that had implicitly or explicitly renounced national Risorgimento (such as Nice and Corsica), and in this case only the *non regnicoli* who came from the former territories should qualify. However, a third opinion—apparently the most widespread of all—was in favor of a generously inclusive interpretation that recognized as *Italiani non regnicoli* those who originated from *any* province that was "Italian from a geographical and ethnographical point of view"—thus making none of these distinctions and including countries or lands such as Malta, Corsica, Ticino and San Marino.[30]

To conclude, the *Italiani non regnicoli* were *sui generis* immigrants because they had national traits in common with the subjects of the 1861 kingdom. The political debates and legal decisions pertaining to the definition(s) of this historical group of aliens pointed to an idea of Italian nationhood that combined cultural and civic elements to varying degrees (i.e., language, history and patriotic will to live together and to contribute, in certain cases, to political unification of the Italian provinces, as the political exiles demonstrate). Also, since the category consisted of Austro-Hungarian and papal migrant subjects as well as of a variety of other foreign citizens who originated from, say, Ajaccio, Lugano and Valletta, it mirrored an idea of *italianità* that was not "state-national" as in France but formulated, constantly, against the territorial framework of the existing Italian state. The *non regnicoli* were seen as components of the Italian nation; indeed, the non-Italian newcomers lacked such an important national link and came from countries that had no connections with Italy. This explains why the former were special foreigners, that is, peculiar Others.

3.2. *ITALIANI NON REGNICOLI*: CITIZENSHIP AS A RIGHT

3.2.a. Legislation and Policy

Italian citizenship policy vis-à-vis the *non regnicoli* was extremely generous during the entire liberal period. In fact, contrary to non-Italian immigrants, they enjoyed a facilitated naturalization procedure—"small naturalization" or "administrative naturalization by royal decree"—based on a short and relatively easy bureaucratic process that required only the discretionary decision of the executive authority, without involving the participation of both chambers of the Italian parliament or the favorable opinion of the Council of State. Also, although both Italian and non-Italian immigrants who naturalized became subjects of the dynasty of Savoy, former *non regnicoli* enjoyed full citizenship status inclusive of active and passive political rights at the national level, which former non-Italians could exercise only exceptionally.[31] Finally and most interestingly, these special aliens were entitled to a very substantial "denizenship status" without naturalizing (while thus holding onto their Austrian, pontifical, French, Swiss or San Marinese citizenship).[32] In effect, despite their juridical alienhood they had the right not to be expelled from the territory of the Italian kingdom for reasons of public security, as well as enjoying active and passive political rights at the communal and provincial levels. Therefore, in opposition to the non-Italians, they did not risk deportation, and in the quality of settled "foreigners of Italian nationality" they could vote and be elected in local and provincial elections as well as being entitled to pursue administrative careers as councilors and vice-mayors, with the only exception, apparently, being head of a municipality.[33] In short, even though all foreign immigrants (Italian and non-Italian) enjoyed civil rights without limiting the latter entitlements to the existence of reciprocal agreements between Italy and the countries of origin, major differences of status existed with regard to the other aspects of citizenship mentioned in this section.[34]

3.2.b. State Official Discourses:
Nationhood, Citizenship and Irredentist Political Objectives

From a historical point of view, the continuity of legislation and policy concerning the peculiar status of the *Italiani non regnicoli* from 1861 until 1922 is telling: it demonstrates that the Italian state showed, consistently, for the entire liberal epoch, a favorable disposition vis-à-vis these special foreigners. Obviously, bearing in mind the first part of this chapter concerning context and definitions, it is not difficult to grasp the ideological reasons behind such a permanent generous state attitude: the *non regnicoli* were regarded as members of the nation. They therefore deserved special citizenship status.

Although the idiom of Italianhood shaped constantly the opinions and judgments of the Italian authorities and decision-making elites who debated the introduction, adoption and application of the norms, the language and tone used when alluding to that national reference varied within state discourse(s) throughout the liberal epoch, according to the strength of irredentist ideology and objectives among state authorities. More particularly, the sources at our disposal demonstrate that the state nationalist rhetoric accompanying discussion of civic inclusion of these special aliens was highly passionate, and even aggressive in certain cases, during the first years of political unification, when the unredeemed territories of Venice and Rome were claimed by the Italian kingdom and still under foreign rule. Indeed, during the first post-unification decade, citizenship policies were clearly linked to further aspirations of statehood and even used as a means to anticipate it. Subsequently, though, despite the fact that, for many Italians, the events of 1870 did not represent the completion of national Risorgimento and that official irredentist ambitions were still rather significant in the peninsula, official discourse about the *non regnicoli* became moderate, lost the highly fervent tones of the first years of post-unification history and was not linked to irredentist political objectives—the only exception being the final nationalist "war legislative eruption," which took place in liberal Italy between 1915 and 1918 in anticipation of the demise of the Austro-Hungarian empire and incorporation of its subjects. Finally, whereas these citizenship issues were openly associated with projects of statehood in reference to the political émigrés of pontifical and Austrian lands before 1870, never was such a link made in our sources by Italian authorities during the liberal period when talking about the arrivals from Ticino, San Marino, Corsica and Malta. Our documents confirm that Italian liberal elites did not use civic inclusion of the inhabitants originating from these countries and territories with a view to realizing the "maximalist project" of making the political borders of the Italian state congruent with the broadest boundaries of the Italian nation.

Historical evidence is provided here to ground all the aforementioned affirmations—including some important archival documentation that, although covering the pre-1866 post-unification period of Chapter One, must be mentioned here as it refers to the imminent incorporations of Venice and Rome to take place in 1866 and 1870.

During the momentous years preceding annexation of Venice and Mantua and proclamation of Rome as Italy's capital, the Italian state advocated and defended its generous citizenship rules touching on the status of the *Veneti* and *Romani* as an instrument to anticipate the accomplishment of Italian unification, that is, to anticipate and push forward what diplomacy and the army had not yet achieved. First, during those early years of national history, liberal Italy allowed some Austrian subjects to sit in the Italian parliament, and exercise national political rights, without having naturalized at all, as Italian law required. This was the case, specifically, of deputies Luigi Silvestrelli, Filippo De Boni and Mattia Montecchi, who were allowed to stand for political elections and enjoy the highest and most solemn of all political entitlements: formulation of the laws of the nation. Obviously, the fact that the door of the Italian parliament was open, even in violation of the law, to certain foreign citizens who were regarded as "Italian brothers" of the *terre irredente* (unredeemed lands), before the latter were annexed, can say a lot about how nationalist application of an aggressive citizenship policy was used by Italian authorities against the political *status quo* and as a way to demonstrate that the inhabitants of the territories from which the three deputies originated deserved to become subjects of the Italian king—in a word, *regnicoli.*[35]

Second, because having only three *non regnicoli* in the Italian parliament was deemed not enough, Italian authorities proposed on various occasions bills that aimed at making the process of naturalization of these special aliens even easier than it was. The proposals—presented in the lower chamber by the radical Left deputy and former patriotic activist Cairoli in 1866 and in 1868—were similar to another project of law that had been formulated in 1862 and provided for automatic and obligatory recognition of full Italian citizenship by the liberal state vis-à-vis a *non regnicolo,* once the individual had asked for it and fulfilled some simple requirements (i.e., registering in a *comune* of his choice as well as providing a birth certificate and a clear criminal record).[36]

Also, the theoretical arguments that were upheld on those occasions by intransigent as well as moderate Left deputies to justify such generous practices of naturalization were very categorical in explaining the ideological underpinnings that, in the eyes of some liberal elites, made an open naturalization policy a "just" and "necessary" measure that would contribute to the ongoing historical process of Risorgimento. For instance, in the words of the proponent Cairoli, the recognition of Italian citizenship through facilitated naturalization procedures was "a right" for the *Italiani non regnicoli* not only because many of them (or many of their relatives) had fought or died in the battlefield and contributed to Italy's national independence but also because of the 1861 decree of the nation, which had proclaimed the birth of the Italian kingdom. Since that date, argued the deputy in blunt language, "all the Italians [were] citizens," and because Italy had declared that the provinces of Venice and Rome belonged to the 1861 state and should be freed from foreign domination, the right of those immigrants to be "recognized" as Italian citizens was incontestable and unquestionable. The project did not "grant" citizenship but only "recognized" a status that existed already *a priori.*[37]

In line with this fervent nationalist argument, the moderate exponent and professor Mancini (already mentioned in our previous chapters) also added a further theoretical justification, which we found in some documents preceding the Venetian annexation of 1866 and which would be defended by the deputy and academic during his entire life. Specifically, using his famous theory on nationality according to which the nation rather than the state was the primary actor in international relations and "the elementary unit," "the rational monad," "the mother idea" of international law,[38] the parliamentarian elaborated on the idea that nationhood (rather than statehood) defined the concept of national citizenship. For him, Italian state legislation had to confer the same citizenship rights on those who belonged to the Italian nation—no matter whether the latter was all united under one state or scattered across numerous political entities. Citizenship did not necessarily follow the political borders of the state but could well go beyond them, should the boundaries of Italianhood require it. This is why every Italian (*regnicolo* and *non regnicolo*) was a citizen in the 1861 kingdom and generous naturalization provisions were highly justified in his view.[39] In this case, and to apply to the Italian peninsula a recent remark made elsewhere in reference to the German context, one could well argue that for Mancini "citizenship [was] quite literally about an *imagined* community; rather than representing the actual composition of society, it represent[ed] its ideal."[40]

Finally, the reference to the nexus between an open naturalization policy and the accomplishment of political unification was also made plainly—with very explicit allusions—during those early years. For instance, deputy (and later minister) Castagnola argued that Cairoli's project was the best way to convince Europe that "the unity of Italy [could] probably be stopped still for some time but not be prevented."[41] Italy's domestic legislation was therefore an additional measure to show to the international community that Italian truncated Risorgimento was to be rectified soon. Mancini as well intervened, again to make the same point—although in a much more temperate style. According to him, the

approval of the proposal would have a strong political signification before the other European states because "the whole Europe will recognize
in it that we do not lose sight, a single day, of our last goal, and that,
faithful interpreters of the national sentiment, we do not avert our gaze
from that aim which is in the aspirations and affections of all the Italians."[42] The final objective of Italian national patriotism had not yet been
achieved; naturalization reforms were a move forward toward that goal.

Admittedly, these highly generous parliamentary bills of 1866 and
1868 (as well as the one of 1862) never became law because the legislative sessions adjourned and also because the norms involved were too
controversial and, if approved, could have been seen with suspicion by
Austrian and papal authorities—thus destabilizing the already tense foreign relations among Italy, Vienna, the papacy and other European powers implicated in the Risorgimento process and in the Roman Question.
Yet they say a lot about Italy's attempt to use its citizenship provisions as
a way of pushing the national unification of the country further ahead.[43]

Subsequently, once Venice and Rome were finally annexed to the
Italian kingdom, the nationalist discourse on the *non regnicoli* throughout the first post-unification decade lost ground and, according to our
sources, was no longer to be heard afterward when thinking and talking
about citizenship issues related to this category. Not surprisingly, explicit or implicit references to the Italian nation and to Italian belonging
continued to be made after 1870 and throughout the liberal epoch. For
example, on the occasion of the presentation of the future 1882 electoral
law, Minister of the Interior Depretis said that the special provision reserved for the *non regnicoli* was in line with Italy's past policy because it
had a "historical and political value which no one [could] miss."[44] Also,
criticizing an article in the initial project of the 1912 citizenship law that
lowered the status of the *non regnicoli* to that of non-Italian immigrants,
a senatorial authority said that the norm concerning "these brothers of
ours" had to be kept unchanged in continuity with Italian tradition; low-
ering their status to the level of the non-Italians could only be condemned
by the "conscience of the entire Nation."[45]

Yet the sources at our disposal show that, in comparison with the official discourse pertaining to the *Veneti* and *Romani*, the explicit mention
of Italian nationhood after 1870 was always very general and shorter
(mainly a few words rather than long speeches), that the language used
was not emphatic or aggressive at all and that citizenship policy was
not used as an irredentist instrument for the realization of Risorgimento.
This does not mean that after the annexation of Rome and the end of the
pope's temporal power irredentism was not widespread in the peninsula;
indeed, anti-Austrian feelings and resentments were at times quite strong
and reached their climax on several occasions, as in 1882 (following

the arrest and execution of the patriotic activist from Trieste Guglielmo Oberdan) or in 1908 (as a reaction to the Austro-Hungarian annexation of Bosnia). We only want to argue that after the events of Porta Pia in 1870, the nexus between the issue of civic inclusion of the *non regnicoli* and the project of extending Italian statehood was no longer made and applied aggressively. Only during the First World War would new nationalist legislation be introduced in liberal Italy for political and military reasons linked to the hoped for the imminent demise of the Austro-Hungarian empire. For example, between 1915 and 1918 "Austro-Hungarian subjects of Italian nationality" were exempted, despite their foreign legal citizenship, from the restrictions a variety of temporary Italian laws put on citizens of enemy states (i.e., on the obligation to reside in a precise locality for reasons of public security). Also, they could be captains or crew members on board Italian merchant ships and send their children to the secondary schools of the Italian kingdom without paying—upon certain conditions—any registration charges.[46]

Finally, whereas the introduction and adoption of citizenship provisions were inspired by explicit irredentist aspirations with regard to Venice and Rome, our sources demonstrate that this was not the case in reference to the extended concept of Italian nationhood and incorporation of Ticino, San Marino, Corsica and Malta into the 1861 Savoy state. As a senatorial authority maintained in 1869, even if Italy had a generous and open naturalization policy vis-à-vis, say, the *Ticinesi* because of common origins, this did not mean liberal Italy wanted to declare war against the state that owned this "Italian land" with a view to reacquiring it.

I believe that none of the Powers owning part of the Italian territory could get cross because Italy gives the rights of citizenship more easily to those whose ancestors were Italian, than to other foreigners.[...] Of course, if for example a Ticinese argued: Ticino, in antiquity, was an Italian land; my father and my forefather were Italian; I would like to be honored with the bestowal of Italian citizenship; who would dare refuse it? [...] But certainly through this act of kindness and sympathy, nourished by the memory of a common origin, we do not intend to declare war on those who possess some Italian territory in order to regain it.[47]

Also, in line with this point, a judicial authority argued in 1884 that the intention of the Italian liberal legislator when shaping citizenship rules was to pay tribute only to the "commonality of *stirpe* (i.e., racial stock) and language" that united all Italian provinces and was by no means based on a desire to keep alive the aspirations of other lands to unite with the Italian kingdom, nor to encourage and foment such aspirations in those citizens who came from Italian lands that were part of other states and were satisfied with their current condition as part of another country.[48] Finally, since we did not find, during our research, any other source in which citizenship discourse about the immigrants from San Marino, Malta and Corsica was linked to nationalist aspirations of future annexations, we personally think that this silence is eloquent, historically speaking. It shows—together with the explicit evidence given here—that liberal Italy did not use (and was determined not to use) its citizenship policy to pursue a political agenda that would have made the borders of the post-1861 Savoy kingdom coincide with the boundaries of the "entire" Italian nation. In the absence of further archival evidence, one could interpret this reticence of the liberal state as prudent lack of interest in actual annexation of these lands; as a way of admitting, implicitly, the Savoy kingdom's weakness within the international system; or perhaps as an Italian variant of the French adage "*Parlez-en jamais. Pensez-y toujours*" ("Never speak about it. Always think about it"). In our view, the first interpretation should be taken as the more appropriate, the last one as the more intriguing.

Having explored and discussed the peculiar citizenship status that was constantly enjoyed, during the liberal era, by the *non regnicoli* for their innate *italianità*, we shall now turn to the non-Italians, to their possible acquired *italianità* and to their Italian citizenship status, which was regarded as a prize rather than as a right.

3.3. NON-ITALIAN IMMIGRANTS: CITIZENSHIP AS A PRIZE

3.3.a. Legislation and Policy

Non-Italian immigrants (e.g., French, German, British, Ottoman migrants) enjoyed very different citizenship status during the liberal epoch from the one reserved, exclusively, to the *non regnicoli*. Contrary to the latter category, they could indeed be expelled from the Savoy state under specific conditions, were not allowed to exercise municipal political rights while holding their foreign citizenship (and without having naturalized) as well as being subjected to a very complex and restrictive naturalization policy for half a century—despite a few timid liberal reforms having been introduced on several occasions by the Italian governments. Also, although as of 1912 their process of naturalization was finally simplified and made less restrictive, a difference of treatment continued to be kept in force to distinguish them from the *non regnicoli*.

It is precisely the peculiar complexity and ungenerous nature of the naturalization norms concerning these "aliens of non-Italian nationality" as well as the slow and controversial introduction of a simpler and more expansive policy that deserve to be examined here. In our view, this makes the contrast between the respective status of the two types of external Others stand out even more prominently. Until 1912, the non-Italians could naturalize—like the *non regnicoli*—through the process of "small naturalization." In opposition to the latter group, though, they acquired Italian citizenship inclusive only of local political rights. And in fact, to be entitled to vote and be elected at the national level, they were obliged to go through the additional as well as much longer and demanding procedures of "grand or legislative naturalization"—introduced, exclusively, for them and involving the solemn intervention and approval of both legislative chambers.[49]

From a wider European perspective, the distinction between what was called in Italian *"piccola e grande naturalizzazione"*—between "small" and "grand," or "administrative" and "legislative," naturalization—was not attributable to the 1861 Italian peninsula since similar concepts had been in use in France since 1814. More particularly, after Napoleon's fall and the collapse of the empire, the Bourbon King Louis XVIII and his royalist parliamentary bodies decided, unsurprisingly, to return to Old Regime vocabulary and practices of naturalization and introduced not only *"lettres de declaration de naturalité"*(letters of declaration of naturalization) but also a system of *"grande et simple naturalisation"* (grand naturalization and naturalization proper) allowing an analogy to be drawn with the peninsula. The very first type ("declarations of naturalization"), conferred specifically on former soldiers and on property owners and merchants (born in the territories annexed to France since 1791 and detached from the empire in 1814–1815), did not really transform foreigners into Frenchmen but basically recognized retroactively their existing quality of Frenchness. The second and the third types, by contrast ("grand naturalization" and "naturalization proper"), were granted to all the other worthy aliens who had settled in the Hexagon but, despite making a foreigner a French citizen, only the former process (*grande naturalisation*) entitled the naturalized French to sit in the Chamber of Peers and that of Deputies. This French distinction would be abolished in 1848, reestablished the following year, abolished again from 1867 until 1889 and then finally erased from French national legislation only in 1984.[50] What is peculiar, though, about the Italian case study is that the long and complex second practice (grand naturalization) was never applied to the *non regnicoli,* who from a legal point of view were as foreign as the non-Italian immigrants.

The procedure of "small naturalization" was seen by the authorities of the Savoy kingdom as an initial step through which the state could strengthen the existing bonds with the former alien; indeed, by proclaiming the person Italian and letting that person take part in public life at the local level, small naturalization contributed to deepening the attachment between the ex non-Italian migrant and the new adopting state.[51] On the contrary, the second process, "grand naturalization," was regarded as a subsequent and most advanced step of integration, which in the words of a parliamentary commission served the purpose of "refining and completing the quality [of Italian citizen]."[52] However, as this last procedure led to full citizenship, it was applied extremely rarely. In effect, within the context of an already limited political suffrage around the peninsula, the exercise of national political rights by a former non-Italian was seen as an exceptional "prize" to be awarded, only exceptionally, by Italian authorities. This is why full citizenship had to be bestowed on extremely worthy non-Italian foreigners who deserved it for having lived for, and devoted their life in various ways and with special merit to, the benefit of the country. After all, the solemn involvement of the highest representative body of the nation (the parliament) in the procedure of grand naturalization necessarily required corresponding exceptional qualities of the non-Italian alien.[53] This was justified on moral grounds (linked to the high value attached to the concept of full *status civitatis*, and therefore to caution in granting it) as well as on political and security reasons (which excluded foreigners from the highest positions and political functions of a state).[54] As we have seen, naturalization of the *non regnicoli* was not at all linked with these concerns.

Interestingly, this complex policy pertaining to the aliens of non-Italian nationality was repeatedly criticized for its restrictive nature, and various calls were made for reforms in both Italian chambers from the late 1880s to soften it and to abolish the second procedure altogether.[55] To this end, additional naturalization norms were introduced in 1901 and in 1906, allowing acquisition of full citizenship by non-Italians, without the requirement of involving long parliamentary discussion. These generous new rules were defended and approved on the basis of two arguments: state interest on the one hand, due to the high social, intellectual and moral stature of the resident non-Italians at that period; and liberalism and the "spirit of the time" on the other, in reference to the fact that naturalization was seen as a symbol of individual freedom and of free agency that had to be cherished in the name of liberal ideology.[56] However, both the 1901 and the 1906 rules had important limits: the first provision could be applied only to two specific categories of non-Italian foreigners, whereas the second norm—applicable to all aliens of non-Italian nationality—introduced the significant restrictive state guarantee of allowing the naturalized to sit in parliament only after six years from acquisition of Italian citizenship.[57] Non-Italians continued, therefore, to be treated differently from the *non regnicoli*.

Only in 1912 would all the differentiated naturalizations be abolished so as to allow a non-Italian to acquire full citizenship (inclusive, immediately, of local and political rights) via one single procedure. However, the liveliness of the 1911–12 parliamentary debates leading to approval of the norm, as well as the variety of the arguments and reticence among some official authorities to grant full citizenship straightaway to a former non-Italian, demonstrates that the introduction of an open and expansive naturalization policy vis-à-vis the "outright foreigners" was a controversial issue, whereas no doubts existed on the generosity the Italian state had to show vis-à-vis the *non regnicoli*.[58] Also, although strong counterarguments were made in favor of liberalizing the whole process and the final approved provisions of the 1912 law were more generous than the previous ones, the naturalization procedure concerning aliens of non-Italian nationality continued to be slightly more restrictive than the one of the *non regnicoli* since the latter category did not need the favorable opinion of the Council of State; nor was it submitted to the same residence requirements associated with the non-Italians.[59]

The outright foreigners and the *non regnicoli* deserved being treated differently because of their differing alien nature: a Dane and an Italian-speaking Istrian were not foreigners in the same way. As we shall see below, the *italianità* that was innate in the *non regnicoli* and that made them full Italian citizens relatively easily was acquired by the non-Italians after a long, difficult and exceptionally demanding process of social, civic, cultural and political integration within the new adopting state. Nationhood (nation membership) made the difference.

3.3.b. Individual Files Concerning "Grand Naturalization": Italianness and Full Status Civitatis

Throughout nineteenth-century post-unification Italian history and up to 1912 (that is the period in which the norms concerning "grand naturalization" were in force), the number of non-Italian foreigners who acquired full Italian citizenship did not even reach twenty; apparently, only fifteen applications were processed.[60] By taking the Italian state perspective, we can attempt to do a systematic analysis of the official discourse emerging from these files in view of providing further insights on the concepts of alienhood, *italianità* and citizenship during the liberal decades.[61]

The primary sources at our disposal are actually unique documents within the entire history of Italian citizenship since "legislative naturalization" was a specificity of the liberal period that, abrogated in 1912, was never re-introduced—neither during the fascist decades nor in the post–World War Two years. The historical value of these individual dossiers is therefore immense. Moreover, they are particularly interesting not only because they are a reservoir of official comments made on the concept of Italian citizenship but also because they excluded female foreigners *a priori*: readers surely recall from our previous chapter that women did not have the right to vote in Italy and therefore could not apply for "grand naturalization" since it led to acquisition of national political rights.

Which factors, according to Italian state authorities, demonstrated a "complete assimilation of an individual's feelings and interests, with the feelings and interests of the nation," thus making the person finally worthy of acquiring full citizenship?[62] Not surprisingly, the ideals of deep attachment and devotion to Italy were the first introductory elements to be emphasized by state officialdom in assessing the foreigners' applications. General profound affection for the country could be expressed by the alien in a variety of ways that were repeatedly listed together (as complementary factors) to show how a combination of numerous indicators of integration made a person particularly valuable as a full member of the national community. The former non-Italians had, for instance, long years of residence in the peninsula, their upbringing and education had taken place in Italy and they had also acquired property in the country, married an Italian woman, had children in the kingdom and in most cases previously acquired Italian citizenship via the procedure of small naturalization. These were the cases, among others, of the British subjects Evelino Waddington and Ernesto Nathan, both from London, as well as of the Swiss citizen Edmondo Mayor, from the French-speaking Canton of Vaud.[63]

With regard to this general attachment to Italy—which was constantly emphasized at the beginning of state reports—the rhetoric of liberal authorities made explicit reference to some related or additional factors, such as knowledge of the Italian language and any possible link between the foreigner's family background and the peninsula, thus adding a stronger cultural content to the notion of Italian citizenship. For instance, when proposing to grant full membership status to a Dutch professor, Giacomo Moleschott, of the University of Turin, Minister of the Interior Desiderato Chiaves mentioned the alien's profound knowledge of the Italian idiom.[64] Also, in the case of an application by an Austrian subject named Arnaldo Cantani, attention was paid to the fact that the alien's ascendants were of Neapolitan origin, had been forced to emigrate from the peninsula to Bohemia in the second half of the eighteenth century (during the reign of the Bourbon Charles III) and had always kept in their heart the desire to return to Italy. Thus good knowledge of the Italian language as well as distant Italian family memories and background transmitted through blood relations were regarded as additional fundamental indicators of the "worthiness" of the applicant.[65]

Interestingly, though, such factors concerning the alien's general attachment to the country were never sufficient to make an application successful; other important elements were repeatedly mentioned, which explains the highly exceptional and infrequent bestowal of full citizenship upon former non-Italians. First, the philanthropic and civic feelings of the foreigner vis-à-vis Italy, its society and its local communities held a special place within official state discourse. In this respect, the applications of Giovanni Meyer, from Tsarist Saint Petersburg, and of the Greek subject Matteo Schilizzi were particularly worth considering. The former had distinguished himself for his "pious acts" by financing creation of a hospital for children in Florence as well as donating it to the municipality, so gaining the esteem of the entire local community. The latter, in turn, had contributed to the institution of an aid organization in the Tuscan city of Livorno, as well as providing moral and material assistance to the poor victims of Naples during the calamitous cholera epidemic that devastated the southern city in the autumn of 1884.[66] Obviously, persistent reference to these factors illustrated a concept of full Italian citizenship that involved solidarity, civism and cohesion between the alien and the Italian community.

A second complementary factor that state official authorities highlighted in their analysis was the foreigner's personal participation and input into the economic, institutional, political and cultural spheres of Italian state and society. With regard to a contribution to Italian economy, the individual files of the Austrian subjects Alberto and Edoardo Amman as well as of the Hungarian brothers Luigi Teodoro and Francesco Kossuth (sons of the famous patriot Lajos Kossuth) were very instructive. In fact, the two Ammans co-owned a textile factory in the northern Italian city of Pordenone (providing employment and bread to more than a thousand industrial workers), whereas the brothers Kossuth held executive positions in the southern Italian metallurgic industry and, as engineers, had been involved in various Italian public railway works as well as in the national governmental project for the construction of the Cenisio Tunnel across the Alps. Their contribution to Italy's economy was unquestionable.[67]

As for the reference to the alien's active participation in state institutions and civil services as well as within Italy's intellectual and cultural life, the successful applications of some former non-Italians were particularly illuminating. For instance, Cantani, already mentioned, had been teaching medicine in numerous Italian universities as well as having been appointed to various governmental positions within the Supreme Council of Public Education and the Supreme Council of Public Health. Former non-Italian Schilizzi had participated actively as a councilor within the municipality of Naples, thus demonstrating "uncontested civic virtues" and "trust" among his fellow citizens. Finally, Prince Aslan D'Abro Pagratide, born in the Cyclades island of Syros of an Armenian father (Prince Stefano D'Abro) and an English lady (Emma Sparkes), had not only achieved the position of vice-mayor in Naples but had also been very active within Italy's literary and artistic circles by becoming a member of the Italian Society of Fine Arts.[68] Clearly, all these arguments as to

the active participation of the alien in the economic, institutional, political and intellectual spheres of Italian society echoed a concept of post-
unification Italian full citizenship similar to the civic republican ideal of
active service for the *res publica* as it was expressed during the Renais-
sance period.[69]

The third and final element that emerges, plainly, from our sources
as an indicator of deep *italianità* was the ideal of patriotism and of service *pro patria*. Obviously, due to the contemporary historical context of
national Risorgimento, being patriotic during the liberal period meant
having participated in, or contributed in various ways to, the process of
Italian nation-statehood. This contribution to the national cause varied:
it could involve the alien's political participation in the "new order of
things" following the political and military events of the post-1859 period; it could be stretched to include the patriotism of the alien's family
and ascendants; or finally, it could involve the personal sacrifice of one's
life on the battlefield for the liberation of the "oppressed" Italian nation.

The first example was represented by the aforementioned Waddington,
who had in fact participated in organizing the plebiscite for the union
of Umbria with the Savoy kingdom in 1860, thus demonstrating clearly
"his patriotism and his cooperation vis-à-vis the new order of things accomplished in that province."[70] The second model, involving transmission
of patriotic feelings through family blood and relations, was embodied
in the applications of Ernesto Nathan, the brothers Kossuth and Count
Marescalchi. Nathan—whose family name will ring a bell for experts
on Giuseppe Mazzini—was the son of Sara Levi Nathan, the English
lady who had given assistance and hospitality to many Italian patriots
living in exile in England, including Mazzini himself. This is why the
patriotic merits of the applicant's family were magnified on several occasions by Italian authorities.[71] For related reasons, the applications of the
two Kossuths deserved success: sons of the great Hungarian exile who
had constantly upheld the ideals of "redemption" and "resurgence" of
the Magyar and Italian nations, they had been encouraged to show their
devotion vis-à-vis adopting the Italian *patria*, which had given refuge to
their father and shared solidarity with the Magyars in fighting against a
common enemy (Austria). The applicants' family was therefore seen as
a fertile ground where special feelings of affection for the new country
could be cherished.[72] And in the case of Count Marescalchi, the applicant had a paternal ascendant, Count Ferdinando Marescalchi, who had
been an Italian Jacobin, been educated to liberal ideas and contributed
with his liberalism and patriotism to the political events that had taken
place in the Italian peninsula at the end of the eighteenth century and the
beginning of the nineteenth by organizing in Bologna the revolutionary
movements from which the Cisalpine Republic originated, thus giving

form to one of the first projects of Italian unification within the peninsula.[73] Finally, the third and last example, of patriotic attachment involving the military dimension of the heroic sacrifice of one's life *pro patria*, was epitomized in the person of the Hungarian General Stefano Türr, who had become honorary lieutenant general in the Italian Royal Army and general aide-de-camp of His Majesty Vittorio Emanuele II. Indeed, having fought in the name of the historical principle of nationality and shared military experiences even with Giuseppe Garibaldi, the Hungarian general deserved full consideration despite a lack of continuous residence in the country.[74] Obviously, this reference to *amor patriae*—expressed by non-Italian foreigners in different ways—mirrored a concept of liberal Italian citizenship reminiscent of classical notions of patriotism, analyzed and discussed, among others, by Maurizio Viroli and Massimo Rosati.[75]

To conclude, in opposition to the *Italiani non regnicoli* who could acquire full Italian citizenship via a facilitated and rapid process of naturalization—involving neither the exemplary individual profiles and actions explored above nor attentive scrutiny by both chambers of the Italian parliament—the non-Italian immigrants were deemed worthy of the same status only after a very long process of integration and socialization in the peninsula and only if their *cursus* included extraordinary accomplishments and services rendered at various levels and in various spheres of Italian life. Also, their individual files were processed by virtually all Italian authorities, and participation of the legislative power in the discussions was obligatory. The *non regnicoli* shared innate feelings of Italian national belonging that allowed them to enjoy privileged status. The non-Italians did not—by definition. They had to develop these Italian national sentiments. As a consequence, exercise of full citizenship was for them a highly exceptional and honorary award.

3.4. *JUS SOLI* FROM THE CIVIL CODE TO 1922: ASCRIPTION OF CITIZENSHIP TO THE GENERATIONS BORN IN ITALY

Study of naturalization patterns and policy (concerning first-generation immigrants) must be done in conjunction with the even more important analysis of the ascriptive *jus soli* rule (concerning further generations born in the peninsula) because, as Brubaker has put it, "ascription constitutes and perpetually reconstitutes the citizenry; naturalization reshapes it at the margins."[76] Examining within this chapter the provisions pertaining to the aforementioned generations therefore allows us a complete picture of incorporation of foreigners within the institutional history of Italian citizenship during the liberal decades. Also, this makes possible an examination of the evolution that took place, in this respect, since the 1865 civil code was introduced in Italy, as we saw in Chapter One of the book.

Apparently, the territorial norm applied in the peninsula affected the status of the children issued from both types of immigrants, Italian and non-Italian alike. In all the sources at our disposal, nothing is said about the existence of specific provisions for the second generation of the *non regnicoli*—although, indirectly, the minor children of this category did enjoy a privileged position due to family law, since the less demanding and less time-consuming naturalization procedure of a *non regnicolo* entailed quick naturalization of his dependents (i.e., offspring and wife alike), who became Italian subjects upon the father/husband's acquisition of the new status.

As we explained in Chapter One, the 1865 Italian code embraced a substantial element of territoriality by taking into account birth and prolonged residence in the kingdom. More particularly, fulfilling two requirements (the child's birthplace and the father's domicile over the previous ten years) made the children of aliens citizens at birth—with a right to change status via a declaration to be made within one year from majority. On the contrary, if only the territorial requirement of birth were fulfilled (and the father had not been living in the country for a decade), then the children were aliens but could become citizens at majority, by making a declaration, or alternatively by accepting a job in the Italian public service, joining the army or the navy, or responding to the call to arms. Since no rule contained the double *jus soli* principle, the status of the third generation was not regulated.[77]

In 1912, though, with introduction of the new citizenship law abrogating the 1865 provisions, an important evolution took place since the policy concerning the second generation born in the country became more restrictive. In fact, Italian citizenship was no longer to be ascribed at birth (per the specific conditions discussed above) but acquired only at majority by one of the following tacit or explicit manifestations of will: military service, acceptance of a public job, residence in the kingdom at the age of majority (and declaring a wish to take Italian citizenship), or ten years of residence (and no declaration made to keep the original foreign status).[78] This means that, from 1912 onward, all children of foreign parents would be, and remain, aliens at least until the age of twenty-one.

The 1911–12 parliamentary discussions related to this provision were also less open vis-à-vis the children of immigrants than they had been in the past. Admittedly, an amendment was proposed at the Senate to reproduce the double territorial principle of the 1865 rule and limit it to the second and third generations of offspring.[79] However, in the end neither the government nor the senatorial central bureau accepted the proposition. Basically, there were two reasons underlining such a change of policy: the major one, as emphasized by Senator Polacco, was directly linked to demography. In 1865, Italy had just achieved unification, possessed a relatively small population (compared to the statistics of 1910–11) and could therefore use any means to increase its demographic condition. Fifty years later, though, such concern disappeared since the country had become very prolific.[80] Also, apart from the consideration about Italian demographic growth, the new restrictive rule was to be introduced because it was more in line with the much-praised principle of the "unity of nationalities within the household." In effect, by defining a child—born in Italy—as an Italian citizen at birth once the foreign father had ten continuous years of domicile in the kingdom, the civil code contributed to increasing the number of foreign immigrant parents whose children held Italian citizenship. This is why, "as a tribute to the oneness of citizenship, desirable among the members of a same family, it is natural [...] that, without harming the country already well-supplied with population, the ancient presumption of citizenship be abandoned."[81]

To conclude, Italy's citizenship policy, as introduced after the first decade of the twentieth century, affords no evidence of exclusively descent-based provisions since some elements of conditional *jus soli* were adopted. In comparison with the previous norms of 1865, though, a significant change occurred toward a more restrictive stand as the rule concerning attribution of citizenship at birth was erased from national legislation and Italian membership status was acquired only at majority. Despite this fundamental change with the past, the juridical situation of this particular category of offspring continued to differ from that held by its counterpart in early-twentieth-century Germany. In fact, as the 1913 Wilhelmine citizenship law continued to attribute German citizenship, as in the previous post-unification period, exclusively on the basis of *jus sanguinis*, the children of non-German foreign immigrants born in the country could become German only through naturalization. Also, in reference to the debates surrounding this 1913 law, it seems that unconditional, conditional and double *jus soli* were all unthinkable and that no particular voice was heard in favor of any form of territoriality.[82] This was due to the special concern of preserving ethnic Germanness in the eastern border of the Reich, against a double historical threat: the *Reichspolen* (two and a half million German citizens of Polish origin incorporated in the Prussian East and toward whom a hostile Prussian-German *Polenpolitik* was practiced) and the unwanted Slavic and Jewish immigration from the east into Germany. It was this dual context that at the time shaped an ethnonational discourse and influenced Germany's stance vis-à-vis citizenship issues.[83] In the peninsula, on the contrary, the 1912 citizenship law and its related parliamentary hearings show that Italian citizenship tradition still had some room for the territorial tenet.

Wilhelmine Germany and Giolitti's Italy therefore held contrasting positions from this perspective. Consequently, and to continue our historical journey through the notion of *italianità*, we can argue that the imaginary contours of Italianness as drawn by these citizenship norms in 1912 continued to be less rigid and more open than those pertaining to contemporary Germanness, so as to incorporate a relatively more flexible stand vis-à-vis foreignness.

3.5. CONCLUSION

The differentiated use of citizenship strategies and formulation of political discourses pertaining to Italian and non-Italian immigration expressed, and were constantly informed by, concepts of "the nation" and "outsiders of the nation." The significant assimilationist policies and debates vis-à-vis the *Italiani non regnicoli* pointed to an idea of Italian nationhood that was not "state-national," as in France—where the nation was defined in relation to the territorial framework of the state—but "ethnonational," as in Germany—where the nation, seen as a cultural and linguistic community, had preceded creation of the state and was regarded as a community of descent, independent of and defined against the framework of statehood.[84] In particular, while reiterating that a specific citizenship norm does not reflect in and of itself any notion of nationhood, we need to emphasize that what reflected Italianhood and outright foreignhood was not the specific juridical provision as such but the fact of adopting, adapting and applying the latter to a specific Italian context and of choosing one norm for the "special aliens" because they were regarded as Italians and another norm for the "non-Italians" because they did not share any common national traits with the subjects of the peninsula. So both rules (for the "Italian" and for the "non-Italian" immigrants) might well have been borrowed, from a juridical point of view, from past legal traditions and from foreign countries through legal transfers that tell us nothing about concepts of nationhood. What counts, though, for our present argument is that, within the Italian case study, these norms were not only borrowed but used in a certain way by Italian authorities to realize political nationalist objectives and defend particular nationalist discourses. For Italian authorities, the existence and persistence of differentiated juridical rules to be applied vis-à-vis the two groups of aliens mattered, and mattered a lot politically. It is the significant contrast between differentiated citizenship provisions as well as their peculiar application within the specific Italian context that, in our view, mirrors—in tandem with all the more explicit political debates explored in this chapter—the interrelated concepts of the ins and the outs, "us" and "them," "nationhood" and "its outsiders."

Also, as is clearly shown by the historical evidence concerning definitions of the *non regnicoli,* the specific traditions of national self-understanding shaping this issue echoed not only the reference of "the nation in search of a state" but also a more extensive interpretation stretching over territories and populations that shared traits of *italianità* in different ways but were not directly involved in the Risorgimento process.

Thirdly, and by changing the angle of observation, we have also found that until 1912 (when the procedure of grand naturalization for non-Italian aliens was finally abrogated) two specific concepts of being Italian were taking shape on the peninsula: one involving "thick citizenship" inclusive of political rights, the other referring to a "thinner" and less demanding form of membership. Clearly, this further aspect regarding alienhood shows that Italianness was again a dual and multiple concept. The same point was actually argued when talking about women vis-à-vis men in the previous chapter, and an analogous argument can be put forward here when thinking, from another perspective, about "Italian special aliens," "non-Italian aliens," foreignness in general and naturalization policies in particular.

Finally, as shown by Italian incorporation of conditional *jus soli* in 1912—an aspect totally absent in the 1913 German citizenship law—one can argue that the lines shaping the boundaries of Italian national identity and drawn by this specific citizenship rule continued to be distinctly more inclusive than the ones drawn at the German (imperial) level. The notions of Italianness and Germanness were being shaped differently on account of the relations vis-à-vis foreignhood and territoriality in the two respective countries. From this viewpoint, *italianità* continued to be relatively more open to foreign diversity—although less than in the past—and to distinguish itself from the post-unification German example.

In the next chapter, we carry on our analysis of Italian national citizenship and identity by exploring there the state nationality policies that were formulated vis-à-vis the millions of Italian emigrants who left the peninsula in search of bread, and vis-à-vis their descendants who were born and settled abroad.

CHAPTER FOUR

"O migranti o briganti"
Italian Emigration and Nationality Policies in the Peninsula

Between 1876 and 1914, Italy witnessed the largest mass exodus of expatriates ever registered in its entire post-unification history. Those years represent the epoch when "the beautiful country" (*il bel paese*) was a land of emigration, and more particularly when the Italians were "the Albanians" of many destination countries, to paraphrase the title of a recent Italian publication about migration and xenophobic stereotyping.[1] Millions left the peninsula as permanent or temporary migrants, pushed by a despair that was well summarized at the time: "What do you want! Here I cannot have hope [...], I cannot have any hope of improving my condition; I have only my hovel as a palace and, my father as a lord, 'poor farmer in the fields of others'."[2]

The increasing number of Italian emigrants abroad as well as the growing size of the second generations born in the countries of destination created "beyond the sea and over the mountains, among foreign peoples [...], a new great Italy outside Italy," which by 1910 had to confront a complex process of accommodation and integration within the host countries as well as raised fundamental citizenship and identity issues in the peninsula.[3]

After providing a short historical excursus on Italian mass emigration during the liberal era, this chapter analyzes—on the basis of Tintori's and Pastore's works—Italy's citizenship debates and changes of policy concerning the national membership status of its Italian communities living outside the country.[4] Also, by providing additional related evidence, this study shall demonstrate that in line with our findings regarding the immigrant *non regnicoli*, the concepts of citizenship, nationality and Italianness were linked in a peculiar way when thinking and talking about the Italian emigrants and that Mancini's teachings shaped citizenship policies not only on immigration but also on emigration. Finally, bearing in mind recent scholarly research that has been carried out from a political science perspective on "external citizenship" in contemporary states,[5] this chapter aims to examine, in historical perspective, the vicissitudes Italian international migrants had to go through, both as resident foreigners abroad and as external citizens of their country of origin. The objective is once more to stimulate the healthy interdisciplinary conversation that characterizes the field of citizenship and that has inspired our book.

4.1. HISTORICAL CONTEXT: MIGRATORY FLOWS FROM THE ITALIAN PENINSULA (1876–1914)

In almost forty years (between 1876 and the beginning of World War One), more than fourteen million Italians left the country in search of bread, work and a better life. More impressively, although irregular fluctuations occurred, the number of emigrants increased at a rhythm that intensified with the passing of the years; in fact, more than one million Italians emigrated in the 1876–1885 period, more than two million in the subsequent decade, more than four million from 1896 to 1905, and almost six million from 1906 to the beginning of the Great War hostilities.[6]

Writing in 1890, the contemporary Italian observer Attilio Brunialti stated bluntly: "I have asked our emigrants and, only one is the answer, always the same, everywhere, on every tongue, and it's summarized in one word: misery."[7] Economic and social problems at home were in fact the major causes—the "push factors"—of Italian emigration. In particular, the increase of national population from twenty-two million inhabitants in 1861 to more than thirty-five million by 1911 accentuated an already serious shortage of resources and land. Salaries, especially in the agricultural field, were extremely low and precarious, making everyday life unbearable for many Italian families. Also, the system of small property had undergone important structural changes—upsetting the whole sector—and, since a profound economic crisis had occurred during the 1880s due to a sudden fall of world prices in wheat production, many Italians had no choice but to leave and become *migranti* (migrants) or stay and join the *briganti* (bandits).[8]

"Pushed" to emigrate, this mass exodus concerned, to varying degrees, all the regions of the peninsula (including those in the north) and involved two major destinations, namely, continental Europe and the Americas—although, with the colonial scramble for Africa, and up to the debacle at Adwa in 1896, some Italian migratory flows were also planned and unsuccessfully organized to create emigrant overseas settlements in Italian Africa.[9] The migratory movements to continental Europe and to the

Americas varied considerably. The migrants who originated from central Italy kept a balanced position between the two continents and, overall, did not show any special preference between their respective labor markets, but the majority of the southern Italians—especially from Sicily, Campania, Calabria and Basilicata—emigrated mainly to the New World (Brazil, Argentina, and the United States) and those of northern Italy— generally, from Veneto, Friuli, Piedmont and Lombardy—left for the European continent (especially, for France, Switzerland, Austria-Hungary and Germany), although a small percentage also crossed the Atlantic. Obviously, job opportunities, demand for labor and availability of land were significant "pull factors" attracting the Italians in those receiving countries. Also, geography, cost of transportation and family chain migration were additional elements helping to explain the phenomenon.[10]

With the exception of a small minority of educated, bourgeois Italian migrants pursuing mainly commercial and financial activities, the majority of those who left the peninsula shared the disturbing status of illiteracy as well as very harsh migratory experiences—usually in the agricultural and plantation sectors, in construction and mining, in the hotel and restaurant business, or in the worst cases in the streets as itinerant musicians and boot polishers.[11] Undoubtedly, having to start a new life from scratch, many Italian emigrants, including those for whom migration was temporary, went through a very difficult initial process of accommodation within their host society. Also, with the passing of time, as settlement took on a more permanent character for large groups of expatriates (following the birth of children abroad), this initial process of accommodation took the road toward deeper integration within the receiving state, raising peculiar conflicts of citizenship(s) and identity issues for both generations, calling for a state reaction on the part of the mother country and, as emphasized by the scholar Pastore, making the interaction between nationality law and migration politics quite intense in Italy.[12]

In particular, there was one national question, unknown in the first post-unification years, that began to attract the attention and concern of the Italian liberal state: since emigration provided an undeniable soothing to Italy's chronic poverty and domestic social unrest and, since the full participation of the emigrants (and of their descendants) in the countries of destination (and birth) were being seen positively by Italian authorities for a variety of political, economic and social reasons, pertinently discussed by Tintori,[13] how could Italy accept and even encourage the integration in new lands of immigration of its Italian communities without, at the same time, losing national citizens and weakening their *italianità*? Speaking before the Italian parliament in 1912, Deputy Pasquale Grippo went straight to the point:

We find ourselves in a contradictory situation because while, on the one hand, we maintain that it is necessary to facilitate participation in the political and administrative affairs for Italians residing abroad especially in South America, on the other hand, we wish to retain a sense of Italianness, we wish to seek not to lose this great mass of Italians who go to America.[14]

Confronted with this new and complex international situation, the liberal state approved in 1912 introduction of significant modifications in the existing citizenship policies that concerned its Italian subjects living outside the country. This took place with the citizenship law that, adopted under the government of Giolitti, abrogated the previous provisions of 1865, became the second great pillar in the history of Italian citizenship (after the civil code) and remained in force for eighty years until adoption of a new citizenship law in 1992.[15] Before reaching the year 1912, though, it is instructive to go back to the late nineteenth century and explore the various controversial citizenship issues that were to be brought to the attention of Italian officialdom thanks in particular to the debates held in international conferences and congresses on Italian migrant communities living outside Italy.[16]

In this chapter we first examine and discuss the citizenship issues pertaining to Italian emigrants and subsequently focus on those that touched on the status of their offspring. Both groups (i.e., expatriates and their descendants) are part of Italy's "diaspora," to use a debated and controversial term within recent migration scholarship.[17] It is, however, important to distinguish, within Italy's diasporic communities, the first generations on the one hand and their offspring on the other, because the experiences and the issues concerning the expatriates and those of the subsequent generations born abroad shared many similarities but were also different in fundamental ways. Emigrants were those who had actually left Italy and moved to other countries by crossing international borders; their descendants, on the contrary, born in the country of destination, never really "packed their cases" and "moved" as their parents had. This fundamental distinction is also reflected in the structure of the sections following.

4.2. FIRST-GENERATION EMIGRANTS: BETWEEN NATURALIZATION ABROAD, AND LOSS AND REACQUISITION OF ITALIAN CITIZENSHIP AT HOME

According to the 1865 civil code, which was in force in Italy during this period of mass emigration, Italian citizens who emigrated and naturalized in the country of destination (thus acquiring foreign citizenship) would automatically lose their Italian juridical status—the underlying principle being to prevent cases of "dual citizenship."[18] Compared to their German counterparts, Italian migrants were actually in a slightly different, and better, position in this respect because in contemporary Germany, according to a Prussian law extended throughout the empire, loss of national citizenship at home was also occasioned simply by prolonged absence from the territory. In fact, the *Auslandsdeutsche*—unlike the Italian émigrés—would lose their citizenship after ten years' residence in the country of destination and settlement, unless they took the special step of registering with a German consulate. So, in Germany, the right to emigrate was penalized more radically since, as a general principle and bearing in mind the exception, Germans could not reside abroad indefinitely *and* retain their citizenship of origin.[19]

Even though luckier than the *Auslandsdeutsche*, the Italians of the peninsula were obliged nevertheless to lose their Italian citizenship if they naturalized and acquired new national membership status in another country. From a wider European perspective, this was not a peculiarity of the Italian case study; indeed, in other states as well, naturalization abroad would entail loss of membership status at home (with the usual, national variations). For example, the 1804 French civil code provided that French emigrants who acquired foreign status outside the Hexagon would lose their French citizenship. Contrary to liberal Italy, though, an additional special provision was introduced in 1889 according to which the *émigrés français* would still continue to lose their French citizenship by naturalizing in another state, but Frenchmen between the ages of twenty-one and fifty had to ask for an authorization from the French government. The underlying justification for this new norm was to avoid having French males naturalize abroad, on purpose, just to avoid doing compulsory military service at home.[20] Even in Great Britain—the country where traditionally the notion of "perpetual and indissoluble allegiance" was born and defended for centuries, at home and abroad, thus creating and tolerating cases of dual citizenship when new status was acquired by a British subject—changes of policy started taking place from the second half of the nineteenth century. In fact, according to the Naturalization Act of 1870, any British subject becoming voluntary naturalized in another state thereupon lost British subjecthood and became an alien—the same principle being enshrined in the subsequent British Nationality Act of 1914 as well.[21]

Why a certain convergence of policies was gradually taking place at the international level to prevent, as much as possible, cases of dual citizenship will become clear later in this chapter. What interests us here is that application of the provision concerning loss of Italian citizenship upon naturalization outside the peninsula soon collided with a variety of social realities and raised fundamental issues both for the émigrés involved and for the liberal state. From the point of view of the Italian migrants, the issue was related to the fact that many of them wanted to acquire the foreign citizenship of the host country—perceiving naturalization as a necessary step for improving their economic and social status—while at the same time they wished to keep their juridical link with the mother country for practical as well as emotional reasons. As the Italian delegate Giulio Cesare Buzzati argued at the Second Congress of the Italians living abroad, Italy's expatriates had emigrated by necessity but they desired to remain Italian, and their return to the peninsula, which occurred often, was a demonstration of this.[22]

Various factors explained why acquisition of the citizenship of the destination country was perceived as important by Italian migrants. Apart from the general fact that national citizens would not be subject to deportation, acquisition of the new membership status in the immigration country was seen by the arrivals as a necessary juridical instrument of inclusion that would rectify certain legal discriminations and that made the economic integration of the person concerned less difficult. For instance, as argued by a contemporary Italian observer, the foreigners who lived in some parts of the United States could not be owners of real estate; they were discriminated against in the labor market—they could not apply for public sector jobs (even for simple manual labor within the public services) without having naturalized—and received different treatment as aliens should they be entitled to social indemnities for accidents in the workplace.[23] Also, being in the position of a noncitizen was a fundamental cause of the difficulty of their accommodation within mainstream society. Thus, becoming citizens through naturalization would provide the Italians with a situation of legal equality, essential for more facilitated integration in the receiving state.[24]

Second, the fact of naturalizing and acquiring full citizenship inclusive of political rights (at least by the small minority of economically successful and educated Italian migrants) was a positive element because, according to a representative speaking on behalf of the Italians living in Brazil, the immigrants' participation in municipal public life was advisable and even necessary to make their voice heard and have their requests fulfilled. In this respect, the example of the German immigrant community living in certain Brazilian municipalities was very instructive.[25] Moreover, as Franzoni argued in 1909, naturalization allowed the most prosperous Italians not only to increase their power through participating in the public affairs of the host country but also, through their feelings of national solidarity, to make less frequent the numerous abuses that were often perpetrated, even by local authorities, especially against the illiterate Italian immigrants living in isolated regions outside urban centers where the control of mistreatment was weaker.[26] This was the situation in some agricultural and mining areas of the United States, in the *fazendas* of the regions of Espiritu Santo and Sao Paulo in Brazil and in other dispersed zones of Argentina and Chile. Referring to the situation in the United States, Franzoni could not help arguing that there was indeed an "immense and overwhelming need for some authoritative voices to rise in the North American Parliament too, in defence of so many poor pariahs of our people."[27] Obviously, becoming citizens in the receiving state and exercising full *status civitatis* would allow settled Italians to participate in the public sphere and, consequently, defend not only their own interests but also those of the Italian communities at large.

Finally, one could argue as well that naturalization may have been perceived at the individual psychological level as being an additional measure that would contribute to making the Italian immigrant accepted "more easily" and "quickly" by an often hostile, and in certain cases xenophobic, local population. "Informal racism" or xenophobic reactions from certain strata of the local people were, in fact, recurrent at that time, in numerous receiving countries, against various immigrant communities—including the Italians. This is a counterphenomenon to migration that is not unusual in those societies where large groups of "desirable" and "undesirable" foreigners arrive and settle.[28] To take some examples, in the society and workplaces of many North American regions, there was a widespread and ingrained stereotype that singled out the "negritude" of the Italians; at the same time that the Sicilian migrants who worked in the sugar plantations of Louisiana were called *niggers* by their employers, the Italian immigrants in general were associated with the black minority because they did not find it "repugnant" to mix with "colored people," or work with them or live with a black woman. Also, as is well known, negative generalizations were often made to define the migrants from the peninsula as "all *mafiosi* and criminals"—without distinguishing one from the other.[29] Clearly, if we think about Italian expatriates being "thirsty for assimilation" to the point of even changing their names and surnames because the latter ended with "funny" vowels and were therefore too easily recognized by the xenophobic eye,[30] we might say that naturalization could well have been perceived, by some, as another step to be taken for the same purpose.

Disadvantaged as immigrants, as poor, as foreigners and as different, the Italians saw acquisition of the national citizenship of their country of destination as a means of inclusion and a way of facilitating their upward social and economic mobility within an often unfriendly environment. This is a pragmatic approach to citizenship by no means confined to the specific epoch and migrant group under study here. Indeed, to varying degrees, pragmatic considerations and a practical outlook on citizenship very often characterize émigré communities in general, no matter the nationality or the historical period under consideration. To take just one recent example among many, this phenomenon has been observed and analyzed in a qualitative research concerning Kyrgyzstani emigrants and their conceptions of citizenship in post-Soviet Kazakhstan and Russia.[31]

Perceiving acquisition of citizenship as a matter of material benefits, advantages, security and convenience, liberal Italy's expatriates spoke of a "harsh battle" (in reference to their migratory experience), of a "painful necessity" to naturalize and of the clement "understanding" by their mother country that they requested openly.

Do not prevent us from procuring the political and legal instruments that are fundamental, if the need arises, to effectively fight the hard battle in the country where we live.[...] And if, compelled by a painful necessity, we acquire the local citizenship, do not consider this act to be contrary to the fatherland.[32]

So the Italians living abroad saw naturalization as a necessary, needed and looked-for instrument for integrating in the host country. Also, from all the historical arguments and motives surrounding naturalization issues at the time that are described here, it is instructive to address again the fertile interdisciplinary dialogue among researchers and concur with those political scientists who have considered the subjective attachments of first-generation immigrants to the host and origin countries as not mutually exclusive but instead much more complex phenomena involving a variety of feelings.[33]

Naturalization, though, was of particular concern for the mother country. From the perspective of the Italian state, the question was whether it was advantageous, within the context of this mass exodus, to lose so many millions of citizens through naturalization in the countries of immigration and consequently risk weakening their *italianità*.[34] Indeed, the whole issue had become even more significant because of the generous citizenship policies of numerous destination countries, particularly in North and South America, which regulated naturalization procedures without setting restrictive requirements—thus, facilitating acquisition of foreign nationality, encouraging their immigrants to naturalize, and contributing directly to increasing the actual number of ex-Italian citizens.[35]

Many of these host countries had constantly applied expansive naturalization policies in a rather aggressive way since the late nineteenth century. Because they usually lacked population, possessed vast territories and had a high percentage of settled aliens living in their society, they regarded assimilationist practices of acquiring citizenship as useful demographic instruments that would help to increase the circle of their national citizenry and strengthen the process of nation-statehood.[36] An Italian immigrant might be transformed into an Argentine, Bolivian, or Columbian citizen only after a very short period of residence (usually one or two years), or alternatively through acquisition of property or most interestingly by marrying a native woman—this latter requirement making one pause, bearing in mind the discussions and findings on women explored in Chapter Two of this book. Also, in the specific case of Brazil, the Italians who, in accordance with an 1889 decree, were resident in the country on the day of the proclamation of the South American Republic (15 November 1889) were declared, automatically, Brazilians—unless they made a declaration to the contrary within six months. Since the period available to reject Brazilian citizenship was very short and, as we know, a large part of the Italian community was illiterate and therefore could not appreciate the importance of such a formality (or even be aware of it), many Italian migrants became Brazilian citizens—with official complaints from Italian authorities accusing the South American state of basically "imposing" citizenship upon its immigrant population. Finally, the proposition of a new "menacing theory"—regarding naturalization as well, and discussed at the Conference on Pan-Americanism held in Rio de Janeiro in 1906—made the issue even more critical. Known as "*dottrina Drago*" (from the name of Luis Maria Drago), it suggested that any European immigrant resident in the countries of the New World for two years should be obliged to become a citizen of the host state regardless of his or her will. This was only a proposal, but supported by the government of Washington at the conference in Rio, it was perceived as a further expression of the New World's anti-Europeanism, and as a menace to the national citizenship(s) of Old World states. Obviously, the simultaneous combination of these policies and propositions, the strong desire of the Italian emigrants to naturalize and the increasingly massive outflow of Italian expatriates called for a response by the Italian fatherland.[37]

How did the liberal state react to this complex international question, which, as we have said, linked the issue of its emigrants' naturalization abroad with automatic loss of Italian national citizenship at home? Interestingly, since Cicero's much-praised principle regarding the "impossibility of being a citizen of *two* political communities" (*duarum civitatum civis esse jure nostro civili nemo potest*) was well ingrained at the time, liberal Italy did not radically modify the 1865 norm then current so as to let its emigrants naturalize without losing their original status.[38] This means that the Italians living outside the country continued to lose their Italian citizenship upon naturalization—although the letter of the new 1912 law was softer than the rigid formula of the 1865 civil code because the former specified that only "voluntary" naturalization would lead to such loss. However, to counterbalance a rule that still transformed many Italian migrants into foreigners, the liberal state introduced a novelty within its citizenship policy, namely, generous reacquisition provisions. Representing a significant break with the past, these norms aimed at facilitating the process of readmission to Italian citizenry so as to encourage those who had lost their original juridical link with the mother country to reacquire it.[39]

Accepting the notion of "dual citizenship" as a general rule to let all Italian emigrants naturalize in another country *and* keep their original status was almost unthinkable in the peninsula during that period. Nowadays dual citizenship is accepted in Italy and in many other countries. The twenty-first century is seeing an expansion of the phenomenon worldwide, as observed and discussed, for instance, in a recent scholarly article offering a global contemporary overview of the issue.[40] However, at the time it was almost unimaginable. Admittedly, some experts on nationality issues representing the interests of the Italians living especially in South America made and defended a special proposal that would have allowed a migrant to acquire foreign status while maintaining, at the same time, a sort of "sleeping" Italian citizenship—at least during the period of emigration abroad and until the return of the migrant to the country of origin.[41] Yet when the 1912 law was discussed in the Italian parliament, neither the Lower Chamber nor the Senate supported the concept under study.[42] "Dual citizenship," said Deputy Grippo, was a "political and juridical absurdity";[43] a "legal pathological status," continued Deputy Vittorio Scialoja;[44] and a "juridical monster," echoed another parliamentarian.[45] No one could at the same time have been a citizen of two political communities: "Nobody [could] simultaneously participate in the *res publica* of two States, nobody [could] be a citizen of two different political entities," reiterated the *rapporteur* Alfredo Baccelli in making a direct reference to the maxim of Cicero.[46] Since citizenship represented the link between the individual and the fatherland, it could not have had "a double face" or possessed "two contemporary forms of existence," said a ministerial representative.[47]

To strengthen these criticisms, Italian officialdom explained that the notion of *doppia cittadinanza* (dual citizenship) was unacceptable in juridical terms because in international law it would entail the right of the individual to two diplomatic protections; in penal law, it would mean having the right not to be extradited or incur the risk of double extradition; and in family law, it would make possible application of two types of national legislation within the same household—causing great confusion.[48] Moreover, as recapped by the contemporary writer Cesare Facelli, observance of Cicero's maxim helped to

prevent an individual from being forced to fail in his duties and to betray one or the other country, should the duties towards [one fatherland] be in collision with the duties vis-à-vis the other. A natural consequence of this principle is that to register one's name in the official civil records of a foreign State shall constitute an explicit and formal renunciation of Italian citizenship.[49]

So the liberal state continued to endorse this tenet as a general rule— although, as we have said, and in reaction to Brazilian policies in particular, it did not apply to cases of "involuntary" naturalization.[50]

Obviously, from the point of view of the mother country, this meant continuing to lose national citizens who willingly acquired foreign status— citizens who made up a substantial number, bearing in mind the statistics of the massive phenomenon of Italian emigration mentioned at the beginning of this chapter. This is why, to make up for such unavoidable loss, a new and generous reacquisition policy was formulated. In this way, the phenomenon of naturalization of Italian migrants abroad was transformed, through a policy of the sending state, into a "temporary" fact that would have lasted, for many expatriates, only for the period of actual migration abroad and that would have ended with return to Italy and facilitated reacquisition of Italian citizenship.

Indeed, the severity and indispensability of the norm concerning loss of the original status were clearly acknowledged by Italian authorities, as was the need to offset the provision with introduction of a compensating and milder one.[51] After all, such a need was understandable because "as the capacity to develop new ties with the countries [of destination] [...] has grown for the emigrants, so in the same way the facility for them to regain the bonds, interrupted with the country of origin, [...] should be increased when they return."[52] Facilitating reacquisition of the citizenship of origin was "a duty" for a country with a population of expatriates, and for this moral reason Italy would always have kept its arms wide open—as a "gentle mother"—vis-à-vis its children.[53] This "maternal act" was particularly important, and no one could have denied that "it is always sweet for the homeland to regain the son who preserved the flame and [that] the homeland must reopen its arms so as to take comfort from this renewed energy."[54]

Hence, a new reacquisition policy was approved by the Italian legislators, making the bureaucratic process of reacquiring the original status shorter, less troublesome and less expensive for the emigrant.[55] In fact, in contrast to the previous period, from 1912 onward Italian citizenship was to be reacquired after two years of residence in the peninsula; a migrant's return to the kingdom was no longer to be subjected to the special permission of the Italian government and the entire process was exempted from taxes and other charges. Finally and most interestingly, a special regulation was also introduced to take into account the new phenomenon of Italian migration *within* the South America continent. In effect, as emphasized in both legislative chambers, this was because of the great number of Italian emigrants who, for economic and commercial reasons linked to the international market, abandoned one South American country (where they had first naturalized) and moved to another, within the same continent—for instance, Italian expatriates emigrating from Argentina to Uruguay, Brazil or Venezuela.[56] If, in these special cases, the ex-Italian citizens did not naturalize *for a second time* in the other immigration state, they could reacquire Italian citizenship—upon the previous permission of the Italian government—after only two years of residence in the *second* receiving country. This means that return to the Italian kingdom was *not* required for them. Obviously, with this final, generous rule, the number of Italian ex-citizens who could qualify for reacquisition increased markedly.[57]

From a wider European perspective, it is instructive to learn that in 1913 Wilhelmine Germany as well introduced fundamental modifications as far as the citizenship status of German emigrants was concerned. This took place with adoption of the 1913 citizenship law to which we referred in our previous chapter. Less lucky than their Italian counterparts in the preceding years because, as we have said, prolonged residence abroad had a bearing on their German citizenship, from 1913 the *Auslandsdeutsche* saw their legal position improve significantly in this respect. In fact, thanks to the vocal nationalist demands of the Pan-German League and of various international associations of emigrants aiming at "the preservation of German *Volkstum*," the German state erased the provision and facilitated—like liberal Italy—reacquisition of national membership status for its former citizens. Also, while providing—again like the 1912 Italian liberal state—for the loss of national citizenship upon "voluntary" naturalization, Germany made possible in this latter case preservation of German citizenship under special conditions, a norm that was not contemplated in Italy. More particularly, by obtaining the authorization of the German government—granted upon their acceptance of doing military service—the *Auslandsdeutsche* were now allowed to keep their German citizenship upon becoming citizens of other states. This expansive and nationalist-inspired policy toward German emigrants reflected an important historical break with the previous period, as well as causing major diplomatic reactions and disputes during the First World War because, for military and security concerns, numerous European receiving countries as well as the United States—where German citizens had naturalized—viewed maintenance of their German original citizenship with great suspicion.[58]

Sharing generous reacquisition policies with contemporary Germany, the Italian case study is enriched by an additional factor that is worth examining: formulation of open readmission policies vis-à-vis the *emigrati italiani* was accompanied by the gradual emergence of specific state discourse that transformed the "sad" phenomenon of naturalization abroad into a "positive" fact that had to be accepted and even encouraged by Italy, as already noted and discussed in Tintori's research.[59] In particular, and by providing further archival evidence on this theme, we are able to argue that after acknowledging the necessity of naturalization—the latter being a phenomenon that, realistically, could no longer be prevented or stopped by the sending country—the liberal state encouraged it, openly, for various social, economic, moral and political reasons as well as by formulating a unique cultural argument concerning the notion of *italianità*. In this way, acceptance by the Italian state of naturalization of its emigrants was counterbalanced not only with the generous reacquisition policy (applicable at the end of the naturalization experience) we have just explored but also by a new state attitude vis-à-vis naturalization itself (when the latter was in place during the migratory experience). Through this "two-faceted policy"—based on new reacquisition norms on the one hand and on new positive state attitudes vis-à-vis naturalization on the other—the weak, young and unstable liberal state made the best of its mass Italian emigration.

To begin with, Italian officialdom reassured its citizens (and former citizens) that the mother country would not regard their naturalization abroad as a sign of "apostasy":

[Italy] will not condemn its children as apostates if they unhesitatingly acquire the new citizenship; it will instead greet them as pioneers of its ancient civilization transplanted there.[60]

Thus acquisition of foreign status was no longer to be seen as a rejection, by the emigrants, of their original country.

Second and more importantly, Italy did not refrain from verbally encouraging its expatriates to acquire foreign citizenship, supporting such apparently antipatriotic inducements with three complementary arguments: one concerning the emigrants' status, another related to the mother country and the third touching on the concept of *italianità*.[61] The argument about the usefulness of naturalization as an instrument for raising the economic and social status of the Italian migrants as well as for making them respected in their country of destination was finally acknowledged as realistic and endorsed by Italian officialdom. Said one parliamentarian, "If the immigrant in the United States does not become an American citizen, he does not deserve any consideration, any respect, any regard: he is considered to be a beast of burden, like a Chinese coolie and nothing more."[62] Italy should not, therefore, "prevent [these migrants] from acquiring the citizenship of the countries where they go, to be respected therein."[63] Also, as emphasized in the Senate and as already argued in the various international congresses concerning the Italian communities living outside the country, naturalization was a unique means to influence local politics, make the immigrants' voices heard and consequently improve their social conditions within the host country.[64] Acquiring foreign status would therefore have a positive impact on the migrant's economic and social position.

In addition to these considerations pertaining to the emigrants themselves, the deeper integration of the Italians through naturalization was seen as an instrument that would provide the mother country with significant political and economic benefits.[65] As Deputy Grippo argued, Italy would gain many positive advantages by having large Italian communities actively participating in the public life of their new states, especially in terms of widening and strengthening Italy's influence in the South American continent.[66] As he put it:

I believe that, given the conditions of the exuberant Italian population and the need for these great and continuing emigrations, it is better to have, in those States, a transfusion of Italian elements taking part in political and administrative life. In this way, they could not only assert the historical bond and the link of their Italian origin but also represent [...] that conformity of views and traditions which can be very useful for us in the competitions taking place among the various European states that aim at acquiring influence in the regions of South America.[67]

Also, Italy's commercial, economic and moral power would increase significantly thanks to the presence of integrated and consequently well-accepted Italian communities living in various parts of the world. It is Deputy Baccelli who was most eloquent on this point:

We must try, as much as we can, to keep high the number of Italian citizens. But where this is not possible, we must say frankly to the emigrants: Be good and loyal citizens of your host countries. So, without arousing any suspicion in foreign nations, you will be able to keep alive the love for the motherland, to safeguard the language and to become promoters of trade. In this way Italian emigration will certainly be surrounded by an atmosphere of sympathy, from which our country will derive greater moral and economic strength . . . (Most vivid approvals—Many MPs come to congratulate the speaker).[68]

Therefore, clear state interests made naturalization of Italian expatriates highly desirable for the Italian state, in line with the contemporary vision of economist Luigi Einaudi about an "Italy" that, peacefully established in the Americas, would contribute to the commercial successes of the mother country.[69]

Finally, and most fascinatingly from the perspective of the citizenship-identity link, was the fact that according to official discourse naturalization of Italian expatriates and their actual loss of Italian (juridical) citizenship would not have necessarily a negative impact on the concept of Italianness, as one would have thought. In fact, legal Italian citizenship—that is, the invisible juridical cord linking an individual to the Italian state—was not regarded within this context, by Italian authorities, as a *necessary* condition of Italianness. The "nationality of the heart and of the spirit" that, of course, it was important to keep alive could well be nourished, within settled Italian communities abroad, by other state-promoted institutions such as Italian language schools and related cultural organizations.[70] Italian citizenship (juridical) could therefore be lost without much harm to the concept of Italian national identity.[71]

Put differently, and to pay attention to terminology, Italian emigrants could acquire the "citizenship" of their country of settlement (thus losing their juridical link with Italy) while keeping their Italian "nationality" (the latter meaning here nation membership and *not* state membership) because "nationality is one thing, citizenship is another, and the latter is not a necessary exponent of the former."[72] Italian "nationality"—referred to, by Scialoja, as an ensemble of ethnological bonds with Italy and deprived, in this context, of any legal connotation—was one specific concept.[73] "Brazilian, Argentine or Bolivian (legal) citizenship" referred to another and was not necessarily an essential element of "nationality." Therefore, there was nothing wrong with Italian expatriates acquiring foreign citizenship and breaking the juridical link with the Italian state. "It may be evil, and it is a necessary evil," said the same senatorial authority, but "to become a citizen of another state does not mean giving up one's own nationality."[74]

This thought-provoking argument, widespread at the official level (as one can appreciate in Tintori's work),[75] was clarified at that time with the help of an illuminating analogy touching on the citizenship-nationality situation of the category of the *non regnicoli*, analyzed in our preceding chapter. The reader will recall that these immigrants were citizens of foreign states from a legal point of view, and yet they were of "Italian nationality" from cultural, linguistic, historical and geographic perspectives. By distinguishing the legal concept (i.e., citizenship) from the ethnological one (i.e., nationality), one would say that the special aliens of the Italian kingdom had a legal citizenship linking them to a foreign state (for instance, Austria-Hungary) and a nationality linking them to Italy. In short, their "Italian nationality" did not depend on their legal citizenship; indeed, despite being foreigners from a juridical point of view, they were regarded as Italian and as belonging to the Italian nation. By analogy, continued Senator Scialoja in 1911, the same argument could well be applied to the Italian emigrants who wanted to naturalize abroad: they could acquire (legal) foreign "citizenship" that linked them to their host country (thus losing their juridical Italian citizenship) while keeping their "nationality" and cultural belonging to the Italian nation. Italian national identity was not therefore dependent, necessarily, on Italian *juridical* citizenship and could well be maintained despite acquisition of foreign status abroad and despite the actual loss of the juridical link with the country of origin.[76] Here, the echoes of Mancini's teachings as explored in our previous chapter are evident, in particular the way in which citizenship and nationality were seen as two linked but separable notions, two linked but separable facets of the same historical concept.

In conclusion, to face the complex phenomenon of emigration and the citizenship issues related to it, Italy continued to uphold the traditional prescription of Cicero regarding "one single citizenship"—although the norm entailing loss of Italian (juridical) status upon naturalization was clearly limited to cases of voluntary acquisition of foreign citizenship. Also, to offset the latter phenomenon, which had become more significant owing to the scale of Italian emigration and to the expansive naturalization policies of many immigration countries, the liberal state made radical changes of policy and attitude. It introduced a more open reacquisition policy (to reacquire its "lost" former citizens) and, in the meantime, before reacquiring them, it started valuing and encouraging the necessary phenomenon of naturalization in the country of destination and settlement to make the most out of its Italian mass exodus from an economic, social and political point of view. Even the concept of *italianità* was safe because, theoretically linked within this specific context to "nationality," it could be separated from the concept of juridical "citizenship" and therefore allow Italian emigrants to acquire foreign citizenship status abroad without losing their Italianness. In the next section we set aside the first generation of expatriates and focus on their offspring born outside the peninsula to bring to light further important insights.

4.3. THE SECOND GENERATIONS: BETWEEN *JUS SOLI* IN THE COUNTRY OF BIRTH AND *JUS SANGUINIS* IN THE PARENTS' SENDING COUNTRY

The subjects of the Italian kingdom who left the peninsula during this period made the Italian communities abroad substantial in size not only through their massive arrival but also, and most evidently, by settling and giving birth to a second generation of Italian children. The offspring of Italian fathers were in fact Italian citizens at birth—even when born abroad—because of the principle of *jus sanguinis*, which, as we know, was enshrined in Italy's 1865 civil code and which, as emphasized by the contemporary lawyer and professor Felice De Deminicis, was interpreted with a certain rigor and applied in "omni loco et omni tempore" no matter the birthplace of the children.[77]

In numerous countries of immigration, though, where national citizenship was ascribed at birth not only to children of citizens (as everywhere) but also to children born in the country to foreign parents, the child of an Italian emigrant was, say, Argentine (according to Argentine law, because of birth in the South American Republic) *and* Italian (according to Italian law, because of birth from an Italian father). So, following the growth in migration from the Old World to the New, the birth of dual nationals, simultaneously claimed as citizens of more than one country, became common.

Just as numerous *jus sanguinis* states used the principle of descent abroad to transmit their citizenship over generations and in this way keep a link with their emigrants and families as well as increase their national citizenry, immigration countries were keen on applying the *jus soli* norm at home for demographic and political reasons. In particular, as already emphasized in talking about naturalization in our previous section, destination countries had large territories to be populated and massive numbers of aliens to be accommodated. So, easy naturalization procedures for first-generation newcomers were very often combined with the rule of birthplace to be used unconditionally, thus making all children born in the territory national citizens regardless of parentage. Like naturalization, the use of unconditional *jus soli* was seen as an assimilating instrument to admit people of any ethnic origin or culture to the national citizenship of the country and in turn strengthen the process of nationhood and statehood.[78]

Applying the *jus sanguinis* norm abroad (on the part of emigration states such as Italy) in combination with the *jus soli* principle (in force in numerous receiving countries, especially in the Americas) became the cause of specific practical problems related to citizenship, such as double obligations for male citizens to do military service in both countries. Generally, this issue was tackled through international bilateral agreements, and in fact from the 1880s numerous treaties were signed by Italy and other states in view of guaranteeing the exemption, for the second generations born abroad, from doing military service in one country, should they have done it already in the other state. However, by 1910 the question related to the progeny of Italian migrants had become more complex than before, as it involved other aspects of citizenship, identity and integration within the country of birth that went well beyond the military aspect.

As discussed in the Italian parliament in 1911–12, the second generations living especially on the other side of the Atlantic had gone through a gradual and deep process of "attachment," "acculturation" and "full integration" within their societies, as is often common and understandable in these cases of birth and permanent settlement in geographical areas distant from the "mother country." Indeed, this cultural, social and psychological process, taking place at the individual level, could no longer be denied by Italian authorities; as emphasized in both parliamentary chambers, these children preferred speaking Spanish, Portuguese and English rather than Italian; they regarded themselves as Argentine, Brazilian and American citizens (and were proud of it); in some cases they even concealed their Italian origin, since many of them (who had studied in their country of birth) viewed their parents' illiteracy with a sense of mortification and embarrassment and found it difficult to be proud of a country

that had let its population emigrate in such conditions; and finally, there
was a widespread desire among them to be declared citizens only of their
country of birth and have a right to acquire Italian citizenship, if they
wished, by making a declaration at the age of majority.[79]

Italian officialdom was well aware of all these facts not only through
the news coming from consular authorities and other state institutions
but also through the direct personal experiences of some deputies and
senators who had noticed this attitude among the second generations
when the latter made temporary journeys to Italy to see the rest of the
family in the peninsula.[80] Moreover, the whole question was discussed at
great length (together with the one concerning the first generation of expatriates) during the two Congresses of the Italians Abroad and reported
before the Lower Chamber. For instance, summarizing what some representatives had argued in the international conferences, *onorevole* (the
Honorable MP) Fusinato made these assertions in parliament on 4 June
1912:

And as for the children of Italians, born in America, you should accept a situation which neither we nor you have the power to change. Certainly it would be
infinitely better if it were not so; but it is so: [these children], born in a foreign
country, where they must and wish to live, also want to belong to it.[...] But this
vain attempt [from us] to impose a citizenship that they do not want, does not
give to Italy a soldier more, and instead gives to it many less hearts.[81]

Reiterating this point one week later, the same authority was again very
clear: "I still have memories of the second Congress of Italians abroad.
It was our most ardent patriots, emigrants living overseas, who told me:
there is nothing to do; our children born in America, who want and need
to live in America, wish to be Americans!"[82]

Obviously, this new social international context questioned directly
the current citizenship policy of the liberal state and called for reforms
at home. The issue, however, was as problematic for the mother country
as the one concerning the first-generation emigrants. Indeed, to fulfill
the desire of the largest part of the second generations, Italy should have
stopped declaring them Italian citizens at birth, thus giving up applying
its much-praised *jus sanguinis* norm abroad. Alternatively, from a state
interest and national point of view, it could have continued to uphold
the principle of descent and made the generations of Italian emigrants
Italian *ad infinitum*—thereby provoking the continuous complaints of
the individuals concerned. As we shall see below, in 1912 the liberal state
found a middle position between the two solutions: it continued to embrace the *jus sanguinis* provision at home and outside the peninsula, but
in *jus soli* countries it gave the right to the Italian child to renounce Italian citizenship at the age of twenty-one. In other words, contrary to the

previous period a concession was made to the second generations who were born in certain immigration states since for this special category of offspring the principle of ancestry could be limited by the liberal tenet of individual will.

The first radical solution according to which the child should have been declared only a citizen of the country of birth was indeed proposed in the Italian chamber of deputies by Fusinato, who also argued in favor of giving a right to acquire Italian citizenship at majority.[83] According to him, this rule was more convenient from a juridical and political point of view because it would not have made the child a dual national (and so avoiding all the legal problems mentioned in our previous section) and would not have imposed citizenship at birth upon children who, as was recognized, did not really want it.[84]

Fusinato's proposition, however, did not find the consensus of the majority and was criticized on a variety of grounds. To argue that a child of an Italian emigrant was a foreigner at birth was inconceivable, according to one authority, and neither honorable nor just because it would represent a fundamental blow to Italy's well-ingrained juridical tradition of *jus sanguinis* and passive acceptance, by the mother country, of the foreign state's norm on the *jus soli*, with serious consequences for the entire phenomenon of Italian emigration abroad.[85] Moreover, the norm would not be in line with the universally accepted axiom about the unity of the family in nationality matters because the children (of an Italian father) would, in most cases, have citizenship different from the status of their parent—causing deep conflict within the household in terms of family law.[86] Finally, by rejecting Fusinato's amendment, Italy would prevent those cases in which an individual would not ask for Italian citizenship at majority in order to avoid military service for the Italian state. This was indeed a dangerous trend for Italy's interests and had to be averted at all costs.[87] Hence, for all these reasons, the 1912 Italian state should not (and did not) give up claiming the children of its emigrants as its own citizens.

From the opposite perspective, the other radical solution—*jus sanguinis ad infinitum*—was also criticized. In particular, by upholding the principle of the perpetuity of Italian citizenship through paternal lineage, Italy could have continued making every generation belong to the Italian citizenry, and as a result counterbalancing rapid assimilation of these children in their country of birth by the nationalist response of keeping them attached to the mother country through the juridical link of national citizenship.[88] This solution, though, would have overlooked completely the realities and the state of mind of many Italian second generations living overseas, as well as undermined the liberal principle of respect for the individual will of the person concerned.

This is why the 1912 legislation confirmed the rule on indefinite transmission of Italian membership status via descent but, in the specific case
of *jus soli* countries, tried to accommodate the request of the emigrants'
offspring by conceding priority to the Italian child's will at majority. This
last factor was actually discussed at great length in both legislative chambers, as also emphasized by Tintori.[89] According to the initial project presented by Minister of Justice Scialoja, these Italian children would have
lost their Italian citizenship *automatically* at majority unless they made a
declaration within one year to keep it.[90] However, finding this proposal
too severe vis-à-vis the mother country and too open with respect to the
foreign state's *lex loci*, the senatorial central bureau preferred a more
nationalistic solution, which was eventually approved: Italian citizenship
was *not* to be lost automatically at the age of twenty-one, but a declaration had to be made if the person wanted to renounce it.[91] Clearly, the
senatorial counterproposal was more patriotic than Scialoja's first proposition because the second generations could lose Italian juridical status
only by a voluntary act.

Despite the choice in favor of the nationalist-inspired provision,
though, the liberal principle regarding individual will was applied anyway
and Italian juridical citizenship was not imposed at majority as the Italian
child was allowed to renounce it. Indeed, according to Italian officialdom,
it was important to value such a "liberal option" because if the child of
an Italian expatriate were sincerely attached to the country of birth, no
imposition of Italian citizenship should take place. Senator Polacco made
this point plainly:

If those born of Italian parents, in America or in another country where the *jus
soli* is predominant, feel themselves bound by a sincere patriotic love for that
country [...] while having the maximum feelings of sympathy [...] for Italy, we
should not close our eyes to reality and should not want [these offspring] to keep
our Italian citizenship at all costs.[...] Do not insist on an indefinite tribute to the
jus sanguinis principle by imposing Italian citizenship on those who, by now, no
longer feel it, nor desire it.[92]

After all, as the same senatorial representative argued in metaphorical
terms (by referring to the ancient concept of *nexum* in Roman law involving the image of the insolvent debtors held in bondage by their creditors),
Italian juridical citizenship was not a "shirt of Nexus" that no one could
take off; a person was therefore free to renounce it.[93]

Finally, and most importantly from the point of view of the citizenship-identity link, Italian officialdom extended to the second generations
the terminological difference, discussed earlier, applied to their emigrant
parents between "citizenship" on the one hand and "nationality" on the
other. In this way, liberal authorities did not regard eventual loss of the

expatriates' offspring born abroad, should they renounce Italian citizenship, as so damaging for Italy—as one, again, would have thought. Senator Polacco and lawyer Ricci-Busatti were once more influential on this point:

What really matters—let us insist on this concept—is not so much that our emigrants and their children retain the citizenship of the kingdom [of Italy] as [the fact that they keep] the Italian sentiment. Let them have new bonds with the country where they live, and let them feel the pride vis-à-vis the new fatherland that received them or saw them being born.[...] But let us make possible that these feelings be associated with a sense of dignity for their origin and with the affection to the ancient *patria*.[94]

Thus it did not matter whether the children of Italian expatriates renounced Italian juridical citizenship at majority; what really counted was that *il sentimento italiano*—the feelings of belonging to the Italian nation—be kept alive even when these children held the foreign citizenship of their country of birth. In short, like their Italian parents who were encouraged to naturalize abroad, the second generations could be "Argentine citizens" while keeping their "Italian nationality" because the latter could be "independent" from Italy's juridical citizenship and "survive" despite acquisition of a foreign status. Obviously, this state discourse demonstrates, again, that the image and the vocabulary concerning the immigrant *non regnicoli* as well as the related teachings of the deputy and professor Mancini were clearly ingrained within Italian citizenship tradition as to shape not only immigration but also emigration policies.

As in Italian state rhetoric it was the cultural bonds and linguistic ties that really united all the Italian diasporas abroad to peninsular Italy and peninsular Italy to all its diasporas, the liberal state paid particular attention to promoting and subsidizing a "national" identity worldwide. This was to be done through a variety of channels, which, as discussed in Choate's meticulous research,[95] included schools, patriotic banquets, choirs and bands, the Italian Chambers of Commerce Abroad, the Dante Alighieri Society, and the Catholic Scalabrinian missionaries. The ultimate intent was not only the cultural safeguarding and preservation of an Italian identity on the part of migrants and subsequent generations, but also mobilization of culturally attached overseas Italian communities in the interest of Italy's domestic and foreign policies. In fact, liberal Italy soon came to count on its diasporic groups for their regular remittances and essential contribution to the economic development of many backward areas in the country. It came to count on them, as previously emphasized, to increase the country's sphere of influence worldwide through trade, the export-import market and the image of "made in Italy." It was to count on them for aid relief in a number of natural disasters and earthquakes, like the ones occurring in Sicily and Calabria in 1908. Finally, it ultimately counted on them in time of war as more than three hundred thousand emigrant reservists returned to Italy from abroad to fight during World War One—something Fascism and Mussolini's regime were not really capable of doing twenty-five years later when Italy entered World War Two.[96]

4.4. CONCLUSION

Faced with the phenomena of Italian migration and settlement abroad, the liberal state "played" with its policies and vocabulary concerning national citizenship with a certain ease and flexibility. On the one hand, it emphasized the importance of introducing generous reacquisition provisions that would readmit its lost *regnicoli* within the circle of its citizenry as well as keeping the *jus sanguinis* rule at birth and preferring the nationalistic counterproposal of the senatorial central bureau that allowed an Italian child to renounce Italian citizenship rather than making the child lose it automatically. This demonstrates that (juridical) citizenship was seen by liberal officialdom as a fundamental state institution and, valued from this perspective, for its evident link and impact on the strengthening of Italianness.

On the other hand, the Italian state also emphasized that Italy's (juridical) citizenship could well be separated, within this specific international context, from the concepts of *italianità* and of "Italian nationality," defined in nonlegal terms as nation membership. In this case, "citizenship" did not really matter because it was "nationality" in the latter sense that had to be given precedence. This is why, if the legal cord linking the individual to the 1861 Italian kingdom was lost through the necessary naturalization of Italian expatriates or through the understandable changes of mind of the second generations, these facts were not regarded by Italian authorities as harmful to the concept of Italianness. After all, the latter could be kept alive even without legal citizenship status because, as the greatest ideologue of Italian citizenship in the liberal period—Mancini— had already argued since the midnineteenth century, Italian national self-understanding was not "state-framed" but a "nation-defined entity" that could well go beyond the juridical framework of Italy's statehood and citizenship regime.

By playing with this "double language" and by emphasizing the simultaneous importance of "juridical citizenship" and "cultural nationality," young and weak liberal Italy, too poor to feed its prolific population and in desperate need of its migrants' remittances, could make the most out of mass exodus. It facilitated integration of the emigrants and descendants in the host countries and kept alive and justified theoretically the sentiment of *italianità*—with or without the juridical link binding the person to the peninsula. An "emigrant nation," embracing population at home and abroad, liberal Italy could also be seen as "a global nation," in the sense that it was not limited to its territorial boundaries and functioned as a "transnational community" held together by a variety of economic, social, cultural and political networks tied worldwide to the Italian peninsula.[97]

In the next and final chapter of Part One, we take the reader to Italy's colonized and occupied territories to examine the nonmetropolitan dimensions of Italian national citizenship and cast light on a further historical aspect pertaining to the notion of being Italian subjects.

CHAPTER FIVE

Liberal Italy's Expansionism and Citizenship Issues (1880s–1922)

Colonial Subjects, Citizens of Tripolitania and Cyrenaica and Dodecanesini

Latecomer to the world of nation-states and pushed by a variety of national objectives, including pursuit of power politics and international prestige, along with the quest for markets and investment opportunities as well as the search for lands for Italian emigrants, liberal Italy undertook an expansive foreign policy from the 1880s that continued, in successive phases, during the 1910s until the end of the Great War. Throughout these forty years of post-unification history, the Savoy state acquired colonial territorial possessions in East and North Africa as well as occupying militarily some lands in the Mediterranean Orient. Through diplomacy, military adventures and war, the Italians landed on the coasts of the Red Sea, the Indian Ocean and the Southern and Eastern Mediterranean Sea, thus opening an era of Italian territorial ambitions ultimately ending in 1947.

The purpose of this chapter is to provide a comprehensive account of the citizenship policies that were introduced during the liberal decades by an expanding colonial Italy vis-à-vis the native populations that lived in Eritrea, Somalia, Libya and the Aegean Islands. In this way, the still relatively unknown citizenship issues of the Dodecanese will be fully discussed, for the first time, with the citizenship situation of Italy's African subjects on which there is already a substantial literature.[1] Also, by examining the official discourse pertaining to civic incorporation of these autochthones into Italy's institutional framework, the chapter aims at exploring the liberal variant of notions of "civilization" and "race" as they were extended from the peninsula to the African colonial natives. Finally, it will bring to light the historical reference of the "myth of

Rome" as it was evoked in the citizenship debates about *Eritrei, Somali* and *Libici* as well as let the historical paradigm of the "maritime Republics," evoked in discussions about the *Dodecanesini*, emerge fully from the Italian archives.

5.1. ITALIAN EXPANSIONISM IN AFRICA AND COLONIAL CITIZENSHIP STATUS

5.1.a. Eritrea and Somalia

Following long diplomatic and commercial transactions that led to the transfer of the Bay of Assab on the Red Sea from the Italian private navigation company Rubattino to the Italian state, liberal Italy acquired this first official colonial possession in 1882 under the Minister of Foreign Affairs Mancini. The area, left over from the European scramble for Africa, was extremely poor from an economic point of view, but it enjoyed a strategic position of enormous value, especially after completion of the Suez Canal in 1869, which had made possible communication between the Mediterranean Sea and the Indian Ocean, thus opening a direct route to India and China. During the subsequent decade, with the aim of extending the territory of this tiny colony from the coast to the hinterland toward the millenarian Abyssinian empire, Italy took a variety of other military and diplomatic actions, but whereas Italian troops succeeded in occupying the port of Massawa in 1885 and the city of Asmara along with the Ethiopian plateau up to the river Mareb in 1889, Italian diplomacy was less successful. In fact, Crispi's expansionist project to deprive Menelik's empire of its independence through creation of an Italian protectorate soon became an illusion and, owing to the controversy over the 1889 Treaty of Uccially and to the disastrous defeat of Adwa, Italy's "primogenitary colony"—officially called Eritrea from 1890 onward—was not to be given an "Ethiopian sister" during the liberal era.[2]

In the meantime, while the Eritrean-Abyssinian policy was taking its course, the young Italian state attempted to realize its territorial ambitions in the southern part of East Africa as well by carrying out military battles and diplomatic negotiations in the *Aromatica Regio* of the ancients[3]—that is, in those lands that would become known by the name of Somalia. Here the Italians acquired a second colonial possession in successive political-territorial stages by obtaining gradually a number of protectorates and administrative cessions. In particular, they were granted three protectorates on the northern coast (over the Sultanate of Obbia in 1889, the Sultanate of Migiurtini from 1889 to 1901 and the territory of Nogal in 1905), four commercial concessions on the southern coast or Benadir region (over the seaports of Barawa, Merca, Mogadishu and Uarscheich, 1893) and finally, extension of an Italian sphere of influence in the hinterland in agreement with Great Britain. When in 1908 the Benadir region was united administratively with the three northern protectorates, the entire area took the official name of *Somalia italiana*.[4]

Upon their arrival, the Italian colonizers encountered (in many cases for the first time) a variety of East African populations. Bearing in mind the changes of borders of the territorial possessions concerned, the number of natives living in the Eritrean lands under Italian rule rose from about 160 inhabitants of the Bay of Assab in 1882 to 1,000 people in the 1885 extended territory, to 275,000 in 1905. In Somalia, by contrast, after the 1908 administrative unification of Benadir with the northern area, the total indigenous population was estimated at about 300,000–400,000 people.[5] Apart from differing from a demographic point of view, the two colonies also enjoyed ethnic and religious heterogeneity. In Eritrea, for instance, three major languages were spoken (i.e., Arabic, the Tigris language and Amharic). Also, from a religious point of view, the population was divided into a Muslim majority (living predominantly on the coast and on the western lowland), a large minority of Christians (i.e., Ethiopian Christian Copts, Catholics and Protestants) and a large group of pagans. The *Aromatica Regio* of the ancients, on the contrary, was inhabited mainly by tribes of Somalis (who belonged to the oriental Hamitic stock), by some Negroid groups of Bantù (living mainly along the Juba and the Uebi Scebeli rivers) and by Arab and Indian immigrants who had settled in the small cities along the coasts. Finally, with respect to religious affiliation, almost the totality of the population was Muslim, followers of the Shafitic rite.[6]

Within this historical and cultural context, the Italian colonizers who had to deal with organizing and running the administration of the new overseas lands started categorizing people by introducing into the national vocabulary a territorial reference that would constantly characterize the history of post-unification Italian colonialism. The general concept of "Italian subjecthood" that we saw in Chapter One and that referred to the monarchical status linking all Italians to the Savoy dynasty was enriched with an additional geographical element and divided into two interrelated but somehow distinct concepts. On the one hand was the "*sudditanza o cittadinanza italiana*" (Italian subjecthood or citizenship), also called "*metropolitana*" and shared by the Italians of the peninsula (the colonizers). On the other hand was the "*sudditanza coloniale*" (SC, colonial subjecthood) uniting the natives to Italy. Different in content, both juridical statuses incorporated the right to diplomatic protection by the Italian state and were ultimately linked together by the institutional figure of the Italian monarch.[7] Also, throughout the years, whereas outside the colonial context the Italians were referred to as Italian subjects or Italian citizens synonymously (from the centuries-old use in the peninsula of the words *sudditanza* and *cittadinanza* as interchangeable terms), in the colonies the two words acquired a specific meaning thanks to a clear demarcation line between the colonizers and the natives, inspired by widespread anthropological-evolutionist theories constantly emphasizing the inferior civilization of the colonial populations.[8] Consequently, within the colonial milieu, the word *citizen* designated automatically the Italian of the metropole, while the word *subject* was used for the *Eritrei* and *Somali*. The notion of citizenship thereby gained its full significance and was to be used to distinguish the higher and thicker status of the Italians from the lower one held by the native subjects.

From a wider European perspective, this categorizing system was by no means a peculiarity of the Italian case study. Similarities existed, for instance, with neighboring colonial France, where a distinction was made between *les Français de France* (the French of France), being *citoyens français* (French citizens), and *les indigènes des colonies* (the indigenous peoples of the colonies), holding the status of *sujets français* (French subjects) and living, to take some specific examples, in the territories of Madagascar under French sovereignty since 1896, and French Somalia, officially incorporated into the French empire in 1862. As in liberal Italy, the two categories of *citoyens* and *sujets* were distinct in many important respects but united under a common political allegiance.[9]

A rapid overview of the relevant citizenship provisions introduced in the two Italian East African colonies throughout the liberal decades will give us an initial sense of "where the line of separation passed between the colonizers and the colonized" and "how its layout moved over time."[10] During the liberal epoch, the juridical link uniting the indigenous populations to the metropole was generally dealt with in disparate norms concerning mainly administration of justice and, in the particular case of Eritrea, in a civil code used by Italian authorities as a reference guide in the eastern colonies, although the text never entered into force because it was never published in the three required languages (i.e., Italian, Arabic and Amharic).[11] In accordance with these rules, colonial status was ascribed by a blend of *jus soli* and *jus sanguinis* to the individuals who were natives born in the colony or who belonged to one of the colony's tribes or ethnic stocks.[12] Subjects at birth, these Africans basically kept their native status all their life, as they could naturalize and become metropolitan citizens only exceptionally. In fact, naturalization was made possible by law, but in reality it was extremely rare. This was due to the fact that it was regarded as extraordinary, made very restrictive and reserved exclusively for those indigenous colonial subjects who deserved such a civic prize for eminent personal qualities or for special services rendered to the Italian state. The new citizenship status acquired by a formal colonial subject was inclusive only of civil rights (so it was actually lower than the metropolitan one), was strictly personal and was not transmissible in that it could not be extended to the family members of the new citizen.[13] Civilizational concerns and power relations, to be elucidated later in this chapter, shaped and inspired such a restrictive colonial policy.

Between the white Italian citizens and the black African subjects, or between the colonizers and the colonized, there was a "gray zone," to use Barbara Sòrgoni's metaphorical expression: the *meticci*.[14] These children of mixed race issued from an Italian metropolitan parent and an African native and are of particular interest for the study of citizenship within the colonial setting. How were they treated by the Italian liberal authorities? Thanks to recent colonial studies, we know that as a general rule the liberal state embraced the practice of assimilating these kids into the Italian metropolitan community on the basis of paternal lineage. In fact, the *meticci* born from a regular marriage were automatically Italian citizens—although this was only an exiguous minority compared to the large number of mixed-race offspring born within temporary unions and kept in illegitimate status. Because of this specific Italian colonial context, alongside the fact that the number of *meticci* was increasing together with their social marginalization, the Italian legislators also attempted to encourage and make it possible for an Italian father to legitimize his progeny without obliging the citizen to marry the mother (as this was the norm in the peninsula). Finally, even without full legitimization, legal recognition was to be taken as a sufficient criterion so that a métis, acknowledged by the Italian father and registered in the official birth records of the colony, was automatically ascribed Italian citizenship. In this case, the status of Italian could only be acquired with paternal acknowledgment and excluded in any event the right of the child to inheritance because only legitimate or legitimized children were heirs at the time.[15]

These open and relatively generous norms, though, inspired only a minority of Italian fathers, among whom we should mention the well-documented case of Alberto Pollera, a colonial official who recognized and took care of his six children, born from two successive unions with East African natives.[16] In fact, the majority of the Italians sent to the colonies refused to take the responsibility of fatherhood and basically abandoned these offspring; apparently, in Eritrea alone there were almost one thousand illegitimate children by 1926.[17] This situation of abandoned children, often in needy conditions, generated a certain uncomfortable embarrassment within the Italian colonial administration, which had to safeguard the notion of prestige and which regarded these Italo-Eritreans as Italian no matter the paternal recognition. So in 1917, certain that the Italian state had a special responsibility toward this progeny, the

Regent Governor of Eritrea Camillo De Camillis instructed all colonial commissaries to attribute Italian citizenship automatically to the métis of unknown Italian paternal parenthood, even in the absence of paternal legal acknowledgment. As a result, by being registered as children of "unknown Italian fathers" these unacknowledged kids became Italian metropolitan citizens by law, obtaining the citizenship they were supposed to "deserve."[18]

Directly linked to the birth of métis and to their citizenship status was the important issue of interracial unions (either "informal unions" or "marriages") between Italians and native women. Indeed, both forms of interracial relations were highly sensitive issues within the colonial context because sexuality, the control of the body and the question of intimacy between citizens and subjects always enjoyed a central place within colonial ideology and strategies, not only in the Italian colonies but also in all the other European empires.[19] With a few exceptions, the Italian colonizers preferred generally the practice of so-called *madamato* to actual marriage with the native. *Madamato* was a new form of conjugal union taking shape specifically in colonial settings—a "new" form, both for the colonizers and for the colonized.[20] A type of interracial concubinage, which some Italian representatives saw as "damaging" the metropole's prestige, it was by and large practiced and tolerated for the entire liberal epoch.[21] These temporary, but not occasional, unions concerned mainly Italian male citizens and female colonial subjects (the "black Venus," to use a widespread image and metaphor in Italian colonial exotic literature),[22] while interracial intimate relations between Italian women and natives were practically nonexistent at the time.

Turning now to formal marriages, we know that they were not frequent (and actually were extremely rare). Also, these unions were not explicitly forbidden by the Italian state but were subject, in any event, to the judgment of the Italian colonial authority, which would give its permission in rare occasions, and "in cases absolutely exceptional" should the marriage unite a white woman with a black subject.[23] Interestingly, if an Italian metropolitan citizen married a native woman, the latter would acquire Italian metropolitan status automatically because of the already known principle of family unity in nationality matters, which in this case was extended to the colonial lands too. However, if an Italian woman were to marry a black colonial subject, she would keep her Italian citizenship, would not need marital authorization and would also be responsible for legal guardianship of her children. In other words, for additional racial considerations (which will be discussed later in the chapter) the Italian woman "could not" have been dependent upon a husband who happened to be a native. Race and protection of the white race were more important than gender arguments.[24] Moreover, with the introduction of the 1914 decree, Italian authorities discouraged colonial civil servants from marrying indigenous women by making the metropolitan citizen resign from his position in case of marriage with a colonized partner.[25] Yet the final, definitive prohibition of intimate relations between citizens and subjects was to take place only in the late fascist period, as we shall see in Chapter Seven.

Obviously, to explain who, how and when a person was a colonial subject of the Savoy dynasty as well as a potential metropolitan citizen, it is not enough to understand what it meant to be a *suddito coloniale* under Italian dominion. This is why we shall now turn to issues of content and substance of rights, discuss them and conclude this section concerning East Africans in the Italian territories.

The major characteristic of Italian colonial subjecthood—shared by *Eritrei* and *Somali* alike—is that it was an extremely "thin" status. East Africans were in fact entitled to very few rights, and these, mainly related to the civil sphere, were never coupled with, or extended to incorporate, other substantial political or social dimensions. For instance, the colonizers made clear since their arrival on the Red Sea and on the Indian Ocean that respect for local customs and traditions as well as freedom of religion would be guaranteed. That is why these important civil entitlements were enshrined in numerous colonial provisions, the only exception being abolition of certain "barbaric" local customs such as cutting off the hand of a thief, and lapidation and talion, which could not be tolerated by Italian authorities.[26] Most importantly, in the name of respecting the natives' religious affiliations the Italian colonizers introduced a concept of colonial subjecthood that was inclusive of the "personal statute" (*statut personnel*) of the individual. This guaranteed that property and inheritance rights as well as issues of family law (i.e., marriage, polygamy, divorce, separation, paternity, adoption, age of majority and paternal tutelage) were determined by the religious laws and tribunals of each native. Thus, fundamental spheres of indigenous life continued to be regulated by shariatic, Orthodox and Jewish principles to which the African populations were particularly attached for historical, social and cultural reasons.[27]

The liberal accommodation of this religious heterogeneity and cultural diversity was considered necessary by Italian metropolitan officialdom not only from an ideological point of view but also for pragmatic reasons. In effect, bearing in mind that local and religious customs were profoundly ingrained within the natives' societies, only a tolerant policy could make possible the metropole's occupation and colonization. In particular, the risk that a perceived menace to Islam and to Islamic law could have united all the native tribes against the colonizers in Italian Somalia was regarded as serious by Italy's authorities.[28] So acceptance of this diversity by the colonizers was transformed basically into an instrument of colonial rule.

Though entitled to certain rights within the civil sphere, the *Eritrei* and *Somali* did not really see any change concerning their thin status; the political as well as social spheres of their colonial subjecthood were kept quite empty. In fact, neither in Eritrea nor in Somalia were colonial subjects granted any political right at the local or national colonial level. Admittedly, exclusion of colonial indigenous people from the exercise of public functions was never absolute since liberal Italy, like other European states, continued to maintain the tribal institutions of the territories concerned, in particular their judiciary organs (i.e., native judges). However, these cases were only small exceptions, and the right to more substantial political entitlements was never contemplated during the forty years of liberal colonialism—not even for a limited class of indigenous individuals and despite the positive developments that took place, in this respect, in Tripolitania and in Cyrenaica and that are analyzed in the next section of this chapter.[29] Also, although a fragmented and timid policy was introduced as to state education for the natives of Eritrea, this issue was not apparently discussed for the populations of Somalia. In particular, regarding the territory on the Red Sea, we know that initially the Italian colonizers were very reluctant to open schools for the natives because education was seen as a perilous policy that could endanger the power relations in the colony. Subsequently, a limited and modified ad hoc school curriculum was introduced, but only for the first three years of elementary levels, and only by taking into account the special needs of Italian colonial rule for interpreters, domestic workers and so on. Finally, no attempt was really made by the Italians to introduce a secondary school system, as France and England had for instance done in some of their colonies, contributing to creation of African cultivated elites who would play an important role in the future struggle for decolonization within the French and British empires.[30]

Apart from being extremely thin, Italian colonial subjecthood incorporated two further historical facets that now merit analysis. By focusing first on Somalia, it is instructive to learn that the colonial subjecthood formulated by the metropole took shape within a specific historical context characterized by the slave trade. The latter continued to be tolerated by Italian liberal authorities for a long time, since what had been defined as an inhuman phenomenon, in Italy and elsewhere, did not raise universal condemnation among Italian metropolitan representatives.

A social phenomenon that had accompanied European expansionism since the first Portuguese naval adventures in Africa in the fifteenth century, the slave trade was officially abolished, on the international level, at the 1890 Conference of Brussels—although some European states, such as Great Britain, had already outlawed it within their empires in the 1830s in the name of humanitarian and liberal tenets. As a matter of fact, despite Italy's official acceptance of the 1890 Brussels Act, Italian anti-slavery norms were introduced in the lands of the Somalis quite late, only in 1903. Also, apart from being tolerated *in loco* by Italian colonial authorities such that, in Benadir, slaves were "freely purchased, sold, inherited, offered as a present, exploited, chained, deported,"[31] the phenomenon was not to be abolished "right away" according to some high-ranked Italian representatives. Its abolition lacked, in fact, consistent and univocal support by colonial liberal Italy. For instance, during the vociferous anti-slavery campaign undertaken in the metropole to push the Italian government to outlaw the phenomenon in southern Somalia, Minister of Foreign Affairs Tommaso Tittoni intervened in parliament by arguing against its sudden eradication for two pragmatic reasons: the end of slavery would turn against the Italian colonizers all the tribes that had lost their slaves, and serious economic problems would be caused by the sudden freedom of thousands of ex-slaves who were not prepared to "look after themselves."[32] Moreover, according to an Italian deputy, though it was just to implement antislavery rules in the Italian colonies when the slaves concerned were Italian colonial subjects, some questions and doubts could be raised about the obligation of Italy to free the subjects of other states—especially if this could have had additional negative economic consequences in the Italian colonial territories.[33] In fact, cases were frequent in which African caravan guides traveled to, and through, Italian Somalia with slaves and merchandise. Yet, argued the Italian representative, whereas the slaves who held Italian colonial status would be freed in the name of the Brussels Act, and also because the Italian press would not be slow to accuse the Italian colonial governor of being *"barbaro e negriero,"* strict application of antislavery norms vis-à-vis all other foreign slaves would lead to economic losses because the traders would prefer traveling to neighboring colonies, where apparently antislavery rules were applied less rigorously.[34]

Moving our analysis from Somalia to Eritrea, we can add that the colonial subjecthood of both *Eritrei* and *Somali* (examined again together) came into being with further significant events. First, the internal situation of each colony was extremely insecure because of frequent guerrilla revolts against the Italians, such as those taking place in the Eritrean region of Agordat in 1890–1894, the various attacks of the patriotic Somali Mullah Mohammed ben Abdallah Hassan in Northern Somalia and the violent rebellions of the Somali Bimal tribe in the southern region of Benadir. Also, apart from the fact that both colonies had uncertain

borders owing to constant controversies with Ethiopia and with neighboring European colonial powers, a widespread and persistent hostility
against the colonizers existed among the natives in general, from the Italians' insufficient knowledge about the local populations, the metropole's
inexperience in colonial affairs, its bad administration and frequent contradictory actions and its forced expropriations of agricultural land.[35]
Obviously, within such a context the whole concept of colonial subjecthood—uniting the natives with the metropolitans to one and the same
state and to one and the same king—took on a peculiar dimension. Finally, it has already been well demonstrated by post-1970 Italian colonial
historiography that Italy's colonialism in Africa was not more humane
and gentler than other colonialisms: the familiar notion of Italians as
"brava gente" ("good people," "good colonizers") is only a hypocritical
myth used in the peninsula during the two decades following the Second
World War to obfuscate the issue and keep from coming to terms with
Italy's aching past.[36]

To conclude, following liberal Italy's first colonial adventures on the Red
Sea, the Italian state introduced a nonmetropolitan status called *sudditanza
coloniale* that was shared by *Eritrei* and *Somali* throughout the entire liberal era. This thin colonial status added a new nonmetropolitan dimension
to the history of Italian citizenship, enriching the existing system and official discourse with new geographic and colonial references. In the next
section, we move to North Africa and see how liberal Italy incorporated
the *Libici* into the political framework of its expanding state.

5.1.b. Tripolitania and Cyrenaica

Following Italy's ultimatum to the Ottoman empire in September 1911
and the subsequent declaration of war, Italian military troops landed in
the North African cities of Tripoli, Homs, Bengasi and Derna, occupying the *vilayets* of Tripolitania and Cyrenaica. Under the government
of Prime Minister Giolitti, liberal Italy embarked on a new colonial experience, pushed in particular by the strong and well-organized domestic pressure of Italian nationalists. In October 1912, the two Ottoman
provinces came under Italian full sovereignty—in accordance with the
Treaty of Ouchy, which closed the Italo-Turkish war for the conquest
of Libya—and were extended slightly in 1919, after some minor border
changes took place as compensation by British and French allies to Italy
for the latter's participation in World War One against the central powers. Colonizers in North Africa, the Italians could now extend the territorial expansionist foreign policy they had started in the previous century in
the eastern part of the African continent by adding a new Mediterranean
dimension.[37]

As a direct result of this aggressive expansionism, the liberal state met a variety of new indigenous populations, which, in this territory, amounted to almost 750,000 people—more than half living on the Mediterranean coast and the rest being scattered on the Gebel, on the uplands and around the oases. From an ethnic point of view the colony was inhabited by Arabs, Berbers, Arabo-Berbers and Jews as well as by African black minority groups of Cologhli and Tebu, whereas from a religious perspective the affiliation of the majority was Islam and the largest minority, represented by Jewish peoples, was followed by Christians.[38]

Confronted with the task of accommodating these North African natives, Italy introduced additional citizenship policies that deserve particular consideration if one also bears in mind what we have just said about the *Eritrei* and *Somali* under Italian rule. In the previous section we saw that East Africans shared the same juridical link uniting them to the Italian state (SC, *sudditanza coloniale*) and kept this thin status throughout the entire liberal epoch. By contrast, the Libyans not only were granted an initial colonial membership status that was "thicker" than the corresponding one introduced on the Red Sea and on the Indian Ocean but also saw it evolving, within just six years, from "colonial subjecthood" to "colonial citizenship."

When Tripolitania and Cyrenaica came under Italian rule in 1912, the natives concerned—who had been Ottoman—were transformed into Italian subjects and united to the metropole via a juridical link of indigenous subjecthood called "*sudditanza degli indigeni della Libia*" (henceforth SIL). This colonial membership status pertaining to the North African inhabitants was officially proclaimed and regulated by an Italian national decree introduced as early as 1913. According to this metropolitan policy, in Libya as in East Africa the natives acquired this status on the basis of a combination of *jus sanguinis* and *jus soli*—principles which linked the quality of subject to native parenthood and birth in the colony. Also, children of mixed unions (Italo-Libyan offspring) followed the same criteria as the *meticci* in Eritrea and Somalia, being ascribed metropolitan citizenship, as a general rule, according to paternal bloodline and if acknowledgment of the child by the metropolitan father had taken place. In addition, whereas colonial subjecthood could be acquired in the North African territory by a foreign woman who married a Libyan colonial subject, acquisition of metropolitan citizenship by the Libyan natives was not fully regulated in 1913. So in the absence of further archival documents, one can suppose that the Italian legislature left this issue to a later norm, which in fact was introduced in 1919, as we shall see in the next pages.[39]

The content of rights formulated in relation to the 1913 status is also worth analyzing in detail. Compared to the colonial subjecthood of the Eritreans and Somalis, SIL was different and slightly thicker. For instance, whereas in Eritrea and Somalia the indigenous peoples were entitled mainly to a limited number of civil rights, the 1913 subjecthood of Italy's North African natives incorporated more substantial entitlements. Both Libyans and East Africans enjoyed the "personal statute" and related civil rights according to religion; yet the former population could also exercise a variety of public functions within the colonial administration—at the governmental, regional and municipal levels—that the latter never could. In particular, the head of a Libyan administrative region (i.e., the regional commissioner) was to be a metropolitan, but the heads of other administrative units (i.e., the district delegates and county agents) could be chosen from among the indigenous notables. The North African natives were also entitled to join various consultative organs, such as the Council of the Region and the Councils of the Districts, as well as taking up the position of mayor and councilor at the municipal level. Finally, from 1917, through creation of two indigenous committees in Tripoli and Bengasi, the indigenous subjects had the right to send their delegates to the metropole as members of the Central Joint Consultative Committee, which was part of the Ministry of the Colonies in Rome. Clearly, almost all these positions filled by the *Tripolitani* and *Cirenaici* were consultative and therefore had not much say in the policy-making process; they were appointed by a metropolitan governor rather than elected, and their power was seriously limited by the supervising authority of the colonizers.[40] However, compared to the much less substantial indigenous participation in the administration of Eritrea and Somalia, the Libyan situation stands out within liberal Italy's citizenship system. By 1913, the existing civic hierarchy, which was made up of metropolitan citizens (at the top) and colonial subjects (at the bottom), was enriched with an additional status, located in our imaginary line, above the *Eritrei* and *Somali* and below the *metropolitani*.

Most importantly, within just six years of the Italians' arrival in North Africa and in stark contrast with the subjects of East Africa, the indigenous inhabitants of Libya saw their juridical link to the Italian state change in name and content as their membership evolved from "*sudditanza*" (SIL) in 1913 to "*cittadinanza italiana in Tripolitania e Cirenaica*" (CITC) in 1919. This civic evolution took place not only on the basis of civilizational considerations, which will be fully discussed in the third section of this chapter, but also for a variety of important reasons connected to the international system and to specific colonial domestic politics. More particularly, following the Great War and the ideological influence of President Woodrow Wilson's democratic tenets upon the peninsula, numerous voices supported elevating the Libyans from the quality of colonial subjects to the status of colonial citizens with introduction of a local representative system and of an autonomous government to be enshrined in the so-called Libyan

Statutes. Also, clear political imperatives encouraged the Italian state to grant a higher civic position: concession of autonomy and of a more substantial colonial citizenship was seen as a useful instrument through which Italy would keep the rebels at bay and reestablish some state authority in a colony that had been under guerrilla warfare for years.[41] Readers should in fact bear in mind that following the Arab rebellions of 1914–15 against the Italian troops who had tried to move toward the internal part of the Libyan territory, occupying Fezzan, Ghibla and Gebel, the Italians suffered serious defeats and were obliged to retreat to the coast.[42] So although Italy would have to wait for the violent fascist repressions of 1932 before being able to recuperate these lost territories of the Libyan hinterland, it regarded citizenship policy as an additional tool that could help face a hostile colonial environment. Finally, by allowing more substantial participation by the natives within their own territory, the metropole would thank those Arabs who contributed to the "pacification" of the colony after so many uprisings. "Our Arabs," argued Italy's Minister of Colonies Gaspare Colosimo in 1919, in reference to the Libyans, "were holding out their hand to come closer to us, to march under one and the same flag"; it was therefore politically convenient to reciprocate and "to shake with loyalty and cordiality the [...] outstretched and invoking hand."[43] Consequently, granting colonial citizenship was perceived by the metropole as contributing to the fecund collaboration between metropolitans and autochthones with the ultimate goal of strengthening Italian colonial rule.

This particular membership status that the liberal state introduced right after the First World War was regulated in accordance with some of the same principles that we saw in 1913 but in a more detailed and comprehensive way. For instance, a native would hold CITC on the basis of Libyan paternal bloodline and birth in the colony as general norms (with the exclusion of those who had Italian metropolitan citizenship or any other status as subjects or citizens of other states). Also, the Italo-Libyan progeny continued to be assimilated into the Italian metropolitan citizenry via paternal *jus sanguinis*, and the principle of the unity of the family in citizenship matters would be upheld so that alien women marrying male Libyan natives acquired CITC and female Libyans holding CITC acquired Italian metropolitan citizenship by marrying Italian colonizers.[44] Finally, if a Libyan wanted to become a metropolitan citizen through naturalization, the latter was very restrictive, as we also saw in the eastern African territories. In fact, the Libyan had to be monogamous or single, have five years of residence in Italy or in the colony and be in one of six situations: (1) have served with loyalty and honor within the royal army or navy, (2) have successfully completed at least Italian elementary school, (3) have exercised a governmental public function, (4) have been invested with a public elective mandate, (5) be in possession of an honorary title or decoration from the Italian government, or (6) be born to a native Italian citizen of Tripolitania or Cyrenaica who also naturalized and became a metropolitan citizen. Most importantly, by acquiring metropolitan status the Libyans—as did their East African counterparts— had to follow all the laws of the Italian kingdom; this means they automatically lost the "personal statute" to which they were very attached.[45] Although sharing a higher colonial juridical status than East Africans, Libyans as well would not become metropolitan citizens so easily.

Finally, as far as content of citizenship is concerned, one should emphasize that the 1919 Libyan colonial status was more substantial, *de jure*, than the colonial subjecthood of 1913—thus making the civic accommodation of the Libyans stand out all the more in comparison with the juridical position that Italy reserved for *Eritrei* and *Somali* during the same years. For instance, in 1919 the civil rights to which the North African natives were entitled increased as to include not only equality before the law, freedom of conscience and respect for the indigenous *statut personnel* but also individual liberty, inviolability of domicile and property, freedom of press and freedom of association. Also, the Libyan position improved from the perspective of political participation because, with the introduction of a colonial elective parliamentary system, (male) Libyan natives started enjoying active and passive electoral rights in the respective colonial parliaments of Tripolitania and Cyrenaica as well as the right of petition to Italy's National Assembly. Lastly, since a variety of social entitlements were guaranteed as well (i.e., the right to free exercise of profession in Italy and obligatory primary education for male natives), the difference between the Libyan status and that of the East Africans could not have been more evident.[46]

Bearing these civic developments in mind, one should, however, add that even though the *de jure* link uniting North Africans to Italy evolved in six years into a fuller colonial participatory citizenship that *Eritrei* and *Somali* never had, the exercise of such a status was seriously complicated and undermined in practice by the colonial context of those years. Most importantly, the 1919 parliamentary system (and related colonial citizenship) remained partly a dead letter because a local parliament was created only in Cyrenaica, whereas the rebels' activities in Tripolitania prevented formation of a local assembly in the western part of the colony.[47] Moreover, despite the apparent "pacification" within the colonial possession, local hostility never really disappeared, and the risk of rebellions continued to be so high as to make colonial civic membership an institution often only on paper. So, although the formal and juridical positions of the natives living in Libya and in East Africa were clearly distinct, exercise of colonial status was similarly shaped in the respective territories within a context of instability and of native opposition to colonial rule.

To conclude, liberal Italy's territorial expansionism in the African continent up to 1922 led to introduction of a *sudditanza coloniale* for Eritreans and Somalis and also of a *sudditanza per gli indigeni della Libia* and of a *cittadinanza italiana della Tripolitania e Cirenaica*, both reserved for the Libyans. Each status enjoyed its own geographical specificity and content as well as being part of a hierarchical system of nonmetropolitan positions that would be used by the liberal state with a certain ease in order to accommodate its native populations.

Leaving now the coast of North Africa, we take the reader to the Eastern Mediterranean and see how the notions of metropolitan and nonmetropolitan membership(s) were given an Aegean flavor.

5.2. ITALY'S FOREIGN POLICY IN THE MEDITERRANEAN ORIENT AND ISSUES OF MEMBERSHIP STATUS: THE AEGEAN ISLANDS

During the colonial war between Italy and the Ottoman empire that led to the Italian conquest of Libya, the liberal state extended its military operations by opening a naval front in the Aegean Sea in May 1912 and occupying during the same month thirteen islands that were under Ottoman sovereignty: Rhodes, Stampalia, Chalki, Karpathos, Kassos, Piscopi, Nisyros, Kalymnos, Leros, Patmos, Lissos, Simi and Kos. Extension of the colonial war to the eastern part of the Mediterranean as well as the military occupation were deemed necessary in the Italian peninsula for the purpose of attacking the enemy in a most vulnerable part of its empire (and finally ending a conflict that had become too long and too expensive to justify at home) as well as capturing a pawn (i.e., the occupied islands) that could then be used in the future peace settlement. Keeping the status of a military occupying power for the entire liberal period, Italy expanded its *occupatio* over a fourteenth island in 1921—Kastellorizo—and had to wait for the fascist period before the *de jure* acquisition and transfer of sovereignty of all these territories took place in accordance with the 1923 Lausanne Treaty. Already colonizers in East and North Africa, by occupying what became known improperly as *Dodecaneso*, the Italians enriched their expansionist foreign policy on the Red Sea and on the Southern Mediterranean with an additional Oriental (Aegean) agenda.[48]

As a result of this Eastern Mediterranean military policy, Italian troops landed on territories that before 1922 were inhabited by roughly a hundred thousand native people. The latter were mainly Greek from an ethnic point of view and professing Greek Orthodoxy, although small minorities of Muslim Turks, Jews and Roman Catholics were present as well. Also, on the largest island of Rhodes, besides the majority (Greek) language one could hear a Spanish dialect (*spaniolo*) spoken by those

Jewish inhabitants whose ancestors had left the Iberian peninsula in the fourteenth and fifteenth centuries to escape persecution.[49]

Bearing in mind our previous sections concerning the way in which liberal Italy accommodated its (East and North) African populations, it is appropriate to raise the same issue here and see how the Italian state dealt, in this respect, with the *Dodecanesini* or *Egei* (the terms being used here synonymously). Interestingly, our findings show that compared to Eritreans, Somalis and Libyans, who became colonial subjects of the Italian king (and the North African natives also saw their membership improve from colonial subjecthood to colonial citizenship), the Dodecanese people were in a completely different juridical situation, thanks to the political-administrative context of the islands and the arrangements that took place at the international level. More particularly, since the fourteen Aegean islands were only occupied militarily by Italian troops, and from an international legal point of view these territories continued to be part of the Ottoman Empire, the *status civitatis* of the native populations did not change.[50] This means that the *Egei* under consideration continued to be Ottoman subjects throughout the entire liberal epoch, as they had been before Italy's military occupation started in May 1912. Also, as Ottomans, they continued to follow an 1869 Turkish nationality law whose application was formally acknowledged and guaranteed by Italian authorities, as well as to enjoy membership status regulated by Ottoman legislation and, in some cases, by "the system of capitulations," to which we shall come back in a moment.[51] This legal situation would last for the entire liberal era and change only in August 1924—during the fascist period—when the Lausanne Treaty sanctioning the formal transfer of the islands to Italy entered into force in the peninsula.[52]

Since the *Dodecanesini* held Ottoman subjecthood under Italian occupation, this also means that they were automatically foreigners vis-à-vis the Italian state and the Italian militaries that were stationed in the occupied islands. Most revealingly, though, we were able to discover a variety of historical documents demonstrating Italy's special concern for these aliens and its attempt to use certain "citizenship instruments" with the objective of making sure the natives of the islands concerned would not be "lost" as potential citizens, especially within the context of the imminent demise of the Ottoman empire and the peace settlement in the Orient (1920–1922). Two specific "citizenship tools" were used by liberal Italy up to 1922 with a clear foreign policy objective: the system of capitulations, and a generous policy of individual naturalizations.

The former, first introduced in the Christian states of the Orient (i.e., Antiochia and Jerusalem) at the end of the eleventh century in favor of the ancient naval powers of Genoa, Venice and Marseilles, was applied in the Ottoman state following an international treaty of 1535 between the French king François I and Sultan Suleiman I. It basically consisted of special status granted by Ottoman authorities to the nationals of those European states that were signatories of a treaty of capitulation with Turkey because the Koran and sharia law—constitutional foundations of the Ottoman Empire—could not be applied to regulate all spheres of life for its non-Muslim inhabitants. As a result, the affected European citizens enjoyed inviolability of domicile as a form of immunity from the local authority, followed special fiscal and judiciary norms and were entitled to diplomatic protection of their state of origin (protection that, upon request, the same European state could also extend to non-Muslim Ottoman subjects and their families).[53]

The important thing about this system—formally abolished in 1923 following the Treaty of Lausanne—is that by the end of the nineteenth century it had become an instrument of foreign policy used by many European powers to extend their influence in the Ottoman area through creation of substantial groups of "protected persons" (*protégés*). This was indeed the case with post-unification Italy as well, which had been very keen on extending its state protection, especially vis-à-vis so-called *Levantini* (Levantines). The latter were Jews and other non-Muslims, the majority of whom were descendants of those "Italians" who had moved to the Orient with their commercial activities during the period of the ancient Republics of Genoa, Amalfi, Pisa and Venice.[54] Subsequently, upon Italian occupation of the Aegean Islands in 1912, the liberal state continued to use this "citizenship instrument" by according protection to some non-Muslim *Dodecanesini* who were living this time outside the islands. The documents at our disposal say a lot about how these *Egei* used the system of consular protection for personal and opportunistic reasons: some of them wanted Italy's protection to avoid being drafted during the Great War as Ottoman subjects living in Germany, and others wished to avoid the laws concerning enemy subjects (i.e., expulsion, political detention or forced transfer to prisoner of war camps) as Ottomans living in Wales, South Africa, Russia and France. However, the fact that Italy agreed to protect them without reservation, and that in some of these documents reference is also made to French and Greek consulates abroad having been authorized by their respective governments to protect Christian Ottomans (i.e., Maronites, other Roman Catholics and Greek Orthodox), says a great deal about the will of a state to continue being open vis-à-vis the natives of this area in competition with other European powers.[55]

Diplomatic protection, though, was not enough. Within the evident final collapse of the Ottoman empire and the context of the peace settlement (1920–1922), Italy formulated a generous policy concerning individual naturalizations, which basically aimed at reintroducing the easy procedure of "*la piccola naturalizzazione*" (small naturalization), discussed in Chapter Three and, as we know, abolished in the peninsula with the 1912 citizenship law. Admittedly, during the first years of Italian occupation, when the latter was deemed to be temporary and the Aegean islands were to be given back to Turkey, Italian Minister of Foreign Affairs and President of the Council of Ministers Antonio Salandra emphasized that it was inopportune to grant Italian citizenship to those Ottoman subjects who were resident in the occupied isles and had formally applied for it because this could lead people to "insinuate that, despite our commitments, we are planning to keep the islands."[56] Subsequently, though, as the "sick man of Europe" was dying, the moderate Italian position vis-à-vis this issue changed completely: Italy hurried to propose an urgent naturalization provision to make sure that, with the end of the Ottoman state and the system of capitulations, the liberal state would not have lost its many prestigious, economically active and socially important *protégés* by transforming them into Italian citizens. In this way, the commercial expansion, prestige and international position of the peninsula would be maintained once the Ottoman Empire had disappeared.[57]

As a result, in November 1920 the Italian Ministry of Foreign Affairs proposed a legislative bill concerning a simpler process of naturalization for acquiring Italian citizenship (exclusive of political rights and the duty to do military service) by specific categories of people resident in the Orient. This thin Italian citizenship could have been granted to those resident in the Ottoman state who were enjoying or had enjoyed Italian diplomatic protection as well as to those resident people holding Ottoman, or other foreign, status and whose family originated from an ancient ex-Italian state or who were citizens of the former Austrian-Hungarian empire or of a Balkan state and represented in all cases a special interest for Italian commercial influence in the area.[58] Presented twice in the Italian parliament, in November 1920 and June 1921, this proposition had an impact on the final text of a royal decree that, adopted by the Italian state in September 1922, was to enter into force two months later when Mussolini was already in power.[59]

By 1922, liberal Italy had incorporated *Eritrei*, *Somali* and *Libici* into the framework of its expanding state through a system of "nonmetropolitan subjecthood/citizenship," while treating the *Dodecanesini* as "special aliens" and potential Italian citizens whose status, however, would not have included certain entitlements. The *Egei* were not natives living in a territory under Italian sovereignty, but foreigners under military administration, who by naturalizing individually could have easily acquired the thin citizenship of the Italian peninsula. Indeed, even before 1920 the liberal state's reintroduction of the small naturalization procedure for people living in certain geographical areas of special Italian interest had been proposed on several occasions.[60] Consequently, as far as the Aegean populations are concerned and bearing in mind all the other statuses studied in this chapter, the *Dodecanesini* were supposed to be entitled to thin Italian membership, on an individual basis and as privileged aliens.

In reality, by the time liberal Italy—a latecomer as a colonial power— started its expansionist adventures and formulated all the colonial subjecthood, citizenship and naturalization policies, the recent Italian case study was but a small territorial piece on the world map compared to the centuries-old and vast British empire incorporating as it did overseas territories that stretched from America to Africa and from Asia to Oceania. Also, in contrast with the Italian case study, where metropolitan settlements were relatively more recent and less substantial, the colonial territories under British rule had been inhabited by large populations of British and other European descent, settled in the colonies for several generations. In relation to this latter factor and contrary to the Italian example, it is instructive to learn that since the midnineteenth century a "division" had occurred within the British empire between "white-settler colonies," known also as "Dominions" (with a capital D) and enjoying a large degree of autonomy from the metropole (i.e., Canada, Australia, New Zealand, and later, the Union of South Africa), and "colonial territories," being inhabited by large non-European populations that held subordinated status and were run by a minority of people sent out from Britain. Moreover, within the context of the Dominions' insistence on their own autonomy and subsequent desire for more self-assertion, we learned that several Dominion local governments started deciding on issues that pertained to immigration and nationality matters as well as to exclusion of certain native non-Europeans from the full rights of citizenship because of racial prejudice. As a result, although the British empire was united by a theoretically universal common status of British subjecthood, linking all the populations of the Crown around the globe to the British monarch on the basis of the doctrine of personal allegiance, in practical terms this common membership status was being challenged by introduction of local citizenships and local naturalization policies, developed in various overseas territories and important, in particular, for property rights and immigration legislation.[61]

During the period of liberal Italy that concerns us here, these local memberships within the British empire were still in their infancy, carried weight only in the territory concerned and were designed for administrative convenience to differentiate between classes of British subjects. In this respect, the 1910 and 1921 Canadian Acts are a case in point since they introduced and regulated "Canadian citizenship"—an expression that, at the time, had no meaning in international law as state membership but that was used, locally, as a short and convenient term to denote certain persons having special links with Canada. Even though insignificant from an international legal point of view, such local membership status was of fundamental political importance because it was issued by Dominion governments rather than by the metropole and also because it would contribute to setting in motion the gradual process that in the long run would lead to full independence of the territories from the metropole. So by 1922, while young liberal Italy was attempting to realize its colonial dream for the first time in its post-unification history, Great Britain—the traditional imperial power *par excellence*—had concerns about how to keep its own empire in strength; how to manage and neutralize any centrifugal force that might come especially from its white-settler colonies and, most importantly, how to adjust the local citizenships within and beneath the imperial umbrella of a universal British subjecthood that had been keeping the whole institutional imperial structure together for centuries.[62]

Bearing in mind the diverse status of *Eritrei, Somali, Libici* and *Dodecanesini*, we shall now explore in more detail the official arguments and opinions articulated during the liberal period in relation to citizenship, civilizational concerns and racial thinking about Italy's African natives.

5.3. ITALIAN DISCOURSE ON COLONIAL SUBJECTHOOD, CIVILIZATION AND RACE IN THE AFRICAN TERRITORIES

In the sources we were able to collect on questions of citizenship and subjecthood in Italian Africa, we came across a frequently used and sophistically upheld ideological paradigm, namely, nineteenth-century "liberal imperialism" and the inseparable underlying principle of "the civilizing mission" exercised by the colonizers over their "barbaric populations."

On the occasion of acquisition of the Bay of Assab by the Italian state in 1882, Minister of Foreign Affairs Mancini made a straightforward link between Italy's "mission of civilization and peace" (contributing to the "general cause of humanity") and the membership status of the natives. In his view, the Italians had to fulfill the "task of educators" vis-à-vis their colonial subjects, and by taking the latter "by the hand" lead them "gradually" to full exercise of citizenship (inclusive of political rights) up to the point of allowing them eventually to elect their own representatives and have deputies in the Italian parliament. The initial status granted by liberal Italy to its East African populations was very thin because, according to this rhetoric, the political, social and cultural contexts of the colony were not yet ripe. However, as Minister Mancini argued, Italy's objective was not to keep its colonial subjects in an inferior status of "pariahs" but to elevate them and transform them into "real Italian citizens." Through colonization, the natives' colonial subjecthood would have slowly become full participatory citizenship.[63]

Mancini's image of the Italian educators leading indigenous inhabitants to the status of full citizens came to be enriched later on with a second, similar, metaphor used by Senator Michele Carta Mameli in 1903: the image of a father guiding his children toward civilization, and eventually to full civic membership (including metropolitan citizenship) in view of transforming the natives from "uncivilized colonial subjects" to "civilized citizens." As he put it, "since the races under Italian dominion live in a degeneration of age-old uncivilized standing, may the new offspring be gradually introduced to our *civiltà* and eventually acquire our *nazionalità*."[64]

Before this civic transformation of the natives could take place, though, and their membership status could thicken, some civilizing work had to be done by the Italian colonizers according to the level of civilization found in a colony. The natives' evolution from partial to full members of the Italian state would, in fact, have occurred following not only political and economic development of the territory but also, and most importantly, social and moral advancement of the indigenous peoples. After all, as Vittorio Alhadeff reminds us, the word colonization comes from the Latin *colo/colere* ("to cultivate"), and it was used at the time with a double (literal and metaphorical) meaning: to cultivate the overseas territory (with a view to raising its economic value and making it profitable) and to cultivate the natives (with a view to raising their perceived inferior level of civilization).[65] In reference to the latter point, two essential assumptions were strongly upheld in liberal Italy as in other contemporary European states possessing overseas empires: the existence of barbaric indigenous peoples (who had not yet opened their eyes to civilization) and the presence of differing levels of backwardness; and the duty of the most advanced peoples (the European colonizers) to bring civilization and good administration to the uncivilized colonized subjects on the basis of the Western belief in the responsibility to bear what was known as "the white man's burden."[66]

The Italian civilizational arguments shared by many colonial powers echoed well-developed British liberal imperial thought, on a general level, and the classical writings of John Stuart Mill and James Mill in particular. Defining civilization as "the direct converse of rudeness or barbarism," J. S. Mill had assumed some sort of scale of civilizational hierarchies similar to that elucidated by his father in the *History of British India* and regarded as necessary within the general realization of the British imperial project to lead the Indians toward "the high attainments of civilized life." Within this context, the colonization of backward territories and populations was seen by the two British liberal thinkers as being part of "the effort to move societies along the ascending gradient of historical progress" and therefore an important moral duty. This is why colonial expansionism was legitimized as an instrument for "tutelage" and "progressive superintendence" exercised by the colonizers over the colonized subjects, with a view to ultimately leading them to a higher civilization.[67] Indeed, James Mill's image of India being in the infancy of the "progress of civilization" as well as John Stuart Mill's reference to gradual training of the natives "to walk alone" underpinned one and the same concept: India, the colony, was a child, and Britain, the metropole, a legitimate parent who under the concept of tutelage was responsible for the colony's growth and development in all spheres. This specific point drew its theoretical liberal origin from Locke's ideal of tutelage, seen as a necessary temporary period through which all children had to go before they could become adult and acquire the reason necessary to express consent.[68] Clearly, on the basis of these tenets, British colonial subjects would grow up thanks to the work of their tutors and eventually become full participatory citizens.

The history of Italian and British colonialism, though, was to be much more complicated and much less idyllic than this. In fact, the civilizing mission—so central within this ideological thinking—followed a complex path realized within a colonial milieu that was shaped by power relations separating the colonizers from the colonized. By focusing on the Italian case study and drawing from current scholarly debates, we can discuss this fundamental and highly controversial issue.

As already pointed out by Sòrgoni, the notion of civilization as well as use of this concept in Italian colonial rule were very often ambiguous and so inspired contrasting positions.[69] For instance, some Italian colonial authorities, among them Pollera, constantly emphasized the responsibility of bringing progress to the colonial lands, being firmly convinced by the paternalistic ideal of civilizing the African peoples.[70] Yet evidence also reveals that Italian colonialism was at the same time quite unwilling to create institutions that would facilitate civilizing of the autochthones. One example to be taken among many is native education in Eritrea: as we saw, it was first rejected by Italian authorities as putting at risk the appropriate power relations between the conquerors and the conquered. Later on it was introduced, but only for the first years schooling and with an ad hoc curriculum to take into account mainly the needs of the Italian administration *in loco*.[71] Also, we know that Pollera pointed out very often in his writings and discourse that the inferiority of the native populace was "temporary," "mutable" and "relative"—therefore to be indubitably improved, in his view, and elevated toward civic advancement.[72] However, parallel to this positive and optimistic viewpoint, many other Italians took a more cautious stance in arguing about civilization and the potential assimilation of the natives to citizens, favoring for instance holding up, rescheduling or setting back the whole project to a vague future. This postponement was justified, within official rhetoric, either because immediate assimilation of native status to Italian citizenship was seen as detrimental for the indigenous peoples (the stereotyping myth of the "*buon selvaggio,*" "the kind primitive" who would be traumatized by abrupt integration within the higher civilization)[73] or because, for other Italian authorities, the example of neighboring French assimilationist policies caused a certain anxiety and fear.[74] Finally, in some Italian colonial circles, even if a number of Africans had "embraced the imported civilization" and been granted Italian metropolitan citizenship through naturalization for these reasons, their status nevertheless had to be kept inferior to that of the Italian colonizers because of the political power and prestige of the colonizing authorities needing to be defended and preserved in those regions.[75] No matter whether the locals had reached the high standards of progress, their position had to remain subjugated. And this clearly demonstrates that the defense of the conquerors' prestige, based on the institutionalization of a racial civic hierarchy, was an essential tenet within Italy's colonial politics during the liberal decades, as Sòrgoni rightly emphasizes, and not limited only to the late fascist years.[76]

The concept of *civiltà* (civilization), alongside the related question of which civilizational markers were taken into consideration by the Italian administration whenever a population had to be categorized, changed over time and was not always defined in the same way. For instance, in the African territories notions of alienhood came to mirror these aspects in referring to the foreign immigrants living in the Italian colonies alongside Italy's colonial subjects and Italian metropolitans. Interestingly, faced with the necessity of defining those who were neither Eritrean nor Somali nor Italian metropolitan citizens, liberal Italy did not use the words *aliens* or *foreigners*—as it had done previously before the colonial adventures started—but it expanded the concept of foreignness by making a distinction between the foreigners who were "more similar" to the African native subjects of Eritrea and Somalia and those who, on the contrary, were "more similar" to the Italians. In this way, the new legal expression "*assimilati ai sudditi coloniali*" ("assimilated to the colonial subjects") was introduced and distinguished from the already known and used category of "*straniero*" (foreigner) applied when referring to non-Italian Europeans.[77] At the time Italian authorities were specifically confronted with the presence of substantial groups of Indians, Egyptians and Arabs living in those eastern colonies. How did liberal Italy categorize them? On the basis of which civilizational indicators was the whole issue dealt with? Did the metropole take into account the peoples' skin color? Did it pay attention to their social and cultural levels? Were all these factors together to have an impact on the final official decision? This issue, characterizing the entire liberal period, came to be resolved throughout the decades in different ways and therefore without a clear consistency; in fact, whereas initially the three groups were treated as foreigners, from 1908 onward they came to be assimilated to colonial subjects.[78] According to the first categorization, they followed Italian metropolitan legislation as far as justice, nationality matters and content of citizenship were concerned; by contrast, when assimilated to colonial subjects they kept their personal statute and followed the religious customary laws that regulated many spheres of the natives' life.[79]

Changing over time, the notion of civilizational level was also intertwined very often with discourses about race and with concepts of racialized gender, discussed at the time in conjunction with the notion of the colonizers' prestige.[80] For instance, during the liberal decades the term *race* was often used interchangeably with the word *civiltà* and was generally not defined on strictly biological terms, as would be the case during the 1930s, but on similarly important cultural, social, linguistic and religious differences.[81] However, in some cases the intermingling of race (in its biological sense) with the impact of culture and the environment emerged in colonial rhetoric, as for example in the debates pertaining to interracial unions. In this respect, we know that on the Red Sea the practice of marriage (almost nonexistent) between white women and native men was nevertheless regarded as more undesirable by Italian authorities than union between a white man and a colonial subject because, on the basis of widespread socio-anthropological principles, a white woman who married a black subject was perceived as committing a grave action, uniting with him not only "her own dignity" but also "the dignity of her own race."[82] Within the colonial context, the tenet of racial prestige was the key factor in explaining these sexually based considerations. Also, the interrelation between race and gender took on an additional peculiar dimension in the Italian colonies because, within mixed marriages, we can see again that the ideologies of race and gender were related and applied in a specific way. In fact, we have already remarked (in Chapter Two) that in the peninsula Italian women were dependent on their husbands as far as matters of nationality were concerned. So in this case, the ideology of gender was predominant. By contrast, in the colonies the racial ideology upholding the superiority of the white race and of European civilization overcame that of gender so as to upset completely the nationality issues pertaining, even if only in theory, to Italian women married to colonial subjects.[83]

In some instances, the notions of civilization and civilizational gap separating citizens and subjects were also to be called into question entirely. For example, when discussing whether all mixed marriages in general should be prohibited, two parallel and diametrically opposed discourses were upheld by Italian officialdom. On one side of the debate, some would argue about prohibition of these unions because of the existence of a civilizational gap dividing citizens and subjects; on the other side, others would still be against such unions but for the opposite reason—that the civilizational gap was not so wide and therefore interracial marriages could actually be seen as dangerous within a context of colonial power relations.[84] This latter argument, questioning the low level of *civiltà* among the East African inhabitants and emphasizing their "similarity" with Europeans, was inspired by the "Hamitic Hypothesis," a topic of discussion at the international level that in the 1890s involved the Italian anthropologist Sergi as well.[85] The question concerned the anthropological origins of the populations living on the African continent and the fundamental distinction made at the time between "the Hamites" and the "real Negroes."[86] The Hamites (descendants of Ham, the second son of Noah) were peoples defined in this discourse by their lighter skin color, fine facial features and a high level of civilization, as well as being depicted as the ancestors of Egyptians and East Africans. The real Negroes, by contrast, were basically the black, inferior, and backward races of the rest of Africa. For Sergi, the first group belonged to the superior *Homo eurafricus*, the second to inferior *Homo sudanensis* or *Pigmeus africus*.[87] Since the population living in the Italian colonies around the Red Sea and the Indian Ocean were believed to belong to the Hamitic race and were therefore held to be different from the other Africans, standard civilizational concerns were questioned and contested as in the case described above.

Highly debated and contested over time, the whole issue of civilizing the African was also complicated in Italy by the fact that the Italian state was actually struggling at home to civilize the southern part of its own population, as we saw in Chapters One and Two. So the ironical paradox of "still uncivilized Italians" trying to "civilize the backward Africans" could not but be stressed at the time, as emphasized by Wong.[88] In this particular respect, the Italian discussion of the civilizing mission in Africa intertwined with the language and tropes of the Southern Question and further intensified political debates on imperialism. For instance, several opponents of colonial expansionism made use of this language in order to criticize and condemn Italian aims in the African continent. In their minds and discourse, how could Italy bring progress to autochthones and try to eliminate their barbaric mores when in point of fact some barbaric practices were not at all absent in certain areas of the peninsula, as in various distant zones within the regions of Sardinia and Basilicata? Clearly, if the

Italian colonizers had to civilize themselves back home owing to massive illiteracy, chronic destitution and deep-rooted criminality, then one might well wonder how they could disembark on the African coasts to educate and enlighten the wild African populace.[89] For the anti-imperialists the Italian state had to cease these military colonial campaigns and "think of the other Africa that we have here in the house and of the marauders who live in Italy."[90]

Besides this discourse, though, the debate came to be enriched with further parallel arguments that, in contrast, were used to justify the quest for empire. Within this rhetoric, imperial wars and racial difference were presented as means to actually unite the Italians of the peninsula—southerners and northerners. How could colonial expansionism be such a unifying factor? According to this rhetoric, colonialism and the civilizing mission in Africa would have strengthened the unification of the Italians in two ways. First, skin color and interracial encounters would have provided the Italians with the image of a distant and very visible Other, making the Italians "more similar" among themselves through the perceived distance separating white Italians from black autochthones.[91] As Wong put it, "little else could make the perceived biological differences between the northern and southern Italian counterparts disappear so quickly as the even more visible racial differences between the European and the African."[92] From this perspective, then, colonial wars, whiteness and the realities of skin color were to unite the "divided" colonizers because of the visible blackness of the natives. Second, Italian imperial conquests would have provided concrete solutions to the Southern Question through agricultural lands and colonial work opportunities for Italy's surplus population. In this way, colonialism and its related mission would have strengthened the Italians' unification from a more economic and social point of view.[93]

Finally, as emphasized recently by Fabrizio De Donno, discussion of colonial citizenship, race and civilization sheds light on the coexistence and intertwining of the "Aryan" and "Mediterranean" ideas in Italian colonial discourse during the liberal years.[94] The "Aryan idea," formulated by other Europeans before Italian unification, was pioneered in Italy in the 1880s by the orientalist Angelo De Gubernatis and was based on an argument that saw the "Italics" as Aryans because of a common Indo-European unity among Greeks, Indians and Italians deriving from the linguistic affinity of Sanskrit, Greek, Latin, and modern European languages. The Italics were therefore Aryans and had also come from India.[95] Anthropologist Sergi, though, diverged from this philological theory and put forward a parallel "Mediterranean idea" that saw the Italics as Eurafrican (and not Indo-European), originating from the Horn of Africa (and not from Asia).[96] The coexistence of these two theories in Italian colonial discourse was reflected for instance in debates concerning mixed-race children and interracial unions within the context of colonialism in East Africa. For example, when explaining why marriage between an Italian woman and a colonial subject should be prohibited, Italian authorities made reference in 1905 to the harmful effect of this union on the children, and to the fact that by spending their childhood in their paternal environment these *meticci* of "Aryan (maternal) descent" could later in life have desired to take vengeance against the Italian conquerors and their violent conquests in (paternal) Africa.[97] Also, in the argument, already discussed, that questioned the low level of civilization of the East Africans and emphasized the similarity of these colonized populations with the Italians, colonial authorities referred indirectly to Sergi's idea of Mediterraneanism and of Mediterranean unity between Italians and the African peoples of the Horn, including Eritreans, Somalis and Ethiopians, because of their common origins as Eurafricans (*Homo eurafricus*).[98] So in liberal colonial discourse pertaining to citizenship issues, Italian officialdom made reference to both the Aryan and the Mediterranean ideas of race, showing that Aryanism was not accepted everywhere in the peninsula and that it actually coexisted with other competing racial arguments. These two ideas interacted with each other in the liberal decades, and, as we shall see in Part Two of this book concerning Fascism, they interacted during the early years of the dictatorship as well, up to 1936, when the two theories started intermingling with Nazi Aryanism and were joined into specific "Aryan-Mediterranean" notions of race, citizenship and membership status.[99]

In the next and final section, we explore Italy's official discourse by focusing on the liberal variant of the myth of ancient Rome as well as on *Dodecanesini* and the Maritime Republics.

5.4. THINKING AND TALKING ABOUT ANCIENT ROME, THE MARITIME REPUBLICS AND ITALIAN CITIZENSHIP IN THE LIBERAL YEARS

When analyzing our sources pertaining to subjecthood and citizenship in Italy's territories, we came across further interesting historical references that warrant discussion as well, in order to prepare the reader for later comparisons with fascist colonialism. In particular, whereas the "myth of Rome" has already been extensively studied in a growing literature pertaining not only to fascist Italy but also to the liberal period,[100] the specific impact of this myth on liberal Italy's formulation of colonial subjecthood is still relatively unknown.

Scholars have already examined in detail how, throughout the centuries, the memory of ancient Rome nurtured the collective consciousness of numerous peoples—"heirs" of the Roman empire and others alike. "Rome, after Rome" (*Roma, dopo Roma*)—that is, a cluster of transmitted mental representations about the ancient city-republic-empire after its fall—has transformed the history of the Eternal City into a myth and made it a vivid ideological reference to be evoked in different ways and with a level of intensity depending on the country under study and the specific historical period. Roman antiquity has evolved into a multifaceted intellectual paradigm and has evoked, simultaneously or separately, a variety of historical and spiritual elements: the idea of a unified administrative space regulated by a clear, codified legal system; the richness of an old civilization that developed from the Etruscan era to the fifth century; the spiritual center of Christianity, on the basis of the martyrdom of the apostles Peter and Paul as well as the historical role of the papacy; the ancient unification of the Italian peninsula, following the first Roman conquests of the Etruscans, the Gauls (in the north) and the Greek *politeia* (in the south); and finally, the grandeur of a city that expanded into a vast colonial empire across Europe, North Africa and the coasts of the Eastern Mediterranean.[101]

The various sources at our disposal pertaining to Italy's citizenship policies in its overseas territories tell us that explicit and clear connections with ancient Roman citizenship and with how the Eternal City accommodated its nonmetropolitan populations were sometimes evoked before 1922 in reference to the membership status introduced by liberal Italy in its East and North African colonies, while remaining absent in the discourse concerning the *Dodecanesini*. So, without enjoying any central position within Italian citizenship discourse, the traditional myth of Ancient Rome was occasionally resurrected in reference to the subjecthood of the native populations of Africa. For instance, in a speech held in the city of Palermo in October 1889, Prime Minister Crispi referred to the international standing of Italy as a country of mass emigration vis-à-vis the distant oceans, and as a young colonial power that, in "mysterious Africa," would develop trade relations and find vast lands for its colonial settlement migration.[102] Within this speech, interrupted at various times by applause and shouts of approval, the Sicilian premier explicitly evoked ancient Roman citizenship: "Not in vain may [the Italian citizen] be able to repeat in front of the other peoples the Civis romanus sum. (*Benissimo, bravo* coming from the audience)."[103] Clearly, when talking about Italian expansionism in the African continent, ancient Rome and its citizenship system were also vivid references within the *imaginaire* of liberal Italy's officialdom.

An additional and stronger connection to the myth of "*Roma docet*" ("Rome teaches us") within Italian colonial citizenship policies was also made in 1907 during a parliamentary debate regarding the natives of Benadir (South Italian Somalia), whose subjecthood was mainly regulated by local customary laws in accordance with the religious affiliation of the individual. As argued in the Lower Chamber, it was important to keep the personal statute of these indigenous peoples—rather than replacing it violently or arrogantly with the national laws of the metropole—because in this way Italy was upholding the great principles of the classical colonial policy "in which Rome was a master."[104] Obviously, in this second case as well, one can see that the Roman paradigm was present in the minds of those who were dealing with colonial citizenship issues during the liberal era.

In an earlier parliamentary report concerning the Eritrean colony, Deputy Leopoldo Franchetti too referred to the same historical reference. While explaining at great length the system of property rights and how important it was to introduce a clear policy concerning this civil aspect of citizenship and subjecthood (especially with a view to encouraging Italian emigration to the colony and exploitation of colonial land), the deputy explicitly mentioned historic Roman colonial provisions and emphasized that property rights and property-related issues had been taught to the colonizing modern states by the Eternal City.[105] Therefore, liberal Italy had to follow the same political road, and in this specific case—pertaining to the civil sphere of citizenship in the colonies—be inspired, once again, by the Roman model.

Finally and most importantly, when Italy introduced the institution of colonial citizenship for the natives of Tripolitania and Cyrenaica in 1919, Minister of Colonies Colosimo referred directly to the Roman past by emphasizing the ancient town's leading role in formulating progressive citizenship policies for civic incorporation of diverse populations within its empire, and by drawing a parallel with the innovative Italian citizenship norms of 1919 concerning the Libyans. As he argued before the chamber:

> The provision submitted to your examination [...] is a bold step. [...] It puts Italy at the head of the movement of progress within colonial politics, as Rome was in the vanguard in olden times when in front of the various peoples of its empire did not hesitate to grant Roman citizenship to all, in varying degrees and with different content.[106]

The point concerning colonial citizenship and ancient Rome was then embraced by the subsequent minister of colonies, Luigi Rossi, who in presenting a related bill at the Lower Chamber did not hesitate to reproduce *in toto* Colosimo's speech and the reference to ancient Roman citizenship quoted above.[107]

When recalling the "Idea of Rome," what Italian officialdom had in mind was the well-developed politics of membership that the ancient

Romans started introducing in the republican period and further developed during the principate and the late imperial epoch. In accordance with this ancient Roman citizenship system, the Prisci Latini, to take one example, living in the *civitates* under Roman hegemony during the fourth century B.C.E., were entitled to intermediate status between full Roman citizenship and foreignness, called Latinity, involving especially the right to *commercium* and *conubium* (i.e. do business with, and marry, a Roman citizen) and, under specific conditions, elevation to the status of *civis Romanus*. Also, a population under Roman rule could change status according to loyalty as well as political and other strategic considerations. This was the case, for instance, with the Sabine peoples in central Italy, the first *municipes* who, after holding the *civitas sine suffragio* (partial citizenship exclusive of political rights), were elevated in the third century B.C.E. to the status of full citizens by the grant of *ius suffragi* and enrollment in a tribe—a juridical and political change that took place within one generation. Beside the *civis Romanus* (holding full citizenship), the *Latinus* (enjoying the partial status of Latinity) and the *civis sine suffragio* (having a membership that would exclude political rights), ancient Rome also introduced further juridical categories of peoples following its foreign relations with neighboring populations and the gradual incorporation of the *Orbis* into the *Urbs*. In particular, it first created the legal status of *socii* to incorporate the Italian allies who had agreed to "respect the majesty of the Roman people," do military service and receive in return some share of the *iura* already enjoyed by the Latini. Then, in the later and successive non-Italian territories that went under its rule and administration, it distinguished the *coloni* (new inhabitants settled in a colonial territory, mainly to cultivate the land) from the *incolae* (the indigenous free peoples of a conquered territory). The former were granted privileged status (inclusive of political entitlements and transmissible to the descendants); the latter enjoyed a lower and thin position similarly held by the foreigners or *peregrini*. In short, the ancient Roman membership policies granted different rights and privileges to a variety of peoples and had, at their foundation, a unity of purpose, namely to bind all populations to Rome by links of loyalty, strengthen the embryonic polities overseas and institutionally fortify a growing territorial state.[108]

Evoked in liberal Italy, now and then, in reference to its East and North African natives, the myth of ancient Rome is actually absent in the sources at our disposal concerning the *Dodecanesini* of the Aegean islands. In our documents, no mention is made of the Roman past; by mainly focusing on modern Italy's commercial and international prestige in the Ottoman area, these sources sometimes include a more recent type of historical reference, namely, the image of the ancient Italian maritime republics (Pisa, Amalfi, Genoa and Venice) as well as of the economic activities of their numerous merchants who extended their commerce in the Orient between the tenth and thirteenth centuries and left many "Italian" descendants in the region.[109] Deputy Ernesto Vassallo, to take just one example in detail, was very clear on this point when talking about the "Italians" or "potential Italians" living in the former Ottoman Empire and linked to the peninsula through history and trade.[110] As he reminded his colleagues:

The wonderful commercial penetration, made by our ancient republics with their trade across the entire eastern Mediterranean basin, has left in Turkey the descendants of numerous families whose Italianness can now be reestablished with the rapid reacquisition of Italian nationality after a long and painful parenthesis of constriction or forced renunciation.[111]

5.5. CONCLUSION

Throughout forty years of expansionism (1882–1922), liberal Italy colonized about one and a half million (East and North) African natives as well as administrating one hundred thousand Dodecanese people. The former became Italian colonial subjects; the latter remained Ottomans for the entire liberal epoch. Also, whereas *Eritrei* and *Somali* were granted the status of colonial subjecthood, the *Libici* were first colonial subjects and then colonial citizens within Italy's institutional framework. Each status was characterized by a particular name, specific entitlements and a precise geographical application within a civic hierarchy of races. The *Dodecanesini*, by contrast, kept their (legal) foreignness—although the Italian state started treating them as special aliens, in line with a foreign policy that had traditionally been very open vis-à-vis the populations of the East Mediterranean.

Clearly all these historical civic developments led to an initial and gradual expansion of the notion of *italianità* so as to incorporate metropolitan and nonmetropolitan dimensions. In fact, to be an Italian subject of the House of Savoy during the last two decades of the nineteenth century and the first two of the twentieth meant a multiplicity of things according to the individual and the territory concerned, within a context of colonial power relations. "Metropolitan Savoy subjects," on the one hand, came from the peninsula as unified gradually throughout the Risorgimento process. As we saw in the findings of all our previous chapters, these metropolitans enjoyed citizenship status that very often differed for men and women; they had some Italian brothers—immigrant *non regnicoli*—who shared many cultural traits with them; large groups had already emigrated and exported *italianità* worldwide; and they were now colonizers, invested with an ambiguous and contested civilizing mission. By contrast, "nonmetropolitan Savoy subjects" originated from their respective geographic overseas lands; were granted a much thinner status than the metropolitan Italians; some of them were even slaves, as in Somalia; others were allowed the right to vote in the local parliamentary assembly, as in Libya, without exercising it in practice; and in most cases, the majority were very often against colonial rule, making colonial nonmetropolitan status seem an imposition from the perspective of the colonized, a special duty from the perspective of the colonizers. In fact, according to the many official political discourses of the time, metropolitan Italians perceived themselves as the civilized conquerors while the other subjects of the Savoy king—the colonial natives—had to be educated and raised to high standards. This official language, though, was not unanimously embraced and in fact was challenged and disputed because of a similarity between East Africans and Europeans upheld in certain anthropological circles, and because of the perceived uncivilized nature of Italian Southerners highlighted and debated at home.

Visibly different, though, from the black Africans, the white Italians found in those faraway lands a distant and savage Other from whom to differentiate themselves, and through whom to make their domestic south-north divisions relatively less significant within an all-encompassing white and civilized European identity. Moreover, shifting from Aryanism (by no means a Nazi invention) to Mediterraneanism, the Italians continued to discuss their origins as a race through imperialism and through their encounter with the colonial subject, especially in cases of intimate relations. From the latter, an increasing number of children were born in the colonies, children of mixed race who were to make up an important "gray zone." All of them—metropolitan subjects, nonmetropolitans and their progeny—were united, juridically, by a common monarchical allegiance and a common king. It goes without saying these metropolitan and nonmetropolitan statuses started transforming the contours and the content of an already multifaceted Italian national identity so as to add new ethnic, cultural and imperial traits to it. In particular, the gray zone would start making the notion of Italianness an interesting and complicated issue within the colonial setting, since cultural difference, civilization, race, blood and skin color were all themes to be shaken by the presence of these small children, making visible in the streets of Asmara or in the center of Mogadishu not only the prolific nature of (often irresponsible) Italians but also the human dimension of colonial rule and imperial encounters.

As we have also seen in this chapter, for civic incorporation of the Eritreans, the Somalis and the Libyans within the Italian state the ancient myth of Rome was sometimes evoked, although much more weight was given by Italian authorities to the contemporary ideological paradigm of liberal imperialism. On the contrary: Italy's citizenship policy vis-à-vis the Aegeans reflected neither the Roman idea nor any civilizational concerns, mirroring instead the urgent reaction to contemporary changes brought about in the European international system by the end of the Ottoman empire as well as modern Italy's historical continuity with the maritime Republics. This means that ancient Rome shaped debate on colonial citizenship only to a small extent—being largely overcome, as a reference, by nineteenth-century liberal concerns for civilization. Also, it was enriched through evocation of the Italian maritime republican tradition, showing another memorable part of liberal Italy's ancient history.

Having reached the year 1922 and explored the liberal epoch of Mancini, Crispi and Giolitti (Part One of the book), we now start Part Two with discussion of the citizenship developments that took place throughout the fascist era of Benito Mussolini. This is done by first moving from the colonies and the Dodecanese islands back to the peninsula again, where we left our Italian (female and male) subjects.

PART TWO

Historical Evolution During the Fascist Epoch (1922–1945)

Citizenship of Women and Their Counterpart Throughout the Ventennium

In liberal Italy female citizenship enjoyed a specificity of its own in comparison with the corresponding male membership status. In Chapter Two, whose purpose was to make the female part of the population visible within the history of Italian citizenship, we saw that Italian women (as wives and mothers) did not enjoy an independent nationality that could be retained upon marriage and be transmitted to the offspring. Fathers and husbands alone determined the national membership status of all members within the household, and this legal situation would change only from the mid-1970s. Also, the pre-1922 Italian female path toward civic, political and social inclusion in the national citizenry had a different dynamic from the civic road that was taken by the male co-citizens. This differentiated history concerning women and men in the peninsula echoed certain social concerns that, as we saw, were widespread within nineteenth-century European societies and that touched on the concepts of family union, social order, morality and ethics as well as on women's traditional role within the domestic realm. Finally, we also saw that in pre-fascist Italy, Italian national citizenship not only had a gender flavor but was also racialized at times, due to divisive discourses circulated in certain quarters of the peninsula about Southerners on the one hand and Jews on the other.

Following the seizure of power by Mussolini in 1922 and gradual establishment of a fascist dictatorial state from 1925 on, women's national membership went through further fundamental developments, trends as well as dilemmas that deserve to be examined in order to grasp the fascist variant of female *status civitatis* vis-à-vis its male counterpart. By focusing on Italian women without forgetting Italian men, this chapter analyzes several aspects of Italian national citizenship, discusses the issue of

racial thinking in the peninsula as it pertained not only to the later years
of the dictatorship but also to the 1920s and early 1930s and highlights
continuities and breaking points between the liberal and post-1922 epochs. By concentrating our analysis on Italian female nationals alongside the other half, and by drawing parallels and contrasts with Nazi
Germany, the chapter completes our historical account on gender and
citizenship issues and provides, it is hoped, a framework of discussion for
further interdisciplinary dialogue.

6.1. BIRTH TO CITIZENS, *JUS SANGUINIS* AND FASCIST *PROLIFICITÀ*: QUANTITY, QUALITY AND REPRODUCTION OF THE ITALIAN NATION

6.1.a. "As a Wife and as a Mother I Have a Fascist Duty . . ."

In Chapter Two, covering the liberal decades, we saw that an Italian
woman, contrary to an Italian man, could well argue that "as a wife and
as a mother I have no country." In fact, there was no legal recognition
of a "nationality of her own" in relation to loss of status and maternal
bloodline. Later, throughout the fascist decades, these two specific aspects
of female citizenship persisted, and in fact no legislation was introduced
in the peninsula in favor of achieving gender equality from these two perspectives. Italian women continued, as spouses and parents, to have no
state really and no national identity fully acknowledged by law.

During Fascism, though, the notions of wife, husband, mother and
father—so inextricably linked already to these nationality issues—were
incorporated into the concept of national citizenship in an additional and
peculiar way so as to lead to the fascist construction of a new citizenship
aspect that was absent in the pre-1922 epoch, namely, the duty of Italian
citizens (women and men alike) to be prolific in the name of the regime
and of the fascist revolution. Apart from having no country recognized by
national legislation, Italian female citizens could also argue that "as wives
and mothers we had to reproduce the fascist nation"—an obligation that,
obviously, was also shared by their male counterpart.

From a general point of view, this new fascist construction, absent
in the liberal era, can be explained by the fact that reproduction issues
concerning women and men touch on the concept of national citizenship in one important respect: the primary way to be a citizen of a state
and to join the national community is by being born into it. One could
well become a citizen via other means—through naturalization and inter-
marriage for instance—but birth to citizens (*jus sanguinis*) remains the
primary means for states to shape, count and define the circle of their

national citizenry. Since human reproduction, citizenship status and national demography are so inextricably linked with each other, the issue of childbearing and the sexuality of citizen parents are often primary targets of state policy, whether to increase or limit the *size* of a country's population or to protect its perceived racial and ethnic *quality* from alien blood "contamination."[1] As a result, "quantitative" and "qualitative" models, both inspired by eugenic thinking, can enrich population policies, moderately or radically, according to the country under study and the historical period to be analyzed.[2]

As regards the Italian peninsula, fascist politics on pronatalism were being spelled out as early as the mid-1920s. The official discourse that underlined the regime's emphasis on Italian population growth and on prolificacy was what Nira Yuval-Davis has called, on a general and theoretical level, the discourse on "people as power."[3] Put simply, according to the revolutionary rhetoric of the fascist state, the strength and future of the nation depended on numerical extension of the country's citizenry. People were, in fact, seen as a source of power because demographic size and quantity mattered in realizing a variety of state-nationalist projects that ranged from political to economic to imperialist objectives. And this also explains why "the number as strength" (*il numero come forza*) was the central thesis of Mussolini's demographic ideology, an expression that came to be used systematically by fascist officialdom throughout the ventennium as a *leitmotiv* of Italian domestic and foreign policy.[4]

Clearly, since the power of a state was perceived to be directly linked with its demographic expansion, *ex adverso* national decadence was automatically associated with a drop in the birthrate. The Duce again made a sharp and incisive comment on this point when he concluded, "If we diminish, gentlemen, we don't create an Empire, we become a colony!"[5] The regime in fact grew concerned about the decreasing Italian birthrate because of the reproductive habits of the townspeople of northern and central Italy (to control and limit their fertility) and the fear that these urban habits would extend over the peninsula and become a national phenomenon. In particular, as the scholar Victoria De Grazia reminds us, interwar Italy was characterized by two fertility situations: in the south and on the islands population growth was strong, especially in the peasant world; by contrast, in numerous urbanized provinces of northern and central Italy the number of births was low or falling because individuals controlled reproduction from general social and economic motivations as well as a particular desire among women for emancipation.[6] The former situation was seen as "traditional"; the latter was stigmatized as "modern" and, in certain cases, defined by the regime as deplorable because in some cities there were basically "more coffins than cradles."[7] This is why, condemning Italy's "horrendous demographic agony," Mussolini exclaimed in 1928:

The declining motion is not only gradual but is accelerating with each passing year.[...] The whole of urban or municipal Italy is in deficit. Not only is there not equilibrium, but deaths exceed births. We have reached the tragic phase of the phenomenon. Baby cots are empty and the cemeteries are widening.[8]

Faced with the domestic demographic situation, the regime launched the so-called *battaglia della natalità* (battle for births), which enriched the concept of Italian national citizenship with the new *dovere fascista* (fascist sense of duty) of being highly productive—a responsibility, shaped in distinct ways and incorporating different dimensions according to whether it concerned the female or the male half of the citizenry.

The first state instrument to be used in constructing this citizenship task and obligation was untiring and systematic propaganda by word and by pen initiated by Mussolini's Italy and coupled with ceaseless publication of press articles and records concerning numbers of births and deaths as well as official messages regarding fertility duties. Population policy and indoctrination strategies were in fact combined in a unique way, making the brainwashing and greatly rhetorical propaganda system an unprecedented phenomenon in post-unification Italian history.[9] Also and most importantly, the regime intervened directly within the sexual, conjugal and family life of its citizens by introducing in the peninsula a variety of "negative" and "positive" legislative measures. The former were aimed at discouraging and punishing all those individual attitudes and behaviors deemed undesirable from a demographic viewpoint; the latter granted support, protection, prizes and state recognition to encourage Italians to fulfill their new pronatalist civic mission.[10] This means that birth to citizens, and implicitly the corollary principle of *jus sanguinis*, was cherished, directly or indirectly, and put at the center of the fascist revolution.

To begin with, the regime tightened the existing laws that the liberal state had introduced to obstruct dissemination of contraceptive measures and formulated additional ones to stop, more radically, the control over fecundity that its citizens were exercising in their sexual life. With a decree law of November 1926, Mussolini's state prohibited display, sale and distribution of anything publicizing contraception; by enshrining this norm in the 1931 penal code, it proclaimed that "impeding the fecundity of the Italian people" was a crime—to be prevented, also, with other laws concerning public safety.[11]

Parallel to this campaign, then, fascist Italy implemented a multilayered national policy that concerned potential and effective mothers, potential and effective fathers and, more generally, large families. Regarding women, the dictatorship continued banning abortion as in the liberal past and defined it not only as a crime against morality but as a crime against the state. In this way, all means of interrupting pregnancies were outlawed. Also, through extension of social benefits and rights (to which we shall come back in the second part of this chapter), it improved substantially the welfare of pregnant and nursing mothers so as to promote childbearing. Finally, female citizens who distinguished themselves for very special maternal service rendered to the fascist state—i.e., providing the regime with fourteen, sixteen or even eighteen (living) children—were awarded public recognition, state gratitude and medals by Mussolini himself since prolific motherhood was now a form of honorary citizenship.[12]

Besides targeting women with such policies, the dictatorship also introduced additional measures pertaining to marriage and fatherhood that were addressed to the male section of the Italian population for the same pro-birth objectives. As early as December 1926, a punitive tax on male celibacy was instituted for all eligible Italians from the age of twenty-five to sixty-five (making the youngest pay more), in addition to deducting a flat rate of 25 percent from gross income—the only exceptions being priests, infirm men and servicemen on duty. The civic message mirrored in this fascist rule was clear: the selfishness implicit in the bachelor's behavior of not wanting to create a family was to be punished. Also, under the terms of a 1929 law, married men (possibly with many children) were to be given preference over their unmarried compatriots within the civil service and as employees in public enterprises, a provision that was then coupled with a 1937 norm making marital status and fatherhood the necessary prerequisites for being appointed town mayor or university professor. Finally, a generous fascist family policy came to be shaped by the Italian government with a view to giving supplementary support, protection and prizes to extensive families, thus indirectly encouraging prolific couples. In 1928, for instance, large families were granted considerable redactions in taxation; also, a variety of grants concerning family allowances were allotted from the mid-1930s to male heads of household according to how many dependents they had. First introduced for industrial workers, these allowances were then extended, from 1937 onward, to the dependents of all employees not only in industry but also in agricultural enterprises and commerce. Lastly, apart from granting marriage loans (whose reimbursement was gradually reduced every time a child was born and totally canceled with the birth of the fourth child), in 1939 the Grand Council of Fascism, the main body of Mussolini's fascist government, approved introduction of *premi di natalità* (cash prizes) to be conferred to prolific fathers, as heads of household, at every successive birth.[13]

These populationist policies, touching on reproduction issues and birth to citizens (*jus sanguinis*), bring into our discussion an issue of significant importance that has recently attracted scholarly attention:

eugenics in Italian history. On the basis of a growing historiographical debate that has finally started shedding some light on the relatively
less familiar Italian case study, we know that eugenic arguments on degeneration, evolutionary fitness, eradication of hereditary diseases and
reproduction of healthy individuals had already been circulating in the
peninsula since the late 1880s and were ardently discussed within the
Italian scientific community from 1912 onward following the first International Congress of Eugenics held in London.[14] What interests us here,
in reference to later comparisons with Nazi Germany, is to learn that
during the fascist decades the Italian scientific community of biologists,
sociologists, criminologists and doctors in a number of disciplines, including psychiatrists and gynecologists, discussed eugenic issues at great
length. Most interestingly, parallel to the demographic campaign organized by the regime after Mussolini's Ascension Day speech in 1927,
scholarly unanimity seems to have prevailed on "quantitative eugenics"
in line with fascist pro-natalist policies. In fact, during those years a
clear dissociation was made among scientists between eugenics and birth
control. Also, certain practical measures, traditionally subjects of controversy and debate, came to be fiercely criticized and not supported as
appropriate solutions, such as voluntary limitation of births as well as
introduction of more invasive policies of control of human reproduction,
notably an obligatory premarital health certificate for couples (attest-
ing to venereal or mental disease) and voluntary or forced castration
of the unfit. In this way, Italy's eugenic tradition could fully embrace
the century-old cult of maternity, childhood and family that was being
magnified by the regime.[15] Speaking in 1929 in this respect, the Italian
gynecologist Ernesto Pestalozza was clear when arguing that "the improvement of the racial stock" (*il miglioramento della stirpe*) was to be
achieved not through "negative eugenics" based on radical limitations,
extreme restrictions and enforced sterilizations but through a program of
"positive eugenics," like the one then being realized by the fascist regime
and based on guaranteed assistance to maternity and infancy, prenatal
medical care and welfare services as well as physical and moral education of youth.[16] As a result, "Latin eugenics" (in opposition to the "Nordic models" represented by the German, Anglo-Saxon and Scandinavian
experiences) was to have an original connotation in the Italian peninsula
and, as a "science of regime," perform two fundamental tasks within domestic politics: giving support and legitimization to Mussolini's populationist stand, and sealing the relationship between the Fascist regime and
the Catholic Church (with the latter's views on births and sexuality).[17]

Clearly, the population and social policies introduced by the regime
and concerning, directly or indirectly, female and male reproduction issues mirrored and put emphasis on the Italians' civic responsibility to

procreate and reproduce the nation as much as possible. Yet whereas this citizenship obligation was shared by female and male citizens alike, major differences distinguished the fascist construction of female and male reproduction functions within the fascist nation: the duty of motherhood and that of fatherhood were not looked at by the regime with the same lens. The first major difference between *maternità* and *paternità* (motherhood and fatherhood) is that, from a fascist perspective, prolific fatherhood was also proof of masculinity and virility, which were cherished by fascist ideology and rhetoric as defining tenets of the "new male Italian" to be forged by the fascist revolution. "Italian Fascists," exclaimed Mussolini in September 1928, "Hegel, the philosopher of the State, has said: whoever is not a father is not a man!"[18] And for a fascist contemporary writer: "The Italian of today, like the Roman in the past, is not a man if he is not a father and a soldier."[19] To be a father and to have numerous children corresponded, therefore, to the ideals of *virilità fascista* (fascist virility) and *romanità* (romanness) that were fundamental and intertwining tenets within the Duce's regime.

A second important differing factor between the two social constructs is that, drawing directly from the past discourse of the liberal period concerning the primary reproductive functions of women and their natural roles as mothers and caretakers, the fascist state transformed the cult of motherhood and the fact of making babies and staying at home into *the* essential duty of female citizenship. Indeed, as emphasized by De Grazia, the regime saw Italian female nationals as having the preeminent responsibility for bearing the nation's offspring; by highlighting this exclusive duty of procreation, it put into question other aspects of female membership status within the public sphere, such as women's rights in the workplace. Basically, female roles were narrowed to include only maternity, whereas feminist movements had regarded the latter as only one aspect of women's social being. By contrast, this was not to be the case for Italian male citizens, for whom fatherhood was only one facet of their personal identity to be coupled with all other statuses enjoyed in the public realm as workers, voters, and so on.[20]

A third and final element pertaining to fascist *maternità* and *paternità* is that the demographic and family policy we explored here basically reinforced the image of the male head of the household at the expense of women since certain important measures favored mainly male workers, fathers and husbands. For instance, the family allowances that were introduced in the mid-1930s were to be paid by state agencies and private employers to heads of household, thus favoring men over their working wives or other family members, who though working still lived at home. Also, the *premi di natalità* were indemnities awarded to the father rather than to the mother, and only unmarried women could receive them directly because of their status as single mothers.[21] So even though aiming at the same demographic objectives, the fascist civic tenet of being sexually productive targeted differing dimensions according to whether the recipient was a female or a male citizen.

6.1.b. Italianità and Racial Thinking in the Peninsula During the 1920s, the 1930s and the Late Fascist Period

While the regime was introducing population policies concerning explicitly or implicitly Italian national citizenship, *jus sanguinis* and prolific nationhood, discourses about race and racial theories—already started during the liberal age and touching on the notion of Italianness—continued throughout the 1920s and the early 1930s. It is therefore instructive to see how, parallel to the politics explored above, a variety of debates could be heard in the peninsula about the origins of the Italians (women and men alike), about their race and about certain Italian citizens whose "foreignness" was to be highlighted. Subsequently, by focusing on the late fascist period, we will explore the radical racist turn of the regime.

Between 1925 and 1935 (that is, in the course of the first years and early decade of the dictatorship), we know that Mediterraneanist scholars, such as the anthropologist Sergi, along with the influential and fascist doctor Nicola Pende, launched an offensive within racial discussions against those Nordicist writers and historians in the peninsula who had agreed with contemporary German rhetoric, calling the Indo-Europeans and Aryans *Indo-Germanic* and basically claiming German superiority over the Mediterranean race for being at the origin of European culture and civilization.[22] So discussion over definitions and origins of the Italians continued throughout the early fascist years as well and oscillated between and across opposing camps, as had been the case in the liberal epoch. Also, racial issues were not absent in the mind of the Duce, who in this respect drew from such debates although his position was at times vague, contradictory and not always consistent. For instance, in an early speech to the population of Bologna made in April 1921 (before he took power), he referred to the Italians as "our Aryan and Mediterranean race."[23] What exactly he meant by this was left without further elucidation. Also, in 1932, speaking to the famous German Jewish journalist Emil Ludwig, Mussolini denied the existence of race, the latter being "a feeling, not a reality"; did not believe that "biologically pure races [could] be shown to exist today"; and indirectly went against anti-Italian Nordic racism, knowing what Nazi ideologues were frequently saying about Italian inferiority.[24] In this case, as in several other occasions and writings of 1932 and 1935, the Duce rejected the Nazi racial theories that embraced the concept of a fixed German biological entity and put emphasis on

Nordic rhetoric.[25] And in fact, when addressing the Black Shirts in Florence in October 1933, Mussolini referred once more to the Italians as "our Latin and Mediterranean race."[26]

Throughout the 1920s and early 1930s, racial considerations were not limited to these debates in the peninsula. From Michele Sarfatti's research,[27] we also know that anti-Semitic convictions, prejudices and attitudes were by no means a characteristic of the late dictatorship but concerned the early years as well—although in a much less systematic manner, and of course in a less radicalized way. For example, no doubt Mussolini himself constantly emphasized throughout the first decade that the Italian regime was not anti-Semitic; this is a public denial to which he was well habituated especially in order to please, convince and reassure foreign governments and the press. Also, it is well known that the Duce maintained relations with Jews, men and women alike. However, he did display some anti-Jewish prejudices as well, since the beginning of his career; anti-Semitic feelings and attitudes were not totally absent in his initial political life. For instance, as early as June 1919, after the creation of the Fasci di Combattimento, he wrote in *Il Popolo d'Italia* to remind readers about "the great Jewish bankers of London and New York, linked by race with Jews in Moscow as in Budapest who seek revenge against the Aryan race."[28] Writing in 1922 in the same newspaper, Mussolini emphasized the nonexistence of a Jewish question in Italy but also added that he hoped there would not be one in the future, "at least not until Zionism poses Italian Jews with the dilemma of choosing between their Italian homeland and another homeland."[29] More to the point, by asking the Jews of the peninsula in 1928 whether they were really "a religion" or "a nation," the head of fascism questioned their Italianness and national patriotism, making an indirect reference to the incompatibility of simultaneous allegiance by the Jewish minority to Italian nationhood and to the Zionist movement.[30] This was an issue that rose again in subsequent years and that, as in 1934, would involve an anti-Jewish polemic in the Fascist press questioning the affection, assimilation and patriotic sentiments of these Italians.[31] So, negative representations of the Jewish minority were circulating in Italy, and as a result some Italian Jews, if not all of them, were being seen as "foreigners in a foreign land," rather than Italian nationals living in their country of origin. This is why, as we think about the roughly forty-five thousand Italian (female and male) Jewish citizens living there during the 1920s and early 1930s,[32] the historical evidence should be borne in mind.

Having said this, we can now fully explain the late radical period by making reference to how the racial thinking that developed from 1936

onward led to introduction of further significant citizenship provisions pertaining to issues of birth to citizens, *jus sanguinis* and *italianità*. Following the conquest of Ethiopia (which we will examine in Chapter Seven) and the need for a stronger Italian racial consciousness necessary within fascist ideology for empire building, and following the strengthening of ties between fascist Italy and Nazi Germany, Italy's fascist measures concerning sexuality, marriage and births started incorporating an explicitly biological racism and clearly moving toward a full embrace of Aryan values. The aim was to institutionalize the "Aryanization" of the Italians, protect it from Jewish and colonial blood and, by constructing the Italian "Aryan-Mediterranean type," emphasize as well the idea of an Italian ethnic unity against the previous view that the Italians were of two races (i.e., the Aryans in the north, the Mediterraneans in the south).[33]

As a result, within this ideological context the regime's new political agenda inevitably impinged on the life of Italian women and men, as well as transforming the national duty of reproducing the Italian nation by adding an increasingly radical racist dimension to it that would characterize the late years of the Italian dictatorship and distinguish Mussolini's Italy from the early years of fascism and from the pre-1922 liberal age. To start with, the regime's propaganda began to remind Italian women in a systematic and extremist way that their primary social function was not just to become mothers of many Italians but of *many and pure* Italians: according to contemporary influential fascist journals, female citizens had to preserve the racial "genus" and serve the state as the "tutelary priestesses of the most sublime of rites—the continuation and salvation of the Race."[34] Italian men as well were not exempted from such brainwashing discourse, and in particular those leaving for the empire (or already settled there) were to be told systematically not to "offend" the Italian stock by mixing, and having sexual relations, with the natives.[35]

Propaganda, though, was not enough. As usual, it was soon coupled with additional legislative provisions that fascist Rome introduced from 1937 on, in order to prevent or punish certain "antifascist" social phenomena deemed incompatible with the racial standpoint of the late dictatorial state. These norms were actually to be applied in the peninsula, and as we shall see in our next chapter concerning colonialism, they were extended throughout the empire as well. Moreover, as citizenship provisions they touched on Italian women and men in different ways, bearing in mind that in certain cases a rule could concern mainly Italian fathers, or Italian men in general, more than Italian women. In April 1937, for fear of "dangerous crossbreeds," Mussolini's regime commenced to punish the Italian metropolitan (female or male) citizen who lived in the Italian kingdom (or in the colonies) with an autochthon or "assimilated to a colonial subject" with one to five years of imprisonment for discrediting the Italian race.[36] Also, following publication of the *Manifesto della razza* in July 1938, Mussolini's regime and its anthropologist Guido Landra moved a step closer to Nazi racial thinking by plainly supporting biological racism. The *Manifesto* clearly stated that "the concept of race [was] a purely biological concept," that "the population of Italy [was] of Aryan origins and its civilization [was] Aryan" and that "Jews [did] not belong to the Aryan race."[37] In this way, according to scholar Mauro Raspanti, fascism transformed the "Aryan cultural idiom," which had circulated in the Italian peninsula since the nineteenth century, into a radical, vocal and structured "state ideology" aiming at totalitarian Aryanization of Italian society.[38]

To implement and complete the institutional Aryanization of the Italian race and citizenship, the dictatorship extended the scope of its legislative racism with the formulation of several rules particularly worthy of mention. For instance, in November 1938, with a decree-law regarding the defense of the Italian race, the marriage of an Italian Aryan with a person of "another race" was declared illicit and null. This means a marriage that had already been celebrated between an Italian citizen of "Aryan race" and a person who belonged to "other racial stock" was made invalid retroactively by the regime; future unions between the two categories of people would no longer be permitted. Also, in the same legislation the notion of Italian citizenship and the traditional principle of descent were racialized because a person was now to be defined as "belonging to the Jewish race" when born to Italian parents under specific conditions:

For the purpose of the law: a) a person is considered to be of the Jewish race who is born from parents who are both of the Jewish race, even if said person professes a religion other than the Jewish; b) [...] who is born from parents of whom one is of the Jewish race and the other is of a foreign nationality; c) [...] who is born of a mother of the Jewish race when the father is unknown; d) [...] who, even if born from parents of Italian nationality, of whom only one is of the Jewish race, professes the Jewish religion, or is enrolled in a Jewish Community, or has, in some other way, manifested his Judaism. A person is not to be considered of the Jewish race who is born from parents of Italian nationality, of whom only one is of the Jewish race, and who on 1 October 1938-XVI, belonged to a religion other than the Jewish (art. 8).[39]

Through propaganda and specific targeted policies, Italian women (and men) were being transformed into procreators of an Italian citizenry that had to be not only numerically strong but also defined in explicitly radical racist terms.[40]

Finally, on the basis of the academic contributions of fascist writers such as Giulio Cogni, Guido Landra, and Julius Evola, the Italians (women and men alike) were considered as Aryans who belonged to the Mediterranean branch that had eventually unified the whole of Italy, Europe and the Mediterranean, with the important exclusion from the Mediterranean race, though, of those light-skinned groups of (African) Hamites and Semites who had been "dangerously" included by previous anthropological theories, as discussed in Chapters Two and Five. Hence the now familiar Aryan and Mediterranean ideas, circulating in early fascist Italy but also in the liberal period, converged in the late dictatorship in a specifically "Aryan-Mediterranean" concept of race that allowed Mussolini's regime to come closer to its Nazi ally, to push dangerous Others outside any theory of similarity with the Italians and to erase the internal difference that had constantly divided (northern and southern) Italian citizens since unification.[41] Indeed, this type of Aryanism focused on the principle of Italian ethnic unity and criticized social scientists such as Sergi, Lombroso and Niceforo who had claimed that in modern Italy the Aryans were prevalent in the advanced north, while the backward southern regions were basically inhabited by a strong Mediterranean and Semitic element.[42] Italian citizens were now "unified" from a theoretical viewpoint and could differentiate their nationhood from two isolated and targeted Others: the Jew and the African.

At this point of our analysis, an additional discussion about Nazi eugenics, population policies, and birth to citizens is instructive to understand specificities, similarities and differences between fascist Italy and the Third Reich. The first aspect to emphasize is that "qualitative models" of coercive eugenics based on "negative programs" were upheld and practiced in Nazi Germany since the beginning of the dictatorship in 1933, while in Mussolini's regime such negative policies were never introduced, in the first years of the dictatorship or in the late period, although from 1938 onward Italian scientists, in particular those writing in the fascist journal *La difesa della razza*, would propose and defend adoption of the radical German, Scandinavian and Nord-American policies of sterilization and the obligatory premarital certificate.[43]

In Nazi Germany, there was an obsessive emphasis on the quality of the German stock as early as Hitler's taking power in 1933. In fact, according to Nazi instructions given by Goebbels's Ministry for Propaganda, "the goal [was] not: 'children at any cost', but 'racially worthy, physically and mentally unaffected children of German families'."[44] Also, in one of the official Nazi brochures distributed to the German population in 1934, one could read that women's task was not to be prolific but to contribute to "regeneration of the race."[45] This is why, starting in 1933, the Nazi regime, contrary to its Italian counterpart, introduced and rigorously carried out the antinatalist measure of compulsory sterilization vis-à-vis female and male "unfit" citizens. The objective was to inhibit—through forced bodily intervention—the conception of offspring that would be regarded as causing German racial deterioration. As a result, after being defined as racially unworthy by special eugenic courts set up by the Nazi state, the feeble-minded, schizophrenics, the blind, the deaf and alcoholics were obliged to be sterilized, together with their existing children. Moreover, in defense of the German *Volk* from internal as well as external "menaces," this program came to include Aryans as well as non-Aryan people such as Jews, Gypsies, blacks and other "aliens." In 1934, the Nazi regime began sterilizing children issued from the Polish minority in Upper-Silesia on the basis of special intelligence tests that were used as an instrument of diagnosis. Subsequently, the same fate was reserved for the small black (and mixed) German population that was born after 1918, generally to a German mother and to a black father serving in the French occupation army, as this minority became a victim of involuntary sterilization from 1937 on.[46]

This antinatalist policy, which was coupled with and replaced by mass murder and genocide from 1939 onward, distinguished Hitler's Germany from Mussolini's Italy because, as we saw, the Italian regime never introduced sterilization measures to force certain categories of Italian citizens not to have children.[47] Furthermore, whereas German scientists sustained these provisions in the Reich and carried them out as doctors, the Italian scientific community—which we know studied Nazi rules with great attention—distanced itself from the German radical programs of castration throughout the dictatorship, though as already noted during the late years of the fascist regime the voices of Landra, Aldo Modica and Lidio Cipriani revived the debate and suggested adoption of these severe measures, citing the National Socialist legislation as a model to imitate.[48]

Indeed, from the ideological standpoint of National Socialism, antinatalism took precedence over pro-natalism, in theory and in practice since the beginning. As a principle, it was already praised by Hitler himself in *Mein Kampf*, when the future Führer argued that

the folkish State [...] has to take care that only the healthy beget children; that there is only one disgrace: to be sick and to bring children into the world despite one's own deficiencies; but one highest honor: to renounce this.[...] He who is not physically and mentally healthy and worthy must not perpetuate his misery in the body of his child.[49]

A similar message was then reiterated and conveyed subsequently by Nazi officialdom, as a quote from a jurist working for the Reich Ministry of the Interior demonstrates:

The German race question consists primarily in the Jewish question. In the second place, yet not less important, there is the Gypsy question.[...] But degenerative effects on the racial body may arise not only from outside, from members of alien races, but also from inside, through unrestricted procreation of inferior hereditary material.[50]

Surely, pro-natalist measures (to encourage "the fit" to have children) were also introduced in the Third Reich as in fascist Italy. For instance, one could mention the provisions concerning the outlawing of birth control, the increasing punishment for abortion as well as introduction of marriage loans, tax reductions and child benefits for large families of Aryan Germans—sharing many similarities with the Italian case. However, the Nazi pro-natalist campaign to encourage "the fit" was never dissociated from the campaign to "prune the unfit," and if a person was encouraged to have children it was because he or she had not been sterilized for eugenic reasons.[51]

To conclude, from 1922 to 1943 Italian women (as well as their male counterparts) were primary targets of fascist pro-natalist policies because of their fundamental role in reproducing the nation and thus in contributing to the strengthening of the fascist state as a growing territorial and revolutionary power. The issue of birth to citizens and implicitly its related tenet of *jus sanguinis* were fully embraced and magnified within the new fascist duty of being prolific, a duty shared by both female and male segments of the population but incorporating different gender dimensions. Also, racial discussions and racializing discourse continued to be formulated in the peninsula during the 1920s and the 1930s as to notions of Italianness, Aryanism, Mediterraneanism and anti-Semitism, before they eventually took the well-known radical turn of the late fascist period. Because of the state's persistent and aggressive demographic politics, an Italian woman and her other half living during the dictatorship were subjected to a variety of strategies that touched, directly or indirectly, on sexuality, motherhood, fatherhood, births, *jus sanguinis*, marriage, and racial descent. This was a multifaceted process, accompanied by expression of specific racial rhetoric and language.

In the next section, we turn to the notion of female citizenship—in reference to rights and entitlements—as developed throughout the dictatorship in comparison with the male counterpart, and then we highlight further racial formulations that continued to mingle and evolve in Italy, specifically around the concept of content of fascist citizenship.

6.2. FEMALE CITIZENSHIP RIGHTS IN THE FASCIST TOTALITARIAN STATE

In light of the dictatorial strategies and tactics of transforming Italy not only into a demographically strong state but also into a totalitarian country, Mussolini's regime shaped and determined numerous aspects of female citizenship entitlements. From a historical perspective, this totalitarian aspect was indeed to represent another break within the history of Italian national citizenship in comparison with the liberal years, as was the emphasis on prolific nationhood and birth to citizens analyzed in the previous sections. Also, analogous to what we have already argued in the preceding pages, the fascist totalitarian agenda certainly had an impact on female citizenship as much as on male *status civitatis*. Yet by drawing on and extending De Grazia's pioneering work on women and fascism, we shall demonstrate that female fascist membership status reflected certain "dilemmas," official "mixed messages," "new opportunities" and "new and old repressions" that characterized the life of Italian women during the fascist epoch in a peculiar way and differently from their male co-citizens.[52] Moreover, as we shall see in the final section, racial thinking persisted throughout the dictatorship and shaped citizenship rights to a different extent in the 1920s, in the 1930s and most radically from 1936 onward. Female citizenship entitlements and related racial discussion were to go through specific historical developments throughout the ventennium.

6.2.a. Italian Women and Men and the Fascistization of Civil, Political and Social Rights

Bearing in mind De Grazia's research,[53] we can argue that an example of "new and old repressions"—characterizing the sphere of citizenship entitlements—is represented by the issue of civil rights, to be explored here first, as we did in the other chapter regarding women in the liberal period. As Mussolini's regime gradually extended state control over politics, society and the individual with a view to taking the totalitarian road and realizing the Fascist Revolution at home, a variety of antidemocratic and antiliberal measures were introduced in the peninsula. Consequently, the right to individual liberty, freedom of expression, freedom of association and freedom of press, all enjoyed during the liberal era without distinction of sex, were seriously hindered and then subsequently abolished by the fascist state as dictatorial, one-party rule intensified. These were "new" measures that concerned women (and men alike) and that limited the sphere of freedoms for both halves of the Italian population, making this sphere of Italian national citizenship much thinner than its previous liberal variant.[54] However, in addition to these new repressive norms, Italian women, contrary to Italian men, continued to be held in a legally inferior position, as in the liberal epoch, as far as certain other civil entitlements are concerned. In fact, even though wives could administer their personal property independently as they had been doing since 1919, Italian husbands enjoyed more liberties with regard to other dowry and property-related matters within the family.

Italian female citizens would have to wait for post-1946 republican Italy to see, in this respect, their full equality finally enshrined in national legislation.[55] So within the framework of Mussolini's totalitarianism, female civil rights were clearly restrained (as were those of men). Yet for Italian women, the fascist "new" repressive provisions came to be added to "old" ones that, as we have already discussed in Chapter Two, touched on gender issues in a fundamental way.

A second aspect (i.e., female political rights and the question of suffrage) to which we now turn, again in line with the analysis carried out on the liberal age, provides us with an important case of "mixed messages" from fascist officialdom and of a "new opportunity" for female citizens, which, however, was to be emptied very soon of all its value as a consequence of "old and new" oppressive factors. As we saw in the pre-1922 era, the economic and social contribution of Italian female citizens to the world war effort of 1915–1918 gave some hope that in compensation for the services rendered during the conflict Italian women would acquire the right to vote at the local and national levels. This, though, was not to be the case since women's participation in public life was not sufficiently supported in parliament, and when Mussolini seized power in 1922 women were still excluded from national and local elections. Interestingly, the initial fascist platform of March 1919 listed, as its first demand, universal suffrage and specified that this meant extending the right to vote to all women over twenty-one. In early summer 1923, when the International Alliance for Women's Suffrage met in Rome, Mussolini mentioned women's voting rights again, but as Claudia Koonz has already emphasized, it soon became obvious that the Duce's speech reflected Mussolini's desire to cultivate a positive image in the international press more than any concern about women's political status.[56] The issue continued to be discussed at the official level in the following months, and eventually the policy that came to be approved by the regime in 1925—the so-called Acerbo law—limited female suffrage to administrative elections and granted it only to specific categories of women (i.e., those decorated for special services to Italy, mothers and widows of war dead, women who were heads of families, those who had a degree, those who paid local taxes and could read and write). Clearly, despite being limited, the granting of local political rights represented a "new opportunity"—at least for a minority of women— bearing in mind the long-unsuccessful suffragist struggles of the liberal past. Mussolini himself should actually get credit for having introduced administrative voting rights for the female part of the Italian population; because of widespread opposition within both parliamentary chambers, the bill was approved thanks to the direct intervention of the Duce, who reassured Italian deputies that female political participation at the local level would not provoke a catastrophe either for the country or for the household.[57] Mussolini's view on female political rights, though, was not consistent throughout the dictatorship; in 1932, speaking with Emil Ludwig, he would revise his initial position completely and argued that

A woman must obey.[...] She is analytical, not synthetic.[...] My opinion about her participation within the State is in opposition to any feminism. Of course she should not be a slave, but if I bestowed electoral rights upon her, people would scoff at me. In our State, she doesn't have to count.[58]

The issue of female suffrage was therefore subject to "mixed signals" from the regime, and often to official changing positions and points of view.

Also, though the law concerning women's local political rights was approved by the fascist state, it could not be implemented easily in the peninsula and was soon to be rendered void of meaning via "old and new" repressive elements. In fact, many obstacles hindered the actual exercise of this political right at the administrative level; for instance, numerous women lacked an identification card that would suffice before the law and allow them to register as voters. Moreover, as in the liberal era, one could talk of a certain "discomfort created . . . by the irony and jokes of the men at home, husbands, sons, brothers, habituated by tradition and atavisms to divide women into two major categories: those good for their own needs; those necessary for their pleasure."[59] Finally, when in September 1926, in conformity with the regime's totalitarian aspirations, the state abolished local elections by making mayors and town-hall councilmen appointees of the central government in Rome, female political participation at the administrative level was over—as was that enjoyed by the male co-citizens.[60] In this respect, by using a touch of irony one could share the view of the historian Alexander De Grand, who noted that with the fascist abolition of elections there was finally equality between the two sexes now that both were basically disenfranchised.[61] Indeed, a similar point could be made if we think that the Fascist Party gradually became the one, the unique and the supreme political organization with no alternatives, making the whole issue of female (and male) political suffrage an interesting topic for discussion within this specific context. During fascism, then, the question of female political citizenship was often accompanied by contradictory and mixed messages; also, even though local suffrage initially provided a number of women with a "new chance" at public participation that they never had during the liberal era, this new opportunity was soon hindered by "old" social gender concerns and completely abolished (together with male suffrage) by "new" totalitarian norms.

Third, and as a final argument of this section, if we examine the developments of female social entitlements we can see that in this sphere as well, numerous "tensions," "dilemmas," "opportunities and exclusions" were to emerge soon. In particular, by looking at successive phases of women's life and by examining in turn the social right to education among young girls, welfare rights of potential and effective mothers as well as the social right to work, we can furnish additional historical evidence.

First of all, the regime's policies concerning the schooling of young women contained an important gender dimension that can illustrate our point. The school reform of 1923 introduced by the Sicilian philosopher and Minister of Public Education Giovanni Gentile was formulated by the Italian state in order to modify the school system and select the nation's elite. Although increasing the number of girls being schooled beyond the elementary level (and therefore extending female education and decreasing illiteracy in comparison with the liberal past), this reform as well as the philosophy underlining it presented numerous biases against women.[62] Granting "new opportunities" to girls, the fascist school system also incorporated fundamental gender issues that transformed them in an important respect into "new exclusions." For instance, Gentile's idealist philosophy, which emphasized how the individual could grasp the life of the spirit through education and reflection, saw women in a peculiar light: as human beings with fewer and more limited abilities than men and unable to have as full an understanding of the spirit as their counterparts.[63] Consequently, this "natural" difference between female and male capabilities meant that the content of education and culture that a girl should receive had to be "adapted" to her sexual characteristics. This is why a precise model of "differential pedagogy" was introduced by the regime from the first years of dictatorial rule. Women could acquire education, but in specific schools separated from those for men and whose courses were "particularly suitable for them." Among the most significant examples, one can mention creation of the *liceo femminile* (women's high school), *scuola femminile d'avviamento* (women's training school) and *magistero professionale per la donna* (teachers training college for women), as well as formulation of annual and biennial courses on domestic work. So, despite providing "new" openings with different schools, the pedagogical fascist objective was not ultimately emancipatory from a gender standpoint because, as one could read later on in the 1939 School Charter of the regime, education had to prepare Italian girls "spiritually for running households"; thus women's sphere was only "at home."[64] Moreover, because of the pedagogical ideas and policies of the time, female citizens were seen as incapable educators. This is why, as early as 1926, they were excluded from competitions for chairs of letters, Latin, Greek, history and philosophy in the classical and scientific *licei* as well as from posts in Italian and history in technical institutes. Since only male educators were "suitable" for these important disciplines, which aimed at creation of the future Italian elite, women had to be barred from teaching in these fields.[65]

Finally, alongside this fascist blend of "new opportunities and exclusions," other "old" issues—inherited from the liberal past—made the social right to education a peculiar one in the peninsula. Despite the fact that the new school laws made attendance obligatory up to the elementary level of fifth grade, local municipalities, in charge of paying for the last two grades, often lacked budgets to provide classrooms and organize courses. Also, as child labor laws were not enforced in rural areas, many children, especially girls of poor peasant families, ended all their schooling with the third grade so as to work in the field. Lastly, regarding female university education, the few Italian women who could achieve this academic level were often discouraged from finishing their degree, and because they were frequently "dogged . . . by an atmosphere of skepticism about the intrinsic value of instructing them," their high dropout rate was often the rule.[66] Hence, the social right to education—as shaped by the fascist regime—incorporated positive aspects as well as a variety of gender discriminations that made Italian young female citizens gain and lose at the same time.

If one now turns to the welfare social rights that Mussolini's state introduced to improve the health and welfare of pregnant and nursing mothers, one is able to highlight various other related gender "tensions." We have already mentioned the regime's emphasis on reproduction issues and on pro-natalist objectives; further, a wide-ranging system of maternity social policies was implemented throughout the ventennium. In this respect, the most ambitious social initiative was, without doubt, creation of the National Agency for Maternal and Infant Welfare (*Opera Nazionale Maternità e Infanzia* or ONMI) in December 1925. This institution dealt in particular with the welfare of unwed mothers, impoverished widows and married women whose husbands could not support them, as well as taking care of the welfare of children up to the age of five (when parents were unable to give them the necessary care) and of abandoned offspring up to the age of eighteen. Between 1929 and 1934, the dictatorship formulated other state-sponsored social measures such as maternity leave for wage-earning mothers and extensive maternity benefits for female factory and office workers.[67]

Obviously, thanks to these institutions, insurances and social entitlements, female social citizenship became more substantial and thicker compared to its pre-1922 liberal variant. However, the fascist policies had, paradoxically, an antifeminist dimension as well. As already anticipated in the first part of this chapter concerning prolificacy, these social rights were shaped by the regime's principle objective of making female procreative duty *the* defining characteristic of women's *status civitatis* at the expense of female participation and emancipation in the public sphere. Thus, along with granting a variety of social entitlements to Italian women, these measures enforced biologically determined roles of *cittadine* (citizens), as mothers and caretakers, on the basis of the traditional concept of the separation of spheres, which we explored in Chapter Two.[68] From the point of view of female emancipation, one can say that, similar to the case of Italian girls within the fascist school system, Italian female adults—as mothers *and* citizens—made some steps forward and some steps back.

By concluding, now, with the social right to work on grounds of sexual equality, we see that a few other fascist "oppressions" and "exclusions" of female citizens from the public sphere emerge in our analysis. Indeed, fascist labor reforms throughout the regime were particularly discriminatory against women as workers, since they aimed at expelling them from the circle of the workforce with a view to securing positions for male heads of household. Actually, elimination of women from the workplace had commenced in the peninsula before the fascists took power, as war veterans' leagues started complaining about female employment and arguing that the jobs women came to fill in wartime while men were called up for war duty had been stolen from them, and that the feminization of the workplace was the primary cause of male unemployment.[69] This is an element of continuity with the previous years. However, by embracing these pre-1922 arguments, fascism came to formulate a variety of anti-female restrictive measures that intensified in the 1930s as high unemployment became a permanent feature of fascist Italy, due to the impact of the worldwide economic and financial crisis of the Great Depression.[70]

For instance, as early as 1926 the regime started cutting the number of women in the bureaucracy and excluding them from permanent civil service positions at the Ministry of Posts. When the *Consiglio nazionale delle donne italiane*, the Italian branch of the International Council of Women, protested against these provisions, the governmental response was that these labor policies were necessary to solve the problem of high unemployment among men.[71] Also, throughout the Great Depression public agencies were authorized to limit the number of female citizens taking civil service examinations, and whereas from 1934 onward the number of female workers was limited in the public administration and in the banking system, in September 1938 the regime also ordered state and private offices to cut back the number of female employees to 10 percent of their total staff and exclude them in business firms having fewer than ten people.[72] Since the presence of middle- and lower-middle-class women in the employment market was a special problem for the fascists because of the class bias of the regime, female social right to work could only be seriously limited and shaped in a fascist way.[73]

Clearly, throughout this detailed overview of civil, political and social entitlements, one can see that female membership status went through peculiar historical developments that manifested important gender issues, in continuity and in discontinuity with the liberal era. In the following section, we enrich our discussion by drawing from additional scholarly debates on racial thinking and racial discrimination, in reference specifically to Italian citizenship rights and entitlements.

6.2.b. Rights, Racial Representations and Discrimination from the 1920s Through the Late Radical Period

Racial discourses and practice touching on Italian membership status, civic emancipation and discrimination were not only a phenomenon of the late dictatorship. To a very different extent they also characterized the 1920s and the early 1930s, although they were relatively marginal in comparison with the central and essential position they would take in the country after 1936. Furthermore, racializing talk—different in content and tone—was to concern not only the Jews but also Italian Southerners, as we saw already in Chapters One and Two.

For example, even though during fascism the Southern Question was not to produce the amount of writing, letters, discussion and theoretical thinking that we explored in relation to the first decades following national unification, the accompanying stereotypes about Southerners did not disappear. The Duce himself, a northerner from the region of Romagna, did not seem to have had great admiration for southern Italians, saying to the playwright and essayist Sem Benelli during the early years of premiership that he had "low esteem for Neapolitans in particular and southerners in general, exclaiming that, from Tuscany on down, the Italians, deep down, were not willing to do anything to be Italians."[74] Also, as pointed out by the scholar Patriarca, prejudice vis-à-vis southerners enriched Mussolini's rhetoric throughout the dictatorship, especially in speeches pertaining to the ideal of a strong, brave and fascist people of Italy, as opposed to the negative image of the Italians, often held abroad, as a "people of mandolin strummers."[75] This prejudice and lack of sympathy in Mussolini's language were also noted at the time by such fascist representatives of the regime as Giuseppe Bottai, who in 1936 reported in his diary this comment by Mussolini: "One day we will have to do a march on Naples to sweep away guitars, mandolins, violins, storytellers and so on."[76] Even if the frequent discourses we heard in the liberal age about the uncivilized and barbarian southern citizens did not have any central theoretical position within the regime, there is no denying that some racializing thinking about this part of the Italian population (women and men alike) was still circulating in certain quarters and was even symbolized by some of the Duce's words since the early years of fascist rule.

Regarding racial discourse and civic discrimination vis-à-vis the Jews between 1922 and 1935, historical evidence is even more telling. For instance, we know that the Jesuit *Civiltà cattolica* continued to publish articles during the 1920s and early 1930s, writing about the Jewish Question in central Europe as anti-Semitism was actually becoming more and more virulent there.[77] Among the major themes recurring in this press at the time, and read in Italy as elsewhere, we should highlight in particular the already-mentioned danger of having emancipated the Jews, who, equal citizens now in their countries, had been made too powerful and dominant, as well as the related issue of proportionality according to which the Jews were only a minority—in Italy only 0.1 percent—and yet were in control of many sectors of public, political and economic life.[78] Also, two further parallel topics were recurrently resurrected: the Jewish "guilt" for being behind the French and Russian Revolutions with their determination to achieve world hegemony, and the frequently made, and still highly controversial, distinction between a "bad, unchristian and violent brand of anti-Semitism" (which the Church condemned) and a "good, Catholic and healthy recognition of the threat posed by the Jews" (which the Church embraced).[79] Clearly, since all these articles and issues were also read and discussed in Italy through the Catholic press, anti-Semitic prejudices could not but continue circulating in some official circles such that one part of the Italian population (i.e., female and male Jews, or some of them) could well be looked at with a certain suspicion or perceived as not totally Italian. As already explained in the first part of our book, some of the themes had already been formulated and sometimes virulently articulated in the liberal decades too.

Second, and moving from general racializing discourse to specific practice, it is instructive to learn that anti-Jewish discrimination was being carried out by the regime in the early 1930s in the cultural sphere, as the evidence provided and discussed by Annalisa Capristo demonstrates.[80] More particularly, this scholar explains how Mussolini not only introduced a number of discriminatory criteria, as early as 1929, to exclude women, senators and deputies from becoming members of the Reale Accademia d'Italia—the highest cultural organ controlled by the government—but also made sure, at least from 1932, that eminent Jewish (male) scientists would not be appointed there.[81] The origin of the candidates (and whether they were Jews or not) mattered for selection and nomination of scholars and professors because the profile of an applicant, discussed within the circle of the academics in charge of the selection procedure, was subject to debate if the scientist had Jewish origins—implying that the admissions of Jews was a "problem" and that it would not be "appropriate" to support such an application.[82] Moreover, we know that the president of the Accademia, Guglielmo Marconi, repeatedly marked the names of Jewish candidates with the letter *E* when going through the list of those who had been selected for the 1932 academic elections.[83] This was not the only annotation, since other words and letters were also written next to the names of those who happened to be deputies ("D., Dep"), Senators ("Sen."), and military generals ("Gen."). In any case, the Italian word for Jew is *Ebreo*. So Capristo is right in emphasizing how "*i candidati ebrei*" (the Jewish candidates) were to be quickly identified on these lists with the marking *E*.[84] Lastly, even if a Jewish scientist could become a finalist in the selection, as was the case in 1933 with the archeologist Alessandro Della Seta, it was then Mussolini himself who would block the appointment by making the final decision and choosing, eventually, a non-Jew.[85] So it is evident that what can be called plainly anti-Semitic discrimination was being practiced in the Accademia d'Italia through careful selection of candidates and elimination of those proposed members who were considered to be "unwanted" and "unwelcome." This is an important revisionist argument contributing to the historiography on anti-Semitism in Italy as it revises, for instance, some aspects of De Felice's *Storia degli ebrei italiani sotto il fascismo*.[86]

With all of this in mind, we can now turn to the late period of the regime (1936–1943) and explore how radicalized state anti-Semitism was to shape and determine the "civil death" of Italian Jewry (women and men alike) as unworthy of citizenship rights. During the final phase of the regime, up to its downfall in July 1943, and following an increasingly virulent anti-Semitic campaign, further historical developments took place for a minority of female and male nationals as far as the content of their citizenship entitlements was concerned. In particular, the community of Jews was to fall victim to an Italian national process of exclusion—unprecedented in the post-unification peninsula—that led to a cruel civil death and eventually either to emigration abroad or internment and forced labor programs at home during the first three years of the Second World War.[87] Finally, to bring in a comparative perspective, additional aspects of race and women's citizenship entitlements in Nazi Germany are also to be pointed out.

Throughout the late fascist years, the Duce's regime formulated and introduced brutal anti-Semitic measures concerning numerous aspects of the citizenship rights that had been enjoyed up to that moment by Italian women (and their counterpart). First of all, Mussolini's state "attacked" those Italian Jews who held Italian citizenship following their naturalization in the peninsula after 1918. To get rid of them in a totalitarian way and deprive them of all citizenship rights at once, the fascist government denaturalized these co-citizens through two decrees of September 1938.[88] Consequently, those who did not hold, or could not claim, the citizenship of another country became stateless people (*apolidi*) by losing Italian citizenship status and found themselves with no protection (or, if lucky enough to get a Nansen passport or similar documents, with only very limited traveling and sojourn rights).[89] Clearly, this policy affected the life of women (as well as men) touched directly or indirectly by these discriminatory regulations.

Seen from a wider geographical perspective, deprivation of citizenship was a drastic measure, usually defended and applied by totalitarian states in general as they seek to cleanse their citizenry of unwanted minorities. In July 1933, a few months after winning the national elections, the Nazis as well—before the Italian fascists—introduced a law that permitted retrospective annulment of numerous Weimar naturalizations that were deemed unwanted and unworthy on the basis of Nazi ethnoracial ideology.[90]

Alongside deprivation of citizenship vis-à-vis naturalized Italian Jews, Mussolini's regime also targeted the rest of the entire Jewish community holding Italian citizenship by gradually reducing the juridical capacities of its female (and male) citizens. The result was to be a humiliating *morte civile* (civil death), which, through intensification of racial politics, would be coupled ultimately with internment (from May 1940) and a policy of forced labor programs (from May 1942).[91]

Regarding civil rights in general, one can say that the right to equality before the law as well as the personal and religious identity of these Italian co-citizens were seriously undermined because, for instance, the regime introduced the rule according to which personal documents had to single out the Jewish affiliation of the individual concerned. True, Italian Jews were not obliged to wear the yellow star as in Hitler's Third Reich. However, some propositions were made by Italian fascist officialdom in this direction, and thanks to the archival findings of De Felice we know that the file containing this question reached the Duce's desk.[92] Also, and in relation to this issue, the fascist regime introduced a 1939 law allowing daughters and sons of a Jewish father and an Aryan mother to abandon the paternal surname and take the maternal one on racial grounds. Eventually, this rule saved many lives because Jews were often recognized by their family surnames; however, initially, when the provision was introduced, it had a strong psychological impact among Italian Jewish families and was seen as a slight, similar to an individual's abjuration.[93] These Italian state attacks against religious freedom and identity in the peninsula were not accompanied, as in Nazi Germany, by systematic outright *physical* violence at least until 1943. In fact, during the period under consideration, the Italian Jewish minority did not have to witness—with only sporadic, isolated and geographically limited exceptions—the arson and blazes that tragically illuminated German towns when the Nazis were systematically destroying synagogues and other Jewish places within German society. The intensity and organized systematic use of physical violence in Nazi Germany is a known phenomenon worthy of mention here again.[94] Finally, apart from the fact that Italian Jews saw their property rights limited at one point as they could no longer be owners of lands and urban buildings of a certain value, one should add that their individual freedom was attacked from many angles, to the point of humiliating the entire community of female (and male) Jews with the ban issued by the Italian Ministry of the Interior on entering public libraries and other places reserved for non-Jews.[95] Hence, during the late years of the ventennium, discrimination, inequality and humiliation were to be the radical norms regarding the sphere of civic entitlements of Italian Jewish women (and men).

If we now turn to the content of social rights, we can see that it was also shaped and shrunk in a new way, since female Jews (and their male counterparts) were gradually pushed out of state schools, the welfare system and the workplace with additional racist provisions. The special position of Italian women in general vis-à-vis their right to education, welfare benefits and work—as seen in the previous section of this chapter—were subject to further limitations if the individual concerned was a Jew. For instance, according to a decree-law of September 1938 concerning the fascist school system, the regime proclaimed immediate exclusion of Jewish girls and boys from state schools as well as expulsion of Jewish teachers from these institutions. Two weeks later, these same children were allowed to study only in special sections of elementary schools for Jewish pupils, and permission was then given to Jewish communities to set up their own schools. In this way, a particular "stab in the back" was inflicted on an Italian minority that had traditionally distinguished itself among the country's national population for the high level of education and culture of its female and male members.[96] Moreover, as emphasized by the scholar Chiara Saraceno, the welfare state rights introduced and defended by the regime for potential and effective Italian mothers since 1925 were gradually racialized from 1938 onward, and as a result not all Italian mothers were encouraged to have children; in fact, those of Jewish religion were excluded from the welfare state and not welcome as reproducers of the nation.[97] Exclusion from the national welfare state was the rule in Nazi Germany as well, where since 1933 none of the social benefits granted to mothers but also to fathers and to large families (as in Italy) were meant to be given universally. In fact, all the categories of the *minderwertig* (the unworthy)—that is the Jews, the Gypsies and the physically and mentally handicapped—were systematically excluded from Nazi welfare and social programs. Only Aryan women, Aryan men and Aryan families could enjoy these social entitlements.[98]

Finally, the workplace was also to be targeted by the anti-Semitism of Mussolini's state. In 1938 and 1939, the regime approved certain provisions excluding female (and male) Jewish employees from public civil administration at all state levels (governmental, provincial and municipal) as well as from the Fascist party, the banks and the insurance institutes. Moreover, the professions of general medical practitioner and obstetrician, which until then had been filled by female citizens too, were to be exercised by Italian Jews only in favor of Jewish patients, and no collaboration or association should take place between Jewish and non-Jewish professionals. This restrictive labor legislation was then coupled with a plethora of other bans that, introduced by the local administrations around the peninsula, added further exclusions from the exercise of numerous jobs in the fields of commerce, trade, tourism and the entertainment sector (i.e., the theater, music, cinema, radio), thus leading ultimately to economic strangulation of the entire Italian Jewish community.[99]

The anti-Semitic Italian program—whose ultimate objectives, direct and indirect causes and underlying principles are still highly debated within the historiography[100]—was to take a further turn with the proximity of World War Two. From 1940 on, as Italy was preparing to join this second world conflict within the Nazi alliance, Mussolini's anti-Semitic machine intensified its work. In May 1940, with the imminent declaration of war by fascist Rome against the democratic "plutocracies," the anti-Jewish campaign became more vociferous. Also, new measures were formulated by the fascist state to abolish basically all the (already limited) rights, discussed above, that were hitherto enjoyed by the female (and male members) of the Jewish minority. In particular, a few weeks before Italy's entry into the Second World War in June 1940, the fascist regime decided to restrict the individual liberty of Jews by stating that apart from internment of foreign Jews as subjects of enemy states, the Italian Ministry of the Interior had to intern—"in case of emergency"—"dangerous" Jews of Italian nationality together with the other antifascists. Subsequently, from May and June 1942 and as the war went on, the regime started appealing to mobilization of the total population for contributing to the war effort. Yet, whereas for non-Jews this was a national civic demand to contribute their labor to the conflict, for the Jews it was not an appeal but a punitive measure. In effect, orders were given from above to send all foreign and Italian Jews, without distinction, to Italian labor camps under police supervision and thus segregate them from the rest of the national population.[101] Eventually, with Mussolini's downfall in July 1943, these latter measures were prevented from being fully realized. However, after the armistice of 1943 and the birth of the Salò Republic, the persecution of the Jews would change course even more tragically: Italian camps, such as the one in Fossoli near Modena, would in fact be used as transit points before sending Jewish females, males and children to German extermination camps.[102] Here, where the Nazi state had basically acquired the right over the sphere of death, Jews of all nationalities (including Italian) were eliminated physically and systematically. The survivors of this tragedy were to be female and male individuals who, like the Italian writer Primo Levi, were lucky enough to get back home from Auschwitz.[103]

6.3. CONCLUSION

During the fascist revolutionary dictatorship led by Mussolini, Italy's citizenship policies and legislation vis-à-vis women and men were characterized by elements of continuity and discontinuity of historical importance with the liberal period. In fact, as wives and mothers, Italian women continued to lack the full juridical recognition of an independent nationality, like their predecessors. The notion of *italianità*, as shaped and defined by this citizenship aspect, continued to be "a divided notion" throughout the dictatorship as well, differing in accordance with the perspective of the half of the Italian population under consideration. During Fascism, though, the concept of "being Italian" came also to incorporate a new civic dimension touching on the correlated issues of birth to citizen parents, *jus sanguinis*, sexuality and marriage unions. Consequently, a novel duty came to be constructed from the early years of the regime: the duty of reproducing a demographically powerful Italian nation, to be shared by women and men alike but also incorporating important gender aspects within an ever more invasive fascist state.

Parallel to this analysis, we emphasized how racial thinking about notions of Italianness continued its course in the peninsula throughout the 1920s and 1930s and in the late radical period. By drawing on related scholarly debates, we saw that during the first decade of the regime, and as in the previous epoch, the notion of being Italian (for women and men alike) oscillated in these racial discourses across theories pertaining to Aryanism and Mediterraneanism. Moreover, the early fascist age was characterized by anti-Semitic prejudices that continued to question in some quarters the Italianness of (female and male) Jews living in the peninsula. Finally, with respect to the late dictatorial period, we saw that through the totalitarian Aryanization of Italian race and citizenship as well as construction of a specific "Aryan-Mediterranean type," notions of Italianhood came to exclude, drastically, categories of Jews and other races.

Moving to the other matter analyzed in this chapter—citizenship rights—we saw that female entitlements too went through major historical breaks while sharing at the same time elements of analogy with the liberal variant. Italian women (and their male matching counterpart) saw their civil rights disappear gradually as Mussolini's regime extended state control over the society and the individual. Women were then granted by the Duce the right to vote locally, but the following year, with abolition of local elections, this right became an empty word for them, as for men. Finally, Italian female citizens were provided with a variety of new entitlements in the social sphere, but in many cases these "new opportunities" covered corresponding "new and old repressions."

In reference to the rhetoric concerning civic membership, rights and *italianità*, we saw that further racial discourse was formulated in Italy not only in the late period but also before. Prejudices and stereotyping against Southern Italians continued to circulate in some quarters in the 1920s and 1930s; emancipation and the citizenship rights of Italian Jews continued to be put into question by some influential circles and anti-Jewish discrimination was taking place in the early 1930s vis-à-vis Jewish candidates at the Reale Accademia d'Italia. Subsequently, in the course of the late fascist years, the history of Italian citizenship rights for Jews (female and male alike) came to be shaped by seven years of humiliation and ultimately civil death. Clearly, all these civic developments contributed as well to construction of a notion of Italianness that was not only "divided" for gender reasons but also somehow questioned, when referring to Southerners, and contested most tragically, when referring to Jews.

Fascism, as a regime and as an ideology, attempted to create a new concept of being Italian and of contributing, as a female or male citizen, to the establishment of a strong totalitarian state that would make the Fascist Revolution at home and export it overseas while creating a Second Roman Empire. This imperial topic is the subject of our next chapter, covering citizenship and identity issues within Mussolini's *comunità imperiale*.

CHAPTER SEVEN

Fascist Italy's Colonized, Annexed and Occupied Territories

Citizenship Policies and Native Populations in Mussolini's Roman Empire

Between 1922 and 1943, together with the fascist priority of introducing and strengthening totalitarianism at home, Mussolini's regime intensified its expansionist foreign policy abroad so as to lead to consolidation and extension of Italian rule over an increasing number of colonized, annexed or occupied territories in Africa (i.e., Eritrea, Somalia, Ethiopia, Libya) as well as in Mediterranean Europe (i.e., the Dodecanese, Albania, France, the Principality of Monaco, Greece and Yugoslavia).

In Chapter Five, concerning citizenship issues vis-à-vis the nonmetropolitan populations of liberal Italy, we explored the civic accommodation of the natives within the Italian state and also discussed the official discourses that were formulated by liberal authorities when thinking and talking about them. As we explained, these debates put particular emphasis on notions of civilization and race within the colonial context as well as making, at times, some references to the myth of ancient Rome and the maritime republics.

In this chapter covering the fascist epoch, we follow the same research approach. In particular, we analyze and discuss for the first time the still partially unknown citizenship policies concerning all the populations of Mediterranean Europe under fascist Italy and examine them together with the civic accommodation of the African natives, which, by contrast, has already attracted the attention of scholars of colonial studies.[1] In this way, our pages aim not only at providing a more comprehensive picture of the citizenship arrangements introduced in Italian Africa and Mediterranean Europe but also at highlighting continuities and discontinuities with the previous liberal decades. Finally, by focusing on the official

language and discourses of the regime, the chapter explores the themes
and historical references evoked within the citizenship debates in the Italy
of the Duce. This again allows us to draw attention to affinities and dissimilarities with pre-1922 arguments.

7.1. FASCIST CITIZENSHIP POLICIES
IN ITALY'S AFRICAN COLONIES
7.1.a. Eritrea, Somalia, Ethiopia

When fascism came to power in 1922, it inherited from its liberal predecessors the two East African colonies of Eritrea and Somalia—still
under weak Italian colonial rule—as well as the memory of the 1896
defeat of Italian military troops by Ethiopians in Adwa. The fascist
regime was to change all this. Its colonial foreign policy became much
more aggressive and provocative than the one pursued by liberal governments, especially from 1929 onward. Also, Italian colonial rule was
consolidated through systematic and violent policies of "pacification"
involving shameful repressions such as those perpetrated in the northern
Somali protectorates of Obbia and Migiurtini. Finally, from a variety
of motives including domestic economic instability, the need for a di-
versionary propagandistic maneuver and the ideological fascist tenet
according to which a strong totalitarian state at home required creation
of an empire abroad, the regime conquered Ethiopia in 1935–36, being
able to revenge Adwa only with prohibited deployment of chemical
weapons and poison gas bombing. As a result, on 4 May 1936, the
Ethiopian emperor Haile Selassie departed from Djibouti aboard a British cruiser bound for Europe. On the following day, Italian military
troops entered Addis Ababa, and Mussolini could finally appear on
the balcony of Palazzo Venezia in Rome to declare, before a vociferous
crowd, that Ethiopia was under Italian sovereignty and that Vittorio
Emanuele III, King of Italy, had taken the title of emperor. Fascist Rome
was now in possession of an empire.[2]

Following this territorial conquest, the formerly separate colonies of
Eritrea and Somalia were united with Ethiopia in one imperial colony,
named *Africa Orientale Italiana* (AOI). Also, new indigenous populations came under Italian rule, increasing the total number of East African
natives to more than nine million people as well as adding other ethnic and religious pieces to Italy's colonial human mosaic. Ethiopia was
in fact inhabited by autochthones of various races, including the Galla,
the Amara people and the Cusciti; it was divided from a religious point
of view into communities of Muslims, Catholics, Monophysite Copts

and small minorities of Jews and Protestants. It was a territory where populations spoke many languages, among them Amharic, Galla and the Tigrinya tongue.[3]

Confronted with the task of accommodating all these indigenous peoples within the Italian fascist state, Mussolini's Rome extended and modified the existing citizenship system of the liberal period. In fact, as we demonstrate below, the Duce's citizenship policies shared certain elements with those formulated during the previous era; however, in important respects, especially during the last years of the dictatorship, they reflected peculiar fascist principles, priorities and objectives that were absent in the pre-1922 decades. Fascism therefore brought about significant changes within the history of Italian colonial citizenship too.

If one focuses first on the official terminology and legal vocabulary used during the ventennium to refer to East African natives, one notices a certain affinity with the liberal years. Fascism, like the pre-1922 Italian governments, continued to use the term *suddito coloniale* (colonial subject) to refer to an individual who was not an Italian metropolitan citizen and did not hold any foreign nationality and was an autochthon of the colony. It employed as well the expression *assimilato al suddito coloniale* (assimilated to the colonial subject) to indicate the person whose traditions, social habits, laws and customs were similar to those shared by Italy's East Africans and totally different from those that had developed in the metropole and other Western countries.[4] Also, until the proclamation of the Italian empire in 1936, the status of *sudditanza coloniale* (SC, colonial subjecthood), held by Eritreans on the one hand and by Somalis on the other, was kept separated by law, as in the liberal era, although the juridical colonial link uniting them to the metropole was basically the same.[5]

In June 1936, though, with the conquest of Ethiopia, and guided by the fascist tenets of "unity, order and authority," the regime introduced a unifying juridical status for all the natives of Italian East Africa: the "subjecthood of AOI" (*sudditanza dell'AOI*, henceforth SAOI).[6] Also, fascist Rome appeared to be much more determined than its liberal counterpart to start "playing" with legal words and use them with some flexibility as a way of thanking and rewarding those indigenous inhabitants who had contributed to establishment of the empire. Despite the new denomination defining *de jure* all East Africans as *sudditi dell' Africa Orientale Italiana* (subjects of Italian East Africa), fascist authorities began differentiating the natives of Italy's old colonies from the newly incorporated subjects of the ex-empire of Selassie by using, in official acts, the terms *Eritrei* and *Somali* on the one hand while applying the expression *colonial subjects* for the Ethiopians on the other.[7] Obviously, this distinction did not have any juridical value; but from a political point of view, it had an important meaning since it reflected the Italian state's willingness to create different levels of subjecthood according to the loyalty of the populations concerned. Both Eritrea and Somalia had contributed to the Ethiopian conquest and to "pacification" of the new territories by providing the fascist metropole with almost 130,000 colonial troops of the so-called *ascari* (black colonial soldiers) and workers. This apparently insignificant terminological distinction was a way of thanking them while applying a more punitive word for the Ethiopian natives. After all, the Italian legislators' decision to divide AOI into six administrative zones, which dismembered completely the entire ex-empire of Selassie while enlarging the territories of the former separate colonies of Eritrea and Somalia, followed the same logic.[8]

If we leave the sphere of official terminology and legal vocabulary and move on to analyze the citizenship principles used during fascism to ascribe colonial status at birth, we can bring to light other interesting parallels and variations between Mussolini's Italy and liberal Italy. Like pre-1922 Italian governments, the fascist regime continued ascribing colonial subjecthood on the basis of a blend of territorial criteria and principles of descent to any individual who was a native and neither an Italian citizen nor a citizen or subject of other states. Also, similar to liberal Italy, the regime pursued—for more than a decade—a relatively open citizenship policy vis-à-vis mixed-race children born to an Italian parent and an East African native. The *meticci* continued being ascribed Italian metropolitan citizenship at birth if they were legitimate offspring or children acknowledged by their Italian father.[9] Moreover, we know that their legitimization continued to be permitted by early jurisprudential colonial praxis without the father having to marry the native mother[10]; and that De Camillis's initiative to register unacknowledged babies of Italian men in the official birth records so as to automatically grant them Italian citizenship continued to be enforced after the fascist seizure of power.[11] Subsequently, from 1933 onward a colonial citizenship law was also introduced and implemented to allow mixed-race unacknowledged children to claim Italian metropolitan status upon coming of age and on the basis of somatic, cultural and meritocratic criteria.[12]

Following the Ethiopian conquest in 1936, then, a radical change of policy took place vis-à-vis the phenomenon of *meticciato*. The métis became a negative target of the regime because of the metropole's imperial emigration projects concerning Italian metropolitan settlements in AOI (thus making the issue of mixed-race births more salient) as well as the fascist policy on protecting the dignity of the Italian race being put into operation in the metropole and in the empire. As a result, fascist Rome attempted to "attack" Italo-African offspring in two interrelated radical ways: by trying to eliminate the cause of *meticciato* (i.e., sexual relations between Italian and African parents) as well as by limiting its consequences (i.e., an increasing number of new Italian metropolitan citizens of mixed blood).

With respect to the first action (preventing "the monstrosity" of sexual crossbreeding between Italians and Africans),[13] Mussolini's Italy introduced severe measures in 1937 against the colonial phenomenon of informal concubinage (*madamato*) as well as prohibiting in 1938 formal marriages between metropolitan Italians and African natives (or "other races").[14] In this respect, it is important to emphasize that until 1936 the fascist regime of the early years had actually shared several similarities with the liberal period. In fact, in the 1920s and early 1930s, interracial informal unions between Italian men and female natives, which undoubtedly continued to be practiced, were tolerated by Italian authorities, although we know that colonial officials (men vested with public functions) had been forbidden from cohabiting with native women since 1909 and from marrying them since 1914, and that military officers had been subjected to similar restrictions on the basis of Rodolfo Graziani's circular of 1932 prohibiting unions between Italian military men and African women.[15] So partial discouragement through official legal prohibition, combined with a relaxed and lenient attitude on the part of the authorities *in loco*, had very often been the rule up to the war on Ethiopia. This had been made possible—as Barrera reminds us—because of the balancing out of the sex ratio in the Italian community itself, and the fact that the racial hierarchy had been solidly in place in the 1920s and the 1930s while being completely shaken with the massive arrival of Italian men in 1935–36 and the booming of interracial concubinage and births.[16]

In reference to the second and related policy (granting metropolitan citizenship to the born métis), the fascist regime abandoned the previous relatively benevolent norm that had allowed mixed-race children to ask for metropolitan status upon majority and did not reproduce this tolerant rule in the final text, which introduced the subjecthood of AOI in 1936.[17] As emphasized by Luigi Goglia, this was indeed a telling case of intended legislative "silence" through "omission" of a previously accepted principle of relative assimilation.[18] Also, and most significantly, Mussolini's Rome formulated and approved in 1940 an additional racist and exclusionary policy that brutally pushed mixed-race children back to their indigenous legal world by prohibiting metropolitan citizenship. In accordance with this 1940 legislation, métis babies (legitimate, illegitimate or born to one or two unknown parents) were colonial subjects, could neither be recognized by the metropolitan parent nor take the latter's surname and could be the dependent children only of the native father or mother.[19] The only exception concerned "past mistakes," in other words, the *meticci* who had already been born in previous years.

However, not all of them; in fact, only those who were over thirteen when the norm was introduced could claim Italian metropolitan citizenship, and only if they had an Italian upbringing as well as good civil, moral and political behavior in line with the regime's fascist tenets.[20] So late fascist legislation vis-à-vis mixed-race children transmitted a fierce message of racial arrogance, encouraged Italian paternal abandonment and denied metropolitan citizenship to current and future *meticci*, excluding the exceptions mentioned here. However, as emphasized by Barrera, this radical fascist turn also coexisted in the late years of the dictatorship with other less radical (even if marginal) messages and outlooks that made the whole fascist strategy vis-à-vis mixed-race offspring not at all univocal but somehow internally inconsistent.[21] First, the 1940 norm on the "past mistakes" could indeed be seen as a partially benevolent provision, clashing theoretically with the radical stand of the dictatorship. Also, from the end of 1937 onward and in the middle of the fascist racist campaign, we know that the governor of Eritrea and the Ministry of Africa argued on several occasions in favor of putting pressure on Italian fathers to legally recognize these children.[22] And we know that a federal vice-secretary of the colony too had favored the emotional paternal link and desire not to abandon this progeny over the severe official policy.[23] Therefore, although fascist rhetoric and practice took the radical path following the conquest of Ethiopia, certain fascist attitudes and positions were also at times contradictory, particularly if biological racism could be in tension with the fascist tenet of responsible fatherhood.[24]

Finally, apart from the citizenship changes that took place with respect to *meticciato*, another parallel can be drawn between fascist Italy and its liberal counterpart, in relation this time to the question of naturalization. In fact, bearing in mind that the process of naturalization for colonial subjects had already been regarded as exceptional in liberal Italy, made very restrictive and reserved exclusively to those natives who deserved such a civic prize (i.e., metropolitan *status civitatis*) for eminent personal qualities or for special services rendered to the Italian state,[25] it is instructive to see that the fascist legislation of 1933 did not contain any norm on natives acquiring metropolitan citizenship. This silence, emphasized by the scholar Sòrgoni, has been interpreted by many commentators as a clear sign, intentionally given by the regime to exclude any possibility of the autochthones becoming citizens.[26] As such, it can therefore be seen as an anticipation of the late radical turn of fascism, which as we saw was soon to occur in the field of colonial citizenship. Indeed, according to a number of contemporary writers living during the dictatorship, the system of naturalization could not but be denied to these populations, given the "gap" between the metropole and the colony as far as race, traditions and customs were concerned and the fact that this "huge gap" could not give "any" chance to East African peoples to be incorporated into the metropolitan citizenry.[27]

Having talked about official terminology, ascription rules, mixed-race issues and naturalization policies, let us now turn attention to the content of colonial status and see which additional historical parallels and contrasts can be drawn between Mussolini's Italy and the liberal years. Generally speaking, the overall status of East Africans continued to be very thin throughout the ventennium, as it had been in the pre-1922 decades. A variety of limited entitlements were still guaranteed *de jure* by the regime: family-related issues were regulated according to the personal statute of the natives and their individual religious affiliations, and respect for local customs was enshrined in various fascist laws and decrees.[28] As in the liberal era, no voting rights were granted to East Africans at any level—local or national—and even though early fascism, like its liberal predecessors, accepted the very marginal participation of the indigenous element within the public sphere, particularly within the local judiciary, gradually the fascist tendency to exclude the autochthones from any public position and segregate them became evident. This was done in consideration of "hygiene and smell" and with the intention "to bring the indigenous peoples back to that proper sense of their natural place."[29] As a result, exclusion, segregation and an Italian variant of apartheid became important aspects of fascist colonial rule as well as being radicalized in the late years of the dictatorship with the introduction of several decrees prohibiting, for the first time, any form of contact between blacks and whites in public places, working places, restaurants, shops, and cinemas.[30]

A second element of comparison and contrast related to content of status concerns the fact that this thin East African subjecthood took shape, as in the liberal years, within a specific context characterized by social and political local factors that deserve attention. The practice of slavery, for example, went on being tolerated during fascism and was tackled by Italian authorities with "judiciousness and graduation" because of the same economic and social concerns that had been raised by liberal officials in the previous decades. Also, whereas violence and repression had already characterized liberal Italy's colonial rule, terror became a systematic norm between 1922 and 1943, achieving a level of cruelty never attained before. In Somalia, for instance, between 1925 and 1927 the governor, Cesare Maria De Vecchi, carried out ferocious massacres in the northern parts of the colony to disarm the natives and keep the guerrilla war at bay. Instability persisted throughout the years and actually increased with the proclamation of the Italian empire because the end of the 1935–36 Italo-Ethiopian war was followed by the beginning of nationalist uprisings by Ethiopian partisans. As a result, orders were given by the fascist regime not only to punish the rebels and the populations who collaborated with them but also to liquidate the young nationalists and intellectuals who could encourage anticolonial revolts. This is why executions were generalized, concentration camps were established in Nocra (Eritrea) and Danane (Somalia) to "deal with" Ethiopian prisoners and violent fascist reprisals were carried out against the Christian Coptic clergy—as in the notorious slaughter that took place in the monasteries of Debrà Libanòs in which more than four hundred monks where liquidated by the Italians on the basis of an accusation of connivance with the rebels.[31] Obviously, within this particular and tragic context, understanding what it meant to be an Italian colonial subject under fascist dominion does not require a lot of imagination.

Having explored the major affinities and dissimilarities of fascist citizenship issues in East Africa in comparison with the pre-1922 era, we now take the reader to Libya, spend some time with Italy's North African subjects and then conclude this first part of the chapter, which we have devoted to the natives of Africa under Mussolini's rule.

7.1.b. Libya

While Mussolini's regime was trying to strengthen Italian colonial rule in East Africa and in 1936 could proclaim the Italian *Impero*, parallel developments were taking place in the North African territories of Tripolitania and Cyrenaica. Here, as in the East African colonies, fascist Italy pursued an aggressive foreign policy and brought about major political changes, with a view to affirm Rome's authority, reconquer the Libyan lands that had been lost to the rebels and eradicate the latter's opposition with all possible means. In particular, it established a centralized colonial system of direct government and abandoned the decentralization and colonial elective systems that had been introduced in Libya with the 1919 statutes; it proceeded to a ten-year, systematic, violent military campaign against Libyan insurgents that ended only in 1932.[32] Also, once "pacification" was in place, the regime formulated significant constitutional reforms. In 1934, as would happen two years later in East Africa as well, Tripolitania and Cyrenaica were united in a single colony (officially called Libya) and divided administratively into four northern provinces (Tripoli, Misurata, Bengasi, Derna) as well as into one southern military territory (Libyan Sahara), with a total indigenous population of 773,000 inhabitants.[33] Subsequently, in 1939, as a tribute to the fascist dream of making the Mediterranean Sea *mare nostrum*, the four littoral regions were annexed to the Kingdom of Italy, thus becoming metropolitan territory.[34]

This active colonial policy implemented in North Africa was coupled with a parallel dynamic strategy concerning accommodation of Libyan natives within the fascist state. Similar to the East African case, the fascist citizenship policies related to Italy's North African subjects shared important aspects of historical continuity with the preceding liberal years; however, they were also characterized by a fascist specificity that represents a major break within the history of Italian colonial tradition.

This blend of historical similarities and differences can be perceived, for instance, by exploring the colonial principles used by Mussolini's regime in order to define who was a Libyan subject and who could naturalize to acquire either colonial status or metropolitan status. With respect to the first issue, fascism continued to ascribe Libyan colonial status at birth on the basis of the application of the *jus sanguinis* and *jus soli* rules to all those born in Libya who were neither Italian metropolitan citizens nor subjects or citizens of other states. What changed, though, from the former period was the name of this colonial membership: from 1927 onward, the latter was no longer called CITC ("Italian citizenship of Tripoliania and Cyrenaica"), as it had been since 1919, but "*cittadinanza italiana libica*" (henceforth CIL), or "Libyan Italian citizenship."[35] This was due to application of the fascist principle of "unity and centralization" (already seen in East Africa), which in 1934 would also lead to territorial and administrative unification of Tripolitania and Cyrenaica under the name of Libya. Interestingly, in this case fascist citizenship policies (uniting all Libyan natives around CIL) anticipated territorial colonial policy: the autochthonous peoples were united before their territories.

In addition to this, even more significant were the modifications that late fascism brought about with the introduction of radical citizenship norms. For fear of miscegenation, in 1939 (slightly later than in AOI) fascist Rome started "tracking down" Italo-Libyan couples by extending the legislation concerning the crime of *madamato* to Libya as well. Also, as in the Eastern part of the African continent, Mussolini's regime introduced—from May 1940—the norms excluding métis children from Italian metropolitan status and classifying them automatically as natives.[36] Finally, with respect to naturalization, the same gradual exclusionary logic was followed by the regime throughout the ventennium, thus leading to major changes compared to the liberal decades and early fascist colonial rule, which can be easily demonstrated with historical evidence. For instance, whereas the regime—like liberal governments previously—pursued an open policy vis-à-vis the African and Asian immigrants who wanted to acquire Libyan colonial status, state attitudes regarding the Libyan inhabitants who desired to acquire Italian metropolitan citizenship changed during the ventennium from a relatively restrictive stand to very racist. The Libyans, who had been granted the possibility of becoming Italian metropolitans via naturalization until 1938 (upon certain, even if rather demanding, conditions), were no longer allowed to do so.[37] This intolerant measure was "necessary" because, according to fascist officialdom, Libyans were Arabs from an ethnic point of view and as such "within the racial sphere [they] would always remain extraneous to the Aryan aggregate whose prestige we want to preserve."[38] Since citizenship was seen as a fundamental instrument to protect the purity of the Italian race from North African menaces, certain racial provisions had to be extended to all colonies of fascist Rome belonging to the African continent, including the northern lands.[39]

If at this point one explores the content of the membership status enjoyed by the Libyans during fascism, one notices, similarly, various other lines of continuity and discontinuity with the pre-fascist era and within the twenty-year-long dictatorship. As far as *de jure* recognition of rights and entitlements is concerned, the regime followed the pre-1922 colonial tradition of enshrining certain fundamental civil rights in national colonial legislation, such as equality before the law, respect of the natives' *statut personnel*, individual liberty and inviolability of domicile.[40] Yet in comparison with the preceding decades, fascist Italy's attitude toward formal recognition of other important civil and local political entitlements changed radically from 1927 onward as Mussolini's regime abolished the "utopian" and "wretched" Libyan Statutes introduced during Giolitti's rule and, together with them, erased all the substantial rights that had distinguished, at least on paper, the Libyans' colonial citizenship from the East Africans' colonial subjecthood.[41] Indeed, these changes of content were deemed indispensable for the regime because, following "pacification" of the colony and the metropole's formulation of totalitarian principles, the pre-1922 Libyan colonial status was inappropriate and detrimental to consolidation of fascist colonial rule, dangerous for the realization of fascist Rome's imperial project, and in stark contrast with the regime's antiparliamentary tenets.[42]

Most importantly, the fascist determination to eradicate liberal aspects within Italy's colonial policies and to break with the past through the fascistization of the content of colonial status is also reflected in another fundamental citizenship policy, introduced in January 1939 following annexation of the four Libyan northern provinces to the Italian kingdom. From that year, Mussolini's regime granted the Muslim Libyans who originated from those annexed littoral lands the possibility to acquire nonmetropolitan colonial status called "special Italian citizenship" (*cittadinanza italiana speciale*, henceforth CIS), through a form of individual naturalization and by fulfilling specific conditions.[43] This CIS status—which despite the name should not be confused with metropolitan

Italian citizenship since it was inclusive of the *statut personnel* of the Muslim native and could be exercised only in Libya and AOI—incorporated typically fascist entitlements. For example, the Libyan Muslims who were successful in acquiring CIS had the right to register within the *Associazione musulmana del Littorio* (linked to the national Fascist Party and to the youth organization *Gioventù Araba del Littorio*), as well as having a right to be appointed to the fascist posts of *podestà* (head of a town) or *consultore* (advisor) at the municipal level.[44]

The fascistization of colonial status contained an additional element of analysis for historical and geographic comparison. As in the liberal years (and as we also saw in East Africa), the Italian state continued using citizenship policy to reward its overseas indigenous populations and to pursue foreign policy objectives throughout the ventennium. For example, documents at our disposal show that this 1939 *cittadinanza italiana speciale* was introduced by fascist Rome to thank the Muslim Libyans for their loyalty and military help since more than nine thousand North African volunteers had fought in the Ethiopian war in 1936. The reader might recall that this citizenship measure had raised expectations among Eritreans and Somalis as well, for their participation in the same conflict. Also, within the wider contemporary international context, Mussolini's regime regarded citizenship as a tool to enhance Italy's standing vis-à-vis the Islamic world at large; after all, following the conquest of the Ethiopian empire, Italy had become a "Muslim power" since the Muslim subjects under Italian rule in Eritrea, Somalia, Libya and Ethiopia were estimated at about nine million in 1936. These open citizenship norms concerning North Africans were therefore an international message Mussolini wanted to send to the world, so as to contrast Italy's open attitude vis-à-vis its subjects with contemporary restrictive French policies in North Africa and British policies in Egypt and Palestine.[45]

Finally, before concluding this section, we should not leave out a short mention of the historical context and local realities in which the Libyan native status was exercised and seriously limited, as in the eastern part of the African continent. Exacerbating the violent tendency of liberal Italy to "pacify" the colony through the means of imprisonments, deportations and confinements of those who were suspected of resisting Italian colonial rule, the fascist regime introduced forms of internment that differed from the liberal-era abuses in scale and brutality. Between 1928 and 1933, under General Graziani, an entire population, the Cyrenaic Jabal inhabitants, was subject to forced deportation and settlement in concentration camps where executions, forced labor and death by starvation occurred daily. According to recent research, during those years sixteen camps operated in the Cyrenaic region as a means of fighting against the anticolonial activities of the Senussi confraternity.[46] Clearly, as in East

Africa, highly contested colonial power relations made exercise of colonial membership status a complicated and sensitive issue.

To conclude this section concerning the African populations living within Mussolini's *comunità imperiale*, we argue that the citizenship policies introduced by the fascist metropole in East Africa and in Libya regarding almost nine million natives of AOI and more than three-quarters of a million North Africans share numerous affinities with the liberal past as well as being characterized by new significant elements of analysis. The major historical continuities relate to official terminology and to certain citizenship principles; to the use of civic policies as a way of rewarding the natives; and to the contested, even impossible, exercise of colonial rights due to peculiar local realities and violent power relations. By contrast, the most important dissimilarities concern two essential tenets that were to be implemented in different ways especially during the late years of the dictatorship: a radicalized state legal racism, and fascist totalitarianism.

Leaving Africa for a moment, we shall now take the reader to Mediterranean Europe and explore the fascist regime's attitude vis-à-vis the European populations of Mussolini's empire to discover how Italy's citizenship system was extended, enriched and modified to incorporate these Europeans within the orbit of fascist Rome.

7.2. FASCIST CITIZENSHIP POLICIES IN ITALY'S EUROPEAN MEDITERRANEAN TERRITORIES

7.2.a. The Aegean Islands

Mussolini's aggressive foreign policy on the African continent was accompanied by important political developments in the Dodecanese. After long and laborious diplomatic discussions concerning the "sick man of Europe" and the related post–World War One peace settlement, the fourteen Aegean Islands that had been under Italian military occupation since May 1912 were ceded to Italy in accordance with the Lausanne peace treaty. Being under full Italian sovereignty from August 1924 (when the international agreement entered into force in the Italian peninsula), they gave the regime an additional strategic basis in the East Mediterranean Sea to be used by fascist Rome for further expansionist adventures.[47]

To accommodate these ex-Ottoman insular territories within the Italian state, the Duce established a metropolitan governorship *in loco* that was put under the direction of the Ministry of Foreign Affairs; the territory continued to be called *Possedimento* (Possession) as in the preceding historical period, and the word *colonia* was never really used by fascist officialdom.[48] With regard to incorporation of the Aegean natives within Italy's citizenship system (roughly 140,000 *Egei*, according to a 1936 census),[49] Mussolini's regime formulated and introduced important nationality policies. As we saw in Chapter Five, under Italian military occupation the populations of these islands kept their Ottoman *status civitatis* and therefore continued to be foreign citizens with respect to Italy. From 1924, though, with the transfer of sovereignty, the autochthones became Italian subjects, with the exception of those adults who opted for Turkish nationality within two years (and by opting agreed tacitly to emigrate from the islands).[50] The Italian subjecthood, though, acquired by these *Egei* was not metropolitan status but a geographically defined membership that incorporated the personal statute of the inhabitants (according to their religion) and that was similar to what Great Britain had introduced in Cyprus or to what the natives of Libya were holding at that time.[51] Clearly, by introducing the "*cittadinanza italiana egea*" (henceforth CIE, "Aegean Italian citizenship"), first regulated with a 1925 national law, the fascist regime extended the list of existing state memberships: metropolitan citizenship for the Italians of the metropole, colonial subjecthood for East Africans, CIL and CIS for Libyans, CIE for *Dodecanesini*.[52]

Through systematic analysis of the civic position reserved for the Aegean people during fascism, we found some important aspects that deserve consideration in light of what we have learned about East and North Africans, about the citizenship issues we shall explore later in this chapter when talking about other European populations living within Mussolini's empire and about the citizenship-related policies that were introduced in the occupied Dodecanese before 1922. First, with respect to their membership status, the *Dodecanesini* were treated differently from their African counterparts not only from general civilizational considerations—shared by fascist and liberal Italy—about the *Egei's* European origins but also from other specifically racial concerns. Moreover, in particular during the late years of the fascist dictatorship, Aegean citizenship policies were incorporated into an imposed program of forced italianization and fascistization of the *Dodecaneso*, thus sharing some affinities with the citizenship projects that were formulated by Italian authorities for the populations of Yugoslavia and that are dealt with at the end of this second part concerning World War Two. Finally, as in the pre-1922 epoch, the Italian state used citizenship in the East Mediterranean Sea as a useful instrument of expansionism, although the tone of Italian fascist officialdom was much more aggressive and radical than that of its liberal predecessors.

When discussing the introduction of CIE, to be held by the ex-Ottoman subjects who had not opted for other citizenship and to be ascribed at birth to those born in the fourteen islands after 6 August 1924,[53] some contemporary observers emphasized our first point on the fascist "differential treatment" reserved for the *Egei*. For instance, as argued by professor Arnaldo Bertola in 1926, the fascist policy of granting "citizenship" rather than "colonial subjecthood" upon *Dodecanesini* was a sign of "wisdom, expediency, justice and equity," bearing in mind "the remarkable degree of civilization reached by the Aegean populations."[54] Even more significant was a comment by Deputy Orazio Pedrazzi in which the official maintained that the autochthones of these islands "[were] not colored peoples [*popolazioni di colore*]; they [did] not need to be civilized and they only [needed] to be assisted."[55] After all, the term *Possedimento* (rather than "colony") served to emphasize, indirectly, the high level of civilization among the Aegeans and their noncolonial character.[56]

Besides these remarks made by contemporary observers, it is also instructive to discover that the fascist regime differentiated the Aegeans from the African colonial natives with respect to naturalization norms and to acquisition of metropolitan citizenship on the basis of the assumption that the Dodecanese people was perceived as assimilable to the Italian metropolitans, whereas, as we have seen in the first part of this chapter, East Africans and Libyans could enjoy such a "privilege" only rarely and lost it completely during the late years of fascist colonial rule. In 1933, the *Dodecanesini* were in fact granted the possibility of naturalizing and acquiring Italian metropolitan status either by royal decree after hearing the governor's decision and the Council of State's opinion or automatically by doing military service. By acquiring metropolitan citizenship, the naturalized Italian would then lose the *statut personnel* enjoyed in the islands since the indigenous person had to respect the same laws as the metropolitans of the peninsula.[57] This citizenship policy, introduced to reward and honor (as in the African colonies) the attachment of the natives vis-à-vis the regime (especially the young Aegeans who had volunteered within the Italian Royal Army), represented, according to fascist officialdom and propaganda, a further step toward complete political assimilation of these inhabitants within the Italian state, by taking into account the significant civilizational differences between the *Egei* on the one side and the Africans on the other.[58]

Finally, the crucial civic factor that distinguished these European nonmetropolitan citizens from their African counterparts (both from AOI and Libya) was the nonapplication of the 1940 citizenship rules concerning mixed-race children. Whereas these exclusionary and racist norms were applied to the babies born to an Italian metropolitan citizen and an African subject, they did not concern the Italo-Aegean progeny. In

addition, according to the fascist state the child born to an Italian metropolitan citizen and a Dodecanese parent was *not* a métis, whereas this
latter term had to be used for the offspring issued from an Aegean parent
and an African (from AOI or Libya) or an *assimilato*. In these last three
cases, the child was excluded from CIE and pushed back to his or her
African or Asian legal world, as a demonstration of "the high consideration" shown by the fascist state for the Dodecanese people in reference
to the regime's racial hierarchy.[59]

All these "open and tolerant" citizenship policies directed toward progressive assimilation of the *Egei* were however incorporated into a broad,
ambitious and intolerant project of forced italianization and fascistization of the *Possedimento* that had an impact on the content of Aegean
membership status, especially during the late years of fascism, when the
regime pursued centralizing and extremist assimilationist programs under
a new governor, De Vecchi (1936–1940). Whereas throughout the first
decade of Mussolini's dictatorship the regime agreed to respect a variety
of civil rights, such as maintenance of the natives' *statut personnel*, individual liberty and religious freedom, during late fascism the Italian state
showed all its aggressiveness toward other civil entitlements, such as freedom of the press, and to realize the forced italianization objective banned
publication and circulation of daily newspapers written in Greek.[60] For
the same reason, it also modified the natives' social right to education
by introducing unilateral and radical policies that replaced Italian as the
teaching language in all schools and changed the academic curricula to
make them identical with those formulated in the Italian kingdom.[61] As a
contemporary writer had argued already in 1927, the ultimate goal of fascism was to make Rhodes and the other islands "a strip of Italian land in
the Aegean Sea."[62] Citizenship policies were contributing to realization of
this fascist project on ethnic homogenization. Moreover, though the *Egei*'s
participation within the public sphere had been substantial at the local
level during the early years of fascist rule (especially within the justice, fiscal and administrative sectors), it decreased progressively afterward as a
result of the regime's policy on political and administrative centralization
within the empire.[63] The Duce's programs about italianization and fascistization were being brutally imposed with the logic consequence of increasing anti-Italian feelings even further among the population concerned.

Finally, as in the liberal period (when the Aegean islands were only
occupied), citizenship strategies continued to be perceived by fascist
authorities as an instrument of foreign policy to strengthen the Italian
state's position in the East Mediterranean area, especially after Ver-
sailles, Lausanne and Locarno. As a parliamentary official argued in December 1925, by settling the administration of the Italian possessions as
well as the citizenship status of the *Egei*, Italy was evincing pride in its

new status as a power.[64] In the course of the speech, the MP also stated in this regard:

[Italy] is standing and presenting itself confidently within the councils of nations. [...] It does no longer pursue a policy of subservience and accommodation, but a policy of its own.[...] Be friends, yes, but servants, never.[...] This is the result of the tenacious, tireless, and passionate work of Benito Mussolini. (Applause)[65]

Accommodating these European inhabitants within the fascist orbit through a clear and precise citizenship policy was therefore a way of showing the "strength" of Italy as a European Mediterranean power, back on the international scene.

Also, a similar allusion to the link between citizenship and expansionism was made in December 1926 during some discussions concerning the *Egei* living abroad. Throughout that month, Governor Lago contacted Italy's Ministry of Foreign Affairs to propose a project about an additional and easy naturalization procedure for the *Dodecanesini* living outside the islands who wanted to acquire CIE status. The governor made reference in particular to those living in Egypt, many of whom were worth considering because of their number, their economically and socially prestigious position and their special attachment to Italy. As he argued, with the extension and intensification of Italy's Mediterranean policy it was highly appropriate to attract influential groups of Aegeans around the Italian state. Granting them metropolitan citizenship could be excessive, said the governor; however, allowing them to acquire CIE without the obligation of renouncing their original nationality was an intelligent move. The project attracted the attention and general approval of metropolitan authorities but never did become law as the major officials involved decided to postpone it for discussion at a later stage. Yet it demonstrates the importance of citizenship for fascism—since its early years in power—to strengthen Italian standing in Mediterranean Europe, as well as providing a further element of continuity with the liberal decades.[66]

Having described and discussed the civic position of the Aegeans, it is now time to move to Albania and see how fascist Italy dealt with the Skipetars (from 1939 onward) with respect to their *status civitatis*.

7.2.b. Albania

On 7 April 1939, as a delayed reaction to Nazi Germany's annexation of Austria, which had given the key of the Danube basin to Berlin and disrupted Mussolini's long-standing foreign policy in the Balkans, Italian troops attacked the seaports of Durres and Vlora to occupy and transform Albania into an Italian protectorate. Ten days later, in line with the "unanimous" decision of the Albanian Constituent Assembly summoned in Tirana, a Skipetar delegation was sent to Rome to "offer" the Skanderbeg crown to the Italian monarch Vittorio Emanuele III and make him "King of Italy and of Albania, Emperor of Ethiopia." On the basis of this monarchical union, linking fascist Rome to the "Land of the Eagles' Sons," the independent Balkan state that had been created in 1912 was incorporated into Mussolini's empire under specific institutional arrangements: an Albanian kingdom (distinguished from, but constitutionally united with, the Kingdom of Italy); a fascist-type regime run *in loco* under the directives of the metropole by the General Lieutenancy for Albania and the Albanian Fascist Party; and a statute and an Albanian national flag incorporating the symbol of the *fascio littorio*.[67]

As a result of the political changes, the Italian empire extended its territory as well as incorporating an estimated population of 1.1 million Albanians, who, from an ethnic point of view, were a non-Slav population of Illyrian origin, divided into three major religious communities: Muslim (70 percent of the total population including the Islamic order of Bektashism), Christian Orthodox (20 percent) and Roman Catholic (10 percent). Also, following the 1941 Vienna Conference and the partition of Yugoslavia by the two Axis allies, Greater Albania was established with the annexation of Kosovo and of ex-Yugoslav western Macedonia— thus extending further the borders of Mussolini's empire and increasing its population by about three-quarters of a million people.[68]

An important fact, still insufficiently noted, is that following acceptance of the Skanderbeg crown by Vittorio Emanuele III, these Balkan inhabitants automatically became subjects of the Italian monarch: "Let us greet the Albanians [...], the new subjects of Vittorio Emanuele III and of his adamant thousand-year House," said Fleet Admiral Paolo Thaon di Revel in the Italian Senate on 15 April 1939.[69] The Albanians' juridical status (linking them to the Italian king and to fascist Rome) was not, though, metropolitan status but instead another new, nonmetropolitan type of membership introduced by fascism to accommodate the Skipetars alongside East Africans, Libyans and *Dodecanesini*. In order to do this, the regime used citizenship policies with a certain flexibility and, by mixing pre-1939 Albanian citizenship norms with post-1939 fascist rules, it formulated a new Albanian *status civitatis* that, as we shall demonstrate, reflected again special racial considerations and represented the most substantial civic position, held *de jure*, by a nonmetropolitan people within Mussolini's imperial community.

With regard to ascription and attribution norms that defined who was, and who could become, an Albanian (thus, a nonmetropolitan subject of the Italian king), fascist Rome continued to keep in force the pre-invasion Albanian civil code that had been introduced in 1929 under the reign of King Zog. This means that during the period of the fascist monarchical union, a person went on being ascribed Albanian status (*shtetësi*) at birth according to paternal descent (as a primary rule) and to maternal lineage (as the exception), and it meant as well that a foreigner could naturalize and become Albanian on specific conditions.[70] Also, apart from the fact that the expression "*cittadinanza albanese*" (Albanian citizenship) was kept in use by fascist officialdom to refer to the juridical status of the Skipetars within the empire, we have found that, following expansion of Albania's borders in 1941, Albanian citizenship was extended to the populations—the *pertinenti*—of the ex-Yugoslav territories that were annexed, by taking into account the lists of the official registers.[71] As a consequence, Albanian citizenship was acquired *en masse*, and many ex-Yugoslavs became new Italian nonmetropolitan subjects having the right to ask Italy's consular authorities for the special passport that was issued for them and for the Skipetars of the former kingdom of Albania invaded in 1939.[72] Finally and most significantly, some of the radical norms the regime was currently implementing in its East and North African colonies were not fully extended to Albania. According to our sources, we found that the November 1938 legislation touching on mixed-race marriages was not to be fully applied to Italo-Albanian unions[73] and no specific concerns were raised by the fact that the 1940 law relating to *meticci* was completely silent about Italo-Albanian progeny.[74] The reason this radicalized type of state legal racism was not entirely introduced and implemented in Tirana might be found in some of the assertions of Italian Minister of Foreign Affairs Galeazzo Ciano. As he emphasized in April 1939 while speaking on the occasion of the offer of the Skanderbeg Crown, a racial similarity united the Skipetars with the Italians since both were of Aryan origin.[75] This means that, within the regime's racial hierarchy, the "pure and noble" Albanian race held a special position, compared to its African counterparts, like the *Dodecanesini* of the Aegean Islands.

Focusing on the content of this status, one can bring to light other important historical evidence since the Skipetars were gradually granted by the regime a thick status that let them enjoy the highest and most substantial civic position ever awarded to a nonmetropolitan population by fascist (and also liberal) Italy. Apart from being entitled to various civil rights that were also enjoyed by other Italian nonmetropolitan subjects (i.e., religious freedom, equality before the law, individual liberty, inviolability of domicile),[76] the Albanians had the "privilege" of seeing geographic extension of the content of their status from their country to the metropole, and subsequently the unprecedented introduction of equality of certain rights between them and the Italian metropolitans. More particularly, only a few days after the fascist invasion of the country in April 1939, an Italo-Albanian convention was signed in Tirana in which it was clearly stated that the Albanian citizens living in Italy and the Italian metropolitan citizens living in Albania enjoyed all civil and political rights to which they were entitled in their country of origin.[77] Also and most importantly, in December 1942, in line with an additional agreement that introduced "the principle of reciprocity" in citizenship matters, fascist Rome allowed a further civic development since, from that moment on, Italian citizens would enjoy, in Albania, all civil and political rights of the Albanian citizens, whereas in Italy the Skipetars would enjoy all civil and political rights of the metropolitan Italians.[78] In short, "equality" between Albanians and metropolitans was achieved in this respect upon condition of emigration. This explains why, as a fascist official also emphasized at the time, there were Albanian deputies sitting on various benches of the Fascist Senate and of the Chamber of Fasci and Corporations in Rome as well as Italian metropolitans being appointed deputies and senators in Tirana.[79] Clearly, to see a Skipetar in the national chambers of the metropole was something new within the entire history of Italian citizenship.

But why were the Albanians so "privileged"? As evidenced in some of our sources, the ultimate objective of these open citizenship policies was to realize a "more intimate collaboration between the two peoples" across the Adriatic, in particular within the "spiritual union" that had already started taking place following the proclamation of Vittorio Emanuele III as king of Albania, fusion of the Italian and Albanian Armed Forces, establishment of an Albanian Fascist Party and the union between the diplomatic services of the two countries.[80] Citizenship was therefore an additional means to achieve this fascist spiritual union, which was of course directed toward the broad goal of strengthening Mussolini's Italy's international position in the Balkan area. Also, during the Second World War these Albanian citizenship norms were perceived by the regime as a diplomatic tool to be used to implement an anti-British foreign policy. In fact, as stated by fascist officialdom in mid-July 1943, such civic openness regarding the Skipetars was a way of distinguishing Italy's fascist imperial project from the "harsh imperialisms of other nations," especially the "British enemy."[81] Like the 1939 introduction of CIS in the Libyan colony, fascist Albanian citizenship norms were seen as a political measure to send international messages from Palazzo Venezia in Rome.

Obviously, similar to the other nonmetropolitan membership statuses we have studied so far, the relatively thick Albanian citizenship was not exercised fully by the Skipetars because of the peculiar historical context of those years and widespread and profound anti-Italian feelings among the population. A number of factors were to create a very tense atmosphere where exercising any citizenship right was doomed from the beginning: the fascist aggression in establishing and keeping, unilaterally,

an Italo-Albanian monarchical union; the specific and tragic Balkan scenario of the Second World War; the Resistance movement led by Enver
Hoxha from 1941 and the forced Albanization of the newly annexed
ex-Yugoslav lands involving violent repressions against minorities on the
part of Tirana's authorities.[82]

We have now reached the Second World War. Italy has decided to join
the conflict alongside Germany, thinking that the victory of the Axis is
approaching and that other territories and populations can be gained
from the spoils. It is to these specific lands and autochthonous peoples of
Mediterranean Europe that we now turn.

7.2.c. Italy's Occupied and Annexed Lands During World War Two: In France, Monaco, Greece and Yugoslavia

Between 1940 and 1943, Mussolini pursued an aggressive territorial
policy against various European Mediterranean countries, although the
actual outcome of this expansionism was mainly determined by the military contribution of his Nazi ally and by the redistribution of territories
to the junior partner of the Axis.[83] Following the French armistice of
June 1940, Italy first occupied a number of French communes along the
western Italian border (including the city of Menton) and then, from November 1942, after the Anglo-American landing in Africa, extended its
military occupation over the island of Corsica, over a number of French
continental *départements* as well as the Principality of Monaco.[84] Italian
fascist aggression, though, was not limited to France and to the *Rocher*
of the Grimaldi family. Greek and Yugoslav territories were also targeted.
After the Greek military defeat of April 1941 by German troops who had
intervened to rescue the Italians *in extremis*, fascist Rome militarily occupied continental Greece (except Greek Macedonia, which went under
German rule, and Thrace, which was annexed to Bulgaria) as well as the
Ionian, Cyclades and Southern Sporades Islands.[85] Also, between April
and July 1941, with the dismemberment of Yugoslavia, the Italian state
annexed a number of Yugoslav cities, adjacent districts and islands to
create the "Province of Ljubljana" and the "Governorate of Dalmatia"
(inclusive of Zara, ceded to Italy in 1920) as well as to enlarge the "Province of Fiume" (under Italian sovereignty since 1924).[86] Finally, apart
from these annexations, Mussolini's regime was allowed to occupy, partially or totally, two new independent Balkan states: the western and
central parts of Ante Pavelic's State of Croatia (including all Herzegovina
and part of Bosnia), after Ustasha crimes had taken place against civilian
populations and the Axis powers feared that Croatian internal instability
could upset the whole Balkan area; and the entire territory of the State
of Montenegro, whose very short independent life was struck down by

a communist revolt only a few hours after the fascist-supported proclamation of Montenegrin independence in July 1941.[87] In short, by 1943 Mussolini's fascist empire included not only the territories of AOI, Libya, the Dodecanese and Albania but also French, Monegasque, Greek and Yugoslav lands that were either occupied militarily or annexed and enlarged *de jure*. The Mediterranean Sea was almost *mare nostrum*.

Clearly, the territorial expansionism meant that new European populations with differing ethnic, linguistic and religious backgrounds had to be accommodated within the orbit of fascist Rome. From a statistical point of view (and taking estimations and data with great caution), Mussolini's imperial community increased during those years by about eleven million inhabitants.[88] Bearing in mind the previous sections of this chapter, it is pertinent to ask what type of citizenship norms and citizenship-related policies were introduced by the regime to incorporate all these new populations. For the purpose of clarity and conciseness, we first deal with the citizenship issues related to the occupied lands (7.2.c.i), and then turn to those that were annexed (7.2.c.ii).

7.2.c.i. Occupied territories

The people who lived in the Italian occupied territories of France, Greece, Monaco as well as the independent states of Croatia and Montenegro did not become Italian (metropolitan or nonmetropolitan) subjects during the years under study but continued to be "foreign citizens" with respect to the Italian state because their territories were only under Italian occupying authority and were not transferred under Rome's full sovereignty. Like the *Dodecanesini* during the liberal era, the populations of the 1940–1943 occupied lands continued to hold the citizenship status they had held before the invasion of Italian troops. In other words, the inhabitants of occupied France, Monaco and Greece continued to be French, Monegasque and Greek citizens; those living in the Italian zones within the State of Croatia were to hold the new "Croatian citizenship" following Croatian statehood in 1941; the inhabitants of the Montenegrin State had to be defined as "ex-Yugoslav citizens" since the July 1941 Statute of Montenegro (containing new citizenship norms for the small independent Balkan country) never entered into force because of the war context and the domestic turmoil provoked by communist insurgents.[89]

Despite the alien status of all these populations, though, one finds that fascist Rome formulated, discussed and in some cases introduced certain citizenship norms aimed at distinguishing these Mediterranean foreigners from other aliens, not only with the precise objective of preparing the ground for future annexations but also with the more general goal of improving the international stature of fascist Italy (especially in the Balkans) and of helping Italian diplomacy and the army with an additional instrument of indirect expansionism, as we saw in the Dodecanese.

For instance, in 1941, within the context of legislation about mixed-race marriages that also required the prior approval of the Ministry of the Interior for formal unions between Italian metropolitan citizens and foreigners, Italian authorities raised the question of the nationality of the inhabitants of those French communes occupied in 1940 along Italy's borders (i.e., Alpes-Maritimes, Basses- and Hautes-Alpes, Savoy) and discussed whether these inhabitants were to be treated as aliens *tout court* and therefore obliged to abide by this norm. Fascist officialdom was very quick to resolve this issue, and with the aim of granting these French inhabitants a special status that would differentiate them from other aliens, it classified them as *Italiani non regnicoli* and exempted them from the rule.[90] As a result, the basket of the *non regnicoli*, which was already full of different populations—as we saw in Chapter Three concerning the liberal period—was filled by the fascist regime with additional French citizens. As in the pre-1922 years, though, some uncertainty continued to persist among the authorities as to extension of this category: whereas the French inhabitants of occupied Nice and Alpes-Maritimes were regarded as ethnically Italian, doubts were raised about those of occupied Savoy. Unfortunately, archival documentation is lacunary. However, we know that even though Gabap (Gabinetto-Armistizio Pace) pointed out that Savoy had actually been excluded in a 1936 circular of the Presidency of the Council of Ministers containing the list of lands inhabited by potential *non regnicoli*, other Italian authorities (i.e., the Ministry of the Interior and the *Servizio affari privati* within the Ministry of Foreign Affairs) were in favor of an extensive interpretation that stretched this legal category to include the *Savoyards* as well. This was due to contingent political reasons linked to the occupation and to the fascist imperial project: fascist authorities were not willing to make a distinction of treatment within the populace of an occupied territory because they wanted to avoid inappropriate differences of status that could alienate the inhabitants even further.[91]

Interestingly, in the course of the following year, the same issue was to be raised in occupied Greece as well. Faced with the identical bureaucratic question concerning, in this case, Italo-Greek marriages, the *Ufficio affari civili delle Jonie*—established *in loco* by the fascist regime—proposed in 1942 to consider the natives of the Ionian Islands as *non regnicoli*.[92] An Italian juridical expert of the Ministry of Foreign Affairs argued that this decision was rather premature[93]; however, the fact that some fascist authorities working on the spot contemplated further extension of this category of special foreigners to incorporate the Greeks of the occupied territories demonstrates the significance, for the Italian state, of distinguishing the populations of the occupied lands from other aliens because the former were now living under the aegis of Rome.

By moving, at this point, to Ante Pavelic's Croatia and to the independent Kingdom of Montenegro, we can find additional citizenship issues and policies pointing in various ways to the regime's determination to use citizenship as a tool to support the cause of fascist imperial territorial projects in the Balkans. In August 1941, Minister of Foreign Affairs Ciano wrote to the legation in Zagreb to express Italy's satisfaction about the acceptance by the Croatian government of the Italian offer to extend Italy's consular assistance over the numerous Croat nationals living abroad who were resident in those countries where Zagreb did not have yet its own diplomatic representative authorities. This consular assistance, especially important for those who wanted to repatriate and needed travel documents, concerned Croatians living in nonoccupied France, Greece, Portugal, Spain and Morocco as well as in Brazil, Chile, Argentina, Uruguay, Peru and Bolivia.[94] The importance given by the fascist regime to extension of its assistance over the Croatians living as far away as Latin America attracted our attention because, as demonstrated by the following passage, fascist Italy was determined to show its openness vis-à-vis the Croat communities living abroad as the latter could become important intermediaries and help, indirectly, fascist foreign policy objectives.

There is an undoubted interest on our part to come to the aid of this Croatian, who first turned to us asking for assistance, because he is a first breach in the Croatian and Dalmatian community resident in Chile which seems to be distinctly hostile to us. I wish in fact to obtain from him confidential information that could be necessary in the course of time, and possibly, to set him to do as well some work of persuasion among his compatriots.[95]

Even an apparently minor consular measure was perceived by the fascist regime as useful to communicate with, help and eventually get information from these ex-Yugoslavs for evident reasons of instrumentality.

With respect to the citizenship policies related to the inhabitants of the independent Kingdom of Montenegro, one can single out further evidence of historical importance. As we said, the Montenegrins were alien citizens vis-à-vis the Italian occupants. However, together with creation of an independent kingdom under the Petrovic dynasty within the orbit of Rome, the regime formulated not only the 1941 statute of the new Balkan state but also a bilateral agreement between Rome and Cettigne incorporating a citizenship policy for the *Montenegrini* that was identical to the one applied in Albania from the end of 1942. Neither document concerning Montenegro entered into force because of the revolt of July 1941; however, from a comparative perspective, it is instructive to learn that the citizens of the new Montenegrin state would have enjoyed basically the same reciprocity of civil and political rights with the Italian metropolitans to which the Albanians would be entitled from the subsequent year.[96] This significant historical discovery on the potentially high civic status that the fascist regime attempted to reserve for the *Montenegrini* demonstrates—as in the Albanian case study—the importance of Montenegro within fascist Balkan foreign policy. Marco Giurovic went straight to the point when he wrote in a contemporary report that the small Balkan country was a state of Orthodox Slavs from which Italy could extend its influence over the whole Balkan region. Albania was also crucial for the fascist regime, but it was not a Slav country—hence the importance of Montenegro.[97]

7.2.c.ii. Annexed territories

The populations of the *occupied* territories were foreigners with respect to the fascist state, but those living in the ex-Yugoslav *annexed* lands between 1941 and 1943 held a more complicated citizenship status—from a historical and juridical point of view—owing to strong uncertainties caused by the war context. Two factors are certain: the inhabitants of the city of Zara (annexed in 1920) had acquired Italian metropolitan citizenship in accordance with the Treaty of St. Germain unless opting for other citizenship; and the same metropolitan status was extended to the people of Fiume (annexed in 1924) on the basis of the international agreements of Rome, Rapallo and Nettuno. Therefore, when Italy unilaterally annexed the other former Yugoslav lands in 1941, a metropolitan citizenship link united already fascist Rome with some inhabitants of the new Governorate of Dalmatia (notably those of Zara) as well as with those living in the old province of Fiume.[98]

Having said this, whereas the *status civitatis* of the *Zaresi* and *Fiumani* was clearly defined and continued to be held by those inhabitants during the Second World War, the civic position of the ex-Yugoslavs who lived in the 1941 territories remained unclear for the entire period of fascist annexation. Of course the Italian inhabitants of these lands, who already had Italian citizenship before the annexation took place, continued to hold this status; however, for the rest of the population, the situation remained blurred. Eventually, they were supposed to become Italian metropolitan citizens as a fascist nationality law was actually under study from May 1941. But because of the unstable war context, the need to postpone final approval after the end of the conflict and the collapse of Mussolini's regime in July 1943, this citizenship policy was never made into law, and consequently the status of the 1941 ex-Yugoslav citizens remained undetermined.[99]

Beyond the details provided here, it is important to explore the citizenship policy that the fascist regime had in mind for these Balkan populations despite the various projects discussed from May 1941 until June 1943 never being approved. One significant point that must be stressed is that contrary to the autochthonous peoples studied so far in our chapter, these former Yugoslavs would have been granted *metropolitan* citizenship rather than nonmetropolitan status. After all, their lands were now an integral part of Italian metropolitan territory, which with the annexation expanded eastward. This explains why the issue was so sensitive at the time and why the fascist regime incorporated this Balkan citizenship policy into the complex, and notoriously aggressive, program of "forced italianization," which—much more than in the Dodecanese—was supposed to realize the ambitious objective of transforming foreign (Slav) regions into completely Italian provinces. Rodogno's findings provide evidence on the importance the regime gave to the italianization of these zones and how fascist Rome attempted, at least until the summer of 1942, to achieve the ethnic homogenization of these new lands through various measures: political and administrative purges of ex-Yugoslav civil servants and school teachers; introduction of Italian as the official language within the administration; removal of the Slav and Habsburg pasts through destruction of monuments and changes of place names; forced expulsion of autochthonous peoples; transfer of German minorities; fascistization of the remaining loyal population through schooling and the Fascist Party; and projects of Italian metropolitan emigration to the new lands.[100] Our sources confirm that citizenship policies were meant to achieve the same radical goal: italianization of the Italian kingdom's new ex-Yugoslav population.

How could this political objective be brought about? The unanimously agreed formula was to propose very restrictive citizenship rules that, by making attribution and acquisition of Italian citizenship a highly selective process, would transform these recently annexed lands into territories eventually inhabited only by Italian metropolitan citizens who would be loyal to Italy and to the fascist regime. Historical evidence abounds in this respect. For instance, in a project concerning annexed Dalmatia (formulated by Governor Giuseppe Bastianini and sent to the Presidency of the Council of Ministers in August 1941), the official proposed to attribute Italian metropolitan citizenship, automatically, only to those former Yugoslavs resident in the annexed province who fulfilled the combined restrictive criteria of *jus soli* and residence of both parents at the moment of the child's birth. Also, if the territorial principle did not apply, then the individual had to have at least fifteen years of residence. As argued by Bastianini, these rigorous criteria were necessary to achieve the *italianità* of those Adriatic regions, bearing in mind the local political situation. In fact, in the Governorate of Dalmatia, anti-Italian feelings and pro-Croatian irredentist aspirations were serious menaces undermining

Italian fascist rule; and in the other annexed territories, the forced expulsion of ex-Yugoslavs carried out by the regime for political reasons had led to strong opposition by the local populace. Therefore, only through a highly exclusionary selection of potentially "good" metropolitan citizens could fascist Rome achieve its goal. More to the point, even though the relatively open rule concerning acquisition of Italian metropolitan status *par option* (by opting) was incorporated into the project, Bastianini diluted it by setting significant restrictions: the resident ex-Yugoslav had to have "good civil and political behavior" as well as "being able to use the Italian language correctly." In other words, fascist conformism and linguistic homogeneity were seen as appropriate principles that the fascist state could have used to inhibit acquisition of Italian metropolitan status by the "unworthy."[101] Finally, in a further proposal put forward by Italy's Ministry of the Interior and concerning the three 1941 annexed territories together, an additional norm was contemplated to give the right to local prefects to deprive a person of acquired Italian metropolitan status "for grave reasons"—with automatic expulsion of that stateless individual from the territory of the kingdom.[102] The totalitarian practice of depriving a person of his or her nationality would therefore have been applied in the annexed lands (as it was, already, in the peninsula).[103]

The ultimate goal of all these citizenship norms was to make sure that the following scenario did not take place: "[A politics of citizenship that] would create, besides a large number of Italian citizens who do not want to be Italian, [...] even worse, a number no less indifferent of citizens who, for political reasons, cannot, indeed must not, become Italian citizens."[104]

The reason for these concerns lay in the fact that, as already emphasized, the new annexed regions were not just part of the "second" Roman Empire but also of the metropole. As a result, the issue of so-called *allogeni* (i.e., inhabitants who did not share the linguistic and cultural background of the majority) was crucial because, as Mussolini enunciated in June 1941, "States must strive to achieve the maximum of their ethnic and spiritual unity so as to make the three factors of race, nation and State coincide at one point."[105] Slav populations could be openly incorporated within the empire as nonmetropolitan members. This is what the case of the Montenegrins, for instance, clearly tells us. However, Slavs could not become part of the metropolitan *ethnie* so easily. There was no space for minorities in Mussolini's metropole.

To conclude this entire section concerning the European populations who lived under the aegis of fascist Rome, we can argue that the regime's appetite for lands in Mediterranean Europe extended the fascist citizenship system to accommodate an overwhelming variety of almost thirteen million inhabitants. The Aegeans and the Albanians were granted nonmetropolitan status that was clearly in contrast with that held by their African counterparts. In fact, the natives of the African continent and the peoples who originated from Europe had to be distinguished within the fascist empire: fascist ideology required it, although such distinction between Europeans and African nonmetropolitan subjects had already been a characteristic of the liberal years too. Moreover, the populations of the territories occupied during the Second World War were regarded as special foreigners by Mussolini's Rome because Frenchmen, Monegasques, Greeks, Croatians and Montenegrins were living within its orbit and, after the victory, would have eventually become part of the empire. Finally, the nationals of the three annexed ex-Yugoslav territories were supposed to become Italian metropolitan citizens and therefore had to be selected in a fascist way to be worthy of this civic title. All together—metropolitan Italians, European nonmetropolitan subjects, European special aliens and African nonmetropolitan subjects—constituted the human mosaic of the Italian empire. The Duce's dream of creating a second Roman empire around *mare nostrum* was gradually being realized. It is the ideological impact of the myth of ancient Rome on the regime's citizenship discourse as well as further fascist official rhetoric that we shall now explore in comparison with pre-1922 arguments.

7.3. FROM ROME TO AFRICA TO MEDITERRANEAN EUROPE: CITIZENSHIP DISCOURSES IN MUSSOLINI'S *COMUNITÀ IMPERIALE*

On the basis of existing literature, it is well known that the myth of ancient colonial Rome, already present at times within the cultural and ideological political *imaginaire* of liberal Italy, was transformed into a systematic cult during the fascist ventennium.[106] Thanks to the unprecedented persistent use of basically all channels of mass communication available at the time (i.e., theatrical speeches by the Duce in crowded squares, cinematography, radio programs, press articles and hyperbolic iconography), the regime attempted to transmit to the masses a "sacralized political liturgy" that, with the help of the "mythological credo" of the Idea of Rome (including its symbols, references and rites), would contribute to the Italians' conversion to fascism as a lay religion, to their union around the same political "faith" and to consolidation of fascist power. Unlike pre-1922 Italy, Mussolini's regime regarded the Roman paradigm as a primary pillar of fascist ideology and culture to be used to mold the masses.[107]

As we saw in Chapter Five, the little-known impact of the Roman myth on the formulation of the citizenship policies introduced during the liberal epoch vis-à-vis Italy's nonmetropolitan populations was not really significant, quantitatively, as it was actually overcome by the stronger influence of nineteenth-century liberal idea on the European civilizing mission overseas. In our sources we also found that the Roman paradigm was sometimes enriched in pre-1922 Italy with additional sporadic references to the ancient Maritime Republics of Venice, Pisa, Genoa and Amalfi. Keeping this in mind, we find it pertinent to ask how and to what extent the fascist cult of *romanità* was reflected in the citizenship policies and discourses that the regime upheld to incorporate its nonmetropolitan autochthonous inhabitants.

As confirmed by our findings, the Idea of Rome was such a central and diffused component within fascism that, contrary to the liberal era, the myth was used frequently during the ventennium in thinking and talking about the membership status of the natives living in Italy's colonies and territories. Moreover, the way in which fascist officialdom evoked the Roman "model" when faced with the issue of accommodating its multiethnic autochthonous populations differed from the pre-1922 decades by virtue of a typically fascist rhetorical and systematically propagandistic style.

For instance, as early as 1924, in a speech pronounced in the Foro Romano, the Duce referred explicitly to the expansion of ancient Rome and to how the ancient Romans had wisely combined "force" and "citizenship policies" to realize their imperial project; citizenship was therefore an important instrument of ancient Roman foreign policy that Mussolini was also determined to use, to make the fascist dream of reestablishing a historical Roman empire come true. This is what the Duce argued:

The fate of humanity was decided here and Rome pursued her dream by following a program of force which was never separated by lines of great wisdom. Justly, Rome wanted to weaken the peoples who were opposed to her; justly, she was severe in the conduct of war.[...] But when the populations recognized her superiority, she welcomed them into her womb; made them citizens of her city; and bestowed upon them legislation [...] which is still with us today, gentlemen! She made the peoples take part in her civilization and, she respected their customs and religion.[108]

Twelve years later, on the occasion of the proclamation of the Italian empire in May 1936, Mussolini could send a similar message by saying to the crowds, convened under his balcony in Piazza Venezia, that fascist Italy was following ancient Rome, which, "after having won, assimilate[d] the peoples to her destiny."[109]

The explicit reference to the ancient Roman "predecessor" was repeatedly made not only by the head of fascism but also by other executive and state authorities dealing with citizenship issues throughout the ventennium. To describe, in a highly rhetoric fascist style, the enthusiasm of a number of Muslim Libyans of Derna, Bengasi, Misurata and Tripoli who had been granted CIS (introduced by the regime in 1939), Governor Italo Balbo sent a telegram to Mussolini on 22 April of that year, explicitly evoking Roman antiquity and the spiritual link that had united the Eternal City to the ancient multiethnic populations conquered during the imperial epoch. As he wrote: "In your name, DUCE, these masses [of Libyans] begin to be animated by a new consciousness, and it is not rhetorical language to affirm that it is the same consciousness which rallied around Rome the most diverse peoples of its imperial conquests."[110]

Also, on the occasion of the offer of the Skanderbeg Crown to Vittorio Emanuele III, which, as we saw, transformed the Skipetars into subjects of the Italian king, the president of the Chamber of Fasci could not avoid evoking the "traditional" place of the Albanian nation within Italian imperial history since the times of the ancient Romans. As he put it:

Resolute, thanks to its sober and brave people,
Proud of its heroic and war-like traditions,
Taking part, since the days of Rome, in the imperial fortunes of Italy,
The Albanian Nation will now no longer stop on its way.[111]

Interestingly, this Roman intellectual paradigm was constantly in the mind of fascist officialdom not only to achieve the ancient model's colonial *grandeur* but also to avoid the institutional collapse that led to the fall of the Roman Empire in the fifth century. In this respect, the "erroneous" citizenship norms that the ancient Romans introduced and that, in the eyes of the fascists, contributed to the end of their ancient imperial adventures were not to be repeated by Mussolini's Italy. For instance, in discussing the type of citizenship status that should pertain to the Libyans once the annexation of the four northern provinces to fascist Italy took place, an Italian authority argued that "the fall of Rome began with the granting of Roman citizenship to the barbarians; the decadence of today's France originates, among various causes, from the assimilation of negroes. If fascist Italy too was to get on that road, its fate might not be different."[112] For this reason, Italian metropolitan citizenship should not be extended by the fascist regime to its North African natives and only a more limited status, be introduced for them.

This same ancient civic error, made by the Romans in olden times, was also criticized in greater detail in a propaganda journal of the regime that directly attacked the "monstrous" Edict of Caracalla (C.E. 212), granting full status to all nonmetropolitans of the provinces.[113] Despite the fact that the old Roman emperor had introduced these citizenship norms for sound political and fiscal reasons (i.e., to acquire new support among the provincials as well as extending inheritance taxes among the *novi cives*), the fascist journal accused the "semi-barbarous" Caracalla—"African by race, Celt by morals"—of introducing a civic policy that led ultimately to the mixing of populations and the decline of the Italic civilization. This great political mistake had to be avoided by fascist Rome.[114]

Another significant aspect of comparison with the pre-1922 references to the myth of Rome is that, during fascism (and contrary to the liberal era), a special link was drawn between "*romanità* at home" (in the metropole) and "*romanità* abroad" (in the overseas empire), between a fascist Roman totalitarian state at home and a fascist Roman imperialistic mission abroad. As a contemporary scholar put it in discussing the creation of AOI and introduction of unifying subjecthood status for all East African natives, these policies were being inspired by the "Roman genius which, as in the reconstitution of the New Italy, [was] shining immortal light through the foundation and the organization of the Empire too."[115] Ancient Rome was therefore the model inspiring both the fascist revolution at home (leading to a New Italy) and the fascist aggressive expansionism abroad (leading to empire and a new world order). These two apparently unrelated concepts (i.e., *romanità* in the peninsula and *romanità* overseas) were peculiarly united throughout the ventennium. The aspect of the multifaceted myth of Rome that we also saw in liberal Italy and that was related to the notion of "imperial power" came to be inextricably linked to another facet of the same Roman myth that in contrast had been absent in the pre-1922 decades: the ancient concepts of *disciplina* and *virtus romana* (i.e., discipline, justice, law, order and cult of the state), which would have transformed the Italians into a strong and disciplined nation, ready for, and deserving of, an everlasting empire. For the fascist regime, the latter element (*disciplina/virtus*) was the prerequisite of the former (imperial power) because without a totalitarian transformation of the Italian people and the Italian state, any imperial aspiration would be disastrous, as in pre-fascist Italy. So the ancient "Roman Revolution" that in old times had transformed an outdated republican constitutionalism into an imperialistic dictatorship under Caesar and Augustus had a parallel with the "Fascist Revolution" whose objective was to achieve and link totalitarianism in the metropole with imperialism abroad. The fascist cult of *romanità* was thus a "global model" that had to be applied in everyday life by the individual, the Party, the whole civil society and the state *as well as* being projected overseas to spread ancient Roman virtues and values across the world.[116]

In relation to this last point, another comparative element reflected in the citizenship discourse concerning fascist Italy's nonmetropolitan peoples should also be discussed further: reference to civilization. As we saw, the differentiated system of *status civitatis* introduced during fascism vis-à-vis its autochthonous inhabitants was formulated, as in the liberal decades, by taking into account the perceived more-or-less-backward civilizational levels of the natives with the objective of leading them toward a superior *civiltà*. The Imperial Community of Rome (*la communità imperiale di Roma*, this Italian expression being used systematically at the time) was a *corpus misticum* that, according to contemporary writers, accommodated through a well-developed civic hierarchy a number of native peoples whose status varied according to geography, race, social customs and morals. Starting from the highest membership status and moving down the civic ladder, one encountered Italian metropolitans first; then the Albanians; some steps below, the *Dodecanesini*; further down, the Libyans; and at the bottom, the subjects of AOI.[117] However, the civilization that the regime wanted to expand among all these autochthones was a fascist concept of *civiltà*, a new and revolutionary idea that distinguished post-1922 Italy from the *Italietta* (weak and little Italy) of the liberal epoch.[118] In particular, as stated in a propaganda journal of the regime, fascism had "its own" notion of civilization:

To Fascism civilization means both the conquest by a people of the supreme values of the spirit—being expressed in the political, civil, legal, moral and social life [of a country]— [...] and, at the same time, the opportunity for expansion and the will to give to the world the fruit of the achieved victories.[...] Fascist civilization [...] is [...] a perpetual act of conquest of the spirit over nature, of a people's genius over its epoch, of a nation's faculties over history. This conquest is realized in the field of arts and thought, of science and social relations: and takes naturally its full form in the system of the State, ultimate expression of the moral, civil and intellectual organization of a people.[119]

Thus, the concept of civilizing mission was shared by liberal and post-1922 Italies, but there were significant differences between the two periods. Mancini and other liberal authorities had persistently upheld the nineteenth-century liberal assumption of the imperial duty to expand a Western or European civilization among backward peoples; Mussolini's regime wanted to spread totalitarianism and other related aggressive fascist tenets around the world, or to use a contemporary term drawn from fascist (and Nazi) vocabulary, across Italy's *spazio vitale*, *Lebensraum*, vital space.[120] Moreover, especially from the 1930s onward, the notion of "low civilization" came to be seen more and more in the colonial context as a fixed and unalterable concept incapable of any "evolution."[121] As a consequence, native acquisition of metropolitan citizenship was to be avoided at all costs, and their future civic development seen as a mere utopian project. Finally, with the radicalized racist turn of 1936, it is evident that the increasing institutionalization of Aryanism would exclude the Jews from this racial fascist hierarchy, not only in the metropole but also in the empire—although in different ways and to differing degrees according to the local context of the imperial territory involved.[122]

To conclude our comparative analysis, we can also add that explicit mentioning of the ancient Roman predecessor by fascist officialdom was accompanied, as in the liberal decades, by short references to the old Italian Republics, especially when thinking and talking about the nonmetropolitan citizens of the Eastern Mediterranean territories. For instance, on the occasion of the fusion of the Italian and Albanian armies in 1939, leaving the Skipetars and the metropolitan citizens of the Kingdom of Italy fighting and dying for the same fascist cause as soldiers of the same monarch, *camerata* (comrade) Giuseppe Francesco Ferrari addressed the senatorial commission to make a clear reference to the way Italy and its civilization would be resurrected in the Orient "for the third time," after *Roma imperiale* (imperial Rome) and *le Repubbliche marinare* (the maritime Republics).[123] Our findings, though, also demonstrate that the fascist regime was much more aggressive than liberal governments in alluding to what has been called "the strategy of occupying Time," aimed at making a twenty-year-old regime legendary, by inserting it within a millenarian history that started with ancient Rome, continued with the Maritime Republics and, by projecting it into the future, gave to it a sense of "eternity" and "immortality."[124]

7.4. CONCLUSION

Between 1922 and 1943, Mussolini's regime put into place an elaborate citizenship system linking roughly ten million Africans and thirteen million Europeans to fascist Rome. Building on what the liberal predecessors had already done, and introducing new fascist modifications to take into account totalitarian and radically racist axioms, fascist Italy established an empire and accommodated all its overseas populations according to geographic location, civilizational level, skin color, loyalty, and state foreign policy objectives. As a result of all these historical civic developments, the contours and the content of the notion of *italianità*—as drawn and shaped by the numerous citizenship policies and discourses of the regime—could not remain similar to those that had emerged in liberal Italy, and in fact they started evolving and being modified. As in the liberal epoch, the concept of Italianness continued to be enriched by metropolitan and nonmetropolitan dimensions. However, throughout the fascist ventennium both dimensions came to be extended geographically so as to incorporate new territories and populations. Moreover, to be Italian (metropolitan and nonmetropolitan) subjects soon entailed, in different levels and degrees, a process of fascistization that, shaped and directed by an increasingly omnipresent regime, aimed at totalitarian transformations of the notions under consideration, with the ultimate goal of exporting the Fascist Revolution from Italy to its empire, and to the outside world.

As we have also tried to demonstrate in this chapter, the "Idea of Rome"—reflected in political discourse concerning the populations of the fascist empire—shared some analogy with the counterpart of the liberal era. Yet as it was transformed into a cult, it came to be characterized by certain historical specificities that made the myth of *romanità* a central and essential tenet of *italianità*—for the first time, within Italy's post-unification national history. Eventually, the fascist imperial project of realizing after victory what the fifth century Roman poet Rutilius Namatianus had written about ancient Rome—"*Fecisti patriam diversis gentibus unam*" (From differing peoples you have made one homeland)—remained a dream.[125] Mussolini, "founder of the Italian empire" and holding this self-bestowed honorary title with his well-known pride, aimed eventually at getting rid of the Savoy monarch and himself becoming the emperor of his multiethnic, multireligious and multilingual *comunità imperiale*. History, though, turned out different, and "Benito *il Duce*" never became "Benito *Augusto Imperatore*." On 25 July 1943, Mussolini was dismissed, the fascist regime collapsed and with the subsequent armistice and change of military alliances the peninsula went through a "war of Liberation" (for some), a "civil war" (for others), to which we shall devote our next chapter concerning citizenship and identity issues in Italy during the six hundred days of the Republic of Salò.

CHAPTER EIGHT

The Armistice of 8 September, Brindisi and Salò

Reflections on Citizenship Issues (1943–1945)

On 8 September 1943, in the midst of the Second World War, the octogenarian institution of Italian national citizenship—which, as we saw, first united the people of the peninsula in 1861—was profoundly and seriously shaken. National citizenship, a special spiritual link vertically binding all citizens to a head of a state and horizontally creating a well defined group of co-citizens, was questioned from a variety of fronts, giving rise to some of the most fundamental, and ever since controversial, issues within the entire history of Italian post-unification civic tradition. Several defining tenets underlying the notion of citizenship, such as the concept of allegiance, the idea of *patria* (homeland), the principle of solidarity among co-nationals and the ideal of sacrificing one's life for the country if necessary, were completely upset.

The purpose of this chapter, ending Part Two of the book, is to focus on the two dramatic years that followed this crucial phase of the Second World War—1943 through 1945—by using the lens of citizenship and identity and by taking the whole peninsula as our geographic and political point of analysis. In this way, citizenship issues will be studied by integrating the history of "the Italians who won" (i.e., the antifascist Resistance movement) with the history of "the Italians who lost" (the fascists of the Republic of Salò) without forgetting "the Italy of all the others."[1] These two contentious years of Italian national history have been the subject of polemical debates among the protagonists as well as extensive research by academics, triggering a rich and growing literature.[2] No study, though, has looked at those unique months by placing special emphasis on the important prism of national citizenship; hence, this chapter is intended to cast new and different light on old and often politicized themes. Also, as our pages cover the final period concluding our history of national citizenship during fascism up to 1945, they allow us to shed light on fundamental citizenship aspects that will provide the reader with the essential background to understand the origins and the first developments of postwar Italian democratic *status civitatis*, to be analyzed in the next and last chapter of the book.

8.1. HISTORICAL AND INSTITUTIONAL CONTEXT: FROM PALAZZO VENEZIA IN ROME (25 JULY 1943) TO PIAZZALE LORETO IN MILAN (29 APRIL 1945)

Within a tense atmosphere of war weariness and imminent military defeat of the Italian Army by British and American forces that reached Sicily in June 1943, Benito Mussolini—in power for more than twenty years—was dismissed in a famous Grand Council meeting of 25 July; following his arrest by Italian *carabinieri*, he was replaced by Marshal Pietro Badoglio, who was appointed head of the government by the king, Vittorio Emanuele III. In the meantime, as the fighting continued and the Anglo-Americans prepared to invade the Italian mainland, secret military negotiations were taking place between the Italian high military command and the allied general headquarters in England and Sicily, ending with the signing of an armistice on 3 September, to be made public five days later, when the surrender terms were announced to the Italian population by a radio broadcast of Prime Minister Badoglio.[3]

German feelings regarding the treachery of the Axis junior partner were well summarized by the words of Nazi leader Joseph Goebbels: "The Duce will enter history as the last Roman, but behind his massive figure a gypsy people has gone to rot. We ought to have realized that sooner."[4] As expected, the Nazi reaction to the Italian surrender was rapid and violent, and within a few days the Germans proceeded with military occupation of the peninsula and several territories of the Italian empire. Hitler's troops occupied Rome as well as northern and central Italy down to Naples; established two special zones of operation around the Alps and on the Eastern Italian borders facing the Adriatic; and occupied Albania, Montenegro and the territories of the Governorate of Dalmatia.[5]

Meanwhile, for fear of being captured by the Nazis, the Italian king, Badoglio and the country's highest military officials left Rome and, after moving precipitately to the Southern city of Brindisi (where no foreign troops had yet arrived), transferred the royal court to a territory that was still under Italian control. Here, they set up a temporary government to run what would soon be known as the Kingdom of the South (with Salerno as its provisional capital), and a few days after their arrival they found themselves under the increasing decision-making authority of the Allied Military Government (AMG) and the Allied Control Commission (ACC), both established in the South of the peninsula.

The institutional picture of the country, though, was not complete because the "defunct" Mussolini—as he personally defined himself during the days of his imprisonment after arrest—was rescued by German parachute troops from the Italian prison in Gran Sasso on 13 September; once back on the political stage, he announced from Radio Munich the establishment of a neo-fascist Italian government.[6] The latter was to take a republican form and, established in October in northern Italy under the direct control of German occupying forces, was named officially Repubblica Sociale Italiana (RSI) the following December. It lasted six hundred days. Its ministries were scattered within a geographic area that included the city of Salò on the lake of Garda, the lagoon of Venice, the lake of Como and several other towns in Lombardy and Veneto.[7]

In short, the observer who was in the Italian peninsula during those days was faced with the following situation. There was *one* Italian state, represented by King Vittorio Emanuele III, and from June 1944 by his son, Prince Umberto, appointed Lieutenant General of the Realm and exercising all royal prerogatives. This state was recognized internationally and, although formally sovereign, had its political, military and diplomatic powers seriously limited by British and American interference as a result of the surrender terms and the Allies' military occupation. Apart from this monarchical state entity, one then found *two* rival governmental authorities. On one side there was the government of the Italian state under allied supervision, headed by Prime Minister Badoglio, and subsequently from June 1944 by Ivanoe Bonomi. This was a government that eventually included the six underground antifascist parties (Liberal, Democratic Labor, Christian Democrat, Action, Socialist and Communist) that, after clandestine activity and with the return of civil liberties, proclaimed themselves the Committee of National Liberation and incited the Italians into "struggle" and "resistance" against fascism. On the other side was a de facto government (and not a state), represented by the Italian Social Republic of Mussolini and basically a *longa manus* of Hitler since Salò was under the political, military and diplomatic control of the Third Reich.[8]

Clearly, in the face of such an international and domestic scenario, one could well share the comment of the Italian partisan Emanuele Artom, also noted by the historian Claudio Pavone: "Half Italy is German, half is English and there is no longer an Italian Italy."[9] "Italian Italy," though, had not disappeared; transformed into a battlefield, it was being covered not only by the rubble of the Second World War but also by the ashes of an Italian national civil conflict that was to last for twenty more months and lead as well to the execution of Mussolini by communist partisan forces and to the macabre exposition of the Duce's corpse in Piazzale Loreto, in Milan, on 29 April 1945.[10] The fascist era was finally over. Its scars were not.

In the next section we explore and discuss the first significant citizenship issue that emerged right after the armistice of 8 September.

8.2. WHEN A KING RUNS AWAY: THE NOTION OF SUBJECTHOOD AND THE "ALLEGIANCE-PROTECTION BINOMIAL"

As we saw in Chapter One, from a theoretical point of view the concept of monarchical subjecthood is based on the fundamental principle of allegiance that the subjects owe to their monarch, and according to which the sovereign in return provides protection and guardianship. This special abstract relationship, created around what we call the "allegiance-protection binomial," draws its origins from the feudal epoch, and despite being an imaginary link, it distinguishes in a very clear way the subjects of a monarchical state from its aliens, the nonsubjects.[11]

The reader recalls that in 1943 this juridical bond united the Italians with the Savoy King Vittorio Emanuele III, grandchild of the first monarch of unified Italy, Vittorio Emanuele II, on the throne since 1900. Following the armistice of 8 September, though, Italian monarchical subjecthood was gravely undermined since, to start with, the Italian king gave an important historical twist to the whole concept by severely upsetting these notions of protection and guardianship. On the morning after announcement of the surrender terms by Prime Minister Badoglio, the Italian monarch fled to the south aboard his royal car together with Queen Elena and Prince Umberto, followed by the head of government and other military officials. The fact that a king runs away to avoid being captured (in this case by the Nazi Germans) is not so much the central issue here since, arguably, kings have to avoid being taken by the enemy during an international conflict, in the name of the well established historical and legal principle of the continuity of statehood. Speaking from exile in Portugal in 1958, former King Umberto II, son of Vittorio Emanuele III, emphasized this point in explaining the major reason his father was pushed to leave Rome on that tragic occasion in 1943: German Marshal Albert Kesselring had already decided on the evening of 8 September to arrest the members of the royal family (and the government) and send them to Germany, as the Nazis had already done with the king's daughter Mafalda, deported to the lager of Buchenwald in September 1943 and killed there by an airstrike in 1944.[12] In those dramatic hours following the broadcast of the armistice, the king thought therefore of appealing to the *fictio juris* of moving the court and the legitimate government to an Italian city that was still free from foreign occupation, in order to avoid being taken to Berlin, and to guarantee the constitutional continuity and functioning of the Italian state.[13]

However—and this is the key point of the whole citizenship question under study—even though "the departure [of the monarch] was an absolute necessity [...] a precise duty," as Umberto II reiterated in another interview,[14] the problem is that the royal transfer to the south was accomplished without giving the Italian army and the entire citizenry around the peninsula clear and unequivocal instructions on the prosecution of the war. The king fled leaving the nation defenseless. It is this unprecedented (even though indirect) *act of abandonment by a head of a state vis-à-vis an entire unprotected population of subjects* that deserves academic attention, from a citizenship perspective, without falling into fruitless and politicized polemics that, on the contrary, have often poisoned the debates in Italy.

The general historical events surrounding the king's acts and responsibilities have already been extensively studied in various important monographic works of military and international history, where all the stages of the gigantic institutional, political and moral crisis of 8 September have been documented and analyzed in great detail.[15] What interests us here is to narrow down the focus of the analysis and go over those unique days of Italian national history by concentrating on the dilemmas, the ambiguities, the decisions, the immediate reactions and the consequences that touched, directly or indirectly, on the theoretical monarchical tenets of guardianship and protection mentioned earlier. For this specific historical examination, we have relied largely on Elena Aga Rossi's findings and conclusions since, arguably, they are the most comprehensive to date, being based not only on Italian archival sources but also on the much richer British and American primary documentation generally neglected by Italian historians.[16] Let us explore and discuss them.

The moral, political and military responsibility of the head of the Italian state (shared by Badoglio and Italy's high military commands) stemmed precisely from the signing of an armistice that was accepted without preparing the country's armed forces for a change of military front, and that was even negotiated with the Western Allies while cooperating with the Germans at the same time until the very last day. This was a dangerous ambiguity that lasted throughout the entire period of the diplomatic and military negotiations preceding the signing of the surrender. It was to emerge tragically in the ambiguous words used to announce the armistice to the Italian army and to the population at large. And it was to continue, once the king had fled to the south, during the crucial hours following announcement of the cessation of hostilities.[17]

Until 8 September, the Italian monarch and his government attempted to keep both doors open—the Anglo-American door on one side and the German door on the other—pretending fidelity to the Axis and seeking contact with the Western powers. In this way, Italian state authorities thought of signing an armistice with the forces of (what was already called since 1942) the United Nations, should the imminent landing of allied troops on the Italian mainland be so massive as to push the Germans to retreat, or in the opposite case of disavowing the surrender negotiations and continuing fighting alongside the Nazis. This ambivalent attitude was then mirrored in the written correspondence of Italian General Vittorio Ambrosio, communicating the text of the surrender to the national armed forces as well as in the radio message of Marshal Badoglio to the Italians, addressing the same issue. As a result, very vague directives were given to the Italian soldiers because the latter were told to stop fighting against British and American troops and only "to react" to any possible German attack, without taking any initiative of organized military resistance vis-à-vis the former Nazi ally. Italy's highest state institutions decided, therefore, to maintain a passive military attitude (because no orders were transmitted to take the offensive as the surrender terms required) and not to act, while waiting to see how the Germans would first behave in response to the Italian "treachery." The consequence was great uncertainty and disorientation among the army, the navy and the air forces as well as loss of precious time.[18]

The complexity of the war context and the difficult positions in which the Italian monarch as well as his executive and military officials found themselves at that time are objectively evident and have been rightly acknowledged by historians. Most probably, the decisions of the king and of Badoglio can be explained by making reference to various motivations, including the desire not to betray a former ally, the hope of being able to save face and the fear of German reactions toward the Italian population. Also and somehow irrationally, the monarch and his prime minister carried on hoping that the Nazis would withdraw their troops without reacting violently, if the Italians did not first attack them. The most tragic consequence, though, of leaving Italy's military commands without precise and unequivocal orders was the nondefense of Rome, as well as the total collapse of Italian military units in the peninsula and in the empire. This is why even though the king's concern about becoming "Hitler's prisoner" could be seen as legitimate, Vittorio Emanuele III—head of the Italian state and of the Italian Armed Forces—did not realize that his flight to Brindisi should have been carried out only *after* having organized the defense of the country from German aggression. As this latter element was tragically missing, the monarchy and all the ministers who left the capital gave the impression of being concerned only about their personal safety rather than about the protection of the whole nation.[19] Here, the notion of guardianship and protection to be exercised by a monarch vis-à-vis his national citizenry comes to the fore, as it was undermined through an act that, although unintentional, appeared to be a dramatic act of neglect.

The feeling of "having been abandoned"—shared generally by Italians at the time—might perhaps surprise foreign observers but has already been described in the beautiful pages of Pavone's classic work on the Italian Resistance.[20] The immediate reactions to the announcement of the armistice were multiple, writes the Italian historian and former partisan and were characterized by a variety of sentiments that ranged from joy and happiness to anxiety and dismay.[21] In Rome, adds the fascist Carlo Mazzantini, who would join the Republic of Salò, outside the Theatre Manzoni a small crowd reacted to the recorded voice of Badoglio with "some applauses, some other shouts singing the praises of peace, then an embarrassed silence, full of shapeless questions, of new fears."[22] Part of the population exulted as if the war were finished; others showed apprehension for what would happen; and soon, all started realizing the tragedy of the situation, with soldiers feeling abandoned by their superiors, the latter by the high commanders, all Italians by the authorities and the institutions that were supposed to protect them.[23] "They have betrayed us, the officers have run off, even the king has marooned us!" cried some Italian soldiers, based in the Northern city of Padova, on 9 September 1943.[24] "But, to sum up, sir colonel, [...] now, what do we have to do?" asked an Italian military man by formulating a question that, unfortunately, was left without answer.[25] "The King has run away!" exclaimed Mazzantini's mother, overwhelmed by the news[26]; and, telling her son the words of another woman whose progeny was fighting on the front, she reported: "Lady Mazzantini, even the father has left us. We are a flock without a shepherd. Who will defend our sons now?"[27] The monarch—who was the head of state and who had been head of state during the fascist dictatorship as well (a point not sufficiently emphasized when thinking about the Italian case study)—had just left the capital and "abandoned" his subjects and soldiers.

Because of these events, thousands of Italian troops in the metropole and in the European lands of the empire were disarmed by the Germans and interned as war prisoners in various camps in Germany and in Poland, unless they agreed to join the *Wehrmacht* and continued fighting on the side of the Reich. Among these Italian soldiers, some accepted taking the Nazi side; some attempted to quit the battlefield to go back home; others decided to resist and join the partisan movement, losing their lives as did the Italian military division *Aqui* in the Nazi massacres that took place on the Greek island of Cephalonia.[28] Basically, the entire defense system crumbled disastrously. If one uses the prism of citizenship, one can see that monarchical guardianship was gravely shaken by the behavior and omissions of the person who was on the throne. Unsurprisingly, because of this unfortunate and catastrophic situation, many Italian subjects started questioning the related moral issue of loyalty to the monarch and asking whether one should continue feeling bound by such a civic link, taking into account all the events occurring in the peninsula. So the notion of allegiance as well—inherently connected with the other tenet, protection—was severely eroded and, as will be shown in the next pages, even rejected and disavowed in some important cases, although from a juridical point of view this royal link continued to exist until abolition of the Italian monarchy in June 1946.

In the next section we explore a second and related civic question that characterized the 1943–1945 biennium and that gave the concept of Italian national citizenship a second powerful jolt.

8.3. DYING FOR WHICH HOMELAND? CO-NATIONALS WITH CONFLICTING VISIONS OF IMAGINED ITALIES

The institution of national citizenship, uniting a people to a specific state, is directly linked to a second fundamental civic aspect: the idea of *patria* (fatherland). From a theoretical perspective, to be a citizen means to share particular feelings with other co-citizens vis-à-vis a country, to be attached to the latter in various ways and with a different level of intensity according to personal choice, to be prepared, ideally and if necessary, to make the ultimate sacrifice by dying for it. The issue can of course become more complex for migrants and expatriates since, in their case, the citizen could well share multiple feelings for more than one state, hold dual or multiple citizenships and have an imagined concept of *patria* that often depends on the person's migratory experience and the individual's psychology. Generally speaking, though, and bearing in mind individual exceptions, there is no denying that the juridical bond linking citizens together incorporates an important spiritual dimension that usually transforms a particular country into a special fatherland—essential for the definition of one's national identity.

Following the armistice of 8 September, the idea of *patria* and the corollary tenet of sacrificing one's life for it were also seriously shaken in the Italian peninsula because two diametrically opposed visions of "national fatherland" were upheld simultaneously around the country, leading one part of the Italian national citizenry to fight a civil conflict in the name of two "homelands" that had, though, the same name: *Italia*. One side, represented by the multifaceted Resistance movement and supported by the Southern governments, fought alongside the Anglo-Americans in the name of "an Italy of rupture" (*"l'Italia della rottura"*) and was motivated—concurrently or separately, according to the individual case—by ideological reasons (i.e., fighting against fascism), or patriotic reasons (fighting against the occupying German enemy) or social reasons (fighting a class struggle against the capitalists).[29] The other side, loyal to Mussolini and the Republic of Salò, continued fighting the Second World War against the Anglo-Americans and alongside the "betrayed" German ally, taking as its major sources of inspiration the fascist republican ideology, the Axis alliance and the sacred memory of all the Italian victims who had died during the 1940–1943 conflict against the British enemy and its allies.[30]

Surely, as has been emphasized elsewhere, the Italians were faced with a clear and radical choice, but this does not mean that clear and radical was the attitude of the protagonists involved (i.e., the Resistance partisans on the one hand, the fascist republicans on the other).[31] Indeed, in a context of war, hunger, psychological exhaustion and a very complex Italian institutional situation, individual behavior was not always well defined and unchanging as one might imagine in a simplistic way. Reactions were multiple and often contradictory. Choices and counter-choices (pro–Western Allies, pro-Salò and pro-Germans) were sometimes made within both fronts in a sea of doubt, perplexity and uncertainty. Also, opportunism, indifference and "active" versus "passive" resistance were not at all precisely defined areas, and a person could easily change sides, back and forth, even more than once.[32] Neither choice was simple to make, especially during the first weeks after 8 September and in the "power vacuum" that followed. As noted by Nuto Revelli in his diary in October 1943, before joining the Resistance movement: "I take fright at those who claim to have always understood everything, who continue to understand everything. Comprehending 8 September was not easy!"[33] This is why the two opposing camps were not just "black" and "white": a vast "gray area" actually existed between the two and, owing to years of destruction and widespread psychological tiredness, the 1943–1945 period should be seen as an epoch of "shades" rather than of clear and "distinguished colors."[34]

Moreover, apart from the oscillations and uncertainties of the protagonists, it is interesting to bear in mind for historical analysis that the two contrasting factions under consideration involved only a minority of Italians. In fact, although statistics are incomplete and highly controversial, one can speak, approximately, of figures that range from 200,000 to 350,000 *"partigiani"* (Resistance partisans) on the one hand, and from

570,000 to 850,000 "fascist republicans" on the other.[35] If one then wants to attempt to do a further calculation of the number involved (including their friends and relatives), as the historian De Felice has done, one could have a total of no more than four million Italians—quite a small number, in comparison to the forty-four million citizens of the peninsula at that time.[36] "What was the other Italy doing, [the Italy] of millions of citizens who would neither become fighters nor supporters of the Resistance or of the Social Republic? [...] It is this one the third Italy of 1943, the Italy ignored by research but largely a majority, the Italy of abstention, of waiting, of disengagement."[37] This "third Italy" that did not take sides in a radical and clear way and preferred a policy of wait-and-see, having been devastated by years of conflict and concerned primarily about the imperative of *primum vivere,* made up the largest part of the gray zone, opting for staying in the "house on the hill" rather than choosing the "partisans' mountain" or the "fascist city."[38]

Despite the blurred borders of the opposing camps as well as their statistical weakness in comparison with the entire Italian population, it is instructive to focus on them from the perspective of national citizenship because, as we shall demonstrate below, the political vocabulary and the national ideals of those who joined the two sides touched on the notion of *patria* in an historically fascinating way, defining and redefining Italian national identity and Italian national citizenship throughout the biennium under study and leaving an important symbolic legacy in the post-1945 period, to which we shall come back in our next chapter. The two national visions (i.e., of the Resistance movement and of the Salò republicans) are explored together because both are part of Italian national history and cannot be erased from the past for ideological reasons, as has often been done in the peninsula when politicizing the discussion. In fact, even though the two "choices" (the antifascist and the fascist) were clearly different and one of them belonged to the "wrong side," we cannot deny that both visions tell us something about the history of the country and of national citizenry; they therefore deserve scientific, rather than polemical and myopic, analysis. Let us explore and discuss our findings.

If we first meditate on the last words written by those Italians who were condemned to death by the opposing camp, as well as on a variety of other contemporary sources left by the protagonists of both sides, we notice that the part and the counterpart (i.e., the antifascists and the fascists) were dying, both, for "an idea." "Mom, I die shot for my idea," wrote the twenty-two-year-old artillery reserve Lieutenant Achille Barilatti, before being executed without trial by Italian fascists and Germans in March 1944[39]; "for an ideal I have been fighting and for an ideal I die," echoed the partisan and engineer of FIAT Lorenzo Viale in a letter to his family before being killed by Mussolini's Republican National

Guard in Turin in February 1945.[40] And exactly for an idea did the fascist republicans kill and pass away on the other side of the mountains: in a description of the Blackshirts of Salò written in a fascist weekly newspaper in May 1944, one reads that "on their flame of combat, the motto: Honor Italy is engraved in letters of blood.[...] At the peak of all their aspirations is the salvation of the Fatherland.[...] Thus we have to love them and learn from them how to fight and be ready to die for the triumph of the Idea."[41]

Interestingly and most controversially, both ideas upheld by the two sides had the same name: "*Italia*." Domenico Fiorani, a thirty-one-year-old partisan killed *manu fascista* in Piazzale Loreto in Milan in August 1944 in reprisal for the explosion of a bomb against a German military vehicle, left these lapidary words for his family (to cry over) and for us (to contemplate):

> A few moments before I die
> To all of you
> The last palpitations of my heart.
> Viva Italy[42]

And *Viva l'Italia* was also the expression that another antifascist, the engineer Umberto Fogagnolo, killed in the same circumstances as partisan Fiorani, had the strength to write on one of his son's photos, a picture that was found on Fogagnolo's corpse at the morgue:

> My last thought is for you
> Viva Italy[43]

But the term *Italia* was invoked by the counterpart as well. The Italians of Salò, fighting from the opposing camp, pronounced it and sang it at the top of their lungs during their neo-fascist adventure in the Northern part of the peninsula: "Italy! Italy! Italy! [...] replied [to Rodolfo Graziani] hundreds and hundreds of sailors and, from their chest, rose high in the azure sky the anthem of their faith, the anthem of their rescue."[44]

Since both sides were dying for an idea and both ideas were called by the same name—Italy—those joining the two opposing factions defined themselves, consequently and logically, as "patriots" because all saw themselves as sacrificing their life for the country. "Remember," wrote the twenty-one-year-old worker Amerigo Duò, executed in Turin by a group of fascist republicans in January 1945, "that I do not die as a delinquent but as a Patriot and I die for the Homeland and for the welfare of all[;] so those who feel up to it, continue my struggle."[45] *La patria*, the mother country: this supreme concept was also ingrained in the imagination of the fascists looking at Lake Garda. "At the top of all our deeds is *la Patria*," we read in a fascist weekly in spring 1944.[46]

And both *partigiani* and *fascisti* shared also a "unique feeling of happiness" for offering their life to the country. In fact, for the patriot "death is beautiful" when life is extinguished in the name of the "beloved motherland." In this respect, this is what the partisan Lieutenant Colonel Costanzo Ebat told his son Mario before being shot by Italian fascists in the Roman military fort of Boccea in June 1944:

But most of all, love and have faith in the Fatherland. Put it before all your affections and if it asks you for your life, offer it singing. You will feel then, as I feel it right now, how beautiful it is to die for the country and that death has a real value. Just know, and never forget it, that your little daddy passes on, smiling, [...] confident to have done his duty to the beloved Fatherland until the last instant.[47]

To be happy to die, echoed a fascist voice from the other side, because "the sacrifice of life is a legacy of eternity for the Cause which we are fighting for."[48]

Apart from using the same national political vocabulary (*idea*, *Italia*, *patriota*, *Patria*), both rival sides looked at, and found inspiration in, the same national past and national Risorgimento. As the historian Pavone put it, "more or less, all the political and ideological positions within the Resistance alignment and, the Fascists themselves, picked their own piece of Risorgimento to which to refer."[49] For instance, looking at the Italian Resistance first, we notice that two of its major movements (the Garibaldi Brigades and the Party of Action) chose, as their official denominations, names that evoked the sides defeated during the Risorgimento process by the moderate liberal-monarchical solution.[50] Also, the past national memory of "Italian resurgence" was shared by those "Badoglio troops" who were deported to German lagers and who sang the nationalist piece of *Va' Pensiero* (by Giuseppe Verdi) at the crossing of the Brenner Pass or who refused to join the Salò Republic because, according to them, a choice had to be made between "the Italian Italy of Risorgimento" and "the Germanized Italy of the fascist myth" (*"l'Italia italiana del Risorgimento"* and *"l'Italia intedeschita del mito fascista"*).[51] Finally, similar national ideals were also evoked by those who continued fighting, such as the twenty-three-year-old Italian partisan and infantry Lieutenant Pedro Ferreira writing before his execution in Turin in January 1945. As he put it, he was dying as Italy's nationalist patriots Attilio and Emilio Bandiera, Ciro Menotti, Guglielmo Oberdan and Cesare Battisti had done before him:

Dearest Mom, Dad and Ico,
By the time this letter reaches you, you will already have been told about the misfortune that has befallen you.[...] But greater will be the chance to react to grief if you think that your son and brother has died with the forehead facing the sun from which he always drew strength and warmth like the Bandiera brothers, Ciro Menotti, Oberdan, and Battisti. He has died for the Patria to which he has devoted *all* his life.[52] [emphasis in original]

In the opposite camp, though, on the other side of the Apennine Mountains, the fascist republicans were also embracing political and cultural references that had a direct link with Italy's national history and with recent Risorgimento. For example, the four military divisions of soldiers and volunteers of the Salò Republic who were sent to Germany for military training and who would return to Italy in August 1944 to fight beside Nazi troops against Italian partisan antifascist "banditry" were called names that alluded clearly to the peninsula's past (i.e., San Marco, Italia, Littorio, Monterosa).[53] Also, apart from the fact that Goffredo Mameli's national anthem was used by fascist republicans for propaganda purposes, a very special place was reserved for Giuseppe Mazzini within the *imaginaire* of the Salò experience. The Genoese's effigy was put on the stamps issued in RSI; Mussolini's Republic was proclaimed by the Duce as the heir of the 1849 Roman Republic and the latter's constitutional text was taken as a model by the Salò government during the discussions concerning formulation of a future constitution for the peninsula that was supposed to be approved in Salò after the fascist final victory (which never came about).[54]

So the two symmetrically rival sides, the antifascists and the fascists, were using exactly the same political terminology and the same ideological-historical paradigms. These shared expressions and references, though, were applied and evoked by the two camps to refer to very different things: two radically different "imagined Italies." From the point of view of the ideologically diverse and multifaceted Resistance movement (i.e., that of its partisan combatants as well as the political institutional voice represented by the six antifascist parties united in the Committee of National Liberation), this imagined Italy would no longer be run by fascism and its totalitarian dictatorial system but through democratic principles. The latter had to be restored in the peninsula in the sphere of individual and parliamentary liberties, according to some (the Liberals); in the workplace, according to others (the Socialists and Communists); or in both spheres, according to those who looked for a synthesis between the demands of classical liberalism and those of socialism and who saw fascism as a "monster with two faces" that had to be destroyed simultaneously with equal energy (the Party of Action).[55] Also, this future Italy—dreamed of by the *partigiani* and by the political representatives of the *Resistenza*—would not necessarily continue being a monarchical state: following the events of 8 and 9 September, the position of the Savoy family was acutely debated, attacked or defended in party meetings, in the press and in society at large during the entire 1943–1945 period. Initially, the antifascist parties even refused to enter Badoglio's government unless the king abdicated. Generally, opinions differed on whether the dynastic principle should be kept or abolished. Monarchists, such as the influential liberal intellectual Benedetto Croce, were in favor of the dynastic institution and argued that it could be purified of its fascist past and recent omissions through abdication, and kept as a fundamental constitutional factor of Italian unity. Republicans, on the contrary, such as Count Carlo Sforza, aimed at abolition because of royal complicity with Mussolini's domestic and foreign policy, because of the humiliating events surrounding the armistice and more generally because of an ideological preference for republicanism. Eventually, during the period that concerns us here in this chapter, a political agreement was achieved on this controversial issue among the antifascist forces. After long months of discord, proposals and counterproposals, it was decided to focus on a united war effort against the Nazis and postpone the monarchical question until the end of the conflict, so as to let the Italian people settle it either through a Constituent Assembly or via a popular referendum once the entire peninsula was liberated from the Germans.[56] In exchange, Vittorio Emanuele III—who had opposed in the meantime any proposal of direct abdication either in favor of his six-year-old grandson Vittorio Emanuele assisted by a regent or in favor of his son Umberto—accepted reluctantly and under Allied pressure another institutional compromise that we have already mentioned: nomination of his son as Lieutenant of the Realm, to be made after the liberation of Rome in June 1944 and involving permanent delegation of royal powers by the king (without formal abdication) and his retirement from public affairs.[57] Hence, in the mind of the Resistance, this imagined Italy would be undeniably antifascist and, eventually, either a monarchic state or a republic.

By contrast, imagined from Lake Garda, the Italy of Salò would be shaped by fascism and by its totalitarian agenda through the activities of the newly established Fascist Republican Party, although curiously the adjective *fascista* was not incorporated into the official denomination of RSI.[58] Also, this rival, imagined, Italy would end the Second World War alongside its Nazi ally and continue collaborating with Germany in a future New Order where radically racist tenets and outright anti-Semitic extermination would most probably have cleared it of Jewish "impurity" by extending the directives of the "final solution" to the entire peninsula, as German authorities were then doing in Northern Italy throughout the six hundred days of Mussolini's neo-fascist adventure.[59] Third, despite the fact that the Salò government and the "prisoner of the lake" were "temporarily" obeying orders from Berlin, the Italy conceived from the North of the peninsula would recover its due place on the international stage and "resurrect" as a world power after the tragic "treachery" of the fascist Grand Council of 25 July ("duly avenged" through the famous trial of Verona in January 1944, where the major traitors, including Mussolini's son-in-law, were executed).[60] Lastly, apart from introducing

important programs of so-called *socializzazione* (i.e., economic socialization) in favor of the working classes and against the "masonic capitalist
bourgeoisie" who had abandoned Mussolini, this envisaged Italy would
most importantly be republican, with no space for divergent views on
this issue because the monarchical principle of the "treacherous and fugi-
tive king" (*"re fellone e fuggiasco"*) was inherently antithetical to RSI.[61]
In short, while sharing in some cases an antimonarchist flavor, the two
imagined Italies—seen from the South and from Salò—were completely
different and in conflict with each other as regards their other defining
characteristics.

Interestingly, this great divergence of national visions was also illustrated
in a fundamental way in the two contrasting concepts of "Italian citizenship," which, still insufficiently noted by scholars today, were discussed
at the time by the successive governments in the South of the peninsula
on the one side and by Mussolini's government in Salò on the other. In
the South of the peninsula, an embryonic new Italian citizenship link—
being shaped during the 1943–1945 biennium and introduced legally via
various reforms—pointed to two important interrelated aspects of the
Resistance ideals: antifascism and democracy. More particularly, in January 1944 the Southern Italian government abolished the notorious 1938
fascist laws and related regulations that, during the late dictatorship, had
governed the deprivation of Italian citizenship with respect to naturalized Jews as well as the marriages between Italian Aryans and Jewish
people or other races. The concept of Italian citizenship upheld by the
antifascist authorities of the South started therefore to be purged of its
previous radically fascist connotations.[62] Moreover, in February 1945,
when the peninsula was still occupied and the Second World War had
not yet ended, the Italian Council of Ministers, back in Rome since June
1944 and headed by Bonomi, introduced the right of political suffrage
for women to be exercised at the national level beside their male counterparts. Thus the democratic principle of gender equality in reference to
political participation was also slowly being enshrined in Italian citizenship policy.[63] Finally, already in August 1943, the king and Badoglio
had issued some important decree-laws that abolished the Fascist Grand
Council, the Fascist Party and the Chamber of Fasci and Corporations as
well as stipulating that after the cessation of the war, a new Chamber of
Deputies would be elected. The institutional edifice Mussolini had built
throughout the ventennium in order to realize the totalitarian and revolutionary agenda of fascism was therefore gradually destroyed, with the
aim of eventually taking the difficult democratic road.[64]

Apart from this antiracist, antifascist and democratic Italian citizenship formulated from the South of the country, a totally different imagined Italian citizenship was being dreamed of and discussed in Salò during the same months—although the various constitutional projects containing citizenship provisions were never approved because of the war context and Mussolini's decision to postpone their introduction until the end of the world conflict, and the end of an imposed and never really accepted Nazi occupation of the Italian Alpine and Adriatic regions. Just as the imagined Italy of the North was shaped by the neo-fascist triad of "Italian," "Social" and "Republic," the related new citizenship link that was debated around Lake Garda was also defined by the same three concepts. In fact, this citizenship link was not called "Salò citizenship" (or anything similar) but "Italian citizenship" (as in the South) because RSI claimed to *be* Italy, and therefore its related citizenship was automatically seen as Italian—the citizenship of the whole peninsula.[65] This civic bond incorporated also a strong social component because, according to the Verona Manifesto of 14 November 1943 (the first approved "national" program of the Republican Fascist Party), work (whether manual, technical or intellectual) was the basis of the Salò Republic and important fascist social programs were formulated with the ultimate objective of admitting the workers to the decision-making process within their workplace. "Fascist socialism," though, had to be distinguished from "Marxist socialism" and from the radical Soviet model; this is why the Verona Manifesto defined private property as inviolable, keeping alive an important historical civic right.[66] Third and logically, this new citizenship link was necessarily republican, therefore binding the Italians to a president of the Republic who, according to a constitutional project formulated by Salò Ambassador and Senator Vittorio Rolandi Ricci, would have been elected every ten years.[67] And lastly, even though this Italian citizenship—shaped in RSI—would also have included female national suffrage, as its counterpart in liberated Rome did in February 1945,[68] it remained distinctly anti-Semitic and blatantly racist when it came to racial groups, in line with the Nazi ally's program and with the Italian citizenship policies of the late pre-1943 dictatorship. For example, according to the Verona Manifesto the Jews were foreigners and, during the war, would be regarded as enemy subjects. Moreover, in the constitutional project of Biggini, it was clearly stated that Italian citizenship would be reserved only for those who belonged to "Italian Aryan stock" and could not be acquired by those who belonged to "the Jewish race and to colored races."[69] Finally, in a number of highly restrictive proposals made by Giovanni Preziosi (general inspector of the race in Salò), one can see that there was an attempt to elaborate definitions of "Italian blood," "blood similar to the Italian," "foreign blood" and *"meticci"* with the aim of declaring the Italian Aryans to be the superior race. Marriages with foreign citizens and with *meticci* would also have been prohibited, and foreign citizens as well as métis would have been excluded from military service and from the right to own and inherit property from Italian citizens.[70] In short, two contrasting imagined Italies and two divergent imagined Italian citizenships were simultaneously being shaped and upheld in the peninsula.

To conclude, after the September armistice and the division of Italy (symbolized by the names of Brindisi, Salerno, Salò), part of the Italian national citizenry—holding the citizenship of the same state, from a juridical point of view—went through dramatic months of questioning, defining and redefining Italian national identity by using the same political vocabulary and the same historical references but with clearly opposing and conflicting meanings. Even though millions of Italians followed a policy of wait-and-see and kept the stance of exhausted passive spectators on both sides of the peninsula, two camps took active part in the military and political struggle and attempted to delineate a process of Italian national self-identification that, defined differently from each side, automatically pushed the other in the direction of "anti-Italy." Despite the minority status of the two factions, their symbolic value was to be enormous and would shape post-1945 Italy in a significant way.

In the next section we make some further reflections on the fact that during the 1943–1945 biennium, in the name of these two divergent Italian fatherlands and of these two competing and hostile Italian national identities, citizens *killed* co-citizens in a war of liberation (according to the Partisans), or in a civil war (as the Fascists argued at the time).

8.4. CIVIL WARS AND THE KILLING OF PEOPLE HOLDING
OUR OWN NATIONAL CITIZENSHIP:
THE SPECIFICITY OF THE ITALIAN CASE STUDY

Since De Felice's challenging argument, according to which what happened between 1943 and 1945 was not the brave resistance of a majority of Italians against Nazi Germany and its fascist supporters in Salò but a "civil war," a vigorous debate has occurred in the peninsula about the significance of the Resistance movement, about the history of antifascism and about the Italians' facing up to their own fascist past.[71] If we look at this debate more closely, through the lens of national citizenship, it is instructive to see that the latter term actually combines and summarizes these historiographical discussions. In fact, the notion of citizenship, together with its various historical meanings, seems to reflect both opposing camps in a fascinating way, shedding new light on a long debate that has characterized the history of post–World War Two Italy.

If one sees citizenship as a juridical link uniting a population, then one can understand why the 1943–1945 conflict was a "civil war." Italians holding the same citizenship status fought against each other: citizens killed co-citizens, leading to tragic days for both sides because, as Pavone reminds us, a "war against a foreign nation" and a "war within the same nation" were not the same thing; actually, they were two very different things.[72] Contrarily, if one looks at the notion of citizenship in terms of content and rights, then one can well see that during those two crucial years a "war of Liberation" was fought against Fascism, a regime and an ideology that had given Italians many social entitlements but erased civic and political rights from the peninsula, as well as adding a radicalized racist and anti-Semitic dimension to the notion of *italianità*. From this second perspective, the citizen taking arms in the name of liberty against fascist oppression, fascist uniformity, fascist antiliberalism and fascist antidemocracy was indeed fighting a war of freedom. And a powerful one because, as Pavone also noted, we might wonder in this case whether Franco Venturi was right when he said that civil conflicts are the only wars that "really deserve to be fought."[73] By using citizenship as a source of inspiration and historical analysis, we can see that the opposing camps and historical interpretations are epitomized by the same word. From one viewpoint, Italians sharing the same nationality were fighting against each other. From the other point of view, Italians were freeing each other from twenty years of dictatorial rule in which the healthy linking of civil, political and social rights had been lost. Let us attempt to grasp the profound psychological traumas of those days and the specificity of the Italian case study.

To realize the ultimate patriotic ideal of giving one's life for one's country, the Italian citizens of the peninsula, no matter how many, fought against other co-citizens in a two-year, fratricidal civil conflict where "the other side" was seen as the internal enemy, the non-Italian, the mental foreigner to be associated, and eliminated physically, with the external enemy—namely, the troops of Nazi Germany (if one was pro-Resistance) or of the Anglo-Americans (if one was pro-Salò). In certain cases, this Italian national civil war touched on the microcosm of Italian households since brothers could well be fighting alongside opposing camps having opted for one or the other cause. This is actually what happened to a protagonist who recounts this in one of his books: the aforementioned Mazzantini had in fact two younger brothers joining the Salò Army and his eldest brother fighting for the Italian monarchical troops beside the Western Allies.[74] Arguably, and bearing in mind our first perspective concerning national citizenship, the killing of co-citizens to eliminate them physically (no matter whether the person belongs to the same family or not) is the ultimate and most dramatic scenario one can contemplate.

This fratricidal dimension of the 1943–1945 Italian conflict was felt tragically by both sides around the peninsula, understandably causing profound emotions among those who took part in the war. For example, in a moving letter, written by a sixteen-year-old soldier of the Republican National Guard of RSI to his mother, the young author could not avoid saying that a partisan at whom he had fired a shot lest the other would have shot first, spoke the same language as his and was an Italian "brother."

"Mom," invoked the partisan whom I myself had to carry in my arms to the medication post. During the trip his only thought was his mother. He insistently asked me if we would also hurt his *mamma*.[...] I wish that the many people who so easily discuss and speak about 8 September without even knowing the disaster and the collapse [...] which has caused to our Homeland had seen the whole thing. Because, you see, that partisan, the one on whom I had to shoot otherwise he would have fired at me first, spoke my own language, was saying "*mamma*" as I now say it; he was a brother of mine![75]

Analogous sad feelings were also shared by those who were on the other side of the mountains, and sometimes even in a more complex way, since the widespread argument according to which partisans were fighting against the Germans because the latter were Nazis and against the other Italians only because the latter were fascists could be upheld only ideally or with difficulty. In practice, it effectively led to doubts and uncertainties linked to the fact that, as already noted, a war against foreigners and a war within the same nation are not the same thing.[76]

Consequently, because of the specificity of civil wars in comparison with international conflicts, a variety of personal reactions took place among the people involved, ranging from horrendous "ferocity" to a sense of "dismay" to the "willingness to discuss" with the Italian counterpart.[77] Fierceness is sadly documented by the various executions that were carried out by both sides. Dismay emerges, for instance, in the attitude of a fascist republican who, in a gunfight taking place in Rome, fired off with a machine gun along a footpath; after coming back, the following happened.

Upset, wearing a black leather jacket [...], to the women who look at him with terror and indignation he says: "If you only knew how I feel as well! I can't take it any more! How could we Italians do this among ourselves!"—and bursts into tears, throws away the weapon, crumples onto the floor, half-senseless.[78]

So both camps felt the fratricidal aspect of the conflict with great desolation, especially because it generated massacres and bereavement in the same nation. However, and this is a fundamental point to emphasize, one should not forget those who experienced the civil war as a tragedy (of course) but also as an event to face with pride and strength, in the name of "the choice made" and the responsibility linked to the consequences of such a choice. From this perspective, the civil war is not just seen as a negative and tragic fact, but as something to be worth fighting for, because of its profound psychological dimension, demanding individual reflection and questioning.[79]

Like domestic wars taking place in other countries, the 1943–1945 struggle among the Italians was characterized by suspension of the state's monopoly of legitimate violence. In fact, with the institutional crisis that took place following the fall of fascism on 25 July and creation of multiple authorities in the South and in the North, the use of force was transferred to the single individual. This led to a "license to kill" that was absent before, or in the words of the Italian intellectual Norberto Bobbio, to the "contrast, never solved, between the duty not to kill and the obligation to kill in case of necessity or of legitimate self-defense, [...] [between] offensive and defensive violence, just and unjust violence."[80] And this necessarily pushes one to reflect, within the Italian case study, on the assassination of the philosopher Giovanni Gentile outside his house in April 1944, or on the macabre exposition of Mussolini's and Clara Petacci's cadavers in April 1945.[81] From a psychological point of view, violence became much "closer" than the violence of a regular war because the fighting no longer took place on a distant military front, but on the street. Moreover, as with other civil conflicts, Italy's national war was characterized by the "invisibility of the enemy": of course, one could recognize a soldier of RSI or the armed partisan, but less identifiable were the numerous spies, the informers and the "traitors" who moved about at the time, creating a vicious spiral of suspicion and fear that increased the scale of brutality and atrocities since anyone could betray us and assassinate us "next."[82]

Apart from the common ground between the Italian case study and civil conflicts in general, Italy's domestic war held a specificity of its own that deserves to be emphasized. Contrary to what happened in the civil conflicts fought during the Second World War in France and in the territories of Yugoslavia by their respective Resistance movements, the winners and losers of the Italian national struggle were "already known" from the beginning of civil hostilities. The Nazis were retreating, the victorious Anglo-Americans were already in Southern Italy, and the Red Army, which had arrived in numerous Eastern European countries, was moving southward. Obviously, there was some uncertainty as to *how long* the Italian civil war would last, but all could feel and guess, right from the start, *who would win*. As the writer and fascist follower of RSI Stanis Ruinas put it in his book on the Republic of Salò:

The war was lost and we were involved for the sake of national dignity. We knew actually that this was a lost war right from the beginning; if we stayed in the groove, it is because we wanted to demonstrate and affirm in front of Man and History [...] that not all the Italians followed, applauding, the bandwagon.[83]

Indeed, the awareness of being "the defeated party side" was widespread among the fascists in the North; the fact of fighting "a cause without a future" and of knowing it from the beginning pushed them into a state of psychological exasperation, isolation, funereal anguish and frustrated sense of death that made the 1943–1945 Italian war a distinctive one, different from those taking place at the same time in many parts of Europe.[84] Moreover, as the Italian antifascist militant and founder of the liberal-socialist movement Enzo Enriques Agnoletti has rightly argued, in those countries such as France that had not had a fascist regime before the Second World War, the essential motivation of the Resistance movement was the presence of the hated Nazi invader, and second the important phenomenon of French collaboration with the Germans. Therefore, in France the word *Résistance* meant to "resist" the foreign oppressor and continue fighting after the defeat of 1940, in the name of a preexistent political and ideological patrimony. By contrast, in Italy the term *Resistenza* did not mean "resisting" in view of keeping a preexistent (pre-1943) system but attacking the latter and overthrowing it.[85]

8.5. CONCLUSION

During the historical period that ran from July 1943 to April 1945, the institution of Italian national citizenship was critically questioned and attacked from a variety of directions. The monarchical notions of protection and guardianship underlying the concept of Italian subjecthood and linked to the tenet of allegiance were undermined; the national concepts of *patria*, *Italia*, *patriota* and *identità* were put to the test in a dramatic way, to the point of pushing co-citizens to kill each other in the name of antifascism or the cause of Salò. Two contrasting national projects and national visions took form concurrently, leaving behind dead, survivors and deep scars around the country but also incorporating strong hopes for the post–World War Two future reconstruction of the peninsula.

Everyone knows that the Salò experience "ended" with the capture of Mussolini by partisan forces in a German military vehicle near the northern city of Como, and with the exhibition of the Duce's corpse, hung head downward from the roof of a petrol station in Milan. Less known is that physical elimination of Mussolini did not end the Italian civil war: it actually continued for several months through numerous episodes of "insurrectional justice" that took place in the North of the peninsula right after the total liberation of the country in April 1945. Quick trials, summary executions and, in some cases, private acts of revenge were carried out by the winners against the losers, transforming an already controversial program of *epurazione* (i.e., the purge of fascist collaborators, spies and war criminals) into a "day of reckoning" (*resa dei conti*) on which more archival research should be done.[86]

To conclude our Part Two of the book, covering the entire fascist epoch from 1922 until 1945, we can argue that the notion of Italianness, as it emerged from the citizenship policies and discourses of the liberal decades, went through further significant events and developments of historical importance. Many points of similarity have been highlighted with the liberal years. However, we have also seen that, from other angles, a number of breaks, discontinuities and novelties occurred, particularly within the context of a fascist, revolutionary, increasingly totalitarian and ultimately racist regime that collapsed in 1943. Being an Italian subject of the Savoy House between 1922 and 1945 involved a composite array of meanings and factors, including the fundamental gender dimension (made visible in Chapter Six), the historical nonmetropolitan aspect (discussed in Chapter Seven) and all the conflicting issues regarding allegiance, patriotism, identity and the killing of co-citizens (explored in this chapter). The notion of being Italian from the rise of Fascism to the final liberation of the country from the Nazis was without doubt a "dual" and "multiple" one, as in the liberal era. However, it came to be a much more "complex and contested" concept than in pre-1922 Italy because of the changes brought about by an ever more ubiquitous Duce and state apparatus; because of individual choices in accepting, supporting, resisting or having a passive attitude toward the regime; and because of the conflicts that eventually came to the fore between fascists and antifascists, monarchists and republicans, winners and losers. All were Italian citizens belonging to an exhausted "Italian Italy."

From the ashes of the Second World War and of more than twenty months of Italian civil conflict, a new Republic of Italy was to be proclaimed in June 1946, giving birth to a democratic republican citizenship that we discuss in the next and final chapter.

The Birth and First Developments of Italy's Democratic Republican Citizenship (1946–1950)

Following the psychological civic traumas that seriously put into question the unifying institution of national citizenship during the years 1943–1945, the juridical link binding the people of the peninsula evolved again by going through additional major developments. The monarchical dimension of Italy's *status civitatis* characterizing the liberal and the fascist periods came to an end and was replaced by a republican one, as a direct consequence of the fall of the Savoy monarchy and the birth of the Italian republic taking place after the controversial institutional referendum of 2 June 1946. In addition to this constitutional change, the metropolitan and nonmetropolitan facets of the Italian civic bond, as they had developed throughout the monarchical epoch, were upset through a gradual geographical juridical shrinking that originated from the loss of metropolitan and nonmetropolitan lands and populations by Italy, as a result of the Allied peace settlement of 1947. Republican and geographically truncated, post-1946 Italian citizenship was to be defined by a variety of antifascist and democratic tenets that marked a major historical break with the fascist past and an important civic advancement in comparison with the liberal era.

This final chapter, ending our historical journey, aims at exploring the first five years that followed the end of the Second World War (1946–1950) by focusing on the genesis of Italy's republican citizenship and on the most significant points of rupture and continuity regarding the corresponding fascist and liberal citizenship variants of monarchical Italy. As we shall demonstrate, the major civic developments that took place in the peninsula were determined by important factors of Italian domestic politics as well as by fundamental international pressures and political events deriving from the specific course of World War Two, from the European territorial settlement concerning the "defeated nations" and from the first symptoms of an emerging Cold War mood.

9.1. THE TORMENTED BIRTH OF THE ITALIAN REPUBLIC AND THE END OF MONARCHICAL SUBJECTHOOD FOLLOWING THE REFERENDUM OF JUNE 1946

From the political unification of the peninsula under the Savoy monarchy in March 1861 to the eve of the proclamation of the Republic of Italy in June 1946, the Italians came to be linked, as monarchical subjects, to four subsequent sovereigns: Vittorio Emanuele II and Umberto I (Italian kings from 1861 to 1878 and from 1878 until 1900), Vittorio Emanuele III (on the throne until 1946) and Umberto II (Lieutenant of the Realm from June 1944 until May 1946 and last King of Italy for just over a month). In June 1946, though, the Italian dynastic question—which, as we saw, had been postponed until the total liberation of the country from the Nazis—was finally resolved, and as a result of specific events the Savoy House left for exile, the republic was proclaimed and the Italians ceased to be monarchical subjects. With official abolition of this monarchical aspect, enshrined in the Constitution of 1948, Italian citizens were no longer loyal to the Savoy Crown from a juridical viewpoint but united around the principle of "republican allegiance," which involved fidelity to the republic, observance of the constitution and of the laws, loyalty to an elected president and acceptance of the republican form as a permanent institutional feature of the country with no possibility of changing it since the republican order could not (and cannot) be submitted to any constitutional revision.[1]

As emphasized by the essayist Gloria Chianese, the fall of the Savoy monarchy represents a fundamental rupture within Italian national history, bearing in mind the important role that the House of Savoy played during the liberal and fascist epochs in reference to the process of Italian statehood and to the related developments of a post-unification national identity. As she put it, in June 1946 "the caesura within the history of the country [was] definite."[2] From a citizenship perspective, this major break within the national history of the peninsula deserves to be explored in detail not only for *what* happened but also because important civic issues clearly emerge in discussing *how* and *why* the birth of the Italian republic and automatic death of monarchical subjecthood came about in a certain way. As we shall see below, the 1946 Republic of Italy had a very complicated and tormented birth, due to a particular internal political situation and a complex international context. The origins of its related Italian republican citizenship are therefore of particular historical interest.

An initial matter that was to raise and intensify tensions at the domestic level and lead to passionate debate among the protagonists concerned first of all the institutional method through which the dynastic issue had to be resolved. The question was apparently quite simple: Should the choice between republic and monarchy be made through the "direct" participation of the Italian citizens via a referendum, or should the form of the state be decided by "indirect" popular vote via an elected Constituent Assembly? Though the question seemed to be simple, the answer was quite complex because of the political implications related to each method and the political motivations that were shared by those who preferred one way to the other. The two types of civic participation (i.e., direct and indirect) had in fact profound political dimensions that could not be overlooked by the institutional actors involved. More particularly, while the Actionists, the Socialists and the Communists—clearly republican—strongly supported the second solution (i.e., that the choice be made by an assembly), the conservative parties together with the monarchist circles were more in favor of the plebiscite road. From the perspective of the first three political groups, an assembly would have secured a republican majority more easily, as there was fear that reactionary influences could operate in a referendum where an easily manipulable, and in some cases still illiterate, Italian populace had to vote directly. *Ex adverso*, the conservative forces were well aware that the chances for survival of the monarchy would be much greater through a plebiscite ballot, having in mind in particular the expected votes of the Italian citizens living in the Southern Mezzogiorno where the attachment to the monarchy seemed to be stronger than in the North of the peninsula.[3]

Eventually, in March 1946, during the first government of Alcide De Gasperi, the conservatives succeeded in having the proposal on the referendum officially embraced—with the unofficial, but important, backing of the British and the American allies, still highly influential in the peninsula because of the existing international situation and the fact that the peace treaty concerning Italy had not yet been finalized. As De Gasperi told his cabinet, "the use of a referendum was held by international circles as the most democratic way of ascertaining the will of the people."[4] In addition to this democratic dimension, the referendum was seen in the country as most appropriate and opportune because of the deep ideological divisions within Italy, the complexity and the diversity of experiences of the Italian Resistance movement and the legacy linked to the vicissitudes of the defunct Social Republic of Salò. Clearly, within a context of deep scars left by the Italian civil war, calling on a large portion of the Italian people to express their views would furnish the country with a more legitimate electoral decision.[5] Finally, as noted by Antonio Gambino and Paolo Pombeni, De Gasperi's move in favor of accepting the direct participation of the Italian voters was most probably motivated by additional considerations of partisan politics in view of gaining an advantage for his Christian Democratic Party, whose leadership was republican but whose electorate was largely monarchist.[6] So after animated political debate that fueled the antagonisms and tensions within an already unstable post-war Italian domestic political context, it was finally decided that the continuity of the Savoy monarchy (or its fall) would be determined by the response of about twenty-eight million eligible Italian voters.[7]

Apart from the contentious issue related to the electoral method, the Italian republic had a tormented gestation owing to a general situation of uncertainty, political anxiety and, in some cases, electoral irregularities that contributed to creating a cloudy atmosphere before the vote was to be cast. As emphasized by Pier Luigi Ballini, the outcome of the referendum remained uncertain until the very last day because in many instances the voters' orientation did not always correspond to the position of their party lines.[8] Also, the electoral campaign took place in a context regarded as quite "alarming," for a variety of reasons: lack of a democratic mentality and of a political culture among the Italians in general after more than twenty years of fascist dictatorial rule; the "scaring" and "destabilizing" enlargement of the Italian electorate, which doubled overnight with the granting of national political rights to Italian women; circulation of weapons among the population (many arms had not yet been handed over to the authorities); and the fact that political assassinations were not a thing of the past.[9] Finally, as pointed out by Aldo G. Ricci, certain electoral irregularities were denounced before the referendum took place.[10] For instance, in reference to distribution of the electoral certificates, evidence shows that numerous tribunals, police stations and even the Allied Commission received various protests by some Italian citizens who complained about not having received an electoral certificate, while others were given more than one. This fact then had important implications related to the uncertainty about the total number of people entitled to vote and about the actual number of certificates issued and distributed by the Ministry of the Interior. Obviously, the fact that these written complaints were made mainly by people of a clear monarchical political affiliation might be interpreted as an act of support for a successive request to repeat the balloting; however, no matter the intention of the citizens who protested, there is no denying that, historically, on the basis of the verifications made by the police authorities, the inefficient electoral machine was leaking in many places like a vessel and often functioning not impartially.[11]

Within this peculiar Italian context, the balloting took place on 2 and 3 June. The Italians—male and female citizens aged twenty-one and over—voted on two political issues: choosing between establishment of a republic and maintenance of the Savoy monarchy, and electing a Constituent Assembly that would be in charge of drawing up the new constitution of the country. Not all Italian citizens entitled to vote, though, could take part in the ballot. This is a further aspect we would like to explore as it gives us additional historical evidence to understand why the end of Italian monarchical subjecthood and the origins of Italian republican citizenship were highly complex and tormented. The Italian electorate living in the Upper Adige (i.e., in the province of Bolzano) and in other various metropolitan cities of the Venetian-Julian, Istrian and Dalmatian regions (Trieste, Gorizia, Pola, Fiume, Zara) could not exercise their voting rights simply because in June 1946 no referenda and political elections could be organized in those provinces by the Italian authorities, owing to the uncertain international and political situation of the lands concerned. The latter had been in fact under allied military occupation since the last months of the Second World War, or in the case of the towns of the Upper Adriatic under Tito's troops and subject to Yugoslav expansionist foreign policy claims. Also, aside from these Italians, the prisoners of war (POW) holding Italian nationality and still to be repatriated in 1946 could not take part in the ballot because of their absence from the peninsula. Many of them would return home only after 1947, after being released from the allied camps set up, during the war, in the United States, the British Dominions and the Soviet Union to intern enemy service personnel. So the institutional question was resolved in June 1946 in a "truncated Italy," and with the important exclusion of a substantial number of Italian citizens who could not put a cross on the ballot for reasons of international politics linked to the complex liberation of the northern part of the country from the Nazis by the Allies, the presence of Yugoslav troops on the eastern border and the fate of thousands of Italian servicemen still to be sent home.[12]

The complexity of the situation surrounding the birth of the Republic of Italy did not end here. In fact, once the polling stations were closed in the afternoon of 3 June, other black clouds were to appear over the horizon to announce an imminent political storm. During the hours that followed the end of the referendum and in which the votes were being counted, some people voiced suspicion that further manipulations and irregularities were taking place owing to the slowness in communicating the results and the widespread diffusion of contradictory news as to which side had won. Also and most importantly, a major and controversial juridical issue was raised by a group of professors from the University of Padova, risking invalidation of the final electoral results. The question concerned the definition of the "required majority" that was necessary to proclaim the republic. Should this majority be calculated by taking into account only the number of the valid votes? Or should it be counted in reference to the total number of voters who actually put their cross on the ballot paper (thus including the spoiled votes and the blank ones), as required by law and as the monarchists argued?[13] The serious legal implications of this controversy appeared very clear to all the protagonists involved at the institutional level (i.e., the king, the antifascist parties and the Ministry of the Interior) because the 1946 lieutenant-general legislative decree concerning the referendum clearly stated that the republic would be proclaimed "should the majority of the voters cast a ballot for the Republic" (in the original language, so much debated at home, *"qualora la maggioranza degli elettori votanti si pronunci in favore della Repubblica"*).[14] Obviously, one would think, and rightly in our view, that the expression *elettori votanti* meant all those who had cast a vote, no matter how. Soon, though, it became clear that the Supreme Court of Cassation (*Corte Suprema di Cassazione*), responsible for announcing the final official results, was not in a position to transmit accurately *all* the required data. The court had in fact the number of valid votes in favor of the republic (more than twelve million) and the number of those in favor of the monarchy (more than ten million); but while possessing the number of spoiled ballot papers, it did not have the complete statistics concerning blank ones. The court could not have the latter number, and therefore could not confirm it, because numerous electoral reports, issued by the various polling bureaus, had not been sent in their complete forms; the results were sometimes written in pencil and therefore not trustworthy; and most important of all, they were not always accompanied by the boxes containing the blank voting papers (necessary for the double-checking process), as many of them had been destroyed or gone astray. So the actual calculation of *all* the votes (i.e., valid, spoiled *and* blank) could not be carried out.[15]

Interestingly, since the formal legal aspects of this question risked annulling the referendum and making possible a victory of the monarchy (should more transparent and less chaotic balloting be reorganized at a later date), the whole situation was resolved "politically" by the Italian executive simply through sidestepping the unquestionable validity of the juridical argument concerning the blank votes and carrying out—under constant pressure from numerous representatives of the Italian Left—a variety of unilateral political acts. They aimed at ending "quickly" this institutional storm and proclaiming the victory of the republican side on the basis of the data that were available. The epilogue leading to the birth of the Republic of Italy and the related republican citizenship was approaching its end.

On 10 June, Prime Minister De Gasperi informed King Umberto II that the government was unanimous in thinking that even though the

official results of the referendum were not yet complete and definitive, the republican majority—as expressed by the known valid votes
at hand—entailed the provisional transfer of powers from the monarch
to the prime minister and the birth of the republican state. The king,
though, did not seem to share this view, and after reiterating that he
would respect the will of the Italians as expressed by the number of the
elettori votanti and confirmed by the court, he counterproposed a temporary delegation of powers, pending a decision from the *Corte Suprema*.
Faced with this royal statement in respect to all legal formalities, then,
the executive had a choice: wait until the final report of the Court (to be
issued on 18 June) with the high risk of nullifying the plebiscite balloting,
or proceed immediately to unilateral assumption of the powers of head
of state by De Gasperi, with the responsibility for any consequences that
this hazardous move might have. Eventually, a less risky, but still politically symbolic, solution was embraced by the government following a
suggestion made by several representatives of the Party of Action: rather
than transferring "the powers" of the head of state, there would be a
transfer of "functions." Obviously, everyone could sense the juridical
fragility of such an act, but the political message was quite clear since it
was an initiative taken by the executive to start pushing the monarch out
of the institutional framework of the Italian state despite the lack of complete electoral results.[16] At this point, confronted with the government's
unilateral decision, and without listening to all the royal advisors who
were in favor of further legal appeals and constitutional action against
the executive branch, the king left the country for Portugal to join, like
his father in Egypt, the ranks of monarchs in exile. His explicitly declared
aim was to avoid the use of force against a governmental illegal act, and
therefore another civil war. As he told the Italians in his farewell address:
"Since I do not want to oppose force to abuse, nor make myself an ac-
complice to the illegality that the Government has committed, I leave
the soil of my Country, in the hope of warding off from the Italians new
griefs and new pains."[17]

Once the monarch had left the peninsula, the last clouds of the political storm moved to the halls of the Supreme Court, where the issue concerning the quorum was still being debated. The magistrates were divided
on this question but eventually, thanks to political pressure exercised at
the time over the judges, the majority of the court approved the argument
concerning valid votes. On 18 June, the final report of the *Corte Suprema
di Cassazione* was issued:

12,717,923 valid votes had been cast in favor of the republic;

10,719,284 valid votes, in favor of the monarchy;

1,498,136 were spoiled votes, and no separate figure was provided on the blank
    ballots.[18]

As the Italian minister of the Royal House, Lucifero, bluntly noted in his diary on that day: "With all the fraud they have done, there is no majority!"[19]

Born within a highly controversial juridical context, the Italian republic was now a fact, and the Savoy kingdom together with its related monarchical subjecthood were things of the past.[20]

To conclude, a major historical break took place in June 1946 as the Savoy monarchy was abolished, a Republic of Italy proclaimed and, consequently, a new juridical (republican) link created. These events were highly complex and tormented on account of a combination of domestic, international and juridical aspects. In the next section we explore a further change that took place, from a citizenship perspective, following the 1947 Paris peace treaty with the Allies.

9.2. THE GEOGRAPHICAL SHRINKING OF ITALIAN CITIZENSHIP WITH THE POST–WORLD WAR TWO PEACE SETTLEMENT

As we saw in Chapters Five and Seven, covering Italy's expansionist foreign policy during the liberal and fascist periods, the Italian state introduced in successive phases an elaborate system of juridical links with the objective of accommodating, in different ways and according to political, cultural and civilizational criteria, all the autochthones living in the territories under Italian rule. The institution of Italian monarchical subjecthood came to be divided, therefore, into a metropolitan and a nonmetropolitan link, the first uniting the Italians of the peninsula, and the second binding the natives living overseas; both involved loyalty to the same monarch. Also, as a fundamental juridical component of Italian statehood, the institution of Italian subjecthood expanded geographically to follow the nonmetropolitan and metropolitan territorial acquisitions of the Savoy kingdom. As a result, from the first colonial experiences of liberal Italy until the final fascist developments that led to the creation of a vast *comunità imperiale* within Mussolini's Roman Empire, the Italian state created a pyramid of membership statuses containing a number of citizenship links: "colonial subjecthood" (extended to the natives of the East African colonies); "colonial subjecthood," "colonial citizenship" and "special Italian citizenship" (concerning the Libyans); "Aegean Italian citizenship" (regarding the *Dodecanesini*); "Albanian citizenship" with additional special rights (for the Albanians, after the 1939 monarchical union); special status as "foreigners" (for the populations of the occupied territories of Greece, France and Yugoslavia); "metropolitan citizenship" (for the peoples of Zara and Fiume after the annexations of 1920 and 1924); and a "potential [because never approved] metropolitan citizenship" (for the Yugoslavs of the 1941 annexed territories of the Governorate of Dalmatia, the Province of Ljubljana and the enlarged Zona Fiumana).

In 1947, though, this complex system of civic bonds underwent a geographical transformation as it started shrinking following the loss, by Italy, of all nonmetropolitan territories and of some metropolitan lands as well. This major historical break within the history of Italian citizenship came about as a direct consequence of the Paris Peace Treaty, which was signed in February 1947 and went into effect in the peninsula in the following September. In accordance with this postwar settlement, drawn up by the Allies and the Associated Powers, republican Italy was obliged to lose, first of all, all the nonmetropolitan and metropolitan lands that had been acquired during Mussolini's dictatorship. This was a logical outcome bearing in mind that the Second World War had been fought against fascism and against fascist aggression. So, paying for the sins of the fascist Savoy kingdom, postwar Italy had to cede the Dodecanese Islands to Greece (annexed by Italy in 1924); recognize and respect the sovereignty and the independence of the state of Ethiopia and of the state of Albania (invaded in 1935 and 1939 respectively); and give to Yugoslavia the metropolitan lands that constituted the Province of Fiume, the Governorship of Dalmatia and the Province of Ljubljana (the first, annexed in 1924 and enlarged in 1941; the last two, incorporated into the kingdom in the latter year).[21]

Apart from losing the territories that were acquired by fascist Rome, postwar Italy was also compelled to renounce a variety of other nonmetropolitan and metropolitan lands that had been colonized or annexed before Mussolini's seizure of power. The punitive spirit of the settlement went, therefore, beyond its antifascist dimension, and as we shall demonstrate below, it came to reflect other important factors related to the international context and to the emerging rivalries among the Big Powers: the United States, the USSR, Great Britain and France. First of all, the Republic of Italy had to hand over the African colonies of Eritrea and Somalia (acquired in the nineteenth century) as well as Libya (colonized in 1912). Interestingly, though, as the Powers could not find a neat solution for the disposal of these African territories—thanks to wartime promises to native leaders and to considerations of power politics in the Mediterranean—the peace treaty took them away from Italy, kept them under British military occupation and was subsequently followed by several UN decisions. The result was that Libya became an independent state in October 1951; Eritrea, an autonomous territory federated with

Ethiopia in the subsequent year but to be annexed by the latter in 1962 after dissolution of the federation; and Somalia, a trust territory under Italian administration for a period of ten years. So with the exception of the special trusteeship over former Italian Somaliland, postwar Italy lost all the African possessions of the liberal decades.[22] Moreover, important geographical changes were to take place as regards Italy's metropolitan frontiers. In particular, the Italian republic had to make some minor border rectifications by ceding to France four small Alpine areas—especially important for their hydroelectric installations—and, most controversially, hand over to Yugoslavia the Dalmatian city of Zara and the Istrian peninsula (both attributed to Italy in 1920 following the First World War) as well as losing the city of Trieste through creation of a Free Territory under the supervision of the United Nations. These major metropolitan modifications were mainly due to Tito's international standing, to aggressive Yugoslav claims and related Soviet support, as well as to power rivalries among the United States, the USSR, Great Britain and France. As a result, post–World War Two Italy had to accept not only the end of Italian colonial rule in the African continent but also amputation of important metropolitan lands, regarded in the peninsula as integral parts of the Risorgimento process.[23]

A significant historical consequence of all these territorial modifications related to the fascist and liberal epochs is that postwar Italy started losing not only lands but also the various populations that were living in those territories and that had been linked to Rome through a variety of subjecthood bonds and metropolitan citizenship links. As a general rule, the European and African inhabitants who had lived under Italian full sovereignty only during Mussolini's dictatorship (i.e., the Dodecanese people, Ethiopians, Albanians, the population of Fiume and the people of the Governorate of Dalmatia and the province of Ljubljana) went through a process of collective naturalization and thereby acquired Greek, Albanian, Ethiopian or Yugoslav citizenship(s) on the basis of specific conditions and according to the territory concerned.

More particularly, following the cession of the Aegean islands to the Greek state, the inhabitants who were domiciled in those lands on the date of the declaration of war by Italy (10 June 1940) acquired Greek citizenship (together with their children born after this date), with the exception of those who opted for Italian citizenship on the basis of age (majority status), language requirements (use of Italian as the customary idiom), and domicile in Italy.[24] Also, as republican Italy abolished all the international agreements signed between fascist Rome and Tirana between April 1939 and September 1943, the Skipetars ceased to be Italian subjects, no longer enjoyed the special rights that had been introduced by the Duce and kept as their only status citizenship of the state of Albania.[25]

As for the populations of the Ethiopian Empire (Italian colonial subjects since 1936), they became citizens of the state of Ethiopia and acquired this new status according to a citizenship law that, to the best of our knowledge, was in force before Italian invasion and then reintroduced in Addis Ababa following demise of Italian colonial rule.[26] Finally, the inhabitants of the Upper Adriatic—living in the lands that had been annexed by Italy as metropolitan provinces in 1924 and 1941—became citizens of the People's Federal Republic of Yugoslavia according to the same principles that were applied to the Aegean Islands, including a right to opt for Italian citizenship granted to those whose mother tongue was Italian.[27]

The civic vicissitudes of the nonmetropolitan and metropolitan populations of the African and European territories of liberal Italy were to be even more complex. As regards the natives of the pre-fascist African possessions (i.e., Eritrean people, Somalis and Libyans), their loss of Italian colonial status and acquisition of new citizenship became complicated issues because of the fate that was reserved to the final disposal of their lands by the Powers and, subsequently, by the United Nations General Assembly. In fact, from the renouncement of the three territories by Italy to their final settlement by UN resolutions, the status of these autochthons remained uncertain from a juridical point of view as they stopped being Italian colonial subjects and Italian colonial citizens but no new citizenship status could be defined for them in a precise way. Only after the destiny of their lands was finally shaped in London, New York and Geneva did a new juridical situation emerge. Specifically, the Eritrean natives became nationals of their autonomous state within an unstable Ethiopian-Eritrean federal union that was created after a United Nations resolution. The Somalis came to enjoy special status as a population administered by Italy under the UN international trusteeship system. Finally, Italy's former colonial citizens in North Africa became subjects of the Kingdom of Libya, following creation of the new Libyan state in 1951 and introduction of the first postcolonial citizenship law of 1954, which however discriminated against the Libyan Jews and made them, in most cases, stateless.[28]

If we now leave the African natives and move to the lost metropolitan lands of the liberal period, the whole picture is finally complete. The juridical situation of the Italian citizens who were living in the communes of the four Alpine areas that were unified with France in 1947 was not so complicated: they simply became French citizens on the basis of domicile on 10 June 1940, and like the *Dodecanesini* and the Balkan populations of fascist Italy mentioned previously, they were granted a right to decline acquisition of new citizenship (and remain Italian) on the basis of age and language requirements.[29] By contrast, the gradual loss of the Italian citizens living in Zara, in the Istrian peninsula and in the city of Trieste was much more complicated in certain cases and, on account of the lands involved, highly emotional. The inhabitants of Zara and the Istrian peninsula became citizens of the People's Federal Republic of Yugoslavia and lost their Italian citizenship—except those who had the right to opt for it within one year from when the treaty entered into force, like all the other populations already mentioned.[30] In the Istrian case, though, the role of the other state involved in these option processes (Yugoslavia) proved to be crucially important, as noted by the scholar Ballinger, because very often Yugoslav authorities created difficulties or refused option requests.[31] Also, the *Triestini*, were to go through a turbulent civic odyssey that was determined by international political controversies concerning the status of the city and by the ups and downs of an emerging Cold War mood. As we saw, Trieste was internationalized through establishment of a Free Territory (*Territorio Libero di Trieste*, TLT) under the supervision of the United Nations. This free land was supposed to be a separate and independent state entity with a specific territory, population and government; with several official languages (i.e., Italian and Slovene and, in some circumstances, Croatian as well); with a constitution, monetary system and flag; and finally, with "citizenship of the Free Territory" (*cittadinanza del Territorio Libero di Trieste*)—different from Italian, and Yugoslav, citizenship. This new *status civitatis* was defined by the Powers in the Permanent Statute that was annexed to the peace treaty of 1947. The Italian citizens who were domiciled in the TLT on 10 June 1940 were supposed to acquire this new citizenship link with full civil and political rights and, by becoming "citizens of the Free Territory," lose their Italian nationality. Also, those over the age of eighteen (or married people, whether under or over that age) whose customary language was Italian had the right to reacquire Italian citizenship within six months from enactment of the constitution of the Free Territory, and be required to move to Italy. However, because the Western and Eastern Powers could not agree on the appointment of a UN governor for Trieste, the permanent statute never entered into force, and therefore establishment of the Free Territory and introduction of its related *status civitatis* were never realized. As a result, this contentious area of the Upper Adriatic and hotspot of Cold War rivalries was divided into two zones: "Zone A," the smaller but more populous part of the territory, contiguous to Italy and inclusive of the city of Trieste, was under British and American military administration, and "Zone B," the larger and southern portion, continued to be occupied by Yugoslav troops. Moreover, regarding the populations, they continued to hold Italian citizenship for the entire period of the foreign occupation of Zones A and B since military occupation of a territory does not have an impact on the citizenship status of the inhabitants concerned—a point we have already emphasized in other parts of this book. However, when in 1954, following the Memorandum of Understanding between Rome and Belgrade, Zone A was transferred again under the full sovereignty of the Italian state and Zone B was given to Yugoslavia, the many Italians of Zone B who had hoped their homes would remain within Italy opted for Italian nationality and emigrated through what became known as the "*grande Esodo.*"[32]

Besides these aspects of citizenship within the context of Italy's 1947 territorial losses, it is instructive to bring into the picture further diplomatic and political domestic dimensions surrounding the loss of so many lands and peoples by Italy at the time of the Treaty. The punitive component of the postwar settlement and the gradual loss of all the lands were a sour pill to swallow for the young Italian republic. Before the text of the treaty was finalized, the Italian government was allowed to express its viewpoint as the various international peace negotiations transpired. On every occasion, the Italian delegates criticized the "harsh" terms and attempted to convince the other representatives that certain "unacceptable clauses" should be modified. In general, there was a widespread feeling among the Italians that Italy was not being given credit for "having worked her passage home"—to use Churchill's phrase—by fighting alongside the allies during the twenty months of co-belligerency and contributing to the war effort.[33] Also, apart from this general argument, the Italian state felt that a distinction should be made between pre-fascist and fascist colonies, and that if it was to pay just for the crimes of fascist Italy, the young republic should be allowed to retain the African lands acquired before the advent of fascism. With the hope of finding some clemency among the Powers and being able to modify some of the territorial provisions concerning the liberal era, a variety of discourses—some valid, others less convincing—were articulated by the Italian representatives during the negotiations. In particular, an attempt was made to point out that the pre-fascist colonies had been obtained by Italy with the consent of the European powers and that, despite some drawbacks in Italian colonial policy, much had been done by the metropole to advance the well-being of the native populations. As the influential intellectual Croce would reiterate during discussions concerning approval of the peace treaty by the Italian Constituent Assembly, these were colonies that Italy "had acquired with her blood as well as administered and brought to civilized and European life with acumen and with disbursement of no abounding funds."[34] Furthermore, apart from the fact that sentimental ties linked the Italians to the African possessions, the latter were a substantial outlet for Italy's surplus population as well as being lands where Italy had invested money in the last half century, thus deserving to take legitimate profits. Finally, loss of the Istrian peninsula as well as the internationalization of the city of Trieste were to be strongly opposed with reference to the history and *italianità* of these lands.[35]

As expected, the political leaders of the United Nations in discussion around the peace table did not show much appreciation for the Italian viewpoints—with the major exception of the United States. The American delegates were, in fact, influenced by domestic pressures from the large Italian communities of immigrants and descendants who were living there. Also, as fascist aggressive foreign policy had not really threatened any vital interest of Washington, it was not so difficult for the Americans to be more sympathetic to the Italian cause than any other foreign representatives were. By contrast and understandably, too many countries wanted to punish Italy for the aggressive foreign policy of the fascist regime. Britain had almost lost its predominant position in the Mediterranean because of the Duce's project of a Second Roman Empire. As Prime Minister De Gasperi said in January 1946: "On the eve of new negotiations [...] my trepidation is great. The British Empire cannot forget that one day Italians threatened to cut its route to India."[36] Besides the hostile position of the United Kingdom, strong anti-Italian feelings were shared by France, Yugoslavia, Greece, Albania and Ethiopia, which could not forget the invasions that had taken place between 1935 and 1941; thus postwar Italy had to be reduced to never being a threat again. Also and most importantly, the various meetings and conferences that led to the final text of the treaty had the objective of reaching an agreement *among* Britain, the United States, the USSR and France rather than *with Italy*. Italian interests were in fact sacrificed and concessions granted only as part of reaching a *modus vivendi* among the Western and the Eastern Powers. When concessions were made, it was not done just in the name of the post-1943 Italian contribution to the war effort but because Italian friendship could be useful within the larger context of the political "cold hostilities" that were emerging in international relations at the systemic level. Within this context, the position of the Soviet Union at the various peace talks was particularly important. First, Soviet support of Yugoslav aspirations could be realized only at Italy's expense; second, the concessions that Italy could secure thanks to the support of the United States were often used by the USSR as a diplomatic weapon to get similar concessions for countries such as Rumania, Bulgaria and Hungary, which were under the Soviet sphere of influence. Finally, since the Cold War was just emerging and the rivalries among the Powers were not yet very deep, the concessions granted to the Italian state were less generous than those to be given to Japan and Germany within a much more polarized world.[37] So even if Italy was allowed to express its point of view as the international meetings were being held, not much consideration was eventually given to its position because the Italian peninsula was just a small pawn on the chessboard of the Big Powers.

Eventually, when the treaty was presented to Italy for signature, there was some talk in the peninsula of a refusal to sign. However, as the United States made it clear that economic aid would be cut off if the postwar settlement was not accepted, the Italians had no choice but to give their approval by signing and later ratifying it. As a result, though, revisionism via diplomacy was to become a fundamental aspect of Italian foreign policy during the first decades of the postwar period. Also and most interestingly, a particular citizenship measure, introduced in 1948, was to embody Italy's criticism of the political status quo as well as its willingness to rectify a situation regarded as unacceptable, especially in reference to the punitive clauses concerning Trieste, Istria and the Venetia-Julian area.

This special citizenship rule, still insufficiently noted within the literature, was based on a fundamental historical civic principle that, as we saw in Chapter Three, had characterized the peninsula since the time of Risorgimento and been embraced by the Italian post-unification state since the liberal epoch. The principle concerned the special status granted by Italy to the *Italiani non regnicoli*, namely, ethnic Italian immigrants holding foreign citizenship and originating, in the majority of cases, from the lands that were left out of the political unification of the country. Mindful of this category of "special foreigners of Italian nationality," the members of Italy's Constituent Assembly who were responsible for writing the Constitution of the Italian republic incorporated a citizenship norm concerning the *"Italiani non appartenenti alla Repubblica"* (Italians who do not belong to the Republic). This expression basically replaced the one just mentioned and used during the monarchical period (i.e., *Italiani non regnicoli*), since in 1946 the Savoy kingdom was abolished and a republic established. As enshrined in the 1948 constitutional text, these ethnic Italians continued to have the right to take up public functions within the civil service as well as elective positions that were reserved for Italian citizens. Therefore they clearly held a foreign status that was more privileged than the one concerning other aliens.[38] The significant thing about the discussion on the approval of this citizenship issue is that a number of constituents emphasized the enormous moral and political significance of the provision under consideration, especially because "unfair treaty" had unjustly deprived the Italian *patria* of many of "our Italian brothers." Giuseppe Codacci Pisanelli was very clear on this aspect:

I would point out the political importance of the proposal.[...] It concerns the constitutional enshrinement of a tenet which has been welcomed throughout the entire history of our Risorgimento. In a moment in which an iniquitous treaty tears our brothers from the bosom of our Fatherland, I believe it is a just recognition. And I urge the House to consider the consequences of rejecting the proposed principle. I think it is fair to acknowledge that everyone, including those who have been torn from the mother country, continue to be part of the Italian family.[39]

Clearly, as various international events dictated by Big Power politics had detached important metropolitan cities from the Italian state, the young republic felt a "duty" to make sure that the inhabitants of these lands who acquired foreign citizenship continued to partake in the *italianità* of the peninsula. Just as the 1861 Savoy kingdom had a moral and political duty vis-à-vis the *non regnicoli*, the 1946 Italian republic felt obliged toward the *non appartenenti*. Citizenship policies were a useful diplomatic instrument in this respect.

To conclude, whereas the Italian monarchical subjecthood of the Savoy kingdom expanded from a geographical point of view throughout the liberal and the fascist periods as well as being enriched with colonial and nonmetropolitan flavors, the post-1946 Italian republican citizenship went through an opposite shrinking process. In fact, it lost completely the colonial and nonmetropolitan dimension that had developed during the monarchical era, as well as being reduced in comparison with the metropolitan counterpart of the late liberal period since the northeastern part of the peninsula was, again, "truncated."

9.3. POST-WAR ITALY'S *CITTADINANZA REPUBBLICANA*: ANTIFASCISM, DEMOCRACY AND CITIZENSHIP RIGHTS

Alongside the republican change and the geographical transformations of Italian national citizenship, further civic developments took place in the peninsula during the first years of life of the new republic. This latter evolution echoed in particular postwar Italy's unequivocal rejection of fascist ideology and policies as well as its determination to take the democratic journey (begun, slowly, during the liberal period and abandoned completely by the fascist state), with a view to making Italian citizenship a primary instrument for realizing democracy. Postwar Italian *status civitatis* therefore came to represent a major point of rupture with the fascist past and a fundamental civic improvement in comparison with the liberal epoch.

The first significant citizenship reform pointing to the antifascism of the Republic of Italy concerned abolition of the racist legislation that, since 1940, had categorically excluded mixed race children (*meticci*) from acquiring or being ascribed Italian citizenship. As we saw in our previous chapter concerning the 1943–1945 period, the antifascist legitimate government in the South of the peninsula abolished the racist citizenship measures that had concerned Jews during Mussolini's late dictatorship with the objective of reintegrating them into the Italian political community. After the war, pursuing further the same antifascist policy line, the republican state dismantled the notorious civic barriers that had been built by the fascist regime against the offspring of an Italian parent and an African, Arab or Indian native. Consequently, this specific category of children was reincorporated into the circle of Italian citizenry, by granting the *meticcio* the right to Italian membership status if legitimized or recognized by the Italian parent and by guaranteeing the right of the child, born to unknown parents, to acquire Italian nationality via the decision of a competent tribunal, under the condition that the candidate concerned was not polygamous.[40] In the words of Italian Prime Minister De Gasperi, there was no room in postwar Italy for fascist racist norms because the latter were based on gravely reprehensible and inhuman principles that contradicted not only the most elementary tenets of natural law but also any moral axiom.[41] Furthermore, argued the premier, acknowledgment and reintroduction of the rights of the métis into the country's legislation were more "in line with Italian traditions and ethics" that fascism had seriously mutilated; state racism was a sad and ignominious parenthesis that had to be definitely closed in the Italian peninsula.[42]

In addition to rejection of restrictive citizenship policy, republican Italy broke with its fascist past by introducing certain fundamental constitutional guarantees that were to abolish all the citizenship provisions Mussolini had formulated in order to transform "weak liberal Italy" into a strong totalitarian state where the Italian citizen was obliged to conform to the regime's directives. To start with, the constituents who were in charge of drafting the constitutional text in 1947 unanimously embraced the important right of a person not to be deprived of his or her juridical capacity, citizenship and name because of political affiliation and ideas. Therefore, political conformity—so important within fascist ideology—was no longer to be the rule, and all Italian citizens were free to hold political views without risking being punished through "statelessness," as the Duce's regime used to do when distinguishing "good" and "bad" citizens—the first to be part of the fascist state, the second (the *fuoriusciti*) to be eliminated through civic death.[43] The constituents also made sure that all the individual freedoms the pre-1943 dictatorship had gravely undermined or completely abolished were to be restored and explicitly recognized as full constitutional entitlements. This is why, in the name of classical liberalism, post–World War Two Italy reintroduced in the peninsula all the fundamental civil rights that had already been enjoyed in the country before the seizure of power by the fascists: individual liberty, religious freedom, inviolability of domicile, freedom of expression and correspondence, freedom of movement within the country and freedom of emigration.[44]

This unequivocal and profound aversion to the past fascist era also encouraged a national process of democratization, which enriched Italian citizenship with further antifascist ingredients as well as deepening and widening the (very limited) democratic dimension that had characterized the *status civitatis* of the Italians during the liberal decades.[45] As we saw in our previous chapter, the democratic ideal had been the unifying force of the ideologically diverse and politically multifaceted Resistance movement, as well as inspiring formulation of the first citizenship norms to be introduced by the governments of the South during the 1943–1945 biennium. Continuing along this political road, the constituents made democracy the founding rock of postwar republican citizenship—meaning by *democracy* a set of principles, rules and institutions that involve the citizens' greatest participation in all public spheres and in the control of state powers.[46]

The emergence of an Italian *democratic* national citizenship—completely different from its fascist counterpart and more substantial than the juridical link uniting the Italian people before 1922—can be grasped by looking at the numerous citizenship provisions introduced by the Republic of Italy between 1946 and 1948 in order to increase the involvement of male and female Italian citizens in the political, social and economic spheres. In particular, mindful of the electoral excesses of fascism and of Mussolini's gradual erosion of political rights, the constituents ensured that political participation of the electorate would become a reality again. This is why they defined Italy as a "democratic republic" and emphasized that sovereignty was a principle, finding its sole origin in "the people" who exercised it either indirectly (through elected representatives) or directly (through referenda and people's legislative initiatives). In stark contrast with the fascist era, Italian citizens were also granted the right to associate freely in political parties and, most important of all, to vote and be elected at the national level independently of sex, since universal suffrage was enshrined in the constitution, in line with the 1945 legislation that we saw in our preceding chapter.[47]

Introduction of measures concerning "direct democracy" (i.e., referenda and legislative initiatives) as well as extension of political rights to women at the national level represented fundamental changes in comparison with the liberal years as well. Another important factor, absent during the fascist and the pre-fascist epochs, was the introduction of regional autonomy, which extended the participation of the Italians in the public sphere from the center to the periphery through creation of territorial subdivisions (i.e., regions, provinces and communes). Postwar Italy remained a unitary state:

one and indivisible. Yet political decentralization was embraced as a fundamental principle, to avoid any fascist return to a strong centralized state and to extend the Italians' public involvement at all institutional levels.[48] Finally, postwar political citizenship was clearly more democratic than the civic variants of fascist and liberal Italies because Italian citizens had now the political right to choose a president of the republic through their parliamentary representatives (rather than having a hereditary monarchical head of state) and to have a second elected chamber (in contrast with the royally nominated senators of the monarchical period).[49]

The *social* dimension of Italian republican citizenship was also very visible, especially compared to the liberal years. Thanks in particular to the size and strength of the Left parties within the Constituent Assembly, great importance was given to the concepts of "social justice" and "social rights" in drafting the constitution of the country and defining a new national citizenship for the republic.[50] As the author Paolo Vercellone reminds us, the economic and political context in the peninsula did not allow the Constituent Assembly to be silent on social issues, for a variety of reasons. First, the economic plight of most Italians was very serious because of the war, and changes were needed. Moreover, elections were due in the spring of 1948 and therefore, because of partisan politics, each political party wanted to have an electoral program that incorporated questions of social equality. Finally, the largest Italian party, Christian Democracy, had an important electoral base that, while rejecting radical revolutionary claims, wanted greater changes in the social and economic spheres; thus the party could not risk disappointing a large segment of its voters.[51] As a result, the constituents introduced significant provisions aimed at thickening the postwar social citizenship of the Italian people. For instance, they emphasized the special duty of the new republican state to remove those economic and social obstacles that, by limiting the equality of all citizens, prevented full development of the person. Also, apart from guaranteeing some general social rights related to education and health, they underlined the importance of effective participation of all workers within the economic and social organization of the country by enshrining in the constitution the right to work, freedom of social association, the right to strike, the right to take part in management of firms, the workers' right to social insurance benefits and the right of female workers to enjoy the same entitlements and salaries as their male counterparts. Finally, social assistance was also guaranteed for citizens who were in special economic need, such as the indigent and those unfit for work and without the necessary means to live.[52]

Interestingly, even though Italy's republican citizenship was clearly enriched in a substantial way with all these political, social and economic entitlements, the extent of this democratic thickening was shaped, determined and limited by the parameters of a polarized international context, where Italy came to join the Western camp of representative democracies under the leadership of the United States. Thanks to the incorporation of the peninsula within the Western sphere of influence and to the political strength of the United States in shaping postwar Italian domestic politics, the national process of democratization that took place in Italy after the end of the Second World War could not avoid the impact of an emerging Cold War climate and therefore had to keep—at a good distance—any radical democratic formulas that could have led to a Communist Italy "lost" to the Soviet camp. This was indeed a fundamental issue at the time, given the strength of the Italian Communist party within domestic politics—although the Italian Marxist left under the leadership of Togliatti was in favor of gradualist methods and hoped thereby to obtain a majority in Parliament and achieve socialism through democratic, rather than revolutionary, means.[53]

So within this context, how could Italian republican citizenship be enriched with democratic ingredients without becoming "too red"? With a view to avoiding this political risk, the constituents took a variety of "precautions." To start with, some of the most radical constitutional proposals, which could have sounded "too communist" or have brought about extreme social changes, were basically watered down. For instance, the first article of the constitutional bill was to begin with "Italy is a workers' republic"—a phrase that recalled socialist formulas—but the text that was eventually adopted sounded much more moderate: "Italy is a democratic republic founded on labor."[54] Also, in discussing the extent to which much social democracy and social rights should be introduced in the peninsula, the conservative and the moderate parties within the assembly accepted inclusion of certain social clauses so long as the left parties gave up their demands for immediate changes.[55] In some important cases, the constituents also used the additional method of laying down vague social principles and leaving to future laws the task of specifying their content—thus making the citizenship article a programmatic aspiration to be realized in the future, and only by parliamentary discussions and approved legislation. This was the case, for instance, concerning the right to strike, which could be exercised in the peninsula "within the framework of the laws regulating it," as well as the right of the workers to participate in management of their firms "in the ways and within the limits laid down by law." This means any substantial change in more socialist terms was to be postponed to a later and unspecified date and made possible only through parliamentary and democratic methods.[56] Finally, what the constituents could not do, the Americans did—by exercising political and economic pressures that ultimately shaped the context where Italian democratic citizenship was to be exercised. In the Atlantic Charter, the Allies declared that the peoples of the occupied and liberated territories would have the right to choose any type of democratic government they wished. Later, in a message to the Italian people delivered in June 1943, President Franklin Delano Roosevelt reiterated this point in a stronger way:

I think it is fair to say that all of us—I think I can speak for all the United Nations—are agreed that, when the German domination of Italy is ended and the Fascist regime is thrown out, we can well assure the Italian people of their freedom to choose the non-Fascist, non-Nazi kind of Government they wish to establish.[57]

Clearly, the underlying democratic principle implied, at least in theory, that the Italians could choose between a monarchical and a republican state, between a capitalist and a socialist economic and political system, or among combinations of them. The choice was to be—ideally—a "free" one.[58] Theory, though, was to be very different from reality. In fact, because of an emerging division of the world into two ideological, political and social blocs, the United States intervened, directly or indirectly, in the internal affairs of the peninsula, in order to preserve conservative forces and traditional property relationships and in this way avoid the loss of Italy to the opposite side. The Soviet Union was using the same tactics in its sphere of influence, for the same political objective. Bearing in mind the international context, this phenomenon was inevitable. Just to give one Italian example among many: during the political campaign preceding the Italian national elections of 18 April 1948, as the elections drew nearer, American threats to stop all economic aid in the event of a communist victory became frequent instruments of persuasion.[59] From a citizenship perspective, it is important to highlight the existence of the economic and political pressures exercised at the time because this means that the concept of democracy, the corollary tenet of having the right to choose *any* type of government and the related ideal of a democratic citizenship, were shaped in Italy, as in other countries, by the polarization of world politics.

9.4. CONCLUSION

Between 1946 and 1950, the Italians of the peninsula were confronted with important changes concerning their national citizenship. Thanks to the fall of the Savoy monarchy, they came to enjoy republican membership status, for the first time since 1861 at the national (peninsular) level; Salò was a short-lived republican experience that concerned only one part of the country and the population, and its constitutional projects never entered into force. Also, within the context of the postwar settlement concerning the defeated nations of the Second World War, the Italians lost all their nonmetropolitan and colonial counterparts as well as being detached from a substantial group of metropolitan "brothers" of the Upper Adriatic. Finally, in the name of antifascism and democracy, they started to enjoy a variety of citizenship rights that reflected the end of an epoch—Fascism—and the beginning of a long and difficult democratic journey that, as with all ideals, is never-ending.

Consequently, the boundaries and the content of the concept of *italianità*, as drawn and shaped by these historical civic developments, started evolving again. At the beginning of the postwar period, to be Italian meant being part of a republican system and sharing certain political constitutional principles with one's co-citizens—although, of course, monarchical feelings could not (and did not) disappear or fade away overnight. It also meant having to come to terms with a colonial and imperial past, as well as embracing an Italianness that, despite the "loss" of some co-citizens to the east in the Adriatic, would still incorporate them thanks to their shared national traits. Most importantly, the notion under consideration came to involve in an explicit way a full embrace of antifascism, while at the same time having to confront itself with the preceding fascist epoch and heal all the deep scars left from years of dictatorship, conflict and civil war. This would indeed be a most challenging task for postwar Italy. Finally, to be Italian in the 1946 republic meant exercising a new democratic membership status that would be fashioned in a significant way not only by domestic politics but also by the international context.

In 1951, Italy together with France, Germany and the Benelux countries was one of the founding states of the European Coal and Steel Community. This joint economic move represented the first important institutional step of a European project that, four decades later, would see creation of the European Union, following implementation of the Maastricht Treaty in November 1993. Since that time, in line with the political deepening of European integration, a new membership status has been held by all nationals of every member state: citizenship in the European Union. Consequently, the Italians, who were monarchical subjects during the liberal and fascist epochs and have been republican citizens since 1946, acquired an additional European *status civitatis* involving a variety of rights to be exercised within the EU.[60] Also, the Italians' national identity is now enriched with a European dimension that, according to a recent qualitative analysis, makes their collective identification a complex and dynamic phenomenon where local, regional, national and European attachments seem to be intertwined, contextual, contested and often in need of reaffirming their vitality.[61] The history of Italian national citizenship and of Italian national identity continues. Our historical journey, though, has ended. And it is now time to conclude the book.

National Citizenship and *Italianità* in Historical Perspective

Invited to define the Italians, students at Princeton replied: "artistic, impulsive, passionate."[1] This is a stereotype that, together with many other formulas such as "the Italian is good, [...] bright, [...] lazy, [...] an anarchist, [...] a saint, a hero," is not infrequently heard when trying to capture the "Italian character."[2] Leaving aside these curious portraits, and having reached the end of our voyage (the *ad quem* of our research), we now draw some conclusions and discuss fully the vision(s) of Italian national identity that emerge from analysis of the citizenship policies and related official discourse carried out in our history.

To this purpose, we will go back to the two metaphors introduced at the start (i.e., citizenship as a mirror and citizenship as a pencil) because it is through them that we have written this political history of Italian citizenship, and it is through them that we finally provide and discuss the full details about notions of Italianness. The first metaphor (citizenship as a mirror) has given us guidance to answer an important question: What types of national self-identification are reflected, as a mirror, in appropriating and applying certain differentiated membership policies by Italian authorities, and in the political debates pertaining to the status of the Italians from monarchical subjects to republican citizens and throughout the liberal and the fascist eras of their national history? In other words, which traditions of nationhood and which concepts of the nation have clearly shaped in the peninsula contingent adoption of certain citizenship strategies, the choice of a particular policy, the running of a discussion?

Second, and moving from mirrors to pencils, the other metaphor has provided us with assistance and support to answer a further historical question of significant importance. Since citizenship norms, legislation and debate can be a useful pencil for the historian in attempting to sketch and give form to meanings of being Italian, what findings analyzed in the *longue durée* are of particular significance in this respect? Put differently, as Italian national citizenship evolved from 1861 to 1950, how did the contours, the boundaries and the content of Italianness change, develop, adjust and end up defined in the historical epochs under consideration? National citizenship, understood both as status in law and as practice, can indeed be a mirror and a pencil for the scholar and be used as such in order to comprehend, today, notions of national identity in historical perspective. Bearing these two allegorical arguments in mind, let us start our concluding discussion.

The historical sources pertaining to the first years of national statehood (1861–1866) constitute a rich reservoir of civic aspects for understanding the origins of post-unification Italianness. As we saw in Chapter One, in 1861 the peoples of the peninsula were unified around one and the same notion of monarchical allegiance, and transformed into Italian subjects sharing one and the same state, one and the same monarch. The contours and content of *italianità* therefore started being defined and shaped in monarchical, territorial and geographical terms—more particularly, in reference to the Savoy kingdom, which from 1859 was extending its borders and was ultimately to change its name from Kingdom of Piedmont-Sardinia to Kingdom of Italy once national unification had been achieved. This means that the origins of the national notion of Italianness are marked in a fundamental way by the process of statehood that took place, both from a historical and a juridical point of view. Also, this clearly indicates that among the first important defining features of Italian national self-identification, one should highlight the unifying figure of the king and the existence of a historic territory. The first aspect—the unifying role of the Crown—refers to the historical function of the monarchy as a national cement binding all the Italians together, bearing in mind the specific, and often divisive, regional contexts of the country, as well as referring to the contribution of the monarchical institution to development of a national identity within large sections of the population.[3] Regarding the second aspect—the historic land—one can well agree with Smith's point that "the earth in question cannot be just anywhere; it is not any stretch of land. It is, and must be, the 'historic' land, the 'homeland', the 'cradle' of our people."[4] In our Italian case study, it is the peninsula— although in 1861 it was a "truncated" peninsula.

This concept of being Italian, as it began to emerge following unification and the birth of Italian monarchical subjecthood, took on a peculiar profile during the first years of Italy's national history since it was simultaneously one and many, unique and multiple, uniform and variable,

stretching over the entire post-unification Savoy state, and yet changing its contours according to the juridical landscape of the cacophonous
citizenship rules inherited from the Restoration period and kept in force
until 1865. The fact that the provisions concerning *jus soli*, naturalization
and loss of subjecthood, to name just a few, were applied according to
geography points to an important identity issue because, under these circumstances, the interrelated notions of *italiano* and *straniero* were being
fashioned in an uneven and nonhomogeneous way.

In effect, since in juridical terms it looked as if there were "many national citizenship(s) and many *italianità*" rather than "one national citizenship and one *italianità*," our case study might indeed seem *sui generis*,
especially if analyzed from the perspective of nation-statehood. Clearly,
the existence and persistence of heterogeneous and chaotic citizenship
provisions was, to say the least, atypical and not advisable within a context of political union because the populations of the peninsula, divided
already from the point of view of linguistic dialects, regional cultural
traditions and economic-social geography, were additionally separated
by invisible civic borders, making the Italians almost foreigners among
themselves. This is why introduction of a national civil code, inclusive of
uniform citizenship norms valid for all, was seen as an additional state instrument to start "making the Italians" and strengthening the interrelated
processes of statehood and nationhood.

When this citizenship unification was achieved in 1865–66, one further
factor occurred and should be highlighted because it draws additional
fascinating contours around the notion of *italianità*. This important aspect refers to the principle of descent not being contemplated at the time
in an exclusive way; as we saw, Italy diluted it in 1866 with an important
level of territoriality that, by contrast, was not taken into account in post-
unification nineteenth-century Germany. So, in this respect, we can well
argue that the lines defining the boundaries of inclusion and exclusion, as
drawn by the Italian civil code, were more inclusive than those emerging
from the citizenship norms of the German counterpart pertaining to the
children of non-Germans born in Germany.

Hence the findings at our disposal regarding the origins of Italian monarchical subjecthood (1859–1866) contain a number of initial elements
to shed light on the topic of our inquiry. During those first years of Italian
history, national identity was at its inception on the peninsula and was
therefore in the making. As we have demonstrated, major components
were significantly framing its foundation, among them the presence of a
unifying monarchical link, reference to the geographic Italian boot and
formulation of a national membership status based on descent but also
open to *jus soli*. However, we also saw that this unifying and in-the-
making Italian nationhood was by no means uncontested. In fact, it had

to compete from the very beginning with a variety of divisive discourses that touched on racializing arguments about internal Otherhood when referring to the perceived uncivilized status of the Southerners and to their non-Italianness.

If we now turn to the history and evolution of national citizenship throughout the liberal decades (1866–1922), further civic developments and details can be discerned. This citizenship evolution was examined and discussed in the four chapters of Part One, devoted respectively to female citizens and their male counterparts within the liberal state, the immigrants of the Italian kingdom, its emigrants and its nonmetropolitan populations. The historical evidence pertaining to these four themes is also particularly revealing when thinking and talking about notions of being Italian. For instance, as we have noted, during the liberal age Italian women went through a differentiated civic path compared to men, in terms of national-ity matters and content of *status civitatis*. As a result, the invisible juridical cord, linking female and male citizens to the same state, differed accord-ing to historical gender considerations. This finding clearly indicates that from the point of view of national self-identification, both women and men were Italian, but no liberal government would be ready or willing to give full legal recognition to females' national identity in the capacity of spouse and parent. Moreover, the fact that in the sphere of rights Italian female nationals were usually held to be inferior points again to a separate notion of Italianhood when referring to exercise and content of citizen-ship as practice. This is why, as emphasized in our historical account, the notion of national identity, drawn and shaped by the citizenship pencil of the numerous norms analyzed in the chapter, but also reflected as a mirror in the related discourses regarding women, had a significant gender flavor that merits being made visible in comparison as well with the British and French case studies.

Though holding differentiated status in the quality of Italians, women also shared with their male counterparts a notion of national identity that was subject to further racialized discursive representations. In par-ticular, we saw that throughout the liberal decades the Italians of the South, no matter whether female or male, continued to be pointed out as inferior and semibarbarous strangers, belonging to a primitive Medi-terranean race in opposition to a northern Aryan element. Likewise, the unifying idea of Italianness was challenged, on another front, by the ag-gressive language of anti-Semitic prejudices circulating in certain quar-ters of the peninsula; as a result, female and male Italian Jews were not unanimously seen as full Italians but actually perceived and portrayed by some co-nationals as a suspicious foreign race, undeserving of its citizenship emancipation.

Different but also similar *qua* national citizens, Italian women and men shared the same external Others—the same "special foreigners" to look to for similar traits of national identification, and also the same "outright foreigners" from whom to differentiate themselves, together, as a nation in the making. This was illustrated through our analysis of the differentiated citizenship policies and lively debates of the liberal years vis-à-vis the *Italiani non regnicoli*, on the one hand, and the non-Italian immigrants on the other. As we saw, the official discourses pertaining to the definition of the former category reflected a variety of components of Italian nationhood that are very useful within our present discussion in order to grasp the multidimensionality of Italian national identity. To start with, the image of the *non regnicoli* clearly reveals a "pre-political" vision of national self-identification, as well as a "counter-state model" of nationhood rather than a "state-framed" type. In other words, it mirrors an Italian *natio* whose existence preceded creation of the 1861 state, one that, rather than being congruent with and territorially framed by the latter as in France, was conceived as distinct from, and often in opposition to, the existing state entity, as in Germany.[5] Historically, the Italian nation—in search of a state—shared this "pre-political aspect" with its German counterpart since in both countries the "imagined community of nationhood" and "the realities of statehood" were clearly distinct. This was due, on the one hand, to the political fragmentation and the continuous foreign occupations of the peninsula before 1861, and on the other hand to the disparity between the supranational empire and the subnational sovereign units in Germany. Moreover, the two countries' models of national self-understanding shared an analogous "counter-state aspect" within their post-unification history, owing to the "truncated" Risorgimento of the peninsula, which excluded from the 1861 Italian political unification a variety of lands and populations, and to nonincorporation of the German-speaking peoples of Austria and Bohemia by Bismarck's state in 1871.

These Italian national characteristics were reflected in particular in the eloquent speeches of Mancini. The reader will surely remember that for the nineteenth-century professor the citizenship regime followed the nation rather than the political borders of statehood and therefore could well go beyond the latter, should the boundaries of Italian nationhood require it. This explains why in the Italian archives we found that citizenship policies were very generous and assimilationist in regard to the immigrants of "Italian nationality" (meaning here nation membership, and being deprived of any legal connotations) while being simultaneously more restrictive vis-à-vis the non-Italians. Clearly, the official discourses

as well as the differentiated application and adaptation of specific citizenship rules within the particular Italian context reflect idioms of Italian
nationhood. Our findings tell us that the political debates, as well as the
choice of applying certain rules to the *non regnicoli* and other norms to
the other migrants, were shaped and determined in a significant way by
notions of the nation. Put it differently, they were not completely autonomous from conceptions of nationhood. This is why, as a mirror, they
reflected in this case concepts of Italian national identity.

"Pre-political" and "counter-state," the notion of *italianità* embodied
in the figure of the *non regnicoli* was characterized by two further important aspects that must be highlighted. The first concerns the fact that the
Italianness of these special Others was defined by making explicit references to ethno-cultural, linguistic, historical and geographical considerations *as well as* to more spiritual factors, such as the patriotic will to live
together and contribute, in the case of the "unredeemed populations,"
to unification of their lands with the "free Italian provinces" of the 1861
Savoy state. This indicates that even though Italian nationhood shared a
"pre-political" nature with the corresponding notion of Germanness, it
was also distinct from the latter in an important respect. To use Federico
Chabod's famous lectures on the "Idea of the Nation," where the Italian
professor applied "the naturalistic-voluntaristic dichotomy,"[6] we can say
that Germany traditionally had a more ethnic (naturalistic) vision of national self-identification than Italy, while in the peninsula more emphasis
was put on voluntaristic connotations. Specifically, whereas the German
philosopher and ideologue Johann Gottfried von Herder (1744–1803) focused on naturalistic aspects and saw the *Volk* or nation as the possessor
of innate and unique characteristics such as language, culture, religion and
customs, the Italian counterpart represented by Mazzini defined linguistic
traits, culture, history and geography as important objective elements linking men together but never making them a nation if the paramount subjective aspect—the "consciousness of nationality"—was lacking.[7] So, in line
with the writings of these ideologues, we can argue that the Italian nation,
illustrated by the political discourses pertaining to the *non regnicoli*, was
clearly more inclusive and less ascriptive than the German *Volksnation*.[8]

The other aspect worth highlighting is that besides being a blend of
ethnic/naturalistic and civic/voluntaristic components, the notion of Italianness personified in the *non regnicoli* enjoyed another peculiarity. It did
not have precise borders, precise contours. In fact, apart from incorporating immigrant *Veneti* and *Romani*, Italian nationhood—as evoked in the
sources at our disposal—included at times *Goriziani, Triestini, Istriani*
and *Fiumani* as well as the interesting cases of *Maltesi, Corsi, Tirolesi,
Nizzardi, Ticinesi* and *San Marinesi*, while excluding the *Savoiardi*.
The elusiveness of many officials as well as the lack of unequivocal and

unanimous definitions are of particular interest because they leave us with two highly sensitive and debated historical questions. Where does the Italian nation end? What are the precise mental and geographical boundaries of *italianità*? These are historical questions that remained unanswered at the time and that are still open today, particularly when thinking and talking about Italy's Oriental frontiers in the Adriatic and the historical references to nationhood with respect to Zara, Fiume, Pola, the Istrian peninsula and parts of Dalmatia, where a clear-cut line, really, could not then and cannot now be drawn so easily—not even with President Wilson's pen used at the Paris Peace Conference.

Finally, the Italian idiom of nationhood, as clearly reflected in adoption of citizenship policies concerning alienhood and in the conduct of related political debates, must be enriched with a further point of analysis, this time regarding the notion of *italianità* as drawn by the citizenship norms pertaining to the second generations issued from non-Italian immigration and born in the peninsula. As we saw, these provisions became more restrictive in 1912 in comparison with the previous period since Italian citizenship was no longer ascribed at birth under specific conditions on children of foreign fathers but could be acquired only at majority. This aspect represented an important change from the past policies of 1865–66; however, the fact that the territorial tenet was not erased completely from Italian legislation so as to become absent, as in 1913 Wilhelmine Germany, points again to a concept of Italian national identity whose boundaries continued to be shaped in a less restrictive way than in the German example.

Study of citizenship policies regarding immigration was then followed by examination of the civic issues and provisions touching on the large communities of Italian first-generation emigrants abroad and their offspring born and settled outside the peninsula. As we argued, the liberal state found itself confronted with a political and cultural dilemma. How could the "mother country" make sure that its "sons and daughters" (together with their children) would have the least painful process of accommodation and integration in their countries of destination (and birth), but without losing national citizens and weakening the notion of *italianità* abroad?

The most significant factor for our present discussion is that naturalization of the first generations of expatriates and the related loss of Italian citizenship, on the one hand, as well as renunciation of the Italian juridical link by their offspring at majority on the other, were not necessarily seen by Italian officialdom as having a negative impact on *italianità*. Indeed, by applying a double language that shared a similar historical vocabulary with contemporary Germany (i.e. *Staatsangehörigkeit* and *Nationalität*), the Italian state linked theoretically the notion of Italianness to the term *nazionalità* (meaning here nation membership and being deprived again of any legal value) and separated it, in this context, from the word *cittadinanza* (referring to juridical citizenship). In this way, it introduced an additional idea into our political history: the sentiment of Italianness not only was linked to national legal citizenship (the latter shaping and having an impact on the former) but could also be detached from it. National identity could therefore be kept alive with or without the juridical bond linking a person to the Italian state. As we saw, this historically interesting but somehow ambiguous national discourse was backed theoretically with Mancini's teachings and with the analogy concerning the *non regnicoli*. In practical terms, it was certainly most welcome, especially from an economic and political standpoint, bearing in mind the fundamental contribution of Italian emigration to alleviating the chronic poverty of liberal Italy and the strategic importance of keeping cultural ties with the diaspora worldwide.

An emigration country throughout the liberal decades, Italy was also a late colonial power. This historical phase, explored in the last chapter of Part One, enriched the notion of Italian national citizenship with a new aspect: a nonmetropolitan dimension incorporating a hierarchical system of membership status granted to Eritreans, Somalis and Libyans, while paying particular attention to the status of the *Dodecanesini* as "special aliens" under military occupation.

This juridical situation embodied the beginning of a gradual transformation of the notion of *italianità* that lasted until 1947. The general concept of Italianhood whose boundaries and content had been shaped by specific citizenship norms and policies since the unification of the country began to take on a particular profile because at the same time that the Italian state incorporated, politically, all the nonmetropolitan populations under its rule, it attempted to categorize them as well as distinguish "the core" (the Italians of the peninsula) from the "periphery" (the natives). The members of the core and the periphery were all subjects of the Italian king. However, they were considered and treated differently on the basis of civilizational and racial considerations. As a result, the notion of Italianness came to involve a complex overseas-colonial facet that was further complicated by the realities of colonial rule.

This point can actually be grasped and further illuminated by making reference to some specific findings. For instance, we have seen that the liberal state continued to apply the *jus sanguinis* rule at home and abroad, including in the colonial setting; thus Italian citizenship was conferred on the mixed-race children of the Italian colonizers who were either born within legitimate unions or recognized by the male metropolitan parent. Many of these children were actually abandoned, but the legal possibility and even the encouragement by the liberal state to recognize the mixed-race progeny and grant them Italian citizenship are important political and juridical factors to highlight because they point to the fact that the notion of *italianità*—as drawn by this specific civic policy—was slowly evolving, although still only on paper, to adjust to the new social and cultural context. From a theoretical point of view, the idea of Italianness was being stretched to accommodate, alas with difficulty, those mixed-race children who, born in the colonies, necessarily held a complex double identity, spoke more than one language (Italian, Amharic, Arabic), could well have a Catholic father and a Christian Copt mother, and very often were victims of social or psychological exclusion within the community of one or of both parents, especially in East Africa, where they were perceived as "too dark to be Italian" or "too pale to be African."

Second, by analyzing the official discourse pertaining to the nonmetropolitan peoples of liberal Italy, we were able to appreciate other revealing aspects that can again cast a different light on the notion under consideration. For example, as the "myth of ancient Rome" was sometimes evoked in the peninsula before 1922 when thinking and talking about civic incorporation of Eritreans, Somalis and Libyans, this means that post-unification Italy found inspiration on several occasions in its Roman past, thus suggesting that the reference to *romanità* was regarded as an important, although not essential and exclusive, defining component of Italianness. Also, the historical image of the Italian maritime republics—found in the sources concerning the Aegean people—points to a notion of Italian national identity whose common myths and shared historical memories touch on a further aspect of the history of the peninsula, namely, its republican maritime tradition. Consequently, we can say that the intellectual evocation of the Idea of Rome illustrates the significance of *romanità* and *latinità* as defining characteristics of Italianhood, and that both the Roman and the maritime republican pasts shed light on the *mediterraneità* of Italian national self-identification.[9] Last and most important, shaped by this unique past and geography, the notion of post-unification Italianness was also enriched with an ideological historical paradigm that drew its origins from liberal imperialism. Consequently, the notion of being Italian (or rather, a metropolitan Italian) before 1922 was complemented with a civilizational facet making those who were part of the core responsible for and having the duty of bringing the periphery to enjoy a higher civilization within "the Italian house." This mission was by no means uncontested, thanks to a certain ambiguity surrounding the notion of civilization in the Italian context; to the "Hamitic hypothesis" making the Italian African subjects not so much different from the Italians of the metropole as part of the same Mediterranean race; to the domestic national issue of uncivilized Italians civilizing the Africans; and to discourse concerning the distant origins of the Italics either from Aryanism or from Mediterraneanism. As we saw, questions pertaining to the colonizers' national identity through the prism of colonialism had also been discussed across the Channel. However, in comparison with the British imperial counterpart, the colonial dimension of Italian national identity—a blend of Roman, Mediterranean and civilizing components—looked quite pale. This was because Italy, a late colonial power, was still trying to realize its expansionist dream by 1922 while Great Britain had already shaped a notion of common British imperial identity uniting all the populations of its vast empire to the British monarch.

So the sources at our disposal regarding Part One of the book (1866–1922) illuminate the concept of *italianità*, once again through mirrors and pencils. They suggest a vision of Italian national identity that incorporated a specific gender dimension, as explained in the pages concerning female citizenship. They illustrate the "pre-political" and "counter-state" facet of Italianhood—analogous with Germanness—but also a more inclusive nature than the latter because of the Italian emphasis on spiritual, voluntaristic and territorial elements, as discussed in the chapter pertaining to the foreigners living in Italy. They point to a concept of Italianness that contained a peculiar cultural and psychological dimension linked to the word *nazionalità* and not necessarily to (juridical) *cittadinanza*, as shown in relation to the Italian communities living abroad. And they cast light on the metropolitan and colonial contours and content of the notion under consideration, as explored in the pages concerning Italy's expansionism. In short, our findings mirror in some specific respects as well as draw in others a "multidimensional" image of "liberal *italianità*" that defies any simplistic definition, can be grasped in all its complexity by bearing in mind all these components together and, most importantly, was by no means untouched by various racial questions concerning, in different ways, Italian Southerners, Italian Jews, Italian colonial subjects and the historical origins of the Italics.

✳ ✳ ✳

This multifaceted liberal notion of Italianhood emerging from our political history could not remain the same following the coming to power of Fascism and the revolutionary agenda of the regime. The blend of continuities and discontinuities between the citizenship policies and issues of the liberal and fascist eras was examined and discussed in the three chapters of Part Two devoted to the period from 1922 to 1945—and encompassing, respectively, the membership status of women and men, civic incorporation of all the populations of Mussolini's *comunità imperiale* and citizenship and identity issues in the peninsula following the armistice with the Western Allies.

The findings concerning these themes, analyzed within their fascist context, are also very instructive in attempting to comprehend the evolution and changes of the concept of Italianness as reflected and shaped according to our two metaphorical arguments. As noted, during the fascist dictatorship Italian women continued to lack that important legal recognition of their national identity, as spouses and mothers, which their female predecessors had also been deprived of. From this viewpoint, throughout the ventennium the notion of being Italian continued to incorporate significant gender tenets when thinking about the female and male halves of the Italian population.

Sharing this peculiarity with the liberal variant, post-1922 *italianità* was characterized by further aspects of comparison as well as contrast with the previous decades. For example, the formulation and implementation by law of a new citizenship component (i.e., prolificacy), touching directly or indirectly on the related issues of birth, sexuality, *jus sanguinis* and marriage, clearly indicates that the notion of Italianness began to undergo a process of fascist transformation, being imbued, in this first case, with the Duce's totalitarian principle of demographic national strength. By contrast, the fact that *maternità* and *paternità* integrated additional gender connotations points again to the shaping of an Italian national identity that, as previously, was evidently different according to sex. Also, as emphasized in the chapter, this civic situation was enriched with certain racial discourses that did not characterize only the late years of the dictatorship but the 1920s and the early 1930s too, although in very different ways and to a very different degree. This racial rhetoric of the early decade touched in particular, as in previous years, on the origins of the Italics and on anti-Semitic prejudices, although not in a systematic manner and without being in the center of public debate or political life. From 1936 onward, then, a radical change took place as political language and related citizenship strategies were infused and saturated with aggressive racist tenets. As a consequence, Mussolini's citizenship rules started redrawing and reshaping the contours of inclusion and exclusion by magnifying the Aryan race, pushing the Jews (as well as other "non-Aryan stocks") outside the boundaries of Italianness, and upholding the idea of an Italian ethnic unity through construction of an "Aryan-Mediterranean type."

These fascist developments had an impact not only on the contours of *italianità* but also on its content. The totalitarian agenda of the regime shaped a new concept of female citizenship, understood here as practice, which like its male counterpart was transformed according to antidemocratic, antiparliamentarian, revolutionary and ultimately radical racist principles. Being a mélange of new and old repressions, dilemmas, new opportunities and new exclusions, the fascist notion of rights and entitlements began to mold a particular concept of being Italian that once more incorporated significant gender issues, as in the liberal age, but also important old and familiar racial aspects taking a new twist in the late fascist years. In effect, negative images about the Southern citizens continued to circulate in some quarters throughout the ventennium, including in the Duce's Palazzo Venezia; also, anti-Semitic prejudicial preconceptions characterized some official circles, and anti-Semitic civic discrimination was practiced within the cultural sphere from the early 1930s behind the distinguished doors of the Accademia d'Italia. Finally, owing to the radical racist turn of the regime and the coming of World War Two, fundamental breaking points occurred within the history of Italian rights, entitlements and identity, distinguishing early fascist Italy from the late dictatorship as well as late fascism from liberal Italy.

Prolific, fascist in the making and with specific domestic racial idioms, the Italians of the ventennium, as imagined and forged by the regime, came to have a mission: to create, finally, a Second Roman empire made of a multiplicity of native populations living within the orbit of Mussolini's Rome. As we have seen, fascist Italy's expansionist appetite widened the geographical borders of the Italian empire and led to civic incorporation (or special status) not only of the peoples of liberal Italy but also of the Ethiopian natives in East Africa, and of the inhabitants of Mediterranean Europe who lived in Albania, in the occupied French, Monegasque, Greek and ex-Yugoslav lands as well as in the annexed provinces of Dalmatia, Ljubljana and the enlarged *zona fiumana*. Consequently, important changes were taking place as far as the notion of *italianità* is concerned, in its nonmetropolitan and metropolitan variants. In particular, the nonmetropolitan facet (with its African and Mediterranean-European flavors) evolved as it was stretched to integrate new East African and Balkan peoples. Also, the metropolitan component underwent modification since the frontiers of peninsular Italy changed eastward. Obviously, following all these developments and events, the boundaries of Italianness were extended and given a much stronger and clearer Mediterranean tint than before.

Moreover, while expanding geographically and following the borders of an enlarging empire, the notion of what can be called fascist imperial Italianness was complemented with totalitarian and racist ingredients, which, in the overseas territories and new metropolitan lands, paralleled the situation discussed earlier in dealing with female and male citizenship on the peninsula. In particular, we have in mind the fascist tenets affirming Rome's authority and exporting the fascist revolution abroad through introduction of unifying citizenship systems in Libya and in AOI;

abolition of the 1919 Libyan Statutes with the related local parliamentary systems; introduction of new fascist citizenship provisions in Albania; forced projects of italianization implemented in the Aegean islands; the restrictive citizenship norms discussed in reference to the annexed territories of ex-Yugoslavia; and continuities with the liberal years—as far as racial thinking and colonial power relations are concerned—but also the radical breaking points represented by the legislation on *madamato* and *meticciato*.

Finally and most importantly, this fascist notion of *italianità* could not but be based on the myth of *romanità*, which, transformed into a cult, was for the regime the defining characteristic of being Italian. So, whereas the Idea of Rome—as reflected in the political discourses of the time— was an element of continuity within Italy's national self-identification across the liberal and fascist epochs, the position of the Roman paradigm within the multifaceted concept of Italianhood changed radically during the ventennium. It was marginal in liberal Italy; it was central and essential in fascist Italy. Also, it was to be enriched with references to civilization and to the Maritime Republics as in the pre-1922 years, but with a totally different rhetoric that was aggressive, brainwashing . . . fascist.

This complex, revolutionary and ever since debated transformation of pre-1922 "liberal *italianità*" into a "fascistized" new concept lasted for about two decades and was interrupted in July 1943 when Mussolini was dismissed, the fascist regime collapsed and Italian national history set off on a peculiar course. By studying the intense biennium of 1943–1945, we were able to explain how a people holding the same national citizenship, from a juridical point of view, went through months of defining and redefining notions of Italianness. Indeed, what it meant to be Italian during those days was, and still is, a further controversial, contested and sensitive issue. The expression "Italian subjects of the Savoy king" was not to be the same again; the words *patria, patriota, Italia* and *identità* all had dual and conflicting meanings according to whether they were pronounced or invoked from anti-fascist Italy or from the fascist Republic of Salò. Two radically different Italies were simultaneously being upheld. Clearly, this ideological conflict did not erupt out of the blue since it had actually started during the fascist ventennium, represented for instance by the clandestine activities of the antifascists living in the peninsula and abroad. Also, it comes to our mind that before 1943 it was embodied in the famous battle of Guadalajara during the Spanish civil war, where Italian Blackshirts and soldiers sent by Mussolini to fight alongside the Nationalist forces of Francisco Franco found themselves shooting Italian antifascist volunteers who had joined the International Brigades to fight for the Spanish Republicans. However, it is during the 1943–1945 biennium that these conflicting notions of "fascist and antifascist *italianità*" emerged fully and took a national, military and political-institutional dimension.

Finally, we also learned from our findings that at the institutional level two contrasting concepts of Italian citizenship were discussed during those months by the successive governments of the South and by Salò authorities. The first Italian citizenship link, which was actually introduced, was purged of its previous fascist, radically racist and totalitarian connotations while waiting for the institutional monarchical-republican issue to be sorted out after the end of the war. The second, formulated from Lake Garda and never approved, was defined not only as republican but also as anti-Semitic and violently racist. In the end, it was the imagined Italy of the multifaceted antifascist camp as well as the new Italian citizenship link introduced by the governments of the South that were to shape post-1945 Italy and its citizenship regime.

The policies, issues and debates pertaining to Part Two of the book (1922–1945) reflect, from one angle, as well as help us draw, from others, a notion of Italian national identity that appears to be more intriguing, complicated and contested historically than the one of the liberal decades. The findings regarding the fascist ventennium up to 1943 point to a multifaceted vision of Italianhood containing some elements of continuity with the liberal era as well as many significant historical discontinuities. In particular, the gender dimension as well as the metropolitan and colonial facets persisted throughout the dictatorship, but most important of all, they took a singular fascist profile that distinguished them from the liberal variant because of the regime's strong emphasis on totalitarian objectives, fascist revolutionary changes, exclusionary ethnic discourses as well as systematic and brain-washing references to *romanità*. Also, since racial talks continued their course throughout the ventennium, Italianness was shaped by notions of race touching on the same pre-1922 categories of peoples we have discussed: Southerners, Jews, colonial subjects, and Italics. The difference, in this respect, with the earlier Italy was of course the systematic indoctrination organized by the regime and the brutally exclusionary policies of Fascism vis-à-vis Africans and the Jews. Subsequently, the findings concerning the 1943–1945 biennium illustrate all the conflicting and dividing meanings of a notion that was being questioned, shaped and reshaped at a crucial point of Italian national history.

"Liberal" at first, and then under a process of "fascistization," the concept of post-1861 Italianness was to adapt and evolve again with the proclamation of the Republic of Italy in 1946 and the birth of a republican citizenship that is the founding pillar of today's *status civitatis* in

Italy. The years 1946–1950 were also full of interesting happenings that can help us conclude our discussion on the notion of *italianità*. For instance, as the monarchical dimension came to an end, a new concept of Italian was being reflected by the citizenship norms pertaining to republican allegiance and loyalty in regard to the constitution and the republican order. Also, as the genesis of Italian republican *status civitatis* was characterized by a gradual geographical juridical shrinking owing to the terms of the peace settlement, we were able to sketch the new contours of the notion under consideration by using citizenship policies as pencils, and see that Italianness was truncated again—with the loss of certain metropolitan lands and populations—as well as deprived of its historical nonmetropolitan colonial dimension. Finally, infused with many democratic tenets, and kept under check for evident reasons of Cold War logic, the content of the juridical link binding the Italians from 1946–1948 onward marked a major break with the fascist past and a significant advancement in comparison with the liberal years, reflecting a further characteristic of post–World War Two national identification.

The artistic, impulsive, and passionate citizens of the peninsula—Italian, European, and holding homegrown traditions of racial thinking—celebrated the 150th anniversary of Italian unity in March 2011.[10] Since 1861 they have gone through a history of national citizenship and identity that continues today through contemporary domestic debates concerning the mounting institutional visibility and racializing language of the Northern League,[11] the unprecedented historical rise of immigration into Italy,[12] and an ever-larger settled population of foreign origins with a right to Italian citizenship.[13] Between mirrors and pencils, our history of national citizenship has shown that *italianità* is by no means a fixed notion; it can be dual, multidimensional, variable in historical perspective and constantly under construction, to borrow an expression from Geoff Eley.[14] Without doubt, it currently faces major challenges and will have to adapt and adjust, as it has done in the past.

Abbreviations Used in the Notes

ACS   Archivio Centrale dello Stato, Rome

AOI   Africa Orientale Italiana

AUSSME   Archivio dell'Ufficio Storico dello Stato Maggiore dell'Esercito, Rome

b.   box

C 124   C, followed by a number, refers to a bill presented in the Chamber of Deputies

C 124-A   C, followed by a number and a letter, indicates the chamber's report on the bill

C disc. 8/7/1865
     Chamber, discussions, hearing of 8 July 1865

C disc. 8/7/1865(ii)
     Chamber, discussions, second hearing of 8 July 1865

CC   Civil Code

CCD   Consiglio del Contenzioso Diplomatico (Council of Diplomatic Disputes)

CFC   Camera dei Fasci e delle Corporazioni (Chamber of Fasci and Corporations; it replaced the Chamber of Deputies from 1939 to 1943)

CFC, AP disc.
     Camera dei Fasci e delle Corporazioni, Assemblea Plenaria, Discussioni

CFC, CLAE disc.
     Camera dei Fasci e delle Corporazioni, Commissione Legislativa degli Affari Esteri, Discussioni

CFC, CLFA disc.
     Camera dei Fasci e delle Corporazioni, Commissione Legislativa delle Forze Armate, Discussioni

CIAF   Commissione Italiana di Armistizio con la Francia

CIE	Cittadinanza italiana egea (Aegean Italian citizenship)
CIL	Cittadinanza italiana libica (Libyan Italian citizenship)
CIS	Cittadinanza italiana speciale (Special Italian citizenship)
CITC	Cittadinanza italiana in Tripolitania e Cirenaica (Italian citizenship of Tripolitania and Cyrenaica)
CS	Consiglio di Stato (Council of State)
CTLT	Cittadinanza del Territorio Libero di Trieste (Citizenship of the Free Territory of Trieste)
d. l. l.	decreto legislativo luogotenenziale (Lieutenant-general legislative decree)
EU	European Union
f.	fascicle
FCCD—SCD (1857–1923)	Fondo Consiglio del Contenzioso Diplomatico, Serie Contenzioso Diplomatico (1857–1923)
FCCD—SCD (1924–1937)	Fondo Consiglio del Contenzioso Diplomatico, Serie Contenzioso Diplomatico (1924–1937)
F-CIAF	Fondo Commissione Italiana di Armistizio con la Francia— Commissariato Civile di Mentone e Ufficio Informazioni
FD-3	Fondo D-3, Somalia
FD-7 CIAF	Fondo D-7, Commissione Italiana per l'Armistizio con la Francia
FDDAS	Fondo Serie "D"—Direzione dell'Archivio Storico (1861–1953)
FGABAP	Fondo Carte del Gabinetto del Ministro e della Segreteria Generale (1923–1943), Serie Ufficio Armistizio Pace (AP)
FL-7	Fondo L-7, Eritrea
FL-8	Fondo L-8, Libia
FM-3	Fondo M-3, Documenti Italiani restituiti dagli USA
FMAI	Fondo Ministero Africa Italiana—Gabinetto—Archivio Segreto 1°
FMICat. 1	Fondo Ministero dell' Interno—Direzione Generale della Pubblica Sicurezza—Divisione Affari Generali e Riservati—Cat. A1
FMIGpc	Fondo Ministero dell'Interno—Gabinetto—Progetti di Codici (1861–1863)
FMIM	Fondo Ministero dell' Interno—Direzione Generale della Pubblica Sicurezza—Divisione Affari Generali e Riservati— Massime (1880–1954)
FPCM	Fondo Presidenza del Consiglio dei Ministri
FSAP	Fondo Serie Affari Politici (1931–1945)

FSMERI	Fondo Scritture del Ministero degli Esteri del Regno d'Italia dal 1861 al 1887
FSPD	Fondo Segreteria Particolare del Duce—Carteggio Ordinario Serie Numerica
FSPP	Fondo Serie Politica "P" (1891–1916)
Gabap	Gabinetto—Armistizio Pace
MAE	Ministero degli Affari Esteri (Ministry of Foreign Affairs)
MAEASD	Ministero degli Affari Esteri—Archivio Storico Diplomatico, Rome
MI	Ministero degli Interni (Ministry of the Interior)
PCM	Presidenza del Consiglio dei Ministri (Presidency of the Council of Ministers)
r. d.	regio decreto (royal decree)
r. d. l.	regio decreto-legge (royal decree-law)
RSI	Repubblica Sociale Italiana
S 124	S, followed by a number, refers to a bill presented in the Senate
S 124-A	S, followed by a number and a letter, indicates the senatorial report on the bill
S disc. 2/9/1938	Senate, discussions, hearing of 2 September 1938
S disc. 2/9/1938(ii)	Senate, discussions, second hearing of 2 September 1938
SAP disc.	Senate, Assemblea Plenaria, Discussioni
S-CAESC disc.	Senate, Commissione degli Affari Esteri, degli Scambi Commerciali e della Legislazione Doganale, Discussioni
S-CFA disc.	Senate, Commissione delle Forze Armate, Discussioni
S-CR disc.	Senate, Commissioni Riunite, Discussioni
SAOI	Sudditanza dell'Africa Orientale Italiana (Subjecthood of Italian East Africa)
SC	Sudditanza coloniale (Colonial subjecthood)
SIL	Sudditanza degli indigeni della Libia (Subjecthood of the indigenous peoples of Libya)
TLT	Territorio Libero di Trieste (Free Territory of Trieste)

Notes

INTRODUCTION

1. Dante, *Divine Comedy*, vol. 3, *Paradiso*, canto XVII, lines 58–60 (*"Tu prov-erai sì come sa di sale lo pane altrui, e come è duro calle lo scendere e 'l salir per l'altrui scale"*).

2. Dante, *Divine Comedy*, vol. 1, *Inferno*, canto XXIII, lines 94–95 (*"I' fui nato e cresciuto sovra 'l bel fiume d'Arno a la gran villa"*).

3. The Latin quote is from Dante's letters V, VI and VII, in *Dantis Alagherii Epistolae/Le Lettere di Dante: Testo, versione, commento e appendici*, ed. A. Monti (Milan: Ulrico Hoepli, 1921), 92, 134 and 180. See also C. Honess, "Feminine Virtues and Florentine Vices: Citizenship and Morality in *Paradiso* XV–XVII," in *Dante and Governance*, ed. J. Woodhouse (Oxford: Clarendon Press, 1997), 102–120; as well as G. Petronio, *L'attività letteraria in Italia: Storia della lettera-tura* (Florence: Palumbo, 1980), 82–84.

4. H. Nelson Gay, "Garibaldi's American Contacts and His Claims to Ameri-can Citizenship," *American Historical Review* 38, no. 1 (1932): 1–19.

5. Ibid. Also, Garibaldi could not have become an American citizen anyway because, despite having received an American passport in 1851 and living on American soil in 1851 and 1854, he did not fulfill the five-year residence require-ment for an alien to naturalize in the United States. Ibid., 6–7 and 16–19.

6. P. Magnette, *La citoyenneté: Une histoire de l'idée de participation civique* (Brussels: Bruylant, 2001); and P. Riesenberg, *Citizenship in the Western Tradi-tion: Plato to Rousseau* (Chapel Hill: University of North Carolina Press, 1992).

7. See the collection of essays by G. Shafir, ed., *The Citizenship Debates: A Reader* (Minneapolis, London: University of Minnesota Press, 1998); as well as the concise article of W. Kymlicka and W. Norman, "Return of the Citizen: A Sur-vey of Recent Work on Citizenship Theory," *Ethics* 104, no. 1 (1994): 352–381.

8. P. Weis, *Nationality and Statelessness in International Law*, 2nd ed. (Alphen aan den Rijn, Netherlands, Germantown, Md.: Sijthoff and Noordhoff, 1979), 4–5.

9. J. Rawls, "Justice as Fairness in the Liberal Polity," in Shafir, *Citizenship Debates*, 53–72.

10. On the communitarian approach, see A. Oldfield, *Citizenship and Com-*

282   *Notes to Introduction*

munity: Civic Republicanism and the Modern World (London: Routledge, 1990). For Aristotle's concept of citizenship, J. G. A. Pocock, "The Ideal of Citizenship Since Classical Times," in Shafir, *Citizenship Debates*, 31–41.

11. P. J. Conover, "Citizenship Identities and Conceptions of the Self," *Journal of Political Philosophy* 3, no. 2 (1995): 133–165.

12. See the classic work of T. H. Marshall, *Class, Citizenship and Social Development: Essays* (Garden City, N.Y.: Doubleday, 1964).

13. P. Costa, *Civitas: Storia della cittadinanza in Europa*, vol. 1, *Dalla civiltà comunale al Settecento* (Rome, Bari: Laterza, 1999), ix.

14. Ibid.

15. Costa, "Il discorso della cittadinanza in Europa: Ipotesi di lettura," in *Cittadinanza. Individui, diritti sociali, collettività nella storia contemporanea: Atti del convegno annuale SISSCO (Società Italiana per lo Studio della Storia Contemporanea), Padova, 2–3 dicembre 1999*, ed. C. Sorba (Rome: Ministero per i Beni e le Attività Culturali-Direzione Generale per gli Archivi, 2002), 21–22.

16. See D. B. Heater, *Citizenship: The Civic Ideal in World History, Politics, and Education* (London, New York: Longman, 1990); Riesenberg, *Citizenship*; D. Zolo, ed., *La cittadinanza: Appartenenza, identità, diritti* (Rome, Bari: Laterza, 1994); S. Veca, *Cittadinanza: Riflessioni filosofiche sull'idea di emancipazione* (Milan: Feltrinelli, 1990); E. Grosso, *Le vie della cittadinanza: Le grandi radici, i modelli storici di riferimento* (Padova: Cedam, 1997).

17. J. H. Carens, "Membership and Morality: Admission to Citizenship in Liberal Democratic States," in *Immigration and the Politics of Citizenship in Europe and North America*, ed. R. Brubaker (New York, London: University Press of America, 1989), 31–49.

18. R. Bauböck, *Transnational Citizenship: Membership and Rights in International Migration* (Aldershot: Edward Elgar, 1994); Y. N. Soysal, *Limits of Citizenship: Migrants and Postnational Membership in Europe* (Chicago, London: University of Chicago Press, 1994).

19. Kymlicka, *Multicultural Citizenship: A Liberal Theory of Minority Rights* (Oxford, New York: Clarendon Press, 1995); W. Kymlicka and W. Norman, eds., *Citizenship in Diverse Societies* (Oxford: Oxford University Press, 2000); C. Taylor, *Multiculturalism and "The Politics of Recognition,"* ed. A. Gutmann (Princeton: Princeton University Press, 1992).

20. A. MacIntyre, "Is Patriotism a Virtue?" in *Theorizing Citizenship*, ed. R. Beiner (Albany: State University of New York Press, 1995), 209–228.

21. J. Löfström, "Historical Apologies as Acts of Symbolic Inclusion—and Exclusion? Reflections on Institutional Apologies as Politics of Cultural Citizenship," *Citizenship Studies* 15, no. 1 (2011): 93–108.

22. On citizenship in France, see R. Brubaker, *Citizenship and Nationhood in France and Germany* (London, Cambridge, Mass.: Harvard University Press, 1992); P. Weil, *Qu'est-ce qu'un Français? Histoire de la nationalité française depuis la Révolution* (Paris: Bernard Grasset, 2002); M. Feldblum, *Reconstructing Citizenship: The Politics of Nationality Reform and Immigration in Contemporary France* (Albany: State University of New York Press, 1999); P. Sahlins, *Unnaturally French: Foreign Citizens in the Old Regime and After* (Ithaca, London: Cornell University Press, 2004); Sahlins, "La nationalité avant la lettre: Les

pratiques de naturalisation en France sous l'Ancien Régime," *Annales: Histoire, sciences sociales* no. 5 (September–October 2000): 1081–1108; M. Vanel, *Histoire de la nationalité française d'origine: Évolution historique de la notion de Français d'origine du XVI siècle au code civil* (Paris: Ancienne Imprimerie de la Cour d'Appel, 1945). On citizenship in Germany and in Great Britain: G. Eley and J. Palmowski, eds., *Citizenship and National Identity in Twentieth-Century Germany* (Stanford: Stanford University Press, 2008); Brubaker, *Citizenship and Nationhood*; Weil, *Qu'est-ce qu'un Français?* ch. 7; M. Fulbrook, "Germany for the Germans? Citizenship and Nationality in a Divided Nation," in *Citizenship, Nationality and Migration in Europe*, ed. D. Cesarani and M. Fulbrook (London, New York: Routledge, 1996), 88–105; M. Ruby, *L'évolution de la nationalité allemande d'après les textes (1842 à 1953)* (Baden-Baden: Wervereis, 1954); Cesarani, "The Changing Character of Citizenship and Nationality in Britain," in Cesarani and Fulbrook, *Citizenship, Nationality and Migration*, 57–73; A. Fahrmeir, *Citizens and Aliens: Foreigners and the Law in Britain and the German States, 1789–1870* (London, New York: Berghahn Books, 2000).

23. See G. Brochmann and I. Seland, "Citizenship Policies and Ideas of Nationhood in Scandinavia," *Citizenship Studies* 14, no. 4 (2010): 429–443.

24. Among the most comprehensive Italian legal analyses, see L. Bussotti, *La cittadinanza degli italiani: Analisi storica e critica sociologica di una questione irrisolta* (Milan: Franco Angeli, 2002). Despite the claim made in this title for a historical analysis and a sociological critique, Bussotti's book provides a detailed historical overview of mainly juridical clauses and principles from the unification of the country to the present day. See also S. Bariatti, *La disciplina giuridica della cittadinanza italiana*, 2 vols. (Milan: Giuffrè Editore, 1989–1996); and R. Clerici, *La cittadinanza nell'ordinamento giuridico italiano* (Padova: Cedam, 1993). For a sociological and political science approach to Italian citizenship, turn to P. Donati, *La cittadinanza societaria* (Rome, Bari: Laterza, 2000); and G. Zincone, *Da sudditi a cittadini: Le vie dello stato e le vie della società civile* (Bologna: Il Mulino, 1992).

25. G. Tintori, "Cittadinanza e politiche di emigrazione nell'Italia liberale e fascista: Un approfondimento storico," in *Familismo legale: Come (non) diventare italiani,* ed. G. Zincone (Rome, Bari: Laterza, 2006), 52–106.

26. F. Pastore, "A Community out of Balance: Nationality Law and Migration Politics in the History of Post-Unification Italy," *Journal of Modern Italian Studies* 9, no. 1 (2004): 27–48; and Pastore, "Droit de la nationalité et migrations internationales: Le cas italien," in *Nationalité et citoyenneté en Europe*, ed. P. Weil and R. Hansen (Paris: La Découverte, 1999), 95–116.

27. M. Koenig-Archibugi, "National and European Citizenship: The Italian Case in Historical Perspective," *Citizenship Studies* 7, no. 1 (2003): 85–109.

28. P. Ballinger, "Borders of the Nation, Borders of Citizenship: Italian Repatriation and the Redefinition of National Identity After World War II," *Comparative Studies in Society and History* 49, no. 3 (2007): 713–741.

29. S. Berger, "A Return to the National Paradigm? National History Writing in Germany, Italy, France, and Britain from 1945 to the Present," *Journal of Modern History* 77 (2005): 629–678; R. Pertici, "Storici italiani del Novecento," *Storiografia: Rivista annuale di storia* 3 (1999): 7–53.

30. Berger, "A Return to the National Paradigm?" 638–639; Pertici, "Storici italiani," 23–25.

31. Berger, "A Return to the National Paradigm?"

32. Brubaker, *Citizenship*; Brubaker, "The Manichean Myth: Rethinking the Distinction between 'Civic' and 'Ethnic' Nationalism," in *Nation and National Identity: The European Experience in Perspective,* ed. H. Kriesi, K. Armingeon, H. Siegrist, A. Wimmer (Chur, Zurich: Verlag Rüegger, 1999), 55–71; Weil, *Qu'est-ce qu'un Français?* ch. 7; Weil, "Access to Citizenship: A Comparison of Twenty-Five Nationality Laws," in *Citizenship Today: Global Perspectives and Practices,* ed. T. A. Aleinikoff and D. Klusmeyer (Washington, D.C.: Carnegie Endowment for International Peace, 2001), 17–35.

33. Weil, *Qu'est-ce qu'un Français?* ch. 7; Weil, "Access to Citizenship," 17–35; Brubaker, *Citizenship.*

34. Weil, *Qu'est-ce qu'un Français?* 187–197.

35. Eley and Palmowsky, *Citizenship and National Identity.*

36. A. D. Smith, *National Identity* (Reno: University of Nevada Press, 1993), 15.

37. A. Triandafyllidou, "Popular Perceptions of Europe and the Nation: The Case of Italy," *Nations and Nationalism* 14, no. 2 (2008): 261–282.

38. S. Patriarca, *Italianità: La costruzione del carattere nazionale* (Rome, Bari: Laterza, 2010).

39. Ibid., ix–xii.

40. I owe this reflection to Magnette, *La citoyenneté,* 9–10. In another context, Magnette's comments echo the considerations of Italian historian Federico Chabod on the use of the words *nation, state* and *patria* (fatherland) in different historical times: F. Chabod, *L'idea di nazione,* ed. A. Saitta and E. Sestan (Rome, Bari: Laterza, 1998), 139–190.

41. Weis, *Nationality and Statelessness,* 3–12.

42. See D. Gosewinkel, "Citizenship, Subjecthood, Nationality: Concepts of Belonging in the Age of Modern Nation States," in *European Citizenship Between National Legacies and Postnational Projects,* ed. K. Eder and B. Giesen (Oxford: Oxford University Press, 2003), 18–23; and Brubaker, *Citizenship,* 50.

43. See Gosewinkel, "Citizenship, Subjecthood, Nationality," 23–27; A. Dummett and A. Nicol, *Subjects, Citizens, Aliens and Others: Nationality and Immigration Law* (London: Weidefeld and Nicolson, 1990), 20–38, 121–127; and Weis, *Nationality and Statelessness,* 3–6.

44. Magnette, *La citoyenneté,* 182–202.

45. See Gosewinkel, "Citizenship, Subjecthood, Nationality," 28–30; as well as Brubaker, *Citizenship,* 35–50.

46. Magnette, *La citoyenneté,* 7–8.

47. As cited by Riesenberg, *Citizenship,* 142.

CHAPTER ONE

1. See N. Rich, *Great Power Diplomacy, 1814–1914* (New York, London: McGraw-Hill, 1992), 123–146; J. A. Davis, ed., *Italy in the Nineteenth Century 1796–1900* (Oxford: Oxford University Press, 2000); F. Barbagallo, "Italy: The

Idea and the Reality of the Nation," *Journal of Modern Italian Studies* 6, no. 3 (2001): 388–401.

2. R. Sarti, "Giuseppe Mazzini and His Opponents," in Davis, *Italy in the Nineteenth Century*, 75.

3. See G. Mazzini [1849], "La Santa Alleanza dei Popoli," in *Scritti editi e inediti*, ed. Edizione Nazionale (Imola: Galeati, 1906–1981), 39: 215; Mazzini [1850], "Comitato Nazionale Italiano. Agli Italiani," in Edizione Nazionale, *Scritti*, 43: 219–227; Mazzini [1871], "Politica Internazionale," in Edizione Nazionale, *Scritti*, 92: 144–145; A. Levi, *La filosofia politica di Giuseppe Mazzini* (Bologna: Zanichelli, 1922).

4. V. Gioberti, *Del primato morale e civile degli italiani*, 2 vols. (Brussels: Meline Cans, 1843); and A. C. Jemolo, *Chiesa e Stato in Italia negli ultimi cento anni*, rev. ed. (Turin: Einaudi, 1990), ch. 1.

5. See A. Cardoza, "Cavour and Piedmont," in Davis, *Italy in the Nineteenth Century*, 108–131.

6. See "Costituzione della Repubblica Romana (1849)," in *Le Costituzioni italiane*, ed. A. Acquarone, M. D'Addio and G. Negri (Milan: Edizioni di Comunità, 1958), 614–624; and G. Monsagrati, "La Repubblica romana del 1849," in *Almanacco della Repubblica: Storia d'Italia attraverso le tradizioni, le istituzioni e le simbologie repubblicane*, ed. M. Ridolfi (Milan: Mondadori, 2003), 84–96.

7. The Piedmontese use of the word *regnicoli*, meaning literally "belonging to the kingdom," corresponded to the French term *regnicoles*, applied during the Old Regime to refer to all French male and female subjects of the French monarch. See Sahlins, "La nationalité avant la lettre," 1082–1083.

8. See G. Azzolini, "Principali lineamenti storici del diritto di cittadinanza in Italia: Periodo moderno," *Lo stato civile italiano* nos. 17–18 (1927): 136–137; nos. 19–20 (1927): 146–148; nos. 23–24 (1927): 179–183; as well as nos. 1–2 (1928): 1–6; nos. 3–4 (1928): 22–26; and nos. 5–6 (1928): 37–40. Also, see the civil codes that regulated citizenship in all Restoration states (except in Tuscany) in *Collezione completa dei moderni Codici Civili degli Stati d'Italia secondo l'ordine cronologico della loro pubblicazione* (Turin: Libreria della Minerva Subalpina, 1845); as well as *Codice Civile per gli Stati Estensi* (Modena: Eredi Soliani Tipografi Reali, 1852). On Tuscany, see the law on "Regolamento della nobiltà e cittadinanza" of 31 July 1750, in force in the grand-duchy since the fall of the Napoleonic system in 1814, in *Repertorio del diritto patrio toscano vigente ossia spoglio alfabetico e letterale delle più interessanti disposizioni legislative veglianti nel Granducato* (Florence: Giuliani, 1837), 6: 126–142; and, with comments, in *Legislazione toscana raccolta ed illustrata dall'avvocato Lorenzo Cantini* (Florence: Stamperia Albizziniana, 1806), 26: 231–280.

9. For an overview and discussion about these events, see Cardoza, "Cavour and Piedmont," 126–130; as well as L. Riall, "Garibaldi and the South," in Davis, *Italy in the Nineteenth Century*, 142–147.

10. Detailed descriptions and discussions concerning collective naturalizations in general can be found in E. Gordon, "Les cessions de territoires et leurs effets sur la nationalité des habitants," in B. Akzin, M. Ancel, S. Basdevant, M. Caleb, R. Drouillat, M. Gégout, E. Gordon, R. Kiefé, P. de La Pradelle, R. Maunier, B. Mirkine-Guetzévitch, J. Ray, *La nationalité dans la science sociale et dans le*

droit contemporain (Paris: Sirey, 1933), 127–145; Weis, *Nationality and State-lessness*, 135–160; C. Facelli, *Saggio sui diritti delle persone: Commento al primo titolo del codice civile italiano, godimento dei diritti civili e cittadinanza* (Turin: Unione Tipografico-Editrice, 1892), 182–189.

11. On all these changes and citizenship acquisitions, see Peace Treaty Between Austria and France (art. 12), Treaty Between France and Sardinia on the Cession of Lombardy (art. 2), and Peace Treaty Between Austria, France and Sardinia (art. 12), all signed on 10 November 1859, in *La formazione dello stato italiano: Il Risorgimento*, ed. E. Zamuner (Turin: Giappichelli, 2002), 96–109; "Cittadinanza," in *Repertorio generale annuale di giurisprudenza, bibliografia e legislazione in materia di diritto civile, commerciale, penale e amministrativo*, 5 (1880): 208–209; and the Report of Piedmontese Ministry of Foreign Affairs to CCD, 5 December 1860, in MAEASD, FCCD—SCD (1857–1923), b. 1, f. 13.

12. The quote is by jurist Carlo Francesco Gabba as cited in Zamuner, *La formazione dello stato italiano*, 3.

13. The quote by Gabba summarizes concisely a juridical debate concerning creation of the 1861 Italian state, which has been going on in the peninsula since the end of the nineteenth century and which deserves to be mentioned because, as we have just seen, it does have a bearing on the origins of Italian subjecthood as well. The issue is whether the process of Italian political unification created a "new" state from an international point of view or whether it simply led to extension of the geographical borders of an existing state (Piedmont-Sardinia), which in 1861 took a new name (*Regno d'Italia*). Today, Italian legal scholars are in agreement on this second interpretation, although the latter was much criticized in the beginning for being "unpatriotic." See Zamuner, *La formazione dello stato italiano*, 2–56; D. Anzilotti, "La formazione del Regno d'Italia nei riguardi del diritto internazionale," *Rivista di diritto internazionale* 1, no. 1 (1912): 1–33; S. Romano, "I caratteri giuridici della formazione del Regno d'Italia," *Rivista di diritto internazionale* 1, no. 3 (1912): 337–367; and P. Biscaretti di Ruffià, "Problemi, antichi e nuovi, circa la natura giuridica del 'procedimento di formazione' dello Stato italiano," *Rivista trimestrale di diritto pubblico* no. 1 (1962): 3–21.

14. R. Kiefé, "L'allégeance," in Akzin et al., *La nationalité dans la science sociale*, 50.

15. The expression "legal superior and legal inferior" is from W. W. Willoughby, "Citizenship and Allegiance in Constitutional and International Law," *American Journal of International Law* 1, no. 4 (1907): 915. The Latin phrase is by the seventeenth-century English jurist and judge Sir Edward Coke, quoted in Kiefé, "L'allégeance," 51. For a detailed discussion of this issue, see also J. W. Salmond, "Citizenship and Allegiance," *Law Quarterly Review* 17 (1901): 270–282 and 18 (1902): 49–63.

16. Gosewinkel, "Citizenship, Subjecthood, Nationality," 23–24.

17. See C. Ghisalberti, *Unità nazionale e unificazione giuridica in Italia: La codificazione del diritto nel Risorgimento*, 9th ed. (Rome, Bari: Laterza, 2002); and S. Gianzana, ed., *Codice Civile: Preceduto dalle relazioni ministeriale e senatoria, dalle discussioni parlamentari, e dai verbali della commissione coordinatrice . . .* (Turin: Unione Tipografico-Editrice, 1887–88), 4: V–LXXII and LXXIII–LXXVIII.

18. See Piedmontese CC (art. 19, 22–24), Austrian CC (art. 28), Parmese CC (art. 13, 16, 17), Two Sicilies CC (art. 11–13) and Lucca CC (art. 9, 10), in *Collezione completa dei moderni Codici Civili*; *Codice Civile per gli Stati Estensi* (art. 16, 19, 20); and on Tuscany turn to Opinion of CCD (Mancini, *rapporteur*), 22 May 1864, in MAEASD, FCCD—SCD (1857–1923), b. 1, f. 34.

19. See the archival documentation covering the period October 1861–July 1864 in MAEASD, FCCD—SCD (1857–1923), b. 1, f. 34.

20. See Council of State, 5 June 1863, "Naturalizzazione degli stranieri (Parere, adottato)," *Manuale degli amministratori comunali e provinciali* no. 3 (1 February 1864): 41–42.

21. On all these norms, see "Legge per la naturalizzazione degli stranieri" n. 1024, 17 December 1817, promulgated under the kingdom of Ferdinand I and in force in southern Italy until December 1865, in *Collezione delle leggi e decreti reali del Regno delle due Sicilie* (Naples: Stamperia Reale, 1822), Year 1817 (II Semester—July–December): 454–456; Austrian CC (art. 29, 30) and Piedmontese CC (art. 26, 42), in *Collezione completa dei moderni Codici Civili*.

22. See Two Sicilies CC (art. 20, 25), Piedmontese CC (art. 34, 35), Lucca CC (art. 17, 21), Parmese CC (art. 20, 22) and Austrian CC (art. 32), in *Collezione completa dei moderni Codici Civili*; *Codice Civile per gli Stati Estensi* (art. 23); as well as Azzolini, "Principali lineamenti storici," 181.

23. See Piedmontese CC (art. 34) and Two Sicilies CC (art. 20), in *Collezione completa dei moderni Codici Civili* as well as the Opinion of CCD (Mancini, *rapporteur*), 20 July 1864, in MAEASD, FCCD—SCD (1857–1923), b. 1, f. 34. As international law professor and deputy Pasquale Stanislao Mancini reminds us in this opinion, nonexemption from military service for a person who had nevertheless lost his citizenship of origin was due the link of subjecthood being seen as a contract with bilateral obligations from which the individual could not be exempted at will. Thus, an Italian who naturalized abroad without the sovereign's approval would lose his rights but would still have the duty to do military service as if the original status had not been completely erased.

24. C 276-A (Pisanelli, *rapporteur*), *Atti Parlamentari*, 12 January 1865, 8.

25. M. D'Azeglio, *I miei ricordi*, ed. A. M. Ghisalberti, new ed. (Turin: Einaudi, 1971), 368.

26. See Cassinis' project on the civil code for the Kingdom of Italy (April 1861) in ACS, FMIGpc, b. 2, f. 21; Miglietti's proposal (January 1862) in ACS, FMIGpc, b. 2, f. 24; Pisanelli's text (November 1863) in ACS, FMIGpc, b.3, f. 25, f. 26 and f. 27; C 276, 24 November 1864, 1–18; S 45 bis (Vigliani, De Foresta and Vacca, *rapporteurs*), 26–29 June 1864, 1–251; Gianzana, *Codice Civile*, 4: LXXIX–XCV.

27. C 276, 24 November 1864, 1.

28. C 276-A, 12 January 1865, 5; as well as the senatorial report S 45 bis, 26 June 1864, 1–3 and 117.

29. C 276-A, 12 January 1865, 1–2; Minister Vacca in S 195, 23 February 1865, 2–3.

30. S disc. 16/3/1865, 2572.

31. C disc. 21/2/1865, 8431.

32. C disc. 11/2/1865, 8170.

33. C disc. 14/2/1865, 8210.
34. C disc. 9/2/1865, 8114.
35. C disc. 17/2/1865, 8307–8308.
36. S 195 bis (De Foresta, *rapporteur*), 6 March 1865, 19.
37. See C 276-A, 24 November 1864, 26–44; the senatorial commission report on the 1862 Miglietti project in ACS, FMIGpc, b. 2, f. 22; the senatorial report about Pisanelli's text in S 45 bis, 26 June 1864, 3–7; Ghisalberti, *Unità nazionale e unificazione giuridica*, 111–146 and 223–255; Weil, *Qu'est-ce qu'un Français?* 193–197.
38. Here we are following Weil's argument in *Qu'est-ce qu'un Français?* 197 and in "Access to Citizenship," 19–21.
39. See art. 4 and 7 of *Codice Civile del Regno d'Italia* (Turin: Stamperia Reale, 1865). For a detailed explanation and discussion of the various articles pertaining to citizenship, see also Bussotti, *La cittadinanza degli italiani*, 31–41.
40. C disc. 16/2/1865, 8299; and C disc. 17/2/1865, 8313.
41. C disc. 17/2/1865, 8313.
42. Weil, *Qu'est-ce qu'un Français?* 193–197; Weil, "Access to Citizenship," 19–21.
43. See *Codice Civile del Regno d'Italia* (art. 8 and 6).
44. C disc. 16/2/1865, 8299.
45. C disc. 16/2/1865, 8276.
46. Ibid.
47. See Miglietti's proposal (art. 14, 15) in ACS, FMIGpc, b. 2, f. 24; and Pisanelli's project (art. 6, 9) in ACS, FMIGpc, b. 3, f. 25.
48. On Pisanelli's project, see S 45 bis, 26 June 1864, 14–20; S 45 ter, 1 October 1864, 1–24; S 45 ter (supplement), 8 November 1864, 1–12 and S 45 quater, 12 November 1864, 1–12. On Miglietti's text, see the related senatorial reports kept in ACS, FMIGpc, b. 2, f. 22 and f. 23.
49. Brubaker, *Citizenship*, 114–137; A. Fahrmeir, "Nineteenth-Century German Citizenships: A Reconsideration," *Historical Journal* 40, no. 3 (1997): 721–752.
50. See for example R. Grew, "Culture and Society, 1796–1896," in Davis, *Italy in the Nineteenth Century*, 206–234; and, from the same edited book, Davis, "Economy, Society, and the State," 235–263.
51. A. S. Wong, *Race and the Nation in Liberal Italy, 1861–1911: Meridionalism, Empire, and Diaspora* (New York, Basingstoke: Palgrave Macmillan, 2006).
52. Ibid., 11–23.
53. As reported in ibid., 15.
54. Ibid., 21.
55. A. Bianco di Saint Jorioz, *Il brigantaggio alla frontiera pontificia dal 1860 al 1863* (Milan: Daelli & Co., 1864), 12, quoted in P. P. Poggio, "Unificazione nazionale e differenza razziale," in *Nel nome della razza: Il razzismo nella storia d'Italia (1870–1945)*, ed. A. Burgio, 2nd ed. (Bologna: Il Mulino, 2000), 92.
56. D. T. Goldberg, "Introduction," in *Anatomy of Racism*, ed. D. T. Goldberg (Minneapolis: University of Minnesota Press, 1990), xiii.
57. Wong, *Race and the Nation*, 16–21.
58. As cited by Wong, *Race and the Nation*, 18.

59. See A. Burgio, "Per la storia del razzismo italiano," in Burgio, *Nel nome della razza*, 9–29.

60. Wong, *Race and the Nation*, 25.

CHAPTER TWO

1. The words in quotation marks are by Eric Cohen, quoted in N. Yuval-Davis, *Gender and Nation* (London, New Delhi: Sage, 1997), 1.

2. R. Bridenthal, C. Koonz and S. Stuard, eds., *Becoming Visible: Women in European History* (Boston: Houghton Mifflin, 1987).

3. The title of this section is a paraphrase of J. Bhabha, F. Klug and S. Shutter, eds., "'As a Woman I Have No Country': Women and Nationality," *Worlds Apart: Women Under Immigration and Nationality Law* (London: Pluto Press, 1985), 10–23; also republished in J. Bhabha and S. Shutter, *Women's Movement: Women Under Immigration, Nationality and Refugee Law* (London: Trentham Books, 1994), 15–28.

4. The Latin expression is cited by Facelli, *Saggio sui diritti delle persone*, 166.

5. Bhabha, Klug and Shutter, "'As a Woman I Have No Country'," 10.

6. See *Codice Civile del Regno d'Italia* (art. 11 and 14); Citizenship law n. 555 of 13 June 1912 (art. 10 and 11), in Bariatti, *La disciplina giuridica*, 1:53-58; Facelli, *Saggio sui diritti delle persone*, 163–169 and F. Degni, *Della cittadinanza* (Naples: Marghieri; Turin: Unione Tipografico-Editrice Torinese, 1921), 160–178.

7. See *Codice Civile del Regno d'Italia* (art. 4 and 7); the 1912 citizenship law (art. 1); Facelli, *Saggio sui diritti delle persone*, 124–140 and Degni, *Della cittadinanza*, 54–71.

8. See *Codice Civile del Regno d'Italia* (art. 4, 7, 9 and 10) as well as the 1912 citizenship law (art. 1, 10 and 11).

9. See Bhabha, Klug and Shutter, "'As a Woman I Have No Country'," 10–17 as well as L. F. Crane, "The Nationality of Married Women," *Journal of Comparative Legislation and International Law* 7, no. 1 (1925): 53–60.

10. See Weil, *Qu'est-ce qu'un Français?* 211–221.

11. S 164-A (Polacco, *rapporteur*), 29 May 1911, 14.

12. See "Osservazioni della commissione del Senato del Regno sul progetto di codice civile presentato dal ministro guardasigilli Miglietti nella tornata del 9 gennaio 1862," 4, in ACS, FMIGpc, b. 2, f. 22; and C 966-A (Baccelli, *rapporteur*), 30 March 1912, 6.

13. See "Relazione sul progetto del Primo Libro del codice civile presentato al Senato dal ministro guardasigilli (Pisanelli) nella tornata del 15 luglio 1863," 3–4, in ACS, FMIGpc, b. 3, f. 25 as well as M. Ancel, "Le changement de nationalité," in Akzin et al., *La nationalité dans la science sociale*, 261–274.

14. See "Relazione sul progetto del Primo Libro del codice civile presentato al Senato dal ministro guardasigilli (Pisanelli)" as well as C disc. 4/6/1912, 20325–20326.

15. See for instance U. Vogel, "Marriage and the Boundaries of Citizenship," in *The Condition of Citizenship*, ed. B. van Steenbergen (London: Sage, 1994), 76–89; N. F. Cott, "Marriage and Women's Citizenship in the United States, 1830-1934," *American Historical Review* 103, no. 5 (1998): 1440–1474.

16. "Relazione sul progetto del Primo Libro del codice civile presentato al Senato dal ministro guardasigilli (Pisanelli)" as well as C disc. 4/6/1912, 20325–20326.

17. S 45 bis, 26 June 1864, 83.

18. Facelli, *Saggio sui diritti delle persone*, 129 and 163.

19. Ibid., 228 as well as the parliamentary document C 966-A (Baccelli, *rapporteur*), 30 March 1912, 5.

20. See Vogel, "Marriage and the Boundaries of Citizenship," 76–89.

21. Ibid., 80–81.

22. S disc. 17/3/1865, 2594. The legal definition of *adultery* was also different in nineteenth-century Italy, according to whether the concept was applied to the husband or the wife; indeed, an adulterous married woman was someone who had had a sexual encounter with a man other than her husband whereas an adulterous married man was defined as someone who had a concubine and kept her without discretion. See J. J. Howard, "The Civil Code of 1865 and the Origins of the Feminist Movement in Italy," in *The Italian Immigrant Woman in North America: Proceedings of the Tenth Annual Conference of the American Italian Historical Association held in Toronto, Ontario (Canada), October 28 and 29, 1977, in conjunction with the Canadian Italian Historical Association*, ed. B. B. Caroli, R. F. Harney and L. F. Tomasi (Toronto: Multicultural History Society of Ontario, 1978), 19.

23. See Vogel, "Marriage and the Boundaries of Citizenship," 81; as well as Vogel, "Is Citizenship Gender-Specific?" in *The Frontiers of Citizenship*, ed. U. Vogel and M. Moran (London: Macmillan, 1991), 71–75.

24. S 164-A (Polacco, *rapporteur*), 29 May 1911, 13.

25. See K. Augustine-Adams, "'With Notice of the Consequences': Liberal Political Theory, Marriage, and Women's Citizenship in the United States," *Citizenship Studies* 6, no. 1(2002): 15–18. The quoted passage is on page 18.

26. C disc. 17/2/1865, 8314.

27. See Report n. 3, hearing of 15/4/1865, in Gianzana, *Codice Civile*, 3:16–18.

28. Report n. 2, hearing of 14/4/1865, in Gianzana, *Codice Civile*, 3:11.

29. Ibid., 11–12.

30. S disc. 19/6/1911, 5758–5759.

31. C 966-A (Baccelli, *rapporteur*), 30 March 1912, 14. See also S disc. 19/6/1911, 5771; S 164-A (Polacco, *rapporteur*), 29 May 1911, 22; S disc. 20/6/1911, 5785 as well as Minister of Justice Camillo Finocchiaro-Aprile in C 966, 7 July 1911, 6.

32. As cited by Bhabha, Klug and Shutter, "'As a Woman I Have No Country'," 14–15.

33. Quoted in Cott, "Marriage and Women's Citizenship," 1460–1461.

34. Bhabha, Klug and Shutter, "'As a Woman I Have No Country'," 15.

35. Ibid.

36. See M. Page Baldwin, "Subject to Empire: Married Women and the British Nationality and Status of Aliens Act," *Journal of British Studies* 40, no. 4 (2001): 522–556.

37. See Weil, *Qu'est-ce qu'un Français?* 217–221.

38. See Bariatti, *La disciplina giuridica*, 1:5–6 and 32–34; Bhabha, Klug and Shutter, "'As a Woman I Have No Country'," 10 and 20–23; Weil, *Qu'est-ce qu'un Français?* 222–224.

39. See Marshall, "Citizenship and Social Class," in Shafir, *Citizenship Debates*, 93–111; and B. S. Turner, "T. H. Marshall, Social Rights and English National Identity," *Citizenship Studies* 13, no. 1 (2009): 65–73.

40. See Zincone, *Da sudditi a cittadini*, 201–213; C. Pateman, *The Disorder of Women: Democracy, Feminism and Political Theory* (Stanford: Stanford University Press, 1989), 184–185; A. Del Re, "Le genre comme paradigme de la citoyenneté," in *Citoyenneté(s): Perspectives internationales*, ed. M. Spensky (Clermont-Ferrand: Presses Universitaires Blaise Pascal, 2003), 134–136; as well as B. Siim, *Gender and Citizenship: Politics and Agency in France, Britain and Denmark* (Cambridge: Cambridge University Press, 2000).

41. See M. Roggero, "The Meaning of Literacy: An Italian Reappraisal," *Journal of Modern Italian Studies* 14, no. 3 (2009): 346–356.

42. Davis, "Economy, Society and the State," 235–263.

43. References to electoral malpractice during the premierships of Francesco Crispi and Giovanni Giolitti are made by D. Mack Smith, *Modern Italy: A Political History* (London, New Haven: Yale University Press, 1997), 199.

44. D. I. Kertzer, "Religion and Society, 1789–1892," in Davis, *Italy in the Nineteenth Century*, 200–201. The Jews of Rome's ghetto, though, will have to wait for 1870, when Italian forces finally freed them, following the annexation of Rome to the new secular kingdom of Italy and the end of papal temporal power. Canon law and pontifical legislation had in fact "kept the Jews in their place" for centuries to "protect" Catholic society from them. See Kertzer, *The Popes Against the Jews: The Vatican's Role in the Rise of Modern Anti-Semitism* (New York: Vintage Books, 2002), 25–37, 60–85, 125–130.

45. On these aspects pertaining to civil rights, see the constitution of the Kingdom of Italy in Gianzana, *Codice Civile*, 4:1–11 and Howard, "The Civil Code of 1865," 15.

46. Howard, "The Civil Code of 1865," 15; Zincone, *Da sudditi a cittadini*, 205.

47. Weil, *Qu'est-ce qu'un Français?* 217.

48. See C. Gini and E. Caranti, "The Family in Italy," *Marriage and Family Living* 16, no. 4 (1954): 357; as well as M. Castellani, *Les femmes italiennes*, trans. C. Belin (Rome: Editrice Novissima, 1939), 111.

49. See C. Duggan, "Politics in the Era of Depretis and Crispi, 1870–1896," in Davis, *Italy in the Nineteenth Century*, 174–175.

50. Reference to universal manhood suffrage in the past national plebiscites is made by various senators and ministers during the discussions concerning the 1912 Italian electoral law in S disc. 24/6/1912, 9025–9026 and in S disc. 26/6/1912, 9085–9086. On this see Ghisalberti, *Storia costituzionale d'Italia 1848–1994*, new ed. (Rome, Bari: Laterza, 2002), 97–100. On the various Italian electoral reforms, see "Legge elettorale n. 593 del 22 gennaio 1882," together with comments, in A. Brunialti, *Legge elettorale politica* (Turin: Unione-Tipografica Editrice, 1882); "Legge sulla riforma della legge elettorale politica n. 665, 30 giugno 1912" and "Legge n. 666, 30 giugno 1912, contenente il nuovo testo

unico della legge elettorale politica," together with comments, in G. Fragola, *La legge elettorale politica* (Milan: Società Editrice Libraria, 1913); Zincone, *Da sudditi a cittadini,* 67–76; D. Caramani, *The Societies of Europe: Elections in Western Europe Since 1815* (Basingstoke, Oxford: Macmillan, 2000), 607–612.

51. See the report concerning the electoral law approved in 1882 in C 38-A (Zanardelli, *rapporteur*), 21 December 1880, 1:32; as well as the recent publication of the Italian Chamber of Deputies, *Cinquanta anni dal voto alle donne (1945–1995): Atti del convegno svoltosi alla Camera dei Deputati il 24 febbraio 1995 e documentazione allegata* (Rome: Camera dei Deputati, 1996), 40.

52. See for instance art. 8 of the 1882 electoral law as also noted and discussed by Zincone, *Da sudditi a cittadini,* 205–206.

53. This issue pertaining to the final years of liberal Italy is addressed and discussed by V. De Grazia, *How Fascism Ruled Women: Italy, 1922–1945* (Berkeley, Los Angeles and Oxford: University of California Press, 1992), 26–30; and by A. De Grand, "Women Under Italian Fascism," *Historical Journal* 19, no. 4 (1976): 948–949.

54. See P. Orman Ray, "The World-Wide Woman Suffrage Movement," *Journal of Comparative Legislation and International Law* 1, no. 3 (1919): 220–238; A. K. Smith, *Suffrage Discourse in Britain During the First World War* (Aldershot: Ashgate, 2005); as well as S. Stanley Holton, *Suffrage Days: Stories from the Women's Suffrage Movement* (London, New York: Routledge, 1996).

55. Mack Smith, *Modern Italy,* 230–232.

56. See U. Ascoli, "Le caratteristiche fondamentali del Welfare State italiano," in Sorba, *Cittadinanza,* 221; Zincone, *Da sudditi a cittadini,* 210–211.

57. Zincone, *Da sudditi a cittadini,* 211.

58. Ascoli, "Le caratteristiche fondamentali del Welfare State italiano," 216.

59. See J. Lewis, "Models of Equality for Women: The Case of State Support for Children in Twentieth-Century Britain," in *Maternity and Gender Policies: Women and the Rise of the European Welfare States, 1880s–1950s,* ed. G. Bock and P. Thane (London, New York: Routledge, 1991), 76–77.

60. See A. Buttafuoco, "Motherhood as a Political Strategy: the Role of the Italian Women's Movement in the Creation of the *Cassa Nazionale di Maternità,*" in Bock and Thane, *Maternity and Gender Policies,* 187–191.

61. Bock and Thane, "Introduction," in Bock and Thane, *Maternity and Gender Policies,* 6.

62. This point is also emphasized by Siim, *Gender and Citizenship,* 3.

63. This expression is used by Cott, "Marriage and Women's Citizenship," 1450.

64. Senator Giovanni Siotto Pintor in S disc. 17/3/1865, 2587.

65. Zincone, *Da sudditi a cittadini,* 214.

66. Ibid., 195–199 and 211–213.

67. See Deputy Francesco Restelli in C disc. 17/2/1865, 8327–8329.

68. Deputy Oreste Regnoli in C disc. 17/2/1865, 8327.

69. Ibid.

70. Deputy Roberto Mirabelli in C disc. 7/5/1912, 19106.

71. C disc. 13/2/1865, 8191.

72. Vogel, "Is Citizenship Gender-Specific?" 58–60.

73. Ibid.

74. C disc. 10/2/1865, 8136–8137.

75. Ibid. as well as Report n. 28, hearing of 11/5/1865, in Gianzana, *Codice Civile*, 3:236.

76. M. E. Wiesner, *Women and Gender in Early Modern Europe* (Cambridge: Cambridge University Press, 1993), 108–110.

77. C 38-A, 21 December 1880, 34. In line with this view, see also Senator Vittorio Rolandi Ricci in S disc. 27/6/1912, 9137.

78. C 38-A, 21 December 1880, 34–35.

79. Ibid.

80. Ibid.

81. See for instance C disc. 2/5/1912, 18979; C disc. 2/5/1912, 18973; C disc. 2/5/1912, 18983; S disc. 24/6/1912, 9028–9029; S disc. 26/6/1912, 9093 and S disc. 26/6/1912, 9099–9100.

82. C disc. 2/5/1912, 18979; S disc. 27/6/1912, 9144 and S 813, 28 May 1912, 2.

83. C disc. 2/5/1912, 18979.

84. C disc. 2/5/1912, 18973.

85. Deputy Francesco Ciccarone in C disc. 2/5/1912, 18983.

86. See Senator Raffaele Garofalo in S disc. 24/6/1912, 9028–9029; Senator Giovanni Faldella in S disc. 26/6/1912, 9093; and Senator Paolo Emilio Bensa in S disc. 26/6/1912, 9099–9100.

87. C disc. 2/5/1912, 18979.

88. S disc. 27/6/1912, 9144 and S 813, 28 May 1912, 2.

89. De Grazia, *How Fascism Ruled Women*, 26–30.

90. Wong, *Race and the Nation*, 25–77.

91. Ibid.

92. Ibid., 25–45.

93. Ibid., 26–32.

94. Ibid., 32.

95. Ibid., 35.

96. Ibid.

97. Ibid., 38–39.

98. Ibid., 47–77.

99. On this criticism concerning nineteenth-century anthropology, see ibid. as well as A. Gillette, *Racial Theories in Fascist Italy* (London, New York: Routledge, 2002), 3 and 21.

100. See Wong, *Race and the Nation*, 51–54; Patriarca, *Italianità*, 92–93; Gillette, *Racial Theories*, 26–27.

101. On Cesare Lombroso's writings and criminal science, see D. Pick, *Faces of Degeneration: A European Disorder, c. 1848–c. 1918* (Cambridge: Cambridge University Press, 1996), 109–152.

102. See Wong, *Race and the Nation*, 52–58.

103. Ibid., 58–65.

104. Ibid., 57 and 66.

105. Ibid., 39. For further discussion about Colajanni's critique of anti-Southern racism, see A. Goussot, "Alcune tappe della critica al razzismo: Le riflessioni di G. Mazzini, N. Colajanni e A. Ghisleri," in Burgio, *Nel nome della razza*, 136–137.

106. Wong, *Race and the Nation*, 43. Also, on European representations depicting the whole of Italy as the "South" of Europe, see Patriarca, *Italianità*, xvi–xviii and 3–8.

107. Wong, *Race and the Nation*, 70–77.

108. Patriarca, *Italianità*, xxiv.

109. Kertzer, *Popes Against the Jews*, 133–151.

110. Ibid.

111. *Civiltà cattolica*, 1880, as cited by Kertzer, *Popes Against the Jews*, 137.

112. Father Raffaele Ballerini, 1891, as cited by Kertzer, *Popes Against the Jews*, 144.

113. This point on the Jews and Italian national consciousness in the nineteenth century is discussed in M. Sarfatti, *The Jews in Mussolini's Italy: From Equality to Persecution*, trans. J. Tedeschi and A. C. Tedeschi (Madison, London: University of Wisconsin Press, 2006), ix–x and 3–6.

114. Kertzer, *Popes Against the Jews*, 136–137 and 144–145.

115. *Civiltà cattolica*, 1880, quoted in Kertzer, *Popes Against the Jews*, 136–137.

116. Milan daily newspaper *L'Osservatore cattolico*, 1885, emphasis in original, as cited by Kertzer, *Popes Against the Jews*, 149–150.

117. Kertzer, *Popes Against the Jews*, 142–144.

118. The Catholic daily *L'Osservatore romano*, 1898, quoted in Kertzer, *Popes Against the Jews*, 149.

119. Kertzer, *Popes Against the Jews*, 264–267.

120. Ibid., and Sarfatti, *Jews in Mussolini's Italy*, 13–14.

121. Detailed statistics of Italian Jews in the liberal (and fascist) period can be found in Sarfatti, *Jews in Mussolini's Italy*, 20–22.

122. For further discussion, see G. Miccoli, "Santa Sede, 'Questione Ebraica' e Anti-Semitismo alla fine dell'Ottocento," in Burgio, *Nel nome della razza*, 215–246.

123. All these topics are discussed in Kertzer, *Popes Against the Jews*.

124. Mazzini [1860], *The Duties of Man*, in *The Duties of Man and Other Essays* (London, Toronto: J. M. Dent, 1907), 122.

125. C. L. Bredbenner, *A Nationality of Her Own: Women, Marriage, and the Law of Citizenship* (Berkeley: University of California Press, 1998).

CHAPTER THREE

1. See Triandafyllidou, "National Identity and the 'Other'," *Ethnic and Racial Studies* 21, no. 4 (1998): 593–612.

2. See for instance M. I. Choate, *Emigrant Nation: The Making of Italy Abroad* (Cambridge, Mass., London: Harvard University Press, 2008); G. Rosoli, ed., *Scalabrini tra vecchio e nuovo mondo: Atti del convegno storico internazionale (Piacenza, 3–5 dicembre 1987)* (Rome: Centro Studi Emigrazione, 1989); Rosoli, ed., *Un secolo di emigrazione italiana: 1876–1976* (Rome: Studi Emigrazione, 1978); E. Sori, *L'emigrazione italiana dall'unità alla seconda guerra mondiale* (Bologna: Il Mulino, 1979); L. De Rosa, "Italian Emigration in the Post-Unification Period,

1861–1971," in *European Expansion and Migration: Essays on the Intercontinental Migration from Africa, Asia, and Europe*, ed. P. C. Emmer and M. Mörner (New York, Oxford: Berg, 1992), 157–178.

3. For a partial exception, see L. Einaudi, *Le politiche dell'immigrazione in Italia dall'unità a oggi* (Rome, Bari: Laterza, 2007). This detailed volume, based on meticulous research, contains a chapter on foreigners in Italy between 1861 and 1961. It does not, however, deal with the *non regnicoli*, mentioning the peninsula's political émigrés only *en passant* on page 27.

4. C 184-A (Imbriani, *rapporteur*), 18 July 1862, 2.

5. Incorporation of the populations living in the Austrian and later Austro-Hungarian empire into the Italian citizenry following 1866 and World War One was regulated by the Treaty of Vienna (concerning the inhabitants of the provinces of Venice and Mantova) as well as by several international treaties (related to the change of nationality of the peoples originating from Trentino, Süd Tirol, Gorizia, Trieste, the Istrian Peninsula and the Dalmatian city of Zara): the Peace Treaty of St. Germain-en-Laye with Austria, the Treaty of Trianon with Hungary and the Treaty of Rapallo with the Kingdom of the Serbs, Croats and Slovenes. See *The Consolidated Treaty Series*, ed. C. Perry, vol. 133, Year 1866–1867 (New York: Oceana), 210–217; as well as Bariatti, *La disciplina giuridica*, 1:119–124 and 183–184. Regarding the ex-pontifical subjects of the territories that were annexed to Italy in 1870, their change of status took place automatically following the breach of Porta Pia and the *debellatio* of the papal state and was not regulated by any international agreement. See circular letter of MAE, 30 October 1870, in *Raccolta delle circolari e istruzioni ministeriali* (Rome: Ministero degli Affari Esteri), 1:142–143.

6. Einaudi, *Le politiche dell'immigrazione in Italia*, 3–4.

7. Ibid., v and 3–16.

8. S 178-A (Di San Giuliano, *rapporteur*), 4 July 1905, 1.

9. The terms and concepts of "*non regnicoli*" and "non-Italians" go back to Piedmontese Royal Edict of 17 March 1848 concerning election of the chamber of deputies. As the edict became the basis of all subsequent electoral laws of the Savoy state and its content was also reproduced in post-unification legislation, the differentiation became a fundamental feature of liberal Italy. See G. C. Buzzati, "Note sulla cittadinanza: La concessione della cittadinanza agli italiani non regnicoli," *Rivista di diritto civile* (1916): 485–506.

10. See C. Bufardeci, "Gli italiani non regnicoli nel nostro diritto positivo," *Rivista di diritto pubblico* (1923): 607–609.

11. See the speeches of Senator Raffaele Conforti, Senator Enrico Poggi and Italy's Minister of the Interior Gerolamo Cantelli in S disc. 14/6/1869, 2207–2209.

12. See Council of State, 6 February 1866, "Naturalizzazione italiana (Parere, adottato)," *Manuale degli amministratori comunali e provinciali* no. 4 (15 February 1866): 56–57; Opinion of CCD, 24 December 1868, in MAEASD, FCCD-SCD (1857–1923), b. 1, f. 63; Bufardeci, "Gli italiani non regnicoli," 602–609.

13. See for instance a note of MAE to CCD, 2 November 1868, and the corresponding opinion by CCD, 24 December 1868, in MAEASD, FCCD-SCD (1857–1923), b. 1, f. 63. The absence of a clear definition and the presence of a

variety of interpretations are also emphasized by Bussotti, *La cittadinanza degli italiani*, 121.

14. See C disc. 26/3/1863, 6041; C disc. 3/2/1863, 985–986; and C disc. 25/3/1863, 6013.

15. See Court of Appeal of Venice, 11 October 1887, "Elezioni amministrative—Cittadini della Gorizia—Iscrizione nelle liste," *Il Foro italiano: Raccolta generale di giurisprudenza* 12 (1887): 1164–1166.

16. See C disc. 25/3/1863, 6020 and C disc. 26/3/1863, 6041.

17. See the discussions concerning the case of Carlo Schanzer in C disc. 19/12/1903, 10139–10179. On other previous occasions, birth in an Italian land (rather than residence) had been regarded by several Italian authorities as the criterion to be used for defining a *non regnicolo*. See Minister of Interior Cantelli in C disc. 30/11/1868, 8193, and in line with his argument a previous opinion of Italy's CS, 6 February 1866, "Naturalizzazione italiana (Parere, adottato)," 56–57.

18. Court of Appeal of Ancona, 2 August 1912, "Avvocato e procuratore—Italiano non regnicolo e non naturalizzato—Iscrizione nell'albo dei procuratori," *Il Foro italiano* 37 (1912): 1420–1423.

19. S disc. 19/4/1899, 926.

20. C disc. 25/3/1863, 6013.

21. Ibid.

22. See Court of Cassation in Rome, 23 April 1896, "Elezioni amministrative—Cittadino della Savoia," *Il Foro italiano* 21 (1896): 836–837.

23. See Deputy Nino Bixio in C disc. 25/3/1863, 6020.

24. S disc. 14/6/1869, 2209.

25. See Court of Cassation in Rome, 17 November 1884, "Elettorato amministrativo—Cittadino della svizzera italiana—Art. 17 legge comunale e provinciale," *Giurisprudenza italiana: Raccolta generale, periodica e critica di giurisprudenza, legislazione e dottrina* 37 (1885): 26–27; and Court of Appeal of Turin, 16 June 1884, "Elettorato amministrativo—Cittadino svizzero del Cantone Ticino—Iscrizione nelle liste—Art. 17 legge comunale e provinciale," *Giurisprudenza italiana* 36 (1884): 427.

26. See Bufardeci, "Gli italiani non regnicoli," 602–604 as well as parliamentary hearings C disc. 25/3/1863, 6020; C disc. 26/3/1863, 6041; C disc. 26/3/1863, 6046 and S disc. 14/6/1869, 2207.

27. See Council of State, 31 March 1905, "Medico condotto—Nomina—Cittadinanza italiana—Cittadini di provincie geograficamente italiane—Ammissibilità della nomina—Obbligo e diritti—Contributo alla Cassa pensioni," *Il Foro italiano* 30 (1905): 107–110.

28. See Deputy Cairoli in C disc. 25/3/1863, 6012, and the commission's report in C 184-A, 18 July 1862, 3–4. The quote is by Deputy Mauro Macchi speaking before the Low Chamber in C disc. 26/3/1863, 6032.

29. C 184-A, 18 July 1862, 3.

30. In chronological order, see the previously mentioned judicial sources: Court of Appeal of Turin, 16 June 1884; Court of Cassation of Rome, 17 November 1884; Court of Appeal of Venice, 11 October 1887; Court of Cassation in Rome, 23 April 1896; Court of Appeal of Ancona, 2 August 1912.

31. Bufardeci, "Gli italiani non regnicoli," 609–616. Obviously, not every *non*

regnicolo who had naturalized enjoyed national political rights, but only those who fulfilled the census, literacy and gender requirements that characterized liberal Italy and that we discussed in the preceding chapter.

32. The term *denizenship*, used in past centuries to describe a halfway status between a citizen and a noncitizen, was first applied by Thomas Hammar in 1990 to refer to the status of contemporary migrant workers as quasi-citizens who enjoy particular rights in the country of immigration despite their legal foreignness. See T. Hammar, *Democracy and the Nation-State: Aliens, Denizens, and Citizens in a World of International Migration* (Aldershot: Avebury, 1990).

33. Bufardeci, "Gli italiani non regnicoli," 612–616; Bussotti, *La cittadinanza degli italiani*, 121–123. This finding concerning local political entitlements for the *non regnicoli* during the liberal period contributes to the growing contemporary literature on the particular history of local political participation of resident noncitizens in European countries. It is commonly argued that Sweden was the first European state to grant this right in 1976, followed by Denmark, the Netherlands and the United Kingdom. See O. Le Cour Grandmaison and C. Wihtol de Wenden, eds., *Les étrangers dans la cité: Expériences européennes* (Paris: La Découverte, 1993). Clearly, within the historical limits of male suffrage and of a notion of shared nationhood, liberal Italy preceded all these states as it allowed some resident noncitizens to vote at the local level despite their foreign citizenship. For a theoretical discussion concerning the much-debated issue of alien suffrage in today's nation-states, see S. Song, "Democracy and Noncitizen Voting Rights," *Citizenship Studies* 13, no. 6 (2009): 607–620.

34. The privileged position of the *non regnicoli* living in the Italian kingdom is also demonstrated by the fact that apart from the rights mentioned above and in addition to the position of councilor, they could be appointed to certain state jobs—reserved exclusively for citizens—without the need to naturalize. For instance, they could apply within the civil service, exercise the profession of chartered accountant and, from 1911, be appointed general practitioner in a *comune* of the kingdom.

35. On these three cases, see the speeches of Deputy Stefano Castagnola in C disc. 25/3/1863, 6014–6015 and of Deputy De Boni in C disc. 25/3/1863, 6020.

36. See Cairoli's proposals in C 184, 3 February 1862, 1 and C 196, 1 June 1868, 1. For a concise overview, Buzzati, "Note sulla cittadinanza," 491–494.

37. See C 196-A (Cairoli, *rapporteur*), 27 November 1868, 2; Cairoli's speech in C disc. 30/11/1868, 8195; as well as his pre-1866 interventions in C disc. 3/2/1862, 985–987; C disc. 25/3/1863, 6011–6012 and C disc. 26/3/1863, 6034–6035.

38. Mancini, *Della nazionalità come fondamento del dritto delle genti* (Turin: Eredi Botta, 1851), in *Della nazionalità come fondamento del diritto delle genti di Pasquale Stanislao Mancini*, ed. E. Jayme (Turin: Giappichelli, 1994), 19–64.

39. See Deputy Mancini in C disc. 25/3/1863, 6016–6018 and in C disc. 27/3/1863, 6088; as well as his classic *Della nazionalità*, 48 and 51.

40. A. Sammartino, "Culture, Belonging, and the Law: Naturalization in the Weimar Republic," in Eley and Palmowski, *Citizenship and National Identity*, 62.

41. C disc. 25/3/1863, 6014.

42. C disc. 25/3/1863, 6019.

43. The politically and diplomatically sensitive nature of the issue concerning naturalization of *non regnicoli* originating from Austrian and papal lands was emphasized for instance by Minister of the Interior Ubaldino Peruzzi and Minister of Justice Pisanelli in C disc. 26/3/1863, 6035–6040 and 6044–6045 as well as by Deputy Cadorna in Report n. 2, hearing of 14/4/1865, in Gianzana, *Codice Civile*, 3:10. Obvious matters of foreign policy were involved.

44. S 119, 2 July 1881, 4.

45. S 164-A, 29 May 1911, 12.

46. See Bufardeci, "Gli italiani non regnicoli," 628–634.

47. Senator Leopardi's speech in S disc. 14/6/1869, 2209.

48. Court of Appeal of Turin, 16 June 1884, 425–427.

49. See Italy's various electoral laws; the 1865 civil code (art. 10); and Council of State, 6 February 1866, "Naturalizzazione italiana (Parere, adottato)," 56–57.

50. See Sahlins, *Unnaturally French*, 307–320; Weil, *Qu'est-ce qu'un Français?* 42–43, 58–59 and 244–245.

51. See President of Council of Ministers and Minister of the Interior Crispi in S 53, 12 March 1888, 1; and in C 121, 25 February 1888, 1.

52. See the report C 121-A (Nocito, *rapporteur*), 21 May 1888, 1.

53. See C disc. 8/6/1888, 3360.

54. See C 78-A (Nocito, *rapporteur*), 23 February 1888, 3; and C 121-A, 21 May 1888, 2.

55. See for instance the report C 121-A, 21 May 1888, 2; and the hearing S disc. 2/5/1906, 3048.

56. See Sidney Sonnino's speech in C 179, 24 May 1905, 1; senatorial report S 178-A, 4 July 1905, 1; as well as parliamentary commission report C 179-C (Riccio, *rapporteur*), 9 May 1906, 1–2.

57. The 1901 provision introduced acquisition of full citizenship (inclusive of national political rights) being granted without the intervention of the Italian parliament to those who were born in the kingdom or abroad and who became foreigners because they were minor children of a father who had lost Italian citizenship, or to those born in the kingdom or abroad to a father who had lost Italian citizenship before the child's birth. See art. 36 of law on emigration n. 23, 31 January 1901, *Raccolta ufficiale delle leggi e dei decreti del Regno d'Italia* (Florence: Stamperia Reale, 1861–1946), Year 1901, 77. In 1906, on the contrary, Sonnino's law granted full Italian citizenship (except the right to sit in parliament during the first six years) to be bestowed by royal decree after the favorable opinion of Italy's Council of State upon the following categories: foreigners who had six years of residence in the kingdom or in the Italian colonies; foreigners who had rendered four years of service to the Italian state (also abroad); and foreigners with three years of residence in the kingdom (or in the colonies) and who had married an Italian woman or performed significant services for Italy. See art. 1 of Sonnino's law n. 217, 17 May 1906, *Raccolta ufficiale delle leggi e dei decreti*, Year 1906, 1282–1283.

58. See S 164, 22 February 1910, 8; S disc. 3/7/1911, 6583–6584; S disc. 1/7/1911, 6560–6562 and S disc. 19/6/1911, 5751–5752.

59. Following approval of the 1912 citizenship law, non-Italian aliens could acquire full citizenship after five years of residence in the kingdom. Alternatively,

they could become Italian after three years of services rendered to the state (even abroad) or after three years of residence in Italy (combined with important services to the Italian state). See art. 4 of the 1912 citizenship law. Regarding the counter-arguments in favor of liberalizing the whole naturalization process, see S 164-A, 29 May 1911, 13; S disc. 3/7/1911, 6585; and S disc. 20/6/1911, 5783 and 5792.

60. This figure is confirmed by our research in the archives and can also be found in various primary and secondary sources dealing with "grand naturalization." See for instance the senatorial hearing S disc. 2/5/1906, 3048–3051, and the parliamentary document C 179, 24 May 1905, 1. Also, Azzolini, "Principali lineamenti storici," 26.

61. A similar exercise was recently carried out by Sahlins in his concise article concerning French naturalizations under the Ancien Régime from 1660 to 1789. Whereas the author has approached the question from the point of view of the individual and used the foreigners' letters as his sources, our analysis of the Italian case study—never attempted before—is based on state authorities' documentation to see the reasons given by the Italian state for accepting or refusing someone as a full citizen. See Sahlins, "La nationalité avant la lettre," 1081–1108. Unfortunately, the foreigners' letters one would expect to find in an application form for naturalization in Italy seem to have been destroyed, or gone astray, or not been kept in the archival files.

62. The quote is by President of the Council of Ministers Bettino Ricasoli speaking before the Low Chamber in C 13, 21 December 1866, 4.

63. On Waddington, see in particular C disc. 28/1/1864 (ii), 3068; C 13, 21 December 1866, 5; C 60, 13 May 1867, 5; and parliamentary commission report C 13-A (Corsi, *rapporteur*), 11 February 1867, 3. On Mayor and on Nathan, see respectively C 80-A (Ferri, *rapporteur*), 15 March 1888, 1; and C 76-A (Marcora, *rapporteur*), 7 February 1888, 1–2.

64. C 83, 24 March 1866, 1.

65. See S 53-A (Borelli, *rapporteur*), 17 March 1888, 2.

66. See C 79-A (Chiaradia, *rapporteur*), 4 February 1888, 1; C 79, 10 December 1887, 1; S 51-A (Guarini, *rapporteur*), 16 March 1888, 1; as well as C 81, 10 December 1887, 1.

67. On the two Ammans, see C disc. 30/6/1889, 3224; on the Kossuth brothers see Crispi in C 120, 25 February 1888, 1 as well as the parliamentary commission reports C 120-A (Cucchi, *rapporteur*), 24 March 1888, 1 and S 113-A (Guerrieri-Gonzaga, *rapporteur*), 4 July 1888, 1.

68. See C 78-A, 23 February 1888, 2; S 53-A, 17 March 1888, 1; S 54, 12 March 1888, 1; the senatorial commission in S 54-A (Trocchi, *rapporteur*), 15 March 1888, 1; and the parliamentary document C 152, 6 February 1899, 1–2.

69. See Sahlins, "La nationalité avant la lettre," 1091; and Riesenberg, *Citizenship*, 187–199.

70. See letter of MI to CS, 28 November 1864, in MAEASD, FSMERI, b. 1498, f. 12.

71. See for instance Crispi in C 76, 10 December 1887, 1; and in S 52, 12 March 1888, 1.

72. See C 120, 25 February 1888, 1; C 120-A, 24 March 1888, 2; C disc. 8/6/1888, 3357; and S 113, 1 July 1888, 1.

73. See S 252-A (Borgatti, *rapporteur*), 29 June 1882, 1–2.

74. C 77, 10 December 1887, 1; S 74, 22 April 1888, 1; C 77-A (Pais, *rapporteur*), 20 March 1888, 1–2.

75. M. Viroli, *Per amore della patria: Patriottismo e nazionalismo nella storia* (Rome, Bari: Laterza, 2001); M. Rosati, *Il patriottismo italiano: Culture politiche e identità nazionale* (Rome, Bari: Laterza, 2000).

76. Brubaker, *Citizenship*, 81.

77. See *Codice Civile del Regno d'Italia* (art. 8 and 6).

78. See the 1912 citizenship law (art. 3).

79. See Senator Pasquale Fiore in S disc. 1/7/1911, 6544–6545; Jurist and Senator Gabba in S disc. 1/7/1911, 6547; and Senator Lodovico Mortara in S disc. 1/7/1911, 6551.

80. S disc. 20/6/1911, 5783.

81. Senator Polacco in S disc. 20/6/1911, 5783. On the same point, see S disc. 1/7/1911, 6545; and C 966, 7 July 1911, 3.

82. Brubaker, *Citizenship*, 119–137.

83. Ibid.

84. Ibid., 1–17 and 122–125. Here we are following Brubaker's historical account of the nationalisms developed in these two countries, but without embracing his conclusions on the history of citizenship, which in fact were flawed from several legal perspectives, as demonstrated by Fahrmeir and Weil. See Fahrmeir, "Nineteenth-Century German Citizenships," 721–752; and Weil, *Qu'est-ce qu'un Français?* ch. 7.

CHAPTER FOUR

1. G. A. Stella, *L'orda: Quando gli Albanesi eravamo noi* (Milan: Rizzoli, 2003).

2. Contemporary poem cited by Italian Senator Fedele Lampertico in S disc. 22/1/1901, 878, and containing verses of Virgil's *Aeneid*.

3. The quoted phrase is by Deputy Guido Fusinato in C disc. 4/6/1912, 20334.

4. Tintori, "Cittadinanza," 52–106; Pastore, "A Community out of Balance," 27–48.

5. See R. Bauböck, "The Rights and Duties of External Citizenship," *Citizenship Studies* 13, no. 5 (2009): 475–499. By proposing a stakeholder criterion, the author discusses "external citizenship" using this term to mean "a generic concept that refers to the status, rights and duties of all those who are temporarily or permanently outside the territory of a polity that recognizes them as members" (ibid., 478). Bauböck's theoretical discussion covers both first-generation emigrants and subsequent generations.

6. Data are taken from L. Favero and G. Tassello, "Cent'anni di emigrazione italiana (1876–1976)," in Rosoli, *Un secolo di emigrazione italiana*, 21, 25 and 29.

7. Brunialti, "Gli italiani fuori d' Italia," *La rassegna nazionale* 60 (1890): 626.

8. The historical expressions "*O migranti o briganti*" and "*O emigrare o rubare*" (either to emigrate or to steal) were commonly used at the time among the migrants themselves and often repeated by religious and political representa-

tives dealing with the care and the welfare of Italian families during their migratory experiences. Representing an entire epoch, these expressions acquired a special historical meaning and are now part of the national vocabulary of the country, evoked for instance by the Italian Scalabrinian missionaries of the Catholic Church around the world involved in migration issues since Bishop Giovanni Battista Scalabrini founded the order in 1887. See Rosoli, *Scalabrini tra vecchio e nuovo mondo*; the document "Ruolo della Chiesa italiana nell'assistenza ai migranti," available at http://www.cestim.org (accessed 26 March 2012); and the website of the Scalabrini Order, http://www.scalabrini.org. On the causes of Italian emigration during this period, see Sori, *L'emigrazione italiana*, 69–118; and F. P. Cerase, "Economia precaria ed emigrazione," in Rosoli, *Un secolo di emigrazione italiana*, 117–135.

9. See Choate, *Emigrant Nation*, ch. 1, which contributes to the scholarship on Italian emigration by emphasizing the historical initial connection between Italian emigrations abroad and colonialism.

10. Sori, *L'emigrazione italiana*, 28–32 and 62–65, as well as De Rosa, "Italian Emigration," 165–167. The theoretical distinction between push and pull factors in migration studies goes back to the nineteenth-century geographer Ernest George Ravenstein and to the formulation of his statistical laws in 1885 and 1889. It has subsequently been endorsed by neoclassical economic theorists. On the contrary, the role of family chain migration in developing informal social networks that can encourage and facilitate migration flows has been emphasized by so-called migration system theorists. The migratory phenomenon has been approached from a variety of theoretical angles; for an introductory overview of the major theories, see S. Castels and M. J. Miller, *The Age of Migration* (New York: Palgrave Macmillan, 2003), 21–32.

11. De Rosa, "Italian Emigration," 167–169; and Sori, *L'emigrazione italiana*, 32–39, 205–211 and 348–361.

12. Pastore, "A Community out of Balance," 28.

13. Tintori, "Cittadinanza," 52–106.

14. C disc. 4/6/1912, 20322. Also cited in Pastore, "A Community out of Balance," 30–31.

15. See law n. 555 of 13 June 1912 (Disposizioni sulla cittadinanza italiana).

16. For instance, the Fourth National Juridical Congress, organized in Naples in 1897; the First Congress of the Italians Abroad, held in Rome in 1908; the Twentieth Congress of the Dante Alighieri National Society for Italian Language and Culture Outside the Kingdom, taking place in Brescia in 1909; and the Second Congress of the Italians Abroad, organized in the Italian capital in 1911.

17. There is an interesting ongoing discussion in migration studies that focuses on the definition(s) and appropriate use of the term *diaspora*. For some scholars the word is to be applied only restrictively to refer to those ethnic groups that have been territorially dispersed across different countries following an initial violent episode causing the first migratory flows and the exile. In this case, the term would refer to the Jews (the first classic example of diasporic peoples), the Armenians, the Africans, and the Palestinians but would not be appropriate for the Italian case study. Other scholars, by contrast, have extended this initially nar-

row definition and used the term to refer to those communities abroad that were first dispersed not necessarily for ethnopolitical persecutions but for economic factors. It is this "broad definition" that is of course relevant for our analysis on Italian emigration. On this debate, see S. Rosière, "Groupe ethniquement minoritaires et violence politique: Essai de typologie," *Diasporas: Histoire et sociétés* 10, first semester (2007): 11–25; as well as C. Bordes-Benayoun and D. Schnapper, "Entretien: Les mots des diasporas," *Diasporas: Histoire et sociétés* 13, second semester (2008): 11–19. Among the scholars who apply the term to the Italian case, turn to D. R. Gabaccia, *Italy's Many Diasporas* (London: UCL Press, 2000); T. Tsuda, "Ethnic Return Migration and the Nation-State: Encouraging the Diaspora to Return 'Home'," *Nations and Nationalism* 16, no. 4 (2010): 616–636.

18. See *Codice Civile del Regno d'Italia* (art. 11) and Facelli, *Saggio sui diritti delle persone*, 206–207.

19. See Brubaker, *Citizenship*, 114–115; and Facelli, *Saggio sui diritti delle persone*, 190–191.

20. See Weil, *Qu'est-ce qu'un Français?* 256–259.

21. See Kiefé, "L'allégeance," 48–59 as well as Dummett and Nicol, *Subjects, Citizens, Aliens and Others*, 86–87. In the words of the nineteenth-century British jurist William Blackstone, this is how one could explain perpetual and indissoluble allegiance: "Natural allegiance is a debt of gratitude that can neither be subject to limitation, nor be cancelled nor, modified, by any lapse of time, in any place, under any circumstances. It can be wiped out only with the intervention of Parliament or of the King. An Englishman who emigrates to France or to China owes the same allegiance to the King of England as if he resided in his country— and this is the case on the day of his departure as twenty years later.[...] It is in fact a principle of universal law that a prince's subject by birth can neither by his own authority, nor by taking an oath of allegiance to another prince, liberate himself from the natural allegiance that he owed to the first [sovereign]." Taken from Kiefé, "L'allégeance," 54.

22. See hearing of 16/6/1911, in *Atti del secondo congresso degli italiani all'estero (11-20 giugno 1911)*, 2 vols. (Rome: Tipografia Editrice Nazionale, 1912), 2:95.

23. A. Franzoni's report to the Twentieth Congress of the Dante Alighieri Society (Brescia, September 1909), *Cittadinanza e nazionalità* (Rimini: G. Benzi, 1909), 13–16.

24. Hearing of 16/6/1911, in *Atti del secondo congresso*, 2:102. This first point is emphasized by Tintori as well in his "Cittadinanza," 61.

25. Hearing of 16/6/1911, in *Atti del secondo congresso*, 2:115–116.

26. Franzoni, *Cittadinanza e nazionalità*, 8–15.

27. Ibid. The quote is on page 14.

28. Contrary to "institutional or structural racism," which is sustained by state laws and administrative practices, "informal racism" consists of racist attitudes among a population or part of it. The first type of racism is endorsed and perpetrated by the host country through state institutions, while the second concerns the discriminatory behavior of the people in general. Whether "institutional" or "informal," racism can be defined, within the migratory context, as the in-

feriorization and differentiation of certain groups on the basis of phenotypical or cultural markers. I owe these definitions to Castles and Miller, *The Age of Migration*, 35–36.

29. See Stella, *L'orda*, 38–54. Also, on the experiences of these Italians, often called the "Chinese of Europe" in the United States because they were perceived as undesirable, inassimilable and racially inferior, turn to Wong, *Race and the Nation*, 120–124 and 131–136.

30. Stella, *L'orda*, 38.

31. See V. Ruget and B. Usmanalieva, "How Much Is Citizenship Worth? The Case of Kyrgyzstani Migrants in Kazakhstan and Russia," *Citizenship Studies* 14, no. 4 (2010): 445–459.

32. As reported by Deputy Fusinato in the Italian parliament in C disc. 4/6/1912, 20335.

33. See the article by L. Zimmermann, K. F. Zimmermann and A. Constant, "Ethnic Self-Identification of First-Generation Immigrants," *International Migration Review* 41, no. 3 (2007): 769–781, acknowledging this complexity and providing an analysis (of today's foreign nationals in Germany) based on a two-dimensional dependent variable.

34. See V. Polacco and A. Ricci-Busatti, "Il problema della cittadinanza specialmente nei rapporti degli italiani all'estero," in *Atti del secondo congresso*, 1:63–69.

35. Tintori, "Cittadinanza," 59–60.

36. Pastore, "A Community out of Balance," 29.

37. On these expansive naturalization policies, see Buzzati, "Cittadinanza e Servizio Militare," in *Atti del primo congresso degli italiani all'estero (ottobre 1908)*, 2 vols. (Rome: Cooperativa Tipografica Manuzio, 1910), 1:6; and Degni, *Della cittadinanza*, 198–199. Various criticisms by legislative and executive Italian authorities of the Brazilian system of "imposed naturalizations" can be found in C disc. 4/6/1912, 20325; C disc. 7/6/1912, 20530; S 164-A, 29 May 1911, 14; S disc. 19/6/1911, 5751; and in MAEASD, FDDAS, b. 40, f. 405. Finally, see Pastore, "Droit de la nationalité," 98 and Rosoli, "La crise des relations entre l'Italie et le Brésil: La grande naturalisation (1888–1896)," *Revue européenne des migrations internationales* no. 2 (1986): 69–90.

38. The Latin quote can be found in C 966-A, 30 March 1912, 3 and in Facelli, *Saggio sui diritti delle persone*, 206.

39. See the 1912 citizenship law (art. 8, 9, 13). Also, Pastore, "A Community out of Balance," 31 and Tintori, "Cittadinanza," 90–91.

40. See T. B. Sejersen, "'I Vow to Thee My Countries': The Expansion of Dual Citizenship in the 21st Century," *International Migration Review* 42, no. 3 (2008): 523–549.

41. For instance, Buzzati suggested that the "dual nationals" should have enjoyed all rights and duties in the country of immigration; should have had their original Italian citizenship "suspended" partially (as if it were a "citizenship in lethargy"), although political rights could have been exercised in both countries; should not have been drafted by either of their two states in case of war; and finally, could have reactivated their Italian "sleeping citizenship" in the totality of its rights and duties by returning to the Italian kingdom. See *Atti del primo*

congresso, 1:27–28; and *Atti del secondo congresso*, 2:94–96. In line with Buz-zati's point of view, see Franzoni, *Cittadinanza e nazionalità*, 17–27 as well as his intervention in *Atti del secondo congresso*, 2:119–120. Also, on Buzzati's argu-ment and related debate between Buzzati and his colleague Nissim Samama, turn to Tintori, "Cittadinanza," 92–93 and 85–86.

42. See Tintori, "Cittadinanza," 86–97.
43. C disc. 4/6/1912, 20324.
44. C 966-A, 30 March 1912, 3; also Tintori, "Cittadinanza," 88.
45. C disc. 7/6/1912, 20533.
46. C 966-A, 30 March 1912, 3; and C disc. 11/6/1912, 20700.
47. Minister of Justice Finocchiaro-Aprile in S disc. 20/6/1911, 5791.
48. See Deputy Scialoja as quoted in C 966-A, 30 March 1912, 4; and Deputy Baccelli in C disc. 11/6/1912, 20700.
49. Facelli, *Saggio sui diritti delle persone*, 206.
50. See the 1912 citizenship law (art. 8).
51. See for instance Minister Finocchiaro-Aprile in C 966, 7 July 1911, 5.
52. Polacco and Ricci-Busatti, "Il problema della cittadinanza," 68.
53. C disc. 7/6/1912, 20536; and S disc. 20/6/1911, 5787.
54. Baccelli in C 966-A, 30 March 1912, 5.
55. Tintori, "Cittadinanza," 90–91.
56. Finocchiaro-Aprile in C 966, 7 July 1911, 5; and Senatorial Central Bureau in S 164-A, 29 May 1911, 20–21.
57. See the 1912 citizenship law (art. 9 and 13).
58. For this comparative analysis, see Brubaker, *Citizenship*, 114–119; as well as Weil, *Qu'est-ce qu'un Français?* 200–202.
59. Tintori, "Cittadinanza," especially 62–65 and 76–86.
60. Senatorial authority in S 164-A, 29 May 1911, 6. This point was also high-lighted during the Second Congress of the Italians Abroad by a delegate proposing to make clear that the Italian expatriates who participated in the political life of their country of settlement were not "antipatriotic" and did not deny their original *patria* by doing it. *Atti del secondo congresso*, 2:101–102. Finally, see also Italian jurist Luigi Raggi (1903) as discussed in Tintori, "Cittadinanza," 76–77.
61. Encouraging interventions were made, for instance, in S 164-A, 29 May 1911, 6; by Deputy Sonnino, *Quid agendum? Appunti di politica e di economia* (Rome: Direzione della Nuova Antologia, 1900), 19; and by Deputy Lelio Bonin in C disc. 24/11/1900, 461–462 as cited by Tintori, "Cittadinanza," 62–63.
62. C disc. 7/6/1912, 20536.
63. Ibid.
64. Senator Polacco in S disc. 20/6/1911, 5782.
65. Tintori, "Cittadinanza," 63–64 and 93–94.
66. See C disc. 4/6/1912, 20323.
67. Ibid.
68. C disc. 11/6/1912, 20703. Also Tintori, "Cittadinanza," 93–94.
69. Einaudi (1874–1961) was a professor of economics in Turin. With his book *A Merchant Prince: A Study in Italian Colonial Expansion* (1899), he greatly influenced liberal Italy's ruling elites dealing with emigration and interna-tional trade relations. On Einaudi's vision, see Choate, *Emigrant Nation*, 49–56.

70. S 164-A, 29 May 1911, 6.

71. On this point, see ibid.; Senator Scialoja in *Atti del secondo congresso*, 2:117–118; and Senator Polacco and Professor Ricci-Busatti, "Il problema della cittadinanza," 64–65, 84–85. Finally, see "Conclusioni e voti approvati dal Congresso," in *Atti del secondo congresso*, 2:517–518.

72. S 164-A, 29 May 1911, 6.

73. *Atti del secondo congresso*, 2:117–118.

74. Ibid., 117.

75. See for instance the points made by Bonin in 1900. by Samama in 1910, and by Baccelli in 1912, as cited and discussed in Tintori, "Cittadinanza," 63, 84, and 93–94.

76. *Atti del secondo congresso*, 2:117–118. This point was also supported and defended on other occasions during the liberal epoch. For instance, in 1909 the Italian writer Franzoni argued that "one [could] be a national, or rather belong to our nationality, without having ever been an Italian citizen; and an individual [continued] to belong to it even though, due to the vicissitudes of life, [had] successively acquired and lost various foreign citizenships." See Franzoni, *Cittadinanza e nazionalità*, 6. More than a decade later, an Italian academic will maintain the same principle: citizenship meant "State membership" (*appartenenza ad uno Stato*) whereas nationality referred to "membership to an ethnic group" (*appartenenza ad un gruppo etnico*), the latter sharing common origins, territory, language and traditions. The two terms, however, did not always correspond; in fact, "[nationality] may or may not coincide with the concept of citizenship." Degni, *Della cittadinanza*, 59.

77. See Italian civil code (art. 4) and F. De Dominicis, *Commento alla legge sulla cittadinanza italiana del 13 giugno 1912* (Turin: Unione Tipografico-Editrice Torinese, 1916), 35–37.

78. Pastore, "A Community out of Balance," 29.

79. All these points were made by Deputy Grippo in C disc. 4/6/1912, 20324; by Deputy Angelo Cabrini in C disc. 7/6/1912, 20532; by Senator Scialoja in S disc. 19/6/1911, 5772; and in the senatorial report S 164-A, 29 May 1911, 17.

80. C disc. 4/6/1912, 20324.

81. C disc. 4/6/1912, 20335.

82. C disc. 11/6/1912, 20706.

83. C disc. 11/6/1912, 20705.

84. Ibid., 20706.

85. See Deputy Baccelli in C 966-A, 30 March 1912, 10; and in C disc. 11/6/1912, 20701. In line with this criticism, see also the speeches of Minister of Justice Finocchiaro-Aprile in C disc. 11/6/1912, 20710; and of Deputy Secretary of State for Foreign Affairs Pietro Lanza di Scalea in C disc. 11/6/1912, 20698.

86. Baccelli in C 966-A, 30 March 1912, 10; as well as Finocchiaro-Aprile in C disc. 11/6/1912, 20710–20711, in C disc. 7/6/1912, 20543 and in C 966, 7 July 1911, 2–3.

87. See Deputy Luigi Borsarelli in C disc. 7/6/1912, 20539–20540.

88. This argument was defended, for instance, in the volume *Il problema politico dell'emigrazione italiana e la questione della cittadinanza* (Rome: Coop. Tipografica Popolo Romano, 1911), written by "Un Italiano" and published in

preparation for the Second Congress of the Italians Abroad. It is also mentioned in S 164-A, 29 May 1911, 17.

89. Tintori, "Cittadinanza," 88–90.

90. See art. 7 of the project in S 164, 22 February 1910, 8.

91. See S 164-A, 29 May 1911, 17–18 and 28; as well as art. 7 of the 1912 citizenship law.

92. S 164-A, 29 May 1911, 7.

93. See S 164-A, 29 May 1911, 4. The same figurative style was also used by Deputy Cabrini in C disc. 7/6/1912, 20529. For the definition of *nexum* in Roman law, *The New Encyclopaedia Britannica* (Chicago: Encyclopaedia Britannica, 1985), 8:664, s.v. "Nexum."

94. See Polacco and Ricci-Busatti, "Il problema della cittadinanza," 73–74.

95. Choate, *Emigrant Nation.*

96. I owe all these points of analysis to Choate, *Emigrant Nation*, especially ch. 3 and ch.7.

97. Ibid., 2–3, 218–220 and 244.

CHAPTER FIVE

1. See for example B. Sòrgoni, *Parole e corpi: Antropologia, discorso giuridico e politiche sessuali interrazziali nella colonia Eritrea (1890–1941)* (Naples: Liguori editore, 1998); G. Barrera, "Sex, Citizenship and the State: The Construction of the Public and Private Spheres in Colonial Eritrea," in *Gender, Family and Sexuality: The Private Sphere in Italy, 1860–1945*, ed. P. Willson (New York, Basingstoke: Palgrave Macmillan, 2004), 157–172; Barrera, "Patrilinearity, Race, and Identity: The Upbringing of Italo-Eritreans During Italian Colonialism," in *Italian Colonialism*, ed. R. Ben-Ghiat and M. Fuller (New York, Basingstoke: Palgrave Macmillan, 2005), 97–108; Barrera, "Patrilinearità, razza e identità: L'educazione degli Italo-eritrei durante il colonialismo italiano (1885–1934)," *Quaderni storici* 109, no. 1 (2002), 21–53; E. Capuzzo, "Sudditanza e cittadinanza nell'esperienza coloniale italiana dell'età liberale," *Clio* 31, no. 1 (1995), 65–95. Despite the claim made by Capuzzo's title for an analysis of subjecthood and citizenship in liberal Italy's colonial experience, her article covers all the African territories during the liberal era while leaving out the Dodecanese before 1922 (and discussing it only in reference to the fascist period). Also, see the recent monograph of Luca Pignataro, *Il Dodecaneso italiano (1912–1947)*, vol.1, *Lineamenti giuridici: L'occupazione iniziale (1912–1922)* (Chieti: Edizioni Solfanelli, 2011) where the author, though, examines citizenship issues only from 1923 onward, ibid., 21–29.

2. See A. Del Boca, *Gli italiani in Africa Orientale*, vol. 1, *Dall'unità alla marcia su Roma*, 2 tomes (Rome, Bari: Biblioteca Universale Laterza, 1985); Del Boca, *L'Africa nella coscienza degli italiani: Miti, memorie, errori, sconfitte* (Milan: Mondadori, 2002), 3–39; G. Candeloro, *Storia dell'Italia moderna* (Milan: Feltrinelli, 1977), 4:334–342.

3. Del Boca, *Gli italiani in Africa Orientale*, vol. 1, t. 1, 233.

4. See G. Mondaini, *La legislazione coloniale italiana nel suo sviluppo storico e nel suo stato attuale (1881–1940)*, 2 vols. (Milan: Istituto per gli Studi di Politica

Internazionale, 1941), 1:229–260; Del Boca, *Gli italiani in Africa Orientale*, vol. 1, t. 1, ch. 5 and t. 2, ch. 8.

5. "Colonia Eritrea: Censimento della popolazione indigena. Anno 1905," *Bollettino ufficiale della colonia Eritrea*, 12, in AUSSME, FL-7, b. 125, f. 38; Del Boca, *Gli italiani in Africa Orientale*, vol. 1, t. 1, 123, 164, 359; as well as Mondaini, *La legislazione coloniale*, 1:238. As emphasized in various Italian military correspondence and reports of 1888–89, serious problems emerged in the colonies in reference to establishment of a regular *état civil* for the natives and about related collection of statistical data. The difficulty was due in particular to the indigenous peoples' suspicion vis-à-vis the colonizers, to the opposition of the Muslim followers to registering women and children and to the frequent nomadism of the populations. For these reasons, colonial censuses were often approximations and must be read with great caution. See the semestral reports of the Secretariat of Indigenous Affairs, "Massaua, 29 giugno 1888, protocollo n. 1926/130" and "Massaua, 17 dicembre 1889, protocollo n. 4533/54," in AUSSME, FL-7, b. 125, f. 16 and b. 132, f. 18 respectively.

6. See "Colonia Eritrea: Censimento," 12; the report of the colonial civil commissary Ferdinando Martini in C LXII, 14 June 1913, vol. 1, 44–45; Senator Pierantoni's speech in S disc. 14/5/1903, 2156; Mondaini, *La legislazione coloniale*, 1:211 and 362; Del Boca, *Gli italiani in Africa Orientale*, vol. 1, t. 1, 430.

7. See Capuzzo, "Sudditanza e cittadinanza," 65–69.

8. Ibid., 68–69. These arguments are discussed at length in the third section of this chapter.

9. See A.-R. Werner, *Essai sur la réglementation de la nationalité dans le droit colonial français* (Toulouse: Boisseau, 1936), 17–19, 40–46, 175–178 and 187–188.

10. I owe these words to Sòrgoni, *Parole e corpi*, 3.

11. See M. D'Amelio, *L'ordinamento giuridico della colonia Eritrea* (Milan: Società Editrice Libraria, 1911), 241–243.

12. Sòrgoni, *Parole e corpi*, 109; Capuzzo, "Sudditanza e cittadinanza," 72.

13. See D'Amelio, *L'ordinamento giuridico*, 241–246; Romano, *Corso di diritto coloniale* (Rome: Athenaeum, 1918), 1:130–134; Sòrgoni, *Parole e corpi*, 109 and 95.

14. Sòrgoni, *Parole e corpi*, 207. The term *meticcio* (mixed-race) is generally perceived as offensive by the population concerned. It was offensive at the time and it continues to be so today. Yet we cannot do without this historical terminology since it was widely employed in policies and debates.

15. See Sòrgoni, *Parole e corpi*, 91–92, 104–108, 121, 213–214; Barrera, "Patrilinearità, razza e identità," 21; the circular letter of Governo dell'Eritrea—Direzione degli Affari Civili, 22 December 1917, almost entirely reprinted in Capuzzo, "Sudditanza e cittadinanza," 75–77.

16. See Sòrgoni, *Etnografia e colonialismo: L'Eritrea e l'Etiopia di Alberto Pollera (1873–1939)* (Turin: Bollati Boringhieri, 2001). For some other examples of Italian high colonial officials who recognized their children in Eritrea as well as giving them their surname and patrimony, see Barrera, "Patrilinearità, razza e identità," 27–28.

17. As reported in Sòrgoni, *Parole e corpi*, 121.

18. See Sòrgoni, *Parole e corpi*, 122; Barrera, "Patrilinearità, razza e identità,"

39–40; Barrera, "Sex, Citizenship and the State," 164–165; Capuzzo, "Sudditanza e cittadinanza," 75–77.

19. Sòrgoni, *Etnografia e colonialismo*, 230; A. L. Stoler, "Sexual Affronts
and Racial Frontiers: European Identities and the Cultural Politics of Exclusion
in Colonial Southeast Asia," in *Tensions of Empire: Colonial Cultures in a Bourgeois World*, ed. F. Cooper and A. L. Stoler (Berkeley, Los Angeles and London:
University of California Press, 1997), 198–237.

20. See Sòrgoni, *Parole e corpi*, 2, 116–118, 127–138; R. Iyob, "*Madamismo*
and Beyond: The Construction of Eritrean Women," in Ben-Ghiat and Fuller,
Italian Colonialism, 233–244.

21. Sòrgoni, *Parole e corpi*, 2, 116–118, 127–138; Barrera, "Sex, Citizenship
and the State," 157–158, 161–162. Largely tolerated, the phenomenon of *madamato* was nonetheless a subject of legislation too. In fact, with a 1914 decree
that was in line with two previous 1909 and 1910 regulations concerning Eritrea
and Somalia, Italian authorities attempted to limit this phenomenon by explicitly
prohibiting colonial officials from cohabiting with African women. This prohibition was not generalized to all the Italians but limited to those vested with public
functions; for this reason we can explain the policy by making reference to the
general concern about "Italian prestige" having to be safeguarded, especially by
those who represented Italian rule in the colonial territories. In any case, a certain
ambiguity and discordance seemed to emerge in this respect because, as noted by
Sòrgoni and Giulia Barrera, proscription of concubinage appears to have been
selectively enforced, with a number of colonial representatives continuing to live
with Eritrean women. The government introduced legal rules to point out the
political significance of Italian white prestige within the colonial milieu, but it
also turned a blind eye vis-à-vis those who did not display these unions too visibly
and widely. Sòrgoni, *Parole e corpi*, 113–114; Sòrgoni, *Etnografia e colonialismo*,
103–106; Barrera, "Sex, Citizenship and the State," 162; L. Baiada, "Notturno
africano. Libertà sessuale, forze armate, giurisdizione," *Questione Giustizia* 1
(2009): 196–199. The 1909 and 1910 royal decrees pertaining to Eritrea and
Somalia are, respectively, r. d. n. 839, 19 September 1909, "Regio decreto che
approva l'ordinamento del corpo dei funzionari coloniali dell'Eritrea"; and r. d. n.
562, 4 July 1910, "Regio decreto che approva l'annesso regolamento amministrativo per la Somalia italiana," in *Collezione celerifera delle leggi, decreti, istruzioni
e circolari dell'anno 1910 ed anteriori*, ed. D. Scacchi (Rome: Stamperia Reale,
1911), 127–138 and 962–983.

22. Sòrgoni, *Parole e corpi*, 58–60.

23. See D'Amelio, *L'ordinamento giuridico*, 249–251; Sòrgoni, *Parole e corpi*,
110.

24. Sòrgoni, *Parole e corpi*, 109–110.

25. Sòrgoni, *Parole e corpi*, 113–114; Barrera, "Sex, Citizenship and the
State," 162.

26. See law n. 857 of 5 July 1882 (Legge concernente i provvedimenti per
Assab, art. 3), in *Raccolta ufficiale delle leggi e dei decreti*, 66:2247–2248; law n.
205 of 24 May 1903 (Legge portante l'ordinamento della Colonia Eritrea, art. 3),
in *Raccolta dei principali ordinamenti legislativi delle colonie italiane*, ed. A. Parpagliolo (Rome: Istituto Poligrafico dello Stato, 1932), 2:5; the proclamation of the

governor of Italian Somalia, 1 March 1912, annexed to C XXXVIII-ter, 4 December 1912, 211; Mondaini, *La legislazione coloniale*, 1:23–24, 97–98 and 109–110.

27. See C. Conti Rossini, *Principi di diritto consuetudinario dell'Eritrea* (Rome: Tip. Dell'Unione Editrice, 1916); M. Colucci, *Principi di diritto consuetudinario della Somalia italiana meridionale—I gruppi sociali—La proprietà* (Florence: La Voce, 1924); E. Cerulli, "Il diritto consuetudinario nella Somalia italiana settentrionale: Sultanato dei Migiurtini," *Bollettino della Società Africana d'Italia* no. 3 (1918): 120–137, no. 5 (1918): 216–233, no. 1 (1919): 45–56, no. 4 (1919): 177–195, no. 5 (1919): 231–247, no. 6 (1919): 276–286; A. Cicchitti, "Il problema religioso nella legislazione coloniale italiana," *Rivista coloniale* 6 (1926): 476–496.

28. See "Benadir. Domande formulate dal Direttore Centrale degli Affari Coloniali al Comandante Cerrina Feroni sulle più importanti questioni riguardanti la colonia del Benadir," 31 August 1907, 122–127, in AUSSME, FD-3, b. 1bis, f. 9.

29. D'Amelio, *L'ordinamento giuridico*, 86; Costanzo, "Sudditanza e cittadinanza nelle ex colonie italiane," in *Novissimo digesto italiano*, 18:910; Mondaini, *La legislazione coloniale*, 1:208–209 and 358–359.

30. See Sòrgoni, *Parole e corpi*, 96–97.

31. Del Boca, *Gli italiani in Africa Orientale*, vol. 1, t. 2, 783.

32. See his speech in C disc. 15/2/1908, 19241–19242. Also, as Governor Emilio Dulio argued in 1902, it was unthinkable to abolish the phenomenon in Benadir at once because this would have led to a sudden need for cheap labor and caused damage to the cultivation of lands. See Del Boca, *Gli italiani in Africa Orientale*, vol. 1, t. 2, 785.

33. C disc. 15/2/1908, 19238–19239.

34. Ibid.

35. See Del Boca, *Gli italiani in Africa Orientale*, vol. 1, t. 1, 429–430 and 495–499 as well as vol. 1, t. 2, 789–801 and 806–810; Del Boca, *L'Africa nella coscienza degli italiani*, 112; Mondaini, *La legislazione coloniale*, 1:90–93 and 235–238.

36. See the historiographical discussion of N. Labanca, "Il razzismo coloniale italiano," in Burgio, *Nel nome della razza*, 145–163; as well as G. Rochat, *Il colonialismo italiano* (Turin: Loescher, 1973) and the pioneering work of Del Boca, *Gli italiani in Africa Orientale*.

37. See Del Boca, *Gli italiani in Libia: Tripoli bel suol d'amore 1860–1922* (Milan: Oscar Mondadori, 1993); C. G. Segré, "Il colonialismo e la politica estera: Variazioni liberali e fasciste," in *La politica estera italiana (1860–1985)*, ed. R. J. B. Bosworth and S. Romano (Bologna: Il Mulino, 1991), 121–146.

38. See Comando del corpo di occupazione della Libia, Ufficio politico-militare, *Censimento della Tripolitania del 3 luglio 1911*, Tripoli, 1912, as reported in Del Boca, *Gli italiani in Libia*, 86–88.

39. See r. d. n. 315 of 6 April 1913 (Regio decreto che regola i rapporti di sudditanza degli indigeni della Libia), in *Raccolta ufficiale delle leggi e dei decreti*, 1:986–988; as well as S. Villari, *La condizione giuridica delle popolazioni coloniali (la cittadinanza adiectitia)* (Rome: Casa Editrice Ulpiano, 1939), 269–275. Unfortunately, owing to archival lacunas, we are unable to say how the issue of citizenship was regulated in 1913 in the case of marriages between Italian metropolitan citizens and Libyan colonial subjects.

40. See G. Ambrosini, "La condizione giuridica dei libici dall'occupazione all'avvento del Fascismo," *Rivista delle colonie* no. 1 (1939): 81–85.

41. Ibid., 85; and Mondaini, *La legislazione coloniale*, 1:34–36.

42. Del Boca, *L'Africa nella coscienza degli italiani*, 31–32.

43. C 1120, 19 June 1919, 3.

44. Unfortunately, on the basis of the archival sources at our disposal we are unable to say whether in 1919 special citizenship regulations were also introduced or discussed in reference to Italian women marrying natives in Libya (as was the case in East Africa).

45. See r. d. n. 931 of 1 June 1919 (Regio decreto che approva le norme fondamentali per l'assetto della Tripolitania), art. 1, 32–34; as well as r. d. l. n. 2401 of 31 October 1919 (Regio decreto-legge che approva le norme fondamentali per l'assetto della Cirenaica), art. 1, 34–37, in *Raccolta ufficiale delle leggi e dei decreti*, 12:1844–1852 and 14:5702–5712 respectively; Villari, *La condizione giuridica delle popolazioni coloniali*, 269–270.

46. See art. 4–7 and art. 10–18 of the 1919 royal decrees pertaining to Tripolitania and Cyrenaica.

47. Ambrosini, "La condizione giuridica dei libici dall'occupazione all'avvento del Fascismo," 89.

48. See Del Boca, *Gli italiani in Libia*, 171; V. Alhadeff, *L'ordinamento giuridico di Rodi e delle altre isole italiane dell'Egeo* (Milan: Istituto Editoriale Scientifico, 1927), chs. 1 and 2; Mondaini, *La legislazione coloniale*, 2:803–805. Historically, the term *Dodecaneso* was first used during the Middle Ages to refer to the Cyclades. It was only in 1909 that the word started being used in reference to the twelve Southern Sporades islands of the Aegean Sea that enjoyed, at that time, special fiscal, administrative and judiciary exemptions under Ottoman rule. These were the twelve islands among the fourteen that we have just mentioned, except Rhodes and Kos. The term (as it was used during the liberal era) is therefore improper because the Italians occupied fourteen (rather than twelve) insular territories. In this book, we nevertheless use the word, as was widely done at the time, to refer in general to the "*isole egee*" (Aegean islands) under Italian occupation. Also, in our narrative we use the correct Italian spelling *Dodecaneso* and *Dodecanesini* (with one "n"), reminding our readers that in historical sources and legislation these words were often erroneously written with two "n," as one can see in the bibliography (i.e., *Dodecanneso*). On this improper terminology and spelling, see Alhadeff, *L'ordinamento giuridico di Rodi*, 2.

49. See Comando della 6° Divisione Speciale, *Cenni monografici sulle Sporadi meridionali occupate dalle truppe italiane durante la guerra italo-turca*, Rhodes, 1912, in AUSSME, FL-8, b. 231, f. 21; Comando del Corpo di Stato Maggiore—Ufficio Coloniale, *Cenni monografici sull' isola di Rodi*, Rome, 1912, 12, in AUSSME, FL-8, b. 232, f. 2; *Contributo monografico per lo studio politico ed economico dell' isola di Rodi*, Rhodes: Comando della 6° Divisione Speciale, 1913, 6–14 and 84–102, in AUSSME, FL-8, b. 232, f. 2; Alhadeff, *L'ordinamento giuridico di Rodi*, 41.

50. Romano, *Corso di diritto coloniale*, 1:93.

51. See letter of MAE to PCM, 16 May 1914, prot. n. 28027/98, in ACS, FPCM, Year 1914, f. 11/2.

52. Clearly, if the 1920 Sèvres Treaty had been ratified, the *Egei* would have become Italian subjects, probably by the end of the liberal epoch. The treaty regulated, in fact, acquisition of Italian citizenship by the natives of the islands with a right to opt for Ottoman nationality, or in case of minority status, for the nationality of Armenia, Azerbaijan, Georgia, Greece, Hedjaz, Mesopotamia, Syria, Bulgaria or Turkey, and in all cases emigrate to the respective states. However, since the treaty never entered into force, these nationality changes did not take place. See Section XI ("Libye et îles de la mer Egée") as well as Section XII ("Nationalité"), in "Traité de Paix, signé à Sèvres le 10 août 1920," in *Nouveau recueil général de traités et autres actes relatifs aux rapports de droit international* (Leipzig: Weicher, 1924), 12:664–779.

53. *Enciclopedia del diritto* (Varese: Giuffrè Editore, 1960), 6:213–217, s.v. "Capitolazioni (Regime delle)"; and G. Tosti, "Studi recenti di diritto capitolare," *Rivista di diritto internazionale* 1, no. 3 (1912): 428–459.

54. This special category is also mentioned by De Dominicis, *Commento alla legge sulla cittadinanza italiana*, 150–153; and by Degni, *Della cittadinanza*, 327–328.

55. See the telegrams, concerning Ottoman subjects who originated from the Italian occupied Aegean islands and were resident abroad, exchanged between Italy's MAE and the Italian Embassies and Consulates in London, Berlin, Petrograd, Paris, Cardiff, Johannesburg and Marseilles, October–November 1914, in MAEASD, FSPP, b. 171, f. 17/4.

56. See the letter of MAE to PCM, 16 May 1914, prot. n. 28027/98, concerning acquisition of Italian citizenship by Greek and Ottoman subjects living in the Dodecanese, in ACS, FPCM, Year 1914, f. 11/2; and in the same file, the reply by the president dated 20 May 1914.

57. See Minister of Foreign Affairs Carlo Sforza in C 976, 17 November 1920, 1, and in S 118, 18 June 1921, 1; the parliamentary report C 976-A (Vassallo, *rapporteur*), 23 March 1921, 1; as well as Italy's Council of Ministers' deliberation of 2 November 1920 in the appendix of Degni's book, *Della cittadinanza*, 327–328.

58. C 976, 17 November 1920, 1–3.

59. See r. d. l. n. 1387 of 10 September 1922 (Disposizioni sulla cittadinanza italiana) in Bariatti, *La disciplina giuridica*, 1:69–70; as well as Azzolini, "Principali lineamenti storici," 38.

60. See, for instance, C 1320, 21 February 1913, 1–3; C 1320-A (Baccelli, *rapporteur*), 13 March 1913, 1–2; C disc. 3/5/1913, 24960; S 1004, 5 May 1913, 1.

61. For this comparative analysis, see Dummett and Nicol, *Subjects, Citizens, Aliens and Others*, 113–125; E. F. W. Gey van Pittius, "'Dominion' Nationality," *Journal of Comparative Legislation and International Law* 13, no. 4 (1931): 199–202; and T. Baty, "The History of Canadian Nationality," *Journal of Comparative Legislation and International Law* 18, no. 4 (1936): 195–203.

62. See Dummett and Nicol, *Subjects, Citizens, Aliens and Others*, 113–125; Gey van Pittius, "'Dominion' Nationality," 199–202; and Baty, "The History of Canadian Nationality," 195–203.

63. See Mancini, "Provvedimenti per Assab," hearing of 26 June 1882, in *Discorsi parlamentari di Pasquale Stanislao Mancini* (Rome: Camera dei Deputati, 1896), 7:155–156 and 168.

64. S disc. 13/5/1903, 2136.
65. Alhadeff, *L'ordinamento giuridico di Rodi*, 51.
66. The expression originated in Rudyard Kipling's most famous British colonial poem, "The White Man's Burden," in *The Five Nations* (London: Macmillan, 1904), 78–80:

> Take up the White Man's burden
> Send forth the best ye breed
> Go bind your sons to exile
> To serve your captives' need;
> To wait in heavy harness,
> On fluttered folk and wild
> Your new-caught, sullen peoples,
> Half-devil and half-child.

67. See U. S. Mehta, *Liberalism and Empire: A Study in Nineteenth-Century British Liberal Thought* (Chicago, London: University of Chicago Press, 1999), 81–82, 91–92 and 102–106.
68. Ibid., 31–32.
69. See Sòrgoni, *Parole e corpi*, 94–101.
70. Sòrgoni, *Etnografia e colonialismo*, 22–25, 64–66, 232–234.
71. Sòrgoni, *Parole e corpi*, 96–97.
72. Sòrgoni, *Etnografia e colonialismo*, 232–236.
73. Capuzzo, "Sudditanza e cittadinanza," 69.
74. Sòrgoni, *Parole e corpi*, 97–98.
75. Ibid., 95–96.
76. Ibid., 124–125.
77. See r. d. n. 937 of 8 June 1911 (Ordinamento giudiziario per la Somalia italiana), art. 2; law n. 161 of 5 April 1908 (Legge portante l'ordinamento della Somalia italiana), art. 12–13; law n. 205 of 24 May 1903 (Legge portante l'ordinamento della Colonia Eritrea), art. 4; Mondaini, *La legislazione coloniale*, 1:143–144 and 273–274. Also, Sòrgoni, *Parole e corpi*, 109 and 94–95.
78. See Sòrgoni, *Parole e corpi*, 93 and 183; as well as Capuzzo, "Sudditanza e cittadinanza," 72–73.
79. Mondaini, *La legislazione coloniale*, 1:143–144 and 273–274; Cicchitti, "Il problema religioso," 479; D'Amelio, *L'ordinamento giuridico*, 184–185.
80. Sòrgoni, *Parole e corpi*, 102–107, 249–256.
81. Ibid., 251–252.
82. Ibid., 102.
83. Ibid., 106–107.
84. Ibid., 105.
85. Ibid., 105–106 and 38–46.
86. Ibid., 105–106 and 38–46.
87. Ibid., 105–106 and 38–46.
88. See her discussion in Wong, *Race and the Nation*, 79–112.
89. Ibid., 93–95.
90. *Epistolario africano ovvero italiani in Africa. Pagine sparse* (Rome: Tipografia della Buona Stampa, 1887), 255–256, quoted in Wong, *Race and the Nation*, 97.
91. Wong, *Race and the Nation*, 89.

92. Ibid.

93. Ibid., 79–83 and 92–93.

94. F. De Donno, "La Razza Ario-Mediterranea. Ideas of Race and Citizenship in Colonial and Fascist Italy, 1885–1941," *Interventions* 8, no. 3 (2006): 399–400.

95. Ibid., 395–398.

96. Ibid., 398–399.

97. See Sòrgoni, *Parole e corpi*, 103; and De Donno, "La Razza Ario-Mediterranea," 401.

98. Sòrgoni, *Parole e corpi*, 105; and De Donno, "La Razza Ario-Mediterranea," 401.

99. De Donno, "La Razza Ario-Mediterranea," 397 and 405–409.

100. See for instance A. Giardina and A. Vauchez, *Il mito di Roma: Da Carlo Magno a Mussolini* (Rome, Bari: Laterza, 2000); C. Edwards, ed., *Roman Presences: Receptions of Rome in European Culture, 1789–1945* (Cambridge: Cambridge University Press, 1999); Chabod, *Storia della politica estera italiana dal 1870 al 1896*, vol. 1 (Bari: Laterza, 1951).

101. Giardina and Vauchez, *Il mito di Roma*; Edwards, "Introduction: Shadows and Fragments," in Edwards, *Roman Presences*, 1–18; Chabod, *Storia della politica estera italiana*, 1:179–323.

102. F. Crispi, *Scritti e discorsi politici di Francesco Crispi (1849–1890)*, 2nd ed. (Turin, Rome: Casa Editrice Nazionale Roux e Viarengo, n.d., after 1890), 738.

103. Ibid., 737.

104. C 745-A (De Marinis, *rapporteur*), 5 June 1907, 4.

105. C 57-A (Franchetti, *rapporteur*), 7 June 1902, 7.

106. See C 1120, 19 June 1919, 2-3.

107. See C 606, 13 July 1920, 1.

108. See A. N. Sherwin-White, *The Roman Citizenship*, 2nd ed. (Oxford: Clarendon Press, 1973); A. Chastagnol, "*Coloni et Incolae*. Note sur les différenciations sociales à l'intérieur des colonies romaines de peuplement dans les provinces de l'Occident (Ier siècle av. J.-C.—Ier siècle ap. J.-C.)," in *Splendidissima Civitas: Études d'histoire romaine en hommage à François Jacques*, ed. A. Chastagnol, S. Demougin and C. Lepelley (Paris: Publications de la Sorbonne, 1996), 13–25; Riesenberg, *Citizenship*, 56–84.

109. See for instance Minister of Foreign Affairs Sforza in C 976, 17 November 1920, 1–3, and in S 118, 18 June 1921, 1-3; the report C 976-A, 23 March 1921, 1–3; as well as the archival files in ACS, FPCM, Year 1914, f. 11/2 and in MAEASD, FSPP, b. 171, f. 17/4.

110. C 976-A, 23 March 1921, 1.

111. Ibid.

CHAPTER SIX

1. Yuval-Davis, *Gender and Nation*, 29–31; and S. Pryke, "Nationalism and Sexuality, What Are the Issues?" *Nations and Nationalism* 4, no. 4 (1998):540–544.

2. F. Cassata, *Molti, sani e forti: L'eugenetica in Italia* (Turin: Bollati Boringhieri, 2006).

3. Yuval-Davis, *Gender and Nation*, 29–31.

4. B. Mussolini, "Il numero come forza," September 1928, in *Opera Omnia di Benito Mussolini*, ed. E. Susmel and D. Susmel (Florence: La Fenice, 1951–1980), 23:214.

5. Mussolini, "Il discorso dell'Ascensione," 27 May 1927, in Susmel and Susmel, *Opera Omnia*, 22:367.

6. De Grazia, *How Fascism Ruled Women*, 45–52.

7. Ibid.

8. Mussolini, "Il numero come forza," 214.

9. W. Ebenstein, *Fascist Italy* (New York: Russell & Russell, 1973), 128–131.

10. Here we are following C. Saraceno's analysis, "Costruzione della maternità e della paternità," in *Il regime fascista: Storia e storiografia*, ed. A. Del Boca, M. Legnani and M. G. Rossi (Rome, Bari: Laterza, 1995), 485–491.

11. De Grazia, *How Fascism Ruled Women*, 55–56; Saraceno, "Costruzione della maternità," 490–491.

12. De Grazia, *How Fascism Ruled Women*, 55–56 and 71–76; Saraceno, "Costruzione della maternità," 490–491.

13. On all these measures, see De Grand, "Women Under Fascism," 964–965; E. S. Pankhurst, "Women Under Fascism," *Hibbert Journal: A Quarterly Review of Religion, Theology, and Philosophy* 34, no.2 (1935–1936): 222–223; De Grazia, *How Fascism Ruled Women*, 43, 69–71 and 86–88; Saraceno, "Costruzione della maternità," 486–489.

14. See C. Pogliano, "Scienza e stirpe: Eugenica in Italia (1912–1939)," *Passato e presente: Rivista di storia contemporanea* no. 5 (1984): 61–97; Pogliano, "Eugenisti, ma con giudizio," in Burgio, *Nel nome della razza*, 424–432; Pick, *Faces of Degeneration*, 109–152 and 234–240; Cassata, *Molti, sani e forti*, 9–23 and 27–51.

15. Pogliano, "Scienza e stirpe," 74–75; Pogliano, "Eugenisti, ma con giudizio," 432–440; Cassata, *Molti, sani e forti*, 98–113 and 141–176.

16. Cassata, *Molti, sani e forti*, 165.

17. Ibid., 141–144.

18. Mussolini, "Il numero come forza," 216.

19. D. Aringoli, *La famiglia italiana attraverso i secoli* (Bologna: Coop. Tip. Azzoguidi, 1938), 9, quoted in P. Meldini, *Sposa e madre esemplare: Ideologia e politica della donna e della famiglia durante il fascismo* (Rimini, Florence: Guaraldi Editore, 1975), 43.

20. De Grazia, *How Fascism Ruled Women*, 43–44.

21. Ibid., 86–88; Saraceno, "Costruzione della maternità," 486–489.

22. Gillette, *Racial Theories*, 46–49.

23. Ibid., 39.

24. Ibid., 44.

25. Ibid., 44–46.

26. Ibid., 45.

27. Sarfatti, *The Jews in Mussolini's Italy*.

28. Mussolini, *Opera Omnia* (1919), cited by Sarfatti, *The Jews in Mussolini's Italy*, 42.

29. Mussolini, *Il Popolo d'Italia* (1922), quoted in Sarfatti, *The Jews in Mussolini's Italy*, 43.

30. Sarfatti, *The Jews in Mussolini's Italy*, 59–60.

31. Ibid., 67–68.

32. Statistics are taken from ibid., 63.

33. De Donno, "La Razza Ario-Mediterranea," 405–409.

34. E. P. Noether, "Italian Women and Fascism: A Reevaluation," *Italian Quarterly* (Fall 1982): 77; L. Businco, "La donna depositaria dei caratteri della razza," *La difesa della razza* 1, no. 4 (September 1938): 34–36.

35. Del Boca, "Le leggi razziali nell' impero di Mussolini," in Del Boca, Legnani and Rossi, *Il regime fascista*, 329–351.

36. Del Boca, "Le leggi razziali nell'impero," 329–351. On the basis of Sòrgoni's research and of Gianluca Gabrielli's findings, we also know that the regime conducted a census in 1938 to count the (East and North) Africans living in the Italian peninsula, and to start expelling them in line with Mussolini's orders about their immediate repatriation. See Sòrgoni, *Parole e corpi*, 187–189; G. Gabrielli, "Africani in Italia negli anni del razzismo di stato," in Burgio, *Nel nome della razza*, 201–212.

37. De Donno, "La Razza Ario-Mediterranea," 408.

38. M. Raspanti, "Il mito ariano nella cultura italiana fra Otto e Novecento," in Burgio, *Nel nome della razza*, 85.

39. r. d. l. n. 1728 of 17 November 1938 (Provvedimenti per la difesa della razza italiana—Capo II. Degli appartenenti alla razza ebraica), reproduced in the appendix of Collotti's book, *Il fascismo e gli ebrei*, 194–195.

40. On all these racial policies and aspects, see Del Boca, "Le leggi razziali nell'impero," 329–351; R. De Felice, *Storia degli ebrei italiani sotto il fascismo*, rev. ed. (Turin: Einaudi, 1993), chs. 6 and 7; Sarfatti, *The Jews in Mussolini's Italy*, ch. 4; Sarfatti, "Il razzismo fascista nella sua concretezza: La definizione di 'ebreo' e la collocazione di questi nella costruenda gerarchia razziale," in Burgio, *Nel nome della razza*, 321–332; Collotti, *Il fascismo e gli ebrei*, chs. 4 and 5.

41. See De Donno, "La Razza Ario-Mediterranea," 395 and 409.

42. Ibid., 395–397 and 409.

43. See Cassata, *Molti, sani e forti*, ch. 5.

44. Cited by G. Bock, "Anti-Natalism, Maternity and Paternity in National Socialist Racism," in Bock and Thane, *Maternity and Gender Policies*, 240.

45. Ibid., 239.

46. Ibid., 233–240; Bock, "Racisme, stérilisation obligatoire et maternité sous le national-socialisme," in *Femmes et Fascismes*, ed. R. Thalmann (Paris: Tierce, 1986), 108–109; C. Koonz, "The Fascist Solution to the Woman Question in Italy and in Germany," in Bridenthal, Koonz and Stuard, *Becoming Visible*, 521–522.

47. This contrast is also emphasized by De Grazia, *How Fascism Ruled Women*, 53.

48. See Pogliano, "Eugenisti, ma con giudizio," 442; Cassata, *Molti, sani e forti*, 229–230.

49. A. Hitler, *Mein Kampf: Complete and Unabridged, Fully Annotated* (New York: Reynal & Hitchcock, 1939), 608.

50. Cited by Bock, "Anti-Natalism, Maternity and Paternity," 236.

51. Koonz, "The Fascist Solution to the Woman Question," 521–523; Bock, "Anti-Natalism, Maternity and Paternity," 242–247.

52. De Grazia, *How Fascism Ruled Women*.

53. Ibid.

54. N. Bobbio, *Dal fascismo alla democrazia: I regimi, le ideologie, le figure e le culture politiche*, ed. M. Bovero (Milan: Baldini & Castoldi, 1997), ch. 1.

55. See Castellani, *Les femmes italiennes*, 109–112; Gini and Caranti, "The Family in Italy," 350–361.

56. Koonz, "The Fascist Solution to the Woman Question," 505.

57. Mussolini, "Per il voto alle donne," 15 May 1925, *Discorsi del 1925* (Milan: Alpes, 1926), 59–64, as reproduced in the anthological appendix of Meldini's book, *Sposa e madre esemplare*, 136–140.

58. E. Ludwig, *Colloqui con Mussolini*, trans. T. Gnoli (Milan: Mondadori, 1932), 166.

59. The monthly *La donna italiana* no. 4 (April 1926): 332–333, cited by De Grazia, *How Fascism Ruled Women*, 38.

60. See Camera dei deputati, *Cinquanta anni dal voto alle donne*, 122–127; De Grazia, *How Fascism Ruled Women*, 36–40 and 238–240.

61. De Grand, "Women Under Fascism," 955.

62. De Grazia, *How Fascism Ruled Women*, 149–157.

63. Ibid., 151–153.

64. Meldini, *Sposa e madre esemplare*, 52–53.

65. De Grazia, *How Fascism Ruled Women*, 152–153.

66. E. Carrara, "Il presente problema dell'educazione femminile," *Annuario dell'anno scolastico, 1930–1931* (Naples: Siem, 1931), 138, cited by De Grazia, *How Fascism Ruled Women*, 156.

67. See De Grazia, *How Fascism Ruled Women*, 60–68; Castellani, *Les femmes italiennes*, 117–124; Koonz, "The Fascist Solution to the Woman Question," 510.

68. See Saraceno's conclusive remarks, "Costruzione della maternità," 495–497; De Grazia, *How Fascism Ruled Women*, 45.

69. De Grazia, *How Fascism Ruled Women*, 166–173.

70. See Noether, "Italian Women and Fascism," 71–72.

71. De Grand, "Women Under Fascism," 956.

72. De Grazia, *How Fascism Ruled Women*, 178–181.

73. De Grand, "Women Under Fascism," 947–948.

74. Cited by Gillette, *Racial Theories*, 56.

75. Patriarca, *Italianità*, 144–147.

76. Ibid., 147. The quote can be found in G. Bottai, *Diario 1935–1944*, ed. G. B. Guerri (Milan: Rizzoli, 1982), 115.

77. See Kertzer, *The Popes Against the Jews*, 270–276.

78. Ibid.

79. Ibid.

80. See A. Capristo, "L'esclusione degli Ebrei dall'Accademia d'Italia," *La rassegna mensile di Israel* 67, no. 3 (2001): 1–36.

81. Ibid., 11–36.

82. Ibid., 9–10 and 20–21.

83. Ibid., 16–19.

84. Ibid.

85. Ibid., 21.

86. Ibid., 24–26 and De Felice, *Storia degli ebrei italiani*, 236.

87. This chapter is concerned with the fascist period until 1943. Subsequently, though, with the establishment of the Republic of Salò—studied in Chapter Eight—thousands of these Italian Jews would be sent to German extermination camps since the "final solution" was extended to the German-occupied zones of northern Italy as well. See L. Picciotto Fargion, *Il libro della memoria: Gli ebrei deportati dall'Italia (1943–1945)* (Milan: Mursia, 1991); Sarfatti, *The Jews in Mussolini's Italy*, ch. 5.

88. See Sarfatti, *The Jews in Mussolini's Italy*, 138.

89. Issued in 1922 at the suggestion of the Norwegian High Commissioner for Refugees Dr. Fridtjof Nansen, the document of identification—the "Nansen passport"—first concerned the international status of Russian refugees who had fled from their country after the Russian Revolution. Subsequently, it was to be extended to other categories of refugees, including all those generally who had ceased to enjoy the protection of their government, as well as to those persons who did not possess the citizenship of any state (stateless people). See G. S. Goodwin-Gill, *International Law and the Movement of Persons Between States* (Oxford: Clarendon Press, 1978), 42–43; R. Huntford, *Nansen: The Explorer as Hero* (London: Abacus, 1997), 629–639; and G. Coudry, "Note sur le 'passeport Nansen'," *Matériaux pour l'histoire de notre temps* no. 44 (October–December 1996): 19–21.

90. Brubaker, *Citizenship*, 165–166. In fascist Italy, the political practice of depriving a person of his or her Italian citizenship had also been employed since 1926 against those Italian antifascists who were forced to leave the peninsula for their political views (so-called *fuoriusciti*) and who "deserved" civil death because of their antifascist activities abroad and opposition to the regime. In this case, the totalitarian "citizenship instrument" was not applied against a racial minority but against those who did not want to conform to fascism. See parliamentary report C 623-A (Bastianini, *rapporteur*), 27 November 1925, 1–4, as well as law n. 108 of 31 January 1926 (Modificazioni ed aggiunte alla legge 13 giugno 1912 n. 555 sulla cittadinanza) in Bariatti, *La disciplina giuridica*, 1:74–75.

91. Sarfatti, *The Jews in Mussolini's Italy*, ch. 4; Sarfatti, "The Persecution of the Jews in Fascist Italy (1936–1943)," in *The Jews of Italy: Memory and Identity*, ed. B. D. Cooperman and B. Garvin (Bethesda: University Press of Maryland, 2000), 415–424.

92. De Felice, *Storia degli ebrei italiani*, 349.

93. Collotti, *Il fascismo e gli ebrei*, 78.

94. See P. Burrin, "Fascisme, nazisme et génocide," in *Les sociétés en guerre: 1911–1946*, ed. B. Cabanes and E. Husson (Paris: Armand Colin, 2003), 151–173; Burrin, *Fascisme, nazisme, autoritarisme* (Paris: Editions du Seuil, 2000), ch. 9. Some details on the isolated and occasionally violent anti-Jewish action on the part of Italian fascist squads in the peninsula before 1943 can be found in Sarfatti, *The Jews in Mussolini's Italy*, 158–161.

95. Collotti, *Il fascismo e gli ebrei*, 91.

96. Ibid., 69–71.

97. Saraceno, "Costruzione della maternità," 496.
98. Bock, "Anti-Natalism, Maternity and Paternity," 243–247.
99. Collotti, *Il fascismo e gli ebrei*, 75–76 and 84–86; Sarfatti, *The Jews in Mussolini's Italy*, 151–157.
100. See De Felice, *Storia degli ebrei italiani*; Sarfatti, *The Jews in Mussolini's Italy*.
101. See Collotti, *Il fascismo e gli ebrei*, 102–125; and Sarfatti, *The Jews in Mussolini's Italy*, 146–150.
102. Sarfatti, *The Jews in Mussolini's Italy*, 187–202; Picciotto Fargion, *Il libro della memoria*; Picciotto Fargion, "The Persecution of the Jews in Italy, 1943–1945: A Chronicle of Events," in Cooperman and Garvin, *The Jews of Italy*, 443–454.
103. P. Levi, *Se questo è un uomo*, 11th ed. (Turin: Einaudi, 1981).

CHAPTER SEVEN

1. See for instance Sòrgoni, *Parole e corpi*; Barrera, "Patrilinearità, razza e identità," 21–53; G. Gabrielli, "Un aspetto della politica razzista nell'impero: Il 'problema dei meticci'," *Passato e presente* 15, no. 41 (1997), 77–105; Del Boca, "Le leggi razziali nell'impero," 329–351.
2. On all these events, see Del Boca, *Gli italiani in Africa Orientale*, vol. 2, *La conquista dell' impero*, t. 1, chs. 1–3; A. Sbacchi, "Poison Gas and Atrocities in the Italo-Ethiopian War (1935–1936)," in Ben-Ghiat and Fuller, *Italian Colonialism*, 47–56; G. Rochat, "The Italian Air Force in the Ethiopian War (1935–1936)," in Ben-Ghiat and Fuller, *Italian Colonialism*, 37–46.
3. Mondaini, *La legislazione coloniale*, 2:366–389, 398–399, 407–409, 607–615; H. A. Steiner, "The Government of Italian East Africa," *American Political Science Review* 30, no. 5 (1936): 893–895.
4. See for instance r. d. n. 342 of 7 February 1926 (Approvazione dell'ordinamento giudiziario per la colonia Eritrea), in *Raccolta dei principali ordinamenti legislativi delle colonie italiane*, 2:156–157 and 163.
5. See law n. 999 of 6 July 1933 (Ordinamento organico per l'Eritrea e la Somalia. Capo II. Della sudditanza e della cittadinanza), in *Le leggi e decreti reali secondo l'ordine della inserzione nella Gazzetta Ufficiale* (Rome: Società Editrice del periodico Il Foro Italiano, 1861–1945), Year 1933: 951–952.
6. See r. d. l. n. 1019 of 1 June 1936 (Ordinamento e amministrazione dell' Africa Orientale Italiana. Capo II. Della Sudditanza), in *Leggi e decreti reali*, Year 1936:448–449; the speech of Minister of Colonies Alessandro Lessona in C 1501, 2 December 1936, 1–2; and parliamentary report C 1501-A (Bolzon, *rapporteur*), 4 December 1936, 1.
7. Del Boca, *Gli italiani in Africa Orientale*, vol. 3, *La caduta dell' impero*, t. 1, 137–140.
8. Ibid. During our archival research, we were able to find further evidence on the use of citizenship as an instrument of fascist Italy to reward its African populations *and* as an expectation of the colonial subjects to be rewarded. For instance, we know that the introduction of "special citizenship status" for Mus-

lim Libyans in 1939 (which we shall discuss in our next section concerning North Africa) provoked some reactions and aspirations to higher civic status among Eritreans and Somalis for having demonstrated much more loyalty to the Italian state than the Libyans had done. Also, in a reserved note of 3 May 1939, one reads that "The Duce has confirmed the opportunity to study a type of citizenship to be granted to Eritreans and Somalis." Unfortunately, the documentation has many gaps and because of the Second World War it is entirely possible that this policy was put aside. However, these documents are telling because they demonstrate how citizenship policies were used by the metropole *and* by the colonial subjects alike for different but related reasons. See the archival typed document of 9 November 1939 (without signature) in MAEASD, FMAI, b. 167, f. xi–v; as well as "Appunto per la Direzione Generale degli Affari Politici," 3 May 1939, signed by the office head, in MAEASD, FMAI, b. 167, f. xi.

9. Sòrgoni, *Parole e corpi*, 144–145.

10. Ibid., 149; Barrera, "Patrilinearità, razza e identità," 43.

11. Barrera, "Sex, Citizenship and the State," 165.

12. See Barrera, "Patrilinearità, razza e identità," 42–43; A. Bertola, "I meticci nell'ordinamento italiano vigente," *Rivista di diritto pubblico* no. 1 (1941): 492–493; Barrera, "Patrilinearity, Race and Identity," 97 and 105; Costanzo, "Meticci e meticciato," 601; Villari, *La condizione giuridica delle popolazioni coloniali*, 270–271. Also, see law n. 999 of 6 July 1933 (Ordinamento organico per l'Eritrea e la Somalia), art. 18–20. The conditions upon which the *meticcio* could ask for Italian citizenship at the age of majority were as follows: the child's somatic traits had to prove that one of the parents belonged undeniably to the white race; and the person was not polygamous, had a clear criminal record, had passed the exam of the third year of Italian elementary school and had received an Italian upbringing.

13. L. Cipriani, "Razzismo coloniale," *La difesa della razza* no. 2 (1938): 18–20.

14. Del Boca, "Le leggi razziali nell'impero," 336–339.

15. See Barrera, "Sex, Citizenship and the State," 162–163; Baiada, "Notturno africano," 196–199.

16. Barrera, "Sex, Citizenship and the State," 162–163.

17. See r. d. l. n. 1019 of 1 June 1936 (Ordinamento e amministrazione dell'Africa Orientale Italiana), art. 28; Bertola, "I meticci," 493–494; Villari, *La condizione giuridica delle popolazioni coloniali*, 273.

18. L. Goglia, "Note sul razzismo coloniale fascista," *Storia contemporanea* 19, no. 6 (1988): 1237.

19. See law n. 822 of 13 May 1940 (Norme relative ai meticci), art. 1–13, in Bariatti, *La disciplina giuridica*, 1:85–87; Bertola, "I meticci," 496–498; Mondaini, *La legislazione coloniale*, 2: 410–416; Barrera, "Patrilinearity, Race and Identity," 97.

20. Goglia, "Note sul razzismo coloniale fascista," 1262–1263.

21. See Barrera, "Patrilinearità, razza, identità," 44–45.

22. Ibid.

23. Ibid.

24. Ibid.

25. D'Amelio, *L'ordinamento giuridico*, 184 and 241–246; Romano, *Corso di diritto coloniale*, 1:130–134.

26. Sòrgoni, *Parole e corpi*, 149.

27. See A. E. Folchi, "Cittadinanza e sudditanza nell'espansione imperiale italiana," *Rivista di diritto pubblico* no. 1 (1939): 60; R. Monaco, "Caratteri della sudditanza dell'Africa Orientale Italiana," *Rivista di diritto pubblico e della pubblica amministrazione in Italia* no. 1 (1937): 242.

28. See gubernatorial decree n. 4379 of 24 May 1926 (Approvazione del regolamento giudiziario per l'Eritrea), in *Raccolta dei principali ordinamenti legislativi*, 2:205; law n. 999 of 6 July 1933 (Ordinamento organico per l'Eritrea e la Somalia), art. 21; r. d. l. n. 1019 of 1 June 1936 (Ordinamento e amministrazione dell'Africa Orientale Italiana), art. 31; Steiner, "The Government of Italian East Africa," 898–900; Monaco, "Caratteri della sudditanza dell'Africa Orientale Italiana," 245–246; Mondaini, *La legislazione coloniale*, 2: 407–409.

29. Governor Corrado Zoli, quoted in Del Boca, *Gli italiani in Africa Orientale*, vol. 2, t. 1, 28. On native participation in the public sphere see Del Boca, ibid., 24–50; Del Boca, *Gli italiani in Africa Orientale*, vol. 3, t. 1, 143–144; Mondaini, *La legislazione coloniale*, 2: 444–453 and 463–468.

30. Goglia, "Note sul razzismo coloniale fascista," 1249–1250; Sòrgoni, *Parole e corpi*, 153. For further discussion concerning Mussolini's policy of racial segregation in AOI, see Barrera, "Mussolini's Colonial Race Laws and State-Settler Relations in Africa Orientale Italiana (1935–1941)," *Journal of Modern Italian Studies* 8, no. 3 (2003): 425–443.

31. On all these colonial issues and historical events, see Del Boca, *Gli italiani in Africa Orientale*, vol. 2, t. 1 (chs. 3 and 7), vol. 2, t. 2 (ch. 13), vol. 3, t. 1 (chs. 1-3); Del Boca, *L'Africa nella coscienza degli italiani*, 41–57; Labanca, "Italian colonial internment," in Ben-Ghiat and Fuller, *Italian Colonialism*, 29–33.

32. Del Boca, *Gli italiani in Libia: Dal fascismo a Gheddafi* (Rome, Bari: Laterza, 1991), chs. 1–3; Ambrosini, "La condizione giuridica dei libici dall'occupazione all'avvento del Fascismo," 90; Ambrosini, "La condizione giuridica dei libici dall'avvento del Fascismo a oggi," *Rivista delle colonie* no. 2 (1939): 169.

33. Statistics refer to 1936 and are taken from Mondaini, *La legislazione coloniale*, 2:630.

34. See r. d. l. n. 2012 of 3 December 1934 (Ordinamento organico per l'amministrazione della Libia), art. 1 and art. 11, in *Leggi e decreti reali*, Year 1934:1538–1546; as well as r. d. l. n. 70 of 9 January 1939 (Aggregazione delle quattro provincie libiche al territorio del Regno d'Italia e concessione ai libici musulmani di una cittadinanza italiana speciale con statuto personale e successorio musulmano), in *Leggi e decreti reali*, Year 1939:135.

35. See the aforementioned 1919 royal decrees, which were kept in force in the early years of fascist rule: "Regio decreto n. 931 del 1 giugno 1919 che approva le norme fondamentali per l'assetto della Tripolitania" and "Regio decreto-legge n. 2401 del 31 Ottobre 1919 che approva le norme fondamentali per l'assetto della Cirenaica"; also, law n. 1013 of 26 June 1927 (Legge organica per l'amministrazione della Tripolitania e della Cirenaica), art. 29–30; r. d. l. n. 2012 of 3 December 1934 (Ordinamento organico per l'amministrazione della Libia),

art. 33–34; Villari, *La condizione giuridica delle popolazioni coloniali*, 243–247; Ambrosini, "La condizione giuridica dei libici dall'avvento del Fascismo a oggi," 169–173.

36. See law n. 822 of 13 May 1940 (Norme relative ai meticci); Goglia, "Note sul razzismo coloniale fascista," 1262–1264; Costanzo, "Madamato," 11–12; Bertola, "I meticci," 495; Villari, *La condizione giuridica delle popolazioni coloniali*, 270–275.

37. To naturalize, the native had to be twenty-one years of age and monogamous as well as have a clear criminal record and passed the exam of the third year of Italian elementary school. Also, apart from these requirements, the individual had to be in one of these situations: have served within the Italian Army, Navy or Air forces; have a governmental job or pension; have been awarded an honorary title; or have a Libyan father who had also become a metropolitan citizen. See law n. 1013 of 26 June 1927 (art. 33) as well as r. d. n. 2012 of 3 December 1934 (art. 37). The 1939 changes concerning naturalization were brought about by r. d. l. n. 70 of 9 January 1939 (art. 8).

38. "Ministero dell'Africa Italiana. Pro-memoria per il Duce," Rome, 28 February 1939, in MAEASD, FMAI, b. 167, f. xi–v.

39. See Folchi, "Cittadinanza e sudditanza," 68–69 as well as Ambrosini, "La condizione giuridica dei libici dall'avvento del Fascismo a oggi," 194.

40. See law n. 1013 of 26 June 1927 (art. 35–37); Villari, *La condizione giuridica delle popolazioni coloniali*, 243–245; Folchi, "Cittadinanza e sudditanza," 57–58.

41. See Minister of Colonies Luigi Federzoni in C 1439, 2 April 1927, 1–2.

42. See ibid.; C 1439-A (Messedaglia, *rapporteur*), 28 May 1927, 3–4; S 1065-A (Valvassori-Peroni, *rapporteur*), 6 June 1927, 1–2; S disc. 10/6/1927, 9145–9146.

43. The obligatory requirements included age of majority, birth in the annexed Libyan territories, possession of CIL status (*cittadinanza italiana libica*), Muslim affiliation and clear criminal record. Also, the native had to be in one of these conditions: be a war invalid or wounded; have a military award; know how to read or write in Italian; have worked in the public civil service for at least two years; or be a member of the fascist youth organization *Gioventù Araba del Littorio*. See r. d. l. n. 70 of 9 January 1939 (art. 3–7) as well as Villari, *La condizione giuridica delle popolazioni coloniali*, 247–262.

44. See r. d. l. n. 70 of 9 January 1939 (art. 6–7); Folchi, "Cittadinanza e sudditanza," 67; Ambrosini, "La condizione giuridica dei libici dall'avvento del Fascismo a oggi," 188–195; Villari, *La condizione giuridica delle popolazioni coloniali*, 259–262.

45. Reference to the loyalty and military contribution of the Libyan Muslims in the conquest of the empire as well as to the justice of rewarding them with a higher juridical status is made in an archival document, "Appunto per la Stampa," which can be found in MAEASD, FMAI, b. 167, f. xi–v. On the international dimension of this Muslim Libyan citizenship policy, see J. L. Wright, "Mussolini, Libya, and the Sword of Islam," in Ben-Ghiat and Fuller, *Italian Colonialism*, 124–126. Interestingly, the "openness" of the fascist regime vis-à-vis its North African subjects of the four northern provinces did not stretch so far as

granting them Italian *metropolitan* status. After all, the four Libyan regions were now part of Italy's metropolitan territory. When the annexation project and the granting of a special citizenship were being studied, Governor Italo Balbo proposed to grant the Libyans full citizenship; this is also recorded in Ciano's diary. The Fascist Gran Consiglio, however, opposed him and the final 1939 norms eventually introduced only the nonmetropolitan status CIS, which we saw earlier. Various reasons were given in disapproving the granting of Italian metropolitan status to the North African natives. Making them metropolitans was in stark contrast with the racist directives of the regime. In fact, because of the racial diversity of the populations of the fascist empire, and the notion of nationhood as a union of individuals sharing ethnic-cultural affinities, only the people possessing the latter should be members of the metropolitan citizenry. Also, anti-Semitic considerations were entertained by fascist officialdom: extension of metropolitan status to the Libyans would have caused inconveniences such as granting Italian metropolitan citizenship to Libyan Jews while depriving the Italian Jews of the peninsula of the same status. Finally, imperial objectives were at stake because with extension of full Italian status to the Arabs, North African militaries would have had the right to command national troops, thus giving the rights of the dominators to the dominated subjects and undermining the fascist *mito di potenza* (myth of power). See G. Ciano, *Diario 1937–1943*, ed. R. De Felice, 7th ed. (Milan: Biblioteca Universale Rizzoli, 2000), 201–202, entry 26 October 1938; Del Boca, *Gli italiani in Libia: Dal fascismo a Gheddafi*, 240; the two typed documents (without signature) of 6 October 1938 and 11 October 1938 as well as comments added in a report concerning acquisition of metropolitan citizenship by the Libyan natives, in MAEASD, FMAI, b. 167, f. xi–v.

46. Labanca, "Italian Colonial Internment," 27–36; Del Boca, *Gli italiani in Libia: Dal fascismo a Gheddafi*, 174–189.

47. C. Seton-Watson, *Italy from Liberalism to Fascism, 1870–1925* (London: Methuen, 1967), 668–670.

48. Mondaini, *La legislazione coloniale*, 2:801–891.

49. Ibid., 804.

50. See "Traité de paix signé à Lausanne le 24 juillet 1923," art. 30, 31, 33; A. Bertola, "La cittadinanza italiana nelle isole egee," *Rivista coloniale* no. 1 (1926): 59–66.

51. Emphasis on the nonmetropolitan status of the Aegeans and on the need not to confuse the Italian citizenship of those of the peninsula (*i metropolitani*) and the status acquired by the *Dodecanesini* is made in a report of CCD, 25 February 1925, 3 kept in MAEASD, FCCD-SCD (1924–1937), b. 36, f. 80. References to contemporary Cyprus and Libya are also made in parliamentary report C 675-A (Pace, *rapporteur*), 10 December 1925, 2.

52. In some archival documents we also found the expression "*cittadinanza rodia*" referring to the *status civitatis* acquired by the *Egei*; this terminology comes from the name of the largest island (Rhodes). The expression, though, is not geographically appropriate, bearing in mind that Rhodes was only one of the fourteen islands of the Italian Dodecanese. See the report of CCD, "Schema di legge sulla cittadinanza rodia," 25 February 1925, in MAEASD, FCCD-SCD

(1924–1937), b. 36, f. 80, and, in the same file, letter n. 233567 of MAE to the Ministry of Justice, 2 July 1927.

53. See r. d. l. n. 1854 of 15 October 1925 (Acquisto della cittadinanza italiana degli abitanti del Dodecaneso in base alle disposizioni del trattato di Losanna), art. 1.

54. Bertola, "La cittadinanza italiana nelle isole egee," 67.

55. As quoted by Alhadeff, *L'ordinamento giuridico di Rodi*, 55.

56. Alhadeff, *L'ordinamento giuridico di Rodi*, 59.

57. See r. d. l. n. 1379 of 19 October 1933 (Acquisto della piena cittadinanza italiana da parte degli abitanti delle isole italiane dell'Egeo), art. 1; Mondaini, *La legislazione coloniale*, 2:819–821; Bertola, "Confessione religiosa e statuto personale dei cittadini italiani dell'egeo e libici," *Rivista di diritto pubblico e della pubblica amministrazione in Italia* no. 1 (1934): 103–107; and Pignataro, *Il Dodecaneso italiano*, 25–26. Before 1933, fascist legislation was actually silent on this issue. In 1925, Governor Mario Lago included naturalization norms in an initial project, but during the discussions it was decided to regulate the issue in a separate law that was then approved in 1933, as mentioned already. See r. d. l. n. 1854 of 15 October 1925 and the report of CCD, "Schema di legge sulla cittadinanza rodia," 4–5.

58. See C 1870, 11 November 1933, 1–2; C 1870-A (Pellizzari, *rapporteur*), 11 December 1933, 2; S 1737-A (Salata, *rapporteur*), 15 December 1933, 1–2; L. Di Caporiacco, "Cittadini e sudditi del Dodecanneso," *La difesa della razza* no. 15 (1943): 12–13.

59. See law n. 822 of 13 May 1940 (Norme relative ai meticci), art. 1, 12, 13; Bertola, "I meticci," 495–496.

60. Bertola, "Confessione religiosa e statuto personale," 100–104; Folchi, "Cittadinanza e sudditanza," 58–59; Di Caporiacco, "Cittadini e sudditi del Dodecanneso," 12–13.

61. Mondaini, *La legislazione coloniale*, 2:885–886.

62. Alhadeff, *L'ordinamento giuridico di Rodi*, 62.

63. Ibid., 139–142 and 157–191; Mondaini, *La legislazione coloniale*, 2:825–838 and 862–869.

64. Filippo Pennavaria in C disc. 19/12/1925, 5141.

65. Ibid.

66. See the documentation concerning this additional "naturalizzazione rodia" (December 1926–June 1927), in MAEASD, FCCD-SCD (1924–1937), b. 36, f. 80.

67. See B. J. Fischer, *Albania at War, 1939–1945* (West Lafayette, Ind.: Purdue University Press, 1999), 5–58; G. Villari, "Il sistema di occupazione fascista in Albania," in *Gli ebrei in Albania sotto il fascismo: Una storia da ricostruire*, ed. L. Brazzo and M. Sarfatti (Florence: Giuntina, 2010), 93–124; G. Lucatello, *La natura giuridica dell'unione italo-albanese* (Padova: Casa editrice Milani, 1943); and the text of Albania's National Assembly offering the Albanian crown to the Italian monarch, in *Raccolta di provvedimenti di carattere legislativo riguardanti l'Albania*, ed. R. Bertuccioli (Rome: Regio Ministero degli Affari Esteri, 1941), 7.

68. The percentages of the religious communities refer to 1937 and can be found in R. Morozzo della Rocca, *Nazione e religione in Albania (1920–1944)* (Bologna: Il Mulino, 1990), 23, 45 and 62. All the other data refer to 1941 and

are taken from D. Rodogno, *Il nuovo ordine mediterraneo: Le politiche di occupazione dell'Italia fascista in Europa (1940–1943)* (Turin: Bollati Boringhieri, 2003), 505. To these statistics we should also add that according to a 1937 census a tiny minority of fewer than two hundred Jews were living in Albania on the eve of the Italian invasion. For these latter data and the 1937 census, see Brazzo, "Dall'Impero agli stati: Gli ebrei nei Balcani e in Albania fra la seconda metà dell' Ottocento e la vigilia della seconda guerra mondiale," in Brazzo and Sarfatti, *Gli ebrei in Albania*, 51–59.

69. In SAP disc. 15/4/1939, 3.

70. See "Albania—Civil Code," in *A Collection of Nationality Laws of Various Countries as Contained in Constitutions, Statutes and Treaties*, ed. R. W. Flournoy and M. O. Hudson (New York: Oxford University Press, 1929), 5–8.

71. The Italian word *pertinenti* (and the related term *pertinenza*), equivalent to the Austrian *Heimatrecht* (law of settlement), refers to the juridical link uniting the individual to a specific commune on the basis of ethnic and linguistic criteria. The concept is different from the notion of "habitual residence" because, as it is usually translated, it refers to "the possession of rights of citizenship in a commune," meaning therefore more than simple residence. The historical origins go back to nineteenth-century Austrian law, which granted to those individuals who enjoyed *Heimatrecht* in a municipality an absolute right to undisturbed residence (with no risk of expulsion), enfranchisement and eligibility for election and, most importantly, the right to receive poor relief. Extended to the Austro-Hungarian empire, this status was not regulated by uniform norms, and as a matter of fact the institution under consideration did not exist in Bosnia-Herzegovina. See W. Napier, "Nationality in the Succession States of Austria-Hungary," *Transactions of the Grotius Society* 18 (1932): 1–16; J. Redlich, "The Municipality. I. Austria: The Commune System," *Journal of the Society of Comparative Legislation* 8 (1907): 12–40.

72. See the correspondence among Italy's MAE, the Ministry of Interior and the General Lieutenancy in Tirana as well as the consulate in Skopje (February–March 1942) concerning "Riconoscimento cittadinanza albanese ad ex cittadini jugoslavi," in ACS, FMIM, b. 22, f. 5.

73. See the letter of Ministry of the Interior (Divisione Affari Generali e Riservati, Sezione III), 28 December 1940, n. 443/202908, in ACS, FMIM, b. 15, f. A14 Albania.

74. Law n. 822 of 13 May 1940 (Norme relative ai meticci).

75. See Ciano in CFC, AP disc. 15/4/1939, 7: "Comrades! The Albanian people [...] are sober, proud, warrior and made up of [...] a race as pure and noble as the Italian race since both descend from the common Aryan stock. And these are the fundamental qualities which will determine the conditions for such a cordial cohabitation as to become shortly a fraternal relationship." Because of the already wide scope of this chapter, we are leaving out of our analysis the tiny but interesting minority of Albanian Jews who, as non-Aryan, were subjected to anti-Semitism and whose history would deserve a monograph of its own. See Sarfatti, "La condizione degli ebrei in Albania fra il 1938 e il 1943: Il quadro generale," in Brazzo and Sarfatti, *Gli ebrei in Albania*, 125–151.

76. See "Statuto Fondamentale del Regno d'Albania," 3 June 1939, in *Raccolta di provvedimenti di carattere legislativo*, 9–16.

77. See "Accordo stipulato in Tirana fra l'Italia e l'Albania il 20 aprile 1939 relativo ai diritti dei rispettivi cittadini," in *Raccolta di provvedimenti di carattere legislativo*, 17–18.

78. See CFC 2507, 5 July 1943, 2, containing the Italo-Albanian Agreement (Accordo fra i regi governi d'Italia e di Albania) signed in Rome on 30 December 1942.

79. See CFC, CLAE disc. 14/7/1943, 342.

80. See "Fusione delle Forze armate albanesi con le corrispondenti Forze armate italiane," in *Raccolta di provvedimenti di carattere legislativo*, 69; CFC 256, 10 June 1939, 1; CFC, CLAE disc. 16/6/1939, 32 and CFC 259, 10 June 1939, 1–2. Also Villari, "Il sistema di occupazione fascista in Albania," 101–105.

81. CFC, CLAE disc. 14/7/1943, 342.

82. On the growth of Resistance, see Fischer, *Albania at War*, 121–153; on the forced Albanization of the provinces of Kosovo and Dibrano, see Rodogno, *Il nuovo ordine mediterraneo*, 352–359.

83. Rodogno, *Il nuovo ordine mediterraneo*, prologue and ch. 1.

84. The French *départements* of continental Europe occupied by the Italians included Savoie, Hautes-Alpes, Alpes-de-Haute-Provence, Alpes-Maritimes and territories as far off as the river Rhône. On the history of the Principality of Monaco during World War Two, see P. Abramovici, *Un rocher bien occupé: Monaco pendant la guerre (1939–1945)* (Paris: Seuil, 2001).

85. As listed in Rodogno's work, the Greek islands that came under Italian occupying authority were the Ionian Islands (Paxos, Antipaxos, Cephalonia, Santa Maura, Zakynthos, Thiaki and Corfù as well as the minor islets of Fanò, Erikoussa, Mathraki and Meganisi), the Cyclades (Naxos, Andros, Tinos, Mykonos, Delos, Kea, Kytnos, Gyaros, Syros, Seriphos, Sifnos, Paros, Antiparos, Folegrandos, Sikinos, Ios, Iraklia, Schinoussa, Keros, Koufonisia, Amorgos, Kinarose, Levita, Melos, Kimolos, Polinos, Santorini and Anafé) and the Southern Sporades (Samos, Furni and Ikaria). Rodogno, *Il nuovo ordine mediterraneo*, 115.

86. The Yugoslav territories and cities annexed in 1941 were Kotor, Split, the islands of Veglia and Arbe, Ljubljana and central Slovenian lands, as well as the zone from Sušak to Kraljevica. The Dalmatian city of Zara, promised to Italy in the Treaty of London, was ceded to the Italian state in 1920 following the Treaty of St. Germain. Fiume, by contrast, after being declared a Free City under the League of Nations in 1920 (and after the rocambolesque coup by Gabriele D'Annunzio in September 1919 with his year-long "Regency of Carnaro"), was annexed by fascist Italy in 1924 on the basis of the Treaty of Rome, which was signed by Italy and the Kingdom of the Serbs, Croatians and Slovenes without any reference to the league.

87. Rodogno, *Il nuovo ordine mediterraneo*, 31–38 and 124–136.

88. According to data collected by Rodogno, the populations living in the territories annexed and occupied by Italian troops between 1940 and 1943 were approximately 4.2 million inhabitants in occupied France, 23,000 in the Principality of Monaco, 411,000 in occupied Montenegro, 1.8 million in occupied Croatia, 393,000 in annexed Dalmatia, 336,000 in the Province of Ljubljana and 81,000 in the territories annexed to Fiume. Rodogno, *Il nuovo ordine mediterraneo*, 111, 114, 500 and 502–504. The inhabitants living in occupied continental and insu-

lar Greece numbered approximately 4 million, as stated in a typed draft report kept in MAEASD, FGABAP, b. AP22, f. "Rifornimento di grano canadese nella Grecia."

89. See letter of CIAF to Ministry of the Interior (Direzione Generale per la Demografia e la Razza), 19 July 1941, protocol n. 4346, in MAEASD, FGABAP, b. AP20, f. 1; as well as the various letters and telegrams concerning the issue of passports for ex-Yugoslavs in MAEASD, FGABAP, b. AP52, f. "Vukicevis Blazo—Ingegnere residente in Germania—Passaporto jugoslavo" and f. "Montenegrini all'Estero."

90. See the letters and notes of CIAF (Amministrazione dei territori occupati), of MAE (Servizio Affari Privati) and of MAE (Gab. A.P.—Armistizio), July–October 1941, kept in MAEASD, FGABAP, b. AP20, f. 1.

91. See the letters and notes of CIAF (Amministrazione dei territori occupati), of MAE (Servizio Affari Privati) and of MAE (Gab. A.P.—Armistizio), July–October 1941, kept in MAEASD, FGABAP, b. AP20, f. 1.

92. Rodogno, *Il nuovo ordine mediterraneo*, 335.

93. Ibid.

94. See Ciano's telespresso n. 8/03970, 28 August 1941, concerning "Assistenza ai sudditi croati," kept in MAEASD, FGABAP, b. AP44, f. "A. I. 32 Croazia"; and, from the same file, Luca Pietromarchi's telespresso n. 8/02528 to Royal Legation in Zagreb, 4 July 1941.

95. See telespresso n. 3383/560 of Italian Embassy in Santiago to Italy's MAE, 25 November 1941, concerning "Emanuele Franulic Stipinovic—Ex suddito jugoslavo," kept in MAEASD, FGABAP, b. AP44, f. "A. I. 32 Croazia."

96. See "Statuto del Montenegro" (art. 6, 45–50) as well as "Accordo fra l'Italia e il Montenegro per regolare le reciproche relazioni" (art. 2) kept in MAEASD, FGABAP, b. AP48, f. "Montenegro A1-P.G." Also, on the similarity between the Montenegrin and the Albanian cases, see the letter of Gabap—Ufficio Montenegro to PCM, 25 July 1941, concerning "Aspiranti a pubblici impieghi di nazionalità montenegrina," kept in MAEASD, FGABAP, b. AP48, f. "Montenegro A1."

97. See "Relazione sui problemi del Montenegro" by Marco Giurovic, in MAEASD, FGABAP, b. AP48, f. "Montenegro A1."

98. On acquisition of Italian citizenship in these two Adriatic cities, see the legal documentation in Bariatti, *La disciplina giuridica*, 1:60–72, 119–122 and 183–188; the study of A. Fabbri, *Effetti giuridici delle annessioni territoriali con speciale riguardo alle annessioni di Fiume e della Dalmazia nei rapporti Italo-Jugoslavi* (Padova: Casa Editrice Milani, 1931), 144–154; Bussotti, *La cittadinanza degli italiani*, 133–147 and 155–157.

99. This point is confirmed by an overwhelming amount of archival evidence, which we were able to find in Rome. In these sources, issued by the major Italian authorities that dealt with the issue at the time (i.e., Ministry of the Interior, Ministry of Foreign Affairs, Presidency of the Council of Ministers and Ministry of War), one finds systematic and repetitive statements concerning the fact that the new annexed populations did not hold Italian citizenship *yet* and that, although they would acquire it at a later stage, time was needed, and the regime would probably have to wait until the end of the war. See the following files in ACS,

FPCM, Years 1940-1943: f. G7/1 11897/4; f. 1.1.13 16452/23; f. 15-2 15328/8; f. G7/8 12860/5; f. 1.1.13 16452.149. Also, ACS, FMIM, b. 22, f. 5, as well as MAEASD, FSAP, *Serie Jugoslavia*, b. 153, f. 17.

100. See Rodogno, *Il nuovo ordine mediterraneo*, 314–335. Also T. Sala, "Occupazione militare e amministrazione civile nella 'Provincia' di Lubiana (1941–1943)," in *L'Italia nell'Europa danubiana durante la seconda guerra mondiale*, ed. E. Collotti, T. Sala and G. Vaccarino (Milan: Istituto Nazionale per la Storia del Movimento di Liberazione, 1967), 73–93.

101. See letter of Governor Bastianini to PCM (Zara, 22 August 1941, protocol n. 4417) as well as Bastianini's project and Bastianini's reply to PCM and to MI (Zara, 17 November 1941, protocol n. 8134), in ACS, FPCM, Year 1940–1943, f. 1.1.13 16452/40. The project is also discussed by O. Talpo, *Dalmazia: Una cronaca per la storia*, vol. 1, *1941* (Rome: Ufficio Storico dello Stato Maggiore dell'Esercito, 1985), 653–662.

102. See "Schema di provvedimento legislativo concernente l'acquisto della cittadinanza italiana da parte degli ex sudditi jugoslavi residenti od originari dei nuovi territori: Provincia di Lubiana, Dalmazia, Zona Fiumana, annessi al Regno," by Ministry of the Interior, November 1941, in ACS, FPCM, Year 1940–1943, f. 1.1.13 16452/40.

103. The same reference to this typically fascist criterion is also made in a note of the Ministry of Foreign Affairs, Rome, 25 June 1941, in MAEASD, FGABAP, b. AP47, f. "AG Dalmazia 82."

104. Bastianini's letter, 17 November 1941, protocol n. 8134, in ACS, FPCM, Year 1940–1943, f. 1.1.13 16452/40.

105. Mussolini, 10 June 1941, as cited by Sala, "Occupazione militare e amministrazione civile nella 'Provincia' di Lubiana," 78.

106. See E. Gentile, *Il culto del littorio: La sacralizzazione della politica nell'Italia fascista* (Rome, Bari: Economica Laterza, 2001); Gentile, "Fascism as Political Religion," *Journal of Contemporary History* 25, nos. 2–3 (1990): 241–248; Giardina and Vauchez, *Il mito di Roma*; M. Stone, "A Flexible Rome: Fascism and the Cult of *romanità*," in Edwards, *Roman Presences*, 205.

107. Gentile, *Il culto del littorio*; Gentile, "Fascism as Political Religion"; Giardina and Vauchez, *Il mito di Roma*.

108. Mussolini, "La bandiera dei volontari," 4 June 1924, in *Opera Omnia*, 20:305.

109. Mussolini, "La proclamazione dell'Impero," 9 May 1936, in *Opera Omnia*, 27:269. From the same collection of political writings and speeches, one can find other explicit and implicit references made by the Duce to how ancient Rome incorporated the native peoples of its vast empire: see Mussolini, "Prefazione a 'La Nuova Italia d'Oltremare'," 21 July 1933, 26:30; "Le provincie africane," 7 June 1935, 27:84; "Ai capi abissini," 6 February 1937, 28:118; "Ai musulmani di Tripoli e della Libia," 18 March 1937, 28:145–147; "Ai notabili dell'Impero," 8 May 1938, 29:97–98; "Alla missione albanese," 15 April 1939, 29:262; "Alla missione albanese," 3 June 1939, 29:293; "Ai notabili dell'Impero," 11 May 1940, 29:392.

110. See Balbo's telegram in MAEASD, FMAI, b. 167, f. xi–v.

111. CFC, AP disc. 15/4/1939, 2.

112. See the archival typed note of 11 October 1938 concerning the Libyans in MAEASD, FMAI, b. 167, f. xi–v.

113. See G. Almirante, "L'editto di Caracalla: Un semi-barbaro spiana la via ai barbari," *La difesa della razza* no. 1 (1938): 27–29.

114. Ibid.

115. Ambrosini, *Principi fondamentali dell'ordinamento giuridico dell'Impero* (Tivoli: Officine Grafiche Mantero, 1938), 43.

116. See Gentile, *Il culto del littorio*, 129–135; Giardina and Vauchez, *Il mito di Roma*, 216–219; R. Visser, "Fascist Doctrine and the Cult of Romanità," *Journal of Contemporary History* 27, no. 1 (1992): 13–18.

117. Ambrosini, *L'Albania nella comunità imperiale di Roma* (Rome: Istituto Nazionale di Cultura Fascista, 1940), 63–66; Lucatello, *La natura giuridica dell'unione italo-albanese*, 91; Ambrosini, *Principi fondamentali dell'ordinamento giuridico dell'Impero*, 38–43; Di Caporiacco, "Cittadini e sudditi del Dodecanneso," 12.

118. References to fascist civilization in talking about the civil rights of the natives and respect for local customs and traditions in the colonies are made by Minister of Colonies Lessona in C 1501, 2 December 1936, 2, as well as by Deputy Piero Bolzon in C 1501-A, 4 December 1936, 2.

119. R. Pandolfo, "Valore universale della civiltà fascista," *Gerarchia* no. 4 (1942): 158.

120. As Rodogno has emphasized, the notion of Italy's vital space was based on a fascist deterministic assumption according to which the Italians were destined to expand and conquer specific geographic territories, with the aim, as an elected and superior nation, to civilize the conquered populations. From a geographic point of view, the borders of this *spazio vitale* were never defined in a precise way, although the Mediterranean Sea was certainly perceived as its core. The "ideal type" of Italy's *Lebensraum* could be seen as an area consisting of three concentric circles: the first incorporated the Italian peninsula and the central Mediterranean lands, the second included the other European territories of fascist Rome and the third covered African and Middle-Eastern territories ranging from the Italian colonies to Palestine, Iraq and Yemen. Rodogno, *Il nuovo ordine mediterraneo*, 69–80. See also A. Titta, "Concetto di 'Spazio Vitale'," *Gerarchia* no. 12 (1941): 646–648; G. Selvi, "Le basi dell' ordine nuovo (Parte I)," *Gerarchia* no. 4 (1942): 161–165; Selvi, "Le basi dell'ordine nuovo (Parte II)," *Gerarchia* no. 5 (1942): 205–208.

121. Sòrgoni, *Parole e corpi*, 206.

122. The treatment of the Jews by the fascist regime in the overseas territories from 1936 onward is increasingly attracting academic attention, and this fascinating topic still awaits a full monograph covering the whole Italian empire. On the Jews living in European lands under fascist rule, see Rodogno, *Il nuovo ordine mediterraneo*, ch. 11; Rodogno, "Italiani brava gente? Fascist Italy's Policy Toward the Jews in the Balkans, April 1941–July 1943," *European History Quarterly* 35, no. 2 (2005): 213–240; Brazzo and Sarfatti, *Gli ebrei in Albania*.

123. See S-CFA disc. 30/6/1939, 62. A similar reference to ancient Rome and to the Maritime Republic of Venice was also made on the same occasion by *camerata* Angelo Manaresi in CFC, CLFA disc. 15/6/1939, 43. Finally, ancient Rome

and Venice were also evoked in August 1941 within the context of the fascist policy of forced italianization in the annexed Dalmatian territories, which, as we have seen, had an impact on the various citizenship policies formulated by Bastianini and by the Ministry of the Interior to incorporate the ex-Yugoslav citizens of the territories annexed in 1941 within Italy's metropolitan citizenry. As argued in the Italian Senate, Yugoslavia had "slavisized" Dalmatia in less than twenty years, but the Italian government would reestablish the *italianità* of this region rapidly, "at a fascist pace," building on the foundations of Roman and Venetian traditions. See S-CR disc. 29/8/1941, 1111.

124. See Giardina and Vauchez, *Il mito di Roma*, 229; Gentile, *Il culto del littorio*, 132–135; and by the same author, "Fascism as Political Religion," 245.

125. I owe this Latin expression to A. R. Toniolo, "L'unità economica e politica del Mediterraneo," *Geopolitica* no. 3 (1941): 169.

CHAPTER EIGHT

1. G. Oliva, *Le tre Italie del 1943: Chi ha veramente combattuto la guerra civile* (Milan: Mondadori, 2004).

2. See De Felice, *Rosso e Nero*, ed. P. Chessa, 3rd ed. (Milan: Baldini & Castoldi, 1995); De Felice, *Mussolini l'alleato*, vol. 2, *La guerra civile 1943–1945* (Turin: Einaudi, 1997); C. Pavone, *Una guerra civile: Saggio storico sulla moralità nella Resistenza* (Turin: Bollati Boringhieri, 2003); Pavone, *Alle origini della Repubblica: Scritti su fascismo, antifascismo e continuità dello stato* (Turin: Bollati Boringhieri, 1995); G. E. Rusconi, *Resistenza e Postfascismo* (Bologna: Il Mulino, 1995); E. Galli della Loggia, *La morte della patria: La crisi dell'idea di nazione tra Resistenza, antifascismo e Repubblica*, 3rd ed. (Rome, Bari: Laterza, 2003); L. Ganapini, *La repubblica delle camicie nere: I combattenti, i politici, gli amministratori, i socializzatori* (Milan: Garzanti, 2002); C. Mazzantini, *L'ultimo repubblichino: Sessant'anni son passati* (Venice: Marsilio Editori, 2005).

3. See F. W. Deakin, *The Brutal Friendship: Mussolini, Hitler and the Fall of Italian Fascism*, rev. ed. (London: Phoenix Press, 2000), 457–485 and 528–537.

4. J. Goebbels, *The Goebbels Diaries 1942–1943*, ed. and trans. L. P. Lochner (New York: Doubleday, 1948), 437.

5. The two Nazi "Alpine and Adriatic zones of operation" included, respectively, the northern metropolitan provinces of Belluno, Trento and Bolzano (*Operationszone Alpenvorland*) and the oriental metropolitan territories of Friuli, Gorizia, Trieste, Istria, Fiume, Quarnaro and Ljubljana (*Operationszone Adriatisches Küstenland*). In this way, the Brenner Pass and the Adriatic coast line came under full German control. Ganapini, *La repubblica delle camicie nere*, 324–326; Deakin, *The Brutal Friendship*, 532–533 and 613–618.

6. See De Felice, *Mussolini l'alleato*, 2:3–71.

7. Ibid., 345–348 and 355–359; Deakin, *The Brutal Friendship*, 565–566, 581–586 and 607–612.

8. The juridical nature of the Italian Social Republic has been the subject of interesting debates among Italian jurists and should be taken into account by historians as well: Was Salò a state or was it not? In line with the various arguments

that have been put forward, Mussolini's Republic did not enjoy statehood because no split of Italy's state system took place in 1943. RSI was therefore a *"de facto government"* or a *"juridical system."* True, Salò had a territory, a population and international recognition from several countries. However, it enjoyed all these factors as a governmental authority, and not as a state. For instance, in numerous archival documents published in the 1990s concerning the international recognition of Mussolini's neo-fascist entity, one reads that "a new fascist-republican government" was created in Italy and that the "new Italian government" would be "recognized." The word "state" was not used. See for example the letter that Hitler sent to the Rumanian Marshal Ion Victor Antonescu on 25 September 1943 to "encourage" him to recognize the Duce's new government, translated and published in Italian, in N. Cospito and H. W. Neulen, *Salò-Berlino: L'alleanza difficile. La Repubblica Sociale Italiana nei documenti segreti del Terzo Reich* (Milan: Mursia, 1992), 46. On the various debates concerning Salò from a juridical point of view, see the elaborated discussions of M. S. Giannini, "La repubblica sociale rispetto allo Stato italiano," *Rivista italiana per le scienze giuridiche* (1951): 330–417; and of G. Tuzzolo, *L'ultima notte del Fascismo tra diritto e storia. Dall'ultima seduta del Gran Consiglio del Fascismo alla fine dell'esperienza della Repubblica Sociale: Le relative problematiche giuridico-istituzionali* (Foggia: Edizioni Della Vela, 2001), 97–116.

9. E. Artom, *Diari di un partigiano ebreo (gennaio 1940–febbraio 1944),* ed. G. Schwarz (Turin: Bollati Boringhieri, 2008), 57. See also Pavone, *Una guerra civile,* 172.

10. Deakin, *The Brutal Friendship,* 814–817; Ganapini, *La repubblica delle camicie nere,* 16. On the formal illegality of the execution without process against the Duce (who indeed should have been handed over *alive* to the forces of the United Nations in accordance with the surrender terms), see Tuzzolo, *L'ultima notte del Fascismo,* 124–130.

11. See Kiefé, "L'allégeance," 47–68.

12. See the last king of Italy, Umberto II, to Italian journalist and writer Giovanni Artieri, in G. Artieri, *Umberto II. Il re gentiluomo: Colloqui sulla fine della monarchia* (Florence: Le Lettere, 2002), 33–36.

13. Ibid., 45–46. On 14 October 1943, King Vittorio Emanuele III told Marquis Gianbattista Serra di Cassano, a state official within the Ministry of Foreign Affairs in Brindisi: "Now you will certainly wonder why I did not stay in Rome on 8 September. If I had stayed I would have been captured by the Germans and taken to Berlin. The next day the Italians would have heard a voice like mine giving instructions on behalf of Hitler. I could never have accepted an eventuality of the kind." As reported by Artieri, *Umberto II,* 37. On the king's motivations, see also the diary of Paolo Puntoni, aide-de-camp general of Vittorio Emanuele III, *Parla Vittorio Emanuele III* (Bologna: Il Mulino, 1993), 165–166 (entry 9 September 1943) and 170 (entry 10 September 1943).

14. Umberto II to Luigi Cavicchioli, as reported in F. Perfetti, "Vittorio Emanuele, Umberto e il '25 Luglio' mancato," *Nuova storia contemporanea* no. 5 (2002): 39.

15. See for instance E. Aga Rossi, *Una nazione allo sbando: L'armistizio italiano del settembre 1943 e le sue conseguenze,* new and rev. ed. (Bologna: Il

Mulino, 2003); I. Palermo, *Storia di un armistizio* (Milan: Mondadori, 1967); F. Stefani, *8 Settembre 1943: Gli armistizi dell'Italia* (Settimo Milanese: Marzorati Editore, 1991); A. N. Garland and H. McGaw Smyth, *Sicily and the Surrender of Italy* (Washington, D.C.: Office of the Chief of Military History, 1965).

16. Aga Rossi, *Una nazione allo sbando.*

17. Ibid., 10 and 111–121.

18. Ibid., 112–116 and 121.

19. Ibid., 111–179 and 194–197.

20. Pavone, *Una guerra civile,* 14–15.

21. Ibid.

22. Mazzantini, *L'ultimo repubblichino,* 51.

23. Pavone, *Una guerra civile,* 14–15.

24. Testimony reported in Pavone, ibid.

25. Cited in Pavone, ibid.

26. Mazzantini, *L'ultimo repubblichino,* 53.

27. Ibid.

28. Aga Rossi, *Una nazione allo sbando,* ch. 3.

29. The triad of the "civil war," the "patriotic war" and the "social war" is by Pavone, *Una guerra civile.*

30. Ganapini, *La repubblica delle camicie nere*; Oliva, *Le tre Italie,* 41–57.

31. Pavone, *Una guerra civile.*

32. Ibid.

33. Quoted in Pavone, *Una guerra civile,* 34.

34. Pavone, *Una guerra civile,* 32–35 and 246–247. Also, Ganapini, *La repubblica delle camicie nere,* 7–10.

35. These approximations are taken from Oliva, *Le tre Italie,* 63–64.

36. De Felice, *Rosso e Nero,* 45–54.

37. Oliva, *Le tre Italie,* 66.

38. Ibid., 67–70; De Felice, *Rosso e Nero,* 55–65; Ganapini, *La repubblica delle camicie nere,* 253. *The House on the Hill* (*La casa in collina*) is the title of a novel by Cesare Pavese and the metaphorical reference to it is made by Pavone, *Una guerra civile,* 32.

39. P. Malvezzi and G. Pirelli, eds., *Lettere di condannati a morte della Resistenza italiana (8 settembre 1943–25 aprile 1945),* 15th ed. (Turin: Einaudi, 1994), 21.

40. Ibid., 329.

41. "Camicie nere della Repubblica," *Il Ferruccio,* 8 May 1944, quoted in Ganapini, *La repubblica delle camicie nere,* 33.

42. Malvezzi and Pirelli, *Lettere di condannati a morte,* 113.

43. Ibid., 116.

44. G. Rolandino, "Il Maresciallo Graziani sul fronte della San Marco," *Glaudio: Rivista per le forze armate,* 1 April 1945, cited by Ganapini, *La repubblica delle camicie nere,* 119–120.

45. Malvezzi and Pirelli, *Lettere di condannati a morte,* 97.

46. L. Lenzi, "Noi e loro. Ivan il terribile," *Il Ferruccio,* 8 May 1944, quoted by Ganapini, *La repubblica delle camicie nere,* 112.

47. Malvezzi and Pirelli, *Lettere di condannati a morte,* 99.

48. Lenzi, "Noi e loro," quoted by Ganapini, *La repubblica delle camicie nere*, 112.

49. Pavone, *Una guerra civile*, 179–180.

50. Ibid., 180.

51. Ibid., 180–181.

52. Malvezzi and Pirelli, *Lettere di condannati a morte*, 104–105.

53. Ganapini, *La repubblica delle camicie nere*, 12.

54. See Pavone, *Una guerra civile*, 182; Ganapini, *La repubblica delle camicie nere*, 167; De Felice, *Mussolini l'alleato*, 2:416.

55. Bobbio, *Dal fascismo alla democrazia*, 115–119.

56. See N. Kogan, *Italy and the Allies* (Cambridge, Mass.: Harvard University Press, 1956), 50–65; H. McGaw Smyth, "Italy: From Fascism to the Republic (1943–1946)," *Western Political Quarterly* 1, no. 3 (1948): 211–218; F. Catalano, *Storia d'Italia*, vol. 5, *Dalla crisi del primo dopoguerra alla fondazione della repubblica* (Turin: Unione Tipografico-Editrice Torinese, 1965), 511–513.

57. Through the system of the lieutenancy, Vittorio Emanuele III remained king in name but withdrew from the exercise of all public authority. On the proposition concerning abdication through regency, see the letter of Badoglio to the Italian King (24 October 1943) as reported in the diary of the aide-de-camp general Puntoni, *Parla Vittorio Emanuele III*, 179–181 (entry 24 October 1943) and 198 (entry 13 January 1944). References to the Allies' interference in the Italian dynastic question during this period are made by the last king of Italy from his exile, in Artieri, *Umberto II*, 14–17; and by Puntoni, *Parla Vittorio Emanuele III*, 216–218 (entry 3 April 1944) and 220–223 (entry 10 April 1944).

58. Ganapini, *La repubblica delle camicie nere*, 11.

59. On anti-Semitism and deportations from Italy between 1943 and 1945, see Picciotto Fargion, *Il libro della memoria*; Sarfatti, *The Jews in Mussolini's Italy*, ch. 5; De Felice, *Storia degli ebrei italiani*, ch. 8; Collotti, *Il fascismo e gli ebrei*, ch. 7.

60. The metaphorical expression referring to Mussolini (Prisoner of the Lake) can be found in S. Ruinas, *Pioggia sulla repubblica*, 3rd ed. (Rome: Corso, 1979), 178; as well as in Ganapini, *La repubblica delle camicie nere*, ch. 6.

61. Ganapini, *La repubblica delle camicie nere*, 31.

62. See r. d. l. n. 25 of 20 January 1944 (Disposizioni per la reintegrazione dei diritti civili e politici dei cittadini italiani e stranieri già dichiarati di razza ebraica o considerati di razza ebraica), in Bariatti, *La disciplina giuridica*, 1:88.

63. See d. l. l. n. 23 of 1 February 1945 (Estensione alle donne del diritto di voto), in *Raccolta ufficiale delle leggi e dei decreti*, 1:79–80.

64. McGaw Smyth, "Italy: From Fascism to the Republic," 208.

65. The phrase *cittadinanza italiana* can for instance be found in a proposal of Salò Minister of Education Carlo Alberto Biggini concerning the future constitution of RSI, "Progetto di Costituzione di Carlo Alberto Biggini," in F. Franchi, *Le costituzioni della Repubblica Sociale Italiana* (Rome: Edizioni Settimo Sigillo, 1997), 178.

66. Ganapini, *La repubblica delle camicie nere*, 367–370. The Verona Manifesto is published in the appendix of De Felice's book, *Mussolini l'alleato*, 2: 610–613.

67. "Il progetto di Costituzione di Vittorio Rolandi Ricci," in Franchi, *Le costituzioni*, 149.

68. See Franchi, *Le costituzioni*, 149–152 as well as Ganapini, *La repubblica delle camicie nere*, 165.

69. Franchi, *Le costituzioni*, 178.

70. See Ganapini, *La repubblica delle camicie nere*, 132–156.

71. See the historiographical article and discussion by Berger, "A Return to the National Paradigm?" especially 652–654 and 665–667.

72. Pavone, *Una guerra civile*, 266–267.

73. Ibid., 225.

74. Mazzantini, *I Balilla andarono a Salò* (Venice: Marsilio Editori, 1995), 39.

75. Letter of Roberto Nanni, 21 January 1945, as quoted by Pavone, *Una guerra civile*, 58. The same reference to the fratricidal aspect of the war can also be found in an RSI propaganda journal of September 1944, where a young neo-fascist lieutenant said with a certain bitterness: "[Before 8 September] you were teaching us how to fight against the enemies of the fatherland, and now instead we have in front of us some brothers whom we have to hate more than the enemy itself because they betray us ... How sad, Captain G." Lieutenant P. Tura, *Libro e moschetto*, 9 September 1944, cited by Ganapini, *La repubblica delle camicie nere*, 26.

76. Pavone, *Una guerra civile*, 266–267.

77. Ibid., 242–243.

78. F. Calamandrei, *La vita indivisibile: Diario 1941–1947* (Rome: Editori Riuniti, 1984), 137, quoted in Pavone, *Una guerra civile*, 243.

79. Pavone, *Una guerra civile*, 225.

80. Bobbio, *Dal fascismo alla democrazia*, 155.

81. Bobbio, ibid., 156; Pavone, *Una guerra civile*, 512–514; D. Coli, *Giovanni Gentile* (Bologna: Il Mulino, 2004).

82. Oliva, *Le tre Italie*, 77–82.

83. Ruinas, *Pioggia sulla Repubblica*, 82.

84. These specific Italian aspects are emphasized by Pavone, *Una guerra civile*, 40; and by Oliva, *Le tre Italie*, 83–85.

85. E. E. Agnoletti, "Prefazione," in Malvezzi and Pirelli, *Lettere di condannati a morte*, xv–xvi.

86. See Oliva, *Le tre Italie*, 90–94.

CHAPTER NINE

1. See the 1948 Italian Constitution (art. 54, 83–91, 139), in *Commentario sistematico alla Costituzione italiana*, ed. P. Calamandrei and A. Levi (Florence: Barbera Editore, 1950), 1: XXXVI, XL–XLII and L.

2. G. Chianese, "I monarchici nella Repubblica," in *Almanacco della Repubblica: Storia d'Italia attraverso le tradizioni, le istituzioni e le simbologie repubblicane*, ed. M. Ridolfi (Milan: Mondadori, 2003), 262.

3. McGaw Smyth, "Italy: From Fascism to the Republic," 218–222; Bobbio, *Dal fascismo alla democrazia*, 160–165.

4. Allied Commission, *Weekly Bulletin*, 23 February 1946, quoted in Kogan, *Italy and the Allies*, 127.

5. P. L. Ballini, "Il referendum del 2 giugno 1946," in Ridolfi, *Almanacco della Repubblica*, 223-224.

6. A. Gambino, *Storia del dopoguerra dalla Liberazione al potere DC* (Rome, Bari: Laterza, 1978), 149-150; P. Pombeni, "La Costituente," in Ridolfi, *Almanacco della Repubblica*, 234-235.

7. This number is taken from A. Spreafico, "La competizione elettorale e gli esiti del voto," in *La nascita della Repubblica: Atti del convegno di studi storici (Roma, 4-5-6 giugno 1987)*, ed. Presidenza del Consiglio dei Ministri (Rome: Presidenza del Consiglio dei Ministri, 1987), 187.

8. Ballini, "Il referendum," 224-225.

9. Ibid.

10. A. G. Ricci, *La Repubblica* (Bologna: Il Mulino, 2001), 182.

11. Ibid.

12. References to all these categories of Italian citizens can be found in Artieri, *Umberto II*, 221 and 251-252. Also see Spreafico, "La competizione elettorale," 187 and 193. On the Italian POWs turn to L. E. Keefer, *Italian Prisoners of War in America, 1942-1946: Captives or Allies?* (New York: Praeger, 1992) and B. Moore, "Turning Liabilities into Assets: British Government Policy Towards German and Italian Prisoners of War During the Second World War," *Journal of Contemporary History* 32, no. 1 (1997): 117-136.

13. See Gambino, *Storia del dopoguerra*, 225-227; Ballini, "Il referendum," 226-227; Ricci, *La Repubblica*, 187-188; Artieri, *Umberto II*, 263-267. We remind the reader that a "spoiled vote" and a "blank vote" imply two different types of behavior on the part of the electorate: a "spoiled ballot paper" can be the result of an error made by the voter owing to insufficient information or electoral preparation, or it can be used by the person entitled to vote as a tool to express dissent by annulling the vote intentionally. A "blank ballot paper," by contrast, implies the will of the elector not to express any view, usually in facing a problematic and difficult political issue. See Spreafico, "La competizione elettorale," 188.

14. See decreto legislativo luogotenenziale n. 98, 16 March 1946 (art. 2), in A. Cariola with G. A. Ferro, *Le leggi dell'organizzazione costituzionale* (Milan: Giuffrè Editore, 2004), 45-46. A later decree of April 1946 referred to the "valid votes"; however, the fundamental norm regulating the referendum was the one contained in the first decree issued in March. See G. Tamburrano, "Il paese e le forze politiche," in Presidenza del Consiglio dei Ministri, *La nascita della Repubblica*, 85.

15. The impossibility of calculating the number of blank voting papers was acknowledged at the time by Palmiro Togliatti, head of the Italian Communist Party and minister of justice during the period of the referendum, as well as in 1983 by a former president of the Italian Republic (Giovanni Leone) in a letter sent to Minister Falcone Lucifero on 25 November 1983. See Ricci, *La Repubblica*, 188-191; the letter of Giovanni Leone is reproduced and discussed in F. Perfetti, "I voti nulli, le schede bianche e il referendum istituzionale. Un parere di Giovanni Leone sulla questione del 'quorum'," *Nuova storia contemporanea* no. 5 (2002): 84-85; Artieri, *Umberto II*, 252-253.

16. For a detailed description of the various decisions, proposals and counter-proposals involving this arm wrestling between De Gasperi and Italy's Council of Ministers on one side and the Crown and his advisors on the other, see Gambino, *Storia del dopoguerra*, 229–242.

17. Umberto II to the Italians, 13 June 1946, quoted in Artieri, *Umberto II*, 222, footnote 2.

18. See "Corte Suprema di Cassazione—'Referendum' sulla forma istituzionale dello Stato—Verbale relativo al giudizio definitivo sulle contestazioni, le proteste e i reclami di cui all'art. 19 d. l. l. 23 aprile 1946, n. 219," in Cariola with Ferro, *Le leggi dell'organizzazione costituzionale*, 48–49.

19. F. Lucifero, *L'ultimo Re: I diari del ministro della Real Casa 1944–1946*, ed. A. Lucifero and F. Perfetti, 2nd ed. (Milan: Mondadori, 2003), 558.

20. On all these events, see Lucifero, *L'ultimo Re*, especially 481–571; Perfetti, "I voti nulli," 83–90; Ballini, "Il referendum," 222–229; Ricci, *La Repubblica*, 187–198.

21. Because the Dodecanese islands were occupied militarily by liberal Italy in 1912 but were annexed in 1924 when Mussolini was already in power, we have grouped them together with the "fascist territories." On the territorial clauses concerning the lands that came under Italian sovereignty during the fascist period, see "Treaty of Peace with Italy" (Section I and Sections V–VII), in United Nations, *Treaty Series*, 1950, vol. 49, I. n. 747. Also H. Stuart Hughes, *The United States and Italy* (Cambridge, Mass.: Harvard University Press, 1979), 148–152.

22. See "Treaty of Peace with Italy" (Section IV and Annex XI). Also Stuart Hughes, *The United States and Italy*, 148–152.

23. On the territorial clauses concerning the Italo-French border, see "Treaty of Peace with Italy" (Sections I–II and Annexes I–II). On the borders with Yugoslavia and on Trieste, see Sections I, III, IV and Annex I. For a general discussion and overview, Kogan, *Italy and the Allies*, 132–150.

24. See "Treaty of Peace with Italy" (Section II); Italian Ministry of Foreign Affairs, Circular n. 38, "Territori ceduti alla Grecia—Opzioni," 8 September 1948, in *Raccolta delle circolari e istruzioni ministeriali*, 14:252–255; Villari, "Italiani dell'Egeo e sudditi coloniali," *Rivista trimestrale di diritto e di procedura civile* (1950): 668–672.

25. "Treaty of Peace with Italy" (Section VI).

26. See "Ethiopian Nationality Law of 1930," first published in *Berhanena Selam Newspaper* 6, no. 30 (24 July 1930), available on the website of the United Nations High Commissioner for Refugees, http://www.unhcr.org/refworld/docid/3ae6b52ac.html (accessed 27 October 2012).

27. See "Treaty of Peace with Italy" (Section II); Italian Ministry of Foreign Affairs, Circular n. 50, "Opzioni," 6 November 1947, in *Raccolta delle circolari e istruzioni ministeriali*, 14:119–122; Italian Ministry of Foreign Affairs, Circular n. 15, "Articoli 19 e 20 del Trattato di Pace—Opzioni," 27 April 1948, in *Raccolta delle circolari e istruzioni ministeriali*, 14:185–193. The reader might recall that between 1940 and 1942 fascist troops also occupied some *départements* in Southern France and Corsica, the Principality of Monaco and parts of continental and insular Greece as well as some Croatian zones and Montenegro. The inhabitants of these lands did not become Italian citizens or subjects because

their territories were not annexed but only occupied. This is why, once Italian military occupation was over, they kept (respectively) their French, Monegasque and Greek citizenship(s) as well as acquiring Yugoslav membership status, without losing any previous juridical link with Italy.

28. On all these issues, see G. Crifò, E. Cortese and G. Biscottini, "Cittadinanza," *Enciclopedia del diritto* (Milan: Giuffrè, 1960), 7:148; R. Quadri, "Cittadinanza," in Azara and Eula, *Novissimo digesto italiano*, 3:309; Bariatti, *La disciplina giuridica*, 2:8–9; Villari, "Italiani dell'Egeo e sudditi coloniali," 672–674; Bussotti, *La cittadinanza degli italiani*, 188–190.

29. See "Treaty of Peace with Italy" (Section II); Ministry of Foreign Affairs, Circular n. 31, "Territori ceduti alla Francia—Opzioni," 15 July 1948, in *Raccolta delle circolari e istruzioni ministeriali*, 14:221–229.

30. See "Treaty of Peace with Italy" (Section II); Italian Ministry of Foreign Affairs, Circular n. 50, "Opzioni," 6 November 1947; Italian Ministry of Foreign Affairs, Circular n. 15, "Articoli 19 e 20 del Trattato di Pace—Opzioni," 27 April 1948.

31. See Ballinger, "Borders of the Nation," 726–727.

32. See "Treaty of Peace with Italy" (Annexes VI–VII); V. Favilli, "L'attuale situazione giuridica internazionale del territorio di Trieste," *Rivista di studi politici internazionali* no. 3 (1950): 370–372; C. Lipartiti, "Naturalizzazioni collettive," in Azara and Eula, *Novissimo digesto italiano*, 11:69. For a comprehensive analysis concerning the question of Trieste, see C. B. Novak, *Trieste 1941–1954: The Ethnic, Political and Ideological Struggle* (Chicago, London: University of Chicago Press, 1970); and J. B. Duroselle, *Le conflit de Trieste 1943–1954* (Brussels: Editions de l' Institut de Sociologie de l'Université Libre, 1966). On the Esodo, turn to R. Pupo, *Il lungo esodo. Istria: Le persecuzioni, le foibe, l'esilio* (Milan: Biblioteca Universale Rizzoli, 2005). On the realities and sociological dimensions related to these Italian citizenship issues and repatriation, see Ballinger, "Borders of the Nation."

33. Churchill's words are quoted in R. Albrecht-Carrié, "Peace with Italy—An Appraisal," *Political Science Quarterly* 62, no. 4 (1947): 485.

34. B. Croce, *Contro l'approvazione del dettato della pace: Discorso tenuto all'Assemblea Costituente il 24 luglio 1947* (Bari: Laterza, 1947), 9.

35. See Kogan, *Italy and the Allies*, 134–141 and 163–168; A. Varsori, *L'Italia nelle relazioni internazionali dal 1943 al 1992* (Rome, Bari: Laterza, 1998), 27–42.

36. Allied Commission, *Weekly Bulletin*, 26 January 1946, quoted in Kogan, *Italy and the Allies*, 133.

37. See Kogan, *Italy and the Allies*, 132–134, 168, 192–193.

38. See the 1948 Italian Constitution (art. 51). Also, A. Reposo, "Gli italiani non appartenenti alla Repubblica (vecchi e nuovi problemi)," *Diritto e Società* 4 (1973): 906–927; G. Biscottini, "La condizione giuridica degli italiani non appartenenti alla Repubblica," *Annali della Facoltà Giuridica. Università degli Studi di Camerino* 17–18 (1950): 81–124.

39. See *Atti dell'Assemblea Costituente*, vol. 8, hearing of 17 October 1947, 1326. In December 1947, Meuccio Ruini, president of the commission set up for the constitution, would reiterate the same political message by saying that article

51 was the "due acknowledgment of solidarity vis-à-vis our brothers, recently torn from Mother Italy," in *Atti dell'Assemblea Costituente*, vol. 10, hearing of 22 December 1947, 3571.

40. See Decreto Legislativo del Capo provvisorio dello Stato n. 1906, 3 August 1947 (Abrogazione della legge 13 maggio 1940 n. 822 contenente norme relative ai meticci), in Bariatti, *La disciplina giuridica*, 1:88–89.

41. See De Gasperi, hearing of 3 July 1947, in Archivio Centrale dello Stato, *Verbali del Consiglio dei Ministri (luglio 1943–maggio 1948)*, ed. A. G. Ricci (Rome: Istituto Poligrafico e Zecca dello Stato, 1998), 9i: 254.

42. Ibid.

43. See the parliamentary report concerning the fascist law on deprivation of citizenship for political opponents (*fuoriusciti*) in C 623-A (Bastianini, *rapporteur*), 27 November 1925, 1–4; as well as the Italian Constitution of 1948 (art. 22). On this constitutional change, see also the discussion in Bussotti, *La cittadinanza degli italiani*, 219–221.

44. See the Italian Constitution of 1948 (art. 3, 13–16, 19–21).

45. Bobbio, *Dal fascismo alla democrazia*, 168–170; J. C. Adams and P. Barile, *The Government of Republican Italy*, 3rd ed. (Boston: Houghton Mifflin, 1972), 52–58.

46. Bobbio, *Dal fascismo alla democrazia*, 166–170.

47. Ibid., 55–57 and 171; Bussotti, *La cittadinanza degli italiani*, 223–225; A. Tesauro, "The Fundamentals of the New Italian Constitution," *Canadian Journal of Economics and Political Science* 20, no. 1 (1954): 52–53; Italian Constitution of 1948 (art. 1 and art. 48–51).

48. Tesauro, "The Fundamentals of the New Italian Constitution," 44–48; Italian Constitution (art. 5, 114–133).

49. Bobbio, *Dal fascismo alla democrazia*, 172–173; Italian Constitution (art. 83–91 and art. 55–69).

50. S. J. Woolf, "The Rebirth of Italy, 1943–50," in *The Rebirth of Italy 1943–1950*, ed. S. J. Woolf (London: Longman, 1972), 234–235.

51. See P. Vercellone, "The Italian Constitution of 1947–1948," in Woolf, *The Rebirth of Italy*, 123–124.

52. A. Ventrone, "Il cittadino nella Repubblica," in Ridolfi, *Almanacco della Repubblica*, 319–320; Tesauro, "The Fundamentals of the New Italian Constitution," 59–60; Italian Constitution (art. 3, 4, 18, 32–38, 40 and 46).

53. Woolf, "The Rebirth of Italy," 230–231.

54. Vercellone, "The Italian Constitution," 124.

55. Ibid., 123–125.

56. Bobbio, *Dal fascismo alla democrazia*, 168–170; Vercellone, "The Italian Constitution," 126.

57. President Roosevelt, *New York Times*, 12 June 1943, as cited by Kogan, *Italy and the Allies*, 172.

58. I owe these reflections to Kogan, *Italy and the Allies*, 171–173.

59. Woolf, "The Rebirth of Italy," 235–236.

60. See M. Martiniello, "Citizenship of the European Union," in *From Migrants to Citizens: Membership in a Changing World*, ed. T. A. Aleinikoff and D. Klusmeyer, 342–380 (Washington D.C.: Carnegie Endowment for Interna-

tional Peace, 2000); as well as the discussion by R. Bellamy, "Evaluating Union Citizenship: Belonging, Rights and Participation within the EU," *Citizenship Studies* 12, no. 6 (2008): 597–611.

61. Triandafyllidou, "Popular Perceptions of Europe," 261–282.

CONCLUSION

1. R. Brown, *Social Psychology* (New York: Free Press, 1965), 174, quoted in G. Bollati, *L' Italiano: Il carattere nazionale come storia e come invenzione* (Turin: Einaudi, 1996), 34.

2. Bollati, *L' Italiano*, 34.

3. Mack Smith, *Italy and Its Monarchy* (New Haven, London: Yale University Press, 1989).

4. Smith, *National Identity*, 9.

5. See Brubaker, "The Manichean Myth," 55–71; Brubaker, "Myths and Misconceptions in the Study of Nationalism," in *National Self-Determination and Secession*, ed. M. Moore (Oxford: Oxford University Press, 1998), 257–260; Brubaker, *Citizenship*, 1–17.

6. Chabod, *L' idea di nazione*, 68–75.

7. See J. Penrose and J. May, "Herder's Concept of Nation and Its Relevance to Contemporary Ethnic Nationalism," *Canadian Review of Studies in Nationalism* 18, nos. 1–2 (1991): 165–178; Mazzini, "Nazionalismo e Nazionalità," in Edizione Nazionale, *Scritti*, 93:85–96; Mazzini, "Politica Internazionale," 145; Levi, *La filosofia politica*, 195–231.

8. The analytical and normative ambiguities of classifying the various nationalisms through the means of dichotomies, such as "ethnic-civic," "naturalistic-voluntaristic" and "cultural-political," have been the object of much academic discussion. Though we acknowledge that all classifications are inherently limited and can therefore be criticized in one way or another, we do think they are still useful instruments for the scholar. Within this debate see, among others, Smith, *National Identity*; D. Schnapper, *La communauté des citoyens: Sur l'idée moderne de nation* (Paris: Gallimard, 1994); B. C. J. Singer, "Cultural v. Contractual Nations: Rethinking Their Opposition," *History and Theory* 35, no. 3 (1996): 309–337; Brubaker, "The Manichean Myth," 55–71; A. Dieckhoff, "La déconstruction d'une illusion: L'introuvable opposition entre nationalisme politique et nationalisme culturel," *L'année sociologique* 46, no. 1 (1996): 43–55; T. Reeskens and M. Hooghe, "Beyond the Civic-Ethnic Dichotomy: Investigating the Structure of Citizenship Concepts Across Thirty-Three Countries," *Nations and Nationalism* 16, no. 4 (2010): 579–597.

9. On these aspects, see Galli della Loggia, *L'identità italiana* (Bologna: Il Mulino, 1990).

10. See "150° anniversario dell'Unità d'Italia" on the website of the Presidency of the Italian Republic, http://www.quirinale.it/qrnw/statico/eventi/150italia -unita/150anni.htm (accessed 20 April 2011).

11. See I. Diamanti, *Il male del Nord: Lega, localismo, secessione* (Rome: Donzelli editore, 1996); S. Donati, "'La Ligue Nord pour l'Indépendance de la

Padanie': Entre séparatisme et fédéralisme," *Revue militaire suisse,* October 2010: 56–60; P. Berizzi, "Cresce la rabbia della base leghista. 'Ci trattano come i terroni d'Europa'," *la Repubblica,* 10 April 2011, http://www.repubblica.it; S. Bignami, "La Lega: 'Contiamo i musulmani'. E la maggioranza abbandona l'aula," *la Repubblica,* 27 January 2012, http://bologna.repubblica.it.

    12. C. Bonifazi, *L'immigrazione straniera in Italia* (Bologna: Il Mulino, 2007).

    13. "Napolitano: 'È una follia che i figli di immigrati nati in Italia non siano cittadini'," *Corriere della Sera,* 22 November 2011, http://www.corriere.it. Also, Zincone, *Familismo legale.*

    14. Eley, "Some General Thoughts on Citizenship in Germany," in Eley and Palmowski, *Citizenship and National Identity,* 238.

Bibliography

1. GUIDES TO THE ITALIAN ARCHIVES
AND TO RESEARCH MATERIAL

Brugioni, A., and M. Saporiti. *Manuale delle ricerche nell'Ufficio Storico dello Stato Maggiore dell'Esercito.* Rome: Stato Maggiore dell'Esercito, 1989.

Cassels, A., ed. *Italian Foreign Policy 1918–1945: A Guide to Research and Research Materials.* Wilmington, Del.: Scholarly Resources, 1981.

Commissione delle comunità europee. "Italia." In *Guida degli archivi dei ministeri degli affari esteri degli Stati membri, delle Comunità europee e della coo-*

perazione politica europea, 43–47. Luxembourg: Ufficio delle pubblicazioni ufficiali delle Comunità europee, 1991.

Gionfrida, A. "Censimento sommario dell'Archivio dell'Ufficio Storico dello Stato Maggiore dell'Esercito." *Bollettino dell'Archivio dell'Ufficio Storico* 1, no. 1 (2001): 31–70.

Ministero per i Beni Culturali e Ambientali—Ufficio Centrale per i Beni Archivistici. *Guida Generale degli Archivi di Stato Italiani*. Vol. 1. Florence: Le Monnier, 1981.

2. PRIMARY SOURCES

2.a Unpublished archival sources

Ministero degli Affari Esteri—Archivio Storico Diplomatico (MAEASD), Rome:

Fondo Consiglio del Contenzioso Diplomatico, Serie Contenzioso Diplomatico (1857–1923)
   On the origins (1859–1865): b. 1 (f. 13, f. 34)
   On *non regnicoli* and non-Italian immigrants: b. 1 (f. 46, f. 63)
   On European Mediterranean populations (liberal period):
      System of capitulations: b. 1 (f. 23)

Fondo Consiglio del Contenzioso Diplomatico, Serie Contenzioso Diplomatico (1924–1937)
   On European Mediterranean populations (fascist period):
      Aegean Islands: b. 28 (f. 10); b. 36 (f. 80)

Fondo Scritture del Ministero degli Esteri del Regno d'Italia dal 1861 al 1887
   On non-Italian immigrants: b. 1498 (f. 12)

Fondo Serie "D"—Direzione dell'Archivio Storico (1861–1953)
   On non-Italian immigrants: b. 42 (f. 532)
   On Italian emigration: b. 40 (f. 405)

Fondo Serie Politica "P" (1891–1916)
   On European Mediterranean populations (liberal period):
      Aegean Islands: b. 171 (f. 17/4)

Fondo Ministero Africa Italiana—Gabinetto—Archivio Segreto 1°
   On African populations (fascist period):
      Libya: b. 167 (f. xi-v)
      AOI: b. 167 (f. xi-v, f. xi)

Fondo Carte del Gabinetto del Ministro e della Segreteria Generale (1923–1943), Serie Ufficio Armistizio Pace (AP)
   On European Mediterranean populations (fascist period):
      Occupied France: b. AP20 (f. 1)

Occupied Greece: b. AP22 (f. Rifornimento di grano canadese nella Grecia); b. AP24 (f. ag-Ionio 23)

Occupied Montenegro: b. AP48 (f. Montenegro A1, f. Montenegro A1-P.G., f. Montenegro A-17); b. AP50 (f. Giustizia, f. 81); b. AP51 (f. A51-12); b. AP52 (f. Aspirazioni montenegrine, f. Vukicevis Blazo—Ingegnere residente in Germania—Passaporto Jugoslavo, f. Yovanovitch Savo, f. Montenegrini all'estero)

Occupied Croatia: b. AP25 (f. 3); b. AP34 (f. AG Croazia 4); b. AP39 (f. A.G. Croazia 5. Stampati e pubblicazioni); b. AP40 (f. A.G. Croazia 16/1); b. AP44 (f. A. I. 32 Croazia)

Annexed ex-Yugoslav lands: b. AP46 (f. AG Dalmazia P.G. 2); b. AP47 (f. AG Dalmazia 82, f. AG Dalmazia 5); b. AP48 (f. A-27)

Fondo Serie Affari Politici (1931–1945)
Serie Jugoslavia
On European Mediterranean populations (fascist period):
Annexed ex-Yugoslav lands: b. 153 (f. 17)

Archivio Centrale dello Stato (ACS), Rome:

Fondo Ministero dell'Interno—Gabinetto—Progetti di Codici (1861–1863)
On the origins (1859–1865): b. 2 (f. 21–24); b. 3 (f. 25–27)

Fondo Ministero dell'Interno—Divisione Generale della Pubblica Sicurezza—Divisione Affari Generali e Riservati—Massime (1880–1954)
On European Mediterranean populations (fascist period):
Albania: b. 15 (f. A14 Albania); b. 22 (f. 5)
Annexed ex-Yugoslav lands: b. 22 (f. 5)

Fondo Ministero dell'Interno—Direzione Generale della Pubblica Sicurezza—Divisione Affari Generali e Riservati—Cat. A1

Year 1942
On European Mediterranean populations (fascist period):
Annexed ex-Yugoslav lands: b. 2 (f. Cittadini dei nuovi territori annessi)
Year 1943
On European Mediterranean populations (fascist period):
Annexed ex-Yugoslav lands: b. 1 (f. Connazionali per annessione)

Fondo Presidenza del Consiglio dei Ministri
On African populations (liberal period):
Libya: Year 1913 (f. 1 1)
On European Mediterranean populations (liberal period):
Aegean Islands: Year 1914 (f. 11 2)
On European Mediterranean populations (fascist period):
Albania: Years 1940–1943 (f. 15-2 6504; f. 15-2 11102)

Occupied Croatia: Years 1940–1943 (f. 15-2 15328/4)

Annexed ex-Yugoslav lands: Years 1940–1943 (f. G7/1 11897/4; f. G7/8 12860/5; f. G7/8 12860/4; f. 1.1.13 16452/23; f. 15-2 15328/8; f. 1.1.13 16452.157; f. 1.1.13 16452.149; f. 1.1.13 16452/45; f. 1.1.13 16452/39; f. 1.1.13 16452/40; f. 1.1.13 16452.161)

Fondo Segreteria Particolare del Duce—Carteggio Ordinario Serie Numerica
   On European Mediterranean populations (fascist period):
      Albania: f. 187.636

Fondo Commissione Italiana di Armistizio con la Francia—Commissariato Civile di Mentone e Ufficio Informazioni
   On European Mediterranean populations (fascist period):
      Occupied France: b. 1 (f. 1); b. 2 (f. 19, f. 44, f. 47)

Archivio dell'Ufficio Storico dello Stato Maggiore dell'Esercito (AUSSME), Rome:

Fondo L-8, Libia
   On African populations (liberal period):
      Libya: b. 213 (f. 2)
   On European Mediterranean populations (liberal period):
      Aegean Islands: b. 231 (f. 21); b. 232 (f. 2)

Fondo L-7, Eritrea
   On African populations (liberal period):
      Eritrea: b. 125 (f. 16, f. 38); b. 132 (f. 18)

Fondo D-3, Somalia
   On African populations (liberal period):
      Somalia: b. 1bis (f. 5, f. 9)
   On African populations (fascist period):
      Somalia: b. 8 (f. 36)

Fondo M-3, Documenti Italiani restituiti dagli USA
   On European Mediterranean populations (fascist period):
      Occupied Montenegro: b. 4 (f. 13)

Fondo D-7, Commissione Italiana per l'Armistizio con la Francia
   On European Mediterranean populations (fascist period):
      Occupied France: b. 8 (f. 2); b. 48 (f. 5); b. 53 (f. 1, f. 4, f. 5)

2.b Published archival sources

Archivio Centrale dello Stato. *Verbali del Consiglio dei Ministri (luglio 1943– maggio 1948)*. Edited by A. G. Ricci. Vols. 1 and 9. Rome: Istituto Poligrafico e Zecca dello Stato, 1998.

Cospito, N., and H. W. Neulen. *Salò-Berlino: L'alleanza difficile. La Repubblica Sociale Italiana nei documenti segreti del Terzo Reich.* Milan: Mursia Editore, 1992.

De Felice, R. "Documenti." In *Storia degli ebrei italiani sotto il fascismo,* rev. ed., 487–634. Turin: Einaudi, 1993. First published 1961.

———. "Appendice." In *Mussolini l'alleato.* Vol. 2. *La guerra civile 1943–1945,* 555–753. Turin: Einaudi, 1997.

2.c Printed documentary sources

2.c.i Parliamentary materials (kept at the Archivio e Biblioteca della Camera dei Deputati, Rome)

Pisanelli's project of civil code (1864):

S 45bis. Senato del Regno. *Atti Parlamentari.* Sessione del 1863. Documenti. "Relazione della commissione speciale senatoriale sul progetto d'un Codice Civile pel Regno d'Italia (Libro I—Vigliani *rapporteur,* 26 giugno 1864; Libro II—De Foresta *rapporteur,* 29 giugno 1864; Libro III—Vacca *rapporteur,* 29 giugno 1864)," 1–251.

S 45ter. Senato del Regno. *Atti Parlamentari.* Sessione del 1863. Documenti. "Emendamenti proposti al nuovo Progetto di Codice Civile," 1 October 1864, 1–24.

S 45ter (supplement). Senato del Regno. *Atti Parlamentari.* Sessione del 1863. Documenti. "Emendamenti proposti dal senatore Chiesi ad alcune disposizioni del Codice Civile," 8 November 1864, 1–12.

S 45quater. Senato del Regno. *Atti Parlamentari.* Sessione del 1863. Documenti. "Supplemento alla Relazione della commissione speciale pel Codice Civile sopra gli emendamenti proposti (De Foresta, *rapporteur*)," 12 November 1864, 1–12.

Vacca's project of civil code (1864–1865):

C 276. Camera dei Deputati. *Atti Parlamentari.* Sessione 1863–1864. Documenti. "Progetto di legge: Facoltà al Governo del Re di pubblicare e rendere esecutorii in tutte le province del regno alcuni progetti di legge per l'unificazione legislativa del regno," presented by Minister of Justice (Vacca), 24 November 1864, 1–18.

C 276-A. Camera dei Deputati. *Atti Parlamentari.* Sessione 1863–1864. Documenti. "Relazione della commissione intorno alla facoltà al Governo del Re di pubblicare e rendere esecutorii in tutte le province del regno alcuni progetti di legge per l'unificazione legislativa del regno (Pisanelli, *rapporteur*)," 12 January 1865, 1–288.

C disc. 9/2/1865. Camera dei Deputati. *Atti Parlamentari.* Sessione del 1863–64–65. Discussioni. Hearing of 9 February 1865, 8111–8131.

C disc. 10/2/1865. Camera dei Deputati. *Atti Parlamentari.* Sessione del 1863–64–65. Discussioni. Hearing of 10 February 1865, 8131–8152.

C disc. 11/2/1865. Camera dei Deputati. *Atti Parlamentari.* Sessione del 1863–64–65. Discussioni. Hearing of 11 February 1865, 8152–8176.

C disc. 13/2/1865. Camera dei Deputati. *Atti Parlamentari.* Sessione del 1863–64–65. Discussioni. Hearing of 13 February 1865, 8177–8205.

C disc. 14/2/1865. Camera dei Deputati. *Atti Parlamentari*. Sessione del 1863–
64–65. Discussioni. Hearing of 14 February 1865, 8206–8233.

C disc. 15/2/1865. Camera dei Deputati. *Atti Parlamentari*. Sessione del 1863–
64–65. Discussioni. Hearing of 15 February 1865, 8234–8268.

C disc. 16/2/1865. Camera dei Deputati. *Atti Parlamentari*. Sessione del 1863–
64–65. Discussioni. Hearing of 16 February 1865, 8269–8301.

C disc. 17/2/1865. Camera dei Deputati. *Atti Parlamentari*. Sessione del 1863–
64–65. Discussioni. Hearing of 17 February 1865, 8302–8338.

C disc. 18/2/1865. Camera dei Deputati. *Atti Parlamentari*. Sessione del 1863–
64–65. Discussioni. Hearing of 18 February 1865, 8338–8370.

C disc. 20/2/1865. Camera dei Deputati. *Atti Parlamentari*. Sessione del 1863–
64–65. Discussioni. Hearing of 20 February 1865, 8371–8408.

C disc. 21/2/1865. Camera dei Deputati. *Atti Parlamentari*. Sessione del 1863–
64–65. Discussioni. Hearing of 21 February 1865, 8408–8438.

C disc. 22/2/1865. Camera dei Deputati. *Atti Parlamentari*. Sessione del 1863–
64–65. Discussioni. Hearing of 22 February 1865, 8439–8455.

S 195. Senato del Regno. *Atti Parlamentari*. Sessione del 1865. "Progetto di legge
per la facoltà al Governo del Re di pubblicare in tutte le province del regno
alcune leggi per l'unificazione legislativa," 23 February 1865, 1–12.

S 195bis. Senato del Regno. *Atti Parlamentari*. Sessione del 1865. "Relazione
dell'Ufficio Centrale sul progetto di legge per la facoltà al Governo del Re di
pubblicare in tutte le province del regno alcune leggi per l'unificazione legislativa (De Foresta, *rapporteur*)," 6 March 1865, 1–19.

S disc. 14/3/1865. Senato del Regno. *Atti Parlamentari*. Sessione del 1865. Discussioni. Hearing of 14 March 1865, 2539–2552.

S disc. 16/3/1865. Senato del Regno. *Atti Parlamentari*. Sessione del 1865. Discussioni. Hearing of 16 March 1865, 2569–2583.

S disc. 17/3/1865. Senato del Regno. *Atti Parlamentari*. Sessione del 1865. Discussioni. Hearing of 17 March 1865, 2584–2604.

S disc. 18/3/1865. Senato del Regno. *Atti Parlamentari*. Sessione del 1865. Discussioni. Hearing of 18 March 1865, 2605–2620.

S disc. 20/3/1865. Senato del Regno. *Atti Parlamentari*. Sessione del 1865. Discussioni. Hearing of 20 March 1865, 2621–2635.

S disc. 21/3/1865. Senato del Regno. *Atti Parlamentari*. Sessione del 1865. Discussioni. Hearing of 21 March 1865, 2636–2652.

S disc. 22/3/1865. Senato del Regno. *Atti Parlamentari*. Sessione del 1865. Discussioni. Hearing of 22 March 1865, 2653–2672.

S disc. 23/3/1865. Senato del Regno. *Atti Parlamentari*. Sessione del 1865. Discussioni. Hearing of 23 March 1865, 2673–2692.

S disc. 24/3/1865. Senato del Regno. *Atti Parlamentari*. Sessione del 1865. Discussioni. Hearing of 24 March 1865, 2693–2711.

S disc. 25/3/1865. Senato del Regno. *Atti Parlamentari*. Sessione del 1865. Discussioni. Hearing of 25 March 1865, 2712–2733.

S disc. 27/3/1865. Senato del Regno. *Atti Parlamentari*. Sessione del 1865. Discussioni. Hearing of 27 March 1865, 2734–2749.

S disc. 28/3/1865. Senato del Regno. *Atti Parlamentari*. Sessione del 1865. Discussioni. Hearing of 28 March 1865, 2750–2773.

S disc. 29/3/1865. Senato del Regno. *Atti Parlamentari*. Sessione del 1865. Discussioni. Hearing of 29 March 1865, 2774–2792.

Depretis's electoral law (1882):

C 38. Camera dei Deputati. *Atti Parlamentari*. Legislatura XIV. 1° Sessione del 1880. Documenti. "Disegno di legge: Riforma della legge elettorale politica," presented by Minister of the Interior (Depretis), 31 May 1880, 1–13.

C 38bis. Camera dei Deputati. *Atti Parlamentari*. Legislatura XIV. 1° Sessione del 1880. Documenti. "Disegno di legge: Riforma della legge elettorale politica," presented by Minister of the Interior (Depretis), 31 May 1880, 1.

C 38ter. Camera dei Deputati. *Atti Parlamentari*. Legislatura XIV. 1° Sessione del 1880. Documenti. "Allegati al disegno di legge: Riforma della legge elettorale politica," presented by Minister of the Interior (Depretis), 31 May 1880, 1–133.

C 38-A (Vol.1). Camera dei Deputati. *Atti Parlamentari*. Legislatura XIV. 1° Sessione del 1880. Documenti. "Relazione della commissione sul disegno di legge: Riforma della legge elettorale politica, Vol. 1 (Zanardelli, *rapporteur*)," 21 December 1880, 1–467.

S 119. Senato del Regno. *Atti Parlamentari*. Sessione del 1880–1881. Documenti. "Progetto di legge: Riforma della legge elettorale politica," 2 July 1881, 1–141.

S 119-A. Senato del Regno. *Atti Parlamentari*. Sessione del 1880–1881. Documenti. "Relazione dell'Ufficio Centrale sul disegno di legge: Riforma della legge elettorale politica (Lampertico, *rapporteur*)," 24 November 1881, 1–161.

S disc. 9/12/1881. Senato del Regno. *Atti Parlamentari*. Sessione del 1880–1881. Discussioni. Hearing of 9 December 1881, 1913–1938.

S disc. 10/12/1881. Senato del Regno. *Atti Parlamentari*. Sessione del 1880–1881. Discussioni. Hearing of 10 December 1881, 1941–1966.

S disc. 11/12/1881. Senato del Regno. *Atti Parlamentari*. Sessione del 1880–1881. Discussioni. Hearing of 11 December 1881, 1969–1999.

S disc. 12/12/1881. Senato del Regno. *Atti Parlamentari*. Sessione del 1880–1881. Discussioni. Hearing of 12 December 1881, 2001–2022.

S disc. 13/12/1881. Senato del Regno. *Atti Parlamentari*. Sessione del 1880–1881. Discussioni. Hearing of 13 December 1881, 2025–2047.

S disc. 14/12/1881. Senato del Regno. *Atti Parlamentari*. Sessione del 1880–1881. Discussioni. Hearing of 14 December 1881, 2049–2072.

S disc. 15/12/1881. Senato del Regno. *Atti Parlamentari*. Sessione del 1880–1881. Discussioni. Hearing of 15 December 1881, 2073–2100.

S disc. 16/12/1881. Senato del Regno. *Atti Parlamentari*. Sessione del 1880–1881. Discussioni. Hearing of 16 December 1881, 2101–2128.

S disc. 17/12/1881. Senato del Regno. *Atti Parlamentari*. Sessione del 1880–1881. Discussioni. Hearing of 17 December 1881, 2129–2155.

S disc. 18/12/1881. Senato del Regno. *Atti Parlamentari*. Sessione del 1880–1881. Discussioni. Hearing of 18 December 1881, 2157–2194.

S disc. 19/12/1881. Senato del Regno. *Atti Parlamentari*. Sessione del 1880–1881. Discussioni. Hearing of 19 December 1881, 2197–2251.

S disc. 20/12/1881. Senato del Regno. *Atti Parlamentari*. Sessione del 1880–1881. Discussioni. Hearing of 20 December 1881, 2253–2285.

Giolitti's electoral law (1912):

C 907. Camera dei Deputati. *Atti Parlamentari.* Legislatura XXIII. Sessione 1909–1911. Documenti. "Disegno di legge: Riforma della legge elettorale politica," presented by President of the Council of Ministers and Minister of the Interior (Giolitti), 9 June 1911, 1–460.

C 907-A. Camera dei Deputati. *Atti Parlamentari.* Legislatura XXIII. Sessione 1909–1912. Documenti. "Relazione della commissione sul disegno di legge: Riforma della legge elettorale politica (Bertolini, *rapporteur*)," 27 March 1912, 1–158.

C disc. 2/5/1912. Camera dei Deputati. *Atti Parlamentari.* Legislatura XXIII. 1° Sessione. Discussioni. Hearing of 2 May 1912, 18945–18988.

C disc. 3/5/1912. Camera dei Deputati. *Atti Parlamentari.* Legislatura XXIII. 1° Sessione. Discussioni. Hearing of 3 May 1912, 18989–19022.

C disc. 4/5/1912. Camera dei Deputati. *Atti Parlamentari.* Legislatura XXIII. 1° Sessione. Discussioni. Hearing of 4 May 1912, 19023–19069.

C disc. 7/5/1912. Camera dei Deputati. *Atti Parlamentari.* Legislatura XXIII. 1° Sessione. Discussioni. Hearing of 7 May 1912, 19097–19142.

C disc. 8/5/1912. Camera dei Deputati. *Atti Parlamentari.* Legislatura XXIII. 1° Sessione. Discussioni. Hearing of 8 May 1912, 19143–19181.

C disc. 9/5/1912. Camera dei Deputati. *Atti Parlamentari.* Legislatura XXIII. 1° Sessione. Discussioni. Hearing of 9 May 1912, 19183–19226.

C disc. 10/5/1912. Camera dei Deputati. *Atti Parlamentari.* Legislatura XXIII. 1° Sessione. Discussioni. Hearing of 10 May 1912, 19227–19270.

C disc. 11/5/1912. Camera dei Deputati. *Atti Parlamentari.* Legislatura XXIII. 1° Sessione. Discussioni. Hearing of 11 May 1912, 19271–19307.

C disc. 14/5/1912. Camera dei Deputati. *Atti Parlamentari.* Legislatura XXIII. 1° Sessione. Discussioni. Hearing of 14 May 1912, 19349–19392.

C disc. 15/5/1912. Camera dei Deputati. *Atti Parlamentari.* Legislatura XXIII. 1° Sessione. Discussioni. Hearing of 15 May 1912, 19393–19434.

C disc. 16/5/1912. Camera dei Deputati. *Atti Parlamentari.* Legislatura XXIII. 1° Sessione. Discussioni. Hearing of 16 May 1912, 19435–19479.

C disc. 17/5/1912. Camera dei Deputati. *Atti Parlamentari.* Legislatura XXIII. 1° Sessione. Discussioni. Hearing of 17 May 1912, 19481–19524.

C disc. 18/5/1912. Camera dei Deputati. *Atti Parlamentari.* Legislatura XXIII. 1° Sessione. Discussioni. Hearing of 18 May 1912, 19525–19565.

C disc. 21/5/1912. Camera dei Deputati. *Atti Parlamentari.* Legislatura XXIII. 1° Sessione. Discussioni. Hearing of 21 May 1912, 19583–19634.

C disc. 22/5/1912(ii). Camera dei Deputati. *Atti Parlamentari.* Legislatura XXIII. 1° Sessione. Discussioni. Second hearing of 22 May 1912, 19661–19704.

C disc. 23/5/1912. Camera dei Deputati. *Atti Parlamentari.* Legislatura XXIII. 1° Sessione. Discussioni. Hearing of 23 May 1912, 19705–19761.

C disc. 24/5/1912(ii). Camera dei Deputati. *Atti Parlamentari.* Legislatura XXIII. 1° Sessione. Discussioni. Second hearing of 24 May 1912, 19781–19824.

C disc. 25/5/1912. Camera dei Deputati. *Atti Parlamentari.* Legislatura XXIII. 1° Sessione. Discussioni. Hearing of 25 May 1912, 19825–19881.

S 813. Senato del Regno. *Atti Parlamentari*. Legislatura XXIII. Sessione 1909–1912. Documenti. "Disegno di legge: Riforma della legge elettorale politica," 28 May 1912, 1–102.

S 813-A. Senato del Regno. *Atti Parlamentari*. Legislatura XXIII. Sessione 1909–1912. Documenti. "Relazione dell'Ufficio Centrale sul disegno di legge: Riforma della legge elettorale politica (Torrigiani, *rapporteur*)," 19 June 1912, 1–110.

S disc. 24/6/1912. Senato del Regno. *Atti Parlamentari*. Legislatura XXIII. 1° Sessione 1909–1912. Discussioni. Hearing of 24 June 1912, 9009–9036.

S disc. 25/6/1912. Senato del Regno. *Atti Parlamentari*. Legislatura XXIII. 1° Sessione 1909–1912. Discussioni. Hearing of 25 June 1912, 9037–9058.

S disc. 26/6/1912. Senato del Regno. *Atti Parlamentari*. Legislatura XXIII. 1° Sessione 1909–1912. Discussioni. Hearing of 26 June 1912, 9061–9104.

S disc. 27/6/1912. Senato del Regno. *Atti Parlamentari*. Legislatura XXIII. 1° Sessione 1909–1912. Discussioni. Hearing of 27 June 1912, 9105–9153.

S disc. 28/6/1912. Senato del Regno. *Atti Parlamentari*. Legislatura XXIII. 1° Sessione 1909–1912. Discussioni. Hearing of 28 June 1912, 9157–9227.

S disc. 29/6/1912. Senato del Regno. *Atti Parlamentari*. Legislatura XXIII. 1° Sessione 1909–1912. Discussioni. Hearing of 29 June 1912, 9229–9331.

The 1912 Citizenship Law:

S 164. Senato del Regno. *Atti Parlamentari*. Legislatura XXIII. 1° Sessione 1909–1910. Documenti. "Disegno di legge: Sulla cittadinanza," presented by Minister of Justice (Scialoja), 22 February 1910, 1–9.

S 164 (annesso). Senato del Regno. *Atti Parlamentari*. Legislatura XXIII. 1° Sessione 1909–1910. Documenti. "Annesso al disegno di legge 'Sulla cittadinanza n. 164': Elenco delle disposizioni vigenti negli Stati esteri in materia di cittadinanza," presented by Minister of Justice (Scialoja), 22 February 1910, 1–3.

S 164-A. Senato del Regno. *Atti Parlamentari*. Legislatura XXIII. 1° Sessione 1909–1911. Documenti. "Relazione dell'Ufficio Centrale sul disegno di legge: Sulla cittadinanza (Polacco, *rapporteur*)," 29 May 1911, 1–32.

S disc. 19/6/1911. Senato del Regno. *Atti Parlamentari*. Legislatura XXIII. 1° Sessione 1909–1911. Discussioni. Hearing of 19 June 1911, 5749–5776.

S disc. 20/6/1911. Senato del Regno. *Atti Parlamentari*. Legislatura XXIII. 1° Sessione 1909–1911. Discussioni. Hearing of 20 June 1911, 5777–5796.

S disc. 1/7/1911. Senato del Regno. *Atti Parlamentari*. Legislatura XXIII. 1° Sessione 1909–1911. Discussioni. Hearing of 1 July 1911, 6537–6569.

S disc. 3/7/1911. Senato del Regno. *Atti Parlamentari*. Legislatura XXIII. 1° Sessione 1909–1911. Discussioni. Hearing of 3 July 1911, 6573–6606.

S disc. 4/7/1911. Senato del Regno. *Atti Parlamentari*. Legislatura XXIII. 1° Sessione 1909–1911. Discussioni. Hearing of 4 July 1911, 6609–6780.

C 966. Camera dei Deputati. *Atti Parlamentari*. Legislatura XXIII. Sessione 1909–1911. Documenti. "Disegno di legge: Sulla cittadinanza," 7 July 1911, 1–13.

C 966-A. Camera dei Deputati. *Atti Parlamentari*. Legislatura XXIII. Sessione 1909–1912. Documenti. "Relazione della commissione sul disegno di legge: Sulla cittadinanza (Baccelli, *rapporteur*)," 30 March 1912, 1–28.

C disc. 4/6/1912. Camera dei Deputati. *Atti Parlamentari*. Legislatura XXIII. 1° Sessione. Discussioni. Hearing of 4 June 1912, 20321–20337.

C disc. 7/6/1912. Camera dei Deputati. *Atti Parlamentari*. Legislatura XXIII. 1°
Sessione. Discussioni. Hearing of 7 June 1912, 20527–20544.

C disc. 11/6/1912. Camera dei Deputati. *Atti Parlamentari*. Legislatura XXIII. 1°
Sessione. Discussioni. Hearing of 11 June 1912, 20697–20716.

C disc. 11/6/1912(ii). Camera dei Deputati. *Atti Parlamentari*. Legislatura XXIII.
1° Sessione. Discussioni. Second hearing of 11 June 1912, 20717–20766.

Cairoli's projects concerning the non regnicoli:

C 184. Camera dei Deputati. *Atti Parlamentari*. Sessione 1861–1862. Documenti.
"Progetto di legge: Cittadinanza agli emigrati delle province italiane non ancora unite al regno," presented by deputy Cairoli, 3 February 1862, 1.

C 184-A. Camera dei Deputati. *Atti Parlamentari*. Sessione 1861–1862. Documenti. "Relazione della commissione sulla proposta di legge: Cittadinanza agli
emigrati delle province italiane non ancora unite al regno (Imbriani, *rapporteur*)," 18 July 1862, 1–4.

C disc. 3/2/1862. Camera dei Deputati. *Atti Parlamentari*. Sessione 1861–1862.
Discussioni. Hearing of 3 February 1862, 982–1006.

C disc. 25/3/1863. Camera dei Deputati. *Atti Parlamentari*. Sessione 1862–1863.
Discussioni. Hearing of 25 March 1863, 6005–6026.

C disc. 26/3/1863. Camera dei Deputati. *Atti Parlamentari*. Sessione 1862–1863.
Discussioni. Hearing of 26 March 1863, 6027–6048.

C disc. 27/3/1863. Camera dei Deputati. *Atti Parlamentari*. Sessione 1862–1863.
Discussioni. Hearing of 27 March 1863, 6073–6095.

C 196. Camera dei Deputati. *Atti Parlamentari*. Documenti. "Progetto di legge:
Estensione dei diritti civili e politici agli italiani delle provincie che non fanno
ancora parte del regno," 1 June 1868, 1.

C 196-A. Camera dei Deputati. *Atti Parlamentari*. Documenti. "Relazione della
commissione sul progetto di legge: Estensione dei diritti civili e politici agli
italiani delle provincie che non fanno ancora parte del regno (Cairoli, *rapporteur*)," 27 November 1868, 1–4.

C disc. 30/11/1868. Camera dei Deputati. *Atti Parlamentari*. Discussioni. Hearing
of 30 November 1868, 8174–8196.

C disc. 1/12/1868. Camera dei Deputati. *Atti Parlamentari*. Discussioni. Hearing
of 1 December 1868, 8197–8213.

S. disc. 14/6/1869. Senato del Regno. *Atti Parlamentari*. Discussioni. Hearing of
14 June 1869, 2200–2215.

S. disc. 16/6/1869. Senato del Regno. *Atti Parlamentari*. Discussioni. Hearing of
16 June 1869, 2234–2264.

C 196-B. Camera dei Deputati. *Atti Parlamentari*. Documenti. "Progetto di legge:
Estensione dei diritti civili e politici agli italiani delle provincie che non fanno
ancora parte del regno," 18 June 1869, 1–3.

Individual files concerning the "grand naturalization" of foreigners of non-Italian origin:

Moleschott

"Legge 19 giugno 1866 n. 3015: Legge che accorda la cittadinanza italiana al professore Giacomo Moleschott, nato a Bois-le-Duc (Olanda)." In *Raccolta ufficiale delle leggi e dei decreti del Regno d'Italia*. Vol. 15, 941. Turin: Stamperia Reale, 1866.

C 83. Camera dei Deputati. *Atti Parlamentari*. Sessione 1865–1866. Documenti. "Progetto di legge: Cittadinanza italiana al professore Giacomo Moleschott di Bois-le-Duc (Olanda)," presented by Minister of the Interior (Chiaves), 24 March 1866, 1–2.

C 83-A. Camera dei Deputati. *Atti Parlamentari*. Sessione 1865–1866. Documenti. "Relazione della commissione sul progetto di legge: Cittadinanza italiana al professore Giacomo Moleschott di Bois-le-Duc (Olanda) (Macchi, *rapporteur*)," 10 May 1866, 1–2.

C disc. 19/5/1866. Camera dei Deputati. *Atti Parlamentari*. Sessione 1866. Discussioni. Hearing of 19 May 1866, 2316–2339.

S 44. Senato del Regno. *Atti Parlamentari*. Sessione 1865–1866. Documenti. "Progetto di legge per la concessione della cittadinanza italiana a favore del prof. Giacomo Moleschott," 7 June 1866, 1.

S 44-A. Senato del Regno. *Atti Parlamentari*. Sessione 1865–1866. Documenti. "Relazione dell'Ufficio Centrale sul progetto di legge per la concessione della cittadinanza italiana al prof. Giacomo Moleschott (Matteucci, *rapporteur*)," 12 June 1866, 1.

S disc. 17/6/1866. Senato del Regno. *Atti Parlamentari*. Sessione 1865–1866. Discussioni. Hearing of 17 June 1866, 477–497.

S disc. 19/6/1866. Senato del Regno. *Atti Parlamentari*. Sessione 1865–1866. Discussioni. Hearing of 19 June 1866, 520–543.

Waddington

"Legge 4 agosto 1867 n. 3833: Legge che accorda la piena naturalità italiana al cav. Evelino Waddington, nativo di Londra." In *Raccolta ufficiale delle leggi e dei decreti del Regno d'Italia*. Vol. 19, 1279. Florence: Stamperia Reale, 1867.

C disc. 28/1/1864 (ii). Camera dei Deputati. *Atti Parlamentari*. Sessione del 1863–1864. Discussioni. Second hearing of 28 January 1864, 3067–3083.

C 13. Camera dei Deputati. *Atti Parlamentari*. Sessione 1867. Documenti. "Progetto di legge: Concessione della naturalità italiana al signor Waddington Evelino," presented by President of the Council of Ministers and Minister of the Interior (Ricasoli), 21 December 1866, 1–6.

C 13-A. Camera dei Deputati. *Atti Parlamentari*. Sessione 1867. Documenti. "Relazione della commissione sul progetto di legge: Concessione della naturalità italiana al signor Waddington Evelino (Corsi, *rapporteur*)," 11 February 1867, 1–4.

C 60. Camera dei Deputati. *Atti Parlamentari*. Legislatura X. Sessione 1867. Documenti. "Progetto di legge: Concessione della naturalità italiana al signor

Waddington Evelino," presented by President of the Council of Ministers and Minister of the Interior (Rattazzi), 13 May 1867, 1–6.

C 60-A. Camera dei Deputati. *Atti Parlamentari.* Legislatura X. Sessione 1867. Documenti. "Relazione della commissione sul progetto di legge: Concessione della naturalità italiana al signor Waddington Evelino (Puccioni, *rapporteur*)," 5 July 1867, 1–4.

C disc. 13/7/1867 (ii). Camera dei Deputati. *Atti Parlamentari.* Legislatura X. Sessione 1867. Discussioni. Second hearing of 13 July 1867, 2229–2244.

C disc. 15/7/1867. Camera dei Deputati. *Atti Parlamentari.* Legislatura X. Sessione 1867. Discussioni. Hearing of 15 July 1867, 2245–2276.

S 42. Senato del Regno. *Atti Parlamentari.* Sessione del 1867. Documenti. "Progetto di legge per la concessione della cittadinanza italiana al cavaliere Evelino Waddington," 16 July 1867, 1–2.

S 42-A. Senato del Regno. *Atti Parlamentari.* Sessione del 1867. Documenti. "Relazione dell'Ufficio Centrale sul progetto di legge per la concessione della naturalità italiana al cav. Evelino Waddington (Mamiani, *rapporteur*)," 19 July 1867, 1.

S disc. 26/7/1867. Senato del Regno. *Atti Parlamentari.* Sessione del 1867. Discussioni. Hearing of 26 July 1867, 232–246.

S disc. 29/7/1867. Senato del Regno. *Atti Parlamentari.* Sessione del 1867. Discussioni. Hearing of 29 July 1867, 259–276.

Marescalchi

"Legge 5 luglio 1882 n. 884: Legge che accorda la piena naturalità italiana al signor conte Antonio Marescalchi." In *Raccolta ufficiale delle leggi e dei decreti del Regno d'Italia.* Vol. 66, 2650. Rome: Tipografia Regia, 1882.

C 321. Camera dei Deputati. *Atti Parlamentari.* Legislatura XIV. 1° Sessione 1880–1881. Documenti. "Disegno di legge: Concessione della naturalità italiana al conte Antonio Marescalchi," presented by President of the Council of Ministers and Minister of the Interior (Depretis), 29 May 1882, 1–2.

C 321-A. Camera dei Deputati. *Atti Parlamentari.* Legislatura XIV. 1° Sessione 1880–1881. Documenti. "Relazione della commissione sul disegno di legge: Concessione della naturalità italiana al conte Antonio Marescalchi (Guiccioli, *rapporteur*)," 14 June 1882, 1–2.

C disc. 21/6/1882 (ii). Camera dei Deputati. *Atti Parlamentari.* Legislatura XIV. 1° Sessione 1880–1881. Discussioni. Second hearing of 21 June 1882, 11869–11899.

S 252. Senato del Regno. *Atti Parlamentari.* Sessione del 1880-81–82. Documenti. "Progetto di legge: Naturalità italiana al conte Antonio Marescalchi," 24 June 1882, 1–2.

S 252-A. Senato del Regno. *Atti Parlamentari.* Sessione del 1880-81–82. Documenti. "Relazione dell'Ufficio Centrale sul progetto di legge: Naturalità italiana al conte Antonio Marescalchi (Borgatti, *rapporteur*)," 29 June 1882, 1–2.

S disc. 2/7/1882. Senato del Regno. *Atti Parlamentari.* Sessione del 1880-81–82. Discussioni. Hearing of 2 July 1882, 3493–3503.

Meyer, Nathan, Cantani, Schilizzi

"Legge 25 marzo 1888 n. 5296: Legge che accorda la naturalità italiana al signor marchese Giovanni Meyer." In *Raccolta ufficiale delle leggi e dei decreti del Regno d'Italia*. Vol. 88, 670. Rome: Tipografia Regia, 1888.

"Legge 25 marzo 1888 n. 5298: Legge che accorda la naturalità italiana al signor Ernesto Nathan." In *Raccolta ufficiale delle leggi e dei decreti del Regno d'Italia*. Vol. 88, 672. Rome: Tipografia Regia, 1888.

"Legge 25 marzo 1888 n. 5299: Legge che accorda la naturalità italiana al sig. comm. prof. Arnaldo Cantani." In *Raccolta ufficiale delle leggi e dei decreti del Regno d'Italia*. Vol. 88, 673. Rome: Tipografia Regia, 1888.

"Legge 25 marzo 1888 n. 5297: Legge che accorda la naturalità italiana al signor Matteo Schilizzi." In *Raccolta ufficiale delle leggi e dei decreti del Regno d'Italia*. Vol. 88, 671. Rome: Tipografia Regia, 1888.

C 79. Camera dei Deputati. *Atti Parlamentari*. Legislatura XVI. 2° Sessione 1887. Documenti. "Disegno di legge: Concessione della naturalità italiana al signor marchese comm. Giovanni Meyer," presented by President of the Council of Ministers and Minister of the Interior (Crispi), 10 December 1887, 1–2.

C 79-A. Camera dei Deputati. *Atti Parlamentari*. Legislatura XVI. 2° Sessione 1887–1888. Documenti. "Relazione della commissione sul disegno di legge: Concessione della naturalità italiana al signor marchese comm. Giovanni Meyer (Chiaradia, *rapporteur*)," 4 February 1888, 1–2.

S 51. Senato del Regno. *Atti Parlamentari*. Legislatura XVI. 2° Sessione 1887–1888. Documenti. "Progetto di legge: Concessione della naturalità italiana al signor marchese comm. Giovanni Meyer," 12 March 1888, 1–2.

S 51-A. Senato del Regno. *Atti Parlamentari*. Legislatura XVI. 2° Sessione 1887–1888. Documenti. "Relazione dell'Ufficio Centrale sul progetto di legge: Concessione della naturalità italiana al signor marchese comm. Giovanni Meyer (Guarini, *rapporteur*)," 16 March 1888, 1.

C 76. Camera dei Deputati. *Atti Parlamentari*. Legislatura XVI. 2° Sessione 1887. Documenti. "Disegno di legge: Concessione della naturalità italiana al signor Ernesto Nathan," presented by President of the Council of Ministers and Minister of the Interior (Crispi), 10 December 1887, 1–2.

C 76-A. Camera dei Deputati. *Atti Parlamentari*. Legislatura XVI. 2° Sessione 1887–1888. Documenti. "Relazione della commissione sul disegno di legge: Concessione della naturalità italiana al signor Ernesto Nathan (Marcora, *rapporteur*)," 7 February 1888, 1–3.

C disc. 9/2/1888. Camera dei Deputati. *Atti Parlamentari*. Legislatura XVI. 2° Sessione 1887–1888. Discussioni. Hearing of 9 February 1888, 989–1000.

S 52. Senato del Regno. *Atti Parlamentari*. Legislatura XVI. 2° Sessione 1887–1888. Documenti. "Progetto di legge: Concessione della naturalità italiana al signor Ernesto Nathan," 12 March 1888, 1–2.

S 52-A. Senato del Regno. *Atti Parlamentari*. Legislatura XVI. 2° Sessione 1887–1888. Documenti. "Relazione dell'Ufficio Centrale sul progetto di legge: Concessione della naturalità italiana al signor Ernesto Nathan (Marescotti, *rapporteur*)," 16 March 1888, 1.

C 78. Camera dei Deputati. *Atti Parlamentari*. Legislatura XVI. 2° Sessione 1887. Documenti. "Disegno di legge: Concessione della naturalità italiana al signor comm. prof. Arnaldo Cantani," presented by President of the Council of Ministers and Minister of the Interior (Crispi), 10 December 1887, 1–2.

C 78-A. Camera dei Deputati. *Atti Parlamentari.* Legislatura XVI. 2° Sessione 1887–1888. Documenti. "Relazione della commissione sul disegno di legge: Concessione della naturalità italiana al signor Cantani Arnaldo (Nocito, *rapporteur*)," 23 February 1888, 1–4.

S 53. Senato del Regno. *Atti Parlamentari.* Legislatura XVI. 2° Sessione 1887–1888. Documenti. "Progetto di legge: Concessione della naturalità italiana al signor Arnaldo Cantani," 12 March 1888, 1–2.

S 53-A. Senato del Regno. *Atti Parlamentari.* Legislatura XVI. 2° Sessione 1887–1888. Documenti. "Relazione dell'Ufficio Centrale sul progetto di legge: Concessione della naturalità italiana al signor Arnaldo Cantani (Borelli, *rapporteur*)," 17 March 1888, 1–2.

C 81. Camera dei Deputati. *Atti Parlamentari.* Legislatura XVI. 2° Sessione 1887. Documenti. "Disegno di legge: Concessione della naturalità italiana al signor Matteo Schilizzi," presented by President of the Council of Ministers and Minister of the Interior (Crispi), 10 December 1887, 1–2.

C 81-A. Camera dei Deputati. *Atti Parlamentari.* Legislatura XVI. 2° Sessione 1887–1888. Documenti. "Relazione della commissione sul disegno di legge: Concessione della naturalità italiana al signor Matteo Schilizzi (Mel, *rapporteur*)," 27 February 1888, 1–2.

S 54. Senato del Regno. *Atti Parlamentari.* Legislatura XVI. 2° Sessione 1887–1888. Documenti. "Progetto di legge: Concessione della naturalità italiana al signor Matteo Schilizzi," 12 March 1888, 1–2.

S 54-A. Senato del Regno. *Atti Parlamentari.* Legislatura XVI. 2° Sessione 1887–1888. Documenti. "Relazione dell'Ufficio Centrale sul progetto di legge: Concessione della naturalità italiana al signor Matteo Schilizzi (Trocchi, *rapporteur*)," 15 March 1888, 1.

C disc. 2/3/1888. Camera dei Deputati. *Atti Parlamentari.* Legislatura XVI. 2° Sessione 1888. Discussioni. Hearing of 2 March 1888, 1141–1154.

S disc. 20/3/1888. Senato del Regno. *Atti Parlamentari.* Legislatura XVI. 2° Sessione 1887–1888. Discussioni. Hearing of 20 March 1888, 1153–1175.

S disc. 21/3/1888. Senato del Regno. *Atti Parlamentari.* Legislatura XVI. 2° Sessione 1887–1888. Discussioni. Hearing of 21 March 1888, 1177–1205.

The Kossuth brothers

"Legge 15 luglio 1888 n. 5545: Legge che accorda la naturalità italiana ai signori comm. Francesco e Luigi Teodoro di Kossuth." In *Raccolta ufficiale delle leggi e dei decreti del Regno d'Italia.* Vol. 89, 2123–2124. Rome: Tipografia Regia, 1888.

C 120. Camera dei Deputati. *Atti Parlamentari.* Legislatura XVI. 2° Sessione 1887–1888. Documenti. "Disegno di legge: Concessione della naturalità italiana a Luigi Teodoro e Francesco di Kossuth," presented by President of the Council of Ministers and Minister of the Interior (Crispi), 25 February 1888, 1–2.

C 120-A. Camera dei Deputati. *Atti Parlamentari.* Legislatura XVI. 2° Sessione 1887–1888. Documenti. "Disegno di legge: Concessione della naturalità italiana a Luigi Teodoro e Francesco di Kossuth (Cucchi, *rapporteur*)," 24 March 1888, 1–3.

C disc. 8/6/1888. Camera dei Deputati. *Atti Parlamentari*. Legislatura XVI. 2° Sessione. Discussioni. Hearing of 8 June 1888, 3351–3368.

C disc. 9/6/1888. Camera dei Deputati. *Atti Parlamentari*. Legislatura XVI. 2° Sessione. Discussioni. Hearing of 9 June 1888, 3407–3436.

S 113. Senato del Regno. *Atti Parlamentari*. Legislatura XVI. 2° Sessione 1887–1888. Documenti. "Progetto di legge: Concessione della naturalità italiana a Francesco e Luigi Teodoro di Kossuth," 1 July 1888, 1–2.

S 113-A. Senato del Regno. *Atti Parlamentari*. Legislatura XVI. 2° Sessione 1887–1888. Documenti. "Relazione dell'Ufficio Centrale sul progetto di legge: Concessione della naturalità italiana a Francesco e Luigi Teodoro di Kossuth (Guerrieri-Gonzaga, *rapporteur*)," 4 July 1888, 1.

S disc. 5/7/1888. Senato del Regno. *Atti Parlamentari*. Legislatura XVI. 2° Sessione 1887–1888. Discussioni. Hearing of 5 July 1888, 2001–2002.

S disc. 9/7/1888. Senato del Regno. *Atti Parlamentari*. Legislatura XVI. 2° Sessione 1887–1888. Discussioni. Hearing of 9 July 1888, 2037–2064.

Maurogordato

C 121. Camera dei Deputati. *Atti Parlamentari*. Legislatura XVI. 2° Sessione 1887–1888. Documenti. "Disegno di legge: Concessione della naturalità italiana a Matteo Maurogordato," presented by President of the Council of Ministers and Minister of the Interior (Crispi), 25 February 1888, 1–2.

C 121-A. Camera dei Deputati. *Atti Parlamentari*. Legislatura XVI. 2° Sessione 1887–1888. Documenti. "Relazione della commissione sul disegno di legge: Concessione della naturalità italiana a Matteo Maurogordato (Nocito, *rapporteur*)," 21 May 1888, 1–4.

C disc. 8/6/1888. Camera dei Deputati. *Atti Parlamentari*. Legislatura XVI. 2° Sessione 1888. Discussioni. Hearing of 8 June 1888, 3351–3368.

C disc. 8/6/1888(ii). Camera dei Deputati. *Atti Parlamentari*. Legislatura XVI. 2° Sessione 1888. Discussioni. Second hearing of 8 June 1888, 3369–3406.

Türr and Mayor

"Legge 3 maggio 1888 n. 5399: Legge che accorda la naturalità italiana al sig. generale Stefano Türr." In *Raccolta ufficiale delle leggi e dei decreti del Regno d'Italia*. Vol. 88, 1229–1230. Rome: Tipografia Regia, 1888.

"Legge 3 maggio 1888 n. 5400: Legge che accorda la naturalità italiana al sig. cav. Edmondo Mayor." In *Raccolta ufficiale delle leggi e dei decreti del Regno d'Italia*. Vol. 88, 1230–1231. Rome: Tipografia Regia, 1888.

C 77. Camera dei Deputati. *Atti Parlamentari*. Legislatura XVI. 2° Sessione 1887. Documenti. "Disegno di legge: Concessione della naturalità italiana al signor generale Stefano Türr," presented by President of the Council of Ministers and Minister of the Interior (Crispi), 10 December 1887, 1–2.

C 77-A. Camera dei Deputati. *Atti Parlamentari*. Legislatura XVI. 2° Sessione 1887–1888. Documenti. "Relazione della commissione sul disegno di legge: Concessione della naturalità italiana al signor Stefano Türr (Pais, *rapporteur*)," 20 March 1888, 1–3.

S 74. Senato del Regno. *Atti Parlamentari*. Legislatura XVI. 2° Sessione 1887–1888. Documenti. "Progetto di legge: Concessione della naturalità italiana al signor generale Stefano Türr," 22 April 1888, 1–2.

C 80. Camera dei Deputati. *Atti Parlamentari*. Legislatura XVI. 2° Sessione 1887. Documenti. "Disegno di legge: Concessione della naturalità italiana al signor cav. Edmondo Mayor," presented by President of the Council of Ministers and Minister of the Interior (Crispi), 10 December 1887, 1–2.

C 80-A. Camera dei Deputati. *Atti Parlamentari*. Legislatura XVI. 2° Sessione 1887–1888. Documenti. "Relazione della commissione sul disegno di legge: Concessione della naturalità italiana al signor cav. Edmondo Mayor (Ferri, *rapporteur*)," 15 March 1888, 1–2.

S 75. Senato del Regno. *Atti Parlamentari*. Legislatura XVI. 2° Sessione 1887–1888. Documenti. "Progetto di legge: Concessione della naturalità italiana al signor cav. Edmondo Mayor," 22 April 1888, 1–2.

S 75-A. Senato del Regno. *Atti Parlamentari*. Legislatura XVI. 2° Sessione 1887–1888. Documenti. "Relazione dell'Ufficio Centrale sul progetto di legge: Concessione della naturalità italiana al signor cav. Edmondo Mayor (Verga, *rapporteur*)," 28 April 1888, 1.

C disc. 24/3/1888. Camera dei Deputati. *Atti Parlamentari*. Legislatura XVI. 2° Sessione. Discussioni. Hearing of 24 March 1888, 1579–1610.

S disc. 1/5/1888. Senato del Regno. *Atti Parlamentari*. Legislatura XVI. 2° Sessione 1887–1888. Discussioni. Hearing of 1 May 1888, 1461–1464.

The Amman brothers

"Legge 18 luglio 1889 n. 6277: Legge che accorda la nazionalità italiana ai signori conte Alberto ed Edoardo fratelli Amman." In *Raccolta ufficiale delle leggi e dei decreti del Regno d'Italia*. Vol. 94, 3047. Rome: Tipografia Regia, 1889.

C disc. 30/6/1889. Camera dei Deputati. *Atti Parlamentari*. Legislatura XVI. 3° Sessione. Discussioni. Hearing of 30 June 1889, 3213–3226.

C disc. 1/7/1889. Camera dei Deputati. *Atti Parlamentari*. Legislatura XVI. 3° Sessione. Discussioni. Hearing of 1 July 1889, 3227–3259.

S 82. Senato del Regno. *Atti Parlamentari*. Legislatura XVI. 3° Sessione. Documenti. "Progetto di legge: Naturalità italiana ai fratelli Amman," presented by President of the Council of Ministers and Minister of the Interior (Crispi), 1 July 1889, 1–3.

S 82-A. Senato del Regno. *Atti Parlamentari*. Legislatura XVI. 3° Sessione. Documenti. "Relazione della commissione sul progetto di legge: Naturalità italiana ai fratelli Amman (Pecile, *rapporteur*)," 3 July 1889, 1.

S disc. 4/7/1889. Senato del Regno. *Atti Parlamentari*. Legislatura XVI. 3° Sessione. Discussioni. Hearing of 4 July 1889, 1049–1055.

S disc. 6/7/1889. Senato del Regno. *Atti Parlamentari*. Legislatura XVI. 3° Sessione. Discussioni. Hearing of 6 July 1889, 1057–1064.

D'Abro Pagratide

"Legge 27 aprile 1899 n. 161: Legge che accorda la naturalità italiana al principe Aslan D'Abro Pagratide." In *Raccolta ufficiale delle leggi e dei decreti del Regno d'Italia*. Vol. 2, 1252–1253. Rome: Tipografia Regia, 1899.

C 152. Camera dei Deputati. *Atti Parlamentari*. Legislatura XX. 2° Sessione 1898–1899. Documenti. "Disegno di legge: Concessione della naturalità italiana al signor principe Aslan D'Abro Pagratide," presented by President of the Council of Ministers and Minister of the Interior (Pelloux), 6 February 1899, 1–2.

C 152-A. Camera dei Deputati. *Atti Parlamentari*. Legislatura XX. 2° Sessione 1898–1899. Documenti. "Relazione della commissione sul disegno di legge: Concessione della naturalità italiana al principe Aslan D'Abro Pagratide (Falconi, *rapporteur*)," 15 February 1899, 1–2.

C disc. 8/3/1899. Camera dei Deputati. *Atti Parlamentari*. Legislatura XX. 2° Sessione. Discussioni. Hearing of 8 March 1899, 2683–2696.

C disc. 8/3/1899(ii). Camera dei Deputati. *Atti Parlamentari*. Legislatura XX. 2° Sessione. Discussioni. Second hearing of 8 March 1899, 2697–2740.

S 58. Senato del Regno. *Atti Parlamentari*. Legislatura XX. 2° Sessione 1898–1899. Documenti. "Disegno di legge: Concessione della naturalità italiana al signor principe Aslan D'Abro Pagratide," presented by President of the Council of Ministers and Minister of the Interior (Pelloux), 18 March 1899, 1–2.

S 58-A. Senato del Regno. *Atti Parlamentari*. Legislatura XX. 2° Sessione 1898–1899. Documenti. "Relazione dell'Ufficio Centrale sul disegno di legge: Concessione della naturalità italiana al signor principe Aslan D'Abro Pagratide (Tajani, *rapporteur*)," 28 March 1899, 1–2.

S disc. 19/4/1899. Senato del Regno. *Atti Parlamentari*. Legislatura XX. 2° Sessione. Discussioni. Hearing of 19 April 1899, 917–935.

S disc. 20/4/1899. Senato del Regno. *Atti Parlamentari*. Legislatura XX. 2° Sessione. Discussioni. Hearing of 20 April 1899, 937–938.

Sonnino's law on naturalization (1906):

"Legge 17 maggio 1906 n. 217: Legge portante norme per la concessione della cittadinanza italiana." In *Raccolta ufficiale delle leggi e dei decreti del Regno d'Italia*. Year 1906, 1282–1284. Rome: Tipografia Regia, 1906.

C 179. Camera dei Deputati. *Atti Parlamentari*. Legislatura XXI. 2° Sessione 1902–1904. Documenti. "Proposta di legge: Norme per la concessione della cittadinanza italiana," presented by Deputy Sonnino, 24 May 1905, 1–4.

C 179-A. Camera dei Deputati. *Atti Parlamentari*. Legislatura XXII. Sessione 1904–1905. Documenti. "Relazione della commissione sulla proposta di legge: Norme per la concessione della cittadinanza italiana (Sonnino, *rapporteur*)," 6 June 1905, 1–6.

C disc. 2/7/1905. Camera dei Deputati. *Atti Parlamentari*. Legislatura XXII. 1° Sessione. Discussioni. Hearing of 2 July 1905, 5259–5298.

S 178. Senato del Regno. *Atti Parlamentari*. Legislatura XXII. 1° Sessione 1904–1905. Documenti. "Disegno di legge: Norme per la concessione della cittadinanza italiana," 3 May 1905, 1–2.

S 178-A. Senato del Regno. *Atti Parlamentari*. Legislatura XXII. 1° Sessione 1904–1905. Documenti. "Relazione dell'Ufficio Centrale sul disegno di legge: Norme per la concessione della cittadinanza italiana (Di San Giuliano, *rapporteur*)," 4 July 1905, 1.

S disc. 2/5/1906. Senato del Regno. *Atti Parlamentari*. Legislatura XXII. 1° Sessione. Discussioni. Hearing of 2 May 1906, 3045–3062.

S disc. 3/5/1906. Senato del Regno. *Atti Parlamentari*. Legislatura XXII. 1° Sessione. Discussioni. Hearing of 3 May 1906, 3065–3084.

C 179-B. Camera dei Deputati. *Atti Parlamentari*. Legislatura XXII. Sessione 1904–1905. Documenti. "Proposta di legge: Norme per la concessione della cittadinanza italiana," 4 May 1906, 1–2.

C 179-C. Camera dei Deputati. *Atti Parlamentari*. Legislatura XXII. Sessione 1904–1906. Documenti. "Relazione della commissione sulla proposta di legge: Norme per la concessione della cittadinanza italiana (Riccio, *rapporteur*)," 9 May 1906, 1–4.

C disc. 15/5/1906. Camera dei Deputati. *Atti Parlamentari*. Legislatura XXII. 1° Sessione. Discussioni. Hearing of 15 May 1906, 8137–8201.

C disc. 16/5/1906(ii). Camera dei Deputati. *Atti Parlamentari*. Legislatura XXII. 1° Sessione. Discussioni. Second hearing of 16 May 1906, 8227–8269.

C disc. 19/12/1903. Camera dei Deputati. *Atti Parlamentari*. Legislatura XXI. 2° Sessione. Discussioni. Hearing of 19 December 1903, 10139–10179.

Law on emigration (1901):

"Legge 31 gennaio 1901 n. 23: Legge sulla emigrazione." In *Raccolta ufficiale delle leggi e dei decreti del Regno d'Italia*. Year 1901, 50–78. Rome: Tipografia Regia, 1901.

C disc. 24/11/1900. Camera dei Deputati. *Atti Parlamentari*. Legislatura XXI. 1° Sessione. Discussioni. Hearing of 24 November 1900, 460–470.

C disc. 29/11/1900. Camera dei Deputati. *Atti Parlamentari*. Legislatura XXI. 1° Sessione. Discussioni. Hearing of 29 November 1900, 687–727.

C disc. 30/11/1900(ii). Camera dei Deputati. *Atti Parlamentari*. Legislatura XXI. 1° Sessione. Discussioni. Second hearing of 30 November 1900, 747–782.

C disc. 1/12/1900. Camera dei Deputati. *Atti Parlamentari*. Legislatura XXI. 1° Sessione. Discussioni. Hearing of 1 December 1900, 783–833.

C disc. 2/12/1900. Camera dei Deputati. *Atti Parlamentari*. Legislatura XXI. 1° Sessione. Discussioni. Hearing of 2 December 1900, 835–863.

C disc. 3/12/1900(ii). Camera dei Deputati. *Atti Parlamentari*. Legislatura XXI. 1° Sessione. Discussioni. Second hearing of 3 December 1900, 945–984.

S. disc. 21/1/1901. Senato del Regno. *Atti Parlamentari*. Legislatura XXI. 1° Sessione. Discussioni. Hearing of 21 January 1901, 837–859.

S. disc. 22/1/1901. Senato del Regno. *Atti Parlamentari*. Legislatura XXI. 1° Sessione. Discussioni. Hearing of 22 January 1901, 861–881.

S. disc. 25/1/1901. Senato del Regno. *Atti Parlamentari*. Legislatura XXI. 1° Sessione. Discussioni. Hearing of 25 January 1901, 913–942.

S. disc. 26/1/1901. Senato del Regno. *Atti Parlamentari*. Legislatura XXI. 1° Sessione. Discussioni. Hearing of 26 January 1901, 945–972.

S. disc. 29/1/1901. Senato del Regno. *Atti Parlamentari*. Legislatura XXI. 1° Sessione. Discussioni. Hearing of 29 January 1901, 1013–1043.

Deprivation of citizenship (fuoriusciti):

C 623-A. Camera dei Deputati. *Atti Parlamentari*. Legislatura XXVII. Sessione 1924–1925. Documenti. "Relazione della commissione sul disegno di legge:

Modificazioni ed aggiunte alla legge 13 giugno 1912, n. 555, sulla cittadinanza (Bastianini, *rapporteur*)," 27 November 1925, 1–4.

Citizenship statuses and African populations (1880s–1922):
Eritrea and Somalia

C 341. Camera dei Deputati. *Atti Parlamentari*. Legislatura XIV. 1° Sessione 1880–1881. Documenti. "Progetto di legge: Provvedimenti per Assab," presented by Minister of Foreign Affairs (Mancini), 12 June 1882, 1–46.

C 341-A. Camera dei Deputati. *Atti Parlamentari*. Legislatura XIV. 1° Sessione 1880–1881. Documenti. "Relazione della commissione sul progetto di legge: Provvedimenti per Assab (Picardi, *rapporteur*)," 19 June 1882, 1–14.

C disc. 26/6/1882(ii). Camera dei Deputati. *Atti Parlamentari*. Legislatura XIV. 1° Sessione 1880–1881. Discussioni. Second hearing of 26 June 1882, 12177–12228.

C disc. 28/6/1882. Camera dei Deputati. *Atti Parlamentari*. Legislatura XIV. 1° Sessione 1880–1881. Discussioni. Hearing of 28 June 1882, 12281–12329.

S disc. 4/7/1882. Senato del Regno. *Atti Parlamentari*. Legislatura XIV. 1° Sessione 1880–1881–1882. Discussioni. Hearing of 4 July 1882, 3533–3539.

C 57. Camera dei Deputati. *Atti Parlamentari*. Legislatura XXI. 2° Sessione 1902. Documenti. "Disegno di legge: Ordinamento della colonia Eritrea," presented by Minister of Foreign Affairs (Prinetti), 13 March 1902, 1–11.

C 57-A. Camera dei Deputati. *Atti Parlamentari*. Legislatura XXI. 2° Sessione 1902. Documenti. "Relazione della commissione sul disegno di legge: Ordinamento della colonia Eritrea (Franchetti, *rapporteur*)," 7 June 1902, 1–18.

C disc. 18/12/1902. Camera dei Deputati. *Atti Parlamentari*. Legislatura XXI. 2° Sessione 1902. Discussioni. Hearing of 18 December 1902, 4757–4796.

S disc. 13/5/1903. Senato del Regno. *Atti Parlamentari*. Legislatura XXI. 2° Sessione 1902–1903. Discussioni. Hearing of 13 May 1903, 2127–2149.

S disc. 14/5/1903. Senato del Regno. *Atti Parlamentari*. Legislatura XXI. 2° Sessione 1902–1903. Discussioni. Hearing of 14 May 1903, 2151–2172.

S disc. 15/5/1903. Senato del Regno. *Atti Parlamentari*. Legislatura XXI. 2° Sessione 1902–1903. Discussioni. Hearing of 15 May 1903, 2175–2190.

S disc. 26/4/1907. Senato del Regno. *Atti Parlamentari*. Legislatura XXII. 1° Sessione 1904–1907. Discussioni. Hearing of 26 April 1907, 5645–5681.

S disc. 27/4/1907. Senato del Regno. *Atti Parlamentari*. Legislatura XXII. 1° Sessione 1904–1907. Discussioni. Hearing of 27 April 1907, 5685–5709.

C 745. Camera dei Deputati. *Atti Parlamentari*. Legislatura XXII. Sessione 1904–1907. Documenti. "Disegno di legge: Ordinamento del Benadir (Somalia italiana meridionale)," 15 May 1907, 1–11.

C 745-A. Camera dei Deputati. *Atti Parlamentari*. Legislatura XXII. Sessione 1904–1907. Documenti. "Relazione della commissione sul disegno di legge: Ordinamento del Benadir (Somalia italiana meridionale) (De Marinis, *rapporteur*)," 5 June 1907, 1–13.

C disc. 14/2/1908. Camera dei Deputati. *Atti Parlamentari*. Legislatura XXII. 1° Sessione. Discussioni. Hearing of 14 February 1908, 19167–19202.

C disc. 15/2/1908. Camera dei Deputati. *Atti Parlamentari*. Legislatura XXII. 1°
Sessione. Discussioni. Hearing of 15 February 1908, 19203–19250.

S disc. 31/3/1908. Senato del Regno. *Atti Parlamentari*. Legislatura XXII. 1° Sessione. Discussioni. Hearing of 31 March 1908, 8149–8178.

C XXXVIII-ter. Camera dei Deputati. *Atti Parlamentari*. Legislatura XXIII. Sessione 1909–1912. Documenti. "Relazione sulla Somalia Italiana del Gover-
natore Nobile Giacomo De Martino per gli anni 1911 e 1912," presented by
Minister of Colonies (Bertolini), 4 December 1912, 1–220.

Mancini, P. S. *Discorsi parlamentari di Pasquale Stanislao Mancini*. Vol. 7. Rome:
Camera dei Deputati, 1896.

Libya

C 1120. Camera dei Deputati. *Atti Parlamentari*. Legislatura XXIV. Sessione
1913–1919. Documenti. "Disegno di legge: Conversione in legge del regio decreto 1 giugno 1919 n. 931 che approva le norme fondamentali per l'assetto
della Tripolitania," presented by Minister of Colonies (Colosimo), 19 June
1919, 1–12.

C 605. Camera dei Deputati. *Atti Parlamentari*. Legislatura XXV. Sessione 1919–
1920. Documenti. "Disegno di legge: Conversione in legge del decreto reale 31
ottobre 1919 n. 2041 che approva le norme fondamentali per l'assetto della
Cirenaica," presented by Minister of Colonies (Rossi), 13 July 1920, 1–10.

C 606. Camera dei Deputati. *Atti Parlamentari*. Legislatura XXV. Sessione 1919–
1920. Documenti. "Disegno di legge: Conversione in legge del decreto reale
1 giugno 1919 n. 931 che approva le norme fondamentali per l'assetto della
Tripolitania," presented by Minister of Colonies (Rossi), 13 July 1920, 1–11.

Citizenship statuses and European Mediterranean populations (1912–1922):

Aegean Islands

C 1320. Camera dei Deputati. *Atti Parlamentari*. Legislatura XXIII. Sessione
1909–1913. Documenti. "Proposta di legge: Autorizzazione al governo di concedere la piccola cittadinanza," 21 February 1913, 1–3.

C 1320-A. Camera dei Deputati. *Atti Parlamentari*. Legislatura XXIII. Sessione
1909–1913. Documenti. "Relazione della commissione sulla proposta di legge:
Autorizzazione al governo di concedere la piccola cittadinanza (Baccelli, *rapporteur*)," 13 March 1913, 1–2.

C disc. 3/5/1913. Camera dei Deputati. *Atti Parlamentari*. Legislatura XXIII. 1°
Sessione. Discussioni. Hearing of 3 May 1913, 24923–24962.

S 1004. Senato del Regno. *Atti Parlamentari*. Legislatura XXIII. Sessione 1909–
1913. Documenti. "Disegno di legge: Autorizzazione al governo di concedere
la piccola cittadinanza," 5 May 1913, 1.

C 976. Camera dei Deputati. *Atti Parlamentari*. Legislatura XXV. Sessione 1919–
1920. Documenti. "Disegno di legge: Concessione della cittadinanza ad alcune
categorie di persone residenti in Oriente," presented by Minister of Foreign
Affairs (Sforza), 17 November 1920, 1–3.

C 976-A. Camera dei Deputati. *Atti Parlamentari*. Legislatura XXV. Sessione
1919–1920. Documenti. "Relazione della commissione per i rapporti politici
con l'estero-colonie sul disegno di legge: Concessione della cittadinanza ad

alcune categorie di persone residenti in Oriente (Vassallo, *rapporteur*)," 23 March 1921, 1–3.

S 118. Senato del Regno. *Atti Parlamentari.* Legislatura XXVI. 1° Sessione 1921. Documenti. "Disegno di legge: Concessione della cittadinanza ad alcune categorie di persone residenti in Oriente," 18 June 1921, 1–3.

Citizenship statuses and African populations (1922–1943):

Eritrea and Somalia

C 1704. Camera dei Deputati. *Atti Parlamentari.* Legislatura XXVIII. Sessione 1929–1933. Documenti. "Disegno di legge: Legge organica per l'Eritrea e la Somalia," presented by Minister of Colonies (De Bono), 20 April 1933, 1–20.

C 1704-A. Camera dei Deputati. *Atti Parlamentari.* Legislatura XXVIII. Sessione 1929–1933. Documenti. "Relazione della giunta generale del bilancio sul disegno di legge: Legge organica per l'Eritrea e la Somalia (Vassallo, *rapporteur*)," 18 May 1933, 1–19.

C disc. 23/5/1933. Camera dei Deputati. *Atti Parlamentari.* Legislatura XXVIII. 1° Sessione. Discussioni. Hearing of 23 May 1933, 8877–8920.

S 1638. Senato del Regno. *Atti Parlamentari.* Legislatura XXVIII. 1° Sessione 1929–1933. Documenti. "Disegno di legge: Legge organica per l'Eritrea e la Somalia," presented by Minister of Colonies (De Bono), 26 May 1933, 1–13.

S 1638-A. Senato del Regno. *Atti Parlamentari.* Legislatura XXVIII. 1° Sessione 1929–1933. Documenti. "Relazione dell'Ufficio Centrale sul disegno di legge: Legge organica per l'Eritrea e la Somalia (Bongiovanni, *rapporteur*)," 2 June 1933, 1–13.

S disc. 7/6/1933. Senato del Regno. *Atti Parlamentari.* Legislatura XXVIII. 1° Sessione 1929–1933. Discussioni. Hearing of 7 June 1933, 6547–6697.

AOI (Africa Orientale Italiana)

C 1501. Camera dei Deputati. *Atti Parlamentari.* Legislatura XXIX. Sessione 1934–1936. Documenti. "Disegno di legge: Conversione in legge del regio decreto-legge 1 giugno 1936 n. 1019 sull'ordinamento e l'amministrazione dell'Africa Orientale Italiana," presented by Minister of Colonies (Lessona), 2 December 1936, 1–14.

C 1501-A. Camera dei Deputati. *Atti Parlamentari.* Legislatura XXIX. Sessione 1934–1936. Documenti. "Relazione della giunta generale del bilancio sul disegno di legge: Conversione in legge del regio decreto-legge 1 giugno 1936 n. 1019 sull'ordinamento e l'amministrazione dell'Africa Orientale Italiana (Bolzon, *rapporteur*)," 4 December 1936, 1–2.

S 1497. Senato del Regno. *Atti Parlamentari.* Legislatura XXIX. 1° Sessione 1934–1936. Documenti. "Disegno di legge: Conversione in legge del regio decreto-legge 1 giugno 1936 n. 1019 sull'ordinamento e l'amministrazione dell'Africa Orientale Italiana," presented by Minister of Colonies (Lessona), 17 December 1936, 1–9.

S 1497-A. Senato del Regno. *Atti Parlamentari.* Legislatura XXIX. 1° Sessione 1934–1936. Documenti. "Relazione della commissione permanente sul disegno di legge: Conversione in legge del regio decreto-legge 1 giugno 1936 n. 1019 sull'ordinamento e l'amministrazione dell'Africa Orientale Italiana (Gualtieri, *rapporteur*)," 22 December 1936, 1–2.

Libya

C 1439. Camera dei Deputati. *Atti Parlamentari*. Legislatura XXVII. Sessione 1924–1927. Documenti. "Disegno di legge: Legge organica per l'amministrazione della Tripolitania e della Cirenaica," presented by Minister of Colonies (Federzoni), 2 April 1927, 1–18.

C 1439-A. Camera dei Deputati. *Atti Parlamentari*. Legislatura XXVII. Sessione 1924–1927. Documenti. "Relazione della giunta generale del bilancio sul disegno di legge: Legge organica per l'amministrazione della Tripolitania e della Cirenaica (Messedaglia, *rapporteur*)," 28 May 1927, 1–20.

C disc. 3/6/1927. Camera dei Deputati. *Atti Parlamentari*. Legislatura XXVII. 1° Sessione. Discussioni. Hearing of 3 June 1927, 7807–7934.

S 1065. Senato del Regno. *Atti Parlamentari*. Legislatura XXVII. 1° Sessione 1924–1927. Documenti. "Disegno di legge: Legge organica per l'amministrazione della Tripolitania e della Cirenaica," 4 June 1927, 1–11.

S 1065-A. Senato del Regno. *Atti Parlamentari*. Legislatura XXVII. 1° Sessione 1924–1927. Documenti. "Relazione della commissione di finanze sul disegno di legge: Legge organica per l'amministrazione della Tripolitania e della Cirenaica (Valvassori-Peroni, *rapporteur*)," 6 June 1927, 1–11.

S disc. 10/6/1927. Senato del Regno. *Atti Parlamentari*. Legislatura XXVII. 1° Sessione 1924–1927. Discussioni. Hearing of 10 June 1927, 9141–9264.

C 467. Camera dei Deputati. *Atti Parlamentari*. Legislatura XXIX. Sessione 1934–1935. Documenti. "Disegno di legge: Conversione in legge del regio decreto-legge 3 dicembre 1934 n. 2012, riflettente l'ordinamento organico per l'amministrazione della Libia," presented by Prime Minister (Mussolini), 26 February 1935, 1–14.

C 467-A. Camera dei Deputati. *Atti Parlamentari*. Legislatura XXIX. Sessione 1934–1935. Documenti. "Relazione della giunta generale del bilancio sul disegno di legge: Conversione in legge del regio decreto-legge 3 dicembre 1934 n. 2012, riflettente l'ordinamento organico per l'amministrazione della Libia (Pace, *rapporteur*)," 12 March 1935, 1–3.

C disc. 20/3/1935. Camera dei Deputati. *Atti Parlamentari*. Legislatura XXIX. 1° Sessione. Discussioni. Hearing of 20 March 1935, 1039–1083.

S 472. Senato del Regno. *Atti Parlamentari*. Legislatura XXIX. 1° Sessione 1934–1935. Documenti. "Disegno di legge: Conversione in legge del regio decreto-legge 3 dicembre 1934 n. 2012, riflettente l'ordinamento organico per l'amministrazione della Libia," presented by Prime Minister (Mussolini), 21 March 1935, 1–17.

S 472-A. Senato del Regno. *Atti Parlamentari*. Legislatura XXIX. 1° Sessione 1934–1935. Documenti. "Relazione della commissione permanente per l'esame dei disegni di legge per la conversione dei decreti-legge sul disegno di legge: Conversione in legge del regio decreto-legge 3 dicembre 1934 n. 2012, riflettente l'ordinamento organico per l'amministrazione della Libia (Manfroni, *rapporteur*)," 28 March 1935, 1–18.

S disc. 1/4/1935. Senato del Regno. *Atti Parlamentari*. Legislatura XXIX. 1° Sessione 1934–1935. Discussioni. Hearing of 1 April 1935, 1013–1088.

S disc. 2/4/1935. Senato del Regno. *Atti Parlamentari*. Legislatura XXIX. 1° Sessione 1934–1935. Discussioni. Hearing of 2 April 1935, 1089–1109.

CFC 57. Camera dei Fasci e delle Corporazioni. Legislatura XXX. Documenti. "Disegno di legge: Conversione in legge con approvazione complessiva dei regi decreti-legge emanati fino al 10 marzo 1939 e convalida dei regi decreti, emanati fino alla data anzidetta, per prelevazioni di somme dal fondo di riserva per le spese impreviste," 15 April 1939, 1–11.

CFC 57-A. Camera dei Fasci e delle Corporazioni. Legislatura XXX. Documenti. "Relazione della commissione speciale nominata dal presidente sul disegno di legge: Conversione in legge con approvazione complessiva dei regi decreti-legge emanati fino al 10 marzo 1939 e convalida dei regi decreti, emanati fino alla data anzidetta, per prelevazioni di somme dal fondo di riserva per le spese impreviste (Fera, *rapporteur*)," 10 May 1939, 1–16.

S 159. Senato del Regno. Legislatura XXX. Documenti. "Disegno di legge: Conversione in legge con approvazione complessiva dei regi decreti-legge emanati fino al 10 marzo 1939 e convalida dei regi decreti, emanati fino alla data anzidetta, per prelevazioni di somme dal fondo di riserva per le spese impreviste," 18 May 1939, 1–12.

S 159-A. Senato del Regno. Legislatura XXX. Documenti. "Relazione della commissione speciale sul disegno di legge: Conversione in legge con approvazione complessiva dei regi decreti-legge emanati fino al 10 marzo 1939 e convalida dei regi decreti, emanati fino alla data anzidetta, per prelevazioni di somme dal fondo di riserva per le spese impreviste (Berio, *rapporteur*)," 26 May 1939, 1–19.

SAP disc. 30/5/1939. Senato del Regno. Legislatura XXX. Assemblea Plenaria. Discussioni. Hearing of 30 May 1939, 189–267.

Citizenship statuses and European Mediterranean populations (1922–1943):
Aegean Islands

C 675. Camera dei Deputati. *Atti Parlamentari*. Legislatura XXVII. Sessione 1924–1925. Documenti. "Disegno di legge: Conversione in legge del regio decreto 15 ottobre 1925 n. 1854, relativo all'acquisto della cittadinanza italiana degli abitanti del Dodecanneso, in base alle disposizioni del Trattato di Losanna del 24 luglio 1923," presented by Prime Minister (Mussolini), 5 December 1925, 1–3.

C 675-A. Camera dei Deputati. *Atti Parlamentari*. Legislatura XXVII. Sessione 1924–1925. Documenti. "Relazione della commissione speciale nominata dal presidente sul disegno di legge: Conversione in legge del regio decreto 15 ottobre 1925 n. 1854, relativo all'acquisto della cittadinanza italiana degli abitanti del Dodecanneso, in base alle disposizioni del Trattato di Losanna del 24 luglio 1923 (Pace, *rapporteur*)," 10 December 1925, 1–3.

C disc. 5/12/1925. Camera dei Deputati. *Atti Parlamentari*. Legislatura XXVII. 1° Sessione. Discussioni. Hearing of 5 December 1925, 4823–4856.

C disc. 10/12/1925. Camera dei Deputati. *Atti Parlamentari*. Legislatura XXVII. 1° Sessione. Discussioni. Hearing of 10 December 1925, 4891–4924.

364 Bibliography

C disc. 19/12/1925. Camera dei Deputati. *Atti Parlamentari*. Legislatura XXVII. 1° Sessione. Discussioni. Hearing of 19 December 1925, 5117–5144.

C disc. 17/1/1926. Camera dei Deputati. *Atti Parlamentari*. Legislatura XXVII. 1° Sessione. Discussioni. Hearing of 17 January 1926, 5149–5159.

S 374. Senato del Regno. *Atti Parlamentari*. Legislatura XXVII. 1° Sessione 1924–1926. Documenti. "Disegno di legge: Conversione in legge del regio decreto 15 ottobre 1925 n. 1854, relativo all'acquisto della cittadinanza italiana degli abitanti del Dodecanneso, in base alle disposizioni del Trattato di Losanna del 24 luglio 1923," 28 January 1926, 1–3.

S 374-A. Senato del Regno. *Atti Parlamentari*. Legislatura XXVII. 1° Sessione 1924–1926. Documenti. "Relazione dell'Ufficio Centrale sul disegno di legge: Conversione in legge del regio decreto 15 ottobre 1925 n. 1854, relativo all'acquisto della cittadinanza italiana degli abitanti del Dodecanneso, in base alle disposizioni del Trattato di Losanna del 24 luglio 1923 (Perla, *rapporteur*)," 11 March 1926, 1–3.

S disc. 15/3/1926. Senato del Regno. *Atti Parlamentari*. Legislatura XXVII. 1° Sessione 1924–1926. Discussioni. Hearing of 15 March 1926, 4965–5046.

C 1612. Camera dei Deputati. *Atti Parlamentari*. Legislatura XXVII. Sessione 1924–1927. Documenti. "Disegno di legge: Conversione in legge del regio decreto-legge 13 marzo 1927 n. 1378, relativo alle dichiarazioni di eleggere la cittadinanza italiana, presentate in base all'articolo 34 del Trattato di pace di Losanna dagli originari delle isole italiane dell'Egeo stabiliti all'estero," 5 September 1927, 1–3.

C 1612-A. Camera dei Deputati. *Atti Parlamentari*. Legislatura XXVII. Sessione 1924–1928. Documenti. "Relazione della commissione sul disegno di legge: Conversione in legge del regio decreto-legge 13 marzo 1927 n. 1378, relativo alle dichiarazioni di eleggere la cittadinanza italiana, presentate in base all'articolo 34 del Trattato di pace di Losanna dagli originari delle isole italiane dell'Egeo stabiliti all'estero (Solmi, *rapporteur*)," 17 February 1928, 1–2.

S 1350. Senato del Regno. *Atti Parlamentari*. Legislatura XXVII. 1° Sessione 1924–1928. Documenti. "Disegno di legge: Conversione in legge del regio decreto-legge 13 marzo 1927 n. 1378, relativo alle dichiarazioni di eleggere la cittadinanza italiana, presentate in base all'articolo 34 del Trattato di pace di Losanna dagli originari delle isole italiane dell'Egeo stabiliti all'estero," 29 February 1928, 1–2.

S 1350-A. Senato del Regno. *Atti Parlamentari*. Legislatura XXVII. 1° Sessione 1924–1928. Documenti. "Relazione dell'Ufficio Centrale sul disegno di legge: Conversione in legge del regio decreto-legge 13 marzo 1927 n. 1378, relativo alle dichiarazioni di eleggere la cittadinanza italiana, presentate in base all'articolo 34 del Trattato di pace di Losanna dagli originari delle isole italiane dell'Egeo stabiliti all'estero (Artom, *rapporteur*)," 28 May 1928, 1–3.

C 1870. Camera dei Deputati. *Atti Parlamentari*. Legislatura XXVIII. Sessione 1929–1933. Documenti. "Disegno di legge: Conversione in legge del regio decreto-legge 19 ottobre 1933 n. 1379, relativo all'acquisto della piena cittadinanza italiana da parte degli abitanti delle isole italiane dell'Egeo," presented by Prime Minister (Mussolini), 11 November 1933, 1–3.

C 1870-A. Camera dei Deputati. *Atti Parlamentari*. Legislatura XXVIII. Sessione 1929–1933. Documenti. "Relazione della commissione permanente sul disegno di legge: Conversione in legge del regio decreto-legge 19 ottobre 1933 n. 1379, relativo all'acquisto della piena cittadinanza italiana da parte degli abitanti delle isole italiane dell'Egeo (Pellizzari, *rapporteur*)," 11 December 1933, 2.

S 1737. Senato del Regno. *Atti Parlamentari*. Legislatura XXVIII. 1° Sessione 1929–1933. Documenti. "Disegno di legge: Conversione in legge del regio decreto-legge 19 ottobre 1933 n. 1379, relativo all'acquisto della piena cittadinanza italiana da parte degli abitanti delle isole italiane dell'Egeo," presented by Prime Minister (Mussolini), 13 December 1933, 1–2.

S 1737-A. Senato del Regno. *Atti Parlamentari*. Legislatura XXVIII. 1° Sessione 1929–1933. Documenti. "Relazione della commissione permanente sul disegno di legge: Conversione in legge del regio decreto-legge 19 ottobre 1933 n. 1379, relativo all'acquisto della piena cittadinanza italiana da parte degli abitanti delle isole italiane dell'Egeo (Salata, *rapporteur*)," 15 December 1933, 1–3.

S disc. 18/12/1933. Senato del Regno. *Atti Parlamentari*. Legislatura XXVIII. 1° Sessione 1929–1933. Discussioni. Hearing of 18 December 1933, 6811–6828.

Albania

CFC 110. Camera dei Fasci e delle Corporazioni. Legislatura XXX. Assemblea Plenaria. Documenti. "Disegno di legge: Accettazione della corona d'Albania da parte del Re d'Italia, Imperatore d'Etiopia," 15 April 1939, 1.

CFC, AP disc. 15/4/1939. Camera dei Fasci e delle Corporazioni. Legislatura XXX. Assemblea Plenaria. Discussioni. Hearing of 15 April 1939, 1–11.

S 1. Senato del Regno. Legislatura XXX. Documenti. "Disegno di legge: Accettazione della corona d'Albania da parte del Re d'Italia, Imperatore d'Etiopia," 15 April 1939, 1.

S 1-A. Senato del Regno. Legislatura XXX. Documenti. "Relazione della commissione speciale sul disegno di legge: Accettazione della corona d'Albania da parte del Re d'Italia, Imperatore d'Etiopia (Thaon di Ravel, *rapporteur*)," 15 April 1939, 1.

SAP disc. 15/4/1939. Senato del Regno. Legislatura XXX. Assemblea Plenaria. Discussioni. Hearing of 15 April 1939, 1–4.

CFC 256. Camera dei Fasci e delle Corporazioni. Legislatura XXX. Documenti. "Disegno di legge: Fusione delle Forze Armate Albanesi con le corrispondenti Forze Armate Italiane," 10 June 1939, 1.

CFC, CLFA disc. 15/6/1939. Camera dei Fasci e delle Corporazioni. Legislatura XXX. Commissione Legislativa delle Forze Armate. Discussioni. Hearing of 15 June 1939, 39–70.

S 267. Senato del Regno. Legislatura XXX. Documenti. "Disegno di legge: Fusione delle Forze Armate Albanesi con le corrispondenti Forze Armate Italiane," 16 June 1939, 1.

S-CFA disc. 30/6/1939. Senato del Regno. Legislatura XXX. Commissione delle Forze Armate. Discussioni. Hearing of 30 June 1939, 60–68.

CFC 259. Camera dei Fasci e delle Corporazioni. Legislatura XXX. Documenti. "Disegno di legge: Approvazione dell'accordo stipulato in Tirana, fra l'Italia e l'Albania, il 20 aprile 1939 concernente i diritti dei rispettivi cittadini," 10 June 1939, 1–2.

CFC, CLAE disc. 16/6/1939. Camera dei Fasci e delle Corporazioni. Legislatura XXX. Commissione Legislativa degli Affari Esteri. Discussioni. Hearing of 16 June 1939, 31–38.

S 283. Senato del Regno. Legislatura XXX. Documenti. "Disegno di legge: Approvazione dell'accordo stipulato in Tirana, fra l'Italia e l'Albania, il 20 aprile 1939 concernente i diritti dei rispettivi cittadini," 16 June 1939, 1–2.

S-CAESC disc. 1/7/1939. Senato del Regno. Legislatura XXX. Commissione degli Affari Esteri, degli Scambi Commerciali e della Legislazione Doganale. Discussioni. Hearing of 1 July 1939, 28–32.

CFC 2507. Camera dei Fasci e delle Corporazioni. Legislatura XXX. Documenti. "Disegno di legge: Approvazione dell'accordo italo-albanese del 30 dicembre 1942 concernente i diritti dei rispettivi cittadini," 5 July 1943, 1–2.

CFC, CLAE disc. 14/7/1943. Camera dei Fasci e delle Corporazioni. Legislatura XXX. Commissione Legislativa degli Affari Esteri. Discussioni. Hearing of 14 July 1943, 341–345.

S 2433. Senato del Regno. Legislatura XXX. Documenti. "Disegno di legge: Approvazione dell'accordo italo-albanese del 30 dicembre 1942 concernente i diritti dei rispettivi cittadini," 15 July 1943, 1–2.

S-CAESC disc. 23/7/1943. Senato del Regno. Legislatura XXX. Commissione degli Affari Esteri, degli Scambi Commerciali e della Legislazione Doganale. Discussioni. Hearing of 23 July 1943, 453–460.

Dalmatia

S-CR disc. 29/8/1941. Senato del Regno. Legislatura XXX. Commissioni Riunite. Discussioni. Hearing of 29 August 1941, 1105–1113.

Italian Constituent Assembly (1947):

Atti dell'Assemblea Costituente. Vol. 8. Discussioni. Hearing of 17 October 1947, 1299–1332.

Atti dell'Assemblea Costituente. Vol. 10. Discussioni. Hearing of 22 December 1947, 3567–3589.

Croce, B. *Contro l'approvazione del dettato della pace: Discorso tenuto all'Assemblea Costituente il 24 luglio 1947.* Bari: Laterza, 1947.

2.c.ii Government materials

Italian Ministry of Foreign Affairs. Circular 30 October 1870. In *Raccolta delle circolari e istruzioni ministeriali.* Vol. 1, 142–143. Rome: Ministero degli Affari Esteri, 1950.

Italian Ministry of Foreign Affairs. Circular n. 43 "Cittadinanza del Territorio Libero di Trieste," 7 October 1947. In *Raccolta delle circolari e istruzioni ministeriali.* Vol. 14, 109–110. Rome: Ministero degli Affari Esteri, 1950.

Italian Ministry of Foreign Affairs. Circular n. 50 "Opzioni," 6 November 1947. In *Raccolta delle circolari e istruzioni ministeriali.* Vol. 14, 119–122. Rome: Ministero degli Affari Esteri, 1950.

Italian Ministry of Foreign Affairs. Circular n. 15 "Articoli 19 e 20 del Trattato di Pace—Opzioni," 27 April 1948. In *Raccolta delle circolari e istruzioni ministeriali.* Vol. 14, 185–193. Rome: Ministero degli Affari Esteri, 1950.

Italian Ministry of Foreign Affairs. Circular n. 31 "Territori ceduti alla Francia—
Opzioni," 15 July 1948. In *Raccolta delle circolari e istruzioni ministeriali*. Vol.
14, 221–229. Rome: Ministero degli Affari Esteri, 1950.
Italian Ministry of Foreign Affairs. Circular n. 38 "Territori ceduti alla Grecia—
Opzioni," 8 September 1948. In *Raccolta delle circolari e istruzioni ministe-
riali*. Vol. 14, 252–255. Rome: Ministero degli Affari Esteri, 1950.

2.c.iii Civil codes, national legislation and constitutions

1859–1865 period: multiple citizenship norms

Codice Civile per gli Stati Estensi. Modena: Eredi Soliani Tipografi Reali, 1852.
*Collezione completa dei moderni codici civili degli Stati d'Italia secondo l'ordine cro-
nologico della loro pubblicazione*. Turin: Libreria della Minerva Subalpina, 1845.
Collezione delle leggi e decreti reali del Regno delle due Sicilie. Year 1817 (II
Semester: July–December). Naples: Stamperia Reale, 1822.
Gianzana, S., ed. *Codice Civile: Preceduto dalle relazioni ministeriale e senatoria,
dalle discussioni parlamentari, e dai verbali della commissione coordinatrice
colle riferenze sotto ogni singolo articolo agli altri codici italiani, al francese,
alle leggi romane, nonché a tutti i precedenti legislativi coll'aggiunta delle
leggi complementari*. In collaboration with F. Bo and P. Tappari. 7 vols. Turin:
Unione Tipografico-Editrice, 1887–1888.
"Legge 17 dicembre 1817 n. 1024: Legge per la naturalizzazione degli stranieri."
In *Collezione delle leggi e decreti reali del Regno delle due Sicilie*. Year 1817 (II
Semester: July–December), 454–456. Naples: Stamperia Reale, 1822.
Legislazione toscana raccolta ed illustrata dall'avvocato Lorenzo Cantini. Vol.
26. Florence: Stamperia Albizziniana, 1806.
*Repertorio del diritto patrio toscano vigente ossia spoglio alfabetico e letterale
delle più interessanti disposizioni legislative veglianti nel Granducato*. Vol. 6.
Florence: Giuliani, 1837.

Post-1866 peninsula-wide citizenship norms:

Codice Civile del Regno d'Italia. Turin: Stamperia Reale, 1865.
"Legge 13 giugno 1912 n. 555: Disposizioni sulla cittadinanza italiana." In S.
Bariatti, *La disciplina giuridica della cittadinanza italiana*. Vol. 1, 53–58.
Milan: Giuffrè Editore, 1989.

Membership statuses and African populations (liberal period):

Eritrea and Somalia

"Legge 5 luglio 1882 n. 857: Legge concernente i provvedimenti per Assab." In
Raccolta ufficiale delle leggi e dei decreti del Regno d'Italia. Vol. 66, 2245–
2272. Florence: Stamperia Reale, 1882.
"Legge 24 maggio 1903 n. 205: Ordinamento della colonia Eritrea." In *Raccolta
dei principali ordinamenti legislativi delle colonie italiane*. Edited by A. Parpagliolo. Vol. 2, 3–11. Rome: Istituto Poligrafico dello Stato, 1932.
"Legge 5 aprile 1908 n. 161: Legge portante l'ordinamento della Somalia italiana."
In *Raccolta dei principali ordinamenti legislativi delle colonie italiane*. Edited
by A. Parpagliolo. Vol. 2, 59–67. Rome: Istituto Poligrafico dello Stato, 1932.

"Regio decreto 19 settembre 1909 n. 839: Regio decreto che approva l'ordinamento del corpo dei funzionari coloniali dell'Eritrea." In *Collezione celerifera delle leggi, decreti, istruzioni e circolari dell'anno 1910 ed anteriori.* Edited by D. Scacchi. 127–138. Rome: Stamperia Reale, 1911.

"Regio decreto 4 luglio 1910 n. 562: Regio decreto che approva l'annesso regolamento amministrativo per la Somalia italiana." In *Collezione celerifera delle leggi, decreti, istruzioni e circolari dell'anno 1910 ed anteriori.* Edited by D. Scacchi. 962–983. Rome: Stamperia Reale, 1911.

"Regio decreto 8 giugno 1911 n. 937: Ordinamento giudiziario per la Somalia italiana." In *Raccolta dei principali ordinamenti legislativi delle colonie italiane.* Edited by A. Parpagliolo. Vol. 2, 229–254. Rome: Istituto Poligrafico dello Stato, 1932.

Libya

"Regio decreto 6 aprile 1913 n. 315: Regio decreto che regola i rapporti di sudditanza degli indigeni della Libia." In *Raccolta ufficiale delle leggi e dei decreti del Regno d'Italia.* Vol. 1, 986–988. Florence: Stamperia Reale, 1913.

"Regio decreto 1 giugno 1919 n. 931: Regio decreto che approva le norme fondamentali per l'assetto della Tripolitania." In *Raccolta ufficiale delle leggi e dei decreti del Regno d'Italia.* Vol. 12, 1844–1852. Florence: Stamperia Reale, 1919.

"Regio decreto-legge 31 ottobre 1919 n. 2401: Regio decreto-legge che approva le norme fondamentali per l'assetto della Cirenaica." In *Raccolta ufficiale delle leggi e dei decreti del Regno d'Italia.* Vol. 14, 5702–5712. Florence: Stamperia Reale, 1919.

Membership statuses and European Mediterranean populations (liberal period):

Aegean Islands

"Regio decreto-legge 10 settembre 1922 n. 1387: Disposizioni sulla cittadinanza italiana." In S. Bariatti, *La disciplina giuridica della cittadinanza italiana.* Vol. 1, 69–70. Milan: Giuffrè Editore, 1989.

Membership statuses and African populations (fascist period):

Eritrea, Somalia, AOI

"Regio decreto 7 febbraio 1926 n. 342: Approvazione dell'ordinamento giudiziario per la colonia Eritrea." In *Raccolta dei principali ordinamenti legislativi delle colonie italiane.* Edited by A. Parpagliolo. Vol. 2, 155–184. Rome: Istituto Poligrafico dello Stato, 1932.

"Decreto governatoriale 24 maggio 1926 n. 4379: Approvazione del regolamento giudiziario per l'Eritrea." In *Raccolta dei principali ordinamenti legislativi delle colonie italiane.* Edited by A. Parpagliolo. Vol. 2, 185–216. Rome: Istituto Poligrafico dello Stato, 1932.

"Legge 6 luglio 1933 n. 999: Ordinamento organico per l'Eritrea e la Somalia." In *Le leggi e i decreti reali secondo l'ordine della inserzione nella Gazzetta Ufficiale.* Year 1933, 947–956. Rome: Società Editrice del periodico "Il Foro Italiano," 1933.

"Decreto legge 20 giugno 1935 n. 1638: Ordinamento giudiziario per la Somalia Italiana." In *Le leggi e i decreti reali secondo l'ordine della inserzione nella Gazzetta Ufficiale*. Year 1935, 988–1004. Rome: Società Editrice del periodico "Il Foro Italiano," 1935.

"Regio decreto-legge 1 giugno 1936 n. 1019: Ordinamento e amministrazione dell'Africa Orientale Italiana." In *Le leggi e i decreti reali secondo l'ordine della inserzione nella Gazzetta Ufficiale*. Year 1936, 445–452. Rome: Società Editrice del periodico "Il Foro Italiano," 1936.

"Legge 13 maggio 1940 n. 822: Norme relative ai meticci." In S. Bariatti, *La disciplina giuridica della cittadinanza italiana*. Vol. 1, 85–87. Milan: Giuffrè Editore, 1989.

Libya

"Legge 26 giugno 1927 n. 1013: Legge organica per l'amministrazione della Tripolitania e della Cirenaica." In *Le leggi e i decreti reali secondo l'ordine della inserzione nella Gazzetta Ufficiale*. Year 1927, 621–628. Rome: Società Editrice del periodico "Il Foro Italiano," 1927.

"Regio decreto-legge 3 dicembre 1934 n. 2012: Ordinamento organico per l'amministrazione della Libia." In *Le leggi e i decreti reali secondo l'ordine della inserzione nella Gazzetta Ufficiale*. Year 1934, 1538–1546. Rome: Società Editrice del periodico "Il Foro Italiano," 1934.

"Regio decreto-legge 9 gennaio 1939 n. 70: Aggregazione delle quattro provincie libiche al territorio del Regno d'Italia e concessione ai libici musulmani di una cittadinanza italiana speciale con statuto personale e successorio musulmano." In *Le leggi e i decreti reali secondo l'ordine della inserzione nella Gazzetta Ufficiale*. Year 1939, 135. Rome: Società Editrice del periodico "Il Foro Italiano," 1939.

Membership statuses and European Mediterranean populations (fascist period):

Aegean Islands

"Regio decreto-legge 15 ottobre 1925 n. 1854: Acquisto della cittadinanza italiana degli abitanti del Dodecanneso in base alle disposizioni del trattato di Losanna." In S. Bariatti, *La disciplina giuridica della cittadinanza italiana*. Vol. 1, 73. Milan: Giuffrè Editore, 1989.

"Regio decreto-legge 13 marzo 1927 n. 1378: Cittadinanza italiana agli originari delle isole italiane dell'Egeo." In *Raccolta ufficiale delle leggi e dei decreti del Regno d'Italia*. Year 1927, 6536–6537. Florence: Stamperia Reale, 1927.

"Regio decreto-legge 19 ottobre 1933 n. 1379: Acquisto della piena cittadinanza italiana da parte degli abitanti delle isole italiane dell'Egeo." In *Le leggi e i decreti reali secondo l'ordine della inserzione nella Gazzetta Ufficiale*. Year 1933, 1208. Rome: Società Editrice del periodico "Il Foro Italiano," 1933.

Albania

"Albania—Civil Code." In *A Collection of Nationality Laws of Various Countries as Contained in Constitutions, Statutes and Treaties*. Edited by R. W. Flournoy and M. O. Hudson. 5–8. New York: Oxford University Press, 1929.

Raccolta di provvedimenti di carattere legislativo riguardanti l'Albania. Edited by R. Bertuccioli. Rome: Regio Ministero degli Affari Esteri, 1941.

Citizenship and the 1943–1945 biennium:

"Regio decreto-legge 20 gennaio 1944 n. 25: Disposizioni per la reintegrazione dei diritti civili e politici dei cittadini italiani e stranieri già dichiarati di razza ebraica o considerati di razza ebraica." In S. Bariatti, *La disciplina giuridica della cittadinanza italiana.* Vol. 1, 88. Milan: Giuffrè Editore, 1989.

"Decreto legislativo luogotenenziale 1 febbraio 1945 n. 23: Estensione alle donne del diritto di voto." In *Raccolta ufficiale delle leggi e dei decreti del Regno d'Italia.* Vol. 1, 79–80. Florence: Stamperia Reale, 1945.

Citizenship issues and the 1946–1950 period:

"Decreto legislativo luogotenenziale 16 marzo 1946 n. 98: Integrazioni e modifiche al decreto legislativo luogotenenziale 25 giugno 1944 n. 151, relativo all'Assemblea per la nuova Costituzione dello Stato, al giuramento dei membri del Governo ed alla facoltà del Governo di emanare norme giuridiche." In A. Cariola with G. A. Ferro. *Le leggi dell'organizzazione costituzionale.* 45–46. Milan: Giuffrè Editore, 2004.

"Decreto legislativo del Capo provvisorio dello Stato 3 agosto 1947 n. 1906: Abrogazione della legge 13 maggio 1940 n. 822 contenente norme relative ai meticci." In S. Bariatti, *La disciplina giuridica della cittadinanza italiana.* Vol. 1, 88–89. Milan: Giuffrè Editore, 1989.

Constitutions in the Italian peninsula (1848–1948):

"Statuto fondamentale del Regno (1848)." In *Codice Civile: Preceduto dalle relazioni ministeriale e senatoria, dalle discussioni parlamentari, e dai verbali della commissione coordinatrice colle riferenze sotto ogni singolo articolo agli altri codici italiani, al francese, alle leggi romane, nonché a tutti i precedenti legislativi coll'aggiunta delle leggi complementari.* Edited by S. Gianzana in collaboration with F. Bo and P. Tappari. Vol. 4, 1–11. Turin: Unione Tipografico-Editrice, 1887–1888.

"Costituzione della Repubblica Romana (1849)." In *Le Costituzioni italiane.* Edited by A. Acquarone, M. D'Addio and G. Negri. 614–624. Milan: Edizioni di Comunità, 1958.

"Costituzione della Repubblica Italiana (1948)." In *Commentario sistematico alla Costituzione Italiana.* Edited by P. Calamandrei and A. Levi. Vol. 1, XXIX–LIII. Florence: Barbera Editore, 1950.

2.c.iv International treaties

"Peace Treaty between Austria-Hungary and Italy," Vienna, 3 October 1866. In *The Consolidated Treaty Series.* Edited by C. Perry. Vol. 133, 210–217. Dobbs Ferry, N.Y.: Oceana Publications, 1969–1981.

"Trattato di pace tra le potenze alleate ed associate e l'Austria," Saint-Germain-en-Laye, 10 September 1919. In S. Bariatti, *La disciplina giuridica della cittadinanza italiana.* Vol. 1, 119–121. Milan: Giuffrè Editore, 1989.

"Trattato di pace tra le potenze alleate ed associate e l'Ungheria," Trianon, 4 June 1920. In S. Bariatti, *La disciplina giuridica della cittadinanza italiana*. Vol. 1, 122–124. Milan: Giuffrè Editore, 1989.

"Traité de Paix signé à Sèvres le 10 août 1920." In *Nouveau recueil général de traités et autres actes relatifs aux rapports de droit international*. Vol. 12, 664–779. Leipzig: Weicher, 1924.

"Trattato fra l'Italia e lo Stato Serbo-Croato-Sloveno," Rapallo, 12 November 1920. In S. Bariatti, *La disciplina giuridica della cittadinanza italiana*. Vol. 1, 183–184. Milan: Giuffrè Editore, 1989.

"Traité de Paix signé à Lausanne le 24 juillet 1923." In *Nouveau recueil général de traités et autres actes relatifs aux rapports de droit international*. Vol. 13, 342–390. Leipzig: Weicher, 1925.

"Treaty of Peace with Italy," Paris, 10 February 1947. In *Treaty Series*. Edited by the United Nations. Vol. 49, I. n. 747, 126–235. New York: United Nations, 1950.

2.c.v Jurisprudence and legal opinions

"Cittadinanza." *Repertorio generale annuale di giurisprudenza, bibliografia e legislazione in materia di diritto civile, commerciale, penale e amministrativo* 5 (1880): 208–209.

Council of State, 5 June 1863. "Naturalizzazione degli stranieri (Parere, adottato)." *Manuale degli amministratori comunali e provinciali* no. 3 (1 February 1864): 41–42.

Council of State, 6 February 1866. "Naturalizzazione italiana (Parere, adottato)." *Manuale degli amministratori comunali e provinciali* no. 4 (15 February 1866): 56–57.

Council of State, 31 March 1905. "Medico condotto—Nomina—Cittadinanza italiana—Cittadini di provincie geograficamente italiane—Ammissibilità della nomina—Obbligo e diritti—Contributo alla Cassa pensioni." *Il Foro italiano: Raccolta generale di giurisprudenza* 30 (1905): 107–110.

Court of Appeal of Ancona, 2 August 1912. "Avvocato e procuratore—Italiano non regnicolo e non naturalizzato—Iscrizione nell'albo dei procuratori." *Il Foro italiano: Raccolta generale di giurisprudenza* 37 (1912): 1420–1423.

Court of Appeal of Turin, 16 June 1884. "Elettorato amministrativo—Cittadino svizzero del Cantone Ticino—Iscrizione nelle liste—Art. 17 legge comun. e provinciale." *Giurisprudenza italiana: Raccolta generale, periodica e critica di giurisprudenza, legislazione e dottrina* 36 (1884): 425–427.

Court of Appeal of Venice, 11 October 1887. "Elezioni amministrative—Cittadini della Gorizia—Iscrizione nelle liste." *Il Foro italiano: Raccolta generale di giurisprudenza* 12 (1887): 1164–1166.

Court of Cassation in Rome, 17 November 1884. "Elettorato amministrativo—Cittadino della svizzera italiana—Art. 17 legge comunale e provinciale." *Giurisprudenza italiana: Raccolta generale, periodica e critica di giurisprudenza, legislazione e dottrina* 37 (1885): 26–27.

Court of Cassation in Rome, 23 April 1896. "Elezioni amministrative—Cittadino della Savoia." *Il Foro italiano: Raccolta generale di giurisprudenza* 21 (1896): 836–837.

"Corte Suprema di Cassazione—'Referendum' sulla forma istituzionale dello Stato—Verbale relativo al giudizio definitivo sulle contestazioni, le proteste e i reclami di cui all'art. 19 d. l. l. 23 aprile 1946, n. 219." In A. Cariola with G. A. Ferro, *Le leggi dell'organizzazione costituzionale.* 48–49. Milan: Giuffrè Editore, 2004.

2.d Reports and hearings at contemporary international congresses

Atti del primo congresso degli italiani all'estero (ottobre 1908). 2 vols. Rome: Cooperativa Tipografica Manuzio, 1910.

Atti del secondo congresso degli italiani all'estero (11–20 giugno 1911). 2 vols. Rome: Tipografia Editrice Nazionale, 1912.

Franzoni, A. *Cittadinanza e nazionalità.* Rimini: G. Benzi, 1909.

2.e Political, theoretical and other writings

Crispi, F. *Scritti e discorsi politici di Francesco Crispi (1849–1890).* 2nd ed. Turin, Rome: Casa Editrice Nazionale Roux e Viarengo, n.d., after 1890. First published 1890.

Dante. *La Commedia: Secondo l'antica vulgata.* Edited by G. Petrocchi. 4 vols. Verona: Mondadori, 1966–1967.

———. *The Divine Comedy.* Translated with a commentary by C. S. Singleton. 3 vols. Princeton: Princeton University Press, 1977.

Gioberti, V. *Del primato morale e civile degli italiani.* 2 vols. Brussels: Meline Cans, 1843.

Hitler, A. *Mein Kampf: Complete and Unabridged, Fully Annotated.* New York: Reynal & Hitchcock, 1939.

Kipling, R. *The Five Nations.* London: Macmillan, 1904.

Mancini, P. S. *Della nazionalità come fondamento del dritto delle genti.* Turin: Eredi Botta, 1851. In *Della nazionalità come fondamento del diritto delle genti di Pasquale Stanislao Mancini.* Edited by E. Jayme. 19–64. Turin: Giappichelli, 1994.

Mazzini, G. [1832]. "I collaboratori della 'Giovine Italia' ai loro concittadini." In *Scritti editi e inediti.* Edited by Edizione Nazionale. Vol. 3, 27–74. Imola: Galeati, 1906–1981.

———. [1849]. "La Santa Alleanza dei Popoli." In *Scritti editi e inediti.* Edited by Edizione Nazionale. Vol. 39, 203–221. Imola: Galeati, 1906–1981.

———. [1850]. "Comitato Nazionale Italiano. Agli Italiani." In *Scritti editi e inediti.* Edited by Edizione Nazionale. Vol. 43, 219–227. Imola: Galeati, 1906–1981.

———. [1860]. *The Duties of Man and Other Essays.* London, Toronto: J. M. Dent, 1907.

———. [1871]. "Nazionalismo e Nazionalità." In *Scritti editi e inediti.* Edited by Edizione Nazionale. Vol. 93, 85–96. Imola: Galeati, 1906–1981.

———. [1871]. "Politica Internazionale." In *Scritti editi e inediti.* Edited by Edizione Nazionale. Vol. 92, 143–170. Imola: Galeati, 1906–1981.

Monti, A., ed. *Dantis Alagherii Epistolae/Le Lettere di Dante: Testo, versione, commento e appendici.* Milan: Ulrico Hoepli, 1921.

Mussolini, B. *Opera Omnia*. Edited by E. Susmel and D. Susmel. 44 vols. Florence: La Fenice, 1951–1980.

Sonnino, S. *Quid agendum? Appunti di politica e di economia*. Rome: Direzione della Nuova Antologia, 1900.

2.f *Diaries, memoirs, letters, printed testimonies and printed interviews*

Artieri, G. *Umberto II. Il re gentiluomo: Colloqui sulla fine della monarchia*. Florence: Le Lettere, 2002.

Artom, E. *Diari di un partigiano ebreo (gennaio 1940–febbraio 1944)*. Edited by G. Schwarz. Turin: Bollati Boringhieri, 2008.

Bottai, G. *Diario 1935–1944*. Edited by G. B. Guerri. Milan: Rizzoli, 1982.

Ciano, G. *Diario 1937–1943*. Edited by R. De Felice. 7th ed. Milan: Biblioteca Universale Rizzoli, 2000. First published 1946 by Doubleday.

D'Azeglio, M. *I miei ricordi*. Edited by A. M. Ghisalberti. new ed. Turin: Einaudi, 1971. First published 1949.

Goebbels, J. *The Goebbels Diaries 1942–1943*. Edited and translated by L. P. Lochner. New York: Doubleday, 1948.

Levi, P. *Se questo è un uomo*. 11th ed. Turin: Einaudi, 1981. First published 1956.

Lucifero, F. *L'ultimo Re: I diari del ministro della Real Casa 1944–1946*. Edited by A. Lucifero and F. Perfetti. 2nd ed. Milan: Mondadori, 2003.

Ludwig, E. *Colloqui con Mussolini*. Translated by T. Gnoli. Milan: Mondadori, 1932.

Malvezzi, P., and G. Pirelli, eds. *Lettere di condannati a morte della Resistenza italiana (8 settembre 1943–25 aprile 1945)*. 15th ed. Turin: Einaudi, 1994. First published 1952.

Mazzantini, C. *I Balilla andarono a Salò*. Venice: Marsilio Editori, 1995.

———. *L'ultimo repubblichino: Sessant'anni son passati*. Venice: Marsilio Editori, 2005.

Puntoni, P. *Parla Vittorio Emanuele III*. Bologna: Il Mulino, 1993.

Ruinas, S. *Pioggia sulla Repubblica*. 3rd ed. Rome: Corso, 1979. First published 1946.

2.g *Coeval literature*

Akzin B., M. Ancel, S. Basdevant, M. Caleb, R. Drouillat, M. Gégout, E. Gordon, R. Kiefé, P. de La Pradelle, R. Maunier, B. Mirkine-Guetzévitch, J. Ray. *La nationalité dans la science sociale et dans le droit contemporain*. Paris: Sirey, 1933.

Albrecht-Carrié, R. "Peace with Italy—An Appraisal." *Political Science Quarterly* 62, no. 4 (1947): 481–503.

Alhadeff, V. *L'ordinamento giuridico di Rodi e delle altre isole italiane dell'Egeo*. Milan: Istituto Editoriale Scientifico, 1927.

Almirante, G. "L'editto di Caracalla: Un semi-barbaro spiana la via ai barbari." *La difesa della razza* no. 1 (1938): 27–29.

Ambrosini, G. *Principi fondamentali dell'ordinamento giuridico dell'Impero*. Tivoli: Officine Grafiche Mantero, 1938.

———. "La condizione giuridica dei libici dall'avvento del Fascismo a oggi." *Rivista delle colonie* no. 2 (1939): 169–195.

———. "La condizione giuridica dei libici dall'occupazione all'avvento del Fascismo." *Rivista delle colonie* no. 1 (1939): 75–90.

———. *L'Albania nella comunità imperiale di Roma*. Rome: Istituto Nazionale di Cultura Fascista, 1940.

Ancel, M. "Le changement de nationalité." In Akzin, B., M. Ancel, S. Basdevant, M. Caleb, R. Drouillat, M. Gégout, E. Gordon, R. Kiefé, P. de La Pradelle, R. Maunier, B. Mirkine-Guetzévitch, J. Ray. *La nationalité dans la science sociale et dans le droit contemporain*. 223–274. Paris: Sirey, 1933.

Anzilotti, D. "La formazione del Regno d'Italia nei riguardi del diritto internazionale." *Rivista di diritto internazionale* 1, no. 1 (1912): 1–33.

Ascoli, M. "Political Reconstruction of Italy." *Journal of Politics* 8, no. 3 (1946): 319–328.

Azzolini, G. "Principali lineamenti storici del diritto di cittadinanza in Italia: Periodo moderno." *Lo stato civile italiano* nos. 17–18 (1927): 136–137; nos. 19–20 (1927): 146–148; nos. 23–24 (1927): 179–183.

———. "Principali lineamenti storici del diritto di cittadinanza in Italia: Periodo moderno." *Lo stato civile italiano* nos. 1–2 (1928): 1–6; nos. 3–4 (1928): 22–26; nos. 5–6 (1928): 37–40.

Baty, T. "The History of Canadian Nationality." *Journal of Comparative Legislation and International Law* 18, no. 4 (1936): 195–203.

Bertola, A. "La cittadinanza italiana nelle isole egee." *Rivista coloniale* 1 (1926): 59–68.

———. "Confessione religiosa e statuto personale dei cittadini italiani dell'egeo e libici." *Rivista di diritto pubblico e della pubblica amministrazione in Italia* no. 1 (1934): 100–107.

———. "I meticci nell'ordinamento italiano vigente." *Rivista di diritto pubblico* no. 1 (1941): 492–499.

Biscottini, G. "La condizione giuridica degli italiani non appartenenti alla Repubblica." *Annali della Facoltà Giuridica. Università degli Studi di Camerino* 17–18 (1950): 81–124.

Brunialti, A. *Legge elettorale politica*. Turin: Unione-Tipografica Editrice, 1882.

———. "Gli italiani fuori d'Italia." *La rassegna nazionale* 55 (October 1890): 618–638.

Bufardeci, C. "Gli italiani non regnicoli nel nostro diritto positivo." *Rivista di diritto pubblico* (1923): 601–644.

Businco, L. "La donna depositaria dei caratteri della razza." *La difesa della razza* 1, no. 4 (September 1938): 34–36.

Buzzati, G. C. "Note sulla cittadinanza: La concessione della cittadinanza agli italiani non regnicoli." *Rivista di diritto civile* (1916): 485–506.

Cassuto, D. "Della naturalità concessa per decreto reale." *Archivio Giuridico* 13, no. 2 (1874): 152–171.

Castellani, M. *Les femmes italiennes*. Translated by C. Belin. Rome: Editrice Novissima, 1939.

Cerulli, E. "Il diritto consuetudinario nella Somalia italiana settentrionale: Sultanato dei Migiurtini." *Bollettino della Società Africana d'Italia* no. 3 (1918): 120–137; no. 5 (1918): 216–233; no. 1 (1919): 45–56; no. 4 (1919): 177–195; no. 5 (1919): 231–247; no. 6 (1919): 276–286.

Cicchitti, A. "Il problema religioso nella legislazione coloniale italiana." *Rivista coloniale* 6 (1926): 474–496.

Cipriani, L. "Razzismo coloniale." *La difesa della razza* no. 2 (1938): 18–20.

Colucci, M. *Principi di diritto consuetudinario della Somalia italiana meridionale—I gruppi sociali—La proprietà.* Florence: La Voce, 1924.

Conti Rossini, C. *Principi di diritto consuetudinario dell'Eritrea.* Rome: Tipografia dell'Unione Editrice, 1916.

Crane, L. F. "The Nationality of Married Women." *Journal of Comparative Legislation and International Law* 7, no. 1 (1925): 53–60.

D'Amelio, M. *L'ordinamento giuridico della colonia Eritrea.* Milan: Società Editrice Libraria, 1911.

De Dominicis, F. *Commento alla legge sulla cittadinanza italiana del 13 giugno 1912.* Turin: Unione Tipografico-Editrice Torinese, 1916.

de La Pradelle, P. "De la nationalité d'origine." In Akzin, B., M. Ancel, S. Basdevant, M. Caleb, R. Drouillat, M. Gégout, E. Gordon, R. Kiefé, P. de La Pradelle, R. Maunier, B. Mirkine-Guetzévitch, J. Ray. *La nationalité dans la science sociale et dans le droit contemporain.* 209–222. Paris: Sirey, 1933.

Degni, F. *Della cittadinanza.* Naples: Marghieri; Turin: Unione Tipografico-Editrice Torinese, 1921.

Di Caporiacco, L. "Cittadini e sudditi nel Dodecanneso." *La difesa della razza* no. 15 (1943): 12–13.

Donaggio, A. "Caratteri della romanità." *La difesa della razza* no. 1 (1938): 22–23.

Ebenstein, W. *Fascist Italy.* New York: Russell & Russell, 1973. First published 1939.

Fabbri, A. *Effetti giuridici delle annessioni territoriali con speciale riguardo alle annessioni di Fiume e della Dalmazia nei rapporti Italo-Jugoslavi.* Padova: Casa Editrice Milani, 1931.

Facelli, C. *Saggio sui diritti delle persone: Commento al primo titolo del codice civile italiano, godimento dei diritti civili e cittadinanza.* Turin: Unione Tipografico-Editrice, 1892.

Favilli, V. "L'attuale situazione giuridica internazionale del territorio di Trieste." *Rivista di studi politici internazionali* no. 3 (1950): 339–372.

Folchi, A. E. "Cittadinanza e sudditanza nell'espansione imperiale italiana." *Rivista di diritto pubblico* no. 1 (1939): 53–69.

Fragola, G. *La legge elettorale politica.* Milan: Società Editrice Libraria, 1913.

Gey van Pittius, E. F. W. "'Dominion' Nationality." *Journal of Comparative Legislation and International Law* 13, no. 4 (1931): 199–202.

Gordon, E. "Les cessions de territoires et leurs effets sur la nationalité des habitants." In Akzin, B., M. Ancel, S. Basdevant, M. Caleb, R. Drouillat, M. Gégout, E. Gordon, R. Kiefé, P. de La Pradelle, R. Maunier, B. Mirkine-Guetzévitch, J. Ray. *La nationalité dans la science sociale et dans le droit contemporain.* 127–145. Paris: Sirey, 1933.

Gorrini, G. *La concessione della cittadinanza.* Voghera: G. Gatti, 1890.

Jemolo, A. C. *Chiesa e Stato in Italia negli ultimi cento anni.* rev. ed. Turin: Einaudi, 1990. First published 1948.

Kiefé, R. "L'allégeance." In Akzin, B., M. Ancel, S. Basdevant, M. Caleb, R. Drouillat, M. Gégout, E. Gordon, R. Kiefé, P. de La Pradelle, R. Maunier, B. Mirkine-Guetzévitch, J. Ray. *La nationalité dans la science sociale et dans le droit contemporain.* 47–68. Paris: Sirey, 1933.

Kunz, J. L. "Nationality and Option Clauses in the Italian Peace Treaty of 1947." *American Journal of International Law* 41, no. 3 (1947): 622–631.

Levi, A. *La filosofia politica di Giuseppe Mazzini.* Bologna: Zanichelli, 1922.

Longrigg, S. H. "Disposal of Italian Africa." *International Affairs* 21, no. 3 (1945): 363–369.

Lucatello, G. *La natura giuridica dell'unione italo-albanese.* Padova: Casa editrice Milani, 1943.

McGaw Smyth, H. "Italy: From Fascism to the Republic (1943–1946)." *Western Political Quarterly* 1, no. 3 (1948): 205–222.

Monaco, R. "Caratteri della sudditanza dell'Africa Orientale Italiana." *Rivista di diritto pubblico e della pubblica amministrazione in Italia* no. 1 (1937): 239–247.

Mondaini, G. "Il problema della cittadinanza ai sudditi coloniali." *Rivista delle colonie* no. 1 (1939): 51–73.

———. *La legislazione coloniale italiana nel suo sviluppo storico e nel suo stato attuale (1881–1940).* 2 vols. Milan: Istituto per gli Studi di Politica Internazionale, 1941.

Napier, W. "Nationality in the Succession States of Austria-Hungary." *Transactions of the Grotius Society* 18 (1932): 1–16.

Nelson Gay, H. "Garibaldi's American Contacts and His Claims to American Citizenship." *American Historical Review* 38, no. 1 (1932): 1–19.

Orman Ray, P. "The World-Wide Woman Suffrage Movement." *Journal of Comparative Legislation and International Law* 1, no. 3 (1919): 220–238.

Pandolfo, R. "Valore universale della civiltà fascista." *Gerarchia* no. 4 (1942): 155–158.

Pankhurst, E. S. "Women Under Fascism." *Hibbert Journal: A Quarterly Review of Religion, Theology, and Philosophy* 34, no. 2 (1935–1936): 219–232.

Piccioli, A. "Nel prestigio della razza è la salvaguardia dell'Impero." *La difesa della razza* no. 5 (1938): 26–28.

Piovani, P. "Roma e Tirana." *Gerarchia* no. 9 (1942): 371–373.

Redlich, J. "The Municipality. I. Austria: The Commune System." *Journal of the Society of Comparative Legislation* 8 (1907): 12–40.

Romano, S. "I caratteri giuridici della formazione del Regno d'Italia." *Rivista di diritto internazionale* 1, no. 3 (1912): 337–367.

———. *Corso di diritto coloniale.* Vol. 1. Rome: Athenaeum, 1918.

Salmond, J. W. "Citizenship and Allegiance." *Law Quarterly Review* 17 (1901): 270–282; 18 (1902): 49–63.

Selvi, G. "Le basi dell'ordine nuovo (Parte I)." *Gerarchia* no. 4 (1942): 161–165.

———. "Le basi dell'ordine nuovo (Parte II)." *Gerarchia* no. 5 (1942): 205–208.

Sertoli Salis, R. "L'elemento antropico e il nuovo ordine politico mediterraneo." *Gerarchia* no. 2 (1942): 68–73.

Sherwin-White, A. N. *The Roman Citizenship.* 2nd ed. Oxford: Clarendon Press, 1973. First published 1939.

Steiner, H. A. "The Government of Italian East Africa." *American Political Science Review* 30, no. 5 (1936): 884–902.

Titta, A. "Concetto di 'Spazio Vitale'." *Gerarchia* no. 12 (1941): 646–648.

Toniolo, A. R. "L'unità economica e politica del Mediterraneo." *Geopolitica* no. 3 (1941): 165–169.

Tosti, G. "Studi recenti di diritto capitolare." *Rivista di diritto internazionale* 1, no. 3 (1912): 428–459.

[Un Italiano]. *Il problema politico dell'emigrazione italiana e la questione della cittadinanza.* Rome: Coop. Tipografica Popolo Romano, 1911.

Vanel, M. *Histoire de la nationalité française d'origine: Évolution historique de la notion de Français d'origine du XVI siècle au code civil.* Paris: Ancienne Imprimerie de la Cour d'Appel, 1945.

Villari, S. *La condizione giuridica delle popolazioni coloniali (la cittadinanza adiectitia).* Rome: Casa Editrice Ulpiano, 1939.

———. "Italiani dell'Egeo e sudditi coloniali." *Rivista trimestrale di diritto e di procedura civile* (1950): 668–674.

Werner, A.-R. *Essai sur la réglementation de la nationalité dans le droit colonial français.* Toulouse: Boisseau, 1936.

Willoughby, W. W. "Citizenship and Allegiance in Constitutional and International Law." *American Journal of International Law* 1, no. 4 (1907): 914–929.

3. SECONDARY SOURCES
3.a References

Costanzo, G. A. "Madamato (o delitto di relazione d'indole coniugale con nativi dell'Africa italiana)." In *Novissimo digesto italiano.* Edited by A. Azara and E. Eula. Vol. 10, 11–12. Turin: Unione Tipografico-Editrice Torinese, 1965.

———. "Meticci e meticciato." In *Novissimo digesto italiano.* Edited by A. Azara and E. Eula. Vol. 10, 600–602. Turin: Unione Tipografico-Editrice Torinese, 1965.

———. "Sudditanza e cittadinanza nelle ex colonie italiane." In *Novissimo digesto italiano.* Edited by A. Azara and E. Eula. Vol. 18, 909–912. Turin: Unione Tipografico-Editrice Torinese, 1965.

Enciclopedia del diritto. Vol. 6, 213–217. Varese: Giuffrè Editore, 1960. s.v. "Capitolazioni (Regime delle)."

Enciclopedia del diritto. Vol. 7, 127–159. Varese: Giuffrè Editore, 1960. s.v. "Cittadinanza."

Enciclopedia del diritto. Vol. 24, 103–124. Varese: Giuffrè Editore, 1974. s.v. "Legittimazione dei figli naturali."

Enciclopedia del diritto. Vol. 40, 607–632. Varese: Giuffrè Editore, 1989. s.v. "Riconoscimento del figlio naturale."

Lipartiti, C. "Naturalizzazioni collettive." In *Novissimo digesto italiano.* Edited by A. Azara and E. Eula. Vol. 11, 46–72. Turin: Unione Tipografico-Editrice Torinese, 1965.

New Encyclopaedia Britannica. Vol. 8, 664. Chicago: Encyclopaedia Britannica, 1985. s.v. "Nexum."

Quadri, R. "Cittadinanza." In *Novissimo digesto italiano*. Edited by A. Azara and E. Eula. Vol. 3, 306–335. Turin: Unione Tipografico-Editrice Torinese, 1959.

3.b Literature

Abramovici, P. *Un rocher bien occupé: Monaco pendant la guerre (1939–1945)*. Paris: Seuil, 2001.

Adams, J. C., and P. Barile. *The Government of Republican Italy*. 3rd ed. Boston: Houghton Mifflin, 1972. First published 1961.

Aga Rossi, E. *Una nazione allo sbando: L'armistizio italiano del settembre 1943 e le sue conseguenze*. New and rev. ed. Bologna: Il Mulino, 2003. First published 1993.

Aleinikoff, T. A., and D. Klusmeyer, eds. *From Migrants to Citizens: Membership in a Changing World*. Washington, D.C.: Carnegie Endowment for International Peace, 2000.

Ascoli, U. "Le caratteristiche fondamentali del Welfare State italiano." In *Cittadinanza. Individui, diritti sociali, collettività nella storia contemporanea: Atti del convegno annuale della Società Italiana per lo Studio della Storia Contemporanea (SISSCO), Padova, 2–3 dicembre 1999*. Edited by C. Sorba. 214–224. Rome: Ministero per i Beni e le Attività Culturali—Direzione Generale per gli Archivi, 2002.

Augustine-Adams, K. "'With Notice of the Consequences': Liberal Political Theory, Marriage and Women's Citizenship in the United States." *Citizenship Studies* 6, no. 1 (2002): 5–20.

Baiada, L. "Notturno africano. Libertà sessuale, forze armate, giurisdizione." *Questione Giustizia* 1 (2009): 192–202.

Baldocchi, U., and B. Corbellini Andreotti, eds. *Sudditi e cittadini: Per uno studio della storia costituzionale italiana*. Manduria: P. Lacaita, 1997.

Ballinger, P. "Borders of the Nation, Borders of Citizenship: Italian Repatriation and the Redefinition of National Identity After World War II." *Comparative Studies in Society and History* 49, no. 3 (2007): 713–741.

Ballini, P. L. "Il referendum del 2 giugno 1946." In *Almanacco della Repubblica: Storia d'Italia attraverso le tradizioni, le istituzioni e le simbologie repubblicane*. Edited by M. Ridolfi. 222–229. Milan: Mondadori, 2003.

Barbagallo, F. "Italy: The Idea and the Reality of the Nation." *Journal of Modern Italian Studies* 6, no. 3 (2001): 388–401.

Bariatti, S. *La disciplina giuridica della cittadinanza italiana*. 2 vols. Milan: Giuffrè Editore, 1989–1996.

Barrera, G. "Patrilinearità, razza e identità: L'educazione degli Italo-eritrei durante il colonialismo italiano (1885–1934)." *Quaderni storici* 109, no. 1 (2002), 21–53.

———. "Mussolini's Colonial Race Laws and State-Settler Relations in Africa Orientale Italiana (1935–1941)." *Journal of Modern Italian Studies* 8, no. 3 (2003): 425–443.

———. "Sex, Citizenship and the State: The Construction of the Public and Private Spheres in Colonial Eritrea." In *Gender, Family and Sexuality: The Private Sphere in Italy, 1860-1945*. Edited by P. Willson. 157–172. New York, Basingstoke: Palgrave Macmillan, 2004.

————. "Patrilinearity, Race and Identity: The Upbringing of Italo-Eritreans During Italian Colonialism." In *Italian Colonialism*. Edited by R. Ben-Ghiat and M. Fuller. 97–108. New York, Basingstoke: Palgrave Macmillan, 2005.

Bauböck, R. *Transnational Citizenship: Membership and Rights in International Migration*. Aldershot: Edward Elgar, 1994.

————. "The Rights and Duties of External Citizenship." *Citizenship Studies* 13, no. 5 (2009): 475–499.

Beiner, R., ed. *Theorizing Citizenship*. Albany: State University of New York Press, 1995.

Bellamy, R. "Evaluating Union Citizenship: Belonging, Rights and Participation Within the EU." *Citizenship Studies* 12, no. 6 (2008): 597–611.

Ben-Ghiat, R., and M. Fuller, eds. *Italian Colonialism*. New York, Basingstoke: Palgrave Macmillan, 2005.

Berger, S. "A Return to the National Paradigm? National History Writing in Germany, Italy, France, and Britain from 1945 to the Present." *Journal of Modern History* 77 (2005): 629–678.

Bessel, R., ed. *Fascist Italy and Nazi Germany: Comparisons and Contrasts*. Cambridge: Cambridge University Press, 1997.

Bhabha, J., and S. Shutter. *Women's Movement: Women Under Immigration, Nationality and Refugee Law*. London: Trentham Books, 1994.

Bhabha, J., F. Klug and S. Shutter, eds. *Worlds Apart: Women Under Immigration and Nationality Law*. London: Pluto Press, 1985.

Biscaretti di Ruffià, P. "Problemi, antichi e nuovi, circa la natura giuridica del 'procedimento di formazione' dello Stato Italiano." *Rivista trimestrale di diritto pubblico* no. 1 (1962): 3–21.

Bobbio, N. *Dal fascismo alla democrazia: I regimi, le ideologie, le figure e le culture politiche*. Edited by M. Bovero. Milan: Baldini & Castoldi, 1997.

Bock, G. "Racisme, stérilisation obligatoire et maternité sous le national-socialisme." In *Femmes et Fascismes*. Edited by R. Thalmann. 99–113. Paris: Tierce, 1986.

————. "Anti-Natalism, Maternity and Paternity in National Socialist Racism." In *Maternity and Gender Policies: Women and the Rise of the European Welfare States, 1880s–1950s*. Edited by G. Bock and P. Thane. 233–255. London, New York: Routledge, 1991.

Bock, G., and P. Thane. "Introduction." In *Maternity and Gender Policies: Women and the Rise of the European Welfare States, 1880s–1950s*. Edited by G. Bock and P. Thane. 1–20. London, New York: Routledge, 1991.

Bock, G., and P. Thane, eds. *Maternity and Gender Policies: Women and the Rise of the European Welfare States, 1880s–1950s*. London, New York: Routledge, 1991.

Bollati, G. *L'Italiano: Il carattere nazionale come storia e come invenzione*. Turin: Einaudi, 1996.

Bonifazi, C. *L'immigrazione straniera in Italia*. Bologna: Il Mulino, 2007.

Bordes-Benayoun, C., and D. Schnapper. "Entretien: Les mots des diasporas." *Diasporas: Histoire et sociétés* 13, second semester (2008): 11–19.

Bosworth, R. J. B., and S. Romano, eds. *La politica estera italiana (1860–1985)*. Bologna: Il Mulino, 1991.

Brazzo, L. "Dall'Impero agli stati: Gli ebrei nei Balcani e in Albania fra la seconda metà dell'Ottocento e la vigilia della seconda guerra mondiale." In *Gli ebrei in Albania sotto il fascismo: Una storia da ricostruire.* Edited by L. Brazzo and M. Sarfatti. 13–60. Florence: Giuntina, 2010.

Brazzo, L., and M. Sarfatti, eds. *Gli ebrei in Albania sotto il fascismo: Una storia da ricostruire.* Florence: Giuntina, 2010.

Bredbenner, C. L. *A Nationality of Her Own: Women, Marriage, and the Law of Citizenship.* Berkeley: University of California Press, 1998.

Bridenthal, R., C. Koonz and S. Stuard, eds. *Becoming Visible: Women in European History.* Boston: Houghton Mifflin, 1987.

Brochmann, G., and I. Seland. "Citizenship Policies and Ideas of Nationhood in Scandinavia." *Citizenship Studies* 14, no. 4 (2010): 429–443.

Brubaker, R., ed. *Immigration and the Politics of Citizenship in Europe and North America.* New York, London: University Press of America, 1989.

———. *Citizenship and Nationhood in France and Germany.* London, Cambridge, Mass.: Harvard University Press, 1992.

———. "Myths and Misconceptions in the Study of Nationalism." In *National Self-Determination and Secession.* Edited by M. Moore. 233–265. Oxford: Oxford University Press, 1998.

———. "The Manichean Myth: Rethinking the Distinction between 'Civic' and 'Ethnic' Nationalism." In *Nation and National Identity: The European Experience in Perspective.* Edited by H. Kriesi, K. Armingeon, H. Siegrist and A. Wimmer. 55–71. Chur, Zurich: Verlag Rüegger, 1999.

Burgio, A., ed. *Nel nome della razza: Il razzismo nella storia d'Italia 1870–1945.* 2nd ed. Bologna: Il Mulino, 2000.

Burrin, P. *Fascisme, nazisme, autoritarisme.* Paris: Editions du Seuil, 2000.

———. "Fascisme, nazisme et génocide." In *Les sociétés en guerre: 1911–1946.* Edited by B. Cabanes and E. Husson. 151–173. Paris: Armand Colin, 2003.

Bussotti, L. *La cittadinanza degli italiani: Analisi storica e critica sociologica di una questione irrisolta.* Milan: Franco Angeli, 2002.

Buttafuoco, A. "Motherhood as a Political Strategy: The Role of the Italian Women's Movement in the Creation of the *Cassa Nazionale di Maternità.*" In *Maternity and Gender Policies: Women and the Rise of the European Welfare States, 1880s–1950s.* Edited by G. Bock and P. Thane. 178–195. London, New York: Routledge, 1991.

Cabanes, B., and E. Husson, eds. *Les sociétés en guerre: 1911–1946.* Paris: Armand Colin, 2003.

Camera dei Deputati. *Cinquanta anni dal voto alle donne (1945–1995): Atti del convegno svoltosi alla Camera dei Deputati il 24 febbraio 1995 e documentazione allegata.* Rome: Camera dei Deputati, 1996.

Candeloro, G. *Storia dell'Italia moderna.* Vol. 4. Milan: Feltrinelli, 1977.

Capristo, A. "L'esclusione degli Ebrei dall'Accademia d'Italia." *La rassegna mensile di Israel* 67, no. 3 (2001): 1–36.

Capuzzo, E. "Sudditanza e cittadinanza nell'esperienza coloniale italiana dell'età liberale." *Clio* 31, no. 1 (1995): 65–95.

Caramani, D. *The Societies of Europe: Elections in Western Europe since 1815.* Basingstoke, Oxford: Macmillan, 2000.

Cardoza, A. "Cavour and Piedmont." In *Italy in the Nineteenth Century 1796–1900*. Edited by J. A. Davis. 108–131. Oxford: Oxford University Press, 2000.

Carens, J. H. "Membership and Morality: Admission to Citizenship in Liberal Democratic States." In *Immigration and the Politics of Citizenship in Europe and North America*. Edited by R. Brubaker. 31–49. New York, London: University Press of America, 1989.

Caroli, B. B., R. F. Harney and L. F. Tomasi, eds. *The Italian Immigrant Woman in North America: Proceedings of the Tenth Annual Conference of the American Italian Historical Association held in Toronto, Ontario (Canada), October 28 and 29, 1977, in conjunction with the Canadian Italian Historical Association*. Toronto: Multicultural History Society of Ontario, 1978.

Castels, S., and M. J. Miller. *The Age of Migration*. New York: Palgrave Macmillan, 2003.

Cassata, F. *Molti, sani e forti: L'eugenetica in Italia*. Turin: Bollati Boringhieri, 2006.

Catalano, F. *Storia d'Italia*. Vol. 5, *Dalla crisi del primo dopoguerra alla fondazione della repubblica*. Turin: Unione Tipografico-Editrice Torinese, 1965.

Cerase, F. P. "Economia precaria ed emigrazione." In *Un secolo di emigrazione italiana 1876–1976*. Edited by G. Rosoli. 117–152. Rome: Centro Studi Emigrazione, 1978.

Cesarani, D. "The Changing Character of Citizenship and Nationality in Britain." In *Citizenship, Nationality and Migration in Europe*. Edited by D. Cesarani and M. Fulbrook. 57–73. London, New York: Routledge, 1996.

Cesarani, D., and M. Fulbrook, eds. *Citizenship, Nationality and Migration in Europe*. London, New York: Routledge, 1996.

Chabod, F. *Storia della politica estera italiana dal 1870 al 1896*. Vol. 1. Bari: Laterza, 1951.

———. *L'idea di nazione*. Edited by A. Saitta and E. Sestan. Rome, Bari: Laterza, 1998. First published 1961.

Chastagnol, A. "*Coloni* et *Incolae*. Note sur les différenciations sociales à l'intérieur des colonies romaines de peuplement dans les provinces de l'Occident (Ier siècle av. J.-C.—Ier siècle ap. J.-C.)." In *Splendidissima Civitas: Études d'histoire romaine en hommage à François Jacques*. Edited by A. Chastagnol, S. Demougin and C. Lepelley. 13–25. Paris: Publications de la Sorbonne, 1996.

Chianese, G. "I monarchici nella Repubblica." In *Almanacco della Repubblica: Storia d'Italia attraverso le tradizioni, le istituzioni e le simbologie repubblicane*. Edited by M. Ridolfi. 262–273. Milan: Mondadori, 2003.

Choate, M. I. *Emigrant Nation: The Making of Italy Abroad*. Cambridge, Mass., London: Harvard University Press, 2008.

Clerici, R. *La cittadinanza nell'ordinamento giuridico italiano*. Padova: Cedam, 1993.

Coli, D. *Giovanni Gentile*. Bologna: Il Mulino, 2004.

Collotti, E. *Il fascismo e gli ebrei: Le leggi razziali in Italia*. Rome, Bari: Laterza, 2003.

———, T. Sala and G. Vaccarino, eds. *L'Italia nell'Europa danubiana durante la seconda guerra mondiale*. Milan: Istituto Nazionale per la Storia del Movimento di Liberazione, 1967.

Conover, P. J. "Citizenship Identities and Conceptions of the Self." *Journal of Political Philosophy* 3, no. 2 (1995): 133–165.

Costa, P. *Civitas: Storia della cittadinanza in Europa.* 2 vols. Rome, Bari: Laterza, 1999.

———. "Il discorso della cittadinanza in Europa: Ipotesi di lettura." In *Cittadinanza. Individui, diritti sociali, collettività nella storia contemporanea: Atti del convegno annuale della Società Italiana per lo Studio della Storia Contemporanea (SISSCO), Padova, 2–3 dicembre 1999.* Edited by C. Sorba. 12–37. Rome: Ministero per i Beni e le Attività Culturali—Direzione Generale per gli Archivi, 2002.

Cott, N. F. "Marriage and Women's Citizenship in the United States, 1830–1934." *American Historical Review* 103, no. 5 (1998): 1440–1474.

Coudry, G. "Note sur le 'passeport Nansen'." *Matériaux pour l'histoire de notre temps* no. 44 (October–December 1996): 19–21.

Czarnowski, G. "The Value of Marriage for the *Volksgemeinschaft*: Policies Towards Women and Marriage Under National Socialism." In *Fascist Italy and Nazi Germany: Comparisons and Contrasts.* Edited by R. Bessel. 94–112. Cambridge: Cambridge University Press, 1996.

Davis, J. A. "Economy, Society, and the State." In *Italy in the Nineteenth Century 1796–1900.* Edited by J. A. Davis. 235–263. New York: Oxford University Press, 2000.

———, ed. *Italy in the Nineteenth Century 1796–1900.* New York: Oxford University Press, 2000.

De Donno, F. "La Razza Ario-Mediterranea. Ideas of Race and Citizenship in Colonial and Fascist Italy, 1885–1941." *Interventions* 8, no. 3 (2006): 394–412.

De Felice, R. *Storia degli ebrei italiani sotto il fascismo.* rev. ed. Turin: Einaudi, 1993. First published 1961.

———. *Rosso e Nero.* Edited by P. Chessa. 3rd ed. Milan: Baldini & Castoldi, 1995.

———. *Mussolini l'alleato.* 2 vols. Turin: Einaudi, 1997.

De Grand, A. "Women Under Italian Fascism." *Historical Journal* 19, no. 4 (1976): 947–968.

De Grazia, V. *How Fascism Ruled Women: Italy, 1922–1945.* Berkeley, Los Angeles and Oxford: University of California Press, 1992.

De Rosa, L. "Italian Emigration in the Post-Unification Period, 1861–1971." In *European Expansion and Migration: Essays on the Intercontinental Migration from Africa, Asia, and Europe.* Edited by P. C. Emmer and M. Mörner. 157–178. New York, Oxford: Berg, 1992.

Deakin, F. W. *The Brutal Friendship: Mussolini, Hitler and the Fall of Italian Fascism.* rev. ed. London: Phoenix Press, 2000. First published 1962.

Del Boca, A. *Gli italiani in Africa Orientale.* 4 vols. Rome, Bari: Biblioteca Universale Laterza, 1985–1986. First published 1976–1982.

———. *Gli italiani in Libia: Dal fascismo a Gheddafi.* Rome, Bari: Biblioteca Universale Laterza, 1991. First published 1988.

———. *Gli italiani in Libia: Tripoli bel suol d'amore 1860–1922.* Milan: Oscar Mondadori, 1993. First published 1986 by Laterza.

————. "Le leggi razziali nell'impero di Mussolini." In *Il regime fascista: Storia e storiografia*. Edited by A. Del Boca, M. Legnani and M. G. Rossi. 329–351. Rome, Bari: Laterza, 1995.

————. *L'Africa nella coscienza degli italiani: Miti, memorie, errori, sconfitte*. Milan: Mondadori, 2002.

————, M. Legnani and M. G. Rossi, eds. *Il regime fascista: Storia e storiografia*. Rome, Bari: Laterza, 1995.

Del Re, A. "Le genre comme paradigme de la citoyenneté." In *Citoyenneté(s): Perspectives internationales*. Edited by M. Spensky. 131–144. Clermont-Ferrand: Presses Universitaires Blaise Pascal, 2003.

Diamanti, I. *Il male del Nord: Lega, localismo, secessione*. Rome: Donzelli editore, 1996.

Dieckhoff, A. "La déconstruction d'une illusion: L'introuvable opposition entre nationalisme politique et nationalisme culturel." *L'année sociologique* 46, no. 1 (1996): 43–55.

Donati, P. *La cittadinanza societaria*. Rome, Bari: Laterza, 2000.

Donati, S. "'La Ligue Nord pour l'Indépendance de la Padanie': Entre séparatisme et fédéralisme." *Revue militaire suisse*, October 2010: 56–60.

Duggan, C. "Politics in the Era of Depretis and Crispi, 1870–1896." In *Italy in the Nineteenth Century 1796–1900*. Edited by J. A. Davis. 154–180. Oxford: University Press, 2000.

Dummett, A., and A. Nicol. *Subjects, Citizens, Aliens and Others: Nationality and Immigration Law*. London: Weidenfeld and Nicolson, 1990.

Duroselle, J. B. *Le conflit de Trieste 1943–1954*. Brussels: Editions de l'Institut de Sociologie de l'Université Libre, 1966.

Eder, K., and B. Giesen, eds. *European Citizenship Between National Legacies and Postnational Projects*. Oxford: Oxford University Press, 2003.

Edwards, C. "Introduction: Shadows and Fragments." In *Roman Presences: Receptions of Rome in European Culture, 1789–1945*. Edited by C. Edwards. 1–18. Cambridge: Cambridge University Press, 1999.

————, ed. *Roman Presences: Receptions of Rome in European Culture, 1789–1945*. Cambridge: Cambridge University Press, 1999.

Einaudi, L. *Le politiche dell'immigrazione in Italia dall'unità a oggi*. Rome, Bari: Laterza, 2007.

Eley, G. "Some General Thoughts on Citizenship in Germany." In *Citizenship and National Identity in Twentieth-Century Germany*. Edited by G. Eley and J. Palmowski. 233–246. Stanford: Stanford University Press.

————, and J. Palmowski, eds. *Citizenship and National Identity in Twentieth-Century Germany*. Stanford: Stanford University Press, 2008.

Emmer, P. C., and M. Mörner, eds. *European Expansion and Migration: Essays on the Intercontinental Migration from Africa, Asia, and Europe*. New York, Oxford: Berg, 1992.

Fahrmeir, A. "Nineteenth-Century German Citizenships: A Reconsideration." *Historical Journal* 40, no. 3 (1997): 721–752.

————. *Citizens and Aliens: Foreigners and the Law in Britain and the German States, 1789–1870*. London, New York: Berghahn Books, 2000.

Favero, L., and G. Tassello. "Cent'anni di emigrazione italiana (1876–1976)." In *Un secolo di emigrazione italiana 1876–1976*. Edited by G. Rosoli. 9–64. Rome: Centro Studi Emigrazione, 1978.

Feldblum, M. *Reconstructing Citizenship: The Politics of Nationality Reform and Immigration in Contemporary France*. Albany: State University of New York Press, 1999.

Fischer, B. J. *Albania at War, 1939–1945*. West Lafayette, Ind.: Purdue University Press, 1999.

Franchi, F. *Le costituzioni della Repubblica Sociale Italiana*. Rome: Edizioni Settimo Sigillo, 1997.

Fulbrook, M. "Germany for the Germans? Citizenship and Nationality in a Divided Nation." In *Citizenship, Nationality and Migration in Europe*. Edited by D. Cesarani and M. Fulbrook. 88–105. London, New York: Routledge, 1996.

Gabaccia, D. R. *Italy's Many Diasporas*. London: UCL Press, 2000.

Gabrielli, G. "Un aspetto della politica razzista nell'impero: Il 'problema dei meticci'." *Passato e presente* 15, no. 41 (1997), 77–105.

———. "Africani in Italia negli anni del razzismo di stato." In *Nel nome della razza: Il razzismo nella storia d'Italia 1870–1945*. Edited by A. Burgio. 201–212. Bologna: Il Mulino, 2000.

Galli della Loggia, E. *L'identità italiana*. Bologna: Il Mulino, 1998.

———. *La morte della patria: La crisi dell'idea di nazione tra Resistenza, antifascismo e Repubblica*. 3rd ed. Rome, Bari: Laterza, 2003. First published 1996.

Gambino, A. *Storia del dopoguerra dalla Liberazione al potere DC*. Rome, Bari: Laterza, 1978.

Ganapini, L. *La repubblica della camicie nere: I combattenti, i politici, gli amministratori, i socializzatori*. Milan: Garzanti, 2002.

Garland, A. N., and H. McGaw Smyth. *Sicily and the Surrender of Italy*. Washington, D.C.: Office of the Chief of Military History, 1965.

Gentile, E. "Fascism as Political Religion." *Journal of Contemporary History* 25, nos. 2-3 (1990): 229–251.

———. *Il culto del littorio: La sacralizzazione della politica nell'Italia fascista*. Rome, Bari: Economica Laterza, 2001. First published 1993.

Ghisalberti, C. *Storia costituzionale d'Italia 1848–1994*. new ed. Rome, Bari: Laterza, 2002. First published 1974.

———. *Unità nazionale e unificazione giuridica in Italia: La codificazione del diritto nel Risorgimento*. 9th ed. Rome, Bari: Laterza, 2002. First published 1979.

Giannini, M. S. "La Repubblica Sociale Italiana rispetto allo Stato italiano." *Rivista italiana per le scienze giuridiche* (1951): 330–417.

Giardina, A., and A. Vauchez. *Il mito di Roma: Da Carlo Magno a Mussolini*. Rome, Bari: Laterza, 2000.

Gillette, A. *Racial Theories in Fascist Italy*. London, New York: Routledge, 2002.

Gini, C., and E. Caranti. "The Family in Italy." *Marriage and Family Living* 16, no. 4 (1954): 350–361.

Goglia, L. "Note sul razzismo coloniale fascista." *Storia contemporanea* 19, no. 6 (1988): 1223–1266.

Goldberg, D. T., ed. *Anatomy of Racism*. Minneapolis: University of Minnesota Press, 1990.

Goodwin-Gill, G. S. *International Law and the Movement of Persons Between States*. Oxford: Clarendon Press, 1978.

Gosewinkel, D. "Citizenship, Subjecthood, Nationality: Concepts of Belonging in the Age of Modern Nation States." In *European Citizenship Between National Legacies and Postnational Projects*. Edited by K. Eder and B. Giesen. 17–35. Oxford: Oxford University Press, 2003.

———. "Citizenship in Germany and France at the Turn of the Twentieth Century: Some New Observations on an Old Comparison." In *Citizenship and National Identity in Twentieth-Century Germany*. Edited by G. Eley and J. Palmowski. 27–39. Stanford: Stanford University Press, 2008.

Goussot, A. "Alcune tappe della critica al razzismo: Le riflessioni di G. Mazzini, N. Colajanni e A. Ghisleri." In *Nel nome della razza: Il razzismo nella storia d'Italia 1870–1945*. Edited by A. Burgio. 129–142. Bologna: Il Mulino, 2000.

Grew, R. "Culture and Society, 1796–1896." In *Italy in the Nineteenth Century 1796–1900*. Edited by J. A. Davis. 206–234. New York: Oxford University Press, 2000.

Grosso, E. *Le vie della cittadinanza: Le grandi radici, i modelli storici di riferimento*. Padova: Cedam, 1997.

Guild, E. "The Legal Framework of Citizenship of the European Union." In *Citizenship, Nationality and Migration in Europe*. Edited by D. Cesarani and M. Fulbrook. 14–49. London, New York: Routledge, 1996.

Hammar, T. *Democracy and the Nation-State: Aliens, Denizens, and Citizens in a World of International Migration*. Aldershot: Avebury, 1990.

Heater, D. B. *Citizenship: The Civic Ideal in World History, Politics, and Education*. London, New York: Longman, 1990.

Honess, C. "Feminine Virtues and Florentine Vices: Citizenship and Morality in *Paradiso* XV–XVII." In *Dante and Governance*. Edited by J. Woodhouse. 102–120. Oxford: Clarendon Press, 1997.

Howard, J. J. "The Civil Code of 1865 and the Origins of the Feminist Movement in Italy." In *The Italian Immigrant Woman in North America: Proceedings of the Tenth Annual Conference of the American Italian Historical Association held in Toronto, Ontario (Canada), October 28 and 29, 1977, in conjunction with the Canadian Italian Historical Association*. Edited by B. B. Caroli, R. F. Harney and L. F. Tomasi. 14–22. Toronto: Multicultural History Society of Ontario, 1978.

Huntford, R. *Nansen: The Explorer as Hero*. London: Abacus, 1997.

Isnenghi, M. "Il mito di potenza." In *Il regime fascista: Storia e storiografia*. Edited by A. Del Boca, M. Legnani and M. G. Rossi. 139–150. Rome, Bari: Laterza, 1995.

Iyob, R. "*Madamismo* and Beyond: The Construction of Eritrean Women." In *Italian Colonialism*. Edited by R. Ben-Ghiat and M. Fuller. 233–244. New York, Basingstoke: Palgrave Macmillan, 2005.

Joll, J. *Europe Since 1870: An International History*. London: Penguin Books, 1990.

Keefer, L. E. *Italian Prisoners of War in America, 1942–1946: Captives or Allies?* New York: Praeger, 1992.

Kertzer, D. I. "Religion and Society, 1789–1892." In *Italy in the Nineteenth Century 1796–1900.* Edited by J. A. Davis. 181–205. Oxford: Oxford University Press, 2000.

———. *The Popes Against the Jews: The Vatican's Role in the Rise of Modern Anti-Semitism.* New York: Vintage Books, 2002.

Koenig-Archibugi, M. "National and European Citizenship: The Italian Case in Historical Perspective." *Citizenship Studies* 7, no. 1 (2003): 85–109.

Kogan, N. *Italy and the Allies.* Cambridge, Mass.: Harvard University Press, 1956.

Koonz, C. "The Fascist Solution to the Woman Question in Italy and in Germany." In *Becoming Visible: Women in European History.* Edited by R. Bridenthal, C. Koonz and S. Stuard. 499–533. Boston: Houghton Mifflin, 1987.

Kymlicka, W. *Multicultural Citizenship: A Liberal Theory of Minority Rights.* Oxford, New York: Clarendon Press, 1995.

———, and W. Norman. "Return of the Citizen: A Survey of Recent Work on Citizenship Theory." *Ethics* 104, no. 1 (1994): 352–381.

———, eds. *Citizenship in Diverse Societies.* Oxford: Oxford University Press, 2000.

Labanca, N. "Il razzismo coloniale italiano." In *Nel nome della razza: Il razzismo nella storia d'Italia 1870–1945.* Edited by A. Burgio. 145–163. Bologna: Il Mulino, 2000.

———. "Italian Colonial Internment." In *Italian Colonialism.* Edited by R. Ben-Ghiat and M. Fuller. 27–36. New York: Palgrave Macmillan, 2005.

Le Cour Grandmaison, O., and C. Wihtol de Wenden, eds. *Les étrangers dans la cité: Expériences européennes.* Paris: La Découverte, 1993.

Lewis, J. "Models of Equality for Women: The Case of State Support for Children in Twentieth-Century Britain." In *Maternity and Gender Policies: Women and the Rise of the European Welfare States, 1880s–1950s.* Edited by G. Bock and P. Thane. 73–92. London, New York: Routledge, 1991.

Löfström, J. "Historical Apologies as Acts of Symbolic Inclusion—and Exclusion? Reflections on Institutional Apologies as Politics of Cultural Citizenship." *Citizenship Studies* 15, no. 1 (2011): 93–108.

MacIntyre, A. "Is Patriotism a Virtue?" In *Theorizing Citizenship.* Edited by R. Beiner. 209–228. Albany: State University of New York Press, 1995.

Mack Smith, D. *Italy and Its Monarchy.* New Haven, London: Yale University Press, 1989.

———. *Modern Italy: A Political History.* New Haven, London: Yale University Press, 1997.

Magnette, P. *La citoyenneté: Une histoire de l'idée de participation civique.* Brussels: Bruylant, 2001.

Marshall, T. H. *Class, Citizenship and Social Development: Essays.* With an introduction by S. M. Lipset. Garden City, N.Y.: Doubleday, 1964.

———. "Citizenship and Social Class." In *The Citizenship Debates: A Reader.* Edited by G. Shafir. 93–111. Minneapolis, London: University of Minnesota Press, 1998.

Martiniello, M. "Citizenship of the European Union." In *From Migrants to Citizens: Membership in a Changing World*. Edited by T. A. Aleinikoff and D. Klusmeyer. 342–380. Washington, D.C.: Carnegie Endowment for International Peace, 2000.

Mehta, U. S. *Liberalism and Empire: A Study in Nineteenth-Century British Liberal Thought*. Chicago, London: University of Chicago Press, 1999.

Meldini, P. *Sposa e madre esemplare: Ideologia e politica della donna e della famiglia durante il fascismo*. Rimini, Florence: Guaraldi Editore, 1975.

Miccoli, G. "Santa Sede, 'Questione Ebraica' e Anti-Semitismo alla fine dell'Ottocento." In *Nel nome della razza: Il razzismo nella storia d'Italia 1870–1945*. Edited by A. Burgio. 215–246. Bologna: Il Mulino, 2000.

Monsagrati, G. "La Repubblica romana del 1849." In *Almanacco della Repubblica: Storia d'Italia attraverso le tradizioni, le istituzioni e le simbologie repubblicane*. Edited by M. Ridolfi. 84–96. Milan: Mondadori, 2003.

Moore, B. "Turning Liabilities into Assets: British Government Policy Towards German and Italian Prisoners of War During the Second World War." *Journal of Contemporary History* 32, no. 1 (1997): 117–136.

Morozzo della Rocca, R. *Nazione e religione in Albania (1920–1944)*. Bologna: Il Mulino, 1990.

Noether, E. P. "Italian Women and Fascism: A Reevaluation." *Italian Quarterly* (Fall 1982): 69–80.

Novak, C. B. *Trieste 1941–1954: The Ethnic, Political and Ideological Struggle*. Chicago, London: University of Chicago Press, 1970.

Oldfield, A. *Citizenship and Community: Civic Republicanism and the Modern World*. London: Routledge, 1990.

Oliva, G. *Le tre Italie del 1943: Chi ha veramente combattuto la guerra civile*. Milan: Mondadori, 2004.

Page Baldwin, M. "Subject to Empire: Married Women and the British Nationality and Status of Aliens Act." *Journal of British Studies* 40, no. 4 (2001): 522–556.

Palermo, I. *Storia di un armistizio*. Milan: Mondadori, 1967.

Pastore, F. "Droit de la nationalité et migrations internationales: Le cas italien." In *Nationalité et citoyenneté en Europe*. Edited by P. Weil and R. Hansen. 95–116. Paris: La Découverte, 1999.

———. "A Community out of Balance: Nationality Law and Migration Politics in the History of Post-Unification Italy." *Journal of Modern Italian Studies* 9, no. 1 (2004): 27–48.

Pateman, C. *The Disorder of Women: Democracy, Feminism and Political Theory*. Stanford: Stanford University Press, 1989.

Patriarca, S. *Italianità: La costruzione del carattere nazionale*. Rome, Bari: Laterza, 2010.

Pavone, C. *Una guerra civile: Saggio storico sulla moralità nella Resistenza*. Turin: Bollati Boringhieri, 2003. First published 1991.

———. *Alle origini della Repubblica: Scritti su fascismo, antifascismo e continuità dello stato*. Turin: Bollati Boringhieri, 1995.

Penrose, J., and J. May. "Herder's Concept of Nation and Its Relevance to Contemporary Ethnic Nationalism." *Canadian Review of Studies in Nationalism* 18, nos. 1–2 (1991): 165–178.

Perfetti, F. "Vittorio Emanuele, Umberto e il '25 Luglio' mancato." *Nuova storia contemporanea* no. 5 (2002): 31–40.

———. "I voti nulli, le schede bianche e il referendum istituzionale. Un parere di Giovanni Leone sulla questione del 'quorum'." *Nuova storia contemporanea* no. 5 (2002): 83–90.

Pertici, R. "Storici italiani del Novecento." *Storiografia: Rivista annuale di storia* 3 (1999): 7–53.

Petronio, G. *L'attività letteraria in Italia: Storia della letteratura.* Florence: Palumbo, 1980.

Picciotto Fargion, L. *Il libro della memoria: Gli ebrei deportati dall'Italia (1943–1945).* Milan: Mursia, 1991.

———. "The Persecution of the Jews in Italy, 1943–1945: A Chronicle of Events." In *The Jews of Italy: Memory and Identity.* Edited by B. D. Cooperman and B. Garvin. 443–454. Bethesda: University Press of Maryland, 2000.

Pick, D. *Faces of Degeneration: A European Disorder, c. 1848–c. 1918.* Cambridge: Cambridge University Press, 1996.

Pignataro, L. *Il Dodecaneso italiano (1912–1947).* Vol. 1. *Lineamenti giuridici: L'occupazione iniziale (1912–1922).* Chieti: Edizioni Solfanelli, 2011.

Pocock, J. G. A. "The Ideal of Citizenship Since Classical Times." In *The Citizenship Debates: A Reader.* Edited by G. Shafir. 31–41. Minneapolis, London: University of Minnesota Press, 1998.

Poggio, P. P. "Unificazione nazionale e differenza razziale." In *Nel nome della razza: Il razzismo nella storia d'Italia 1870–1945.* Edited by A. Burgio. 87–94. Bologna: Il Mulino, 2000.

Pogliano, C. "Scienza e stirpe: Eugenica in Italia (1912–1939)." *Passato e presente* no. 5 (1984): 61–97.

———. "Eugenisti, ma con giudizio." In *Nel nome della razza: Il razzismo nella storia d'Italia 1870–1945.* Edited by A. Burgio. 423–442. Bologna: Il Mulino, 2000.

Pombeni, P. "La Costituente." In *Almanacco della Repubblica: Storia d'Italia attraverso le tradizioni, le istituzioni e le simbologie repubblicane.* Edited by M. Ridolfi. 230–239. Milan: Mondadori, 2003.

Presidenza del Consiglio dei Ministri, ed. *La nascita della Repubblica: Atti del convegno di studi storici (Roma, 4–5–6 giugno 1987).* Rome: Presidenza del Consiglio dei Ministri, 1987.

Pryke, S. "Nationalism and Sexuality, What Are the Issues?" *Nations and Nationalism* 4, no. 4 (1998): 529–546.

Pupo, R. *Il lungo esodo. Istria: Le persecuzioni, le foibe, l'esilio.* Milan: Biblioteca Universale Rizzoli, 2005.

Raspanti, M. "Il mito ariano nella cultura italiana fra Otto e Novecento." In *Nel nome della razza: Il razzismo nella storia d'Italia 1870–1945.* Edited by A. Burgio. 75–85. Bologna: Il Mulino, 2000.

Rawls, J. "Justice as Fairness in the Liberal Polity." In *The Citizenship Debates: A Reader.* Edited by G. Shafir. 53–72. Minneapolis, London: University of Minnesota Press, 1998.

Reeskens, T., and M. Hooghe. "Beyond the Civic-Ethnic Dichotomy: Investigating the Structure of Citizenship Concepts Across Thirty-Three Countries." *Nations and Nationalism* 16, no. 4 (2010): 579–597.

Reposo, A. "Gli italiani non appartenenti alla Repubblica (vecchi e nuovi problemi)." *Diritto e Società* 4 (1973): 906–927.

Riall, L. "Garibaldi and the South." In *Italy in the Nineteenth Century 1796–1900*. Edited by J. A. Davis. 132–153. Oxford: Oxford University Press, 2000.

Ricci, A. G. *La Repubblica*. Bologna: Il Mulino, 2001.

Rich, N. *Great Power Diplomacy, 1814–1914*. New York, London: McGraw-Hill, 1992.

Ridolfi, M., ed. *Almanacco della Repubblica: Storia d'Italia attraverso le tradizioni, le istituzioni e le simbologie repubblicane*. Milan: Mondadori, 2003.

Riesenberg, P. *Citizenship in the Western Tradition: Plato to Rousseau*. Chapel Hill: University of North Carolina Press, 1992.

Rochat, G. *Il colonialismo italiano*. Turin: Loescher, 1973.

———. "The Italian Air Force in the Ethiopian War (1935–1936)." In *Italian Colonialism*. Edited by R. Ben-Ghiat and M. Fuller. 37–46. New York: Palgrave Macmillan, 2005.

Rodogno, D. *Il nuovo ordine mediterraneo: Le politiche di occupazione dell'Italia fascista in Europa (1940–1943)*. Turin: Bollati Boringhieri, 2003.

———. "Italiani brava gente? Fascist Italy's Policy Toward the Jews in the Balkans, April 1941–July 1943." *European History Quarterly* 35, no. 2 (2005): 213–240.

Roggero, M. "The Meaning of Literacy: An Italian Reappraisal." *Journal of Modern Italian Studies* 14, no. 3 (2009): 346–356.

Rosati, M. *Il patriottismo italiano: Culture politiche e identità nazionale*. Rome, Bari: Laterza, 2000.

Rosière, S. "Groupes ethniquement minoritaires et violence politique: Essai de typologie." *Diasporas: Histoire et sociétés* 10, first semester (2007): 11–25.

Rosoli, G. "La crise des relations entre l'Italie et le Brésil: La grande naturalisation (1888–1896)." *Revue européenne des migrations internationales* no. 2 (1986): 69–90.

———, ed. *Un secolo di emigrazione italiana: 1876–1976*. Rome: Studi Emigrazione, 1978.

———. *Scalabrini tra vecchio e nuovo mondo: Atti del convegno storico internazionale (Piacenza, 3–5 dicembre 1987)*. Rome: Centro Studi Emigrazione, 1989.

Ruby, M. *L'évolution de la nationalité allemande d'après les textes (1842 à 1953)*. Baden-Baden: Werwereis, 1954.

Ruget, V., and B. Usmanalieva. "How Much Is Citizenship Worth? The Case of Kyrgyzstani Migrants in Kazakhstan and Russia." *Citizenship Studies* 14, no. 4 (2010): 445–459.

Rusconi, G. E. *Resistenza e Postfascismo*. Bologna: Il Mulino, 1995.

Sahlins, P. "La nationalité avant la lettre: Les pratiques de naturalisation en France sous l'Ancien Régime." *Annales: Histoire, sciences sociales* no. 5 (September–October 2000): 1081–1108.

———. *Unnaturally French: Foreign Citizens in the Old Regime and After*. Ithaca, London: Cornell University Press, 2004.

Sala, T. "Occupazione militare e amministrazione civile nella 'Provincia' di Lubiana (1941–1943)." In *L'Italia nell'Europa danubiana durante la seconda guerra mondiale*. Edited by E. Collotti, T. Sala and G. Vaccarino. 73–93. Milan: Istituto Nazionale per la Storia del Movimento di Liberazione, 1967.

Sammartino, A. "Culture, Belonging, and the Law: Naturalization in the Weimar Republic." In *Citizenship and National Identity in Twentieth-Century Germany*. Edited by G. Eley and J. Palmowski. 57–72. Stanford: Stanford University Press, 2008.

Sapiro, V. "Research Frontier Essay: When Are Interests Interesting? The Problem of Political Representation of Women." *American Political Science Review* 75, no. 3 (1981): 701–716.

———. "Women, Citizenship, and Nationality: Immigration and Naturalization Policies in the United States." *Politics and Society* 13, no. 1 (1984): 1–26.

Saraceno, C. "Costruzione della maternità e della paternità." In *Il regime fascista: Storia e storiografia*. Edited by A. Del Boca, M. Legnani and M. G. Rossi. 475–497. Rome, Bari: Laterza, 1995.

Sarfatti, M. "The Persecution of the Jews in Fascist Italy (1936–1943)." In *The Jews of Italy: Memory and Identity*. Edited by B. D. Cooperman and B. Garvin. 412–424. Bethesda: University Press of Maryland, 2000.

———. "Il razzismo fascista nella sua concretezza: La definizione di 'ebreo' e la collocazione di questi nella costruenda gerarchia razziale." In *Nel nome della razza: Il razzismo nella storia d'Italia 1870–1945*. Edited by A. Burgio. 321–332. Bologna: Il Mulino, 2000.

———. *The Jews in Mussolini's Italy: From Equality to Persecution*. Translated by J. Tedeschi and A. C. Tedeschi. Madison, London: University of Wisconsin Press, 2006.

———. "La condizione degli ebrei in Albania fra il 1938 e il 1943: Il quadro generale." In *Gli ebrei in Albania sotto il fascismo: Una storia da ricostruire*. Edited by L. Brazzo and M. Sarfatti. 125–151. Florence: Giuntina, 2010.

Sarti, R. "Giuseppe Mazzini and His Opponents." In *Italy in the Nineteenth Century 1796–1900*. Edited by J. A. Davis. 74–107. Oxford: Oxford University Press, 2000.

Sbacchi, A. "Poison Gas and Atrocities in the Italo-Ethiopian War (1935–1936)." In *Italian Colonialism*. Edited by R. Ben-Ghiat and M. Fuller. 47–56. New York: Palgrave Macmillan, 2005.

Schnapper, D. *La communauté des citoyens: Sur l'idée moderne de nation*. Paris: Gallimard, 1994.

Scott, J. W. "Gender: A Useful Category of Historical Analysis." *American Historical Review* 91, no. 5 (1986): 1053–1075.

Segré, C. G. "Il colonialismo e la politica estera: Variazioni liberali e fasciste." In *La politica estera italiana (1860–1985)*. Edited by R. J. B. Bosworth and S. Romano. 121–146. Bologna: Il Mulino, 1991.

Sejersen, T. B. "'I Vow to Thee My Countries'—The Expansion of Dual Citizenship in the 21st Century." *International Migration Review* 42, no. 3 (2008): 523–549.

Seton-Watson, C. *Italy from Liberalism to Fascism, 1870–1925*. London: Methuen, 1967.

———. "Italy's Imperial Hangover." *Journal of Contemporary History* 15, no. 1 (1980): 169–179.

Shafir, G., ed. *The Citizenship Debates: A Reader*. Minneapolis, London: University of Minnesota Press, 1998.

Siim, B. *Gender and Citizenship: Politics and Agency in France, Britain and Denmark*. Cambridge: Cambridge University Press, 2000.

Singer, B. C. J. "Cultural v. Contractual Nations: Rethinking Their Opposition." *History and Theory* 35, no. 3 (1996): 309–337.

Smith, A. D. *National Identity*. Reno: University of Nevada Press, 1993.

Smith, A. K. *Suffrage Discourse in Britain During the First World War*. Aldershot: Ashgate, 2005.

Song, S. "Democracy and Noncitizen Voting Rights." *Citizenship Studies* 13, no. 6 (2009): 607–620.

Sorba, C., ed. *Cittadinanza. Individui, diritti sociali, collettività nella storia contemporanea: Atti del convegno annuale della Società Italiana per lo Studio della Storia Contemporanea (SISSCO), Padova, 2–3 dicembre 1999*. Rome: Ministero per i Beni e le Attività Culturali-Direzione Generale per gli Archivi, 2002.

Sòrgoni, B. *Parole e corpi: Antropologia, discorso giuridico e politiche sessuali interrazziali nella colonia Eritrea (1890–1941)*. Naples: Liguori editore, 1998.

———. *Etnografia e colonialismo: L'Eritrea e l'Etiopia di Alberto Pollera (1873–1939)*. Turin: Bollati Boringhieri, 2001.

———. "Racist Discourses and Practices in the Italian Empire Under Fascism." In *The Politics of Recognizing Difference: Multiculturalism Italian-Style*. Edited by R. Grillo and J. Pratt. 41–57. Aldershot, Hampshire: Ashgate, 2002.

Sori, E. *L'emigrazione italiana dall'unità alla seconda guerra mondiale*. Bologna: Il Mulino, 1979.

Soysal, Y. N. *Limits of Citizenship: Migrants and Postnational Membership in Europe*. Chicago, London: University of Chicago Press, 1994.

Spreafico, A. "La competizione elettorale e gli esiti del voto." In *La nascita della Repubblica: Atti del convegno di studi storici (Roma, 4–5–6 giugno 1987)*. Edited by Presidenza del Consiglio dei Ministri. 181–238. Rome: Presidenza del Consiglio dei Ministri, 1987.

Stanley Holton, S. *Suffrage Days: Stories from the Women's Suffrage Movement*. London, New York: Routledge, 1996.

Stefani, F. *8 Settembre 1943: Gli armistizi dell'Italia*. Settimo Milanese: Marzorati Editore, 1991.

Stella, G. A. *L'orda: Quando gli Albanesi eravamo noi*. Milan: Rizzoli, 2003.

Stoler, A. L. "Sexual Affronts and Racial Frontiers: European Identities and the Cultural Politics of Exclusion in Colonial Southeast Asia." In *Tensions of Empire: Colonial Cultures in a Bourgeois World*. Edited by F. Cooper and A. L. Stoler. 198–237. Berkeley, Los Angeles and London: University of California Press, 1997.

Stone, M. "A Flexible Rome: Fascism and the Cult of *Romanità*." In *Roman Presences: Receptions of Rome in European Culture, 1789–1945*. Edited by C. Edwards. 205–220. Cambridge: Cambridge University Press, 1999.

Stuart Hughes, H. *The United States and Italy*. Cambridge, Mass.: Harvard University Press, 1979.

Talpo, O. *Dalmazia: Una cronaca per la storia.* Vol. 1. *1941.* Rome: Ufficio Storico dello Stato Maggiore dell'Esercito, 1985.

Tamburrano, G. "Il paese e le forze politiche." In *La nascita della Repubblica: Atti del convegno di studi storici (Roma, 4–5–6 giugno 1987).* Edited by Presidenza del Consiglio dei Ministri. 85–88. Rome: Presidenza del Consiglio dei Ministri, 1987.

Taylor, C. *Multiculturalism and "The Politics of Recognition."* Edited by A. Gutmann. Princeton: Princeton University Press, 1992.

Tesauro, A. "The Fundamentals of the New Italian Constitution." *Canadian Journal of Economics and Political Science* 20, no. 1 (1954): 44–58.

Thalmann, R., ed. *Femmes et Fascismes.* Paris: Tierce, 1986.

Thomas, Y. "Le droit d'origine à Rome: Contribution à l'étude de la citoyenneté." *Revue critique de droit international privé* 84, no. 2 (1995): 253–290.

Tintori, G. "Cittadinanza e politiche di emigrazione nell'Italia liberale e fascista: Un approfondimento storico." In *Familismo legale: Come (non) diventare italiani.* Edited by G. Zincone. 52–106. Rome, Bari: Laterza, 2006.

Triandafyllidou, A. "National Identity and the 'Other'." *Ethnic and Racial Studies* 21, no. 4 (1998): 593–612.

———. "Popular Perceptions of Europe and the Nation: The Case of Italy." *Nations and Nationalism* 14, no. 2 (2008): 261–282.

Tsuda, T. "Ethnic Return Migration and the Nation-State: Encouraging the Diaspora to Return 'Home'." *Nations and Nationalism* 16, no. 4 (2010): 616–636.

Turner, B. S. "T. H. Marshall, Social Rights and English National Identity." *Citizenship Studies* 13, no. 1 (2009): 65–73.

Tuzzolo, G. *L'ultima notte del Fascismo tra diritto e storia. Dall'ultima seduta del Gran Consiglio del Fascismo alla fine dell'esperienza della Repubblica Sociale: Le relative problematiche giuridico-istituzionali.* Foggia: Edizioni Della Vela, 2001.

van Steenbergen, B., ed. *The Condition of Citizenship.* London: Sage, 1994.

Varsori, A. *L'Italia nelle relazioni internazionali dal 1943 al 1992.* Rome, Bari: Laterza, 1998.

Veca, S. *Cittadinanza: Riflessioni filosofiche sull'idea di emancipazione.* Milan: Feltrinelli, 1990.

Ventrone, A. "Il cittadino nella Repubblica." In *Almanacco della Repubblica: Storia d'Italia attraverso le tradizioni, le istituzioni e le simbologie repubblicane.* Edited by M. Ridolfi. 314–327. Milan: Mondadori, 2003.

Vercellone, P. "The Italian Constitution of 1947–1948." In *The Rebirth of Italy 1943–50.* Edited by S. J. Woolf. 121–134. London: Longman, 1972.

Villari, G. "Il sistema di occupazione fascista in Albania." In *Gli ebrei in Albania sotto il fascismo: Una storia da ricostruire.* Edited by L. Brazzo and M. Sarfatti. 93–124. Florence: Giuntina, 2010.

Viroli, M. *Per amore della patria: Patriottismo e nazionalismo nella storia.* Rome, Bari: Laterza, 2001.

Visser, R. "Fascist Doctrine and the Cult of *Romanità*." *Journal of Contemporary History* 27, no. 1 (1992): 5–22.

Vogel, U. "Is Citizenship Gender-Specific?" In *The Frontiers of Citizenship.* Edited by U. Vogel and M. Moran. 58–85. London: Macmillan, 1991.

———. "Marriage and the Boundaries of Citizenship." In *The Condition of Citizenship*. Edited by B. van Steenbergen. 76–89. London: Sage, 1994.

Vogel, U., and M. Moran, eds. *The Frontiers of Citizenship*. London: Macmillan, 1991.

Vujosevic, J. "L'occupation italienne." *Revue d'histoire de la IIème guerre mondiale* no. 87 (1972): 33–52.

Weil, P. "Access to Citizenship: A Comparison of Twenty-Five Nationality Laws." In *Citizenship Today: Global Perspectives and Practices*. Edited by T. A. Aleinikoff and D. Klusmeyer. 17–35. Washington, D.C.: Carnegie Endowment for International Peace, 2001.

———. *Qu'est-ce qu'un Français? Histoire de la nationalité française depuis la Révolution*. Paris: Bernard Grasset, 2002.

Weil, P., and R. Hansen, eds. *Nationalité et citoyenneté en Europe*. Paris: La Découverte, 1999.

Weis, P. *Nationality and Statelessness in International Law*. 2nd ed. Alphen aan den Rijn, Netherlands; Germantown, Md.: Sijthoff and Noordhoff, 1979. First published 1956.

Wiesner, M. E. *Women and Gender in Early Modern Europe*. Cambridge: Cambridge University Press, 1993.

Wong, A. S. *Race and the Nation in Liberal Italy, 1861–1911: Meridionalism, Empire, and Diaspora*. New York, Basingstoke: Palgrave Macmillan, 2006.

Woolf, S. J. "The Rebirth of Italy, 1943–1945." In *The Rebirth of Italy 1943–50*. Edited by S. J. Woolf. 212–243. London: Longman, 1972.

———, ed. *The Rebirth of Italy 1943–50*. London: Longman, 1972.

Wright, J. L. "Mussolini, Libya, and the Sword of Islam." In *Italian Colonialism*. Edited by R. Ben-Ghiat and M. Fuller. 121–130. New York: Palgrave Macmillan, 2005.

Wyke, M. "Screening Ancient Rome in the New Italy." In *Roman Presences: Receptions of Rome in European Culture, 1789–1945*. Edited by C. Edwards. 188–204. Cambridge: Cambridge University Press, 1999.

Yuval-Davis, N. *Gender and Nation*. London, New Delhi: Sage, 1997.

Zamuner, E., ed. *La formazione dello stato italiano: Il Risorgimento*. Turin: Giappichelli, 2002.

Zimmermann, L., K. F. Zimmermann and A. Constant. "Ethnic Self-Identification of First-Generation Immigrants." *International Migration Review* 41, no. 3 (2007): 769–781.

Zincone, G. *Da sudditi a cittadini: Le vie dello stato e le vie della società civile*. Bologna: Il Mulino, 1992.

———, ed. *Familismo legale: Come (non) diventare italiani*. Rome, Bari: Laterza, 2006.

Zolo, D., ed. *La cittadinanza: Appartenenza, identità, diritti*. Rome, Bari: Laterza, 1994.

3.c Electronic sources

http://www.quirinale.it (Presidency of the Italian Republic)

http://www.unhcr.org (United Nations High Commissioner for Refugees)

http://www.cestim.org (CESTIM—Centro Studi Immigrazione ONLUS)

http://www.scalabrini.org (Scalabrini Order)
http://www.repubblica.it, http://bologna.repubblica.it, http://www.corriere.it
(Italian daily newspapers *la Repubblica* and *Corriere della Sera*)

Index

Sieyès, Emmanuel J., 10
Silvestrelli, Luigi, 78
Smith, Anthony D., work of: *National Identity*, 8, 262, 338n8
Somalia (liberal period): colonialism and colonial subjecthood in, 119–128; myth of Ancient Rome and its impact on Italian colonial subjecthood, 145–148, 269; naturalization of natives, 122–123, 141; nonmetropolitan status as instrument of colonial rule, 125–126; population statistics, 121; slavery, 126–127, 309n32. *See also* Somalia (fascist period); *Meticci*; Racial thinking (liberal period)
Somalia (fascist period): colonialism and colonial subjecthood in, 184–190; expectation by natives of higher citizenship status, 318–319n8; myth of Ancient Rome and its impact on Italian colonial subjecthood, 209–214; slavery, 189. *See also* Somalia (liberal period); Ethiopia/AOI (*Africa Orientale Italiana*); *Meticci*; Racial thinking (fascist period)
Sonnino, Sidney, and naturalization law, 298n57
Sòrgoni, Barbara, works of: *Etnografia e colonialismo*, 140–143, 308n21; *Parole e corpi*, 123,140–143, 188, 308n21, 315n36
Southerners, Italian. *See* Racial thinking (liberal period); Racial thinking (fascist period)
Storia degli ebrei italiani sotto il fascismo (De Felice), 177, 178
Subjecthood: monarchical, 9–11, 17–20, 21, 22, 23, 26–27, 30, 31, 32, 147, 220, 237, 240, 243, 246, 254, 262–264, 268, 273; status of colonial, 121–123, 125–127, 129–133, 138–144, 145–147, 149, 185–186, 189–190, 246, 248, 268–270. *See also* Great Britain
Da sudditi a cittadini (Zincone), 55–56
Suffrage. *See* Rights, political

Thaon di Revel, Paolo, on Albanians, 199

Ticino. *See* Italiani non regnicoli (liberal period)
Tintori, Guido, work of: "Cittadinanza e politiche di emigrazione nell'Italia liberale e fascista," 4, 95, 97, 106, 109, 114, 303–304n41, 304nn60, 61, 305n75
Tirolo. *See* Italiani non regnicoli (liberal period)
Tittoni, Tommaso, 127
Togliatti, Palmiro, 258, 334n15
Trieste: 81, 243, 248, 252, 253, 295n5, 329n5; citizenship in Free Territory of, 249–251. *See also* Italiani non regnicoli (liberal period)
Tripolitania. *See* Libya
Türr, Stefano, and application for grand naturalization, 89

Umberto I (king), 240
Umberto II (prince, lieutenant of the realm, king), 219, 220, 221, 230, 240, 244, 332n57
United States: cold war and Italy, 240, 250, 252, 257–259, 275; Garibaldi and American citizenship, 1–2; Italian immigrants in, 100–101, 107; racial prejudice in, 101, 302–303n28, 303n29. *See also* Allies, Western

Vacca, Giuseppe, 24, 25, 56
Vassallo, Ernesto, 149
Venice. *See* Italiani non regnicoli (liberal period); Maritime Republics, ancient
Viale, Lorenzo, 226–227
Villari, Pasquale, on Southern Italians, 60
Vittorio Emanuele II (king), 15, 16, 17, 18, 19, 32, 89, 220, 240
Vittorio Emanuele III (king), 184, 199, 201, 211, 218, 219, 220, 222, 230, 240, 330n13, 332n57
Vogel, Ursula, work of: "Is Citizenship Gender–Specific?" 56

Waddington, Evelino, and application for grand naturalization, 86, 88
Weil, Patrick, works of: "Access to Citizenship," 6–7, 26–27; *Qu' est–ce qu'un Français?* 6–7, 26–27, 300n84